D0781382

Beginning Hindi
A Complete Course

प्रारंभिक हिन्दी
एक संपूर्ण पाठ्यक्रम

Joshua H. Pien and Fauzia Farooqui

Georgetown University Press/Washington DC

Library of Congress Cataloging-in-Publication Data

Pien, Joshua H.

Beginning Hindi : a complete course / Joshua H. Pien and Fauzia Farooqui.

p. cm.

Includes bibliographical references and index.

ISBN 978-1-62616-022-4 (pbk. : alk. paper)

1. Hindi language—Textbooks for foreign speakers—English. 2. Hindi language—Spoken Hindi.

3. Hindi language—Self-instruction. I. Title.

PK1933.P43 2013

491.4'3982421—dc23

2013014566

∞ This book is printed on acid-free paper meeting the requirements of the American National Standard for Permanence in Paper for Printed Library Materials.

15 14 9 8 7 6

Printed in the United States

Dedication

For Shaham and Sufi

Table of Contents

Unit 1: Me and My School

Unit 2: My Family and My Home

Unit 3: Daily Life

Unit 4: In the Market

Unit 5: My Childhood

Unit 6: Rules and Responsibilities

Unit 7: A Trip to South Asia

About *Beginning Hindi*

The goal of *Beginning Hindi* is to lead students to the intermediate-mid or high proficiency level in all four skills. Our approach is to promote an enjoyable learning environment in which students actively use the language for genuine communication, and to provide students with the tools that are necessary to do so.

The book begins with an introduction to the sound system and script. This is followed by the core of the book, which focuses on the language and its associated culture. This core is organized around two major components, units and chapters. Units divide the content into broad topics whereas the chapters focus on more specific topics. The core of the book is followed by two appendices, the first of which presents Hindi numbers, and the second of which presents additional grammatical structures to help students proceed to more advanced levels after completing this course. The book also contains Hindi-English and English-Hindi glossaries of the words that are used in the texts.

The book's eight units are defined by themes, which lend continuity to the large amounts of content that the units contain and also provide realistic contexts for communication. The unit themes are appropriate intermediate-level topics, such as: home and family; everyday life; the marketplace; responsibilities at home, work and school; and travel. We have chosen a diverse sampling of themes to broadly represent the targeted proficiency level as a whole.

Each unit culminates in a set of unit activities, which contain tasks, or activities in which the language is employed to reach a realistic and measurable non-linguistic goal. Some examples of tasks that this book contains are: purchasing food and clothing, arranging lodging and transportation, giving and following directions, and visiting a doctor. The unit activities also contain assignments for student-driven projects in which students can further explore and personalize topics related to the overarching theme.

The book contains 41 chapters, each of which focuses on one or two language functions and the structures—grammar and vocabulary—that are required to express them. The chapters are grouped together and distributed among the units so that the contents of the chapters serve as building blocks for the more complex tasks and projects at the end of each unit. The chapters contain straightforward grammar explanations that explain not only the forms of structures, but also their meanings and uses. The chapters also include topically organized vocabulary lists and sequences of exercises that lead students to structurally accurate yet meaningful use of the forms. The exercises address all four skills (reading, writing, listening, speaking) and provide opportunities for actual communication through role plays and games.

The book's 41 chapters cover the grammar and vocabulary that is typically covered in first-year courses. We have organized the grammar by balancing two independent but equally important needs. First, the grammar must be distributed throughout the book so that students have the necessary tools at hand to express what they need and wish to say when they are asked to use the language for a given purpose. Second, complex structures composed of simpler ones should be covered after the simpler ones have already been learned. Organizing the grammar according to these principles is extremely important from the perspective of the student. The language appears less complicated when the level of grammatical complexity increases in smaller increments, and having the tools at hand to express one's desired meaning reinforces the notion that the language is a genuine means of communication and not just a set of rules.

Beginning Hindi contains the resources necessary to maintain a dynamic and student-centered classroom environment, but it also contains tools to encourage students to develop as independent learners. The culminating chapter of each unit includes review activities including tips for increasing fluency and sets of questions to help personalize learning. Students should be encouraged to take charge of their learning by utilizing these resources regularly and developing their own resources according to their own self-assessed needs. Students can also be encouraged to study in pairs to review and repeat the tasks that they have practiced in class.

The book presents culture in a manner that is integrated with the thematic units. Most of the relevant culture is embedded in the texts, situational activities, and tasks. We focus on commonplace aspects of culture related to communication about everyday living and social needs. Students acquire not only explicit knowledge of the culture, but also practicable proficiency in the culture by engaging in culturally authentic situations. Additional notes on culture are included where further explicit explanations are necessary.

We also offer a deeper glimpse into the daily lives as well as the values and ideas of Hindi-speaking communities through our selection of photographs and additional supplementary materials. The photographs that we have included consist of simple signs as well as famous landmarks and typical scenes from South Asian cities. We have also included popular sayings and proverbs that are relatively simple in structure yet convey important cultural values.

Beginning Hindi audio files are available free to download at www.press.georgetown.edu.

How to Use This Book: For Teachers

This book was written to support a student-centered classroom in which Hindi is the primary language and a significant portion of the time is devoted to hands-on interactive activities.

We recommend that grammar explanations and vocabulary be learned by students as homework prior to carrying out the associated activities in class. In addition, grammar-focused reading and writing activities can be assigned as homework. These explanations and activities should sufficiently prepare students to engage in the hands-on meaning-focused activities in class. Activities with a focus on reading, writing, or grammar can be recognized by the following icons:

Reading

Writing

Grammar

If students need additional time practicing structure-focused activities prior to engaging in meaning-focused activities, the grammar activities may be adapted as pair activities and reviewed in class.

The following icons identify activities that have a listening, speaking, or interpersonal component:

Listening

Speaking

Interpersonal

Speaking activities in general, and interpersonal activities in particular are intended to be carried out in class. However, the "Tips for Increasing Fluency" given in each set of unit activities are an exception. They are intended to be used as independent speaking drills by students at home. Students should be encouraged to review these regularly. Many of the interpersonal activities have supporting materials in the form of tables and illustrations. These should be photocopied before class so that the relevant portions can be distributed to the students prior to each activity. This practice will allow students to focus better on the task at hand and will discourage them from referring to their books during these activities.

Beginning Hindi audio files are available free to download at www.press.georgetown.edu. The following icon identifies activities with accompanying audio:

Audio

All audio recordings have accompanying transcripts, yet it is important that students listen to the texts identified by the  icon before reading them. Many audio files are essential to listening activities, whereas others are provided as supplementary review material. For example, vocabulary list recordings can be used by students to review pronunciation or to review the meanings of words. The general questions recordings can be used as speaking drills at home.

The presentation of grammar has been sequenced and situations for communication have been defined in such a way that students should be able to communicate exclusively in Hindi from the first unit. We have included a number of useful classroom management phrases in the first unit to help you and your students continue speaking together in Hindi not only during activities, but also when transitioning between them. These are intended to be learned as fixed expressions without regard to their internal structure. We encourage you to add any additional phrases that you frequently use but are not included in our list.

The book also includes an introduction to the Hindi sound system and script. While this occurs prior to Unit 1 in the textbook, it is intended to be covered concurrently with the first unit. Unit 1 accordingly has a greater focus on speaking and less of a focus on reading and writing. We have included transliteration through Unit 2, but students are expected to have learned the script before proceeding to Unit 3 and beyond.

It is important to note that the chapters and units are of varying length due to the different demands of the content that they contain. Accordingly, some units and chapters will require more time than others to complete. To aid in planning and scheduling class time, we have included a table in appendix 3 that lists the suggested number of class hours to be spent on each activity set.

How to Use This Book: For Students

There are three keys to using this book successfully to learn Hindi; the first is preparation, the second is participation, and the third is regular review. These keys roughly correspond to what you should do at home and what you should do in the classroom. In very general terms, the more you actively use the language in class, the quicker you will acquire it; and the better you prepare and review at home, the more you will be able to participate in class.

It is always a good idea to learn the grammar and vocabulary at home prior to coming to class on the day you will be using it. When learning the grammar, please keep in mind that any complete understanding of a structure should include three points: form, meaning, and function. The form of a structure is its pattern of changes to express different grammatical relations. The meaning of a structure is often easiest to understand by comparing and contrasting it with the closest equivalent English structure. The function of a structure is how it can be used in various contexts. All of these points are addressed in each grammar explanation. The short term aim of learning grammar is to develop the ability to recall these three points about a structure from memory, whereas the long term aim should be to become familiar enough with the structure to use it without thinking.

Vocabulary should also be learned prior to the day in which it will be used in class. When learning vocabulary, it's important to remember that the ability to recognize a Hindi word and tell its English meaning does not automatically translate to the ability to produce the Hindi word from the English. While all words should always be memorized for passive recognition from Hindi to English, it's important to be able to identify the most frequently occurring and functional words to memorize from English to Hindi. These words include core vocabulary items such as pronouns (*I, you, he, she, it, ...*), conjunctions (*and, or, but, that, ...*), postpositions (*in, at, on, by, from, ...*), and any other function words such as interrogatives and relatives (*who, what, when, where,...*). Special attention should also be paid to verbs as it is impossible to form sentences without them. Vocabulary should be reviewed regularly, and eventually all of the words in the book should be learned for both passive and active retrieval.

Preparing regularly before class will allow you to focus more time on using the language in class for real communication and less on the structure of the language. Through the process of actually communicating with the language, using it will become automatic. The more you participate in class, the faster this will happen. We therefore encourage you to be as active as possible in class; you will excel if you have fun and use the language creatively.

It is also important to regularly review what you have already learned. We have provided a number of review activities that include the first three activities in each set of unit activities. In addition, we encourage you to study in pairs with classmates so that you will also be able to review the role plays and other tasks covered in class.

Beginning Hindi audio files are available free to download at www.press.georgetown.edu. We encourage you to download the files and to listen to them frequently.

For Independent Learners

Much of what we recommend for classroom learners also applies to independent learners. Studying will be most efficient and effective if preparation time is devoted to conceptually grasping and committing to memory the grammar and vocabulary prior to carrying out the activities. While written transcripts are provided for each listening text, we recommend first listening exclusively before reading the transcripts. The additional audio files for vocabulary lists and general questions should also be utilized as much as possible.

Although it will not be possible to carry out the role plays if you are learning completely independently, one suggestion that might be useful is that you can write dialogs for the role plays in place of acting them out. The reading and listening texts that we provide can serve as models as you do this. Of course, if you can also find a conversation partner with whom you can practice the role plays, that will be the most useful. Speaking can be practiced without a partner by focusing on the second and third activity in each set of unit activities, "Tips for Increasing Fluency," and "General Questions." The general questions can be listened to and responded to orally.

One of the challenges that independent learners face is managing time. It's better to practice regularly for a short amount of time than to practice for extended lengths intermittently. We recommend setting aside a fixed amount of time every day and devoting that time to Hindi study.

Another challenge is pronunciation. We have provided extensive phonetic descriptions of the sounds of Hindi. It is a good idea to review pronunciation regularly and make full use of the accompanying audio materials as models for pronunciation.

Acknowledgments

There are many people whom we would like to thank for their help in bringing this book to its present form. Aftab Ahmad of Columbia University read the present volume and provided valuable feedback. Surendra Gambhir, Ishrat Afreen, and Rabia Shah reviewed the manuscript of the previous Urdu volume and also provided valuable feedback. Of course, we the authors remain solely responsible for any remaining issues. We would also like to thank Syed Perwaiz Jafri, Rohit Lamba, Parth Mehta, Kishan Shah, Gitanjali Aggarwal, and Azza Cohen for lending their voices and providing help with audio recording. Many people provided beautiful images from their own private collections to be included in the *Beginning Hindi* and *Beginning Urdu* projects. We thank Azza Cohen, Farhan Farooqui, Urfia Farooqui, Fariah Farooqui, Subuhi Firdaus, Natalie Aguayo, and Madhvi Sally for their generosity in sharing their own photographs as well as taking and providing photographs to fit the specific purposes of these books.

We would also like to express our special thanks to Hope LeGro and the entire staff at Georgetown University Press for the hard work, patience, and commitment that brought this book to publication. In addition, we thank our students at the University of Pennsylvania, Princeton University, University of Wisconsin, and University of Michigan. These students used earlier versions of the textbook and provided much useful feedback.

Last but not least, we thank Martha and Paul Pien for their continuous support and encouragement.

About the Hindi Language

Hindi is an Indo-European language, belonging to the same language family as European languages such as French, Spanish, German, and English. While Hindi's relationship to European Romance and Germanic languages is distant, it is more closely related to other South Asian languages, such as Urdu, Panjabi, Bengali, Marathi, Gujarati, Nepali, and Sindhi, all of which share a common ancestor, which was a form of Sanskrit.

Hindi is generally counted among the top five most widely spoken languages of the world. The most recently released Indian Census figures, from 2001, identify more than 422 million people as native speakers of Hindi, a figure that represents 41.03% of the overall population of India (www.censusindia.gov.in). Hindi has a unique relationship with the language Urdu. The grammar and basic vocabulary of Hindi and Urdu are nearly identical, and in many contexts it makes sense to talk about the two languages as a single variety, termed Hindi-Urdu, Urdu-Hindi, or Hindustani. Urdu serves as the native language of an additional 51.5 million in India and several million in Pakistan. Both Hindi and Urdu function as contact languages in India and Pakistan, and are spoken as second languages by millions more South Asians.

This book presents a standard variety of Hindi appropriate for everyday uses of the language. These uses include fulfilling social needs such as exchanging basic biographical information, sharing one's personal experiences, and making future plans; in addition, the uses include carrying out everyday language tasks such as arranging food, clothing, housing, and transportation. The language that this book presents will enable learners to communicate with hundreds of millions of Hindi as well as Urdu speakers throughout northern India and Pakistan, and with members of South Asian heritage communities throughout the world.

Learning Hindi will open access to one of the most culturally rich and diverse regions of the world. Hindi is the primary language of Bollywood, one of the largest producers of films in the world, and one comparable to Hollywood in international popularity. The closely allied music industry is an equally prolific producer of popular music in Hindi. Hindi possesses a rich modern literature that includes many notable writers of short stories, novels, drama, poetry, and non-fiction. While the writing of literature in Modern Standard Hindi began around the beginning of the nineteenth century, literature in related varieties such as Avadhi, Braj Bhasha, and Dakani began several hundred years earlier. In addition, Urdu literature, much of which is understood and enjoyed by Hindi speakers, possesses a history as equally long and rich as Hindi's.

Throughout its history Hindi has had contacts with various languages, and this history of contacts is actually imprinted on the Hindi language itself. Hindi is an Indo-Aryan language, having evolved from a spoken form of Sanskrit. Its core vocabulary consists largely of evolved forms of Sanskrit words, but also contains many loanwords. Hindi's rich vocabulary includes loanwords from Sanskrit, Persian, Arabic, and, increasingly, English. These multiple word sources make possible many different styles of Hindi that include formal Sanskritized Hindi, a style largely shared with Urdu called Hindustani, and a spoken style that contains a high proportion of English loanwords, called Hinglish.

In addition to being the official language of the modern Republic of India, Hindi also serves as an official language in several Indian states, and it also functions as a contact language between many speakers of other Indian languages. It is therefore not surprising that in addition to possessing stylistic variation, Hindi also possesses various regional styles.

Modern Standard Hindi and Urdu are based on a dialect originally spoken in and around the area of Delhi. For many speakers in this region and the broader central Gangetic plane, Hindi and Urdu are representatives of the rich Ganga-Jamuni (Ganges-Yamuna) culture of this region. This culture is a unique mixture of northern Indian and Indo-Persian cultural elements. Hindi is also a major language in several surrounding regions including Rajasthan, Madhya Pradesh, and the Himalayan states of Uttaranchal and Himachal Pradesh. In addition to these regions, other regional varieties include Mumbaiya Hindi and a southern variety of Urdu-Hindi spoken in some Deccan cities such as Hyderabad since the 14th century. Hindi is also spoken by sizable communities of South Asian ancestry in areas including the United States and Canada, South America, the United Kingdom, South Africa, countries of the Persian Gulf, Australia, and Fiji.

Hindi's journey has been a long one with stops in various stations throughout South Asia and the wider world. We welcome you as you embark on your voyage with Hindi and wish you a pleasant journey.

The Sound System and Script of Hindi

Part I: The Sound System of Hindi

Lesson 1: Sounds Similar to English

Hindi has several sounds that are identical or nearly identical to English sounds.

Consonants:

b like 'b' in 'boy'

f like 'f' in 'fox'

g like 'g' in 'gone'

h like 'h' in 'hot'

j like 'j' in 'job'

m like 'm' in 'mob'

n like 'n' in 'not'

s	like 's' in 'sox'
ś	like 'sh' in 'shop'
y	like 'y' in 'yellow'
z	like 'z' in 'zebra'

Vowels:

a	like 'a' in 'about'
ā	like 'a' in 'father'
i	like 'i' in 'in'
ī	like 'ee' in 'keep'
u	like 'u' in 'put'
ū	like 'oo' in 'mood'

Exercise 1

Practice reading the following words aloud. Listen to your audio file and compare your pronunciation with the recording.

bas *sab* *sāf* *sun* *jūn* *nīm* *jīnā* *sāg* *binā* *bahānā*

mahīnā *zamānā* *zamīn* *banānā* *śabānā āzmī*

Exercise 2

The vowel *a* often changes in quality when it occurs next to *h*. The sound that results is similar to the 'e' in 'pet.' Listen to how these words are pronounced in your recording, and then repeat the pronunciation yourself.

bahan *bahas* *zahan* *sahnā* *bahnā* *śahanśāh*

Exercise 3

Now listen to the words in the recording and transcribe them as you hear them pronounced. Check your answers when you are finished. The answers are given at the end of this section, after lesson 7.

Lesson 2: The Sounds *r, l, v, e,* and *o*

The consonants *r, l,* and *v*, and the vowels *e* and *o* are pronounced slightly differently from the closest English equivalents.

The Consonant *r*

This sound resembles Spanish 'r.' It is produced by tapping the tip of the tongue a single time at the location where the tongue contacts the roof of the mouth when pronouncing English 't' and 'd.'

You can produce this sound by beginning with the phrase 'ought to' as pronounced in casual conversation ('otta'). Notice what your tongue does as you pronounce this phrase. It should lightly and very briefly tap the roof of your mouth. This English sound is the closest equivalent to Hindi *r*. Gradually reduce the initial vowel until it is only a few milliseconds in duration. The sound that results should approximate Hindi *r*.

Exercise 1

Listen to the recording of these Hindi words and try to replicate the pronunciation yourself.

rāj *śahar* *rāz* *bār* *hīrā*

The Consonant *l*

This sound is similar to English 'l' in some contexts. English 'l' actually has two variants, which are sometimes called clear 'l' and dark 'l.' Clear 'l' occurs in words such as 'line' and 'list.' The back of the tongue is relaxed and lowered when this 'l' is pronounced. Dark 'l' occurs in words such as 'pool' and 'pull'; its "dark" quality is the result of the back of the tongue being raised during pronunciation. Hindi *l* is similar to the clear 'l' of English. Learning to produce this sound accurately will largely be a matter of unlearning the tendency to produce dark 'l' in certain sound environments.

Exercise 2

Listen to the recording of these Hindi words and try to replicate the pronunciation yourself.

bāl *nal* *gīlā* *bulbul* *lāl*

The Consonant *v*

The sound *v* varies in pronunciation. In some contexts it is pronounced like English 'v.' In other contexts it has some properties of English 'v' and others of English 'w.' It is similar to 'w' in that both lips are involved in producing it, whereas it resembles English 'v' in that the sound produced is more of a vibrating, or buzzing sound; it results from the lips being held closer together than in English 'w.' One way to think about this sound is that it is like an English 'v' pronounced using both lips rather than the bottom lip and the upper teeth.

Exercise 3

Listen to the recording of these Hindi words and try to replicate the pronunciation yourself.

sivā *savā* *ravānā* *havā* *vazan*

Exercise 4

Now listen to the words in the recording and transcribe them as you hear them pronounced. Check your answers when you are finished.

The Vowel *e*

The Hindi vowel *e* is similar to the 'é' in 'café.' However, the English vowel is actually a combination of two sounds, one the pure vowel 'e,' and the other a 'y'-like sound that results from the tongue being raised halfway through the pronunciation of the vowel. To produce Hindi *e*, you must isolate the first sound by preventing your tongue from rising.

Exercise 5

Listen to the recording of these Hindi words and try to replicate the pronunciation yourself.

seb *rel* *ye* *le* *banāe*

The Vowel *o*

The Hindi vowel *o* is similar to English 'o' in 'no.' English 'o' is also actually a combination of two vowel sounds, one the pure vowel 'o' and the other a 'w'-like sound resulting from the lips contracting halfway through the pronunciation of the vowel. To produce Hindi *o*, try to isolate the first sound by preventing your lips from contracting.

Exercise 6

Listen to the recording of these Hindi words and try to replicate the pronunciation yourself.

lo *bano* *suno* *māno* *bolo*

Exercise 7

Now listen to the words in the recording and transcribe them as you hear them pronounced. Check your answers when you are finished.

Lesson 3: Aspirated and Unaspirated Consonants

The Hindi equivalents of the English consonants 'p,' 'ch,' and 'k' are pronounced slightly differently from English. Each of these sounds actually has two Hindi equivalents. The Hindi sounds differ from the English ones in terms of *aspiration*, or breathiness:

Hindi *p* is less breathy than English 'p' in most contexts.
Hindi *ph* is slightly more breathy than English 'p' in most contexts.
Hindi *c* is less breathy than English 'ch' in most contexts.
Hindi *ch* is slightly more breathy than English 'ch' in most contexts.
Hindi *k* is less breathy than English 'k' in most contexts.
Hindi *kh* is slightly more breathy than English 'k' in most contexts.

The Consonants *ph, kh,* and *ch*

Consider the English words 'pot,' 'kin,' and 'chip.' Open your palm and place your hand about an inch in front of your mouth. Now pronounce these words one by one. Note the breath that you feel on your hand when you produce 'p,' 'ch,' and 'k.' This is aspiration. To produce Hindi *ph, ch,* and *kh,* increase the amount of aspiration slightly.

Exercise 1

Listen to the recording of these Hindi words and try to replicate the pronunciation yourself.

phal *khānā* *chāyā* *phūl* *sakhī* *uchalnā*

The Consonants *p, k,* and *c*

Now consider the English words 'spot,' 'skin,' and 'mischief.' Place your open palm in front of your mouth again and pronounce these words aloud. Notice how the amount of breath in the 'p,' 'ch,' and 'k' of these words is significantly diminished. The consonants in these English words are *unaspirated.* They are very similar to Hindi *p, c,* and *k.* Try to pronounce unaspirated *p, c,* and *k* in isolation. You can do this by keeping your hand in front of your mouth (to monitor your breath) and pronouncing 'spot,' 'skin,' and 'mischief,' and then removing the portion of each word that occurs before the target sound.

Exercise 2

Listen to the recording of these Hindi words and try to replicate the pronunciation yourself.

pal *cal* *kal* *pīnā* *bacānā* *pakānā*

The Consonants *bh, jh,* and *gh*

Exercise 3

Hindi also has aspirated versions of *b, j,* and *g.* Listen to what *bh, jh,* and *gh* sound like in these Hindi words:

bhī *jhīl* *ghās* *bhārī* *samajh* *ghulā*

These sounds are similar to *ph, ch,* and *kh,* the only difference being *voicing,* or vibration of the vocal cords during pronunciation. The consonants *ph, ch,* and *kh* are *voiceless,* whereas *bh, jh,* and *gh* are voiced—the vocal cords vibrate while they are pronounced.

One way to learn to pronounce *bh, jh,* and *gh* is to first get the vocal cords vibrating, and then from that state attempt to produce *ph, ch,* and *kh.* First try *bh.* Pronounce a prolonged 'mmmmmmmm' sound. Place your hand on your voice box; the vibration that you will feel is the result of the vocal cords vibrating. Now without stopping the vibration of your vocal cords, release your lips into a *ph*-like sound. The aspiration of the *ph* plus the vibration of the vocal cords should result in *bh.* Repeat these same steps while gradually reducing the 'mmmm' sound until it is only a few milliseconds in length. Now repeat these steps to produce *jh* ('nnnnnnn' releasing into *ch*) and *gh* (from a prolonged 'ng' sound releasing into *kh*). When you are confident producing these sounds, return to the examples above (beginning with *bhī*) and pronounce them aloud. Try to match your pronunciation to that of the recording.

Exercise 4

Now listen to the words in the recording and transcribe them as you hear them pronounced. Check your answers when you are finished.

Lesson 4: Dental and Retroflex Consonants

English 't' and 'd' have four equivalent sounds each in Hindi. In addition to aspirated and unaspirated variants they also have positional variants. *Dental* consonants are produced with the tip of the tongue against the back of the top front teeth. *Retroflex* consonants are produced with the tongue curled back within the mouth. Hindi does not have any 't' or 'd'-like sounds that are produced with the tongue in the same position as English 't' and 'd.'

Dental consonants are transliterated with Roman 't' and 'd': *t, th, d, dh.* Retroflex consonants are transliterated with Roman 't' and 'd' plus a diacritical dot underneath: *ṭ, ṭh, ḍ, ḍh.*

Dental Consonants

Dental *d* can be produced as follows. Pronounce the 'th' sound in the word 'this' continuously. Note where your tongue contacts the back of your teeth. Now gently move your tongue forward to make solid contact with your teeth. This is the dental position. With your tongue in this position, produce a 'd'-like sound. This should be close to a Hindi *d*. To produce *t, th,* and *dh,* place your tongue in this same position and follow the steps you learned in the previous lesson to control your aspiration.

Exercise 1

Listen to the recording of these Hindi words and try to replicate the pronunciation yourself.

dāl *dhīmā* *tārā* *thālī* *dīn* *tīn*

Retroflex Consonants

Retroflex *ḍ* can be produced as follows. Say English 'do' and notice where your tongue contacts the roof of your mouth. Place your tongue against the roof of your mouth in that position. Now slowly slide your tongue backwards. After about a centimeter, you will notice that there is a slight ridge on the roof of your mouth. Continue slowly sliding your tongue back until the tip is lying right on the ridge. Note this position—this is the location from which all retroflex consonants are pronounced. With your tongue in this position, produce a 'd'-like sound. This should very closely approximate Hindi *ḍ*. To produce retroflex *ṭ, ṭh,* and *ḍh,* place your tongue in the retroflex position, and then follow the steps that you learned in the previous lesson to control your aspiration.

Exercise 2

Listen to the recording of these Hindi words and try to replicate the pronunciation yourself.

ḍāk *ṭālnā* *ḍher* *ṭhīk* *ḍūbā* *uṭhnā*

Exercise 3

Now listen to the words in the recording, which contain a mixture of dental and retroflex sounds, and transcribe them as you hear them pronounced. Check your answers when you are finished.

Lesson 5: The Consonants *ṛ* and *ṛh* and the Vowels *ai* and *au*

The Consonants *ṛ* and *ṛh*

The consonants *ṛ* and *ṛh* are called *retroflex flaps*. When producing these sounds, the underside of the tip of the tongue flaps against the roof of the mouth in the retroflex position while moving in a back-to-front motion. You can produce this sound if you begin with the nonsense syllable 'urda' (English pronunciation, emphasis on the second syllable) and then gradually make the motion of your tongue more fluid. Retract your tongue within your mouth behind the retroflex position and then flap it forward making contact with the roof of your mouth in the retroflex position. The sound that results should be similar to Hindi *ṛ*. Now add aspiration to produce *ṛh*.

Exercise 1

Listen to the recording of these Hindi words and try to replicate the pronunciation yourself.

baṛā *baṛhā* *laṛkā* *dāṛhī* *bhīṛ* *ḍeṛh*

The Vowels *ai* and *au*

The vowels *ai* and *au* differ from English vowels. The vowel *ai* is similar to English 'a' as in 'cat' combined with 'e' as in 'pet.' The vowel *au* is similar to British English 'au' as in 'caught' combined with *o*. The best way to learn these vowels is to listen to them and imitate the sound.

Exercise 2

Listen to the recording of these Hindi words and try to replicate the pronunciation yourself.

baiṭh *daur* *pair* *sau* *cain* *kaun*

Exercise 3

Now listen to the words in the recording and transcribe them as you hear them pronounced. Check your answers when you are finished.

Lesson 6: The Consonants *q*, *x*, and *gh*

These consonants do not have direct equivalents in English. The consonant *q* is similar to *k*, but is pronounced further inside the throat. The consonants *x* and *gh* are pronounced from the same position as *k* but in a different manner. The consonant *x* is like the 'ch' sound in 'Bach.' When producing *x*, the back of the tongue does not completely stop airflow, but rather contacts the roof of the mouth lightly so that as air passes between the tongue and the roof of the mouth a scraping sound is produced. The consonant *g̲h̲* is the voiced equivalent of *x*.

Note that the sounds *q*, *x*, and *g̲h̲* only occur in Persian and Arabic loanwords and most Hindi speakers replace these sounds with other ones. For example, *q* is generally replaced with *k*, *x* is replaced with aspirated *kh*, and *g̲h̲* is replaced with unaspirated *g*. In this book we do observe the distinction between these sounds, but it is important to note that many Hindi speakers do not.

It is also important to note that in some speakers' language there is some overlap between the sounds *f* and aspirated *ph* on the one hand, and *z* and *j* on the other. The sounds *f* and *z* are also only found in loanwords. We recommend observing the distinction between *f/ph* and *z/j*, as they exist in English and are also observed by a greater proportion of Hindi speakers, particularly educated Hindi speakers.

Exercise 1

Listen to the recording of these Hindi words and try to replicate the pronunciation yourself.

qānūn *bāqī* *xās* *xair* *g̲h̲alat* *bag̲h̲air*

Note the pronunciation of these words when the sounds *q*, *x*, and *g̲h̲* are replaced with *k*, *kh*, and *g* respectively:

kānūn *bākī* *khās* *khair* *galat* *bagair*

Exercise 2

Now listen to the words in the recording and transcribe them as you hear them pronounced. Check your answers when you are finished.

Lesson 7: Nasalized Vowels, The Sound ṇ, Doubled Consonants, and Word-Final Consonant Clusters

Nasalized Vowels

All of the Hindi vowels have nasalized equivalents as well. Nasalization is indicated in transliteration as a tilde sign (~) above a vowel.

Exercise 1

Listen to the audio and contrast the following pairs of words.

kahā *kahā̃* *cale* *calẽ* *ho* *hõ*

English vowels tend to be nasalized when they occur before a nasal consonant ('n,' 'm,' or 'ng'). To isolate a nasal vowel, begin by pronouncing the word 'on.' Pronounce it slowly so that you can feel your tongue move in slow motion toward the roof of your mouth in order to produce 'n.' Right before your tongue actually makes contact, pause and take note of the quality of the vowel. It should be nasalized. Now try alternately producing this sound and the word 'awe.' After practicing turning on and off nasalization for a few minutes, read the words above and match your pronunciation to the recording.

The Sound *ṇ*

When this sound occurs immediately before another retroflex consonant (*ṭ*, *ṭh*, *ḍ*, or *ḍh*) without any intervening vowel, it is pronounced as a retroflex 'n,' or an 'n'-like sound pronounced from the retroflex position. In other contexts it is pronounced as the nasalized equivalent of the retroflex flap, *ṛ*.

Exercise 2

Listen closely to the pronunciation of the following words, and then reproduce the pronunciation yourself.

bāṇ (*bāṛ̃*) *kāraṇ* (*kāraṛ̃*) *riṇ* (*riṛ̃*) *guṇ* (*guṛ̃*) *aṇḍā* *piṇḍlī*

Doubled Consonants

Doubled consonants are held longer than simple consonants before being released. Consider in English the difference in the pronunciation of the underlined letters in 'He's a natural' and 'He's unnatural.' The 'n' sound in the second example is doubled.

Exercise 3

Listen to the audio and contrast the pairs of examples given.

dilī *dillī* *bacā* *baccā* *pakā* *pakkā*

Now pronounce these words aloud yourself; match your own pronunciation to that of the recording.

Exercise 4

Now listen to the words in the recording and transcribe them as you hear them pronounced. Check your answers when you are finished.

Word-Final Consonant Clusters

Some Sanskrit loanwords end in consonant clusters that at first glance seem difficult to pronounce.

Exercise 5

Listen closely to the pronunciation of the following words, and then reproduce the pronunciation yourself.

tantr *bhasm* *rājy* *praśn* *lakṣy* *mahattv*

Exercise Answers: Sound System and Script, Lessons 1–7

Lesson 1, Exercise 3

jānā	*manānā*	*banī*	*namī*	*nām*
manā	*mānā*	*hāmī*	*ginā*	*sunī*

Lesson 2, Exercise 4

galā	*bavāl*	*rāg*	*jāl*	*sūraj*
sir	*hāl*	*rāl*	*jārī*	*rulānā*

Lesson 2, Exercise 7

lāl	*burā*	*āvāz*	*śer*	*zor*
gorī	*sevā*	*lohā*	*lenā*	*mel*

Lesson 3, Exercise 4

pās	*cār*	*khel*	*bhūlnā*	*phir*	*kār*
ghī	*chūnā*	*jhālar*	*khīr*	*chīlnā*	*calo*

Lesson 4, Exercise 3

tel	*din*	*tīs*	*thā*	*ḍhābā*
ḍākū	*deś*	*dhīre*	*ṭhos*	*ṭamāṭar*

Lesson 5, Exercise 3

sair	*fauj*	*saṛā*	*bail*	*ḍeṛh*
der	*bāṛh*	*bol*	*taur*	*laṛnā*

Lesson 6, Exercise 2

xākī	*faqīr*	*xūn*	*g͟ham*	*bāg͟h*
baqaul	*kelā*	*g͟haur*	*gol*	*xudā*

Lesson 7, Exercise 4

nahī̃	*yahī*	*calū̃*	*izzat*	*mā̃*	*haī̃*
vahā̃	*karo*	*kaccā*	*tājjub*	*abbā*	*hai*

Part II: The Hindi Script

Lesson 8: Introduction to the Hindi Script; The *ka* Series; The Letters *na* and *ma*

Overview

Hindi is written in the Devanāgarī (देवनागरी) script, the most widely used Indian script. The Devanagari script is based on the syllable as the basic unit of sound. One basic feature of Hindi's syllable-based script is that consonants are pronounced with an inherent vowel, *a*.

For example:

स is pronounced *sa*.

ब is pronounced *ba*.

म is pronounced *ma*.

Consonant signs include the inherent vowel except when another vowel sign is added. Other vowel sounds are represented by diacritical marks (called *mātrās*). Note how the diacritical marks below affect the pronunciation of the consonants (for now just try to understand the concept, we will focus on individual diacritical marks later):

सा	बा	मा	सी	बी	मी	सु	बु	मु
sā	*bā*	*mā*	*sī*	*bī*	*mī*	*su*	*bu*	*mu*

The inherent vowel is also dropped in some positions, such as at the end of a word.

For example:

स, *sa*, + ब, *ba*, produces सब, *sab* (not *saba*).
ब, *ba*, + स, *sa*, produces बस, *bas* (not *basa*).
ब, *ba*, + म, *ma*, produces बम, *bam* (not *bama*).

Another important basic feature of the Devanagari script is that there are two types of vowel signs. As explained above, vowels that follow a consonant within a syllable are represented by diacritical marks. Since these diacritics must be added to a consonant sign and they cannot be written independently, they are sometimes called *dependent* vowel signs. Vowels that occur as the initial sound of a syllable are represented by separate *independent* vowel signs.

For example:

अ is the independent vowel sign for *a* (e.g., used when *a* is the first sound of a word).
आ is the independent vowel sign for *ā*.
इ is the independent vowel sign for *i*.

Hindi's script is very closely aligned with Hindi's sound system, so the ability to spell a word generally translates directly to the ability to pronounce it and vice versa. It's generally not necessary to learn irregular spellings as it is in English. Another feature of Hindi's script that facilitates learning it is the systematic ordering of letters, particularly the consonant stops, which are ordered by place of articulation (the part of the vocal tract used to produce the sound) and the manner of articulation (e.g. voiced vs. voiceless, aspirated vs. unaspirated). Here are all of the letters of Hindi's script organized in alphabetical order. The diacritical marks in the second row of vowels are given with the consonant स, *sa*.

Vowels:

अ	आ	इ	ई	उ	ऊ	ऋ*	ए	ऐ	ओ	औ	अं**	अः**
a	*ā*	*i*	*ī*	*u*	*ū*	*ri*	*e*	*ai*	*o*	*au*		
स	सा	सि	सी	सु	सू	सृ	से	सै	सो	सौ	सं	सः
sa	*sā*	*si*	*sī*	*su*	*sū*	*sri*	*se*	*sai*	*so*	*sau*		

*This vowel sign actually represents the consonant *r* followed by a vowel. In Uttar Pradesh, Delhi, and other areas, it is pronounced *ri*. In other regions it is pronounced *ra* or *ru*. We recommend *ri* as the default option.
**These additional diacritical marks are explained below.

Consonants:

क	ख	ग	घ	ङ
ka	*kha*	*ga*	*gha*	*ṅa*[*]
च	छ	ज	झ	ञ
ca	*cha*	*ja*	*jha*	*ña*
ट	ठ	ड	ढ	ण
ṭa	*ṭha*	*ḍa*	*ḍha*	*ṇa*
त	थ	द	ध	न
ta	*tha*	*da*	*dha*	*na*
प	फ	ब	भ	म
pa	*pha*	*ba*	*bha*	*ma*

[*] This represents the sound indicated by the 'n' in words such as 'sing' and 'sink.' While the sound is not uncommon in Hindi, this letter is not very common as there is a much more common alternative to representing this sound. When this letter is pronounced in isolation, it is generally pronounced *aṅga*.

य	र	ल	व	श	ष	स	ह
ya	*ra*	*la*	*va*	*śa*	*ṣa*	*sa*	*ha*

In addition, the Devanagari script also includes a few rules for combining consonant signs to represent consonant clusters (groups of consonants pronounced without vowels between them) and a few irregular conjunct consonant signs. In the traditional alphabet, or *varṇmālā*, the following three conjunct signs are given the status of letters and listed as the final three letters of the alphabet.

क्ष represents क् + ष; its pronunciation will be covered later.
त्र represents त् + र, *tra*.
ज्ञ represents ज् + ञ; it is pronounced *gya* or *gyã* (rather than *jña*).

The remaining consonant sounds of Hindi that are not listed above are represented by adding a dot under other consonant signs:

ड़	ढ़			
ṛa	*ṛha*			
क़	ख़	ग़	ज़	फ़
qa	*xa*	*g͟ha*	*za*	*fa*

These latter five sounds are found in loanwords from Persian and/or Arabic. While *za* and *fa* can be considered part of standard Hindi, many speakers substitute the non-dotted equivalents for क़, ख़, and ग़. It is also not uncommon for some speakers to substitute the non-dotted equivalents for ज़ and फ़, though we recommend that students always maintain the distinction between these sounds.

Hindi's script also includes a few other diacritical marks (illustrated with अ, *a*, and स, *sa*):

अं / सं (*bindī*) represents various nasal consonants in different contexts. It can also represent nasalization (of a vowel) in some contexts.

अँ / सँ (*candrbindu*) is used to represent nasalization in some contexts.

अः / सः (*visarg*) is found in a few Sanskrit loanwords. It is silent in some contexts and pronounced as *h* in others.

स् (*halant*) mutes a consonant sign's inherent vowel, *a*. This sign is relatively uncommon and is only found in a few Sanskrit loanwords.

In terms of dictionary order, *bindī*, *candrbindu*, and *visarg* occur before vowels without these diacritics. For example, अं comes before अ, सँ comes before स, etc.

Hindi numerals also differ from the numerals used in English (which are also commonly used by Hindi speakers).

०	१	२	३	४	५	६	७	८	९
0	1	2	3	4	5	6	7	8	9

The *ka* Series of Consonants, the *ā mātrā*

The first series of consonants in alphabetical order is the *ka* series. This series consists of five consonants.

क	ख	ग	घ	ङ
ka	*kha*	*ga*	*gha*	*ŋa*

It is important to understand how these letters fit into the alphabet. As mentioned above, all consonant stops are organized systematically by the characteristics of their pronunciation. Stops are consonants that are produced by completely blocking and then releasing airflow in the vocal tract. The stops fit into a 5 x 5 chart in which the rows represent the place of articulation starting with the back of the mouth near the throat and moving forward towards the lips. Each column represents a manner of articulation. All consonants that fit into this chart should be memorized according to their place in the chart.

	Voiceless Unaspirated	Voiceless Aspirated	Voiced Unaspirated	Voiced Aspirated	Nasal Consonant
Velar	क *ka*	ख *kha*	ग *ga*	घ *gha*	ङ *ŋa*
"Palatal"	च *ca*	छ *cha*	ज *ja*	झ *jha*	ञ *ña*
Retroflex	ट *ṭa*	ठ *ṭha*	ड *ḍa*	ढ *ḍha*	ण *ṇa*
Dental	त *ta*	थ *tha*	द *da*	ध *dha*	न *na*
Bilabial	प *pa*	फ *pha*	ब *ba*	भ *bha*	म *ma*

Exercise 1

Practice writing the letters of the *ka* series on a separate sheet of paper. Follow the arrows in the illustrations to write the letters in the suggested stroke order. Pronounce each letter aloud as you write it. Repeat until you are familiar with each letter and the sound it represents.

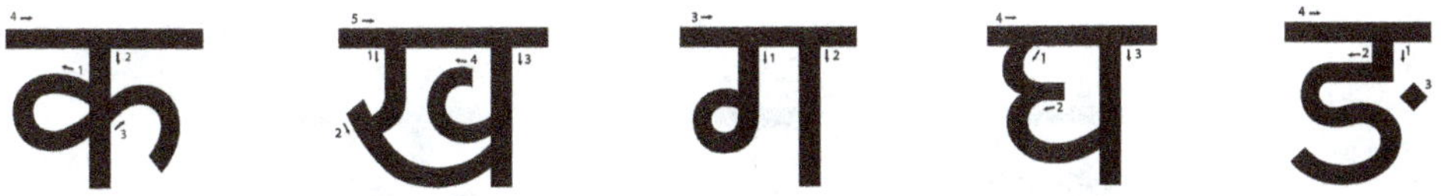

The letter ङ is not very common and is provided here mainly for reference.

The *mātrā* (dependent vowel sign) for the vowel *ā* is written as a vertical line immediately following the consonant it is pronounced after. Practice writing the following syllables containing this *mātrā* and the consonants you have learned already. As always, pronounce each syllable aloud as you write it. Alternate writing each consonant with and without the *mātrā* and repeat until you are familiar with the sound of each syllable.

का	खा	गा	घा
kā	*khā*	*gā*	*ghā*

The *ā mātrā* with a crescent-moon-shaped mark above it is used to represent a similar but rounded vowel found in some English loanwords.

कॉ गॉ

Exercise 2 

Number a blank page 1 to 20. Listen to the audio recording. You will hear various letters pronounced in random order. Write the letters in the order in which you hear them pronounced. Check your answers when finished. The answers are provided at the end of the script introduction (following lesson 16).

The Letters *na, ma,* and *sa*

In this book we will deviate slightly from alphabetical order to introduce a few higher-frequency letters that will allow us to cover the script by using actual words. The sounds *n, m,* and *s* are represented by the following letters:

न	म	स
na	*ma*	*sa*

Exercise 3 

Practice writing the letters *na, ma,* and *sa* on a separate sheet of paper. Follow the arrows in the illustrations to write the letters in the suggested stroke order. Pronounce each letter aloud as you write it. Repeat until you are familiar with each letter and the sound it represents.

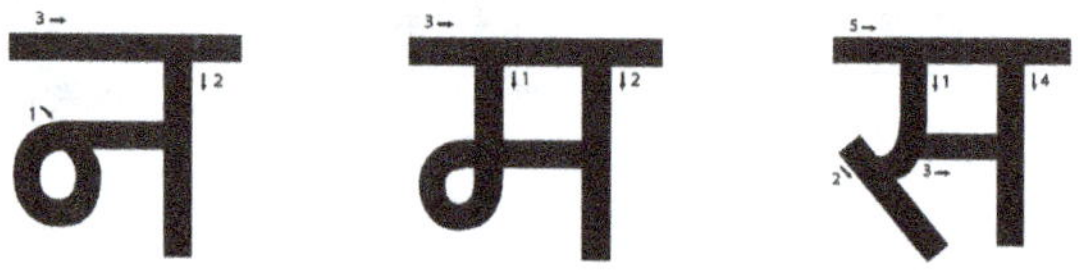

Practice adding the *ā mātrā* to these letters and alternate writing the letters with and without the *mātrā,* pronouncing each syllable aloud as you write it.

ना मा सा

Exercise 4 

Number a blank page 1 to 20. Listen to the audio recording. You will hear various letters pronounced in random order. Write the letters in the order in which you hear them pronounced. Check your answers when finished. The answers are provided at the end of the script introduction.

Exercise 5 

Read the following words aloud. Remember that when a letter representing a consonant sound occurs at the end of the word the inherent vowel *a* is dropped. Check your pronunciation against the transcription given at the end of the script section and match your pronunciation with the audio recording.

का नाम घास काम नाक खाना गाना काना घना साख

Exercise 6 

Listen to the audio recording and write the words exactly as you hear them pronounced. Check your answers when finished.

Lesson 9: The *ca* Series, *i* and *ī mātrās*

Proceeding alphabetically, the series of letters that follows the *ka* series is the *ca* series. The five consonants of this series are:

च	छ	ज	झ	ञ
ca	*cha*	*ja*	*jha*	*ña*

The *mātrās* for the vowels *i* and *ī* are represented as follows (with ज):

जि	जी
ji	*jī*

Note how the short *i mātrā* precedes the consonant in writing. The short *i* vowel is generally pronounced as the ‘i’ in ‘fit,’ but when pronounced as the final sound of an individual syllable Hindi speakers pronounce it as a clipped version of the long vowel *ī*.

Exercise 1

Practice writing the letters of the *ca* series on a separate sheet of paper. Follow the arrows in the illustrations to write the letters in the suggested stroke order. Pronounce each letter aloud as you write it. Repeat until you are familiar with each letter and the sound it represents.

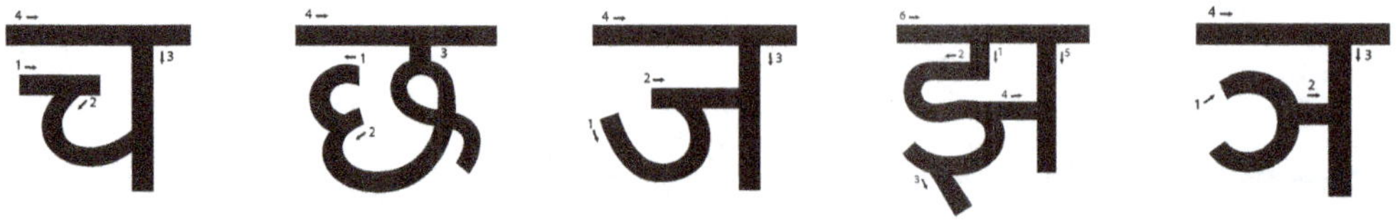

The letter ञ is not very common and is provided here mainly for reference.

After you are comfortable writing the five letters of the च series, practice adding the *ā*, *i*, and *ī* *mātrā*s to them. Pronounce each syllable aloud as you write it.

Exercise 2

Number a blank page 1 to 20. Listen to the audio recording. You will hear a combination of old and newly introduced letters pronounced in random order. Write the letters in the order in which you hear them pronounced. Check your answers when finished. The answers are provided at the end of the script introduction (following lesson 16).

Exercise 3

Read the following words aloud. Remember that when a letter representing a consonant sound occurs at the end of the word the inherent vowel *a* is dropped. You will also find in some of the examples that the inherent vowel is dropped inside the word as well. Check your pronunciation against the transcription given at the end of the script section and match your pronunciation with the audio recording.

चीन झाग जग चना जीना किसान सीखना छीनना

Exercise 4

Listen to the audio recording and write the words exactly as you hear them pronounced. Check your answers when finished.

Lesson 10: The Retroflex *ṭa* Series, The Letters *ṛ*, *ṛh*, *l*, *r*

Proceeding in alphabetical order, the series of letters after the *ca* series is the retroflex *ṭa* series.

The five consonants of this series are:

ट	ठ	ड	ढ	ण
ṭa	*ṭha*	*ḍa*	*ḍha*	*ṇa*

Note that the letters ट, *ṭa*, and ड, *ḍa*, are the default letters for representing 't' and 'd' in English loanwords.

The letters ड and ढ with a dot underneath are used to represent the sounds *ṛ* and *ṛh*.

ड़	ढ़
ṛa	*ṛha*

These sounds never occur as the first sound in a word. When these sounds are pronounced in isolation, a short *a*-like sound is generally added before them to aid in pronunciation.

In addition to these letters, we will also deviate slightly from alphabetical order in this lesson to introduce two additional high-frequency letters:

ल	र
la	*ra*

Exercise 1

Practice writing the letters of the *ṭa* series on a separate sheet of paper. Follow the arrows in the illustrations to write the letters in the suggested stroke order. Pronounce each letter aloud as you write it. Repeat until you are familiar with each letter and the sound it represents.

Practice writing the letters ड़ and ढ़ on a separate sheet of paper. Pronounce the letters aloud as you write them.

When you are comfortable with these letters, practice writing the letters ल and र as indicated in the illustrations.

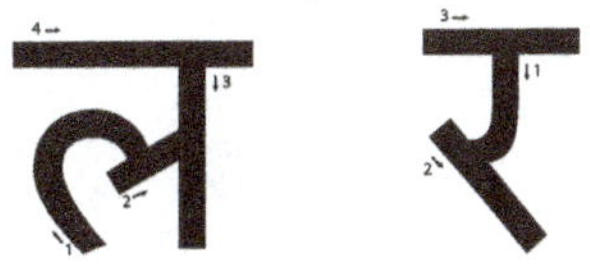

Exercise 2

Number a blank page 1 to 20. Listen to the audio recording. You will hear various letters pronounced in random order. Write the letters in the order in which you hear them pronounced. Check your answers when finished. The answers are provided at the end of the script introduction (following lesson 16).

Exercise 3

Read the following words aloud. Check your pronunciation against the transcription given at the end of the script section and match your pronunciation with the audio recording.

ठग डाक डर कल साड़ी ढाल कण डालना करना मरना

Exercise 4

Listen to the audio recording and write the words exactly as you hear them pronounced. Check your answers when finished.

Exercise 5

Practice writing out the first three rows of the 5 x 5 consonant stop chart in lesson 8. Pronounce each letter aloud as you write it. Repeat until you are able to write out all three rows in the correct order from memory. This exercise should be repeated daily until you comfortably know all the letters. Add new rows of the chart as you learn them.

Lesson 11: The Dental *ta* Series, The *u* and *ū mātrās*, Independent Vowel Signs

The *ta* Series, *u* and *ū mātrās*

The series of letters that follows the retroflex *ṭa* series is the dental *ta* series.

The five consonants of this series are:

त	थ	द	ध	न
ta	*tha*	*da*	*dha*	*na*

Note that the letter थ, *tha*, is the default letter for representing voiceless 'th' (as in 'think') in English loanwords. The letter द, *da* is the default letter for representing voiced 'th' (as in 'this').

The *mātrās* for the vowels *u* and *ī* are represented as follows (with त):

तु	तू
tu	*tū*

The short *u* vowel is generally pronounced as the 'u' in 'put,' but when pronounced as the final sound of an individual syllable Hindi speakers pronounce it as a clipped version of the long vowel *ū*.

Exercise 1 

Practice writing the letters of the *ta* series on a separate sheet of paper. Follow the arrows in the illustrations to write the letters in the suggested stroke order. Pronounce each letter aloud as you write it. Repeat until you are familiar with each letter and the sound it represents.

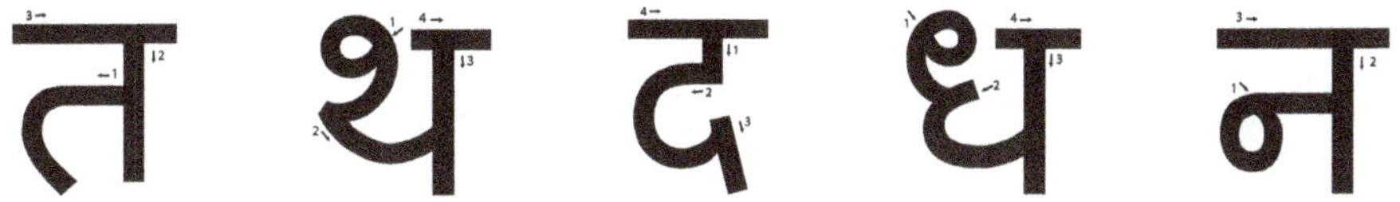

After you are comfortable writing the five letters of the त series, practice adding the *u* and *ū* *mātrās* to them. Pronounce each syllable aloud as you write it.

Exercise 2 

Number a blank page 1 to 20. Listen to the audio recording. You will hear various letters pronounced in random order. Write the letters in the order in which you hear them pronounced. Check your answers when finished. The answers are provided at the end of the script introduction (following lesson 16).

Independent Vowel Signs

As explained earlier, *mātrā* signs are used to indicate non-syllable-initial vowels. There are separate signs for the vowels that do not follow another consonant within a syllable. These are sometimes called independent vowel signs. Here are the independent vowel signs corresponding to the *mātrās* that have already been covered.

अ	आ	इ	ई	उ	ऊ
a	*ā*	*i*	*ī*	*u*	*ū*

Exercise 3

Practice writing the independent vowel signs on a separate sheet of paper. Follow the arrows in the illustrations to write the letters in the suggested stroke order. Pronounce each letter aloud as you write it. Repeat until you are familiar with each letter and the sound it represents.

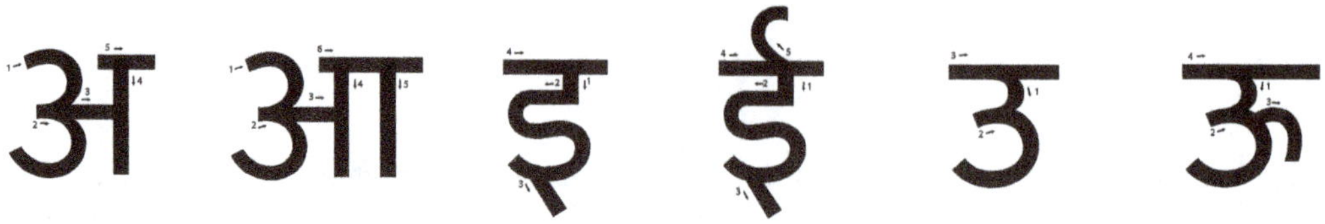

Exercise 4

Number a blank page 1 to 20. Listen to the audio recording. You will hear various letters pronounced in random order. Write the letters in the order in which you hear them pronounced. Check your answers when finished. The answers are provided at the end of the script introduction (following lesson 16).

Exercise 5

Read the following words aloud. Check your pronunciation against the transcription given at the end of the script section and match your pronunciation with the audio recording.

दाल तिल धूम तुम थूक अदा आधा ईसा उस ऊन इधर असर

Exercise 6

Listen to the audio recording and write the words exactly as you hear them pronounced. Check your answers when finished.

Lesson 12: The *pa* Series, The Vowels *ri, e, ai, o,* and *au*

The *pa* Series

Continuing in alphabetical order, the series of letters that follows the *ta* series is the *pa* series.

The five consonants of this series are:

प	फ	ब	भ	म
pa	*pha*	*ba*	*bha*	*ma*

Exercise 1

Practice writing the letters of the *pa* series on a separate sheet of paper. Follow the arrows in the illustrations to write the letters in the suggested stroke order. Pronounce each letter aloud as you write it. Repeat until you are familiar with each letter and the sound it represents.

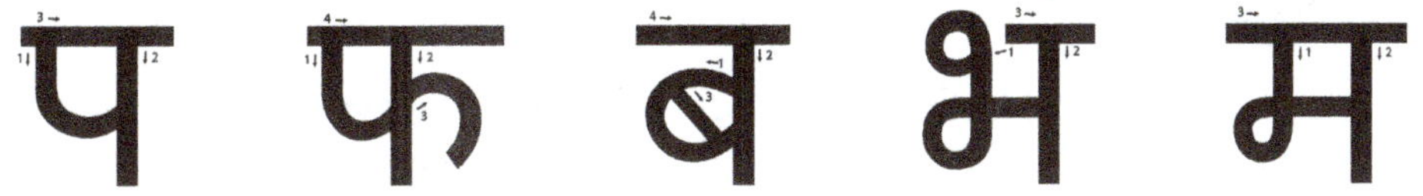

Exercise 2

Number a blank page 1 to 20. Listen to the audio recording. You will hear various letters pronounced in random order. Write the letters in the order in which you hear them pronounced. Check your answers when finished. The answers are provided at the end of the script introduction (following lesson 16).

The Vowels *ri, e, ai, o,* and *au*

The independent vowel signs of the remaining vowels are written as follows:

ऋ	ए	ऐ	ओ	औ
ri	*e*	*ai*	*o*	*au*

The *mātrās* for these vowels are illustrated here with the letter प.

पृ	पे	पै	पो	पौ
pri	*pe*	*pai*	*po*	*pau*

Exercise 3

Practice writing the vowels *ri, e, ai, o,* and *au* on a separate sheet of paper. Follow the arrows in the illustrations to write the letters in the suggested stroke order. Pronounce each letter aloud as you write it. Repeat until you are familiar with each letter and the sound it represents.

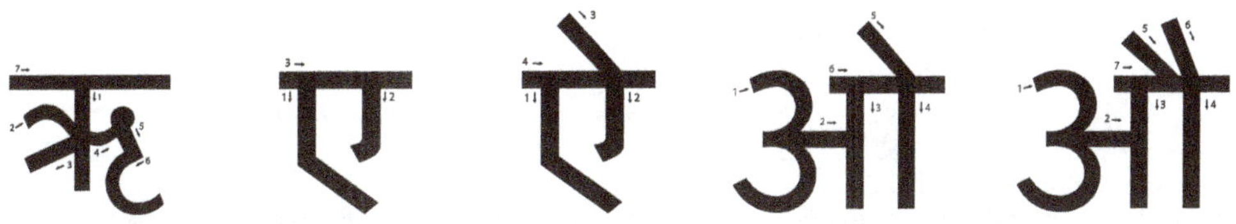

After you are comfortable writing the independent forms of these letters, practice writing their *mātrā* forms by adding them to the consonants that you have learned. Pronounce each syllable aloud as you write it.

Exercise 4

Number a blank page 1 to 20. Listen to the audio recording. You will hear various letters pronounced in random order. Write the letters in the order in which you hear them pronounced. Check your answers when finished. The answers are provided at the end of the script introduction (following lesson 16).

Exercise 5

Read the following words aloud. Check your pronunciation against the transcription given at the end of the script section and match your pronunciation with the audio recording.

पेट देर चैन मृत बैठो बोली ऋण एक और ओस ऐसा जाओ

Exercise 6

Listen to the audio recording and write the words exactly as you hear them pronounced. Check your answers when finished.

Exercise 7

Practice writing out the entire 5 x 5 consonant stop chart in lesson 8. Pronounce each letter aloud as you write it. Repeat until you are able to write out the entire chart in the correct order from memory. Repeat this exercise daily until you comfortably know all the letters.

Lesson 13: The Remaining Letters

The remaining letters of the alphabet are:

य	व	श	ष	ह
ya	*va*	*śa*	*ṣa*	*ha*

The letter ष is generally pronounced identically to श. Historically it represented a 'sh' sound pronounced from the retroflex position.

As mentioned in the overview of the script, the sounds *q*, *x*, *gh*, *z*, and *f* are represented by placing a dot under other letters.

क़	ख़	ग़	ज़	फ़
qa	*xa*	*gha*	*za*	*fa*

Exercise 1

Practice writing the letters introduced above on a separate sheet of paper. Follow the arrows in the illustrations to write the letters *ya*, *śa*, *ṣa*, and *ha* in the suggested stroke order. The other letters can be written by adding a dot under the letters क, ख, ग, ज, and फ, which have already been introduced. Pronounce each letter aloud as you write it. Repeat until you are familiar with each letter and the sound it represents.

Exercise 2

Number a blank page 1 to 20. Listen to the audio recording. You will hear various letters pronounced in random order. Write the letters in the order in which you hear them pronounced. You can assume in this exercise that any 'sh' sound you hear is श. Check your answers when finished. The answers are provided at the end of the script introduction (following lesson 16).

Exercise 3

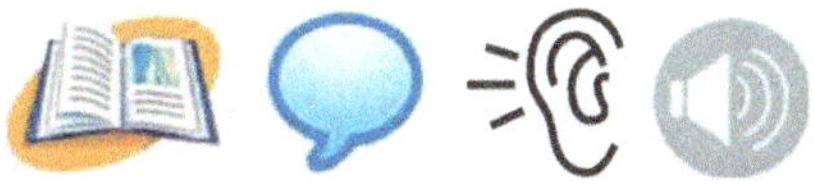

Read the following words aloud. Check your pronunciation against the transcription given at the end of the script section and match your pronunciation with the audio recording.

ये   वन   शेर   हाथ   भाषा   फ़िज़ा   ग़ायब   लायक़   शेष   आइये

Exercise 4

Listen to the audio recording and write the words exactly as you hear them pronounced. Check your answers when finished. Of the two letters that represent the 'sh' sound, श is more common. In this activity you can assume that any 'sh' sound you hear will be written with श.

Lesson 14: Introduction to Conjunct Consonants; *bindī* and *candrbindu*

Deletion of Inherent *a* and the Sign *halant*

As seen earlier, the inherent vowel *a* is deleted when it occurs at the end of a word.

सात	चीन	पैर
sāt	*cīn*	*pair*
(not *sāta*)	(not *cīna*)	(not *paira*)

As also seen in a few examples, the inherent *a* vowel is deleted within words in some positions.

रखना	करना	बचपन
rakhnā	*karnā*	*bacpan*
(not *rakhanā*)	(not *karanā*)	(not *bacapan*)

The rules for the deletion of the inherent vowel *a* are best learned intuitively through exposure to several examples.

In addition to inherent *a* being deleted by virtue of position within a word, it is also possible to mute the inherent *a* vowel manually using the sign *halant*.

क	क्	म	म्	स	स्
ka	*k*	*ma*	*m*	*sa*	*s*

Consonants that have had their inherent *a* vowel muted are referred to using the word आधा, *ādhā*, 'half.'

क्	→	*ādhā ka*, 'half क'
म्	→	*ādhā ma*, 'half म'

Conjunct Consonants: Introduction

Another important feature of Hindi's script is that a half consonant generally joins with the consonant that follows to produce a conjunct consonant.

For example:

स् + त = स्त *s* + *ta* = *sta*

ख़् + व = ख़्व *x* + *va* = *xva*

प् + य = प्य *p* + *ya* = *pya*

The three examples above illustrate the most general pattern for forming conjunct consonants. This pattern applies to consonants that are written with a vertical line on their right side. These consonants are:

ख, ग, घ, च, ज, झ, ञ, ण, त, थ, ध, न,
प, ब, भ, म, य, ल, व, श, ष, स

In most cases these can be linked with the consonant that follows by simply deleting the vertical line on the right side and joining the remaining portion of the letter with the second consonant.

स्वाद → (स् + वाद)
svād → (*s* + *vād*)

ग्लानि → (ग् + लानि)
glāni → (*g* + *lāni*)

प्यास → (प् + यास)
pyās → (*p* + *yās*)

हिन्दी → (हिन् + दी)
hindī → (*hin* + *dī*)

As explained in the introduction to the sound system, Hindi also contains doubled consonants. These are represented by merely repeating the consonant letter.

बच्चा	लज्जा	पन्ना
baccā	*lajjā*	*pannā*

Doubled त takes an irregular form, त्त.

कुत्ता	पत्ती	सत्ता
kuttā	*pattī*	*sattā*

Aspirated consonants cannot be doubled, since the consonant must be released before aspiration can be produced. However, pairings such as the following are common in which an unaspirated consonant is conjoined with the corresponding aspirated consonant:

अच्छा	पत्थर	बग्घी
acchā	*patthar*	*bagghī*

Exercise 1

Take the words apart into their constituent letters and syllables. Use *halant* to indicate a half consonant. Pronounce the words aloud and compare your pronunciation with the recording.

Example:

ग्यारह = ग् या र ह

स्थल प्यार ख़्याल गुस्सा बिल्ली कश्ती पत्ता अग्नि

Exercise 2

Put the syllables and letters together to form words. Put letters muted with *halant* into conjuncts. Compare your words with answers given at the end of the script section and compare your pronunciation with the recording.

Example:

अ ब् बा = अब्बा

प् या ली

ठ प् पा

छ ज् जा

ध् या न

म स् त

ह त् या

व् य स् त

अ भ् या स

bindī and *candrbindu*

In consonant clusters in which the first member is a nasal consonant (ङ, ञ, ण, न, or म), the nasal consonant can be replaced by a dot, called *bindī,* above the right side of the letter preceding the cluster.

गंगा	=	गङ्गा
पंजाब	=	पञ्जाब
अंडा	=	अण्डा
गंदा	=	गन्दा
लंबा	=	लम्बा

Using *bindī* to represent clusters beginning with ङ, ञ, ण, न, and म is both the easiest and the most common method. When learning new words that are written with *bindī*, keep the 5 x 5 consonant stop chart in mind; *bindī* represents the nasal consonant of the same row as whatever consonant follows. For example, if *bindī* is followed by क, ख, ग, or घ, it represents ङ; if *bindī* is followed by ट, ठ, ड, or ढ, it represents ण; if *bindī* is followed by प, फ, ब, or भ, it represents म; *bindī* represents the nasal consonant corresponding to whatever consonant follows.

Note that up to this point we have been using different transliterations for each of the nasal consonants. Hereafter we will use *m* to represent म् and *n* to represent all of the remaining nasal consonants when indicated by *bindī*.

The versatile *bindī* is also used to represent nasalization of vowels in some contexts. More specifically, *bindī* is appropriate with vowel signs in which a portion of the sign extends above the horizontal top line. These signs include the independent signs ई, ऐ, ओ, and औ and the *mātrās* (illustrated here with क) कि, की, के, कै, को, and कौ.

मैं	चलें	हों
maĩ	*calẽ*	*hõ*

Note that when *bindī* occurs with these vowels in the middle of a word, it is ambiguous in terms of whether it represents a nasal consonant or nasalization of the vowel.

बैंगन नींद

It is therefore important to read the transliteration and note what *bindī* represents when learning such words.

For vowel signs that have no portion that extends above the horizontal top line, a separate sign is used to represent nasalization. The sign is called *candrbindu*, or 'moon and dot.' The signs that take *candrbindu* include the independent signs अ, आ, इ, उ, ऊ, and ए, the inherent vowel *a*, and the *mātrās* (illustrated here with क) का, कु, and कू. Nasalization with the vowel ऋ is either extremely uncommon or nonexistent.

हँसना	दाँत	आँख	ऊँचा	हूँ
hãsnā	*dā̃t*	*ā̃kh*	*ū̃cā*	*hū̃*

The distinction between *bindī* and *candrbindu* is not always observed, particularly in modern internet-based texts, in which *bindī* is often used for all nasalized vowels. We recommend that students learn the distinction between the two, but be prepared to encounter *bindī* in both environments in authentic written language.

Exercise 3

For each word write the letter that *bindī* represents. Practice pronouncing the words and compare your pronunciation with the audio recording.

Example:

अंकल = *bindī* represents ङ् (*ŋ*)

बंद   पूंजी   गुंडा   चंदा   बिंब   अंत   घंटा   अंक

Exercise 4

Listen to the audio recording and write the words as you hear them pronounced. Use *bindī* or *candrbindu* where appropriate. Check your answers when finished.

Lesson 15: Conjuncts with क, द, फ़, र, श, and ह; Stacked Conjuncts

क and फ़

The letters क and फ़ both have a hook as their right-most portion. When these are the first member of a compound, the hook becomes clipped and then joins with the letter that follows:

क्या	शक्ल	वक़्त	हुक्म	हफ़्ता	लफ़्ज़
kyā	*śakl*	*vaqt*	*hukm*	*haftā*	*lafz*

As can be seen in the examples above, in most cases dotted letters and their undotted letters behave identically as conjuncts.

The combination क् + त has an alternative form: क्त , for example, शक्ति, *śakti*, 'power.'

Stacked Conjuncts

Some conjuncts are formed by stacking the constituent letters. The consonant that is pronounced first is placed on top.

छुट्टी	चिट्ठी	विद्वान
chuṭṭī	*ciṭṭhī*	*vidvān*

Conjuncts with द

The letter द, which is generally stacked with the following consonant, takes irregular forms in some conjuncts.

मुद्दा	विद्या	उद्भव	पद्धति
muddā	*vidyā*	*udbhav*	*paddhati*

Note that द also takes an irregular form with the *ri mātrā.*

दृश्य	दृष्टि
driśy	*driṣṭi*

Conjuncts with र

Both conjuncts beginning with and ending with र are irregular. When र is the first member of the conjunct, it takes the form of a hook above the second member.

शर्त	गर्व	पूर्ण	कर्म	फ़र्क़
śart	*garv*	*pūrṇ*	*karm*	*farq*

Note the placement of the hook when the second member is followed by a *mātrā* sign.

निर्दोष	कर्ता	भर्ती	ढर्रा
nirdoṣ	*kartā*	*bhartī*	*ḍharrā*

When र is the second member, it takes the form of a small diagonal line attached to the bottom left of the first member.

व्रत	ग्रस्त	प्राण	मुद्रा
vrat	*grast*	*prāṇ*	*mudrā*

The diagonal line has a small extension to the right side with some letters such as ट, ड.

ट्रैफ़िक ड्रामा

ṭraifik *ḍrāmā*

The short *u* and long *ū mātrā*s take irregular forms when added to र.

रुख़ रूप

rux *rūp*

Conjuncts with श

When श is the first member of a conjunct, it sometimes takes as special form. Note the form it takes with र, च, and न in the following examples.

मिश्रित आश्चर्य प्रश्न

miśrit *āścary* *praśn*

श forms conjuncts with other consonants the regular way.

मुश्किल कश्ती अवश्य

muśkil *kaśtī* *avaśy*

Conjuncts with ह

In conjuncts beginning with ह, the second member of the conjunct is sometimes placed inside the hook on the right side of ह.

ह्रास

hrās

Note that ह also takes an irregular form with the *ri mātrā*.

हृदय
hriday

Exercise 1

Take the words apart into their constituent letters and syllables. Use *halant* to indicate a half consonant. Pronounce the words aloud and compare your pronunciation with the recording.

Example:

पट्टा = प ट् टा

प्रिय खट्टा उद्यान निर्देश क्रम उद्देश्य प्रचार उद्धार विश्वास प्राप्त

Exercise 2

Put the syllables and letters together to form words. Put letters muted with *halant* into conjuncts. Compare your words with answers given at the end of the script section and compare your pronunciation with the recording.

Example:

क् रू र = क्रूर

प्	र	सा	द
ग	र्	मी	
भ्	र	म	
स	र्	दी	
ऊ	र्	जा	
श्	वे	त	
भ	द्	दा	
ग	ट्	ठी	

Exercise 3

Listen to the audio recording and write the words as you hear them pronounced. Be sure to use the correct form of र. Check your answers when finished.

Lesson 16: Additional Conjuncts and Signs

The signs क्ष, ज्ञ, and त्र

The signs क्ष, ज्ञ, and त्र are traditionally considered the final three letters of the alphabet though they are also conjunct consonants.

क्ष represents क् + ष. When it occurs word initially, it is pronounced like श/ष.

क्षत्रिय	क्षेत्र	क्षमा
kṣatriy	*kṣetr*	*kṣamā*
(pronounced: *śatriy*)	(*śetr*)	(*śamā*)

When क्ष occurs in other positions, it is pronounced as क् + ष (श).

रक्षा	साक्षी	समीक्षा
rakṣā	*sākṣī*	*samīkṣā*

The sign ज्ञ represents ज् + ञ, but it is always pronounced as *gya* (ग्य). Sometimes the vowel following this sign is nasalized as well. Most, if not all, words containing this sign are derived from the Sanskrit root ज्ञा, 'know' (the Sanskrit root and English word 'know' are actually cognates).

विज्ञान	विशेषज्ञ	ज्ञात	संज्ञा
vijñān	*viśeṣajñ*	*jñāt*	*sañjñā*
(pronounced: *vigyān*)	(*viśeṣagy*)	(*gyāt*)	(*saŋgyā*)

The sign त्र represents त् + र, and it is pronounced as the combination of the consonants all the time.

चित्र	त्रिशूल	पत्र
citr	*triśūl*	*patr*

Exercise 1 

Practice writing क्ष, ज्ञ, and त्र on a separate sheet of paper. Follow the arrows in the illustrations to write the letters in the suggested stroke order.

visarg

Another sign found in Sanskrit loanwords is *visarg*, which resembles a colon. *visarg* is silent in the middle of a word and pronounced as a light *h* at the end of a word.

दुःख निःसंदेह प्रायः प्रातः

This sign is relatively uncommon.

pūrṇ virām

The sign *pūrṇ virām* is used to mark a full stop in a sentence. It corresponds to the period in English. The English period is also commonly used, particularly in modern internet texts.

मेरा नाम राज है। मैं विद्यार्थी हूँ।

As in English, the question mark is used to indicate a question.

तुम्हारा नाम क्या है?

Exercise 2 

Practice reading the following words aloud. Compare your pronunciation with the audio recording.

क्षण कक्षा ज्ञान मात्रा क्षितिज शिक्षा पुत्र आज्ञा

Answer Key

Lesson 8, Exercise 2:

1. ख	2. ग	3. का	4. घ	5. ग	6. ख	7. क	8. ग	9. घ	10. ख
11. घ	12. ख	13. क	14. ग	15. क	16. घ	17. ग	18. क	19. ख	20. ग

Lesson 8, Exercise 4:

1. स	2. म	3. न	4. स	5. क	6. ख	7. म	8. न	9. ग	10. न
11. घ	12. म	13. ख	14. ग	15. स	16. ग	17. क	18. म	19. न	20. म

Lesson 8, Exercise 5:

kā *nām* *ghās* *kām* *nāk* *khānā* *gānā* *kānā* *ghanā* *sākh*

Lesson 8, Exercise 6:

नाग मन साग नम गाम कम नस खान कान माघ

Lesson 9, Exercise 2:

1. च	2. ज	3. छ	4. झ	5. छ	6. च	7. ज	8. झ	9. ज	10. च
11. न	12. म	13. स	14. क	15. ख	16. क	17. च	18. झ	19. घ	20. म

Lesson 9, Exercise 3:

cīn *jhāg* *jag* *canā* *jīnā* *kisān* *sīkhnā* *chīnnā*

Lesson 9, Exercise 4:

जा की छाना खीजना चीनी सिखाना किसी नीम

Lesson 10, Exercise 2:

1. ट	2. ड	3. ड़	4. ठ	5. ढ	6. ढ़	7. ल	8. र	9. ट	10. ल
11. ड	12. ढ	13. ल	14. र	15. ढ	16. ट	17. स	18. ढ	19. ड	20. ट

Lesson 10, Exercise 3:

ṭhag *ḍāk* *ḍar* *kal* *sāṛī* *ḍhāl* *kaṇ* *ḍālnā* *karnā* *marnā*

Lesson 10, Exercise 4:

राल नारी ठीक डाल लाख रीढ़ ढीली लाठी रटना ठिकाना

Lesson 11, Exercise 2:

1. द 2. त 3. थ 4. ध 5. न 6. त 7. द 8. थ 9. त 10. द
11. ट 12. थ 13. द 14. ध 15. ढ 16. द 17. थ 18. ठ 19. म 20. स

Lesson 11, Exercise 4:

1. अ 2. आ 3. इ 4. ऊ 5. आ 6. इ 7. अ 8. उ 9. ई 10. ऊ
11. ई 12. आ 13. अ 14. ऊ 15. इ 16. उ 17. ई 18. आ 19. अ 20. आ

Lesson 11, Exercise 6:

आज तार धूल इस ऊख दिल थका अमर ईद साथ

Lesson 12, Exercise 2:

1. फ 2. भ 3. ब 4. फ 5. प 6. म 7. न 8. क 9. भ 10. झ
11. द 12. ब 13. प 14. भ 15. फ 16. त 17. स 18. म 19. ब 20. भ

Lesson 12, Exercise 4:

1. ऋ 2. ए 3. ऐ 4. ओ 5. आ 6. औ 7. अ 8. ई 9. ए 10. औ
11. ओ 12. ऐ 13. ऊ 14. ए 15. ऋ 16. अ 17. इ 18. ए 19. ओ 20. ऐ

Lesson 12, Exercise 5:

peṭ *der* *cain* *mrit* *baiṭho* *bolī* *riṇ* *ek* *aur* *os* *aisā* *jāo*

Lesson 12, Exercise 6:

दौर मेज़ पौन ओला ऐब पैसे भैस बैरा मेला फैला

Lesson 13, Exercise 2:

1. य	2. र	3. ल	4. व	5. श	6. स	7. ह	8. व	9. ह	10. श
11. य	12. म	13. स	14. ब	15. व	16. ह	17. ल	18. य	19. र	20. श

Lesson 13, Exercise 3:

ye van śer hāth bhāṣā fizā g͟hāyab lāyaq śeṣ āiye

Lesson 13, Exercise 4:

साया हवा ख़ास हार है ग़ालिब वार शाम

Lesson 14, Exercise 1:

स्थल	=	स्	थ	ल
प्यार	=	प्	या	र
ख़्याल	=	ख़्	या	ल
गुस्सा	=	गु	स्	सा
बिल्ली	=	बि	ल्	ली
कश्ती	=	क	श्	ती
पत्ता	=	प	त्	ता
अग्नि	=	अ	ग्	नि

Lesson 14, Exercise 2:

प्याली ठप्पा छज्जा ध्यान मस्त हत्या व्यस्त अभ्यास

Lesson 14, Exercise 4:

हैं चलूँ मेज़ें थीं दें हाँ दोनों लाऊँ

Lesson 15, Exercise 1:

प्	रि	य		
ख	ट्	टा		
उ	द्	या	न	
नि	र्	दे	श	
क्	र	म		
उ	द्	दे	श्	य
प्	र	चा	र	
उ	द्	धा	र	
वि	श्	वा	स	
प्	रा	प्	त	

Lesson 15, Exercise 2:

प्रसाद गर्मी भ्रम सर्दी ऊर्जा श्वेत भद्दा गड्डी

Lesson 15, Exercise 3:

रूस रुको प्रेम मर्द अर्जित ग्राम श्राप कद्दू

Unit 1 Me and My School

In this unit you will learn the following skills:

- Introducing yourself in a culturally appropriate manner.
- Sharing basic information about yourself and seeking information about others.
- Identifying and counting items in the classroom.
- Describing classroom items.
- Giving commands and making requests.

In addition, you will learn commonly used classroom phrases as well as various phrases related to greetings and etiquette.

1

Introductions

In this chapter you will learn how to introduce yourself to new people as well as how to greet acquaintences. You will also learn common etiquette phrases and basic language for classroom survival.

Meeting Somebody New

There are many ways of greeting people in Hindi. The following dialogue presents some typical phrases that people use when introducing themselves and greeting each other.

Exercise 1

Listen to the dialogue of two people meeting and greeting each other.

Note to Student: Throughout the textbook we provide transcripts of listening activities, but it is important to listen to the audio recordings *before* reading the transcripts. This practice will allow you get the full benefit of listening practice. Listening activity transcripts are all enclosed within shaded boxes so they can easily be recognized.

प्रिया	नमस्ते।
रोहन	नमस्ते।
प्रिया	आपका नाम क्या है?
रोहन	मेरा नाम रोहन है। आपका नाम क्या है?
प्रिया	मेरा नाम प्रिया है।
रोहन	आपसे मिलकर ख़ुशी हुई।
प्रिया	मुझे भी।
	...
रोहन	अच्छा प्रिया, फिर मिलेंगे।
प्रिया	ठीक है। नमस्ते।
रोहन	नमस्ते।

Priya	*namaste.*	Hello
Rohan	*namaste.*	Hello.
Priya	*āp kā nām kyā hai?*	What's your name?
Rohan	*merā nām rohan hai. āp kā nām kyā hai?*	My name is Rohan. What's your name?
Priya	*merā nām priyā hai.*	My name is Priya.
Rohan	*āp se milkar xuśī huī.*	Pleased to meet you.
Priya	*mujhe bhī.*	Me too.
	...	...
Rohan	*acchā, priyā, phir milẽge.*	Alright, Priya. See you later.
Priya	*ṭhīk hai. namaste.*	OK. Goodbye.
Rohan	*namaste.*	Goodbye.

Exercise 2

Using the model above, introduce yourself to your classmates and find out their names. Here are some useful sentences that you can use.

नमस्ते	*namaste*	Hello, Goodbye. (a common respectful way of both greeting and saying goodbye)
मेरा नाम ... है।	*merā nām...hai.*	My name is...
आपका नाम क्या है?	*āp kā nām kyā hai?*	What is your name?
आपसे मिलकर ख़ुशी हुई।	*āp se milkar xuśī huī.*	Pleased to meet you.*
मुझे भी।	*mujhe bhī.*	Me too.**
अच्छा	*acchā*	Alright, OK
फिर मिलेंगे	*phir milẽge*	See you later. We'll meet again.
ठीक है	*ṭhīk hai*	OK

*The literal word-by-word translation is, "Having met you happiness happened (to me)."
**Literally, "To me too."

In addition to Hindi *namaste*, it's also useful to know some typical Urdu expressions for meeting and greeting.

आदाब	*ādāb*	Hello. (a secular Urdu greeting)
अस्सलाम अलैकुम	*assalām alaikum*	Peace be upon you. (a common Muslim greeting)
व अलैकुम अस्सलाम	*va alaikum assalām*	And peace be upon you. (the standard response to *assalām alaikum*)
ख़ुदा हाफ़िज़	*xudā hāfiz.*	Goodbye.

Identifying Classroom Items

People and things can be identified using simple sentences such as *This is...* and *That is...* Take a look at the Hindi equivalents of these sentences:

यह ... है।	*ye...hai.**	This is ...
वह ... है।	*vo...hai.*	That is ...

*Note that in this book we represent singular यह in Roman as *ye* and singular वह as *vo*. Plural ये and वे are also represented as *ye* and *vo* following spoken usage.

Though simple, these sentences illustrate an essential difference between the structure of English and Hindi sentences. Whereas English sentences generally follow the pattern SVO, or subject-verb-object, the default Hindi pattern is SOV, or subject-object-verb. In simpler terms, the subject comes first, the verb comes last, and all of the other elements come in between.

Examples:

यह मेज़ है।	*ye mez hai.*	This is a table.
वह दरवाज़ा है।	*vo darvāzā hai.*	That is a door.
यह क़लम है।	*ye qalam hai.*	This is a pen.
वह कुर्सी है।	*vo kursī hai.*	That is a chair.

Vocabulary 1

Note: All Hindi nouns have gender and are either masculine or feminine. We indicate the gender of nouns in all vocabulary lists. Masculine nouns are indicated by 'm,' and feminine nouns by 'f.' Please see chapter 3 for a more detailed discussion of gender in nouns.

School and Classroom

कक्षा	*kakṣā* (f.)	class, classroom
कमरा	*kamrā* (m.)	room (in a building)
क़लम	*qalam* (m., f.)	pen
काग़ज़	*kāghaz* (m.)	paper
कॉपी	*kāpī* (f.)	notepad, blank book for writing
किताब	*kitāb* (f.)	book
कुर्सी	*kursī* (f.)	chair
कूड़ेदान	*kūṛedān* (m.)	trash can
क्लास	*klās* (f.)	class
खिड़की	*khiṛkī* (f.)	window
घड़ी	*ghaṛī* (f.)	clock, watch
चीज़	*cīz* (f.)	thing
छत	*chat* (f.)	ceiling, roof
तस्वीर	*tasvīr* (f.)	picture
दरवाज़ा	*darvāzā* (m.)	door
दीवार	*dīvār* (f.)	wall
नक़्शा	*naqśā* (m.)	map
पेंसिल	*pensil* (f.)	pencil
फ़र्श	*farś* (m.)	floor
मेज़	*mez* (f.)	table, desk
शब्दकोश	*śabdkoś* (m.)	dictionary
स्कूल	*skūl* (m.)	school

Additional Words

यह	*ye*	this, it
वह	*vo*	that, it
है	*hai*	is

Notes:

- *kāpī:* From English 'copy.' English loanwords are frequently used in colloquial Hindi. Some loanwords, such as *kāpī,* differ in meaning from their English source words.
- *ye* and *vo* have multiple meanings. Meanings other than 'this,' 'that,' and 'it' are covered in chapter 2.

Exercise 3

A. Pair up with a classmate. Take turns pointing to and identifying objects in your classroom using complete sentences. How many items can you identify in Hindi?

B. Write the complete sentences that you used to identify the items in your classroom. Pronounce your sentences aloud as you write them.

Asking and Answering Questions

Interrogatives are words that are used to form questions. Most English interrogatives begin with the letter sequence *wh* (e.g., *who, what, when, where, why*). All Hindi interrogatives begin with the letter क, *ka*.

In English, questions are generally expressed not only through the use of interrogatives, but also through a change in word order in which the interrogative is brought to the beginning of the sentence.

What did you eat?

When did they arrive?

Where is everybody?

In Hindi, questions more closely resemble statements. A Hindi interrogative generally occurs in the same position within the question as the word that answers it occurs in the response.

Note the difference in the placement of interrogatives in these Hindi and English sentences. Note also the similarity between Hindi questions and the corresponding responses:

यह क्या है?	*ye kyā hai?*	What is this?
यह किताब है।	*ye kitāb hai.*	It is a book.
वह कौन है?	*vo kaun hai?*	Who is that?
वह मरियम है।	*vo mariyam hai.*	That's Mariyam.

You can begin using these questions immediately to identify items and people in your class.

Vocabulary 2

Interrogatives and Related Words

कहाँ	*kahā̃*	where
कौन	*kaun*	who
क्या	*kyā*	what
यहाँ	*yahā̃*	here, over here
वहाँ	*vahā̃*	there, over there

Notes:

- Many interrogatives occur in sets with related words of similar form and meaning that are not interrogatives. The set *kahā̃, yahā̃, vahā̃* is an example of this.
- Repeating an interrogative gives the sense that the response should take the form of an enumerated list. For example, *kaun-kaun*, 'who (all)'; *kyā-kyā*, 'what (all).' *vahā̃ kaun-kaun hai?* 'Who (all) is over there?'

Exercise 4

A. Pair up with a classmate. Take turns asking each other to identify your other classmates. Respond in complete sentences.

Example:

क. वह कौन है?	A: *vo kaun hai?*
ख. वह पीटर है।	B: *vo pīṭar hai.*

B. Pair up with a classmate. Ask each other to identify the items in your classroom. One partner should point to various items and ask what they are (using *ye* or *vo*) and the other should answer in complete sentences. Take turns asking and answering questions.

Example:

क. यह क्या है?	A: *ye kyā hai?*
ख. यह मेज़ है। वह क्या है?	B: *ye mez hai. vo kyā hai?*
क. वह कुर्सी है।	A: *vo kursī hai...*

C. Take turns with a partner asking questions about the location of various classroom items. The answering partner should point to the objects asked about and answer in complete sentences using *yahā̃* or *vahā̃* as appropriate.

Example:

क. किताब कहाँ है?	A: *kitāb kahā̃ hai?*
ख. किताब यहाँ है। क़लम कहाँ है?	B: *kitāb yahā̃ hai. qalam kahā̃ hai?*
क. क़लम वहाँ है।	A: *qalam vahā̃ hai.*

Exercise 5

Role Play

Role 1: You are a geography teacher in a school in South Asia. One of your students has approached you for help. Answer your student's questions by pointing to the map of South Asia below and identifying the locations you are asked about using complete sentences.

Role 2: You are a child in school in South Asia. You are seeking help from your geography teacher. Ask your teacher where the following places are located:

भारत	पाकिस्तान	श्री लंका	बंग्लादेश	नेपाल	नई दिल्ली	इस्लामाबाद	कोलकाता
bhārat	*pakistān*	*śrī lankā*	*banglādeś*	*nepāl*	*naī dillī*	*islāmābād*	*kolkātā*
कराची	लखनऊ	जयपुर	तिब्बत	चीन	मुंबई	ढाका	चेन्नई
karācī	*lakhnaū*	*jaypur*	*tibbat*	*cīn*	*mumbaī*	*ḍhākā*	*cennaī*

Map of South Asia

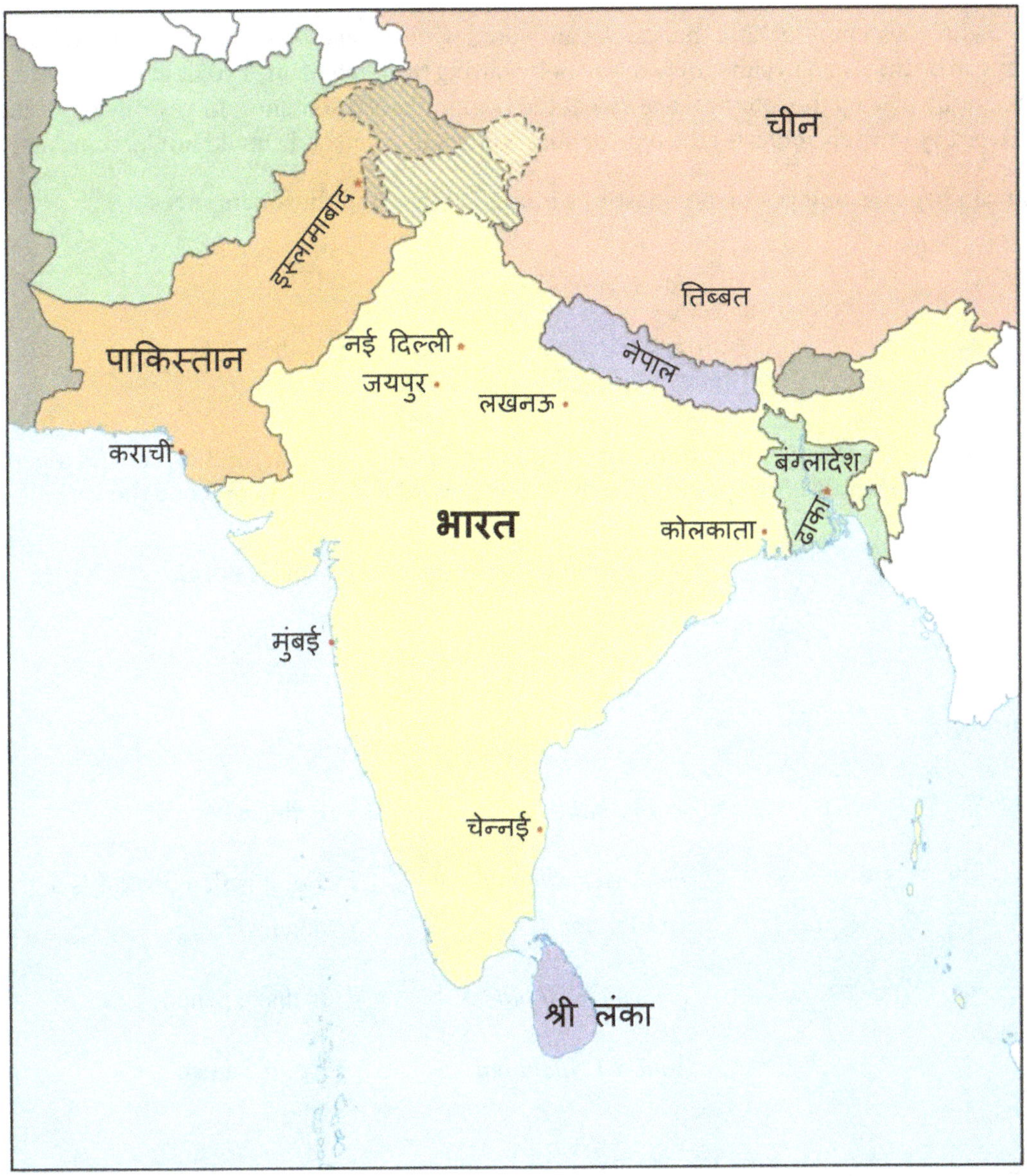

Asking Yes-or-No Questions

Yes-or-no questions are those that can be answered with a single-word response of "yes" or "no." They can be indicated in either of two ways—by raising the pitch of one's voice at the end of a sentence or by placing the interrogative *kyā* at the beginning of a sentence. In yes-or-no questions, the word *kyā* merely indicates the type of question being asked and should not be translated.

You can begin asking yes-or-no questions immediately using these sentences.

क्या यह ... है?	*kyā ye ... hai?*	Is this ...?
क्या वह ... है?	*kyā vo ... hai?*	Is that ...?

The word *nahī̃* expresses negation, corresponding to English *no* as well as *not.* As a general rule, negation words corresponding to the English word *not* directly precede the verb.

यह ... नहीं है।	*ye ... nahī̃ hai.*	This is not ...
नहीं, यह ... है।	*nahī̃, ye ... hai.*	No, this is ...

Examples:

क्या यह किताब है?	*kyā ye kitāb hai?*	Is this a book?
नहीं, यह किताब नहीं है, यह कॉपी है।	*nahī̃, ye kitāb nahī̃ hai, ye kāpī hai.*	No, it isn't a book. It's a notepad.
क्या वह पेंसिल है?	*kyā vo pensil hai?*	Is that a pencil?
नहीं, वह क़लम है।	*nahī̃, vo qalam hai.*	No, it's a pen.

Vocabulary 3

जी	*jī*	yes
जी हाँ	*jī hā̃*	yes
नहीं	*nahī̃*	no; not
हाँ	*hā̃*	yes

Notes:

- The words for *yes* express different degrees of politeness. The word *hā̃* can be regarded as the default word for *yes*; *jī* can also be used to show attentiveness; *jī hā̃* can be used when one wishes to be extra polite.

Exercise 6

Pair up with a classmate. One person should point to objects and ask: *Is this/that a....* The other person should answer in complete sentences. Ask both questions that can be answered with *hā̃* and those that can be answered with *nahī̃*. Take turns playing both roles.

Example:

क. क्या यह मेज़ है?	A: *kyā ye mez hai?*
ख. हाँ, यह मेज़ है / नहीं, यह मेज़ नहीं है, यह कुर्सी है।	B: *hā̃, ye mez hai / nahī̃, ye mez nahī̃ hai. ye kursī hai.*

Greeting an Acquaintance

Earlier in the chapter you learned how to greet and introduce yourself to people you meet for the first time. Listen to these additional dialogues showing ways of greeting people you've met before.

Exercise 7

Listen to the dialogue and refer to the vocabulary list to learn the phrases.

साजिद	नमस्ते, शर्मा जी।
शर्मा	नमस्ते, साजिद साहब। क्या हाल है?
साजिद	मैं ठीक हूँ। आप बताइए।
शर्मा	मैं भी बिल्कुल ठीक हूँ।
साजिद	शर्मा जी, आप कहाँ से हैं?
शर्मा	जी, मैं इलाहाबाद से हूँ। और आप?
साजिद	मैं भोपाल से हूँ।
	...
साजिद	अच्छा शर्मा जी, मैं चलता हूँ।
शर्मा	ठीक है साजिद साहब, फिर मिलेंगे। नमस्कार।
साजिद	जी अच्छा, नमस्कार।

Sajid: Greetings, Mr. Sharma.	*sājid: namaste, śarmā jī.*
Sharma: Greetings, Mr. Sajid. How are you?	*śarmā: namaste sājid sāhab. kyā hāl hai?*
Sajid: I'm good. And you?	*sājid: maĩ ṭhīk hū̃. āp batāie.*
Sharma: I'm also good.	*śarmā: maĩ bhī bilkul ṭhīk hū̃.*
Sajid: Mr. Sharma, where are you from?	*sājid: śarmā jī, āp kahā̃ se haĩ?*
Sharma: I'm from Allahabad. And you?	*śarmā: jī, maĩ ilāhābād se hū̃. aur āp?*
Sajid: I'm from Bhopal.	*sājid: maĩ bhopāl se hū̃.*
…	…
Sajid: Alright, Mr. Sharma. I've got to go.	*sājid: acchā, śarmā jī. maĩ caltā hū̃.*
Sharma: OK, Mr. Sajid. See you later. Goodbye	*śarmā: ṭhīk hai, sājid sāhab, phir milẽge. namaskār.*
Sajid: OK. Goodbye.	*sājid: jī acchā, namaskār.*

Vocabulary 4

Useful Greeting Phrases for Exercise 7

जी	*jī*	an honorific marker appended to names to show respect.
साहब	*sāhab*	an honorific marker appended to male names
क्या हाल है?	*kyā hāl hai?*	How are you? "What is (your) condition?"
मैं ठीक हूँ।	*maĩ ṭhīk hū̃.*	I am fine.
ठीक	*ṭhīk*	fine, OK
बिल्कुल ठीक	*bilkul ṭhīk*	absolutely fine, very well
ठीक-ठाक	*ṭhīk-ṭhāk*	alright, so-so
मैं भी	*maĩ bhī*	I too … (e.g. am also fine.)
आप कैसे / कैसी हैं?	*āp kaise / kaisī haĩ?*	How are you?
आप बताइए।	*āp batāie.*	And you? Literally, "You tell me." (used to ask another person how they are after they have asked you)
आप … हैं।	*āp...haĩ.*	You are...

मैं ... हूँ।	*maĩ...hũ.*	I am...
आप कहाँ से हैं?	*āp kahā̃ se haĩ?*	Where are you from?
मैं ... से हूँ।	*maĩ...se hũ.*	I'm from...
मैं चलता हूँ।	*maĩ caltā hũ.*	I'm going to go. (Similar to "I'm gonna head out.")
नमस्कार।	*namaskār.*	Hello/Goodbye. (Slightly more formal than नमस्ते)

Notes:

- *āp kaise/kaisī haĩ:* Use *kaise* for males and *kaisī* for females.
- *bhī,* 'also,' follows the word that it emphasizes.
- *hāl*: m. condition.

Exercise 8

The dialogue in this audio recording is more informal than the previous one. Listen to the dialogue and refer to vocabulary list no. 5 to learn the phrases.

मरियम	हलो संजना, क्या हाल है?
संजना	ओह, हलो। मैं ठीक हूँ। तुम कैसी हो?
मरियम	मैं भी ठीक हूँ। संजना, वह कौन है?
संजना	वह समीर है।
मरियम	वह कहाँ से है?
संजना	वह इंडिया से है।
	...
संजना	अच्छा, फिर मिलेंगे, बाय।
मरियम	बाय।

Mariyam: Hello, Sanjana. How are you?	*mariyam: halo sanjanā, kyā hāl hai?*
Sanjana: Oh, hello. I'm fine. How are you?	*sanjanā: oh, halo. maĩ ṭhīk hū̃. tum kaisī ho?*
Mariyam: I'm fine too. Sanjana, who is that?	*mariyam: maĩ bhī ṭhīk hū̃. sanjanā, vo kaun hai?*
Sanjana: That's Sameer.	*sanjanā: vo samīr hai.*
Mariyam: Where is he from?	*mariyam: vo kahā̃ se hai?*
Sanjana: He's from India.	*sanjanā: vo inḍiyā se hai.*
...	...
Sanjana: Alright, see you later. Bye.	*sanjanā: acchā, phir milẽge. bāy.*
Mariyam: Bye.	*mariyam: bāy.*

Vocabulary 5

Useful Greeting Phrases for Exercise 8

तुम कैसे / कैसी हो?	*tum kaise / kaisī ho?*	How are you?
तुम ... हो।	*tum...ho.*	You are...

Note:

- *tum* is another word corresponding to English 'you.' The pronouns *tum* and *āp* differ in terms of the level of respect they express toward the addressee. The pronoun *tum* is appropriate for use with friends; *āp* can be used with elders and teachers. Please see chapter 2 for more information on *tum* and *āp*.

Exercise 9

Memorize the sentences given in the dialogues above. When finished, move around your classroom and have short conversations with your classmates. Find out how your classmates are and where they are from. Feel free to use any of the sentences given in the preceding dialogues.

Vocabulary 6

The following phrases and vocabulary items will come in handy in your Hindi classroom. Please use them as much as possible and add to the list any additional words that will help you stay in Hindi.

Classroom Phrases

X को हिन्दी में क्या कहते हैं?	X *ko hindī mẽ kyā kahte haĩ?*	What do you call X in Hindi? (Use when you want the Hindi for an English word.)
X का मतलब क्या है?	X *kā matlab kyā hai?*	What does X mean? (Use when you want the English for a Hindi word.)
बहुत अच्छा।	*bahut acchā.*	Very good.
शाबाश।	*śābāś.*	Bravo! Good job!
ठीक है।	*ṭhīk hai.*	Okay. It's okay.
धन्यवाद, शुक्रिया	*dhanyavād, śukriyā*	Thank you.
कोई सवाल है?	*koī savāl hai?*	Are there any questions?
मेरा एक सवाल है।	*merā ek savāl hai.*	I have a question.
सुनिए।	*sunie.**	Listen! Give me your attention!
पढ़िए।	*paṛhie.**	Read!
लिखिए।	*likhie.**	Write!
बोलिए।	*bolie.**	Speak!
फिर से बोलिए।	*phir se bolie.**	Please repeat ("say it again")!
ज़ोर से बोलिए।	*zor se bolie.**	Speak up! (*zor se*, loudly, forcefully)

खोलिए।	*kholie.**	Open!
बंद कीजिए।	*band kījie.**	Close!
एक मिनट रुकिए।	*ek minaṭ rukie.**	Hold on a minute!
मुझे मालूम नहीं।	*mujhe mālūm nahī̃.*	I don't know.
मुझे याद नहीं।	*mujhe yād nahī̃.*	I don't remember.
मैं नहीं समझा (m.) / समझी (f.)	*maĩ nahī̃ samjhā* (m.) / *samjhī* (f.)	I don't understand ("I didn't understand [what was said]").

*Remember that these words are transliterated and should not be read like English words. *–ie* should be pronounced *–iye* (and it can also be written this way).

Additional Useful Words

अंग्रेज़ी	*angrezī* (f.)	English
उदाहरण, मिसाल	*udāharaṇ* (m.), *misāl* (f.)	example
ग़लत	*ghalat*	wrong, false
जवाब, उत्तर	*javāb, uttar* (m.)	answer
बात	*bāt* (f.)	utterance, a thing that is or has been spoken; a significant thing
मतलब, अर्थ	*matlab, arth* (m.)	meaning
वाक्य	*vāky* (m.)	sentence
शब्द	*śabd* (m.)	word
सवाल, प्रश्न	*savāl, praśn* (m.)	question
सही	*sahī*	correct, true

Notes:

- Hindi contains words from many sources and has many synonyms. In vocabulary lists where multiple Hindi equivalents are given we recommend learning the first word listed for active use and the other equivalents for passive recognition. Eventually all equivalents should be learned for active use.
- *javāb: savāl kā javāb,* the answer to a/the question
- *bāt:* This is one of the most frequently occurring words in Hindi. It occurs in several useful phrases: *merī bāt,* the thing I said; *kyā bāt hai!* What a significant thing! Wow! *kyā bāt hai?* What's the matter? What's the issue? *koī bāt nahī̃,* It's no problem ("It is not a significant thing.")

Exercise 10

Review exercise: Pair up with a classmate. Take turns asking and answering the questions *ye kyā hai, kyā ye...hai,* and *...kahā̃ hai* for all of the items shown in the illustration.

Exercise 11

Review exercise: Pair up with a classmate. Introduce yourself and have a brief conversation in Hindi following the pattern of the dialogue given in exercise 1.

Exercise 12

Review exercise: Pair up with a partner. Assuming you know your partner, have a brief conversation in Hindi following the pattern of the dialogues given in exercise 7.

2

Me and My Classmates

In this chapter you will learn how to exchange basic biographical information with your classmates.

Exchanging Basic Personal Information

Basic information about oneself and others can be expressed with sentences of the form: *I am..., You are..., He is...,* etc. In Hindi as in English there are two closely related structures that are needed to form sentences of this type: personal pronouns, or words such as *I, you, he, she, it,* and the forms of the verb *to be* that accompany them. Take a look at Hindi's personal pronouns below:

Personal Pronouns

	singular	plural
1	मैं *maĩ* I	हम *ham* we
2	तू *tū* you	तुम *tum* you आप *āp* you
3	यह / वह *ye, vo (yah, vah)* he, she, it	ये / वे *ye, vo (ve)* they

Hindi's multiple words for 'you' express varying degrees of respect and intimacy. We will return to these in greater detail later in this chapter. Note also that in casual conversation, singular यह and plural ये are both pronounced *ye* and the pronunciation *vo* is used in place of both singular वह and plural वे. In this book we observe the distinctions in Hindi spelling but assume the pronunciations *ye* and *vo* in all contexts. We will also use the Roman transliterations *ye* and *vo* throughout the book. In more formal styles of the language (such as when reciting poetry), यह and वह can be pronounced as *yah* and *vah*, and वे can be pronounced *ve*. The plural pronoun ये is always pronounced *ye*.

The simple present forms of the verb *honā*, 'to be,' that accompany these pronouns are listed in the table below.

Simple Present Forms of *honā*

person	singular	plural
1	मैं...हूँ *maĩ...hū̃* I am...	हम...हैं *ham...haĩ* We are...
2	तू...है *tū...hai* You are...	तुम...हो *tum...ho* You are... आप ... हैं *āp...haĩ* You are...
3	यह / वह...है *ye, vo...hai* He, she, it is...	ये / वे...हैं *ye, vo...haĩ* They are...

Examples:

मैं अजय हूँ।	*maĩ ajay hū̃.*	I'm Ajay.
मैं अमरीकी हूँ।	*maĩ amrīkī hū̃.*	I'm American.
मैं विद्यार्थी हूँ।	*maĩ vidyārthī hū̃.*	I'm a student.
मैं अध्यापक नहीं हूँ।	*maĩ adhyāpak nahī̃ hū̃.*	I'm not a teacher.
हम विद्यार्थी हैं।	*ham vidyārthī haĩ.*	We are students.
क्या तुम पाकिस्तानी हो?	*kyā tum pākistānī ho?*	Are you Pakistani?
क्या आप शिक्षक हैं?	*kyā āp śikṣak haĩ?*	Are you the instructor?

As seen in the previous chapter, the words *ye* and *vo* correspond to English *this* and *that.* The words *ye* and *vo* have several additional meanings, including the plural meanings: *these* (*ye*) and *those* (*vo*). Compare *ye hai*, 'this is,' and *ye haĩ*, 'these are'; *vo hai*, 'that is,' and *vo haĩ*, 'those are.'

The words *ye* and *vo* also function as third-person personal pronouns, *he, she, it*, and *they*. The words *ye* and *vo* express proximity differences rather than gender differences, so *ye* means *he, she, it, they* (immediately present or close by) and *vo* means *he, she, it, they* (at a distance).

यह कौन है?	*ye kaun hai?*	Who is this/he? (e.g., pointing to a photograph)
वह कौन है?	*vo kaun hai?*	Who is he? (not immediately present)
वह मेरा दोस्त है।	*vo merā dost hai.*	He's my friend.
वे दोनों नेपाली हैं।	*vo donõ nepālī haĩ.*	Both of them are Nepali.

Expressing Respect through Plural Forms

Plural forms are commonly used in Hindi to refer respectfully to individuals. In other words, *vo...haĩ* (plural), 'He/She is...,' is more respectful than *vo...hai* (singular); both plural second-person forms, *āp...haĩ* and *tum...ho*, 'You are...,' are more respectful than the singular form, *tū...hai.*

In the third person ('he/she'), it is generally considered polite to use plural forms when talking about individuals such as elders, teachers, and public figures. For example, plural pronouns and verb forms are generally appropriate when talking about a parent or a peer of one's parents. Using the singular number to describe an elder would often be considered disrespectful. Sentences like the following would therefore be appropriate when describing one's father.

वे डॉक्टर हैं।	*vo ḍākṭar haĩ.*	He is a doctor.
वे भारतीय हैं।	*vo bhāratīy haĩ.*	He is Indian.
वे दिल्ली से हैं।	*vo dillī se haĩ.*	He is from Delhi.

The singular number can be used when talking about people such as friends of equal age and younger—those to whom one does not usually show deference. However, as the plural number is more respectful, it is often used when referring to a person who is immediately present and his or her family members.

In the second person ('you'), Hindi has three degrees of respect. The second person pronouns express different degrees not only of respect, but also of intimacy. The pronoun *tū* is the only second-person pronoun that is singular in number. Both *tum* and *āp* are grammatically plural and hence more respectful.

tū: The singular pronoun *tū* expresses not only the lowest degree of respect but also the highest degree of intimacy. It is commonly used in romantic songs and poetry. We recommend avoiding *tū* altogether as a beginner in order to avoid inadvertently offending anyone.

tum: The plural pronoun *tum* expresses a medium level of both intimacy and respect and is appropriate to use with individuals known on a familiar basis who are either equal or lower in social status. People who fall into this category include friends and casual acquaintances of roughly the same age or younger, and household staff.

āp: The plural pronoun *āp* is the most respectful and least intimate. It should be used with elders, social superiors (teacher, boss, mentor, etc.), and colleagues in a formal work environment. For classroom practice, we suggest using *tum* to address your classmates and *āp* to address your teacher.

आप कहाँ से हैं?	*āp kahā̃ se haĩ?*	Where are you (respectful) from?
क्या आप हिंदुस्तानी हैं?	*kyā āp hindustānī haĩ?*	Are you Indian?
तुम कहाँ से हो?	*tum kahā̃ se ho?*	Where are you (familiar) from?
क्या तुम नेपाली हो?	*kyā tum nepālī ho?*	*Are you Nepali?*
क्या तुम विद्यार्थी हो?	*kyā tum vidyārthī ho?*	*Are you a student?*

In the first person ('I, we'): In certain regions speakers use the first-person plural pronoun, *ham*, 'we,' to refer to themselves as individuals (as 'I'). This does not necessarily signal respect.

हम ठीक हैं।	*ham ṭhīk haĩ.*	I am fine. (regional)

Avoiding ambiguity with plural forms: The practice of using plural pronouns for both individuals and actual groups of people can easily lead to ambiguity. To avoid this ambiguity, speakers often insert an explicitly plural word such as *log* ('people'), *sab* ('all'), or *donõ* ('both') immediately after a plural pronoun when addressing or referring to an actual group of people. When *log* is used in this manner, it can be left untranslated.

तुम लोग कहाँ हो?	*tum log kahā̃ ho?*	Where are you (all)?
क्या आप दोनों भारतीय हैं?	*kyā āp donõ bhāratīy haĩ?*	Are both of you Indian?
वे सब पाकिस्तानी हैं।	*vo sab pākistānī haĩ.*	They are all Pakistani.

Summary

This chapter has presented a significant amount of new information. Here are some pointers to help keep it all in order:

- Memorize the chart of pronouns with accompanying forms of 'to be' and review it regularly.
- Remember *ye* and *vo* have multiple meanings. The meanings of *ye* are: 'this, these; he, she, it, they (proximate),' and those of *vo* are: 'that, those; he, she, it, they (distant).'
- The plural number applied to individuals signals respect.
- There are three respect/intimacy options for 'you.' Singular *tū* is so intimate that it is not used very often. *Tum* is the common word for 'you' to show familiarity, and *āp* is the option that expresses the most respect. **Both *tum* and *āp* are grammatically plural.**

Vocabulary 1

Personal Identifying Information

आदमी	*ādmī* (m.)	man
औरत	*aurat* (f.)	woman
बच्चा	*baccā* (m.)	child (male)
बच्ची	*baccī* (f.)	child (female)
लड़का	*laṛkā* (m.)	boy
लड़की	*laṛkī* (f.)	girl
अध्यापक, अध्यापिका	*adhyāpak* (m.), *adhyāpikā* (f.)	teacher
छात्र, छात्रा	*chātr* (m.), *chātrā* (f.)	student
विद्यार्थी	*vidyārthī* (m./f.)	student
शिक्षक, शिक्षिका	*śikṣak* (m.), *śikṣikā* (f.)	instructor
अफ़ग़ानी	*afghānī*	Afghani
अमरीकी	*amrīkī*	American
ईरानी	*īrānī*	Iranian
चीनी	*cīnī*	Chinese
तिब्बती	*tibbatī*	Tibetan
नेपाली	*nepālī*	Nepali
पाकिस्तानी	*pākistānī*	Pakistani
बंग्लादेशी	*banglādeśī*	Bangladeshi
भारतीय, हिंदुस्तानी	*bhāratīy, hindustānī*	Indian
उदास	*udās*	unhappy, melancholy
ख़ुश	*xuś*	happy
ठीक	*ṭhīk*	fine, OK
दुखी	*dukhī*	unhappy
शादीशुदा	*śādī-śudā*	married

Additional Words

अच्छा	*acchā*	Really! Is that so! (excl.)
और	*aur*	and; else
क्यों	*kyõ*	why
दोनों	*donõ*	both
बहुत	*bahut*	a lot (of); very
बिल्कुल	*bilkul*	completely, absolutely
भी	*bhī*	also
या	*yā*	or
लेकिन, पर	*lekin, par*	but
लोग	*log* (m.pl.)	people
सब	*sab*	all

Notes:

- *acchā:* The basic meaning of *acchā* is 'good,' but it has many additional uses. As an exclamation, it is used to express surprise at something that another person says. It is also used in conversation to acknowledge that one is listening to what the other person is saying.
- *amrīkī:* the word *amrīkan* is also used. Note the difference in pronunciation. Many nationality adjectives are formed by adding *–ī* to the country name. For example, *nepāl, nepālī; hindustān, hindustānī; pākistān, pākistānī.*
- In addition to *chātr/chātrā* and *vidyārthī,* the English word 'student' is also common, especially in informal contexts. English words with an initial combination of 's' plus another consonant are pronounced with an initial short *i* inserted before the *s*. For example, *isṭūḍanṭ.* The short *i* is generally omitted from writing in the Devanagari script.
- *donõ:* The placement of *donõ* differs from that of English 'both.' Compare: 'both Raj and Karan,' vs. *rāj aur karaṇ donõ.*
- *bhāratīy* is pronounced with a clipped short *a* following the *y*.
- Hindi has many words for 'but' and 'however.' These include: *lekin, par, magar, parantu,* and *kintu.*
- *sab: sab log,* 'everybody,' literally means 'all people.'

Exercise 1

G

Read aloud and translate the following sentences into English.

१. मैं अमरीकी हूँ। २. तुम हिंदुस्तानी हो या पाकिस्तानी? ३. मैं हिंदुस्तानी हूँ। मैं दिल्ली से हूँ। ४. अच्छा! मैं भी हिंदुस्तानी हूँ। मैं जयपुर से हूँ। ५. सीमा और निदा दोनों भारतीय हैं। ६. हम सब लोग नेपाली हैं। ७. क्या तुम छात्र हो? ८. मैं छात्र नहीं, अध्यापक हूँ। ९. हम सब छात्र हैं। १०. ये दोनों छात्र अमरीकी हैं। ११. हम कहाँ हैं? १२. यह लड़का कौन है? १३. क्या वह लड़का ईरान से है? १४. नहीं, वह ईरानी नहीं, अफ़ग़ानी है। १५. वे लोग कहाँ हैं? वे यहाँ क्यों नहीं हैं? १६. तुम कौन हो? क्या तुम अमित हो? १७. क्या आप शादीशुदा हैं? हाँ मैं शादीशुदा हूँ। १८. क्या आप लोग ठीक हैं? १९. जी हाँ, हम सब बिल्कुल ठीक हैं। २०. तुम लोग दुखी क्यों हो? हम दुखी नहीं हैं।

Exercise 2

G

Translate into Hindi.

1. Who are you (familiar)?
2. Who is he (respectful)?
3. Who is she (familiar)?
4. Both of us are absolutely fine.
5. All of them are very happy.
6. Are they Indian? Where are they from?
7. Is that woman a teacher?
8. Is everybody OK?

Exercise 3

Pair up with a classmate and take turns asking each other if you are the following things using *kyā tum...ho.* Answer in complete sentences.

ख़ुश	दुखी	छात्र / छात्रा	शादीशुदा	अमरीकी	पाकिस्तानी	भारतीय
xuś	*dukhī*	*chātr / chātrā*	*śādī-śudā*	*amrīkī*	*pākistānī*	*bhāratīy*

Exercise 4

You are attending a professional conference in South Asia. Your classmates will play the role of other attendees. Mingle with your classmates. Introduce yourself and find out who each person is using the appropriate level of respect; ask your classmates questions to find out the information below and note their answers.

Find out from each classmate:

- His/Her name
- Nationality
- From where (which city)?

Exercise 5

Imagine that you have arrived late at the conference and have missed introductions. Your classmates are other attendees. Talk to the person next to you and ask him or her to identify all of the other people in the meeting. Be sure to use the appropriate level of respect.

3

My Classroom

In this chapter you will learn how to describe a physical space, such as your classroom, in terms of the items that it contains.

Listing Items: *There is* and *There are*

In English, sentences of the form *There is...* and *There are...* can be used to state the items present in a space such as a classroom. Hindi does not employ filler words such as *there* or *it* to indicate the presence or existence of an item or person. Sentences of the form *There is a clock in the classroom* and *It's John* should be translated by omitting the words *there* and *it.*

For example, to list the things that are present in a room, you could say:

एक कुर्सी है।	*ek kursī hai.*	There is a chair.
एक मेज़ है।	*ek mez hai.*	There is a table.
एक घड़ी है।	*ek ghaṛī hai.*	There is a clock.
एक कंप्यूटर है।	*ek kampyūṭar hai.*	There is a computer.

The words for *here* (*yahā̃*) and *there* (*vahā̃*) are mainly used for indicating location.

क्या यहाँ कोई कंप्यूटर है?	*kyā yahā̃ koī kampyūṭar hai?*	Is there a computer here?
हाँ, वहाँ एक कंप्यूटर है।	*hā̃, vahā̃ ek kampyūṭar hai.*	Yes, there's a computer over there.

Often it is appropriate to use these words when the word *over* or another adverb is used in English.

मेज़ वहाँ है।	*mez vahā̃ hai.*	The table is over there.
जय यहाँ है।	*jay yahā̃ hai.*	Jay is over here.

Exercise 1

Pair up with a classmate. Take turns asking each other if the items pictured below are present in your classroom. Answer by saying either *Yes, there is a...here*, or *No, there isn't any....*

Note: *koī*, 'any'

क. क्या यहाँ कोई नक़्शा है?	A: *kyā yahā̃ koī naqśā hai?*
ख. हाँ, यहाँ एक नक़्शा है।	B: *hā̃, yahā̃ ek naqśā hai.*
क. क्या कोई तस्वीर है?	A: *kyā koī tasvīr hai?*
ख. नहीं, यहाँ कोई तस्वीर नहीं है।	B: *nahī̃, yahā̃ koī tasvīr nahī̃ hai.*

Discuss these items with your partner:

कुरसी

मेज़

खिड़की

घड़ी

टीवी

तस्वीर

नक़्शा

कॉपी

कंप्यूटर

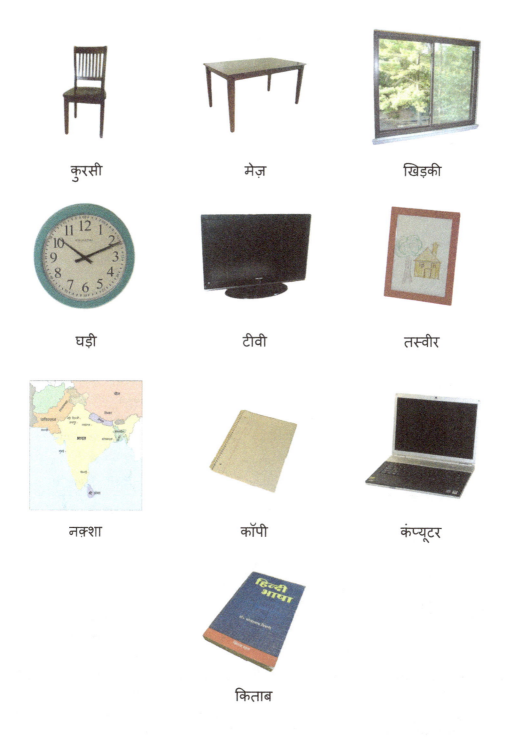

किताब

Noun Types and Forms

In English, forming plural nouns is a relatively straightforward task. The vast majority of nouns are made plural by adding *–s* to the singular form; only a rare noun such as *mouse* or *deer* follows a different pattern. In Hindi, plural forms are slightly more complicated, which makes it necessary to know some basic information about the types of nouns and their properties.

Gender in Nouns

All nouns in Hindi belong to either of two genders—masculine or feminine. The gender of living things is natural in Hindi as in English. People and animals referred to as 'he' in English are masculine and those referred to as 'she' are feminine. Hindi, however, has no neuter ('it') gender. All nouns, including those that name inanimate things, are either masculine or feminine.

It is often possible to predict with reasonable accuracy the gender of a noun by its singular ending. Many, but not all, nouns that end in long *ā* are masculine. Almost all nouns that end in long *ī* are feminine. Nouns that end in most other letters are evenly split between the masculine and feminine gender.

Noun Types and Plural Forms

Based on their singular endings and the patterns that they follow to become plural, masculine and feminine nouns are subdivided into two classes each to produce a total of four noun types.

Noun Forms

	singular	plural
masculine type 1	***-ā*** लड़का, *laṛkā*, 'boy' दरवाज़ा, *darvāzā*, 'door'	***-ā → -e*** लड़के, *laṛke*, 'boys' दरवाज़े, *darvāze*, 'doors'
masculine type 2*	**various endings*** घर, *ghar*, 'house' आदमी, *ādmī*, 'man'	**no change** घर, *ghar*, 'houses' आदमी, *ādmī*, 'men'
feminine type 1**	***-ī*** लड़की, *laṛkī*, 'girl' कुर्सि, *kursī*, 'chair'	***-ī → -iyā̃*** लड़कियाँ, *laṛkiyā̃*, 'girls' कुर्सियाँ, *kursiyā̃*, 'chairs'
feminine type 2***	**various (other than *–ī*)***** मेज़, *mez*, 'table' औरत, *aurat*, 'woman'	**+ *-ẽ*** मेज़ें, *mezẽ*, 'tables' औरतें, *aurtẽ*, 'women'

*Masculine type 2 nouns also include a few nouns that end in *–ā*, for example the word *rājā*, 'king(s)' and some family relation terms (e.g., *pitā*, 'father(s),' *cācā*, 'paternal uncle(s)').

**Also belonging to feminine type 1 nouns are nouns that have singular endings in *–i* as well as those in *–iyā*. All feminine type 1 singular endings are replaced by *–iyā̃* in the plural. Some common examples are: *śakti, śaktiyā̃*, 'power(s),' *vidhi, vidhiyā̃*, 'method(s),' *ciṛiyā, ciṛiyā̃*, 'bird(s),' and *ḍaliyā, ḍaliyā̃*, 'small basket(s).'

***Feminine type 2 nouns also include a sizable number of *ā*-ending nouns. For example, *diśā*, 'direction,' *samāntā*, 'similarity.' The plural forms of these words are formed regularly by adding *–ẽ* to the singular form, e.g., *diśāẽ*, 'directions,' *samāntāẽ*, 'similarities.' Most loanwords from Sanskrit that end in *–ā* are feminine. Note also that long *ū*-ending feminine type 2 nouns shorten the final *ū* before the plural *–ẽ* ending is added, e.g., *ārzū, ārzuẽ*, 'desire(s).'

Vocabulary 1

Common Items from the Classroom and Elsewhere

अलमारी	*almārī* (f.)	wardrobe, closet, cupboard; shelving unit
कंप्यूटर	*kampyūṭar* (m.)	computer
क़ालीन	*qālīn* (f.)	carpet
खाना	*khānā* (m.)	food
गाड़ी	*gāṛī* (f.)	vehicle, car
टीवी	*ṭīvī* (m.)	TV
पंखा	*pankhā* (m.)	fan
पानी	*pānī* (m.)	water
फ़ोन	*fon* (m.)	phone
बोतल	*botal* (f.)	bottle

Additional Words

और	*aur*	and; more, additional
कई	*kaī*	several
कुछ	*kuch*	some, something; a bit (+ adj.)
कोई	*koī*	some, someone; any, anyone
ज़्यादा	*zyādā*	more, (too) many; (+ neg.) not many
बाहर	*bāhar*	outside
सिर्फ़, केवल	*sirf, keval*	only, just

Notes:

- There are a few additional useful rules for predicting the gender of nouns. Most nouns that end in the sound –अत (*-at*) are feminine. For example, *ijāzat*, 'permission'; *sūrat*, 'appearance'; *hālat*, 'condition.' Most nouns that end in –*iś* are also feminine: *bāriś*, 'rain'; *kośiś*, 'effort'; *gunjāiś*, 'scope.' In addition, most nouns of the form *taCCīC* are feminine, in which "C" represents various consonants: *tasvīr*, 'picture'; *taklif*, 'trouble, ailment'; *tahzīb*, 'refinement, culture.'
- *kaī*, meaning 'several,' is often confused with *koī*, meaning 'any.' These words are not related.

- *pānī* is one of the few masculine nouns that ends in *–ī*. A few other common ones are: *ādmī*, 'man,' *dhobī*, 'washerman,' and *ghī*, 'ghee, clarified butter.'
- In addition to *sirf* and *keval*, the word बस, *bas*, can also be used colloquially to mean 'only, just.' In other contexts, this word means 'enough,' or 'stop.'

Cardinal Numbers

Cardinal numbers 1 through 10 are listed here. For the complete list of numbers from 1 to 100, please see appendix 1.

एक	दो	तीन	चार	पाँच	छह	सात	आठ	नौ	दस
१	२	३	४	५	६	७	८	९	१०
1	2	3	4	5	6	7	8	9	10
ek	*do*	*tīn*	*cār*	*pā̃c*	*che*	*sāt*	*āṭh*	*nau*	*das*

Exercise 2 G

A. Indicate whether each word below is singular or plural (or if it could be either) and then translate it.

कमरा, किताबें, खिड़की, नक़्शे, तस्वीरें, क़लम, दीवारें, फ़र्श, अलमारियाँ, कंप्यूटर, कॉपी, दरवाज़ा, छत, मेज़ें

2. Give the plural form of the singular words given above and the singular form of the plural ones.

Exercise 3 G

Read aloud and translate.

१. यहाँ सिर्फ़ चार लोग हैं। २. यहाँ कोई पेंसिल नहीं है, लेकिन पाँच क़लम हैं। ३. क्या यहाँ कोई किताब है? हाँ, तीन किताबें हैं। ४. दो खिड़कियाँ हैं या तीन? ५. सिर्फ़ एक खिड़की है। ६. यहाँ सिर्फ़ ये तीन कुर्सियाँ हैं। ७. वहाँ दो और कुर्सियाँ हैं। ८. यहाँ दो तस्वीरें हैं और दो नक़्शे भी हैं। ९. चार मेज़ें हैं लेकिन सिर्फ़ दो कुर्सियाँ हैं। १०. वहाँ ज़्यादा लोग नहीं हैं। सिर्फ़ एक आदमी और दो औरतें हैं। ११. यहाँ ज़्यादा चीज़ें नहीं हैं। १२. क्या यहाँ कोई छात्र है? हाँ, यहाँ हम सब छात्र हैं।

Exercise 4

Tell your partner about your classroom. How many of the items listed below does it contain, and which of the items listed are not present in your classroom? When listening, note what your partner tells you and then verbally confirm the information by asking him/her yes-or-no questions about the information you recorded.

कुर्सी	मेज़	टीवी	नक़्शा	तस्वीर	किताब
छात्र	लड़का	लड़की	खिड़की	अलमारी	क़लम

Indefinite Words: *koī* and *kuch*

Words such as *koī* and *kuch* are called *indefinite* words. These words express various meanings.

koī and *kuch* as Pronouns

When used independently (as a pronoun), the word *koī* means 'someone, anyone.' The word *kuch* used independently means 'something, anything.'

यहाँ कोई है।	*yahā̃ koī hai.*	Someone is here.
क्या कोई है?	*kyā koī hai?*	Is anyone there?
यहाँ कुछ है।	*yahā̃ kuch hai.*	There is something here.

Generally pronominal *koī* and *kuch* translate as 'someone' and 'something' in positive declarative sentences. They translate as 'anyone' and 'anything' in negative and interrogative sentences.

There are no words in Hindi for 'no one' or 'nothing.' Instead, *koī* and *kuch* are used in negative sentences.

यहाँ कोई नहीं है।	*yahā̃ koī nahī̃ hai.*	No one is here. / There isn't anyone here.
यहाँ कुछ नहीं है।	*yahā̃ kuch nahī̃ hai.*	Nothing is here. / There isn't anything here.

koī and *kuch* as Adjectives

When used as an adjective, *koī* means 'any,' or 'some, a certain...,' and *kuch* means 'some.' The word *koī* is almost always used with singular count nouns and *kuch* is used with plural count nouns and mass nouns (which are grammatically singular). A count noun is a noun that refers to a quantifiable thing (one that can be made plural, e.g., *book, car, television, idea*); a mass noun is a noun that refers to a substance or quality that cannot be counted in discrete units (e.g. *water, air, patience*).

बाहर कोई आदमी है।	*bāhar koī ādmī hai.*	There's a man outside. There's some man outside.
क्या यहाँ कोई डॉक्टर है?	*kyā yahā̃ koī ḍākṭar hai?*	Is there a doctor here?
क्या कोई कुर्सी है?	*kyā koī kursī hai?*	Are there any chairs?*
वहाँ कुछ गाड़ियाँ हैं।	*vahā̃ kuch gāṛiyā̃ haĩ.*	There are some cars over there.
कुछ खाना है।	*kuch khānā hai.*	There is some food.

*Note the difference between the number of the Hindi and English nouns.

Summary of the Uses of *koī* and *kuch*

	pronominal use (used independently)	adjectival use (modifying a noun)
koī	Used to describe human beings. Means "someone, anyone."	Used with singular count nouns. Means "some, a certain; any."
kuch	Used to describe inanimate objects. Means "something, anything."	Used with mass nouns and plural count nouns. Means "some."

Additional Points on Indefinites

There are two additional indefinites. These are:

कहीं	*kahī̃*	somewhere
कभी	*kabhī*	sometime, ever

The word *bhī* following an indefinite gives the sense of 'any... at all.'

कोई भी	*koī bhī*	anyone at all
कुछ भी	*kuch bhī*	anything at all
कहीं भी	*kahī̃ bhī*	anywhere at all
कभी भी	*kabhī bhī*	anytime at all

The word *aur* not only means 'and,' but also 'more, additional.' With an indefinite *aur* gives the sense of 'any...else' or 'some...else.'

और कोई / कोई और	*aur koī / koī aur*	anyone else, someone else
और कुछ / कुछ और	*aur kuch / kuch aur*	anything else, something else
और कहीं / कहीं और	*aur kahī̃ / kahī̃ aur*	anywhere else, somewhere else
और कभी / कभी और	*aur kabhī / kabhī aur*	any other time, some other time

The construction ... *na* ... gives the sense of 'some... or other.'

कोई न कोई	*koī na koī*	someone or other
कुछ न कुछ	*kuch na kuch*	something or other
कहीं न कहीं	*kahī̃ na kahī̃*	somewhere or other
कभी न कभी	*kabhī na kabhī*	some time or other, sooner or later

There are no single-word equivalents of 'for some reason,' 'somehow,' or 'some type of.' Instead, Hindi employs the word *koī* with the words *vajah*, f. and *kāraṇ*, m. 'reason,' and *tarah*, f. 'manner, type.'

किसी वजह से	*kisī** *vajah se*	for some reason
किसी कारण से	*kisī kāraṇ se*	for some reason
किसी तरह से	*kisī tarah (se)*	somehow
किसी तरह का	*kisī tarah kā*	some type of

*The form *kisī* is the oblique form of *koī*. See unit 2 for information on oblique forms.

Exercise 5

G

Read aloud and translate.

१. यहाँ कोई है| २. वहाँ कोई नहीं है| ३. कुछ कुर्सियाँ हैं लेकिन कोई मेज़ नहीं है| ४. क्या वहाँ कोई लड़का है? ५. हाँ, यहाँ कई लड़के हैं| ६. क्या कुछ खाना है? ७. यहाँ कुछ भी नहीं है| ८. यहाँ सिर्फ़ मैं और अमित हैं| और कोई नहीं है| ९. यहाँ कुछ क़लम हैं लेकिन कोई कॉपी नहीं है| १०. क्या कोई छात्र चीनी है?

Exercise 6

Write a paragraph stating the items that are present or not present in your classroom and the number of each item that is present.

4

Describing Classroom Items

In this chapter you will learn how to describe the qualities of classroom items using adjectives such as those that describe size, shape, and color.

Describing Items by Their Qualities: Adjectives

Hindi has two types of adjectives—*variable* and *invariable*.

Variable Adjectives

Variable adjectives, which end in *–ā* in their dictionary form, inflect (change their endings) to reflect agreement with the noun or pronoun that they describe. To say that an adjective *agrees* with a noun is shorthand for saying that the grammatical markers of the adjective—the endings, which indicate gender and number—change to match the properties of the noun that the adjective describes. Take a look at an example with the variable adjective *nīlā*, 'blue.'

नीला दरवाज़ा	***nīlā*** *darvāzā*	a blue door
नीले दरवाज़े	***nīle*** *darvāze*	blue doors
नीली किताब	***nīlī*** *kitāb*	a blue book
नीली किताबें	***nīlī*** *kitābẽ*	blue books

The endings that *nīlā* and other variable adjectives take are these:

Variable Adjective Endings

	singular	plural
masculine	-आ* *-ā*	-ए *-e*
feminine	-ई *-ī*	-ई *-ī*

* Note that throughout the book we use independent vowel signs to represent grammatical endings that begin with a vowel sound. Once the ending is added to the stem it is written as an independent vowel sign, or *mātrā*. For example, the masculine singular form for the adjective 'blue' is नीला, and not नीलआ.

Note that the feminine singular and plural endings are identical. Note also that an adjective agrees with the noun that it describes regardless of the adjective's position within the sentence.

यह बड़ा कमरा है।	*ye baṛā kamrā hai.*	This is a big room.
यह कमरा बड़ा है।	*ye kamrā baṛā hai.*	This room is big.
क्या यह अच्छी किताब है?	*kyā ye acchī kitāb hai?*	Is this a good book?
क्या यह किताब अच्छी है?	*kyā ye kitāb acchī hai?*	Is this book good?

Invariable Adjectives

Invariable adjectives remain the same in all contexts. The adjective *lāl,* 'red,' is an example of an invariable adjective—its form never changes.

लाल दरवाज़ा	*lāl darvāzā*	a red door
लाल दरवाज़े	*lāl darvāze*	red doors
लाल किताब	*lāl kitāb*	a red book
लाल किताबें	*lāl kitābẽ*	red books

Vocabulary 1

General Qualities

अच्छा	*acchā*	good
बुरा	*burā*	bad
ख़राब	*xarāb*	bad, spoiled, in a bad state
नया	*nayā*	new
पुराना	*purānā*	old
सुंदर, ख़ूबसूरत	*sundar, xūbsūrat*	beautiful, handsome
बदसूरत	*badsūrat*	ugly
बढ़िया	*baṛhiyā* (inv.)*	excellent

*The abreviation 'inv.' means 'invariable.'

Physical Characteristics

अण्डाकार	*anḍākār*	oval shaped
आयताकार	*āyatākār*	rectangular
ऊँचा	*ū̃cā*	high
गोल	*gol*	round

Physical Characteristics

चौकोर	*caukor*	square
चौड़ा	*cauṛā*	wide
छोटा	*choṭā*	small
तिकोना	*tikonā*	triangular
नीचा	*nīcā*	low
पतला	*patlā*	thin
बड़ा	*baṛā*	big
भारी	*bhārī*	heavy
मोटा	*moṭā*	thick, fat
लम्बा	*lambā*	long, tall
वज़न	*vazan* (m.)	weight
शक्ल	*śakl* (f.)	appearance; face; shape
हल्का	*halkā*	light

Colors

काला	*kālā*	black
गुलाबी	*gulābī*	pink
नारंगी	*nārangī*	orange
नीला	*nīlā*	blue
पीला	*pīlā*	yellow

बैंगनी	*baĩgnī*	purple
भूरा	*bhūrā*	brown
रंग	*rang* (m.)	color
लाल	*lāl*	red
सफ़ेद	*safed*	white
स्लेटी	*sleṭī*	gray
हरा	*harā*	green

Additional Words

काफ़ी	*kāfī*	quite, rather; enough
ख़ाली	*xālī*	empty
ज़्यादा	*zyādā* (adv.)	more, too much (*zyādā…nahī̃*, not very…)
थोड़ा	*thoṛā*	a little, a bit
बहुत	*bahut*	very, a lot
भी	*bhī*	also, too, either; even (+ negation)
ही	*hī*	only

Notes:

- *nayā*: in the forms other than *nayā*, the य can optionally be deleted: नये/नए, नयी/नई.
- *baṛhiyā*: There are a few adjectival endings that are typically invariable. These include: -इया, *–iyā*, -ईदा, *–īdā*, and -इंदा, *–indā*. Some examples: *ghaṭiyā*, low, inferior; *pasandīdā*, favorite; *sanjīdā*, serious; *zindā*, alive; *cunindā*, choice, select.
- Use caution when learning adjectives such as *bhārī*, which end in *–ī*. A good general practice is to always learn words in their dictionary form. Adjectives that end in *–ā* in the dictionary form should be assumed to be variable unless otherwise noted.
- *bhī* and *hī* always follow the word they emphasize. *bhī* adds inclusive emphasis. For example: *maĩ bhī vidyārthī hū̃*, 'I (in addition to others) am a student.' *maĩ vidyārthī bhī hū̃*, 'I am a student too' (in addition to being other things). The word *hī* adds exclusive emphasis. For example: *maĩ hī vidyārthī hū̃*, 'Only I am a student.' *maĩ vidyārthī hī hū̃*, 'A student is exactly what I am.'

Exercise 1 G

Read aloud and translate.

१. वह मेज़ ज़्यादा भारी नहीं है| वह बहुत हल्की है| २. क्या वह किताब नई है? ३. नहीं, वह बहुत पुरानी है| ४. यह दरवाज़ा काफ़ी ऊँचा है| ५. वह खिड़की कुछ छोटी है| ६. वह बहुत अच्छा छात्र है| ७. वे हरी किताबें कहाँ हैं? ८. यहाँ पाँच लाल कॉपियाँ हैं| ९. ये क़लम बहुत बड़े हैं| १०. ये कुर्सियाँ बहुत ऊँची हैं और यह मेज़ कुछ नीची है| ११. वह तस्वीर बहुत सुन्दर है, ना? १२. वह सुन्दर नहीं है लेकिन बदसूरत भी नहीं है|

Exercise 2 G

Translate into Hindi.

1. This is a good book.
2. These windows are wide.
3. Those notebooks are light blue.
4. Where is the small table?
5. Is the pen red or green?
6. That big beautiful picture is not here?
7. The room is not big enough.
8. Is the room empty?
9. Where is that big square table?
10. The tall (high) chairs are over there.
11. Where are all the black pens?
12. I don't know. There are only blue pens here.

Exercise 3 G

What kinds of items are present in your classroom? Write at least 10 sentences describing the items that are in your classroom. When finished pair up with a classmate. Take turns reading your sentences aloud while the other person listens and translates.

Adjectival Question Words

The question words *kitnā*, 'how much, how many,' *kaun sā*, 'which,' *kaisā*, 'how,' and *kis kā*, 'whose,' are variable adjectives.

कितना	***kitnā***	**How much? How many?**

The question word *kitnā* means 'how much' in the singular (with mass nouns) and 'how many' in the plural (with count nouns).

वहाँ कितना सामान है?	*vahā̃ kitnā sāmān hai?*	How much stuff is over there?
कितनी कुर्सियाँ हैं?	*kitnī kursiyā̃ haĩ?*	How many chairs are there?
यहाँ कितने लोग हैं?	*yahā̃ kitne log haĩ?*	How many people are here?

कौन सा	***kaun sā***	**Which?**
यह कौन सी किताब है?	*ye kaun sī kitāb hai?*	Which book is this?
कौन सा लड़का वहाँ है?	*kaun sā laṛkā vahā̃ hai?*	Which boy is there?

कैसा	***kaisā***	**How? In what state? Of what type?**
वह किताब कैसी है?	*vo kitāb kaisī hai?*	How is that book?
सब लोग कैसे हैं?	*sab log kaise haĩ?*	How is everybody?
अजय कैसा है?	*ajay kaisā hai?*	How is Ajay?

The question word *kaisā* placed before a noun often translates best as 'what kind of,' or 'what sort of.'

यह कैसी किताब है?	*ye kaisī kitāb hai?*	What kind of a book is this / How is this book?
दिल्ली कैसा शहर है?	*dillī kaisā śahar hai.*	What kind of a city is Delhi / How is Delhi as a city?

किसका	***kis kā***	**Whose?**

The form *kis kā*, 'whose' is also a variable adjective as are the words corresponding to English *my/mine* and *your/yours*. These forms will be covered in greater detail in chapter 8.

यह कॉपी किसकी है?	*ye kāpī kis kī hai?*	Whose notepad is this?
यह क़लम मेरा है या आपका?	*ye qalam merā hai yā āp kā?*	Is this pen mine or yours?
क्या यह तुम्हारी किताब है?	*kyā ye tumhārī kitāb hai?*	Is this your book?

Vocabulary 2

आपका	*āp kā*	your, yours
तुम्हारा	*tumhārā*	your, yours
मेरा	*merā*	my, mine
सामान	*sāmān* (m.sg.)	stuff, things
कितना	*kitnā*	how much, how many
किसका	*kis kā*	whose
कैसा	*kaisā*	how, in what state; of what kind
कौन सा	*kaun sā*	which

Note:

- As seen earlier, the words *merā* and *āp kā* mean 'my,' and 'your,' respectively. Both of these words are variable adjectives and so their endings change (*merā / mere / merī; āp kā / āp ke / āp kī*). The word *āp kā* corresponds to the pronoun *āp*. The word *tumhārā* is the form that corresponds to the pronoun *tum*. See chapters 7 and 8 for more information on possessive forms.

Exercise 4

Kabeer and Jaya have just finished working on a joint school project at the library. When they start to pack up their things, they realize that their things have gotten mixed up. Listen to the dialogue and answer the questions about it.

कबीर	यह सब सामान मेरा है या तुम्हारा?
जया	कुछ मेरा है और कुछ तुम्हारा|
कबीर	यह किताब किसकी है?
जया	तुम्हारी है|
कबीर	और कौन सा क़लम मेरा है और कौन सा तुम्हारा?
जया	नीला क़लम मेरा है और काला क़लम तुम्हारा|
कबीर	क्या यह पेंसिल भी मेरी है?
जया	नहीं, वह मेरी है|
कबीर	और यहाँ कौन सी कॉपी मेरी है?
जया	ये दोनों कॉपियाँ तुम्हारी हैं|
कबीर	तुम्हारी कॉपी कैसी है?
जया	मेरी कॉपी नीली है| वह यहाँ नहीं है|
कबीर	क्या मेरी घड़ी भी यहाँ है|
जया	नहीं, यहाँ कोई घड़ी नहीं है|

Questions

A. Which items are Kabeer's?
B. Which items are Jaya's?
C. Which items mentioned are not present and to whom do they belong?

Exercise 5

Pair up with a classmate. Take out five items from each of your bags and place them on the desk in front of you. Imagine that you have lost track of which item belongs to whom. Discuss which items belong to whom and sort them out with your partner. Feel free to use the following phrases:

यह किसका ... है?	*ye kis kā...hai?*
वह मेरा है।	*vo merā hai.*
वह ... किसका है?	*vo...kis kā hai?*
यह तुम्हारा है।	*ye tumhārā hai.*
यह ... मेरा है या तुम्हारा?	*ye...merā hai yā tumhārā?*
कौन सा ... मेरा और कौन सा तुम्हारा है?	*kaun sā...merā aur kaun sā tumhārā hai?*

Exercise 6

Pair up with a classmate. Make a list of eight classroom items. Take turns with your partner asking and answering questions about the items. For each item find out how many of the item there are in the classroom and what the items' qualities are.

उदाहरण

क. यहाँ कितनी किताबें हैं?	A: *yahā̃ kitnī kitābẽ haĩ?*
ख. चार किताबें हैं।	B: *cār kitābẽ haĩ.*
क. किताबें कैसी हैं?	A: *kitābẽ kaisī haĩ?*
ख. किताबें बड़ी और नई हैं।	B. *kitābẽ baṛī aur naī haĩ.*

Plurality and Respect with Adjectives and Nouns

As seen in chapter 2, plural forms such as *tum ho, āp haĩ,* and *ye / vo haĩ* are frequently used to refer to individuals. These plural forms express greater respect than singular forms.

Plural adjective forms must be used with these pronouns and all other words that are plural to convey respect.

तुम कैसे हो?	*tum kaise ho?*	How are you?
तुम कैसी हो?	*tum kaisī* ho?*	How are you?
आप कैसे हैं?	*āp kaise haĩ?*	How are you?
आप कैसी हैं?	*āp kaisī* haĩ?*	How are you?
वे कैसे हैं?	*vo kaise haĩ?*	How is he (respectful)?
वे कैसी हैं?	*vo kaisī* haĩ?*	How is she?

*Feminine singular and plural forms of adjectives are identical, so there is no visible difference between familiar and respectful forms.

Masculine nouns behave similarly to adjectives. When predicated to grammatically plural pronouns such as *tum* and *āp*, they take plural forms.

तुम अच्छे बच्चे हो।	*tum acche bacce ho.*	You are a good child. (not *baccā*)

Feminine nouns, on the other hand, remain singular in this context.

तुम अच्छी बच्ची हो।	*tum acchī baccī ho.*	You are a good child. (not *bacciyā̃*)

Exercise 7 G

Use the words in lists 1–3 below to make at least ten meaningful sentences, and then change the sentences into yes-or-no questions.

ex. *vo acchā chātr hai → kyā vo acchā chātr hai?*

१. यह वह ये वे तू हम तुम मैं आप

२. अच्छा बुरा नया पुराना छोटा बड़ा लम्बा गुलाबी गोल काला ऊँचा सुंदर

३. छात्र/छात्रा अध्यापक/अध्यापिका आदमी औरत लड़का लड़की मेज़ किताब क़लम क्लास

5

Giving Commands and Making Requests

As a matter of basic survival, it is important to be able to understand when somebody asks you to do something in Hindi. One of the forms that you are most likely to hear is the imperative. This chapter introduces imperative forms for the purpose of making commands and requests, but before exploring imperatives, here is a short word on an even more basic form of the verb.

The Infinitive

The infinitive is the form of the verb that means *to* V (e.g. *to do, to eat, to sleep*). We use the capital letter V to represent the verb stem in both English and Hindi. The infinitive is the form of the verb that is listed in dictionaries. It is thus the form that you should memorize whenever you learn a new verb. In Hindi, all verbs have the infinitive form V-*nā*.

V-*nā* to V

Vocabulary 1

Here are some common Hindi verbs. Memorize these along with the vocabulary given later in the chapter.

आना	*ānā*	to come	पूछना	*pūchnā*	to ask
जाना	*jānā*	to go	बताना	*batānā*	to tell
सुनना	*sunnā*	to listen, hear	लेना	*lenā*	to take
देखना	*dekhnā*	to see, look, watch	देना	*denā*	to give
करना	*karnā*	to do	खाना	*khānā*	to eat
होना	*honā*	to be	पीना	*pīnā*	to drink
लिखना	*likhnā*	to write	पढ़ना	*paṛhnā*	to read, to study
बोलना	*bolnā*	to speak, to say	निकालना	*nikālnā*	to take out, remove from

Exercise 1 G

It is important to be able to identify the verb stem since it is the element from which all verb tenses are formed. Examine the infinitives given above, identify the stem in each one, and then fill out the chart below.

Infinitive	Meaning of Infinitive	Verb Stem

The Imperative

The imperative is one of the verb forms used for giving commands and making requests. There are three imperative forms, that correspond to the three second-person pronouns. The imperative is used more frequently in Hindi than in English.

Formation: The imperative is formed by adding the following endings to the verb stem:

āp	V + -इए or -इये	(-*ie* or –*iye*)
tum	V + -ओ	(-*o*)
tū	V (no ending)	

(आप) सुनिए* / सुनिये।	(*āp*) *sunie / suniye.*	Listen!
(तुम) सुनो।	(*tum*) *suno.*	Listen!
(तू) सुन।	(*tū*) *sun.*	Listen!

*Note that if the verb stem ends in a consonant, the imperative endings take their *mātrā* forms (सुनिए, and not सुनइये). The endings appear with independent vowels if the stem to which they are added ends in a vowel. For example, (आप) आइए and (तुम) आओ, both meaning, "Come!"

Negation: The negative imperative (i.e. *Don't...*) is formed by inserting either of two negation words, *na*, or *mat*. As with the word *nahī̃*, the default position of *na* and *mat* is immediately before the verb. Both *na* and *mat* can be used with any of the three imperative forms, though *na* is generally the more polite of the two, and *mat* is more direct.

मत / न कर।	*mat / na kar.*	Don't do that!
मत / न देखो।	*mat / na dekho.*	Don't look!
मत / न जाइए।	*mat / na jāie.*	Don't go!

Politeness Phrases: Hindi does not have any word that directly translates as 'please,' but two common politeness expressions are: *zarā*, 'a little,' and *maharbānī karke*, 'kindly.' The phrase *maharbānī karke* is the more formal of these two options.

ज़रा एक काम करो।	*zarā ek kām karo.*	Please do something for me. ("Please do a task [for me]")
मेहरबानी करके एक काम कीजिए।	*maharbānī karke ek kām kījie.*	Please do something for me. ("Please do a task [for me]")

Two additional formal politeness phrases are कृपया, *kripayā*, and कृपा करके, *kripā karke*, which may be used similarly to *maharbānī karke*.

Verbs with Irregular Imperative Forms

The verbs *karnā*, 'to do,' *lenā*, 'to take,' *denā*, 'to give,' and *pīnā*, 'to drink,' are irregular in the imperative. Their irregular forms are shaded below:

	देना *denā* 'to give'	लेना *lenā* 'to take'	करना *karnā* 'to do'	पीना *pīnā* 'to drink'
आप *āp*	दीजिए *dījie*	लीजिए *lījie*	कीजिए *kījie*	पीजिए *pījie*
तुम *tum*	दो *do*	लो *lo*	करो *karo*	पियो* *piyo*
तू *tū*	दे *de*	ले *le*	कर *kar*	पी *pī*

*Note also that the long vowels ई, *ī*, and ऊ, *ū*, shorten before the *tum* ending –*o* is added. The letter य is also added between the shortened इ and the ending -ओ. For example, जियो (from जीना, 'to live'), छुओ (from छूना, 'to touch'). Final long ऊ is also shortened before the आप ending (e.g., छुइए, from छूना, 'to touch').

Vocabulary 2

Common Verbs

In addition to these verbs, please learn the verbs introduced at the beginning of the chapter.

आराम करना	*ārām karnā* (v.t.)	to rest
उठना	*uṭhnā* (v.i.)	to get up
खोलना	*kholnā* (v.t.)	to open
चलना	*calnā* (v.i.)	to go (with), accompany
जवाब देना	*javāb denā* (v.t.)	to reply, respond, answer
तशरीफ़ रखना	*taśrīf rakhnā* (v.i.)	to sit down
तशरीफ़ लाना	*taśrīf lānā* (v.i.)	to come
बंद करना	*band karnā* (v.t.)	to close (*band*, closed)
बरबाद करना	*barbād karnā* (v.t.)	to ruin; to waste (e.g., *samay*, m. time)
बैठना	*baiṭhnā* (v.i.)	to sit down
रुकना	*ruknā* (v.i.)	to stop, halt
समझना	*samajhnā* (v.i./v.t.)	to understand

Additional Words

अंदर	*andar*	inside
आगे	*āge*	ahead
ऊपर	*ūpar*	up
काम	*kām* (m.)	work, task
गंदा	*gandā*	dirty
जल्दी	*jaldī*	quickly
ज़ोर	*zor* (m.)	force (*zor se*, loudly, forcefully)
धीरे	*dhīre*	slowly (also *dhīre dhīre*)
नीचे	*nīce*	down
पीछे	*pīche*	behind
बाहर	*bāhar*	outside
साफ़	*sāf*	clear, clearly; clean

Notes:

- The letters 'v.i.' and v.t.' stand, respectively, for 'intransitive verb' and 'transitive verb.'
- *taśrīf rakhnā* and *taśrīf lānā* are examples of formulaic speech, common in Urdu, and to some extent in Hindi. These words are often considered more formal or cultivated than their simple, everyday equivalents, *baiṭhnā* and *ānā*.
- *zor* is a noun meaning 'force.' The phrase *zor se*, 'with force, forcefully, loudly' is an example of a very common construction in Hindi in which a noun is used with the postposition *se* in a manner that corresponds to the use of an English adverb. For more information on postpositions, please see unit 2.

Exercise 2

Read aloud and translate the sentences. In addition, indicate a speaker and an addressee that would be appropriate for each sentence.

१. हिन्दी बोलिए। २. किताब खोलो। ३. साफ़ लिखो। ४. अंदर आइए। ५. वहाँ न जाओ। ६. कुछ कीजिए। ७. सवाल पूछिए। ८. ज़रा वह कॉपी दीजिए। ९. कुछ पीजिए। १०. समय बरबाद मत करो।

Exercise 3

Compose sentences that would be appropriate to ask the person indicated in parentheses to perform each action.

A. Wait for a minute. (a friend)
B. Please give me that book. (your teacher)
C. Read this book. (a student in a younger class)
D. Look at that. (a friend of a friend)
E. Sit (very formal). (the father of a friend)
F. Take this pen. (a classmate)
G. Please repeat (what you said). (your teacher)
H. Come here. (a small child)
I. Come inside. (a neighbor)
J. Don't do that. (your friend)

Exercise 4

Listen to the audio passage and follow the Hindi instructions to act out the activities indicated.

१. उठो। २. बैठो। ३. कुछ लिखो। ४. सुनो। ५. किताब खोलो। ६. किताब बंद करो। ७. कुछ खाओ। ८. कुछ पियो। ९. पीछे देखो। १०. आराम करो।

Exercise 5

Your teacher will give additional commands using the vocabulary you have learned so far. Listen to the commands and act them out.

Exercise 6

Pair up with a classmate and take turns giving each other commands and acting out the actions. Use all of the verbs and other words that you learned in this chapter.

6

Unit 1 Review Activities

The goal of this chapter is to review and provide additional opportunities to synthesize the content presented in unit 1.

1. Grammar Review

What grammar have you learned in the chapters of this unit? Try to recall all of the topics that were covered and as many points about each topic as possible.

- Make sure you are able to produce the following tables from memory: personal pronouns, the verb to be in the simple present, variable adjectives.
- What are the three ways of saying you in Hindi and what are the differences among them?
- When is the plural number used to refer to or address individuals in Hindi?
- What are the four noun types and what are their plural forms?
- How is the imperative formed for each of the three second-person pronouns?

2. Listen to the short dialogs and translate them into English.

आधा	*ādhā*	half
आरामदेह	*ārāmdeh*	comfortable
देश	*deś* (m.)	country

मेरा नाम संजय है। और आपका?
मेरा नाम गरिमा है।
आपसे मिलकर ख़ुशी हुई।
मुझे भी।

आप कहाँ से हैं?
मैं भारत से हूँ। और आप?
मैं भी भारत से हूँ।

क्या आप छात्र हैं?
जी हाँ, मैं छात्र हूँ। क्या आप भी छात्र हैं?
नहीं, मैं यहाँ अध्यापक हूँ।

क्या आप नेपाली हैं?
नहीं, मैं तिब्बती हूँ। और आप?
मैं आधा चीनी और आधा भारतीय हूँ।

वे कौन हैं?
वे सिंह साहब हैं।
क्या सिंह साहब प्रोफ़ेसर हैं?
नहीं, वे बहुत बड़े डॉक्टर हैं।

क्या यहाँ कोई क़लम है?
नहीं यहाँ कोई क़लम नहीं है। लेकिन यहाँ एक पेंसिल है।
हाँ, यह पेंसिल ठीक है।

ये अलमारियाँ कैसी हैं?
ये अच्छी हैं लेकिन काफ़ी बड़ी नहीं हैं।
बड़ी अलमारियाँ वहाँ हैं।

वहाँ कोई कुर्सी नहीं है।
यहाँ बैठो। यहाँ काफ़ी कुर्सियाँ हैं।
ये कुर्सियाँ बहुत आरामदेह हैं।

नमस्ते शर्मा जी, कहिए, क्या हाल है?
सब ठीक है। आप कैसे हैं, अकबर साहब?
मैं भी बिल्कुल ठीक हूँ।
तशरीफ़ रखिए।
जी, शुक्रिया।

भारत कैसा देश है?
भारत बहुत बड़ा देश है।
ताज महल कैसा है?
वह बहुत सुन्दर है।

3. Personalization Questions

Take turns asking and answering the following questions with a partner. When asking a question, repeat it aloud until you are able to say it without pausing. Choose the correct masculine or feminine form from the options given. When answering, listen only and respond in a complete sentence without reading.

१. आप कैसे / कैसी हैं?
२. क्या आप छात्र / छात्रा हैं?
३. आप अमरीकी हैं?
४. आप कहाँ से हैं?
५. यह कमरा साफ़ है या गंदा?
६. यह क्लास कैसी है?
७. यहाँ क्या-क्या चीज़ें हैं?
८. ... को हिन्दी में कैसे कहते हैं?

4. Write five sentences in Hindi about yourself. Feel free to write both positive (*I am...*) and negative (*I am not...*) sentences.

5. Write sentences stating the number of each item that appears in the picture below and say anything that you can about the qualities of the items. When finished, write an additional five sentences about the items in the room that you are currently sitting in.

Example:

३ किताबें हैं। किताबें मोटी हैं।

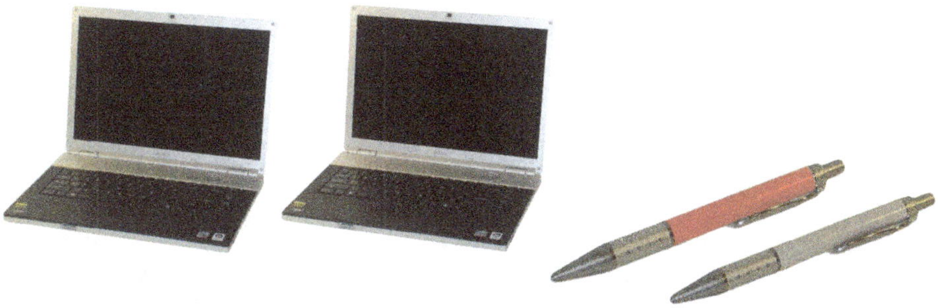

Conversation (Introductions)

6. Listen to the conversation and answer the questions provided. When finished, pair up with a classmate and have a conversation on the same pattern.

थोड़ी देर बाद	*thoṛī der bād*	a little later, after a little while
देर	*der* (f.)	a (short) while; delay

Questions

A. What is the girl's name?
B. What is the boy's name?
C. What does the boy say about the girl's name?
D. Where is the girl from?
E. Where is the boy from?

हर्ष	नमस्ते।
सरिता	नमस्ते।
हर्ष	मेरा नाम हर्ष है। और आपका?
सरिता	मेरा नाम सरिता है।
हर्ष	आपसे मिलकर ख़ुशी हुई।
सरिता	मुझे भी।
हर्ष	सरिता, आपका नाम बहुत सुंदर है।
सरिता	शुक्रिया। क्या आप विद्यार्थी हैं?
हर्ष	जी हाँ। मैं विद्यार्थी हूँ। और आप?
सरिता	मैं भी विद्यार्थी हूँ।
हर्ष	क्या आप अमरीकी हैं?
सरिता	जी नहीं, मैं भारतीय हूँ।
हर्ष	मैं भी भारतीय हूँ।
	...(थोड़ी देर बाद)...
सरिता	अच्छा, मैं चलती हूँ।
हर्ष	फिर मिलेंगे। बाय।
सरिता	बाय।

Sayings and Proverbs

एक अनार, सौ बीमार

कहाँ राजा भोज, कहाँ गंगू तेली

काला अक्षर भैंस बराबर

जैसा देस, वैसा भेस

बद अच्छा, बदनाम बुरा

आ बैल मुझे मार

सुनो सब की, करो मन की

सौ सुनार की, एक लोहार की

Unit 2 My Family and My Home

In this unit you will learn the following skills:

- Describing the locations of places and objects.
- Describing cities: identifying and locating landmarks, reading maps.
- Talking about family: family composition; age, appearance, and traits of family members.
- Describing homes: number and types of rooms, furniture, the layout of rooms.

In addition, you will learn basic information about the structure of South Asian families.

7

Locating Places and Objects

In this chapter you will learn how to locate places and objects in your home as well as your hometown and country.

Locating Places in the City

Postpositions

Locations are commonly expressed in English using phrases such as:

in Delhi
on 1st Street

The key words in these phrases are the prepositions, *in* and *on*. The Hindi equivalents of prepositions are called *postpositions*. Hindi postpositions fulfill the same functions as prepositions in English, but instead of preceding their objects as prepositions do, postpositions follow their objects. The object of a preposition or postposition is the word or phrase that completes its meaning. In the examples above, 'Delhi' is the object of 'in,' and '1st Street' is the object of 'on.'

You can begin using the following postpositions immediately to express location:

में	*mẽ*	in
पर	*par*	at, on

Below are some examples of simple uses of these postpositions. Note the placement of the postpositions relative to their objects.

बॉस्टन में	*bāsṭan mẽ*	in Boston
आगरा में	*āgrā mẽ*	in Agra
अकबर बॉस्टन में है।	*akbar bāsṭan mẽ hai.*	Akbar is in Boston.
ताज महल आगरा में है।	*tāj mahal āgrā mẽ hai.*	The Taj Mahal is in Agra.
मेन स्ट्रीट पर	*men sṭrīṭ par*	on Main Street
घर पर	*ghar par*	at home
वह घर पर है।	*vo ghar par hai.*	She is at home.
बैंक मेन स्ट्रीट पर है।	*baĩk men sṭrīṭ par hai.*	The bank is on Main Street.
मेन स्ट्रीट पर एक बैंक है।	*men sṭrīṭ par ek baĩk hai.*	There's a bank on Main Street.

Note the slight difference in meaning between the final two sentences above.

Vocabulary 1

Places in the City

अजायबघर, संग्रहालय	*ajāyabghar, sangrahālay* (m.)	museum
अस्पताल	*aspatāl* (m.)	hospital
इमारत	*imārat* (f.)	building
केमिस्ट की दुकान	*kemisṭ kī dukān* (f.)	medicine shop
गिरजाघर	*girjāghar* (m.)	church
चिड़ियाघर	*ciṛiyāghar* (m.)	zoo
चौक	*cauk* (m.)	square, central market
डाकघर	*ḍākghar* (m.)	post office
दुकान	*dukān* (f.)	store, shop
पड़ोस	*paṛos* (m.)	neighborhood
पार्क	*pārk* (m.)	park
पुस्तकालय	*pustakālay* (m.)	library
बाग़	*bāgh* (m.)	garden
बाज़ार	*bāzār* (m.)	market
भोजनालय	*bhojnālay* (m.)	traditional vegetarian restaurant
मंदिर	*mandir* (m.)	temple
मस्जिद	*masjid* (f.)	mosque
मार्ग	*mārg* (m.)	road (esp. in proper street names)
मुहल्ला	*muhallā* (m.)	quarter (of town)
मॉल	*māl* (m.)	mall (also, माल, m. goods)
राजमार्ग	*rājmārg* (m.)	highway
रेलवे स्टेशन	*relve sṭeśan* (m.)	train station

रेस्टोरेंट	*resțorenț* (m.)	restaurant
शहर	*śahar* (m.)	city
सड़क	*saṛak* (f.)	road
सिनेमाघर	*sinemāghar* (m.)	cinema, theatre
होटल	*hoṭal* (m.)	hotel; restaurant

Additional Words

कि	*ki* (conj.)	that
नज़दीक	*nazdīk*	near, nearby
पर	*par*	on, at
बहुत सा	*bahut sā*	many, a lot of
में	*mẽ*	in
से	*se*	from, than, by

Notes:

- Note the use of the word *ki* in sentences such as the following: *ye batāie ki aspatāl kahā̃ hai*, 'Tell me where the hospital is,' literally, 'Tell me this, that: "Where is the hospital".' Sentences of this structure will be discussed in greater detail in chapter 35.
- *bahut* by itself means both 'many/a lot of' and 'very.' *bahut sā* is an unambiguous way of saying 'a lot of.' The *sā* portion inflects adjectivally (e.g. *bahut se acche log*, 'a lot of good people').

Exercise 1

Read the following sentences aloud and then translate them into English.

Note: *ye śahar* + *me* → *is śahar mẽ*, 'in this city.' The presence of a postposition causes the word *ye* to change to *is*. We will return to this point in greater detail later in this chapter.

१. वह रेस्टोरेंट कहाँ है? २. वह नेहरु रोड पर है| ३. क्या डाकघर गांधी मार्ग पर है? नहीं, वह नेहरु मार्ग पर है| ४. पहाड़ गंज में बहुत से होटल और रेस्टोरेंट हैं| ५. क्या इस शहर में कोई अस्पताल है? ६. हाँ, जीटी रोड पर एक अस्पताल है| ७. क्या आगरा रोड पर कोई सिनेमाघर है? ८. नहीं, आगरा रोड पर कोई सिनेमा नहीं है लेकिन दिल्ली रोड पर एक है| ९. इस शहर में कितने पुस्तकालय हैं? १०. इस शहर में बहुत सी पुरानी और सुंदर इमारतें हैं| ११. हज़रत गंज में कई अच्छी दुकानें हैं| १२. क्या मीना बाज़ार में कोई रेस्टोरेंट है?

Exercise 2

G

Translate the following phrases and sentences into Hindi. Translating the phrases first will facilitate translating the sentences.

1. on Ambedkar Road. The hospital is on Ambedkar Road.
2. There is a hospital on Gandhi Marg.
3. on Wazir Hasan Road. Is there a mosque on Wazir Hasan Road?
4. in Khatri Bazaar. There are some nice stores in Khatri Bazaar.
5. Where is your house? on Victoria Street. Where on Victoria Street is your house?

When translating the remaining sentences you might find it easier to first extract and translate the postpositional phrases in the manner of the sentences above. This is a good general practice to follow until you get accustomed to using postpositions automatically.

6. Is there a post office on University Road?
7. The railway station is in Badshah Nagar on Faizabad Road.
8. There is a new mall on Raja Bazaar Road.
9. There are a lot of stores in Aminabad Bazaar.
10. Is there a theater in Hazrat Ganj?

Exercise 3

Listen to the dialogue and note the location of each of the places mentioned.

Landmark	Location

क. भाई साहब, ज़रा मुझे बताइए कि अस्पताल कहाँ है।

ख. अस्पताल ग्रैंड ट्रंक रोड पर है।

क. और डाकघर कहाँ है?

ख. डाकघर पुरानी कोतवाली रोड पर है।

क. और यह भी बताइए कि शिव मंदिर कहाँ है।

ख. शिव मंदिर नज़दीक है। वह चारबाग़ में है।

क. और क्या कालीचरण कॉलेज भी चारबाग़ में है?

ख. नहीं, वह सिकन्दर रोड पर है।

क. एक और सवाल है।

ख. हाँ, पूछिए।

क. गोल्डन होटल कहाँ है?

ख. गोल्डन होटल अशोक मार्ग पर है।

क. ठीक है। धन्यवाद।

Exercise 4

You are new to the city and are trying to orient yourself. Pair up with a classmate and take turns playing the roles below.

A. Round 1

Student 1: Ask your partner questions (*Where is...?*) to find out where on the map below the following places are located. Record your findings, and when finished, verify them verbally with your partner by stating in a complete sentence the road on which each place is located.

कालीचरण कॉलेज	पुस्तकालय	डाकघर	अस्पताल
मुग़ल-ए-आज़म रेस्टोरेंट	मंदिर	गोल्डन होटल	पार्क

Student 2: These locations correspond to the numbers on the map below. Answer your partner's questions by reporting the street on which each place is located. As always, speak in complete sentences.

१. कालीचरण कॉलेज २. अस्पताल ३. पार्क ४. डाकघर ५. गोल्डन होटल ६. मुग़ल-ए-आज़म रेस्टोरेंट ७. मंदिर ८. पुस्तकालय

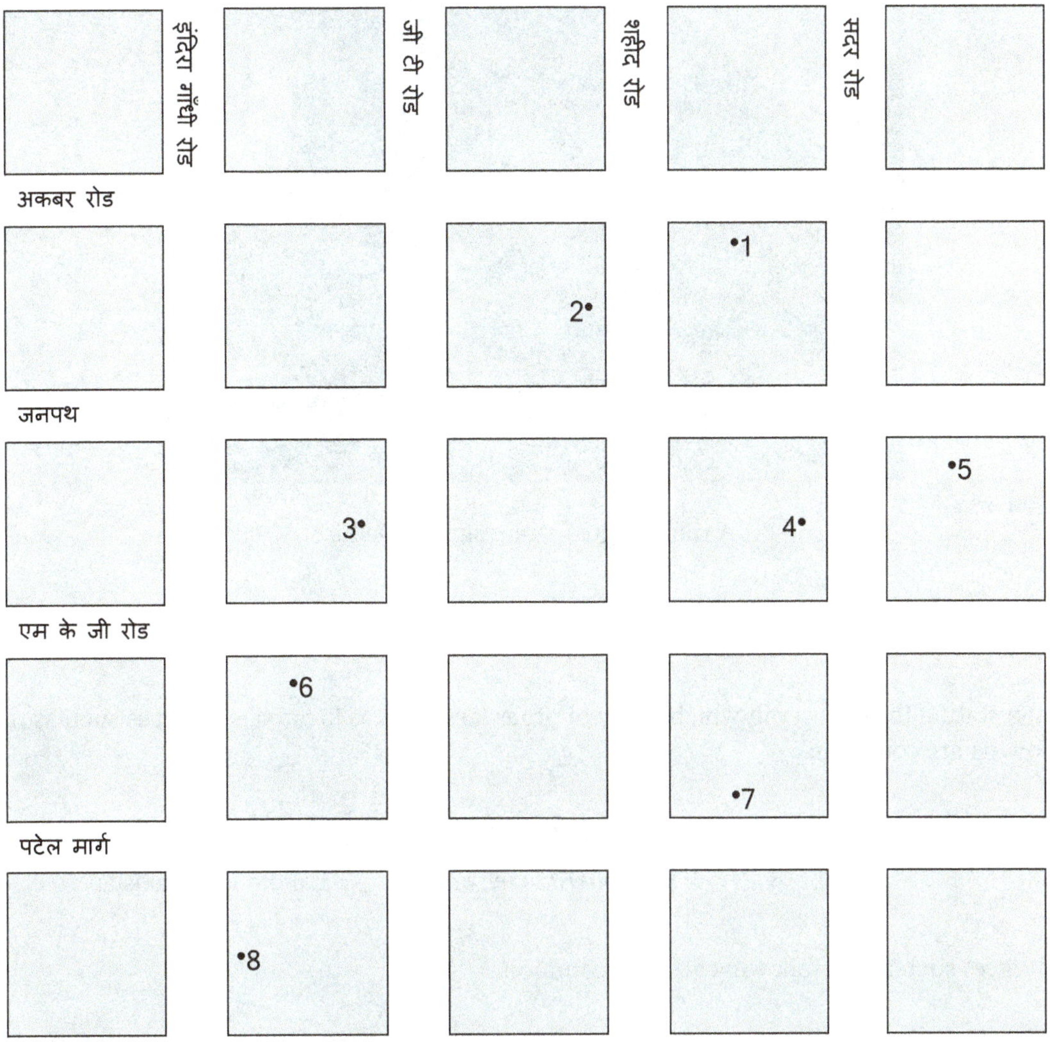

B. Round II

Switch roles and repeat using the same map.

Student 1: Please refer to the "Student 1" instructions under "Round I" above.

मस्जिद	पार्क	डाकघर	सरस्वती भोजनालय
ताज रेस्टोरेंट	सिनेमाघर	अस्पताल	पुस्तकालय

Student 2: Please refer to the "Student 2" instructions under "Round I" above.

१. पार्क २. सरस्वती भोजनालय ३. ताज रेस्टोरेंट ४. अस्पताल ५. पुस्तकालय ६. डाकघर ७. सिनेमाघर ८. मस्जिद

A multilingual street sign in Delhi

Locating Places within Countries

When stating the country in which a city or other landmark is located, sentences such as the following are common:

दिल्ली भारत में है।	*dillī bhārat mẽ hai.*	Delhi is in India.
लाहौर पाकिस्तान में है।	*lāhaur pākistān mẽ hai.*	Lahore is in Pakistan.

Sentences such as the following are also common:

गंगा भारत की एक नदी है।	*gangā bhārat kī ek nadī hai.*	The Ganges is a river in (of) India.
कराची पाकिस्तान का एक शहर है।	*karācī pākistān kā ek śahar hai.*	Karachi is a city in (of) Pakistan.
मुंबई और दिल्ली भारत के दो बड़े शहर हैं।	*mumbaī aur dillī bhārat ke do baṛe śahar haĩ.*	Mumbai and Delhi are two of India's big cities (two big cities of India).

The Postposition *kā*

The sentences above employ the postposition, *kā*, 'of,' which is unusual among postpositions in that its form inflects like an adjective. As can be seen in the examples above, *kā* also takes the forms *ke* and *kī*, depending on the item that follows it. When the masculine noun *śahar*, 'city,' follows, it retains the form *kā*; when the feminine noun *nadī*, 'river,' follows, it takes the form *kī*; when the masculine plural item *do śahar*, 'two cities,' follows, it becomes *ke*. The postposition *kā* has many uses, but for now you will practice using it to identify locations using sentences of the form above.

Vocabulary 2

Locations

भारत, हिंदुस्तान	*bhārat, hindustān*	India
पाकिस्तान	*pākistān*	Pakistan

Please see the exercises for the spelling and pronunciation of additional South Asian places.

Cardinal Directions

उत्तर	*uttar* (m.)	north
उत्तरी	*uttarī*	northern
दक्षिण	*dakṣiṇ* (m.)	south
दक्षिणी	*dakṣiṇī*	southern
पश्चिम	*paścim* (m.)	west
पश्चिमी	*paścimī*	western
पूर्व	*pūrv* (m.)	east
पूर्वी	*pūrvī*	eastern

Additional Vocabulary

इलाक़ा, क्षेत्र	*ilāqā, kṣetr* (m.)	region
क़स्बा	*qasbā* (m.)	town
जगह, स्थान	*jagah* (f.), *sthān* (m.)	place (also, *jagah*, space)

Additional Vocabulary (cont'd)

देश, मुल्क	*deś, mulk* (m.)	country
नदी, दरिया	*nadī* (f.), *dariyā* (m. type 2)	river
प्रदेश, राज्य	*pradeś, rājy* (m.)	state
राजधानी	*rājdhānī* (f.)	capital
शहर	*śahar* (m.)	city

Note:

- In addition to the words for directions given, there are alternatives for some directions. दक्खिन, दक्खिनी, 'south,' 'southern'; पूरब, पूरबी, 'east,' 'eastern'; पच्छिम, पच्छिमी, 'west,' 'western.'

Exercise 5

Listen to the audio while reading the names of the South Asian places listed below. Examine the spelling and pronunciation and then pair up with a partner. With the help of the map below, sort the names of countries, states, and cities.

भारत	हैदराबाद	इलाहाबाद	पाकिस्तान	अफ़ग़ानिस्तान	वाराणसी
मुंबई	तिब्बत	कानपुर	पंजाब	बंग्लादेश	नेपाल
श्री लंका	चीन	भूटान	अमृतसर	उत्तर प्रदेश	कराची
दिल्ली	लाहौर	काठमांडू	गोआ	ढाका	लखनऊ
जयपुर	इस्लामाबाद	गुजरात	राजस्थान	कश्मीर	भोपाल

उदाहरण

क. भारत क्या है?

ख. भारत एक देश है|

क. पंजाब क्या है?

ख. पंजाब एक राज्य है|

क. जयपुर क्या है?

ख. जयपुर एक शहर है| वह भारत में है / जयपुर भारत का एक शहर है|

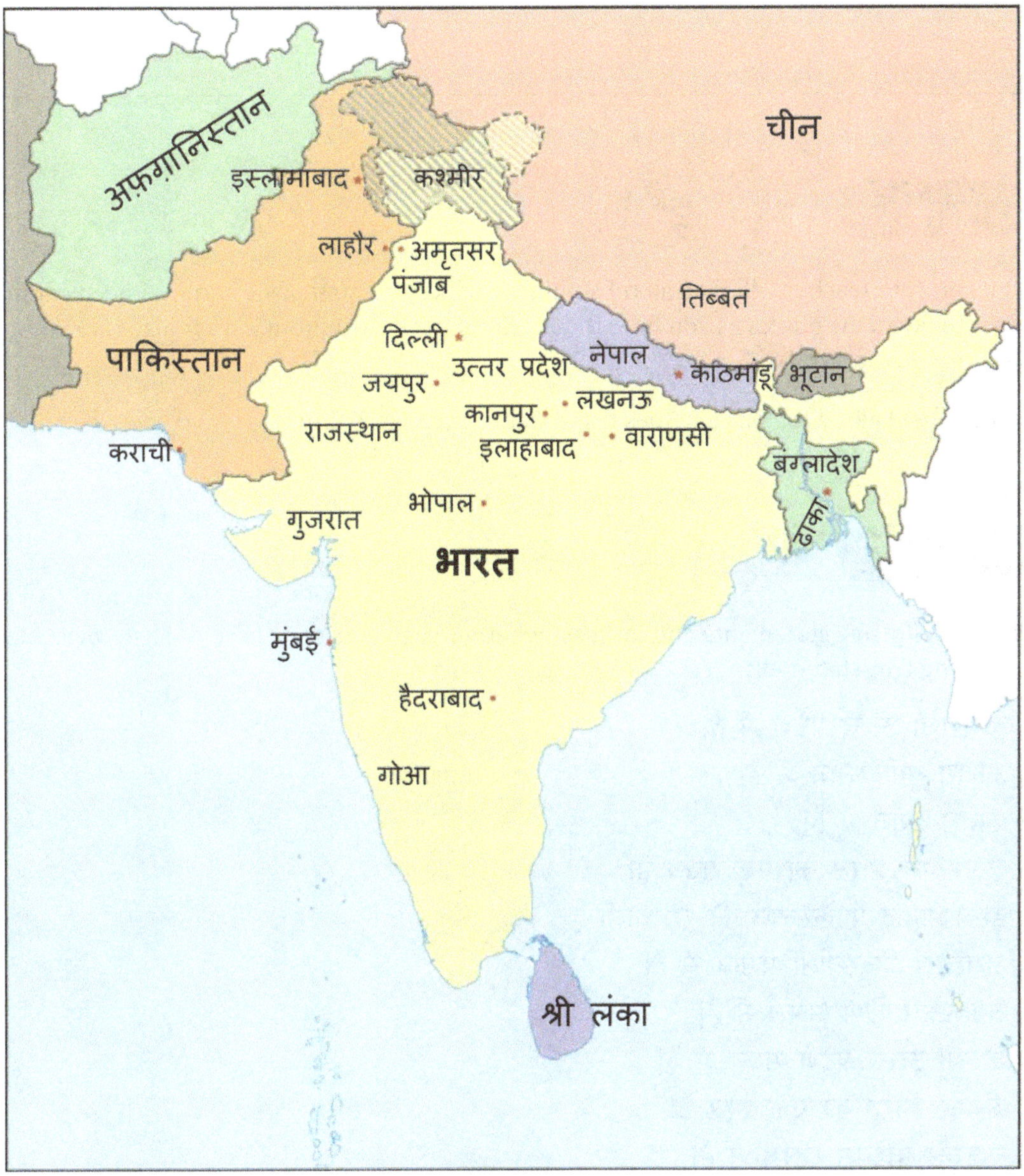

देश	राज्य	शहर

Exercise 6

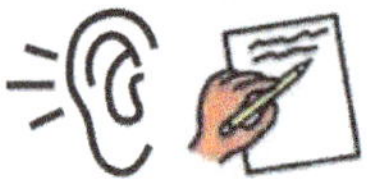

Dictation: Your teacher will read aloud a number of South Asian place names. Listen carefully and write down the names as you hear them pronounced. Also note if each place is a country, state/ province, or a city.

Teacher: Read aloud the place names listed under exercise 5 above.

Exercise 7

Read the following statements and indicate whether each is true or false. If false, write a corresponding true statement.

१. वाराणसी उत्तर प्रदेश में है।
२. आगरा पाकिस्तान में है।
३. काबुल ईरान में है।
४. राजस्थान भारत का एक राज्य है।
५. इस्लामाबाद पाकिस्तान की राजधानी है।
६. अमृतसर हिंदुस्तानी पंजाब में है।
७. लखनऊ दक्षिण भारत में है।
८. दिल्ली उत्तर प्रदेश राज्य में है।
९. जयपुर भारत का एक शहर है।
१०. गुजरात पश्चिम भारत में है।
११. कराची और लाहौर पाकिस्तान के दो बड़े शहर हैं।

Locating Objects in the Home

Earlier in this chapter you learned how to use the postpositions *mẽ* and *par* to locate places within cities and countries. Additional locational relationships can be expressed using other postpositions, such as those corresponding to English 'on top of' and 'next to.' This section will focus on some of these other postpositions and how they can be used to describe the position of objects relative to each other, for example, when describing the location of items within one's home.

Compound Postpositions

All of the postpositions that have been presented till now have been *simple postpositions*, or postpositions that consist of a single word. Most postpositions, however, are *compound postpositions*, meaning they consist of multiple words. Compound postpositions are similar to multiword English prepositions such as 'in front of' and 'to the left of.'

Most compound postpositions begin with either *ke* or *kī*, both of which are forms of the postposition *kā*, 'of.' Here are some examples:

के ऊपर	*ke ūpar*	on top of, above
के बग़ल में	*ke baghal mẽ*	next to
की तरह	*kī tarah*	like; similar to

पलंग के ऊपर एक तस्वीर है|	*palang ke ūpar ek tasvīr hai.*	There is a picture above the bed.
मेज़ के बग़ल में एक गमला है|	*mez ke baghal mẽ ek gamlā hai.*	There's a flower pot next to the table.
सोफ़ा टीवी के सामने है|	*sofā ṭīvī ke sāmne hai.*	The sofa is in front of the TV.

Vocabulary 3

Locational Postpositions

के आगे	*ke āge*	ahead of, beyond
के ऊपर	*ke ūpar*	on top of, above
के दरमियान	*ke darmiyān*	between, in the middle/midst of
के दाईं तरफ़	*ke dāī̃ taraf*	to the right of
के दाहिनी तरफ़	*ke dāhinī taraf*	to the right of

के नीचे	*ke nīce*	under, below
के पास	*ke pās*	near; in the possession of
के पीछे	*ke pīche*	behind
के बग़ल में	*ke ba<u>gh</u>al mẽ*	next to
के बाईं तरफ़	*ke bāī̃ taraf*	to the left of
के बीच	*ke bīc*	between (also *ke bīc mẽ*, between, in the middle of)
के सामने	*ke sāmne*	in front of, facing, opposite from

Household

आँगन	*ā̃gan* (m.)	courtyard
कपड़े	*kapṛe* (m.pl.)	clothes
गमला	*gamlā* (m.)	flower pot
घर	*ghar* (m.)	home, house
चादर	*cādar* (f.)	sheet, bedsheet
डिब्बा	*ḍibbā* (m.)	box, container
पलंग	*palang* (m.)	bed, bedframe
बोतल	*botal* (f.)	bottle
मकान	*makān* (m.)	house
लिहाफ़	*lihāf* (m.)	thick blanket, comforter
सोफ़ा	*sofā* (m.)	sofa

Additional Words

ज़रूर	*zarūr*	certainly
ठीक	*ṭhīk*	right, immediately (with certain compound postpositions)
तरफ़	*taraf* (f.)	direction
तरह	*tarah* (f.)	manner
दायाँ, दाहिना	*dāyā̃, dāhinā*	right (direction)
दूसरा	*dūsrā*	other; second
पानी	*pānī* (m.)	water
पानी की बोतल	*pānī kī botal* (f.)	water bottle
बायाँ	*bāyā̃*	left (direction)

Notes:

- *ṭhīk:* Examples: *ke ṭhīk sāmne,* right in front of; *ke ṭhīk pīche,* right behind, *ke ṭhīk bag͟hal mẽ,* right next to, etc.
- *taraf:* Note the difference between: *is kī taraf,* in the direction of this; and *is taraf,* in this direction.
- *tarah:* Here are some useful phrases featuring *tarah: is tarah,* in this way; *us tarah,* in that way; *is tarah kā,* this sort of ('of this sort'); *us tarah kā,* that sort of; *kis tarah kā,* what sort of; *har tarah kā,* all sorts of.
- *dāyā̃* and *bāyā̃* are both variable adjectives. The final vowel changes as in other variable adjectives, the only difference being that it is nasalized. Note that in the forms other than बायाँ and दायाँ the letter य can be dropped: बायें/बाएँ, बायीं/बाईं, दायें/दाएँ, दायीं/दाईं.
- *pānī kī botal*: Note that where English employs compounding to link two nouns, Hindi often employs the possessive postposition *kā*. Another example of this is *hindī kī kitāb*, 'a Hindi book.'

Additional Postpositions

Here are some additional high-frequency postpositions. These are not used in this chapter but will be useful to learn as soon as possible.

के अनुसार, के मुताबिक़	*ke anusār, ke mutābiq*	according to
के अलावा	*ke alāvā*	apart from, in addition to

के कारण, की वजह से	*ke kāraṇ, kī vajah se*	because of (*kāraṇ*, m., *vajah*, f., reason)
की तरफ़	*kī taraf*	in the direction of (*taraf*, f. direction)
की तरह	*kī tarah*	like, in the manner of (*tarah*, f. manner)
से दूर	*se dūr*	far from, distant from
से पहले	*se pahle*	before
के बजाय	*ke bajāy*	instead of
के बाद	*ke bād*	after
के बारे में	*ke bāre mẽ*	about
के बावजूद	*ke bāvjūd*	in spite of
के लिए / के लिये	*ke lie / ke liye*	for
को लेकर	*ko lekar*	including; regarding
के साथ	*ke sāth*	with, accompanying (*sāth sāth / ek sāth*, adv., together)

Exercise 8 G

Read aloud and translate the sentence pairs.

१. पलंग के ऊपर एक पंखा है| पंखा पलंग के ऊपर है| २. मेज़ के बग़ल में एक लैम्प है| लैम्प मेज़ के बग़ल में है| ३. खिड़की के बाईं तरफ़ एक तस्वीर है| तस्वीर खिड़की के बाईं तरफ़ है| ४. अलमारी के ऊपर एक घड़ी है| घड़ी अलमारी के ऊपर है| ५. पलंग के नीचे एक डिब्बा है| डिब्बा पलंग के नीचे है|

Exercise 9 G

Translate into Hindi. You may find it easier to translate the underlined portion of each sentence first, and then translate the entire sentence.

1. The flower pots are in the courtyard.
2. There are some flower pots in the courtyard.
3. There is a wardrobe closet next to the window.
4. The paper is under the book.
5. There is a notebook next to the bed.
6. The desk is between the window and the closet.

Exercise 10 G

These statements refer to the chart below. Indicate whether each statement is true or false. For all false statements give a corresponding true statement.

१. अलमारी के नीचे टीवी है। २. अलमारी के बग़ल में क़ालीन है। ३. दीवार और अलमारी के बीच घड़ी है। ४. मेज़ के ऊपर कुर्सी है। ५. टीवी के बग़ल में किताब है। ६. किताब और कुर्सी के बीच कंप्यूटर है। ७. पलंग के बग़ल में एक तरफ़ कुर्सी है और दूसरी तरफ़ किताब है। ८. कुर्सी के ऊपर मेज़ है। ९. पलंग के नीचे दीवार है। १०. किताब के नीचे कंप्यूटर है। ११. क़ालीन के बग़ल में एक तरफ़ कंप्यूटर है और दूसरी तरफ़ कुछ नहीं है। १२. कॉपी और क़लम के बीच कुछ नहीं है। १३. कंप्यूटर के ऊपर खिड़की है। १४. कॉपी पलंग के नीचे है। १५. कुर्सी और बोतल के बीच क़लम है। १६. काग़ज़ के ऊपर कुछ नहीं है। १७. काग़ज़ के ऊपर खिड़की है। १८. खिड़की के नीचे कुछ नहीं है। १९. खिड़की और पेंसिल के बीच बोतल है। २०. बोतल पेंसिल के बग़ल में और क़लम के नीचे है।

 मेज़	 दीवार	 घड़ी	 अलमारी
 कुर्सी	 पलंग	 किताब	 टीवी
 क़लम	 कॉपी	 कंप्यूटर	 क़ालीन
 बोतल	 पेंसिल	 खिड़की	 काग़ज़

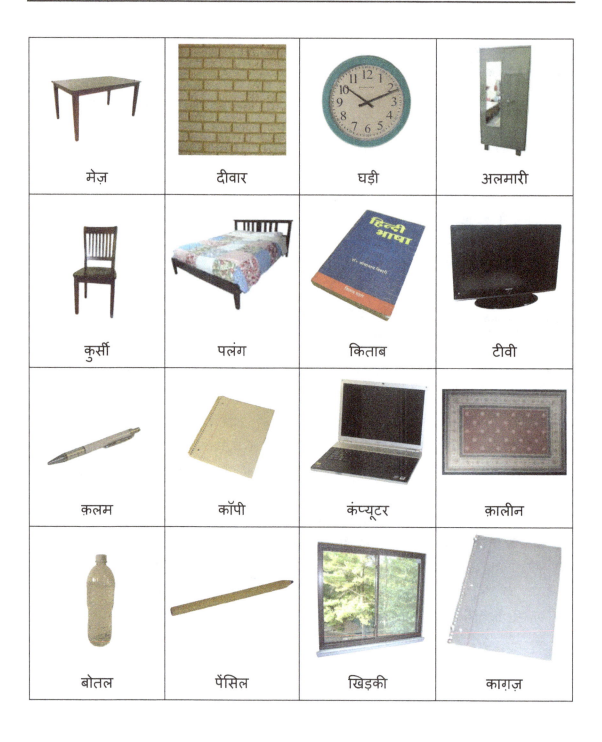

Exercise 11

Listen to the audio and answer the questions about the chart in the previous exercise.

१. अलमारी के बग़ल में क्या है? २. घड़ी के नीचे क्या चीज़ है? ३. क्या मेज़ के ऊपर कुछ है? ४. पलंग किस चीज़* के नीचे है? ५. टीवी और कुर्सी के बीच कौन सी चीज़ें हैं? ६. क़ालीन के ऊपर क्या-क्या चीज़ें हैं? ७. कंप्यूटर के ठीक ऊपर क्या है? ८. क़लम के बग़ल में क्या है? दूसरी तरफ़ क्या है? ९. काग़ज़ के ऊपर कितनी चीज़ें हैं? १०. कॉपी के ठीक ऊपर क्या है?

*किस चीज़, 'which thing.'

Exercise 12

An Indian child has sent his American pen pal a description and a drawing of his room. The drawing has been lost in the mail. Read the passage and then recreate a map of the room's layout.

यह मेरा कमरा है| कमरे में** एक बड़ी खिड़की है| खिड़की के दाईं तरफ़ एक बड़ी मेज़ है| मेज़ पर किताबें हैं| मेज़ के ऊपर, दीवार पर एक तस्वीर है| खिड़की के बाईं तरफ़ एक अलमारी है| अलमारी में कपड़े हैं| अलमारी के सामने मेरा पलंग है| पलंग के नीचे क़ालीन है|

** कमरे में, 'in the room.' The presence of the postposition causes the word *kamrā* to change form as will be explained later in the chapter.

Exercise 13

As you might guess, in addition to describing the locations of objects, postpositions can also be used to describe people's physical positions relative to each other. Listen to the statements about the people standing in line in the picture below. Indicate whether each statement is true or false. For all false statements write a corresponding true statement.

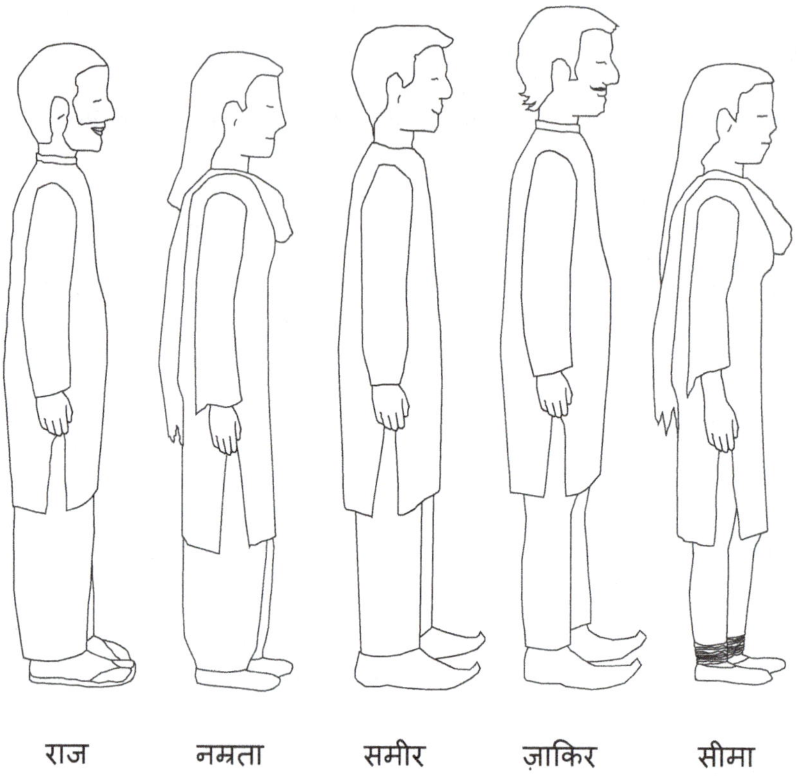

१. ज़ाकिर सीमा के पीछे है।
२. ज़ाकिर और नम्रता के बीच कोई नहीं है।
३. समीर नम्रता के आगे है।
४. सीमा के आगे कोई नहीं है।
५. राज नम्रता के आगे है।
६. समीर नम्रता और राज के बीच है।

Exercise 14

Pair Exercise

Role 1: Ask your partner the questions provided to determine the identities of the people in line. Label each picture with the appropriate name. When finished, compare your results with your partner's information.

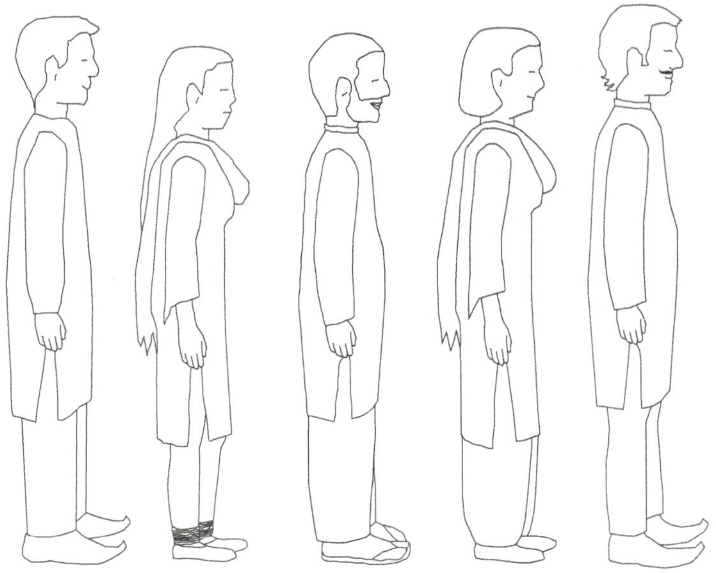

१. रमेश के आगे कौन है?
२. रमेश और हर्ष के बीच कौन है?
३. हर्ष के पीछे कौन-कौन है?
४. निखिल के आगे कौन है?
५. राधा के पीछे कौन-कौन है?

Role 2: This is the order of the people in line. Answer your partner's questions in complete sentences.

पीछे	निखिल	राधा	हर्ष	जया	रमेश	**आगे**

Repeat using the following picture:

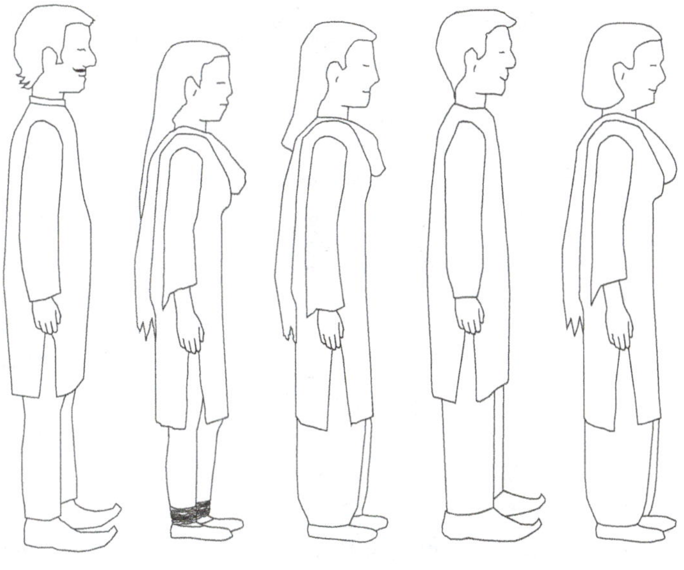

१. क्या बिलाल के आगे कोई है? कौन?
२. क्या उसके आगे* कोई है?
३. बिलाल के ठीक पीछे कौन है?
४. मीरा और तुषार के बीच कौन है?
५ तुषार के आगे और पीछे कौन है?

*उसके आगे, 'ahead of him/her'

Role 2:

पीछे	तुषार	सीमा	मीरा	बिलाल	आशा	**आगे**

Using Postpositions: Oblique Forms

Earlier in the chapter we introduced the concept of the object of a postposition. To recap, the object of a postposition is the word or phrase that immediately precedes the postposition and completes its meaning. This concept is important to understand since many nouns, adjectives, and pronouns take different forms when they become the object of a postposition. The forms that these words take with postpositions are called *oblique case* forms, or as we will call them more simply, *oblique* forms. The forms that nouns, adjectives, and pronouns take in most other circumstances are called *direct* forms. The singular and plural forms of the nouns, adjectives, and pronouns introduced in unit 1 are all direct forms. Direct forms can be regarded as the default forms of these words.

Oblique Noun Forms

Singular oblique forms: The singular oblique forms of all four noun types are given in the table below. The direct forms are also reproduced for easy comparison.

noun type	direct form (form without postposition)	oblique form (form with postposition)
masculine type 1	कमरा *kamrā* room	कमरे में *kamre mẽ* in the room
masculine type 2	पलंग *palang* bed	पलंग के ऊपर *palang ke ūpar* on top of the bed
feminine type 1	अलमारी *almārī* closet	अलमारी में *almārī mẽ* in the closet
feminine type 2	मेज़ *mez* table	मेज़ पर *mez par* on the table

As can be seen in the table, only masculine type 1 nouns change in form when used with post-positions. The final *-ā* vowel of the noun changes to *–e*. All other noun types have identical singular direct and oblique forms.

Plural oblique forms: On the other hand, all plural nouns change when used with postpositions. All nouns take the plural oblique ending *–õ*.

noun type	direct form (form without postposition)	oblique form (form with postposition)
masculine type 1	कमरे *kamre* rooms	कमरों में *kamrõ mẽ* in the rooms
masculine type 2*	पलंग *palang* beds	पलंगों के ऊपर *palangõ ke ūpar* above the beds
feminine type 1**	अलमारियाँ *almāriyā̃* closets	अलमारियों में *almāriyõ mẽ* in the closets
feminine type 2***	मेज़ें *mezẽ* tables	मेज़ों पर *mezõ par* on the tables

*Masculine type 2 nouns that end in *–ā* behave like other masculine type 2 nouns—the ending *õ* is added after the final *ā* noun rather than replacing it. For example, *rājā*, 'kings,' + ppn. → *rājāõ*. Note also the plural oblique forms of masculine type 2 nouns that end in *i*, *ī*, and *ū*. *vyakti*, 'persons,' + ppn. → *vyaktiyõ* (*y* is inserted between *i* and *õ*); *ādmī*, 'men,' + ppn. → *ādmiyõ* (*ī* is shortened to *i* and *y* is inserted); *pahlū*, 'aspects,' + ppn. → *pahluõ* (*ū* is shortened to *u*).

**Words ending in *–iyā*, such as *ciṛiyā*, 'bird,' also have the plural oblique form *–iyõ*: *ciṛiyõ*. Note also: *śaktiyā̃*, 'powers' (from *śakti*) + ppn. → *śaktiyõ*.

***Feminine type 2 nouns that end in *–ā* behave like other feminine type 2 nouns. For example, *mātāẽ* + ppn. → *mātāõ*. Feminine type 2 nouns that end in long *ū* shorten this vowel to *u* before the *õ* ending is added: *ārzuẽ*, 'wishes, longings,' (from *ārzū*) + ppn. → *ārzuõ*.

Oblique Forms of *ye* and *vo*

The object of a postposition is often not a single noun but a multiword phrase. When this is the case, all of the words occurring in the phrase take their oblique form. An example presented earlier in the chapter illustrates this point. When the phrase *ye śahar* became the object of the postposition *mẽ*, the word *ye* changed to *is* (*is śahar mẽ*, 'in this city').

The singular pronoun यह takes the oblique form इस, plural ये takes the oblique form इन, singular वह takes the form उस, and plural वे takes the form उन.

direct form and meaning	direct form (form without postposition)	oblique form (form with postposition)
यह *ye*, this	यह कमरा *ye kamrā* this room	इस कमरे में *is kamre mẽ* in this room
वह *vo*, that	वह कमरा *vo kamrā* that room	उस कमरे में *us kamre mẽ* in that room
ये *ye*, these	ये कमरे *ye kamre* these rooms	इन कमरों में *in kamrõ mẽ* in these rooms
वे *vo*, those	वे कमरे *vo kamre* those rooms	उन कमरों में *un kamrõ mẽ* in those rooms

Some Additional Oblique Forms

The interrogative word *kyā*, 'what,' takes the oblique forms *kis* in the singular and *kin* in the plural. The oblique forms of the word *kaun*, 'who, which' are identical to those of *kyā*.

किस कमरे में	*kis kamre mẽ*	in which room?
किन कमरों में	*kin kamrõ mẽ*	in which rooms?

Vocabulary 4

Household Items

कंबल	*kambal* (m.)	blanket
कटोरी	*kaṭorī* (f.)	small bowl
कपड़े	*kapṛe* (m.pl.)	clothes
काँटा	*kā̃ṭā* (m.)	fork
काग़ज़ात	*kāghzāt* (m.pl.)	papers
कूड़ा	*kūṛā* (m.)	trash
कूड़ेदान	*kūṛedān* (m.)	wastebasket
क़ैंची	*qaĩcī* (f.)	scissors
गिलास	*gilās* (m.)	glass for drinking

चम्मच / चमचा	*cammac/camcā* (m.)	spoon
चाक़ू	*cāqū* (m.)	knife
चादर	*cādar* (f.)	sheet, bedsheet
चाबी, चाभी	*cābī, cābhī* (f.)	key
चूल्हा	*cūlhā* (m.)	stove
डिब्बा	*ḍibbā* (m.)	container
तकिया	*takiyā* (m.)	pillow
तश्तरी	*taśtarī* (f.)	plate
तौलिया	*tauliyā* (m.)	towel
थाली	*thālī* (f.)	metal plate
दरी	*darī* (f.)	carpet, rug
परदा	*pardā* (m.)	curtain
पौधा	*paudhā* (m.)	plant
प्याला	*pyālā* (m.)	bowl
प्याली	*pyālī* (f.)	cup (also, *kap*, m.)
प्लेट	*pleṭ* (f.)	plate
बर्तन	*bartan* (m.)	pots and pans; a cooking or eating vessel
बिस्तर	*bistar* (m.)	bedding
मेज़पोश	*mezpoś* (m.)	table cloth

Notes:

- *kāghzāt* is an irregular plural form.
- *kūṛedān* consists of two parts: *kūṛā*, m. 'trash,' and *–dān*, 'receptacle of...' Other examples with *–dān* are *ātiśdān*, 'fireplace' (*ātiś*, f. fire), and *guldān*, 'vase' (*gul*, m. 'flower, rose').

Exercise 15

Read the statements about the pictures below and indicate whether they are true or false. Explain the reason for all false sentences being so in a complete Hindi sentence.

१. दरवाज़े के बग़ल में डिब्बा है। २. डिब्बे के ऊपर कुछ नहीं है। ३. सोफ़े के ऊपर चादर है। ४. पंखे के नीचे कंबल है। ५. तौलिये और चादर के बीच तकिया है। ६. तकिये के नीचे चम्मच है। ७. प्याला चम्मच के बग़ल में है। ८. प्याले के नीचे कुछ नहीं है। ९. चूल्हे के ऊपर प्लेट है। १०. कटोरी कूड़ेदान के ऊपर है।

 दरवाज़ा	 डिब्बा	 सोफ़ा	 पंखा
 तौलिया	 तकिया	 चादर	 कंबल
 प्लेट	 चम्मच	 काँटा	 चाक़ू
 चूल्हा	 प्याला	 कटोरी	 कूड़ेदान

Exercise 16

G

Translate the following phrases and sentences into Hindi. If you find it easier to break up the sentences into their components as is done in the first four sentences, please do so for the remaining sentences.

1. Room. In the room. The boy is in the room.
2. Tables. On the tables. The Books are on the tables.
3. Pen. Next to the pen. The notebook is next to the pen.
4. Cupboards. In front of the cupboards. The window is in front of the cupboards.
5. The window is to the left side of the door.

6. The fan is above the bed.
7. There is a big cupboard between the pictures.
8. The pencil is under the chair.
9. The chairs are in the rooms.
10. The trash can is in that room.
11. In which box is the pen?
12. What is in these cupboards?

Exercise 17

Listen to the dialogue as you read along with the text below. When finished, create a map of the buildings and locations described. Be sure to also indicate where the conversation is taking place.

क. भाई साहब, क्या यहाँ कोई लाइब्रेरी है?

ख. यह आपके सामने स्कूल है| स्कूल के पीछे एक लाइब्रेरी है|

क. अच्छा, क्या लाइब्रेरी के पास कोई अच्छा रेस्टोरेंट है?

ख. उसके बिल्कुल पास कोई रेस्टोरेंट नहीं है लेकिन उसके दाहिनी तरफ़ कुछ इमारतें हैं| उन इमारतों के बग़ल में एक पार्क है| उसके सामने कबाब की कुछ दुकानें हैं|

क जी, शुक्रिया|

Exercise 18

Listen to the dialogue and note what the person is looking for and whether she finds it. Also list all of the other places where the item was not found.

क. क्या तुमको मालूम है कि मेरी किताब कहाँ है?

ख. कौन सी किताब?

क. मेरी हिन्दी की किताब| वह हरे रंग की है|

ख. अच्छा, क्या वह कमरे में है?

क. हाँ, वह कमरे में ही कहीं है|

ख. क्या वह किताबों की अलमारी में है?

क. नहीं, वहाँ नहीं है|

ख. क्या वह तुम्हारी कपड़ों की अलमारी में है?

क. नहीं, उसमें कोई किताब नहीं है।

ख. क्या वह मेज़ पर है?

क. नहीं, मेज़ पर कुछ काग़ज़ात हैं लेकिन कोई किताब नहीं है।

ख. वहाँ देखो, दरवाज़े के बग़ल में कुर्सी पर। वह क्या है?

क. वह तुम्हारी कॉपी है, मेरी किताब नहीं।

ख. यहाँ देखो। सोफ़े के नीचे कुछ है। क्या यह तुम्हारी किताब है?

क. हाँ, शुक्रिया। यही मेरी किताब है।

Exercise 19

Examine the two sets of pictures below. With a partner take turns pointing out similarities and differences in the two sets.

Set I

 बोतल	 घड़ी	 कंप्यूटर
 पंखे	 चादर	 सोफ़ा
 दीवार	 दरवाज़ा	 किताबें

Set II

 चादर	 पंखे	 सोफ़ा
 दरवाज़ा	 दीवार	 किताबें
 घड़ी	 बोतल	 कंप्यूटर

8

Identifying Family Members

In this chapter you will learn how to talk about your family. Phrases like the following are essential when talking about family, whether expressing family relations or describing one's family members:

मेरा भाई	*merā bhāī*	my brother
तुम्हारी बहन	*tumhārī bahan*	your sister
आपके माता-पिता	*āp ke mātā-pitā*	your parents
हमारा परिवार	*hamārā parivār*	our family
सलमान की माँ	*salmān kī mā̃*	Salman's mother
स्मृति के बच्चे	*smriti ke bacce*	Smriti's children

All of these phrases employ structures for indicating possession. The structures are all variations of the postposition *kā*, 'of,' which was discussed briefly in the previous chapter. This chapter will explore *kā* and related structures in greater detail, focusing on how they can be used to express family relations and describe one's family members.

Using the Possessive Postposition *kā*

The postposition *kā* corresponds to English 'of,' or 'apostrophe, *s*.' Take a look at the following phrases with *kā*:

जॉन का	*jān kā*	John's, of John
जॉन का परिवार	*jān kā parivār*	John's family
जेन का	*jen kā*	Jane's, of Jane
जेन का घर	*jen kā ghar*	Jane's home
सीता का	*sītā kā*	Sita's, of Sita
सीता का भाई	*sītā kā bhāī*	Sita's brother
अकबर का	*akbar kā*	Akbar's, of Akbar
अकबर का बेटा	*akbar kā beṭā*	Akbar's son

As seen in the previous chapter, the postposition *kā* is unusual in that it behaves like an adjective; *kā* takes the following forms that agree in gender and number with the *possessed* noun (the final element in the phrases above):

Forms of the Postposition *kā*

	singular	plural
masculine	का *kā*	के *ke*
feminine	की *kī*	की *kī*

Examples:

वह जॉन का भाई है।	*vo **jān kā bhāī** hai.*	He is **John's brother**.
वे जॉन के भाई हैं।	*vo **jān ke bhāī** haĩ.*	They are **John's brothers**.
वह जॉन की बहन है।	*vo **jān kī bahan** hai.*	She is **John's sister**.
वे जॉन की बहनें हैं।	*vo **jān kī bahnẽ** haĩ.*	They are **John's sisters**.
वह जेन का भाई है।	*vo **jen kā bhāī** hai.*	He is **Jane's brother**.
वे जेन के भाई हैं।	*vo **jen ke bhāī** haĩ.*	They are **Jane's brothers**.
वह जेन की बहन है।	*vo **jen kī bahan** hai.*	She is **Jane's sister**.
वे जेन की बहनें हैं।	*vo **jen kī bahnẽ** haĩ.*	They are **Jane's sisters**.

Vocabulary 1

Family

चाचा	*cācā* (m.)	paternal uncle (father's younger brother)
चाची	*cācī* (f.)	father's younger brother's (*cācā*'s) wife
दादा	*dādā* (m.)	paternal grandfather
दादी	*dādī* (f.)	paternal grandmother
नाना	*nānā* (m.)	maternal grandfather, mother's father

Family (cont'd)

नानी	*nānī* (f.)	maternal grandmother, mother's mother
पति	*pati* (m.)	husband
पत्नी	*patnī* (f.)	wife
परिवार	*parivār* (m.)	family
बहन	*bahan* (f.)	sister
भाई	*bhāī* (m.)	brother
भाई-बहन	*bhāī-bahan* (m.pl.)	siblings, brothers and sisters

Words for Parents

अब्बा	*abbā* (m.)	father
अब्बू	*abbū* (m.)	father
अम्मा	*ammā* (f.)	mother
अम्मी	*ammī* (f.)	mother
पापा	*pāpā* (m.)	father
पिता	*pitā* (m.)	father
बाप	*bāp* (m.)	father (informal, can be disrespectful)
मम्मी	*mammī* (f.)	mother
माँ	*mā̃* (f.)	mother
माँ-बाप	*mā̃-bāp* (m.pl.)	parents
माता	*mātā* (f.)	mother
माता-पिता	*mātā-pitā* (m.pl.)	parents

Additional Words

अभी	*abhī*	right now, at this moment (*ab*, 'now' + *hī*)
का	*kā*	of
दूसरा	*dūsrā*	other, second
दोस्त	*dost*	friend
पूरा	*pūrā*	entire
बाक़ी	*bāqī*	the rest of, the remaining
सहपाठी	*sahpāṭhī*	classmate
सहेली	*sahelī*	female friend of a female

Notes:

- The words *pitā, cācā, dādā, nānā, abbā,* and *pāpā* are all masculine type 2 nouns. In other words, the final *–ā* vowel does not change to *–e* like type 1 nouns. Many masculine family relation nouns that end in *-ā* are type 2 nouns.
- The following words are used when addressing parents (and can also be used when referring to them):

  अब्बा, अब्बू, पापा, अम्मा, अम्मी, मम्मी, माँ

- The following words are used only when referring to parents:

  बाप, माँ-बाप, माता, पिता, माता-पिता

Exercise 1 G

Read aloud and translate.

१. वह रवि की बहन है| २. रवि की बहन का नाम क्या है? ३. क्या वे रोहित के पिता हैं? ४. क्या शंकर की माँ भी इस तस्वीर में हैं? ५. इस तस्वीर में बाक़ी लोग कौन हैं? ६. यह संगीता का बड़ा भाई है और यह उसकी छोटी बहन है| ७. आपका परिवार किस देश से है? ८. इस तस्वीर में सुनीता के माता-पिता नहीं हैं, सिर्फ़ वह और उसके भाई-बहन हैं|

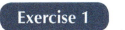

Exercise 2

Take a look at the family tree and read the statements about it. Say whether each sentence is true or false, and if false, explain why.

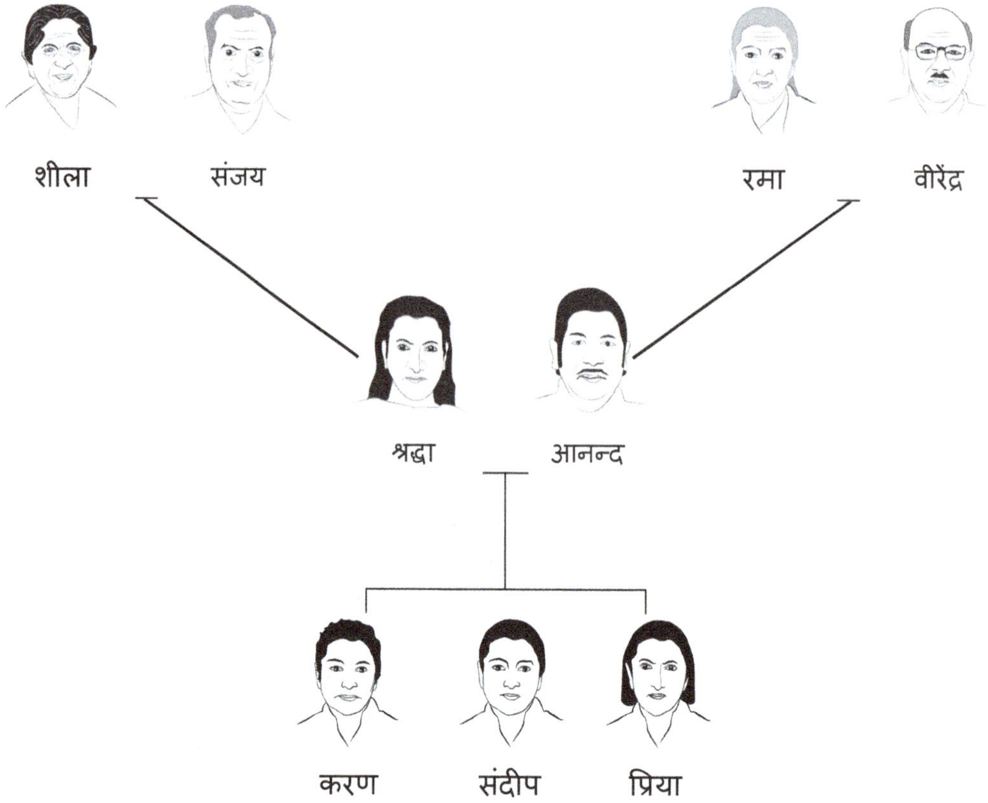

१. करण संदीप का भाई है|

२. प्रिया करण की बहन है|

३. संदीप श्रद्धा का भाई है|

४. श्रद्धा संजय की बेटी है|

५. आनन्द जी संदीप के पिता हैं|

६. संजय शीला का पति है|

७. वीरेंद्र जी की पत्नी का नाम रमा है|

८. प्रिया के दादा-दादी के नाम वीरेंद्र और शीला हैं|

९. संदीप के नाना का नाम संजय है|

१०. आनन्द जी की अम्मा का नाम रमा है|

Possessive Pronouns

The postposition *kā*, in addition to changing its form like an adjective, is also unusual in that it merges with pronouns to produce special words called *possessive pronouns*. These words correspond to the English words 'my,' 'your,' 'his,' 'her,' 'its,' 'our,' and 'their' as well as words such as 'mine,' 'yours,' 'his,' 'hers,' 'its,' 'ours,' and 'theirs.'

Possessive Pronoun Forms

<table>
<tr><th></th><th>singular</th><th>plural</th></tr>
<tr><td>1</td><td>मेरा
merā (maĩ + kā)
'my, mine'</td><td>हमारा
hamārā (ham + kā)
'our(s)'</td></tr>
<tr><td rowspan="2">2</td><td rowspan="2">तेरा
terā (tū + kā)
'your(s)'</td><td>तुम्हारा
tumhārā (tum + kā)
'your(s)'</td></tr>
<tr><td>आपका
āp kā (āp + kā)
'your(s)'</td></tr>
<tr><td>3</td><td>इसका / उसका
is kā (ye + kā)
us kā (vo + kā)
'his/her(s)/its'</td><td>इनका / उनका
in kā (ye + kā)
un kā (vo + kā)
'their(s)'</td></tr>
</table>

The interrogative word *kaun*, 'who,' has the possessive form *kis kā* (pl. *kin kā*), 'whose.' The possessive form of *koī*, 'someone, anyone,' is *kisī kā*, 'someone's, anyone's.'

किसका	*kis kā*, whose (sg.)?	(*kaun* + *kā*)
किनका	*kin kā*, whose (pl.)?	(*kaun* + *kā*)
किसी का	*kisī kā*, someone's	(*koī* + *kā*)

All possessive forms are variable adjectives. The final –*ā* changes to –*e* and –*ī* to reflect gender/number agreement. Possessives always agree with the *possessed* noun, never with the *possessor*.

तुम्हारा भाई किस क्लास में है?	*tumhārā bhāī kis klās mẽ hai?*	Which grade is your brother in? (*tumhārā* agrees with *bhāī*)
मेरी बहन कॉलेज में है।	*merī bahan kālej mẽ hai.*	My sister is in college. (*merī* agrees with *bahan*)
उसके पिता डॉक्टर हैं।	*us ke pitā ḍākṭar haĩ.*	His father is a doctor. (*us ke* agrees with *pitā*)

As seen in chapter 7, compound postpositions are postpositions that consist of multiple words. The first word in most compound postpositions is either *ke* or *kī*. When compound postpositions are used with pronouns, *ke* and *kī* merge with the pronoun as they always do to produce possessive pronoun forms.

मैं + के पीछे = मेरे पीछे (मैं + के = मेरे)

maĩ + ke pīche = ***mere pīche*** *(maĩ + ke = mere)*

तुम + की तरह = तुम्हारी तरह (तुम + की = तुम्हारी)

tum + kī tarah = ***tumhārī tarah*** *(tum + kī = tumhārī)*

Exercise 3 G

Fill in the blanks with the appropriate possessive forms corresponding to the words given in parentheses. When finished, translate the sentences.

Example:

क्या वे (तुम) ___ तुम्हारे ___ पिता हैं?

१. यह (मैं) __________ भाई है।

२. क्या वह (तुम) __________ बहन है?

३. (हम) __________ घर एम. के. जी. रोड पर है।

४. क्या (वह) __________ परिवार भी यहाँ है?

५. वह (मैं) __________ दोस्त नहीं है|

६. (मैं) __________ पत्नी और (वह) __________ पत्नी बहनें हैं|

७. (हम) __________ माँ-बाप अभी घर पर नहीं हैं|

८. क्या (आप) __________ पति घर पर हैं?

Exercise 4

A. Bring a picture of your family to class. Listen to and read along with the dialogue, and then pair up with a classmate. Using the dialogue as a model, find out who each person is in your partner's picture.

क. क्या यह तुम्हारा परिवार है?

ख. हाँ, यह मेरा पूरा परिवार है|

क. क्या ये तुम्हारे माता-पिता हैं?

ख. हाँ, ये मेरे माता-पिता हैं|

क. यह कौन है?

ख. ये मेरे बड़े भाई हैं|

क. और यह?

ख. यह मेरा छोटा भाई है|

क. क्या ये तुम्हारी बहनें हैं?

ख. हाँ, यह मेरी छोटी बहन है और ये मेरी बड़ी बहन हैं|

B. Exchange pictures with your partner. Pair up with another classmate and explain who the people are in your original partner's picture.

Stating the Number of Siblings You Have

Hindi has no verb that corresponds to English 'to have.' In situations where 'to have' is used in English, Hindi employs a number of different constructions, each of which is appropriate in a different context. The following construction can be used to state how many siblings a person has:

X *kā* Y *honā*	**for X to have Y**

The postposition *kā* and the verb *honā* both agree with the Y element in this construction. Here are some examples:

अजय का एक भाई है।	*ajay kā ek bhāī hai.*	Ajay has one brother.
उसकी दो बहनें हैं।	*us kī do bahnẽ haĩ.*	He has two sisters.
तुम्हारे कितने भाई-बहन हैं?	*tumhāre kitne bhāī-bahan haĩ?*	How many siblings do you have?
मेरे दो भाई हैं।	*mere do bhāī haĩ.*	I have two brothers.
मेरी कोई बहन नहीं है।	*merī koī bahan nahī̃ hai.*	I don't have any sisters.

Exercise 5

Read aloud and translate.

१. आपके कितने बच्चे हैं? २. मेरे तीन बच्चे हैं, एक बेटा और दो बेटियाँ। ३. साहिल के दो भाई और तीन बहनें हैं। ४. अक्षय के कितने भाई-बहन हैं? ५. उसकी एक बहन है। उसका कोई भाई नहीं है। ६. मेरी कोई बहन नहीं है। ७. मैं इकलौता बेटा हूँ। ८. क्या तुम्हारे भाई-बहन हैं?

Exercise 6

Compose Hindi questions that you could ask to find out the following information:

- If someone has any siblings
- If somebody has any brothers
- If somebody has any sisters
- How many brothers somebody has
- How many sisters somebody has

In complete Hindi sentences, answer the questions that you have composed.

Exercise 7

You will hear three people introduce themselves and tell about their siblings. Listen to what they say and note what you hear. Compare your results with those of a classmate when finished.

मेरा नाम प्रदीप है। मेरे भाई-बहन नहीं हैं। मैं इकलौता हूँ।
मेरा नाम नम्रता है। मेरी एक बड़ी बहन हैं और दो छोटे भाई हैं।
मैं आशा हूँ। मेरे परिवार में मेरे अलावा दो बच्चे हैं। मेरी दो बहनें हैं। मेरा कोई भाई नहीं है।

नाम	कितने भाई	कितनी बहनें

Exercise 8

Move around your classroom and mingle with your classmates. In five minutes, find out from as many classmates as you can how many brothers and sisters they have. Fill out your findings in the table below. You can record your findings in English, but be sure to ask and answer all questions in complete Hindi sentences. The student who interviews the most classmates wins.

उदाहरण

क. अभिषेक, तुम्हारे कितने भाई-बहन हैं?

ख. मेरा एक भाई है। मेरी दो बहनें हैं।

सहपाठी का नाम	कितने भाई	कितनी बहनें

Exercise 9

Compose two sentences each for three classmates stating how many brothers and how many sisters they have. Be prepared to share what you write if called upon.

9

Describing Family Members

In this chapter you will learn how to describe your family members in terms of their age and appearance.

Describing a Person's Physical Appearance

The construction X *kā* Y *honā*, 'for X to have Y' was introduced in the previous chapter to state how many siblings one has. This construction can be used in other contexts as well. In general, it is appropriate when stating something a person has that is not capable of being transferred to another person (nontransferrable items). This construction is therefore sometimes found in statements about people's physical features.

मेरी बहन के लम्बे बाल हैं।	*merī bahan ke lambe bāl haĩ.*	My sister has long hair.
उसकी बड़ी आँखें हैं।	*us kī baṛī ā̃khẽ haĩ.*	She has big eyes.

Sentences of the following structure are also common when describing a person's physical features:

उसका चेहरा गोल है।	*us kā cehrā gol hai.*	His face is round/He has a round face.
उसकी आँखें हरी हैं।	*us kī ā̃khẽ harī haĩ.*	His eyes are green/He has green eyes.

Vocabulary 1

Body Parts

आँख	*ā̃kh* (f.)	eye
कान	*kān* (m.)	ear
गाल	*gāl* (m.)	cheek
चेहरा	*cehrā* (m.)	face
ठुड्डी	*ṭhuḍḍī* (f.)	chin
तिल	*til* (m.)	mole
तोंद	*tõd* (f.)	belly, gut
दाँत	*dā̃t* (m.)	tooth

दाढ़ी	*dāṛhī* (f.)	beard
नाक	*nāk* (f.)	nose
पेट	*peṭ* (m.)	stomach
पैर	*pair* (m.)	leg, foot
बदन, शरीर	*badan, śarīr* (m.)	body
बाँह, बाज़ू	*bā̃h* (f.), *bāzū* (m.)	arm
बाल	*bāl* (m.)	a strand of hair (*mere bāl,* 'my hair')
मुँह	*mũh* (m.)	mouth, face
मूँछें	*mū̃chẽ* (f.pl.)	moustache
शक्ल	*śakl* (f.)	form, appearance (esp. facial)
सिर, सर	*sir, sar* (m.)	head
हाथ	*hāth* (m.)	hand; arm
होंठ	*hõṭh* (m.)	lip

Physical Appearance

गंजा	*ganjā*	bald
गहरा	*gahrā*	deep, dark (with colors)
गोरा	*gorā*	light-skinned, fair in complexion
गोल	*gol*	round
घना	*ghanā*	thick, dense
घुँघराला	*ghũghrālā*	curly
चौकोर	*caukor*	square in shape

Physical Appearance (cont'd)

चौड़ा	*cauṛā*	wide
तंदुरुस्त	*tandurust*	healthy, fit
दरमियाना	*darmiyānā*	belonging to the middle, medium
दुबला	*dublā*	skinny, thin (people)
दुबला-पतला	*dublā-patlā*	skinny, thin (people)
देखने में	*dekhne mẽ*	in appearance
नाज़ुक	*nāzuk*	delicate
नाटा	*nāṭā*	short (of people)
पतला	*patlā*	thin (things)
बारीक	*bārīk*	fine, thin, threadlike; minute
भरा	*bharā*	full
मज़बूत	*mazbūt*	strong, solid (in build)
मोटा	*moṭā*	fat, heavyset; thick
लगभग, तक़रीबन	*lagbhag, taqrīban*	approximately
लम्बा	*lambā*	long, tall
लम्बाई, क़द	*lambāī* (f.), *qad* (m.)	height
लम्बा-चौड़ा	*lambā-cauṛā*	big and sturdily built ("tall and wide")
साँवला	*sā̃vlā*	dark or dusky in complexion
सीधा	*sīdhā*	straight
सुनहरा	*sunahrā*	golden, blond (with *bāl*, hair)
सेहतमंद, स्वस्थ	*sehatmand, svasth*	healthy
हल्का	*halkā*	light

Exercise 1

You are visiting a friend who lives in another city. Your friend's brother, whom you have never met, is going to pick you up at the airport. Your friend has left you a voicemail describing his brother. Listen to the voicemail and fill out the chart below with the information indicated. In the last two lines fill in any additional information you hear. Be prepared to report what you record if called upon.

लम्बाई	
चेहरा	
बाल	
आँखें	
नाक	
...	
...	

मेरा भाई काफ़ी लम्बा है। उसकी लम्बाई लगभग ६ फुट है। वह कुछ दुबला है। उसका चेहरा छोटा और गोल है। उसके काले घुंघराले बाल हैं। उसकी आँखें गहरी भूरी हैं। उसकी नाक कुछ चौड़ी है। उसकी घनी मूँछें हैं लेकिन उसकी दाढ़ी नहीं है।

Exercise 2

Read the descriptions and match them with the people shown in the pictures. Pair up with a classmate and compare your results.

१. इसका चेहरा चौड़ा है। इसकी आँखें छोटी हैं। इसकी आँखें काली हैं। इसकी नाक चौड़ी और होंठ मोटे हैं। इसके बाल सीधे और हल्के भूरे हैं।

२. इसका चेहरा लम्बा और पतला है। यह गंजा है और इसकी आँखें बड़ी-बड़ी* हैं। इसकी नाक लम्बी है और इसके होंठ बारीक हैं। इसके कान कुछ बड़े हैं। इसकी दाढ़ी है लेकिन मूँछें नहीं हैं।

३. इसका चेहरा गोल है। इसकी आँखें ख़ूबसूरत और कुछ लम्बी सी** हैं। इसके बाल घुँघराले हैं। इसकी नाक पतली है। इसके होंठ छोटे और भरे-भरे हैं।

*Repeating an adjective in this manner intensifies it.

**The form *sā/se/sī* added to an adjective gives a similar sense to the English adjectival suffix *–ish*.

Exercise 3

Write a description of the picture that was not described in the previous activity.

Exercise 4

Pair up with a classmate. Imagine that you need to pick up a sibling or acquaintence of your classmate at the airport. You have never met the person before so you need to find out enough information about the person's appearance to enable you to recognize him or her. Draw a picture of the person your partner descibes. When finished, switch roles and repeat.

Stating a Person's Age

One of the most common constructions for stating a person's age employs the postposition *kā*:

[age] *sāl kā honā.* **to be [age] years old**

Examples:

मैं बीस साल की हूँ।	*maĩ bīs sāl kī hū̃.*	I (f.) am 20 years old.
मैं उन्नीस साल का हूँ।	*maĩ unnīs sāl kā hū̃.*	I (m.) am 19 years old.
आप कितने साल के हैं?	*āp kitne sāl ke haĩ?*	How old are you? (m., *āp*)
तुम कितने साल की हो?	*tum kitne sāl kī ho?*	How old are you? (f., *tum*)

Note that the *kā* portion of this construction agrees with the person whose age is being described. The word *kitnā* always takes the form *kitne* in this construction.

Vocabulary 2

उम्र	*umr* (f.)	age
महीना	*mahīnā* (m.)	month
साल	*sāl* (m.)	year

Notes:

- *umr:* One's age can also be stated by saying: *merī umr* [age] *hai.* Examples: *merī umr pandrah sāl hai.* I am 15 years old. ("My age is 15 years.") *tumhārī umr kyā hai?* What is your age?
- *sāl:* The first portion of the age construction, [age] *sāl kā* (without *honā*), can also be used attributively: *pā̃c sāl kī laṛkī*, a five-year-old girl ("a girl of five years"); *tīs sāl kā ādmī,* a thirty-year-old man. Also note the phrase: *pā̃c sāl kī umr mẽ,* at the age of five.

Prior to beginning these exercises, review Hindi numbers, which are given in Appendix 1.

Exercise 5

Read aloud and translate. Note also if the subject is male or female if it is not evident from your translation.

१. तुम कितने साल के हो? २. मैं बीस साल का हूँ। ३. तुम कितने साल की हो? ४. मैं बाईस साल की हूँ। ५. मेरे माता-पिता दोनों पचपन साल के हैं। ६. मेरा छोटा भाई बीस साल का है। ७. मेरी बड़ी बहन पच्चीस साल की हैं। ८. मेरा बेटा सिर्फ़ दो महीने का है।

Exercise 6

Translate into Hindi.

1. I am [age].
2. How old are you (to an elder female)?
3. How old are you (to a same-age male)?
4. How old is your father?
5. My father is [age].
6. How old is your mother?
7. She is [age].
8. In our class, everybody is 19.
9. How old is your brother.
10. He's 23 years old.

Exercise 7

Listen to the dialogue and note the age of each person mentioned. When finished, compare your results verbally with a classmate by stating each person's age in Hindi.

क. तुम्हारे परिवार में कौन-कौन है?

ख. मेरे परिवार में सात लोग हैं। मेरे माँ-बाप, दो भाई, दो बहनें, और मैं।

क. तुम्हारे माता-पिता कितने साल के हैं?

ख. मेरे पापा साठ साल के हैं और मेरी मम्मी पचपन साल की हैं।

क. तुम्हारे भाई कितने साल के हैं?

ख. मेरे बड़े भाई सत्ताईस साल के हैं और मेरा छोटा भाई सत्रह साल का है।

क. और तुम्हारी बहनें कितने साल की हैं?

ख. एक बहन इक्कीस साल की है और दूसरी उन्नीस साल की है।

क. और तुम कितने साल के हो?

ख. मैं चौबीस साल का हूँ।

Exercise 8

Pair Exercise

Student 1: Imagine that the people listed below are acquaintances of your partner. Find out from your partner how old each person is. Note the answers and then check them verbally with your partner by repeating the age of each person in a complete sentence.

person	फ़ातिमा	सागर	संदीप	नर्गिस	प्रवीण
gender	f.	m.	m.	f.	m.
age?					

Student 2: Your partner will ask you questions about the following acquaintances of yours. Answer the questions in complete sentences:

person	फ़ातिमा	सागर	संदीप	नर्गिस	प्रवीण
gender	f.	m.	m.	f.	m.
age?	19	23	20	18	21

When finished, switch roles and repeat:

Role 1:

person	सुभाष	सना	रश्मि	अमर	दिव्या
gender	m.	f.	f.	m.	f.
age?					

Role 2:

person	सुभाष	सना	रश्मि	अमर	दिव्या
gender	m.	f.	f.	m.	f.
age?	17	25	22	24	26

Exercise 9

Compose ten sentences stating the age (or approximate age) of ten people that you know. Include all of your immediate family members.

Oblique Adjectives

Like nouns and the words *ye* and *vo* (explained in chapter 7), adjectives are also affected by the presence of postpositions. Adjectives take oblique forms when the phrase to which they belong becomes the object of a postposition. Most direct and oblique adjective forms are identical. The one form that differs in the oblique is the masculine singular form; the direct ending –*ā* changes to –*e* in the oblique.

मेरा परिवार	*merā parivār*	my family
मेरे परिवार में	*mere parivār mẽ*	in my family
मेरे परिवार में चार लोग हैं।	*mere parivār mẽ cār log haĩ.*	There are four people in my family.
तुम्हारा छोटा भाई	*tumhārā choṭā bhāī*	your little brother
तुम्हारे छोटे भाई का नाम	*tumhāre choṭe bhāī kā nām*	your little brother's name, the name of your little brother
तुम्हारे छोटे भाई का नाम क्या है?	*tumhāre choṭe bhāī kā nām kyā hai?*	What's your little brother's name?
बड़ा कमरा	*baṛā kamrā*	the big room
बड़े कमरे में	*baṛe kamre mẽ*	in the big room
तुम्हारा सामान बड़े कमरे में है।	*tumhārā sāmān baṛe kamre mẽ hai.*	Your stuff is in the big room.

Masculine plural adjectives as well as both feminine singular and plural adjectives have identical direct and oblique forms.

मेरे भाई	*mere bhāī*	my brothers (without postposition)
मेरे भाइयों के नाम	*mere bhāiyõ ke nām*	my brothers' names (with postposition, no change in adjective)

मेरी बहन	*merī bahan*	my sister (without postposition)
मेरी बहन का नाम	*merī bahan kā nām*	my sister's name (with postposition, no change in adjective)
मेरी बहनें	*merī bahnẽ*	my sisters (without postposition)
मेरी बहनों के नाम	*merī bahnõ ke nām*	my sisters' names (with postposition, no change in adjective)

Vocabulary 3

Personal Characteristics

अक़्लमंद, बुद्धिमान	*aql-mand, buddhimān*	intelligent, having common sense
अजीब	*ajīb*	strange
आम	*ām*	common, commonplace
आलसी	*ālsī*	lazy
ईमानदार	*īmāndār*	honest
ख़ास	*xās*	special
गंभीर, संजीदा	*gambhīr, sanjīdā* (inv.)	serious
ग़ैरज़िम्मेदार	*ghairzimmedār*	irresponsible
चालाक	*cālāk*	cunning
ज़िम्मेदार	*zimmedār*	responsible
तलाक़शुदा	*talāq-śudā* (inv.)	divorced
तेज़	*tez*	sharp, quick, fiery (of people); strong, quick (of things)

Personal Characteristics (cont'd)

थका हुआ	*thakā huā*	tired (both words inflect)
धार्मिक, मज़हबी	*dhārmik, mazhabī*	religious
पढ़ाकू	*paṛhākū*	studious
प्यारा	*pyārā*	cute, dear
बदतमीज़	*badtamīz*	ill-mannered
बदमाश	*badmāś*	wicked, villainous; naughty
बातूनी	*bātūnī*	talkative
बेवक़ूफ़	*bevaqūf*	foolish, a fool
मिलनसार	*milansār*	friendly
मेहनती	*mehantī*	hard working
लापरवाह	*lāparvāh*	careless
शरारती	*śarārtī*	naughty
शर्मीला	*śarmīlā*	shy
शादीशुदा, विवाहित	*śādī-śudā* (inv.), *vivāhit*	married
सख़्त	*saxt*	strict; hard
साफ़-सुथरा	*sāf suthrā*	neat and clean
सीधा	*sīdhā*	simple, ingenuous (of people); straight, direct (of things)
सीधा-सादा	*sīdhā-sādā*	simple, plain, ingenuous

सुस्त	*sust*	lazy; sluggish, slow
स्वभाव, मिज़ाज	*svabhāv, mizāj* (m.)	temperament, disposition
हँसमुख, ख़ुशमिज़ाज	*hãsmukh, xuśmizāj*	fun-loving
होशियार	*hośiyār*	smart, clever

Additional Words

इन्सान, मनुष्य	*insān, manuṣy* (m.)	human being
थोड़ा	*thoṛā*	a little, a bit
व्यक्ति, शख़्स	*vyakti, śaxs* (m./f.)	person, individual

Notes:

- *aql-mand: aql,* f. understanding, good sense. *-mand* is a suffix meaning 'possessed of...'
- *īmāndār: īmān,* m. faith; *-dār,* possessor of...; also *beīmān,* dishonest: *be-* is a prefix meaning 'lacking,' or 'devoid of...'
- *ghairzimmedār: ghair-* in compounds means 'not...'
- *badtamīz: bad-* as the initial member in compounds means, 'one whose...is bad.' *tamīz,* f. manners.
- *mehantī:* cf. *mehnat,* f. hard work.
- *lāparvāh: lā-,* 'lacking...' *parvāh,* f. care, concern.

Exercise 10

Fill in the blank spaces by translating the English words given in parentheses. Make sure to use the correct Hindi form of the words in each phrase.

१. ___________ का नाम अमित है। (my little brother)

२. ___________ के नाम सरिता और मेघना हैं। (his big sisters)

३. क्या ___________ बहुत बड़ा है? (your family)

४. ___________ में बारह लोग हैं। (Manish's family)

५. ___________ बहुत पढ़ाकू है। (my little sister)

६. ___________ के भाई-बहन नहीं हैं। (my friend)

७. ___________ बहुत बड़ा और सुंदर है। (my friend's house)

८. ___________ के सभी लोग बातूनी हैं। (her family)

Exercise 11

A. Read the passage below and fill out the table with key words about each person. Be prepared to report what you record.

मेरा नाम अमित है। मैं पंद्रह साल का हूँ। मैं हाईस्कूल का छात्र हूँ। मेरे परिवार में पाँच लोग हैं, मेरे माता-पिता, एक भाई, एक बहन, और मैं। मेरे पिता का नाम नितिन पाठक है। वे काफ़ी गंभीर स्वभाव के हैं। मेरी माँ का नाम सरिता है। वे बातूनी और हँसमुख हैं। मेरे भाई का नाम सुमित है। वह होशियार है लेकिन कुछ शरारती भी है। मेरी छोटी बहन बहुत प्यारी और सीधी-सादी है। उसका नाम स्नेहा है।

नितिन	
सरिता	
अमित	
सुमित	
स्नेहा	

B. Compose a paragraph about your own family members on the model of the previous paragraph. When finished, pair up with a classmate and share what you have written.

10

My Home, My Belongings

In this chapter you will learn how to describe your home and talk about your belongings.

As seen in the previous chapters, Hindi has no verb corresponding to the English verb 'to have.' In places where 'to have' is used in English, Hindi employs various possession constructions, each of which is appropriate in a different context. The previous two chapters presented the construction for stating the nontransferrable "possessions" that a person has, such as family members and physical features.

This chapter will focus on two additional expressions of possession that can be used to describe the physical possessions that people have and the features that buildings such as homes have. Here are some examples of the expressions that you will be learning to use:

अर्जुन के पास गाड़ी है।	*arjun ke pās gāṛī hai.*	Arjun has a car.
मेरे पास स्कूटर है।	*mere pās skūṭar hai.*	I have a scooter.
हमारे घर में दो बाथरूम हैं।	*hamāre ghar mẽ do bāthrūm haĩ.*	Our house has two bathrooms.
मेरे कमरे में दो खिड़कियाँ हैं।	*mere kamre mẽ do khiṛkiyā̃ haĩ.*	My room has two windows.

In all Hindi expressions of possession, the possessor (the person or thing that *has* something) is marked with a postposition, and the verb agrees with the possessed item (the thing that is *had*).

Features of One's Home

The following construction can be used to describe features of a structure such as a house:

X *mẽ* Y *honā* **for X to have Y**

In general, the construction 'X *mẽ* Y *honā*' can be used when the possessor is inanimate. This construction literally means *for there to be* Y *in* X.

Examples:

मेरे घर में तीन कमरे हैं।	*mere ghar mẽ tīn kamre haĩ.*	My house has three rooms.
मेरे कमरे में पंखा नहीं है।	*mere kamre mẽ pankhā nahī̃ hai.*	My room doesn't have a fan.

Vocabulary 1

Home

आँगन	*ā̃gan* (m.)	courtyard
ए-सी	*e-sī* (m.)	air conditioner, air conditioning
गलियारा	*galiyārā* (m.)	hallway
घर	*ghar* (m.)	home, house
चारदीवारी	*cārdīvārī* (f.)	enclosure wall
छत	*chat* (f.)	roof, ceiling
ट्वायलेट, शौचालय	*tvāyleṭ, saucālay* (m.)	toilet, bathroom
दालान	*dālān* (m.)	interior room open to the air on one side
बरामदा	*barāmdā* (m.)	veranda
बाथरूम	*bāthrūm* (m.)	bathroom
बाथरूम, ग़ुसलख़ाना	*bāthrūm, ghusalxānā* (m.)	bathroom, washroom
बेडरूम	*beḍrūm* (m.)	bedroom
बैठक, ड्रॉइंग रूम	*baiṭhak* (f.), *ḍrāing rūm* (m.)	drawing room, living room
मकान	*makān* (m.)	house
रसोईघर	*rasoīghar* (m.)	kitchen
लॉन	*lān* (m.)	lawn
सोने का कमरा	*sone kā kamrā* (m.)	bedroom (*sonā*, to sleep, sleeping)

Additional Vocabulary

इतना	*itnā*	this much, so much
उतना	*utnā*	that much, so much
ख़ुद, स्वयं	*xud, svayam*	oneself; myself, yourself, himself, etc.

Notes:

- The words *itnā* and *utnā* are related to the interrogative *kitnā*, 'how much.'

Exercise 1

You are looking for a house to rent. Your friend has sent you a note about a house that he has seen. Read the note and answer the questions that follow.

घर में तीन सोने के कमरे हैं। इसके अलावा एक ड्रॉइंग रूम और एक छोटा डाइनिंग रूम भी है। ड्रॉइंग रूम में दो बड़ी खिड़कियाँ हैं। सोने के कमरों में भी एक-एक* खिड़की है। घर के बीच में एक बड़ा आँगन है। बाथरूम सिर्फ़ एक है लेकिन काफ़ी बड़ा है। घर के सामने एक छोटा लॉन भी है।

१. इस घर में कितने कमरे हैं?
२. घर में कितने सोने के कमरे हैं?
३. आँगन कहाँ है?
४. घर में कितने बाथरूम हैं?

*एक-एक, 'one each'

Exercise 2

Pair up with a partner and ask and answer questions about each other's houses. You can use the previous activity as a model. Feel free to ask about the following and any additional things:

- Whether your partner's home has a given feature (courtyard, veranda, garage, lawn, etc.).
- How many of a given feature the home has (bedrooms, bathrooms, etc.).
- Some qualities of those features (size, shape, things they contain, etc.).

Exercise 3

You are going home for the summer and need to find a place to store your things. You have asked your friend if you can store them in her room. Listen to her response and answer the questions about it.

मेरा कमरा बहुत छोटा है। उसमें बहुत सामान है। तीन किताबों की अलमारियाँ हैं। एक कपड़ों की अलमारी है। मेरा पलंग है। एक मेज़ और दो कुर्सियाँ हैं। कमरे में एक छोटा फ़्रिज भी है। एक टीवी भी है। कमरे में इतना सामान है कि ख़ुद मेरे लिए कोई जगह नहीं है।

A. What things does your friend have in her room? List the items in the order they are mentioned.

B. Can your friend store your things? Why or why not?

Exercise 4

Draw a blueprint of the layout of your bedroom. Pair up with a classmate, and using your blueprint, explain all of the furniture items that your room contains. You can also talk about the positions of the furniture items relative to each other.

Expressing What One Has: Physical Possessions

The following construction should be used when talking about people's physical possessions, or the tangible things that they have and don't have.

X *ke pās* Y *honā*	***for* X *to have* Y**

The physical possessions, moreover, must be transferrable to another person. Things such as physical features and body parts are not transferrable.

Examples:

सुरेन्द्र के पास साइकिल है।	*surendr ke pās sāikil hai.*	Surendra has a bicycle.
मेरे पास गाड़ी है।	*mere pās gāṛī hai.*	I have a car.
क्या तुम्हारे पास क़लम है?	*kyā tumhāre pās qalam hai?*	Do you have a pen?
किसके पास मेरी किताबें हैं?	*kis ke pās merī kitābẽ haĩ?*	Who has my books?

Summary of Constructions for Expressing Possession

Three different possession constructions have now been introduced. The following chart summarizes the constructions and the general contexts in which they are used:

X *has* Y
- X is inanimate → X *mẽ* Y *honā*
- X is animate
  - Y is transferrable → X *ke pās* Y *honā*
  - Y is not transferrable → X *kā* Y *honā*

Please keep in mind that this is not an exhaustive list of expressions corresponding to English 'to have.' Additional expressions exist, some of which will be covered later in this book.

Vocabulary 2

कुत्ता	*kuttā* (m.)	dog
चश्मा	*caśmā* (m.)	pair of glasses (*kālā caśmā*, sunglasses)
पालतू	*pāltū* (adj.)	pet (i.e. *pet dog, pet cat*)
फ़ोन	*fon* (m.)	phone
बिल्ली	*billī* (f.)	cat
लिबास	*libās* (m.)	clothing, outfit
साइकिल	*sāikil* (f.)	bicycle

Note:

- The word *pāltū* is an adjective. To say "a pet" (as a noun), use *pāltū jānvar*, literally 'a pet animal.'

Exercise 5

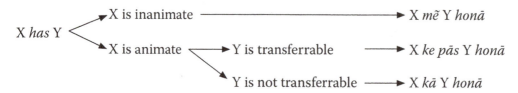

Pair up with a partner and ask each other if you have the items shown in the pictures below.

उदाहरण

क. क्या तुम्हारे पास बहुत किताबें हैं?

ख. जी हाँ, मेरे पास काफ़ी किताबें हैं। क्या तुम्हारे पास गाड़ी है?

क. नहीं, मेरे पास गाड़ी नहीं है ...

 सितार	 गिटार	 कंप्यूटर	 गाड़ी
 बहुत किताबें	 पंखा	 साइकिल	 घड़ी
 टीवी	 क़लम	 फ़ोन	 काला चश्मा
 पानी की बोतल	 पालतू बिल्ली	 पालतू कुत्ता	 कोई भारतीय लिबास

Exercise 6

Pair up with a classmate. Take turns making positive statements guessing what your partner has with him or her at the moment. The first person to guess five items correctly wins.

उदाहरण

क. आपके पास सेलफ़ोन है|

ख. सही, मेरे पास सेलफ़ोन है| आपके पास हिन्दी की किताब है|

क. ग़लत, मेरे पास हिन्दी की किताब नहीं है ...

Exercise 7

Bingo

Find classmates who fulfill the statements given in the grid below. When you find a classmate who fits a description, write the classmate's name in the appropriate square. In order to write a classmate's name, you must first ask a question, even if you know the answer beforehand. The first person to fill five spaces in a row in any direction wins.

Remember to be creative and use the skills that you possess so far to find out the information. For example, to find somebody who "has exactly one brother and one sister" you should not attempt to ask, "Do you have exactly one brother and one sister?" For this question, you might ask, "Do you have any brothers and sisters?" and then "How many brothers and sisters do you have?" Make sure to use the correct 'to have' construction.

Find somebody who:

has a dog	has a car	has brown eyes	has a Hindi book	has no siblings
has a bicycle	has a computer	does not have a pen	whose home has a veranda	has a banana (*kelā*)
does not have a bike	has blue eyes	has brown hair	has exactly one brother and one sister	whose home has a garage
whose home does not have an air conditioner	has two or more sisters	has a cat	has a Hindi dictionary	has a guitar
has four or more siblings	has a water bottle	whose home has four bedrooms	has a pencil	does not have a notebook/ notepad

11

Making Comparisons

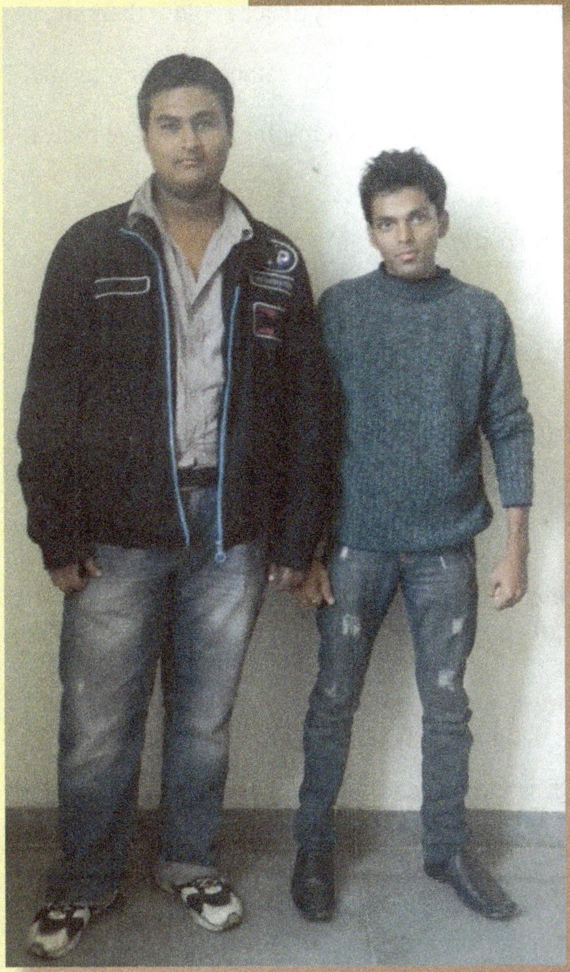

When describing the qualities of people and things, it is common to compare their qualities to those of other people and things. In this chapter, you will learn how to describe the relative qualities of your family members and homes.

Comparative Constructions

The qualities of people and things can be compared using sentences such as these:

मेरी बहन मुझसे बड़ी हैं।	*merī bahan mujh se baṛī haĩ.*	My sister is older than me.
मेरा भाई मुझसे लम्बा है।	*merā bhāī mujh se lambā hai.*	My brother is taller than me.
मेरे परिवार में मैं सबसे बड़ा हूँ।	*mere parivār mẽ maĩ sab se baṛā hū̃.*	In my family, I'm the oldest.
मेरे घर में मेरा कमरा सबसे छोटा है।	*mere ghar mẽ merā kamrā sab se choṭā hai.*	My room is the smallest room in my house.

Adjectives occur in three degrees: *positive* (e.g. *big, smart, beautiful*), *comparative* (e.g. *bigger, smarter, more beautiful*), and *superlative* (e.g. *biggest, smartest, most beautiful*). Hindi expresses the comparative and superlative degrees through constructions that are formed by adding additional words to the positive form.

When using comparative constructions, an important term to understand is the *object of comparison*. The object of comparison is the reference point of the comparison, or the entity against which another is measured. The object of comparison is immediately preceded by the word *than* in English.

Paul is taller *than* Jake.	Jake is the object of comparison
The UK is smaller *than* the US.	The US is the object of comparison
Sarah is older *than* Kristen.	Kristen is the object of comparison

Hindi has two basic comparative constructions: one is most frequently used when the object of comparison is specified and the other is used when the object of comparison is not stated.

Comparatives without an object of comparison: When the object of comparison is understood by context but not specified (when the *than someone/something* portion is not included), the word *zyādā*, 'more,' inserted immediately before an adjective, transforms the adjective into a comparative.

ज़्यादा लम्बा	*zyādā lambā*	longer, taller
ज़्यादा बड़ा	*zyādā baṛā*	bigger, older
ज़्यादा अच्छा	*zyādā acchā*	better
ज़्यादा ख़ूबसूरत	*zyādā xūbsūrat*	more beautiful

जावेद लम्बा है, लेकिन अक्षय ज़्यादा लम्बा है ।	*jāved lambā hai, lekin akṣay zyādā lambā hai.*	Javed is tall, but Akshay is taller.
कौन ज़्यादा गोरा है, तुम या तुम्हारा भाई ?	*kaun zyādā gorā hai, tum yā tumhārā bhāī?*	Who's fairer in complexion, you or your brother?

Comparatives with an object of comparison: On the other hand, the following construction is appropriate when the sentence does include the object of comparison:

X *se* [adjective]　　**more [adjective] than X**

अली से बड़ा	*alī se baṛā*	bigger than Ali, older than Ali
सारा से लम्बा	*sārā se lambā*	taller than Sarah
ऐश्वर्या से सुंदर	*aiśvaryā se sundar*	more beautiful than Aishwarya

Note that the object of comparison has no effect on the gender or number of the adjective.

अली सारा से बड़ा है।	*alī sārā se baṛā hai.*	Ali is older than Sarah. (*baṛā* agrees with 'Ali.')
सारा अली से बड़ी है।	*sārā alī se baṛī hai.*	Sarah is older than Ali. (*baṛī* agrees with 'Sarah.')

Additional Points

It is also possible to use *zyādā* when the object of comparison is specified.

X *se zyādā* [adjective]　　**more [adjective] than X**

This basically means the same thing as the construction without *zyādā*, though it is slightly more emphatic.

राज असलम से लम्बा है।	*rāj aslam se lambā hai.*	Raj is taller than Aslam.
राज असलम से ज़्यादा लम्बा है (कम नहीं)।	*rāj aslam se zyādā lambā hai.* (*kam nahī̃.*)	Raj is taller than Aslam. (Not shorter.)

The word *zyādā* is also used when the comparison is one of quantity rather than of quality.

मेरे पास उससे ज़्यादा सामान है।	*mere pās us se zyādā sāmān hai.*	I have more stuff than him.
उसके तुमसे ज़्यादा भाई हैं।	*us ke tum se zyādā bhāī haĩ.*	He has more brothers than you.

Oblique Pronoun Forms

As seen earlier in chapters 7 and 9, nouns, adjectives, and words like *ye* and *vo* take oblique forms when used with postpositions. Personal pronouns also have oblique forms. A pronoun takes its oblique form when it becomes the object of any of the postpositions *mẽ*, 'in,' *par*, 'at, on,' *se*, 'from, than,' *ko*, 'to,' or *tak* 'till, by (time).'

Oblique Forms of Personal Pronouns

	singular	plural
1	मुझ *mujh* (*maĩ* + ppn.)	हम *ham* (*ham* + ppn.)
2	तुझ *tujh* (*tū* + ppn.)	तुम *tum* (*tum* + ppn.)
		आप *āp* (*āp* + ppn.)
3	इस, उस *is* (*ye* + ppn.) *us* (*vo* + ppn.)	इन, उन *in* (*ye* + ppn.) *un* (*vo* + ppn.)

Most of these forms are identical to ones already encountered. The most important new form to learn is the oblique from of *maĩ*, which is *mujh*, 'me.'

The interrogative words *kaun*, 'who,' and *kyā*, 'what,' have identical oblique forms—*kis* in the singular and *kin* in the plural. The indefinite pronoun *koī* has the oblique form *kisī*.

किस *kis*: oblique singular form of both कौन and क्या

किन *kin*: oblique plural form of कौन and क्या

किसी *kisī*: oblique form of कोई

This chapter will focus on using oblique pronouns in comparisons with *se*, 'than.'

मेरे भाई मुझसे* बड़े हैं।	*mere bhāī mujh se baṛe haĩ.*	My brother is older than me.
मैं उनसे लम्बा हूँ।	*maĩ un se lambā hū̃.*	I'm taller than him.
क्या तुम्हारी बहन तुमसे छोटी है?	*kyā tumhārī bahan tum se choṭī hai?*	Is your sister younger than you?
नहीं, मैं उनसे छोटा हूँ।	*nahī̃, maĩ un se choṭā hū̃.*	No, I'm younger than her.

*Note that postpositions are generally written separately from nouns, whereas they are written together with pronouns (e.g., मेरे दोस्त से vs. उससे).

Exercise 1

Examine the pictures below as you listen to and read the statements about them. Indicate whether each statement is true or false. For all false statements, write a corresponding true statement.

सुशील अहमद

१. सुशील अहमद से लम्बा है|

२. अहमद की आँखें सुशील की आँखों से बड़ी हैं|

३. सुशील के बाल ज़्यादा लम्बे हैं|

४. अहमद का चेहरा सुशील के चेहरे से चौड़ा है|

५. अहमद की नाक सुशील की नाक से छोटी है|

६. अहमद सुशील से मोटा है|

७. सुशील अहमद से दुबला है|

८. अहमद के बाल ज़्यादा घने हैं|

Exercise 2

Read the paragraph below in which Mona compares herself with her sister Maria. Answer the questions that follow in complete Hindi sentences comparing Mona and Maria. When finished, pair up with a classmate and check your answers orally, speaking in Hindi.

मेरा नाम मोना है| मेरी बहन का नाम मारिया है| वह मुझसे दो साल छोटी है लेकिन क़द में वह मुझसे कुछ लम्बी है| उसका रंग ज़्यादा गोरा है| मेरा चेहरा उसके चेहरे से चौड़ा है| उसकी आँखें मेरी आँखों से छोटी हैं| उसके बाल मेरे बालों से लम्बे और काले हैं| मैं उससे कुछ दुबली हूँ|

१. कौन ज़्यादा लम्बी है?

२. कौन उम्र में बड़ी है?*

३. कौन ज़्यादा गोरी है?

४. किसका चेहरा चौड़ा है?

५. किसकी आँखें बड़ी हैं?

६. किसके बाल लम्बे हैं?

७. कौन ज़्यादा दुबली है?

*Also, *kaun umr mẽ zyādā baṛī hai?* The word *zyādā* is sometimes omitted when it is clear from the context that a comparison is being made.

Exercise 3

Write a paragraph introducing one of your siblings and comparing him or her with yourself.

The Superlative Construction

Superlatives are formed by making a comparison with 'all,' *sab.*

***sab se* [adjective]**	**the most [adjective]**

सबसे बड़ा	*sab se baṛā*	the biggest, the oldest
सबसे लम्बा	*sab se lambā*	the longest, the tallest
सबसे ऊँचा	*sab se ū̃cā*	the highest
सबसे अमीर	*sab se amīr*	the richest

हमारी क्लास में जेन सबसे बड़ी है।	*hamārī klās mẽ jen sab se baṛī hai.*	Jane is the oldest in our class.
माउंट ऐवरेस्ट दुनिया का सबसे ऊँचा पहाड़ है।	*māūnṭ aivaresṭ duniyā kā sab se ū̃cā pahāṛ hai.*	Mount Everest is the world's highest mountain.
दुनिया का सबसे अमीर आदमी कौन है?	*duniyā kā sab se amīr ādmī kaun hai?*	Who is the world's richest man?

Vocabulary 1

अमीर	*amīr*	rich
ग़रीब	*g̲h̲arīb*	poor
दुनिया	*duniyā* (f.)	world
पहाड़	*pahāṛ* (m.)	mountain
पैसा	*paisā* (m.)	money
बराबर	*barābar*	equal, equally
बेहतर	*behtar*	better

Note:

The word *paisā* is also used in the plural, *paise,* in the same sense.

Exercise 4

Read aloud and translate.

१. मैं उससे बड़ा हूँ, लेकिन वह मुझसे लम्बा है| २. मेरी सबसे बड़ी बहन का नाम तारा है| ३. तुम्हारे भाई-बहनों में कौन सबसे बड़ा है? ४. मेरे पिता मेरी माँ से पाँच साल बड़े हैं| ५. यश के परिवार में उसका छोटा भाई सबसे होशियार है| ६. अमित सलीम से होशियार है लेकिन सलीम उससे बेहतर छात्र है| ७. तुम्हारी बहन तुमसे बड़ी है या छोटी? ८. तुम्हारे परिवार में सबसे लम्बा कौन है? ९. मेरी बहन के पास पूरी दुनिया में सबसे ज़्यादा कपड़े हैं| १०. उनके पास हमसे ज़्यादा पैसा है लेकिन हम उनसे ज़्यादा ख़ुश हैं|

Exercise 5

Below are the pictures and profiles of four siblings. Examine the profiles and then listen to the questions about them. Answer the questions in complete sentences. Compare your answers with those of a classmate.

 नाम: आभा उम्र: २० साल क़द: ५ फ़ुट ६ इंच	 नाम: ऋषभ उम्र: २२ साल क़द: ६ फ़ुट

नाम: जगत
उम्र: १९ साल
क़द: ५ फ़ुट १० इंच

नाम: अनुपमा
उम्र: २५ साल
क़द: ५ फ़ुट ३ इंच

१. कौन सबसे लम्बा है?
२. कौन सबसे बड़ा है?
३. क्या उम्र में जगत से छोटा कोई है?
४. सही या ग़लत: अनुपमा आभा से लम्बी है|
५. कौन सी बहन छोटी है?
६. किसके बाल सबसे लम्बे हैं?
७. किसकी आँखें सबसे बड़ी हैं?
८. सही या ग़लत: जगत ऋषभ से बड़ा है|
९. आभा जगत से कितने साल बड़ी है?
१०. जगत अनुपमा से कितने साल छोटा है?
११. आभा अनुपमा से कितनी लम्बी है?
१२. सही या ग़लत: अनुपमा और ऋषभ उम्र में बिल्कुल बराबर हैं|

Exercise 6

A. You have received a letter from an Indian pen pal. The following is an excerpt from the letter in which he describes his family. Read aloud and translate the letter.

मेरा नाम संदीप है| मैं बाईस साल का हूँ| मेरे परिवार में मेरे माता-पिता और हम चार बच्चे हैं| मेरे पापा पचपन साल के हैं और मेरी मम्मी उनसे तीन साल छोटी हैं| मेरी बहन दीपिका मुझसे दो साल बड़ी हैं| मेरी दूसरी बहन, जया मुझसे दो साल छोटी है| मेरा भाई, संजय मुझसे चार साल छोटा है| वह हमारे परिवार में सबसे छोटा है| जया हमारे परिवार में सबसे लम्बी है और मेरी बड़ी बहन, दीपिका क़द में सबसे छोटी है| संजय और मैं लम्बाई में बिल्कुल बराबर हैं|

B. Using the passage in the previous activity as a model, write a description of your own family.

12

Unit 2 Review Activities

The goal of this chapter is to review the content of unit 2 and provide additional opportunities to synthesize all of the content presented up to this point.

G

1. Grammar Review

- Brainstorm and recall all of the grammar topics that were covered in this unit. What are the important rules related to each structure? Complete this step before moving on.
- What is the direct case? What is the oblique case?
- Make sure that you are able to reproduce the tables for possessive pronouns and oblique pronouns from memory.
- When do pronouns take possessive forms and when do they take oblique forms?
- What three possession constructions did you learn in this unit? What are the differences between them?

2. Tips for Increasing Fluency: Speaking Drills

You can increase your speaking fluency by regularly performing the following speaking drills. The first few times you carry out each drill, focus on accuracy, and then as you become able to use the structure more automatically, focus on speed.

A. Possessives

a. Wherever you happen to be, name as many of the items around you as you can using complete sentences such as *ye...hai* and *vo...hai.*

b. Make statements about whether or not the items belong to you (e.g. *ye kitāb merī hai / ye merī kitāb hai. ye qalam merā nahī̃ hai / ye merā qalam nahī̃ hai*).

c. Form questions that you could ask a person to determine which of the items are his or hers (e.g. *kyā ye āp kī kitāb hai / kyā ye kitāb āp kī hai*). Form questions using only *āp* first, and then practice using *tum.*

B. X *ke* pās Y *honā*

a. Create questions that you could ask someone to determine if he or she has the items listed below. Create questions using *āp* first, and then form questions with *tum.*

गाड़ी साइकिल कंप्यूटर बहुत किताबें क़लम कॉपी पेंसिल घड़ी

b. Make statements about whether or not you have the items above.

c. Replace the words above with appropriate new words as you learn them. Make sentences about a friend of yours describing things that you know he or she has and does not have.

C. X *kā* Y *honā*

a. Write down the names of ten people about whose families you know. Quickly go through the list, stating how many brothers and sisters each person has.

b. Describe the appearance of somebody you know. You can use both sentences of the type *us ke bāl kāle haĩ* and *us ke kāle bāl haĩ.*

D. Age

Write down the names of ten people of diverse ages that you know. Go quickly through the list and state how old (approximately if you don't know the person's exact age) each person is.

E. Biographical Description

Describe a person whom you know. Include information on: how you know the person (e.g. *merā ek dost hai...*), his or her name, age, appearance, personality traits, family; after unit 3, you can add information on where the person lives and works; after unit 4, you can add information on his or her hobbies and interests.

3. Personalization Questions

Pair up with a partner. Take turns asking and answering the following questions. Answer in complete sentences.

१. आप कितने साल के हैं / की हैं?

२. आपके कितने भाई-बहन हैं?

३. उनके नाम क्या हैं और सब कितने साल के हैं?

४. आपके परिवार में और कौन-कौन है?

५. आपके परिवार में सबसे .... कौन है?
बड़ा, छोटा, लम्बा, मेहनती, होशियार, बातूनी

६. आपके कमरे में क्या-क्या सामान है? सब सामान कहाँ है?

4. You have befriended a man from India and have asked him to tell you about his home city. Listen to his description and then answer the questions provided.

चूँकि ... इसलिए ...	*cū̃ki...islie...*	Since...therefore...
ज़रूरत	*zarūrat* (f.)	necessity
जैसे	*jaise*	like, as
ढाबा	*ḍhābā* (m.)	an open-air, no-frills roadside restaurant

मेरा नाम सचिन है। मेरा घर हिंदुस्तान के एक छोटे क़स्बे में है। इस क़स्बे का नाम मुज़फ़्फ़रपुर है। क़स्बे में ज़्यादा चीज़ें नहीं हैं, लेकिन यहाँ ज़रूरत की सब चीज़ें हैं। जैसे एक छोटा अस्पताल है। एक डाकघर है। एक-दो ढाबे भी हैं। मेरे क़स्बे में दो स्कूल हैं। लेकिन चूँकि क़स्बा छोटा है, इसलिये कोई सिनेमाघर या अजायबघर नहीं है। मेरे क़स्बे में कोई पुस्तकालय भी नहीं है।

१. आदमी का नाम क्या है?
२. उसका घर कहाँ है?
३. वह कैसी जगह है?
४. वहाँ पर क्या-क्या चीज़ें हैं?
५. वहाँ पर क्या-क्या चीज़ें नहीं हैं?

5. Choose one of your classmates and brainstorm on ways in which you could describe their appearance. When called upon by your teacher, come to the front of the class, and without telling your classmates who the person is, describe their appearance. When you are done, your classmates should be able to identify the person you have described.

6. You are working as an aid worker in a refugee camp. The following paragraphs were written by refugees who are trying to locate their family members. Identify which descriptions could and couldn't have been written by members of the same family.

कुल मिलाकर	*kul milākar*	altogether
ढूँढना	*ḍhū̃ḍhnā*	to search for

१. मेरे परिवार में मेरे अलावा छह लोग हैं। मेरे माता-पिता, तीन भाई, और एक बहन। मेरे माता-पिता लगभग साठ साल के हैं। बच्चों में मैं सबसे बड़ी हूँ। मैं सत्ताईस साल की हूँ। मेरे भाई बाईस, अट्ठारह, और तेरह साल के हैं। मेरी बहन सोलह साल की है।

२. मेरे परिवार में कुल मिलाकर सात लोग हैं। मैं, मेरी पत्नी, और हमारे पाँच बच्चे हैं। हमारे दो बेटे और तीन बेटियाँ हैं। हमारी बेटियाँ बीस, अट्ठारह, और सोलह साल की हैं। हमारे बेटे बाईस और चौदह साल के हैं। मेरी पत्नी लगभग पचपन साल की है। वह लम्बी गोरी और दुबली-पतली है।

३. मेरे परिवार में मुझको मिलाकर सात लोग हैं| मैं सबसे छोटा हूँ| मेरी तीन बहनें हैं| सारी बहनें गोरी और दुबली-पतली हैं| उन सबके काले बाल और भूरी आँखें हैं| मेरे एक बड़े भाई भी हैं| वे काफ़ी लम्बे-चौड़े हैं| उनकी हरी आँखें हैं| मेरे पिता क़द में छोटे और मोटे हैं| लेकिन मेरी माँ लम्बी और दुबली-पतली हैं| उनको जल्दी ढूँढिए|

7. Imagine that you are a genealogist. A new customer, Rohit Srivastava, has approached you asking you to research his family history. You have decided to first start with the people in his immediate household. Listen to his description of his family and draw a family tree.

मेरे घर में दस लोग हैं| मेरे माता-पिता हैं| मेरे पिता का नाम गोपीनाथ श्रीवास्तव है और मेरी माता का नाम राधा श्रीवास्तव है| मेरे दादा-दादी भी हैं| दादा का नाम जगन्नाथ श्रीवास्तव है और दादी का नाम सुलोचना श्रीवास्तव है| मेरे परिवार में हम तीन भाई-बहन हैं| मेरा एक छोटा भाई है और एक छोटी बहन| मेरे भाई का नाम सुमित श्रीवास्तव है और बहन का नाम गौरी श्रीवास्तव है| मैं शादीशुदा हूँ| मेरी पत्नी का नाम शालिनी श्रीवास्तव है| हमारे दो बेटे हैं, शशांक और मयंक|

8. You have received a letter from a pen pal in which she talks about her family. Translate the letter into English.

मेरा नाम कामिनी है| मेरे परिवार में हम छह लोग हैं| मेरे माता-पिता, मैं, मेरे दो बड़े भाई और मेरी छोटी बहन| मेरे पिता का नाम कैलाश है| वे डॉक्टर हैं| मेरे पिता गंभीर और सख़्त मिज़ाज के हैं| मेरी माँ का नाम गायत्री है| वे स्कूल में अध्यापिका हैं| वे बहुत सीधी-सादी और हँसमुख हैं| मेरे बड़े भाइयों के नाम गौरव और जीवन हैं| गौरव भैया चौबीस साल के हैं| वे बहुत होशियार और पढ़ाकू हैं| जीवन भैया गौरव भैया से तीन साल छोटे हैं| वे कुछ सुस्त और लापरवाह हैं| मेरी छोटी बहन का नाम सारिका है| उसकी उम्र पंद्रह साल है| वह बहुत बातूनी है|

9. Write a paragraph about your family and your home. Identify the different members of your family and then share some information about them. What are their ages? What are they like? What is your home like? What rooms does it contain? What is the layout like?

10. Below are several additional family relation terms. Hindi's terms for extended family members are much more specific and detailed than those of English. This is perhaps a reflection of the high importance of the extended family in Hindi-speaking communities. While homes consisting of nuclear families are not uncommon, traditional South Asian homes commonly house extended families consisting of three generations of family members. Male children often remain in their parents' home after marrying and having children, whereas women traditionally move to their in-laws' house after marriage.

Take a few minutes to familiarize yourself with the following family relation terms. Make a list showing how the relevant terms apply to your own extended family.

ताई	*tāī* (f.)	wife of *tāū*
ताऊ	*tāū* (m.)	paternal uncle (father's older brother)
दीदी	*dīdī* (f.)	title for older sister
दुल्हन	*dulhan* (f.)	bride
दूल्हा	*dūlhā* (m.)	groom
नाती / नातिन	*nātī/nātin*	grandson/granddaughter (daughter's children)
पोता / पोती	*potā/potī*	grandson/granddaughter (son's children)
फूफा	*phūphā* (m.)	husband of *buā*
बुआ	*buā* (f.)	paternal aunt
भतीजा / भतीजी	*bhatījā/bhatījī*	nephew/niece (brother's children)
भाँजा / भाँजी	*bhā̃jā/bhā̃jī*	nephew/niece (sister's children)
भाभी	*bhābhī* (f.)	sister-in-law (brother's wife)
मामा	*māmā* (m.)	maternal uncle

मामी	*māmī* (f.)	wife of *māmā*
मायका	*māykā* (m.)	parent's home (of a married woman)
मौसा	*mausā* (m.)	husband of *mausī*
मौसी	*mausī* (f.)	maternal aunt
रिश्तेदार	*riśtedār*	a relative
ससुर	*sasur* (m.)	father-in-law
ससुराल	*sasurāl* (m.)	in-laws' (home)
सास	*sās* (f.)	mother-in-law

Additional Vocabulary

तलाक़	*talāq* (f.)	divorce
तलाक़शुदा	*talāq-śudā* (inv.)	divorced
निकाह	*nikāh* (m.)	Islamic wedding
शादी, विवाह	*śādī* (f.), *vivāh* (m.)	wedding

11. Create a family tree of your family. Insert pictures of each of your family members in the tree and label them with the appropriate family relation term. Give a presentation to your class and tell your classmates who the people in your family are, how old they are, and share some information about what they are like.

12. Create a presentation about your home. Draw a blueprint of its layout and also include pictures of various rooms. Using these supporting materials, deliver a presentation on your home to your classmates.

Sayings and Proverbs

आम के आम, गुठलियों के दाम

क़ाज़ी जी दुबले क्यों? शहर के अंदेशे से

जिसकी लाठी, उसकी भैंस

दूर के ढोल सुहावने

धोबी का कुत्ता न घर का न घाट का

मान न मान मैं तेरा मेहमान

मुल्ला की दौड़ मस्जिद तक

चोर चोर मौसेरे भाई

Unit 3 Daily Life

In this unit you will learn how to perform the following skills:

- Provide general information about yourself and others, such as where you live and what you do for a living.
- Describe your daily routine from morning to evening.
- Talk about schedules and regularly occurring events.
- Tell time.
- Talk about weather and climate.
- Narrate ongoing events.

In addition, you will learn some basic information about typical daily life in South Asia.

13

My Daily Routine 1

In this chapter you will learn how to describe your daily routine. You will also learn the basics of telling time and how to provide general information about yourself such as where you live and what you study or do for a living. Here are some examples of things you will be able to say after completing this chapter:

मैं हर सुबह सात बजे उठता हूँ।	I wake up every morning at 7:00.
मैं एक किताब की दुकान में काम करती हूँ।	I work in a bookstore.
मैं रोज़ दो बजे से आठ बजे तक काम करती हूँ।	I work everyday from 2:00 to 8:00.

Saying Where You Live and Work

The verb form that is used to state where people live and what they do for a living is the present habitual verb tense.

The Present Habitual Verb Tense

The present habitual verb tense is used for general statements of fact holding true in the present period of time (e.g. *I live in Chicago*). It is also used to describe actions and events that occur routinely or habitually in the present (e.g. *I get up every day at 7:00*).

Formation: The present habitual is formed by adding two elements to the verb stem (the infinitive minus the *–nā* suffix). The suffix *–tā/-te/-tī* is added directly to the verb stem and agrees with the subject in gender and number like an adjective. The *–tā/-te/-tī* portion of the verb is followed by the appropriate simple present form of the verb *honā*—agreeing with the subject in person and number—which is written separately.

This formula summarizes the formation of the present habitual:

V + ***-tā /-te /-tī*** + ***honā* (simple present)**

Here is the full conjugation of the verb *jānā*, 'to go,' in the present habitual. The structure of this table is the straightforward result of combining two tables learned earlier: the variable adjective endings, and simple present forms of the verb *honā*.

Present Habitual Verb Tense

		singular		plural	
masculine	1	मैं जाता हूँ	I go.	हम जाते हैं	We go.
	2	तू जाता है	You go.	तुम जाते हो	You go.
				आप जाते हैं	You go.
	3	वह जाता है	He/it goes.	वे जाते हैं	They go.
feminine	1	मैं जाती हूँ	I go.	हम जाती हैं*	We go.
	2	तू जाती है	You go.	तुम जाती हो	You go.
				आप जाती हैं	You go.
	3	वह जाती है	She/it goes.	वे जाती हैं	They go.

*Although *ham jātī haĩ* is acceptable, females using the 'we' form generally use the masculine plural form (*ham jāte haĩ*) in practice.

Here are some examples of the present habitual being used to state where people live and work:

मेरा परिवार शिकागो में रहता है।	My family lives in Chicago.
मैं न्यू यार्क में रहता हूँ।	I (m.) live in New York.
तुम यूनिवर्सिटी में क्या पढ़ती हो?	What do you (f.) study at the university?
मैं हिन्दी पढ़ती हूँ।	I (f.) study Hindi.
मेरे पिता बैंक में काम करते हैं।	My father works at a bank.
तुम्हारा दोस्त क्या काम करता है?	What does your friend do for a living?

Please see later in the chapter for examples of the present habitual in use to describe daily routines.

Negation: When a present habitual verb is negated, the auxiliary verb *honā* is generally dropped.

मैं गोश्त नहीं खाता।	I don't eat meat.
हम लोग शराब नहीं पीते।	We don't drink.

However, if the subject of a sentence is feminine and plural, and *honā* is dropped, the –*tī* ending becomes nasalized (-*tī̃*).

मेरी बहनें मेरी कोई बात नहीं सुनतीं।	My sisters don't listen to anything I say.
मेरी माँ अंग्रेज़ी नहीं समझतीं।	My mom doesn't understand English.

Additional Uses of the Present Habitual

Impersonal sentences: The masculine third-person plural form of the present habitual without a subject is used to produce impersonal sentences in Hindi. Impersonal sentences in English generally have "you" or "one" as their subject (e.g. *How do you do this* or *How does one do this?*).

इसको हिन्दी में कैसे लिखते हैं?	How do you write this in Hindi?
इसे हिन्दी में कैसे कहते हैं?	How do you say this in Hindi?

Expressing immediate intentions: The present habitual can also be used to describe an action that one intends to perform in the immediate future. When the present habitual is used in this sense, the subject is often *I* or *we*. This use is frequently signaled by one of the expressions *abhī*, 'right now,' or *calie*, literally, 'let's go.'

मैं अभी आता हूँ।	I'm coming right now.
चलिए, आइसक्रीम खाते हैं।	Let's have some ice cream.

Vocabulary 1

अर्थशास्त्र	*arthśāstr* (m.)	economics
कर्मचारी	*karmcārī*	employee
काम करना	*kām karnā* (v.t.)	to work; to do a task
गणित	*gaṇit* (m.)	mathematics
निवास	*nivās* (m.)	residence
नौकर	*naukar* (m.)	servant, employee
नौकरी	*naukrī* (f.)	job
पढ़ाई करना	*paṛhāī karnā* (v.t.)	to study
पढ़ाना	*paṛhānā* (v.t.)	to teach

पेशा, व्यवसाय	*peśā, vyavasāy* (m.)	profession; occupation
रहना	*rahnā* (v.i.)	to live, reside
राजनीति शास्त्र	*rajnīti śāstr* (m.)	political science
विषय	*viṣay* (m.)	(academic) subject
सरकारी	*sarkārī*	governmental (*sarkār*, f. 'government')

Exercise 1

Read aloud and translate the following sentences. Also note in each sentence whether the subject is male or female and what level of respect is being used.

१. तुम कहाँ रहते हो? २. मैं फ़र्स्ट स्ट्रीट पर रहता हूँ। ३. तुम कहाँ रहती हो? ४. मैं मेन स्ट्रीट पर रहती हूँ। ५. तुम क्या पढ़ती हो? ६. मैं गणित पढ़ती हूँ। ७. तुम क्या पढ़ते हो? ८. मैं हिन्दी और अर्थशास्त्र पढ़ता हूँ।

Exercise 2

Listen to the profiles of the people in the audio clip and note the information that they share in the table.

नाम	उम्र	निवास	पेशा / विषय

१. मेरा नाम जितेन्द्र है। मैं इक्कीस साल का हूँ। मैं मोहनदास रोड पर रहता हूँ। मैं कपड़े की दुकान में काम करता हूँ।

२. नमस्ते। मेरा नाम किशन है। मैं चालीस साल का हूँ। मैं यूनिवर्सिटी के पास रहता हूँ। मैं वहाँ संस्कृत पढ़ाता हूँ।

३. हाय। मेरा नाम सुधा है। मैं तीस साल की हूँ। मैं कमला नेहरु नगर में रहती हूँ और घर के पास ही काम करती हूँ। मैं एक बैंक में काम करती हूँ।

४. हलो। मैं विजय हूँ। मैं उन्नीस साल का हूँ। मैं चौक में रहता हूँ। मैं विद्यार्थी हूँ। मैं राजनीति शास्त्र पढ़ता हूँ।

५. नमस्ते। मेरा नाम सारा है। मैं पच्चीस साल की हूँ। मैं सदर बाज़ार रोड पर रहती हूँ। मैं शादीशुदा हूँ। मेरे पति सरकारी कर्मचारी हैं।

Exercise 3

Mingle with your classmates and find out where each of them lives and what they study. Feel free to model your questions and answers on those in the previous activity.

Exercise 4

Interview a classmate and find out who is in his or her family, where each family member lives, and where they work.

Describing Routine Activities

The present habitual verb tense is also used to describe activities that one performs regularly or habitually. This verb tense is therefore appropriate when describing daily routines. Here are a few examples:

जमीला हर सुबह जल्दी उठती है।	Jameela gets up early every morning.
तुम रोज़ दोपहर को क्या करते हो?	What do you do every afternoon?
मैं घर जाता हूँ और आराम करता हूँ।	I go home and relax.

Vocabulary 2

Daily Routine Verbs

आना	*ānā* (v.i.)	to come
उतारना	*utārnā* (v.t.)	to take off (*kapṛe utārnā*, to get undressed)

कसरत / व्यायाम करना	*kasrat / vyāyām karnā*	to exercise (*kasrat*, f. = *vyāyām*, m., exercise)
खाना	*khānā* (v.t.)	to eat; also, m., food (*khānā khānā*, to eat)
जाना	*jānā* (v.i.)	to go
चलना	*calnā* (v.i.)	to move, go, accompany; to run, operate
टहलना	*ṭahalnā* (v.i.)	to stroll
दौड़ना	*dauṛnā* (v.i.)	to run
नहाना	*nahānā* (v.i.)	to bathe
नाश्ता करना	*nāśtā karnā* (v.t.)	to have breakfast
पकाना	*pakānā* (v.t.)	to cook
पहनना	*pahannā* (v.t.)	to put on (*kapṛe pahannā*, to get dressed)
पहुँचना	*pahũcnā* (v.i.)	to arrive; to reach (somewhere)
बदलना	*badalnā* (v.t./v.i.)	to change (*kapṛe badalnā*, to change clothes, get dressed)
बनाना	*banānā* (v.t.)	to make
लगाना	*lagānā* (v.t.)	to put on, apply to, attach to (*par/se*)
सोना	*sonā* (v.i.)	to sleep (*so jānā*, to fall asleep, go to sleep)

Time-Related Words

अक्सर	*aksar*	often
आमतौर पर	*ām taur par*	usually, generally
कभी-कभार	*kabhī-kabhār*	once in a while
कभी-कभी	*kabhī-kabhī*	sometimes
क़रीब	*qarīb* (adv.)	near, about (cf. *taqrīban*, 'approximately')
के बाद	*ke bād*	after
जल्दी	*jaldī*	early; quickly (*jaldī mẽ*, in a hurry)
तक	*tak* (ppn.)	up till, until; by (time) (...*se lekar...tak*, from...to...)

Time-Related Words (cont'd)

तुरंत, फ़ौरन	*turant, fauran*	immediately
तो	*to*	so, then
दिन	*din* (m.)	day
देर	*der* (f.)	a while, length of time; delay
दोपहर	*dopahar* (f.)	afternoon (*dopahar ko*, in the afternoon)
पहले	*pahle*	first; previously
फिर	*phir*	then; again
बार	*bār* (f.)	time (*i.e.*, one time, two times)
रात	*rāt* (f.)	night (*rāt ko*, at night)
रोज़, रोज़ाना	*roz, rozānā*	daily
शाम	*śām* (f.)	evening (*śām ko*, in the evening)
समय, वक़्त	*samay, vaqt* (m.)	time
सुबह	*subah* (f.)	morning, in the morning
से पहले	*se pahle* (ppn.)	before
हमेशा	*hameśā*	always
हर	*har*	each, every

Additional Words

ख़ासतौर पर	*xās taur par*	especially, particularly
खेल	*khel* (m.)	game, sport
चाय	*cāy* (f.)	tea
ज़्यादातर	*zyādātar*	most, mostly
दिनचर्या	*dincaryā* (f.)	daily routine
पैदल	*paidal*	on foot, by foot

मील	*mīl* (m.)	mile
वापस	*vāpas*	back (*vāpas ānā*, to come back; *vāpas jānā*, to go back, return; *vāpas denā/karnā*, to give back, return)

Notes:

- There are some differences between verbs of motion in Hindi and English. The verb *ānā* is used for movement towards the speaker/addressee from a distant place. The verb *jānā* is used for movement away from the speaker/addressee, and therefore *jānā* is also used for 'to leave.' The verb *calnā*, which basically means 'to move,' is used for 'going/coming with' or 'accompanying' the speaker/addressee. Compare: *tum akele jāo*, 'Go by yourself,' and *mere sāth calo*, 'come with me.'
- Another important point related to verbs of motion is that the destination of a verb of motion generally occurs in the oblique case without a postposition. Sometimes it is said that the word or phrase representing the destination is followed by an implied postposition (*ko*) or a "ghostposition." For example: *maĩ har roz skūl ke bād uske ghar jātā hū̃*. 'I go to his house every day after school,' in which *uske ghar* is oblique.
- *kapṛe pahannā/badalnā* to get dressed; *kapṛe utārnā*, to get undressed
- *kām par jānā*, to go to work
- *phir: phir bhī*, still, nevertheless; *phir se*, again
- *fauran: us ke fauran bād*, right after that
- *bār* means 'time' as in *kitnī bār*, 'how many times.' The general words for time are *samay* and *vaqt*.
- *roz: har roz*, every day
- *hameśā ke liye*, forever

Exercise 5 G

Read aloud and translate the sentences. Note in each sentence whether the subject is male or female and what level of respect is used.

१. मैं रोज़ सुबह जल्दी उठता हूँ। २. मैं आमतौर पर नाश्ता नहीं करता, सिर्फ़ कॉफ़ी या चाय पीता हूँ। ३. क्या तुम नाश्ता करते हो? ४. तुम नाश्ते में क्या लेते हो? ५. क्या तुम स्कूल जाती हो? ६. तुम कौन-कौन से विषय पढ़ती हो? ७. मैं हिन्दी और संस्कृत पढ़ती हूँ। ८. आप कहाँ रहते हैं? ९. मैं शहर में रहता हूँ। आप कहाँ रहती हैं? मैं यहाँ से क़रीब रहती हूँ। १०. तुम रोज़ाना सुबह से लेकर शाम तक क्या-क्या करते हो? ११. पहले मैं उठता हूँ। फिर नहाता हूँ*। उसके बाद स्कूल जाता हूँ। १२. फिर मैं घर वापस आता हूँ और थोड़ी देर आराम करता हूँ। १३. मैं शाम को टीवी देखता हूँ या कोई किताब पढ़ता हूँ। फिर सोता हूँ।

*Subject pronouns are often dropped, particularly when the subject is already clear from the context.

Exercise 6

Translate into Hindi.

1. I drink coffee every morning.
2. I go to class in the morning.
3. I work in the evening.
4. I go to the library every day.
5. What do you usually do after school?
6. I go home; I change clothes there.
7. After that, I go to the gym.
8. I exercise for one hour.
9. After that I usually have something to eat (eat something).
10. Then I go back home and sleep.

Exercise 7

The following paragraphs were written by Indian primary school students, Sangeeta and Ajay, about their daily routines. Compare their routines and note the similarities and differences by filling out the Venn diagram. When finished, pair up with a partner and compare your results. As always, speak only in Hindi.

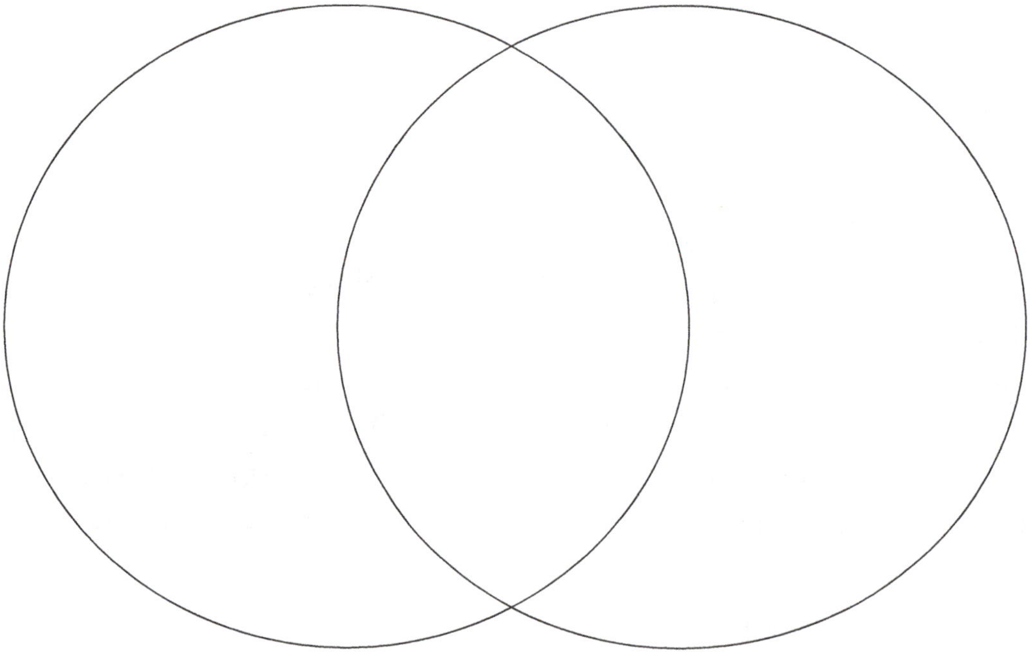

संगीता अजय

मैं हर रोज़ क्या-क्या करती हूँ।

पहले मैं उठती हूँ। फिर नहाती हूँ। फिर नाश्ता करती हूँ। मैं नाशते में अंडा और पराठा खाती हूँ। उसके बाद मैं स्कूल जाती हूँ। स्कूल में मैं पढ़ाई करती हूँ। मेरी सब सहेलियाँ भी स्कूल जाती हैं। स्कूल के बाद हम पैदल घर जाते हैं। सीमा मेरे पड़ोस में रहती है इसलिए हम एक साथ वापस आते हैं। फिर पापा काम से वापस आते हैं तो मैं सबके लिए चाय बनाती हूँ। रात का खाना हम सब साथ खाते हैं। उसके बाद मैं सोती हूँ।

मेरी दिनचर्या क्या है।

मैं सुबह जल्दी उठता हूँ। फिर नहाता हूँ। उसके बाद मैं कपड़े बदलता हूँ। फिर मैं नाश्ता करता हूँ। नाश्ते में मैं टोस्ट खाता हूँ और दूध पीता हूँ। फिर मैं स्कूल जाता हूँ। स्कूल में मैं कई विषय पढ़ता हूँ। स्कूल के बाद मैं दोस्तों के साथ समोसे खाता हूँ और क्रिकेट खेलता हूँ। फिर मैं घर वापस आता हूँ। मेरी माँ और बहन खाना पकाती हैं। हम सब लोग एक साथ खाना खाते हैं। उसके बाद मैं थोड़ी देर पढ़ाई करता हूँ और फिर सो जाता हूँ।

Exercise 8

Listen to the dialogue and answer the questions.

रजनी	अरे सादिया तुम यहाँ! क्या हाल है?
सादिया	सब ठीक है। आप कैसी हैं?
रजनी	मैं भी ठीक हूँ।
सादिया	मैं अक्सर आपको यहाँ देखती हूँ।
रजनी	अच्छा, मैं अक्सर इस समय* लाइब्रेरी जाती हूँ। तुम यहाँ क्या करती हो?
सादिया	मैं यहाँ पढ़ती हूँ।
रजनी	तुम क्या पढ़ती हो?
सादिया	मैं अर्थशास्त्र पढ़ती हूँ।
रजनी	तुम यहाँ कैसे आती हो?
सादिया	मैं ज़्यादातर साइकिल से** आती हूँ। लेकिन कभी-कभी बस से भी आती हूँ।
रजनी	तुम कहाँ रहती हो?

सादिया मैं लिबर्टी स्ट्रीट पर रहती हूँ।

रजनी तुम्हारे साथ कौन रहता है?

सादिया मेरे साथ मेरी दोस्त रहती है।

रजनी उसका नाम क्या है?

सादिया उसका नाम जया है।

रजनी अच्छा सादिया, मैं चलती हूँ। मैं आज ज़रा जल्दी में हूँ। फिर मिलेंगे।

सादिया जी अच्छा, नमस्ते।

रजनी नमस्ते।

*इस समय, 'at this time.'

**साइकिल से, 'by bike.' The postposition *se* is generally the postposition of choice with modes of transportation.

सवाल

१. सादिया क्या पढ़ती है?

२. वह लाइब्रेरी कैसे आती है?

३. सादिया कहाँ रहती है?

४. वह किसके साथ रहती है?

Exercise 9

Sequence the following verbs in a written chronological narrative of what you do every day. For example, *First I get up, then I bathe. After that I have breakfast...* Use the phrases *pahle, phir,* and *us ke bād* to sequence the actions. When you are finished, repeat the exercise as a speaking drill.

उठना, नहाना, नाश्ता करना, स्कूल जाना / काम पर जाना, घर वापस जाना / आना, टीवी देखना, खाना खाना, सोना

Exercise 10

Interview a partner to determine his or her daily routine. Begin with the first thing your partner does in the morning and continue in chronological sequence. When describing your own routine, pause after each sentence to allow your partner to ask what you do next.

उदाहरण

क. तुम रोज़ सुबह सबसे पहले क्या करती हो?

ख. सबसे पहले मैं उठती हूँ|

क. उसके बाद तुम क्या करती हो?

ख. उसके बाद मैं नहाती हूँ|

क. फिर क्या करती हो?

ख. फिर मैं कपड़े बदलती हूँ|

Clock Time

...baje, 'at...o'clock'

When talking about one's routine, it is also common to describe it in terms of specific clock times. One of the most common ways to state the time an action or event occurs is *...baje*, 'at...o'clock.'

एक बजे	at 1:00
दो बजे	at 2:00
नौ बजे	at 9:00
मैं सात बजे उठता हूँ|	I get up at 7:00.
मैं ग्यारह बजे सोती हूँ|	I go to sleep at 11:00.

The following words can be used to state clock times in increments of 15 minutes:

साढ़े	*sāṛhe*	number plus one half; half past	(e.g., *sāṛhe das*, 10 ½; 10:30)
पौने	*paune*	number minus one quarter; quarter to	(e.g. *paune das*, 9 ¾; 9:45)
सवा	*savā*	number plus one quarter; quarter past	(e.g. *savā das*, 10 ¼; 10:15)

The word *sāṛhe* is not used with the number *ek*, 'one,' or *do*, 'two.' Instead there are specific words that are used for 'half past one' and 'half past two.'

डेढ़	*ḍeṛh*	half past one (with *baje*); one and a half
ढाई	*ḍhāī*	half past two (with *baje*); two and a half

साढ़े छह बजे	at 6:30
मैं साढ़े छह बजे उठता हूँ।	I get up at 6:30.
पौने नौ बजे	at 8:45
मैं पौने नौ बजे काम पर जाता हूँ।	I go to work at 8:45.
डेढ़ बजे	at 1:30
हम लोग डेढ़ बजे दोपहर का खाना खाते हैं।	We eat lunch at 1:30.

Telling Time

The preceding section covered how to tell the time at which an action occurs. The forms used to state the current time are similar. There are two forms that are used to tell time by the hour.

एक बजा है	*ek bajā hai*	used to say 'It's one o'clock.'
...बजे हैं	*baje haĩ*	used to tell all other times.

Examples:

एक बजा है।	It's one o'clock
दो बजे हैं।	It's two o'clock.
तीन बजे हैं।	It's three o'clock.
पाँच बजे हैं।	It's five o'clock.
बारह बजे हैं।	It's twelve o'clock.

The form *bajā hai* should be used for all times that have the number 'one' as their reference (12:45, 1:00, 1:15, 1:30). The form *baje haĩ* should be used for all other numbers.

पौने एक बजा है।	It's a quarter to one. It's 12:45.
सवा एक बजा है।	It's a quarter past one. It's 1:15.
डेढ़ बजा है।	It's half past one. It's 1:30.
पौने दो बजे हैं।	It's a quarter to two. It's 1:45.
सवा तीन बजे हैं।	It's a quarter past three. It's 3:15.
साढ़े चार बजे हैं।	It's half past four. It's 4:30.
पौने छह बजे हैं।	It's a quarter to six. It's 5:45.
साढ़े बारह बजे हैं।	It's half past twelve. It's 12:30.

There are many ways to ask the time in Hindi. A couple of the most common ways are:

कितने बजे हैं?	What time is it?
क्या बजा है?	What time is it?

Vocabulary 3

Time-Related Expressions

कब	*kab*	when
कितने बजे	*kitne baje*	at what time
डेढ़	*ḍeṛh*	half past one; one and a half
ढाई	*ḍhāī*	half past two; two and a half
पौने	*paune*	quarter to; number minus a quarter

बजना	*bajnā (v.i.)*	to sound, resound, be struck (a bell)
...बजा है	*...bajā hai*	It's...o'clock (with times having 'one' as their reference)
...बजे	*...baje*	at...o'clock
...बजे हैं	*...baje haĩ*	It's...o'clock
लगभग, क़रीब, तक़रीबन	*lagbhag, qarīb, taqrīban*	approximately
सवा	*savā*	quarter past; number plus a quarter
साढ़े	*sāṛhe*	half past; number plus one half

Exercise 11

Write complete Hindi sentences stating what time it is using the following times:

a. 4:00 b. 11:00 c. 1:00 d. 7:15 e. 7:45

f. 1:30 g. 1:45 h. 12:30 i. 12:45 j. 2:30

Exercise 12

Take turns with a partner asking the time and responding in complete sentences. When responding, use the following times:

a. 5:00 b. 6:30 c. 8:45 d. 11:30 e. 1:30

f. 2:00 g. 2:45 h. 3:45 i. 6:30 j. 7:15

Exercise 13

At what time do you do the following activities? Write a complete Hindi sentence for each activity.

get up bathe eat lunch return home sleep

Exercise 14

Interview a classmate to find out the time he or she usually does the activities below. When answering, speak in complete sentences without reading your responses from the previous activity.

उठना, स्कूल / क्लास जाना / काम पर जाना, दोपहर का खाना खाना, घर वापस जाना, सोना

उदाहरण

क. तुम कितने बजे उठते हो?

ख. आमतौर पर मैं साढ़े छह बजे उठता हूँ।

क. तुम कितने बजे स्कूल जाते हो?

ख. मैं नौ बजे स्कूल जाता हूँ।

Using Postpositions with Verbs

Some of Hindi's rules for marking direct and indirect objects differ from those of English.

Indirect Object

The indirect object is the element of the sentence that is marked with 'to' in English, most typically with verbs of giving and speaking. In Hindi, the indirect object is marked with the postposition *ko*.

यह किताब अमर को दीजिए।	Give this book to Amar.
आशा को यह बात मत बताओ।	Don't tell this to Asha.

Sometimes 'to' is omitted from English sentences and the word order is rearranged. For example, the above sentences could also be phrased, *Give Amar this book* and *Don't tell Asha this.* In Hindi, dropping the postposition *ko* from the indirect object is not possible.

Direct Object

The direct object is the element of the sentence that the verb acts most directly upon. In English, direct objects are not marked with any preposition. Here are some examples of direct objects in English sentences:

I saw *him.*
Open *the book.*
I know *her.*
John ate *a banana.*
He saw *me.*
Give *these papers* to him.

In Hindi, any time the direct object is a specific human being, it must be marked with the postposition *ko.*

उस आदमी को देखो।	Look at that man!
बच्चों को यहाँ मत छोड़िये।	Don't leave the kids here.
क्या आप क़ासिम को जानते हैं?	Do you know Qasim?
ज़्यादातर लोग उसको बेवक़ूफ़ समझते हैं।	Most people consider him a fool.

If the direct object is not a human being, or is a nonspecific human being (e.g., *send a servant*), *ko* is optional. The postposition *ko* is also sometimes used with nonhuman direct objects to add emphasis or avoid grammatical ambiguity.

उस किताब को उठाओ।	Pick up that book.

Verbs that Require Other Postpositions

Many Hindi verbs require that a postposition other than *ko* (most often *se*) be used to mark a specific element in the sentence. Verbs of this type should be memorized along with their accompanying postposition.

Examples:

X से मिलना	to meet X; meet up with X, see X (socially)
X से पूछना	to ask X (a person)
X से बात करना	to talk to X

क्या आप उससे अक्सर मिलते हैं?	Do you see him often?
फ़ैसल से पूछो।	Ask Faisal.
क्या तुम हर रोज़ श्रुति से बात करती हो?	Do you talk to Shruti every day?

Vocabulary 4

Common Verbs

कहना	*kahnā* (v.t.)	to say, call (by name)
X से कहना	X *se kahnā*	to say to X
छोड़ना	*choṛnā* (v.t.)	to leave; to drop off
जानना	*jānnā* (v.t.)	to know
डरना	*ḍarnā* (v.i.)	to fear, be afraid
X से डरना	X *se ḍarnā*	to fear X, be afraid of X
पिलाना	*pilānā* (v.t.)	to serve (a beverage) to
पुकारना	*pukārnā* (v.t.)	to address as, call as
पूछना	*pūchnā* (v.t.)	to ask (someone, X *se*)

Common Verbs (cont'd)

X से पूछना	X *se pūchnā*	to ask X
फ़ोन करना	*fon karnā* (v.t.)	to call (by phone)
बात करना	*bāt karnā* (v.t.)	to talk, converse
X से बात करना	X *se bāt karnā*	to talk to X, converse with X
बुलाना	*bulānā* (v.t.)	to invite, call, summon
मानना	*mānnā* (v.t.)	to believe; to regard
मिलना	*milnā* (v.i.)	to meet; to see (socially)
X से मिलना	X *se milnā*	to meet X; to see X socially
लाना	*lānā* (v.i.)	to bring (also *le ānā*)
ले चलना	*le calnā* (v.i.)	to take with
ले जाना	*le jānā* (v.i.)	to take (someone/something somewhere)

Additional Words

अख़बार, समाचार पत्र	*axbār, samācār patr* (m.)	newspaper
कम	*kam*	less, fewer
कम से कम	*kam se kam*	at least
भैया	*bhaiyā* (*bhayyā*) (m.)	brother
मेज़बान	*mezbān*	host
मेहमान	*mehmān*	guest

Notes:

- Similar to *kam se kam*, 'at least,' is *zyādā se zyādā*, 'at most.'
- *bhaiyā* is a diminutive form of the word *bhāī*.
- The words *lānā* (*le ānā*), *le jānā*, and *le calnā* parallel *ānā*, *jānā*, and *calnā*. The verb *lānā* means 'to bring,' or 'to come bearing...' In spoken English, the verb 'bring' can be used both for movement toward the speaker and movement away from the speaker. For example: 'When you come, bring the CD with you.' and 'When you leave, remember to bring (take) your suitcase with you.' In Hindi, *lānā* is only used for movement toward the speaker. The verb *le jānā* means 'to take away,' or 'to go bearing...' The verb *le calnā* is similar to *le jānā* but is used in contexts in which *calnā* would be more appropriate than *jānā*, for example when the addressee is accompanying the speaker.

Exercise 15

Read aloud and translate into English.

१. मेरे पिता मुझको सुबह ७ बजे स्कूल पर छोड़ते हैं। २. मेरे बड़े भाई मुझको साढ़े ३ बजे घर लाते हैं। ३. मैं राज को अक्सर फ़ोन करता हूँ। ४. मैं हर हफ़्ते कम से कम एक बार उससे बात करता हूँ। ५. क्या तुम राज को जानती हो? ६. मेरे पापा हर रोज़ तीन अख़बार पढ़ते हैं। ७. मेरी माँ हमेशा मेहमानों को चाय पिलाती हैं। ८. क्या आप किसी आदमी से डरते हैं? ९. मेरे दो बड़े भाई हैं। मैं एक भाई को भाई साहब और दूसरे को भैया कहता हूँ। १०. मैं उन दोनों से छोटा हूँ, इसलिए वे मुझको मेरे नाम से पुकारते हैं।

Exercise 16

Translate the following sentences into Hindi.

1. Look at that man.
2. Look at this.
3. How many times a year ("How many times in a year") do you see him?
4. Do you know her?
5. He knows her; ask him.
6. Call him (by phone). Tell him immediately.
7. Read this book. It's interesting.
8. I know Jaswant but I don't see (meet) him often.

14

My Daily Routine 2

In this chapter you will learn how to sequence actions in a description of your daily routine. You will also learn additional structures that are useful for describing routine activities.

Uses of the Infinitive

Citation Form

As explained earlier, the infinitive translates as 'to V' and is the citation form of the verb—the form that is listed in dictionaries and used when talking about verbs. For example, the infinitive would be the appropriate form to use when asking what a verb means or asking how it is spelled.

"टहलना" का मतलब क्या है?	What does "*ṭahalnā*" mean?

The Infinitive as a Verbal Noun

The Hindi infinitive also functions as a verbal noun, or gerund, which in English has the form V-*ing* (e.g. *running, swimming, traveling*). As a verbal noun, the infinitive functions as a regular masculine type 1 noun; its final vowel changes from –*ā* to –*e* in the oblique case.

The infinitive as the object of a postposition: The infinitive, functioning as a verbal noun, may become the object of a postposition such as *ke bād* or *se pahle*.

V-*ne ke bād*	after V-ing	(e.g. after getting up, after eating)
V-*ne se pahle*	before V-ing	(e.g. before starting, before leaving)

उठने के बाद	after getting up
पहुँचने के बाद	after arriving
सोने से पहले	before going to sleep
जाने से पहले	before leaving

नहाने के बाद मैं नाश्ता करता हूँ।	After bathing, I have breakfast.
मैं आमतौर पर क्लास जाने से पहले एक कप कॉफ़ी पीती हूँ।	I usually have a cup of coffee before going to class.
क्या तुम हमेशा सोने से पहले टीवी देखते हो?	Do you always watch TV before going to sleep?
घर पहुँचने के बाद मैं थोड़ी देर आराम करता हूँ।	After getting home, I rest for a little while.

Vocabulary 1

के अलावा	*ke alāvā* (ppn.)	apart from
के बजाय	*ke bajāy* (ppn.)	instead of
के बाद	*ke bād* (ppn.)	after
ख़त्म होना	*xatm honā* (v.i.)	to end
खुलना	*khulnā* (v.i.)	to open
ठीक	*ṭhīk* (adv.)	*ke ṭhīk bād*, 'right after,' *se ṭhīk pahle*, 'right before
दुबारा	*dubārā*	again
धोना	*dhonā* (v.t.)	to wash
बातचीत	*bātcīt* (f.)	conversation
रखना	*rakhnā* (v.t.)	to put, to place; to keep
शुरू होना	*śurū honā* (v.i.)	to begin, to start
से पहले	*se pahle* (ppn.)	before

Days of the Week

सोमवार	*somvār* (m.)	Monday
मंगलवार	*mangalvār* (m.)	Tuesday
बुधवार	*budhvār* (m.)	Wednesday
गुरुवार	*guruvār* (m.)	Thursday
बृहस्पतिवार	*brihaspativār* (m.)	Thursday
शुक्रवार	*śukrvār* (m.)	Friday
शनिवार	*śanivār* (m.)	Saturday
रविवार	*ravivār* (m.)	Sunday
इतवार	*itvār* (m.)	Sunday

Exercise 1

G

Read aloud and translate the passage below.

मैं रोज़ सुबह छह बजे उठता हूँ। उठने के बाद नहाता हूँ और कपड़े बदलता हूँ। उसके बाद नाश्ता करता हूँ। नाश्ता करने के बाद मैं स्कूल जाता हूँ | क्लास शुरू होने से पहले मैं दोस्तों से थोड़ी बातचीत करता हूँ। मेरी क्लासें नौ बजे से लेकर तीन बजे तक होती हैं। उसके बाद मैं घर वापस आता हूँ और चाय पीता हूँ। चाय पीने के बाद थोड़ी देर टीवी देखता हूँ। कभी-कभी टीवी देखने के बजाय मैं कोई किताब पढ़ता हूँ। लगभग आठ बजे मैं रात का खाना खाता हूँ। फिर सोता हूँ। आमतौर पर सोने से पहले मैं दुबारा नहाता हूँ।

Exercise 2

Interview a classmate and find out what his or her daily routine is. Begin by asking when your classmate wakes up and continue in chronological order. After every sentence ask, *what do you do after* V-*ing?* When being interviewed, answer all questions in complete sentences using the same structure. After going through one partner's entire daily routine, switch roles and repeat.

उदाहरण

क. तुम सुबह कितने बजे उठते हो?

ख. मैं साढ़े छह बजे उठता हूँ।

क. उठने के बाद तुम क्या करते हो?

ख. उठने के बाद मैं नहाता हूँ।

क. नहाने के बाद क्या करते हो?

...

Exercise 3

Write a paragraph on your daily routine. Begin with the time you wake up and then proceed in chronological order, using V-*ne ke bād*, *us ke bād*, and *phir* to sequence the actions.

Reflexive Pronouns

Reflexive pronouns are words such as *myself, yourself, himself, ourselves,* as well as *my own, your own, his own,* etc. Reflexive pronouns are used to replace the second mention of the subject within a single clause.

For example, consider the English sentence, *John cut himself.* The subject of the sentence is *John*, and *John* is also the object of the verb. Instead of saying *John cut John*, we use the reflexive pronoun *himself* to replace the second mention of *John* since it occurs within the same clause. Similarly, rather than saying *I bought a cake for me*, we say *I bought a cake for myself.* The subject of the sentence is I and it is mentioned a second time in the same clause.

As you will see, many of Hindi's rules regarding reflexive pronoun use are similar to English ones. However, there are also a few key differences that are important to understand.

Using the Reflexive Pronouns *xud* and *apnā*

Hindi's main reflexive pronouns are ख़ुद, *xud*, स्वयं, *svayam*, and अपना, *apnā*. The words *xud* and *svayam* are identical in the contexts in which they are used, though *svayam* can be considered slightly more formal. In the explanation that follows, we will assume that *xud* and *svayam* are stylistic variants of the same reflexive pronoun. The word *apnā* differs from *xud/svayam* in how it is used.

Placing special emphasis on the subject: As in English, a reflexive pronoun can be used to place special emphasis on the subject of a sentence (e.g. *You yourself know better than anyone else. I myself am to blame*). The reflexive pronoun *xud/svayam* is appropriate in this use.

मैं ख़ुद ज़िम्मेदार हूँ।	I myself am responsible.
तुम ख़ुद जानते हो कि ऐसा नहीं है।	You yourself know it's not like that.
वह ख़ुद भी मानता है कि यह सच नहीं है।	He himself acknowledges that it isn't true.

Replacing the second mention of the subject (non-possessive): In English a reflexive pronoun is also appropriate when the subject of a sentence is mentioned a second time in the same clause and the second mention occurs as the object of a preposition (e.g. *The executive gave a bonus to himself. Why don't you believe in yourself?*). Hindi reflexives have a similar use. When the second mention of the subject occurs as the object of a postposition other than *kā/ke/kī*, either *xud/svayam* or *apnā* may be used.

वह ख़ुद को हर चीज़ का माहिर समझता है।	He considers himself an expert on everything.
वह अपने को हर चीज़ का माहिर समझता है।	He considers himself an expert on everything.
मैं ख़ुद को आम आदमी समझता हूँ।	I consider myself an ordinary person.
मैं अपने को आम आदमी समझता हूँ।	I consider myself an ordinary person.

A variant of *apnā*, *apne āp*, can also be used in this context.

मैं अपने आप को आम आदमी समझता हूँ।	I consider myself an ordinary person.

Replacing the second mention of the subject (possessive): Hindi requires an additional use of reflexive pronouns that is not found in English. When the second mention of the subject occurs as a possessive pronoun, the pronoun is replaced with *apnā*. In other words, in the Hindi equivalents of sentences such as "Are you at your house," and "He lives with his parents," the underlined words, "your" and "his," are expressed using the word *apnā*.

क्या तुम अपने घर पर हो?	Are you at your house?
मैं अपने पिता की कंपनी में काम करता हूँ|	I work in my father's company.
वह अपने माता-पिता के साथ रहता है|	He lives with his parents.

Note that in the first two of the preceding examples a non-reflexive possessive pronoun would be ungrammatical, whereas in the third sentence a non-reflexive pronoun produces a different meaning. Compare with the following sentence:

वह उसके माता-पिता के साथ रहता है|	He lives with his (somebody else's) parents.

While *apnā* is more natural in this use, it is also possible to use *xud/svayam* in this context, particularly when the use is emphatic.

वह ख़ुद का सबसे बड़ा दुश्मन है|	He is his own worst enemy.

The reflexive *apnā* also replaces possessive pronouns being used with compound postpositions that have *ke* or *kī* as the initial element.

तुम यह किताब अपने पास रखो|	Keep this book with you. (*apnā* + *ke pās* → *apne pās*)

Points of Caution When Using Reflexive Words

Accurately identifying the subject is essential. The subject of a sentence need not be an individual noun; it may be a group of nouns joined together by a conjunction such as *aur*, 'and.' The subjects in the following examples have been underlined:

वह और **उसका परिवार** घर पर हैं|	He and **his family** are at home.
वह **अपने परिवार** के साथ घर पर है|	He is at home with **his family**.
मैं और **मेरा भाई** दोनों डॉक्टर हैं|	Both **my brother** and I are doctors.
मैं **अपने भाई** के साथ एक ही दफ़्तर में काम करता हूँ|	I work with **my brother** in the same office.

The subject and its second mention must occur in the same clause. For example, in the following sentence the subject is mentioned twice in the same sentence, but the second mention occurs in a new clause.

वह कहता है कि **उसका भाई** बीमार है।	He says that his brother is ill.

The subject need not be explicitly stated. It might merely be understood. For example, more often than not, the subject of an imperative verb (*āp, tum,* or *tū*) is left unstated.

(आप) **अपना ख़्याल** रखिए।	(You) take care of yourself.
(तुम) **अपना कमरा** साफ़ करो।	(You) clean your room.

Additional Related Words and Expressions

The phrase *ek-dūsre* means 'each other.'

मैं और अकबर एक-दूसरे को अच्छी तरह जानते हैं।	Akbar and I know each other well.
हम एक-दूसरे से रोज़ बात करते हैं।	We talk to each other daily.

The phrases *apne āp, apne se,* and *xud-baxud* have the meaning of 'on its/their own' (without outside interference).

यह दरवाज़ा हमेशा अपने से / अपने आप / ख़ुद-बख़ुद खुलता है।	This door always opens by itself.

Vocabulary 2

अपना	*apnā*	one's own (reflexive)
अपने से, ख़ुद-बख़ुद	*apne se, xud-baxud*	on one's own, without outside influence
एक-दूसरे	*ek-dūsre*	each other (reciprocal)
ऐसा	*aisā*	like this, of this type
कि	*ki* (conj.)	that
ख़ुद, स्वयं	*xud, svayam*	self (reflexive)
खेलना	*khelnā* (v.t.)	to play
गली	*galī* (f.)	lane, alley
जेब	*jeb* (f.)	pocket
दफ़्तर, कार्यालय	*daftar, kāryālay* (m.)	office

दाँत	*dā̃t* (m.)	tooth, teeth
बीमार	*bīmār*	ill, sick
महीना	*mahīnā* (m.)	month
माहिर	*māhir*	expert
वैसा	*vaisā*	like that, of that type
सच	*sac*	true
सप्ताहांत	*saptāhānt* (m.)	weekend
साफ़ करना	*sāf karnā* (v.t.)	to clean
साल, वर्ष	*sāl, varṣ* (m.)	year
हफ़्ता, सप्ताह	*haftā, saptāh* (m.)	week

Notes:

- *aisā* and *vaisā* are related to the question word *kaisā*, 'how, of what type.'
- The word *ki* differs in a few important respects from the English word 'that.' Please refer to chapter 35 for details.

Exercise 4 G

Choose the correct forms from the options given and translate the resulting sentences. In some sentences, both forms might be possible. When this is the case, give both possible translations.

१. मैं रोज़ दो बार __________ (मेरे / अपने) दाँत साफ़ करता हूँ।

२. तुम __________ (तुम्हारे / अपने) कपड़े धोते हो या कोई और तुम्हारे कपड़े धोता है?

३. वह __________ (उसके / अपने) भाई के साथ सिनेमाघर में है।

४. आप आमतौर पर __________ (आपके / अपने)* घर शाम को कितने बजे वापस जाते हैं?

५. वह और __________ (उसका / अपना) भाई घर पर हैं।

६. तुम महीने में कितनी बार __________ (तुम्हारे / अपने) माँ-बाप से बात करती हो?

७. वह और __________ (उसके / अपने) दोस्त अक्सर मॉल जाते हैं।

८. मैं साल में सिर्फ़ एक-दो बार __________ (मेरे / अपने) भाई-बहनों से मिलता हूँ।

९. मुझको __________ (तुम्हारा / अपना) क़लम दो।

१०. __________ (मेरे / अपने) भाई को मत बताइए।

*Note that the word that occurs here must be oblique. Destinations of verbs of motion take the oblique case without an explicitly stated postposition. Sometimes it is said that an implied postposition, or "ghostposition," is present. In this sentence, the word *ghar* is thus oblique and any modifiers must agree with it in case (i.e., in being direct vs.oblique).

Exercise 5

Translate these English sentences into Hindi. Before translating each sentence, determine whether or not *apnā* is appropriate.

1. He is with his parents at home.
2. He and his parents are at home.
3. I meet my friends often for coffee.
4. My friends and I meet often for coffee.
5. I clean my room only once a month.
6. I see my brother often, but I only see my parents once in a while.
7. Do you talk to your grandparents often?
8. He and his family live near my house.
9. He lives with his parents.
10. Tell me your name.

Exercise 6

Take turns asking and answering the following questions with a partner:

१. तुम अपने माता-पिता से महीने / साल में कितनी बार मिलते हो?
२. तुम दिन में कितनी बार अपने दाँत साफ़ करते हो?
३. तुम हफ़्ते / महीने में कितनी बार अपने कपड़े धोते हो?
४. तुम अपने कपड़े ख़ुद धोते हो या कोई और धोता है?
५. तुम अपना कमरा हफ़्ते में कितनी बार साफ़ करते हो?
६. क्या तुम अपने भाई-बहनों से अक्सर मिलते हो?
७. तुम अपने भाई-बहनों से कितने बड़े या छोटे हो?

Exercise 7

Jaya is a housewife with two children. A relative of hers is going to be watching her children for a few days and Jaya has left the relative a voicemail explaining what her kids do every day. To help the babysitter, listen to the voicemail and make a schedule of what her kids do.

समय	दिनचर्या
सुबह	
दोपहर	
शाम	
रात	

बच्चे छह बजे उठते हैं। उसके तुरंत बाद वे नहाते हैं और अपने दाँत साफ़ करते हैं। फिर वे नाश्ता करते हैं। वे अपना नाश्ता नहीं बनाते। मैं हमेशा उनके लिये ऑमलेट बनाती हूँ। नाश्ते के बाद वे स्कूल जाते हैं और वहाँ तीन बजे तक रहते हैं। दोनों बच्चे अपने दोस्तों के साथ स्कूल से पैदल वापस आते हैं। तीन बजे से चार बजे तक वे अपना होमवर्क करते हैं। शाम पाँच से साढ़े छह बजे तक वे अपने दोस्तों के साथ बाहर गली में खेलते हैं। लगभग आठ बजे वे रात का खाना खाते हैं। उसके बाद वे अपने कपड़े बदलते हैं फिर सोते हैं।

15

Describing Events in Progress

In this chapter you will learn how to describe a scene in terms of events that are currently unfolding.

The Present Continuous Verb Tense

In English, actions that are in progress at the time of speaking can be described with sentences such as:

I am studying.

John is sleeping.

My father is watching TV.

What are you cooking?

The equivalent verb tense in Hindi is the present continuous. This verb tense is appropriate when describing events that are currently happening, for example, when describing a scene as it unfolds in front of you, or describing what the people around you are in the process of doing as you speak.

Formation: The present continuous is formed as follows:

V + *rahā / rahe / rahī* + *honā* [present]

Both *rahā* and *honā* are written separately from the verb stem. Here is the full conjugation of the verb *jānā*, 'to go,' in the present continuous.

The Present Continuous Verb Tense

		singular		plural	
masculine	1	मैं जा रहा हूँ।	I am going.	हम जा रहे हैं।	We are going.
	2	तू जा रहा है।	You are going.	तुम जा रहे हो।	You are going.
				आप जा रहे हैं।	You are going.
	3	वह जा रहा है।	He/it is going.	वे जा रहे हैं।	They are going.
feminine	1	मैं जा रही हूँ।	I am going.	हम जा रही हैं।*	We are going.
	2	तू जा रही है।	You are going.	तुम जा रही हो।	You are going.
				आप जा रही हैं।	You are going.
	3	वह जा रही है।	She/it is going.	वे जा रही हैं।	They are going.

* In practice, females using the 'we' form more often use the corresponding masculine form: *ham jā rahe haĩ.*

Like conjugation in the present habitual verb tense, present continuous conjugation is the straightforward result of combining two agreement patterns already covered: the *rahā/rahe/rahī* portion of the verb behaves like an adjective in following the pattern of gender/number agreement, and the auxiliary verb *honā* follows the person/number agreement pattern (*hū̃, hai, hai, haĩ, ho, haĩ, haĩ*). The only new information to learn is that the continuous marker (corresponding to *-ing* in English) is *rah-*.

Examples:

तुम्हारे घर में इस समय क्या हो रहा है?	What's happening* in your house right now?
मेरे पापा अख़बार पढ़ रहे हैं।	My father is reading the paper.
मेरी मम्मी चाय बना रही हैं।	My mother is making tea.
अजय सो रहा है।	Ajay is sleeping.
सीमा टीवी देख रही है।	Seema is watching TV.
तुम क्या कर रही हो?	What are you doing?
मैं कुछ पढ़ाई कर रही हूँ।	I am doing some studying.
मैं कुछ नहीं कर रहा हूँ।	I am not doing anything.

**honā* in the present continuous often translates as *happening,* or *becoming.*

Additional Points

Expressing future actions: In addition to its basic use of describing actions and events currently in progress, the present continuous can also be used for future actions that have already been set in motion or decided upon.

तुम आज दोपहर क्या कर रही हो?	What are you doing this afternoon?
मैं कुछ नहीं कर रही हूँ। मैं घर जा रही हूँ।	I'm not doing anything. I'm going home.

Verbs that differ from their English equivalents: There are a few verbs that are commonly used in the present continuous in English yet in Hindi convey different meanings in this tense.

For example, the verb *baiṭhnā* means 'to sit down.' Consider the following sentence:

सब लोग बैठ रहे हैं।	Everybody is (in the process of) sitting down.

To convey the meaning 'Everybody is sitting (seated),' a different form of *baiṭhnā* is used, *baiṭhā*, which means 'seated.'

सब लोग बैठे हैं।	Everyone is sitting (seated).

To say that a person is standing (statically), use the adjective *khaṛā*, 'standing,' with the appropriate simple present form of *honā*.

सब लोग खड़े हैं।	Everybody is standing (in a standing state).

Contrast this with the following sentence:

सब लोग खड़े हो रहे हैं।	Everybody is (in the process of) standing up.

Vocabulary 1

आज	*āj*	today
आजकल	*ājkal*	these days
आस-पास	*ās-pās*	nearby
इम्तिहान, परीक्षा	*imtihān* (m.), *parīkṣā* (f.)	test, examination
खड़ा	*khaṛā*	standing (*khaṛā honā*, to stand)
ख़रीदना	*xarīdnā* (v.t.)	to buy
गाना	*gānā* (m.)	to sing (v.t.); song
चढ़ना	*caṛhnā* (v.i.)	to climb (X *par*), to ascend
चहल-क़दमी	*cahal-qadmī* (f.)	walk, stroll
चाहना	*cāhnā* (v.t.)	to want (V-*nā cāhnā*, to want to V)
ठेला	*ṭhelā* (m.)	cart
नाचना	*nācnā* (v.i.)	to dance
फल	*phal* (m.)	fruit
फूल	*phūl* (m.)	flower

बजाना	*bajānā* (v.t.)	to play (an instrument); to make ring
बरबाद	*barbād*	ruined
बरबाद करना	*barbād karnā*	to ruin, to waste (e.g., time)
बैठा	*baiṭhā*	seated (cf. *baiṭhnā*)
मदद	*madad* (f.)	help (X *kī madad karnā*, to help X)
मशहूर	*maśhūr*	famous
मुग़लई खाना	*mughlaī khānā*	North Indian Muslim food
मेहमान	*mehmān*	guest
व्यस्त	*vyast*	busy
शायद	*śāyad*	perhaps, maybe
शोर	*śor* (m.)	noise, commotion
शोर मचाना	*śor macānā*	to make a lot of noise
सफ़र, यात्रा	*safar* (m.), *yātrā* (f.)	journey
सीढ़ी	*sīṛhī* (f.)	stair

Notes:

- *ājkal* is a compound of *āj*, 'today,' and *kal*, 'tomorrow, yesterday.'
- *imtihān denā*, 'to take a test.'

Exercise 1 G

Read aloud and translate.

१. तुम्हारे घर के सब लोग इस समय क्या कर रहे हैं? २. मेरे पिता चाय पी रहे हैं और बैठक में मेहमानों से बात कर रहे हैं। ३. मेरी माँ रसोई में खाना पका रही हैं। ४. वे दाल बना रही हैं। ५. मेरी बहन उनके साथ है। वह उनकी मदद कर रही है। ६. मेरे सबसे बड़े भाई कुछ पढ़ रहे हैं। ७. मेरा दूसरा भाई अपने कमरे में सितार बजा रहा है। ८. तुम्हारे घर में क्या हो रहा है? सब लोग किन कामों में व्यस्त हैं? ९. मेरी बहन गा रही है। १०. मेरा भाई उसके साथ बैठा है। वह गिटार बजा रहा है।

Exercise 2

Imagine that it's a typical evening at 8:00 at your home or in your dorm. You are writing a letter to a pen pal. Describe to your pen pal what everybody is currently doing around you. You might use the following verbs or any other ones that you need:

खाना पकाना, पढ़ना, किताब पढ़ना, टीवी देखना, फ़ोन पर बात करना, सफ़ाई करना, बर्तन धोना

उदाहरण

मेरी माँ इस समय खाना पका रही हैं और मेरे पापा किताब पढ़ रहे हैं...

Exercise 3

You overhear the following conversation between Indian students in your dormitory. Listen to the conversation and then answer the questions.

फ़िज़ा	कुसुम! कुसुम! तुम क्या कर रही हो?
कुसुम	मैं पढ़ रही हूँ। अगले हफ़्ते मेरा इम्तिहान है।
फ़िज़ा	ज़रा यहाँ आओ।
कुसुम	अच्छा भई, आ रही हूँ। क्या बात है? इतना शोर क्यों मचा रही हो?
फ़िज़ा	यहाँ बैठो। यह देखो, यह टीवी पर कितना अच्छा शो आ रहा है। आओ मेरे साथ देखो।
कुसुम	नहीं, मैं पढ़ रही हूँ।
फ़िज़ा	और सारिका क्या कर रही है?
कुसुम	वह खाना पका रही है।
फ़िज़ा	वह खाने में क्या पका रही है?
कुसुम	वह आलू-गोभी पका रही है। और शायद कुछ पूड़ियाँ भी।
फ़िज़ा	मैं यह मज़ेदार शो किसी के साथ देखना चाहती हूँ। अच्छा, साहिल क्या कर रहा है?
कुसुम	वह कपड़े धो रहा है।

फ़िज़ा ओफ़्फ़ोह! सब लोग काम कर रहे हैं।

कुसुम मैं भी जा रही हूँ। तुम मेरा वक़्त बरबाद कर रही हो।

सवाल

१. कुसुम क्या कर रही है और क्यों?

२. फ़िज़ा क्या कर रही है?

३. सारिका क्या कर रही है?

४. साहिल क्या कर रहा है?

Exercise 4

Charades

Form two teams. One team chooses a verb already learned and writes it on a slip of paper. The other team chooses a representative who will read the verb and then act it out silently for his or her team. The members of the guessing team must then guess what action their teammate is acting out. They should guess by asking complete sentences: *Are you doing…?* The representative should respond to each question in a complete sentence: either *No, I'm not…* or *Yes, I'm…* For each correctly guessed action (using correct complete sentences) teams will receive one point. The team with the most points wins.

Exercise 5

An American student, James, is currently in India. He is writing a blog from Delhi for his Hindi classmates in America. Read the entry and answer the questions below.

मेरा नाम जेम्स है। मैं यूनिवर्सिटी आफ़ वर्जीनिया का छात्र हूँ। आजकल मैं भारत की यात्रा कर रहा हूँ। इस समय मैं पुरानी दिल्ली में हूँ। मेरे सामने मशहूर जामा मस्जिद है। बहुत से लोग मस्जिद की सीढ़ियाँ चढ़ रहे हैं। शायद नमाज़ का वक़्त है। आस-पास मुग़लई खानों की बहुत सी दुकानें हैं। एक तरफ़ फलों के ठेले हैं। बहुत से लोग खा रहे हैं। बच्चे सड़क पर खेल रहे हैं और कुछ औरतें फल ख़रीद रही हैं। यहाँ उर्दू की किताबों की कई दुकानें हैं। इन दुकानों में लोग चाय पी रहे हैं और ज़ोर-ज़ोर से बातें कर रहे हैं। मैं अभी एक दुकान में जा रहा हूँ। मैं उर्दू की कुछ किताबें ख़रीदना चाहता हूँ।

१. आजकल जेम्स क्या कर रहा है?
२. बच्चे कहाँ खेल रहे हैं?
३. औरतें क्या कर रही हैं?
४. लोग किताबों की दुकानों में क्या कर रहे हैं?
५. जेम्स कहाँ जा रहा है और क्यों?

Conjunct Verbs

Conjunct verbs are a special class of verbal constructions that consist of multiple words yet convey a single unified verbal idea. Many conjunct verbs correspond to simple (single-word) verbs in English. You have already run across a few examples of conjunct verbs.

आराम करना	to rest
काम करना	to work
मदद करना	to help
कसरत करना	to exercise

Conjunct verbs always contain at least two elements: a nonverbal element, generally a noun or an adjective, which comes first, and a common simple verb, most often *karnā*, 'to do,' or *honā*, 'to be.'

Here are some examples of conjunct verbs consisting of an adjective followed by a verb:

गरम करना	to heat (literally, 'to make hot')
परेशान करना	to bother (literally, 'to make worried')

मैं पानी गरम कर रहा हूँ।	I'm heating up some water.
मुझको परेशान मत करो। अपना काम करो।	Don't bother me. Mind your own business.

The conjunct verbs *ārām karnā* and *kām karnā*, which have already been introduced, are examples of conjunct verbs consisting of a noun and a verb:

आराम करना	to rest
आराम	rest (m.)
काम करना	to work
काम	work (m.)

Conjunct Verbs with Associated Postpositions

Many noun-based conjunct verbs require a postposition to link the noun to other portions of sentence. A postposition filling this function should be considered an essential part of the conjunct verb construction and learned along with it. Conjunct verbs can easily be memorized with their postpositions using constructions like the following:

X का इंतज़ार करना	to wait for X (literally, 'to do X's wait')
V-ने की कोशिश करना	to try to V (literally, 'to make the effort of V-ing')

The variables in these constructions (the Xs and Vs) are just placeholders for actual words. Using a construction is simply a matter of replacing the variable with an actual name or word and then conjugating the verb as you would normally.

X का इंतज़ार करना	to wait for X
जॉन का इंतज़ार करना	to wait for John
मैं जॉन का इंतज़ार कर रहा हूँ।	I'm waiting for John.

As explained in chapter 14, the infinitive, which has the general form V-*nā*, can become the object of a postposition. When an infinitive becomes the object of a postposition, it takes its oblique form, V-*ne*. Some conjunct verb constructions such as the following include a place for an oblique infinitive. To use constructions like this, just replace V-*ne* with an actual oblique infinitive.

V-ने की कोशिश करना	to try to V
सोने की कोशिश करना	to try to sleep
मैं सोने की कोशिश कर रहा हूँ।	I'm trying to sleep.

Here are some additional examples:

तुम किसका इंतज़ार कर रहे हो?	Who are you waiting for?
मैं तुम्हारा इंतज़ार कर रहा हूँ।	I'm waiting for you.
वह पढ़ने की कोशिश कर रही है।	She's trying to study.

Conjunct Verbs without Postpositions

Some noun-based conjunct verbs function as if the noun and verb are a single unit—no postposition is used to link the noun to other elements in the sentence. One example of this type of conjunct verb is *śurū karnā*.

शुरू करना	to begin

Note how this two-word verbal phrase functions as a single unit in the following sentence. No postposition is used to link the noun *śurū* with the direct object.

तुम काम जल्दी शुरू करो।	Start the work quickly.

Conjunct Verbs with Optional Postpositions

Still other conjunct verbs can be used either with or without a postposition. An example of this type of conjunct verb is *istemāl karnā*, 'to use.'

इस्तेमाल करना	to use
X का इस्तेमाल करना	to use X

मैं तुम्हारी पेंसिल इस्तेमाल कर रहा हूँ।	I am using your pencil.
मैं तुम्हारी पेंसिल का इस्तेमाल कर रहा हूँ।	I am using your pencil.

Vocabulary 2

Some Common Conjunct Verbs

इंतज़ार	*intazār* (m.)	wait, act of waiting
X का इंतज़ार करना	X *kā intazār karnā*	to wait for X
इस्तेमाल	*istemāl* (m.)	use
X (का) इस्तेमाल करना	X (*kā*) *istemāl karnā*	to use X
कम	*kam*	less, fewer; little, few
कम करना	*kam karnā*	to lower, to lessen, to decrease
कसरत / व्यायाम करना	*kasrat / vyāyām karnā*	to exercise (*kasrat*, f. = *vyāyām*, m., exercise)
कोशिश	*kośiś* (f.)	effort
V-ने की कोशिश करना	V-*ne kī kośiś karnā*	to try to V
ख़त्म	*xatm* (m.)	end
ख़त्म करना	*xatm karnā* (v.t.)	to finish (e.g. "The teacher is finishing class.")
ख़त्म होना	*xatm honā* (v.i.)	to finish (e.g. "Class is finishing/ending.")
चिंता, फ़िक्र	*cintā, fikr* (f.)	worry, thought, preoccupation
चिंता, फ़िक्र करना	*cintā, fikr karnā*	to worry (about X, X *kī*)
ज़िक्र	*zikr* (m.)	mention
X का ज़िक्र करना	X *kā zikr karnā*	to mention X (to, *se*)
नफ़रत	*nafrat* (f.)	hatred
X से नफ़रत करना	X *se nafrat karnā*	to hate X
पढ़ाई	*paṛhāī* (f.)	study
पढ़ाई करना	*paṛhāī karnā*	to study
पता	*patā* (m.)	address, whereabouts
(X का) पता करना	(X *kā*) *patā karnā*	to find out (about X)

Some Common Conjunct Verbs (cont'd)

परेशान	*pareśān*	worried, distressed
परेशान करना	*pareśān karnā*	to bother
पूरा	*pūrā*	completed, complete
पूरा करना	*pūrā karnā*	to complete
प्यार	*pyār* (m.)	love; affection
X से प्यार करना	X *se pyār karnā*	to love X
बंद	*band*	closed
बंद करना	*band karnā*	to close, to stop (discontinue doing sthg.)
बात	*bāt* (f.)	matter, a piece of speech
X से (Y की) बात करना	X *se* (Y *kī*) *bāt karnā*	to talk to X (about Y)
भरोसा	*bharosā* (m.)	trust
X पर भरोसा करना	X *par bharosā karnā*	to trust X; have faith (not religious) in X
मदद	*madad* (f.)	help
X की मदद करना	X *kī madad karnā*	to help X
माफ़	*māf*	excused; forgiven
माफ़ करना	*māf karnā*	to excuse, to forgive (*māf kījie*, excuse me, sorry)
विश्वास, यक़ीन	*viśvās, yaqīn* (m.)	certainty, confidence
विश्वास / यक़ीन करना	*viśvās / yaqīn karnā*	to believe
शुरू	*śurū* (m.)	beginning
शुरू करना	*śurū karnā* (v.t.)	to start, to begin (e.g. "The teacher is starting class.")
शुरू होना	*śurū honā* (v.i.)	to start, to begin (e.g. "Class is starting.")
सफ़ाई	*safāī* (f.)	cleaning
X की सफ़ाई करना	X *kī safāī karnā*	to clean X

Additional Words

देर से	*der se*	late (*der*, f. [a short] while, delay)

Exercise 6

Read the following sentences aloud and then translate them into English.

१. मेरे लिए एक कप दूध गरम कीजिए। २. मैं व्यस्त हूँ। मैं काम करने की कोशिश कर रहा हूँ। ३. मुझको अभी परेशान मत करो। ४. क्लास कितने बजे शुरू होती है? ५. वह आमतौर पर आठ बजे शुरू होती है लेकिन अध्यापक कभी-कभी देर से शुरू करते हैं। ६. तुम किसका इंतज़ार कर रहे हो? ७. आप अपने भाई से महीने में कितनी बार बात करती हैं? ८. मेरा क़लम कहाँ है? माफ़ कीजिए मैं इस्तेमाल कर रहा हूँ। ९. क्या तुम दुनिया में किसी से नफ़रत करते हो? नहीं, मैं सबसे प्यार करता हूँ। १०. ज़रा दरवाज़ा बंद करो। ठीक है, सुनो। किसी पर भरोसा मत करो और हमारी बातचीत का ज़िक्र भी किसी से न करो।

Exercise 7

Translate the sentences into Hindi.

1. Are you waiting for me? No, I'm waiting for someone else.
2. Try to come early.
3. Turn off the TV. I'm trying to sleep.
4. Don't worry. Trust me.
5. Please don't talk to me about him.
6. She's trying to sleep. Don't bother her.
7. I'm busy. I'm helping him. Ask somebody else.
8. I'm fine. Don't worry about me.

16

Weather and Climate

In this chapter you will learn how to describe the current weather as well as the overall climate of a region.

Describing the Weather

In English, many weather-related expressions follow a similar pattern:

It is sunny today.
It is cold today.
It is hot today.

In Hindi, many of the same expressions follow a slightly different pattern:

आज धूप है।	It is sunny today. ("There is sunshine today.")
आज सर्दी है।	It is cold today. ("There is cold weather today.")
आज गर्मी है।	It is hot today. ("There is hot weather today.")

As the examples show, the structure of these sentences is actually the *there is*-type sentences encountered in chapter 3. The weather-related words in these sentences are nouns rather than adjectives.

धूप	sunshine
सर्दी	cold weather, cold
गर्मी	hot weather, warmth, heat

In general, weather-related expressions that use the word 'it' in English are phrased differently in Hindi. For example, note how the verbs for 'to rain' and 'to snow' are used in Hindi.

बारिश होना	to rain
बर्फ़ पड़ना	to snow

बारिश हो रही है।	It's raining. "Rain is happening."
बर्फ़ पड़ रही है।	It's snowing. "Snow is falling."

Vocabulary 1

Weather

कुहरा	*kuhrā* (m.)	fog
ख़राब	*xarāb*	bad, gone bad, in a bad state
गर्म	*garm* (adj.)	hot
गर्मी	*garmī* (f.)	hot/warm weather
जलवायु	*jalvāyu* (f.)	climate
ठंड, ठंडक	*ṭhanḍ, ṭhanḍak* (f.)	cold weather; cold
ठंडा	*ṭhanḍā* (adj.)	cold
तूफ़ान	*tūfān* (m.)	storm (*tūfān ānā*, for a storm to come, for there to be a storm)
तेज़	*tez*	sharp, strong
धूप	*dhūp* (f.)	sunshine
बरसात	*barsāt* (f.)	rains, rainy season
बर्फ़	*barf* (f.)	snow (*barf paṛnā,* to snow)
बादल	*bādal* (m.)	cloud
बारिश, वर्षा	*bāriś, varṣā* (f.)	rain (*bāriś honā*, to rain)
मौसम	*mausam* (m.)	weather, season
सर्दी	*sardī* (f.)	cold weather

Weather (cont'd)

साफ़	*sāf*	clean, clear
सुहावना, सुहाना	*suhāvnā, suhānā*	pleasant
सूरज	*sūraj* (m.)	sun
हवा	*havā* (f.)	wind; air

Additional Words

आसमान	*āsmān* (m.)	*sky*
धरती, ज़मीन	*dhartī, zamīn* (f.)	land, earth

Exercise 1

Read the weather descriptions and match them to the pictures provided.

१. मौसम सुहावना है|

२. बहुत सर्दी है|

३. बारिश हो रही है|

४. तेज़ गर्मी है|

५. बर्फ़ पड़ रही है|

६. कुहरा है|

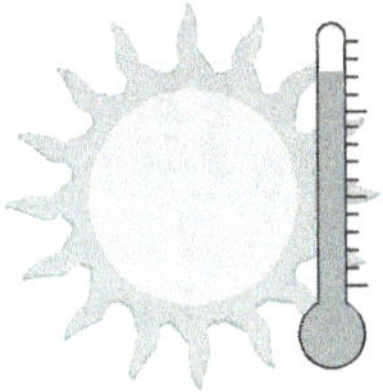

Exercise 2

Look up the weather in five world cities and write sentences describing the current weather in each.

Describing the Climate

Consider the following English sentences:

It's sunny today in San Diego.
It's generally sunny in San Diego.

These sentences have the same basic structure: *It's sunny in San Diego.* The different time frame in each is expressed through the insertion of the additional words, *today* and *generally*, which indicate whether the statement applies to current conditions or general conditions.

Hindi possesses words corresponding to *today* and *generally*, and they are employed in a manner similar to English. However, distinctions between current and general conditions are also expressed through grammatical distinctions in Hindi.

Indicating Current versus General Conditions with *honā*

The forms for describing conditions at the *present moment* in time have already been introduced. These are the simple present forms of the verb *honā*.

आज मौसम बहुत सुहाना है।	The weather is very pleasant today.
यहाँ बहुत गर्मी है।	It's really hot here (at this moment).

Statements about *general conditions* are expressed by using *honā* in the present habitual verb tense.

पहाड़ों का मौसम सुहाना होता है।	The weather in the mountains is pleasant (in general)
सिएटल में बहुत बारिश होती है।	It rains a lot in Seattle.

While the focus of this chapter is on distinguishing between current weather and overall climate, the distinction between simple present and present habitual forms of *honā* must be observed in any context in which a distinction is possible between current and general conditions.

Vocabulary 2

Seasons

गर्मियाँ	*garmiyā̃* (f.pl.)	hot season, summer
जाड़ा	*jāṛā* (m.)	winter
पतझड़	*patjhaṛ* (m.)	fall
बसंत	*basant* (m.)	spring
मौसम	*mausam* (m.)	season; weather
सर्दियाँ	*sardiyā̃* (f.pl.)	cold season, winter

Months of the Year

महीना	*mahīnā* (m.)	month
जनवरी	*janvarī* (f.)	January
फ़रवरी	*farvarī* (f.)	February
मार्च	*mārc* (m.)	March
अप्रैल	*aprail* (m.)	April
मई	*maī* (f.)	May
जून	*jūn* (m.)	June
जुलाई	*julāī* (f.)	July
अगस्त	*agast* (m.)	August
सितंबर	*sitambar* (m.)	September
अक्तूबर / अक्टूबर	*aktūbar/akṭūbar* (m.)	October
नवंबर	*navambar* (m.)	November
दिसंबर	*disambar* (m.)	December

Additional Words

X के दौरान	X *ke daurān*	during X
अंत, आख़िर	*ant, āxir* (m.)	end
ख़ाली	*xālī*	empty, available; free, not occupied
गिनना	*ginnā* (v.t.)	to count
घंटा	*ghanṭā* (m.)	hour
छुट्टी	*chuṭṭī* (f.)	break, day off, weekend, holiday, vacation time
तो	*to*	so, then; indeed [emphatic particle]
न...न...	*na...na...*	neither…nor…
पड़ना	*paṛnā* (v.i.)	to fall, to befall
मिनट	*minaṭ* (m.)	minute
शताब्दी, सदी	*śatābdī, sadī* (f.)	century
शुरू	*śurū* (m.)	beginning

Notes:

- The word *to* can also express the notion that a statement is in contrast or at variance with a previous statement. For example: *sab log itne udās kyõ haĩ? maĩ to xuś hū̃*, 'Why is everybody so melancholy. I'm happy.'

Exercise 3

Read aloud and translate.

१. मेरे शहर में जनवरी से मार्च के शुरू तक सर्दी पड़ती है| २. अप्रैल, मई, और जून में गर्मी पड़ती है| ३. जुलाई से सितंबर तक बरसात होती है| ४. सितंबर के अंत से दिसंबर तक मौसम अच्छा होता है| ५. क्या तुम्हारे शहर में बर्फ़ पड़ती है? ६. कुहरा किस-किस महीने में होता है? ७. जनवरी और फ़रवरी में भारत का मौसम कैसा रहता है? ८. भारत बहुत बड़ा देश है इसलिए हर जगह मौसम एक सा* नहीं होता| ९. गर्मी की छुट्टियों के दौरान आप लोग क्या करते हैं? १०. हम अपने रिश्तेदारों के घर जाते हैं, किताबें पढ़ते हैं, फ़िल्में देखते हैं या फिर बस आराम करते हैं|

*एक सा, 'the same'

Exercise 4

Translate into Hindi.

1. It's usually rainy in December.
2. It's generally cold from October to March.
3. What is the weather like ("How is the weather") in your city in February?
4. Is your country's weather nice?
5. What is Lucknow's weather like in October?
6. In which month is the weather best in Delhi?
7. Where are you usually at 12:00?
8. I'm usually in class at that time.

Exercise 5

Role Play

Role 1: You are planning to spend next year in Varanasi studying Hindi. You don't know much about the city, so you have decided to ask a friend of yours who is from there about its weather. Your partner will play the role of your friend. Ask him about Varanasi's weather in each month of the year and note his responses. When you are finished, verbally review what you have noted with your partner.

उदाहरण

जनवरी में वाराणसी का मौसम कैसा होता है ?

Role 2: You used to live in Varanasi and a friend of yours who is planning to study there next year wants to learn about its weather throughout the year. Answer your partner's questions based on the information given below. Answer in complete sentences.

दिसंबर - फ़रवरी	सर्दी, सुबह के समय कुहरा
मार्च और अप्रैल	सुहावना मौसम, न ज़्यादा सर्दी न ज़्यादा गर्मी
मई और जून	गर्मी
जुलाई और अगस्त	तेज़ बारिश
सितंबर और अक्टूबर	रात में हल्की सर्दी, दिन में सुहावना मौसम
नवंबर	सर्दी शुरू होती है।

Exercise 6

Listen to the audio passage and note what the weather is like throughout the year in northern India. Pair up with a partner and discuss what you think the best months are for visiting the region.

जनवरी	फ़रवरी	मार्च	अप्रैल
मई	जून	जुलाई	अगस्त
सितंबर	अक्टूबर	नवंबर	दिसंबर

भारत के उत्तर मैदानी इलाक़े में एक साल में चार तरह के मौसम होते हैं| सर्दी, बसंत, गर्मी, और बरसात| नवंबर, दिसंबर और जनवरी के दौरान सर्दियों का मौसम होता है| दिसंबर और जनवरी में अक्सर कड़ाके की सर्दी पड़ती है| सुबह के समय काफ़ी कुहरा भी होता है| फ़रवरी, मार्च, और अप्रैल के शुरू में बसंत का मौसम होता है| ख़ासतौर पर फ़रवरी और मार्च में मौसम काफ़ी सुहावना रहता है| अप्रैल के अंत से गर्मियों का मौसम शुरू होता है| मई और जून में तेज़ गर्मी पड़ती है और गरम हवाएँ चलती हैं| ऐसी हवा को लू कहते हैं| जुलाई, अगस्त, और सितंबर के दौरान बरसात का मौसम होता है| जुलाई और अगस्त में तेज़ बारिश होती है जिसे* मानसून भी कहते हैं| अक्टूबर में मौसम अच्छा रहता है| न ज़्यादा गर्मी पड़ती है और न ज़्यादा सर्दी|

*जिसे, 'which.'

Exercise 7

Using the previous audio passage as a model, describe the climate of your home region.

17

Unit 3 Review Activities

The goal of this chapter is to review the content of unit 3 and provide additional opportunities to synthesize all of the content presented up to this point.

G

1. Grammar Review

- Be able to conjugate any verb in the present habitual.
- Be able to conjugate any verb in the present continuous.
- When is the present habitual used and when is the present continuous used?
- What does *honā* in the present habitual mean?
- When is it appropriate to use *apnā*?
- When must the postposition *ko* be used to mark a direct object?
- Name two uses of the infinitive.

2. Tips for Increasing Fluency: Speaking Drills

In this unit you learned some important skills, that include describing events that are happening around you and describing your daily routine. Mastering these and other tenses will contribute to raising your level of fluency. You can practice them by going through the steps below. When you first do these drills, focus on accuracy; then as they begin to become more automatic, focus on increasing your speed.

A. Present Continuous

When you are sitting in a location where there are several people around you, describe where everybody is in relation to you and what everybody is doing. For example, you might describe what your family members are doing next time you are home; if you live in a dorm, you might describe what your dorm mates are doing; or you might describe a scene in a library or a coffee shop. Repeat this activity regularly.

B. Present Habitual

Refer to the following verbs:

उठना, नहाना, कपड़े बदलना, नाश्ता करना, कॉफ़ी पीना, स्कूल / क्लास जाना / काम पर जाना, पढ़ना / काम करना, दोपहर का खाना खाना, घर वापस जाना, शाम / रात का खाना खाना, सोना

1. Describe the time at which you do all of the above activities. Describe the activities in chronological order but make no effort to link sentences.
2. Sequence the activities in chronological order. Begin the first sentence with *pahle* and link all subsequent sentences with either *phir* or *us ke bād*. If your actual daily routine differs from the order of actions above, change the order to reflect what you actually do daily. Feel free to add additional verbs.

3. Sequence the activities in chronological order using V-*ne ke bād* to introduce each new sentence.
4. Describe your daily routine alternating your use of linking and time-telling devices. Alternating your use of ...*baje*, *phir*, (*aur*) *us ke bād*, and (*phir*) V-*ne ke bād* will lend a natural flow to your description. After you are comfortable with step 4, repeat regularly.

3. Personalization Questions

Take turns with a partner asking and answering the following questions in complete sentences.

भाषा	*bhāṣā* (f.)	language

१. आप रविवार को कितने बजे उठते हैं / उठती हैं?
२. क्या आप हर रोज़ कॉफ़ी पीते हैं / पीती हैं?
३. आप कॉफ़ी या चाय दिन में कितनी बार पीते हैं / पीती हैं?
४. आपके माता-पिता क्या काम करते हैं?
५. आपके कितने भाई-बहन हैं?
६. आपके भाई-बहन कहाँ रहते हैं और क्या काम करते हैं?
७. आप कौन-कौन सी भाषाएँ जानते हैं / जानती हैं?
८. क्या आप ज़्यादातर ठीक समय पर क्लास / दफ़्तर पहुँचते हैं / पहुँचती हैं?
९. आप हफ़्ते में कितनी बार अपने कमरे की सफ़ाई करते हैं / करती हैं?
१०. क्या आप अक्सर फ़िल्में देखते हैं / देखती हैं?
११. आप रोज़ कितने घंटे पढ़ाई करते हैं / करती हैं?
१२. यह क्लास कितने बजे शुरू होती है और कितने बजे ख़त्म होती है?

4. Interview a classmate. Find out as much as you can about his or her best friend. Find out his or her name, age, appearance, where he or she lives, what he or she does for a living, how often your classmate sees him or her, and what they do together when they see each other.

5. Write a paragraph in Hindi describing one of your friends. Include all of the information requested in the previous exercise.

6. Listen to the audio passage and make a schedule of the routine that is described.

मैं सुबह छह बजे उठता हूँ। उसके तुरंत बाद मैं नहाता हूँ, फिर कपड़े बदलता हूँ। लगभग साढ़े छह बजे मैं नाश्ता करता हूँ। मेरी माँ मेरे लिए नाश्ता बनाती हैं। नाश्ते के साथ मैं चाय भी पीता हूँ। मैं आमतौर पर सात बजे स्कूल जाता हूँ। मेरी क्लासें दोपहर के तीन बजे तक होती हैं। हमारे स्कूल के पास एक अच्छी चाय की दुकान है। स्कूल के बाद मैं अपने दोस्तों के साथ चाय पीता हूँ और समोसे खाता हूँ। मैं साढ़े छह बजे घर वापस आता हूँ। फिर थोड़ी देर आराम करने के बाद कुछ पढ़ाई करता हूँ। सोने से पहले मैं अपने परिवार के साथ रात का खाना खाता हूँ। फिर थोड़ी देर चहल-क़दमी करता हूँ और आमतौर पर साढ़े दस बजे तक सो जाता हूँ।

7. You have become pen pals with a young Indian student. You have just received your first letter from him. Study the following vocabulary and then read the passage and answer the questions.

आज़ादी	*āzādī* (f.)	freedom, independence
आपस में	*āpas mẽ*	mutually, together, with each other
किराने की दुकान	*kirāne kī dukān* (f.)	general store
ज़माना	*zamānā* (m.)	era
दिल	*dil* (m.)	heart
दिल का अच्छा होना	*dil kā acchā honā*	to be good at heart
प्यार, मुहब्बत	*pyār* (m.), *muhabbat* (f.)	love
मिलना	*milnā* (v.i.)	to be available, "to be gotten"
हर तरह का	*har tarah kā*	all types of, "of all types"

नमस्ते। मेरा नाम अक्षय है। मैं बीस साल का हूँ। मैं दिल्ली में रहता हूँ और यहाँ के एक कॉलेज में इंजीनिरिंग पढ़ता हूँ। मेरा परिवार सिंध से है पर हम लोग आज़ादी के समय से इंडिया में रहते हैं। हमारे परिवार में हम आठ लोग हैं, मैं, मेरा छोटा भाई, मेरी बड़ी बहन, माँ-बाप, चाचा-चाची,

और दादी| मेरे पापा की किराने की दुकान है| उनकी दुकान में हर तरह का सामान मिलता है और तीन आदमी काम करते हैं| मेरे चाचा भी वहीं काम करते हैं| हमारे पड़ोस में सब लोग उनको जानते हैं| हमारे मुहल्ले का नाम विकास नगर है| यह अच्छी जगह है क्योंकि सब लोग दिल के अच्छे हैं और आपस में बड़े प्यार से रहते हैं|

१. अक्षय कितने साल का है?

२. वह क्या करता है?

३. अक्षय का परिवार कहाँ रहता है?

४. अक्षय के परिवार में कितने लोग हैं?

५. अक्षय के पिता क्या काम करते हैं?

६. क्या अक्षय का मुहल्ला अच्छा है? क्यों?

8. Your pen pal's letter continues below. Read the next paragraph and then summarize what it contains.

जीवन	*jīvan* (m.)	life
झाड़ू लगाना	*jhāṛū lagānā*	to sweep
दैनिक	*dainik*	daily
धोबी	*dhobī* (m.)	washerman

मेरे परिवार में बहुत लोग हैं इसलिए हर समय कुछ न कुछ होता रहता है| इस समय मेरे पापा दुकान पर हैं लेकिन मेरे चाचा घर पर हैं| वे बैठक में पड़ोसियों के साथ बैठे चाय पी रहे हैं और ज़ोर-ज़ोर से बातें कर रहे हैं| जब भी कोई आता है तो हम उसको चाय पिलाते हैं| मेरे घर में बाक़ी लोग भी व्यस्त हैं| मेरी दादी, मम्मी, और बहन रसोईघर में हैं| मेरी दादी सब्ज़ियाँ काट रही हैं| मेरी बहन खाना पकाने में मेरी मम्मी की मदद कर रही है| मेरा भाई टीवी देख रहा है| हमारे घर में नौकर भी आते हैं| रोज़ सुबह एक लड़की आती है और घर की सफ़ाई करती है| इस समय वह झाड़ू लगा रही है| आँगन में हमारा धोबी कपड़े गिन रहा है| तुम भी अपने परिवार के बारे में कुछ लिखो| तुम्हारे घर का दैनिक जीवन कैसा है?

9. Write a response to Akshay's letter. Tell him about your own family and life in your home.

10. Due to your language skills, you have been hired by your school's study-abroad office to brief a group of South Asian exchange students in Hindi on daily life in America. Prepare a presentation on a typical week in the life of an American student and deliver it to your class.

Sayings and Proverbs

आटे के साथ घुन भी पिसता है

एक मछली सारे तालाब को गंदा करती है

काठ की हांडी बार-बार चूल्हे नहीं चढ़ती

टेढ़ी उंगली से ही घी निकलता है

प्यासा कुएँ के पास जाता है, कुआँ प्यासे के पास नहीं आता

अपनी-अपनी डफ़ली, अपना-अपना राग

ख़रबूज़े को देख कर ख़रबूज़ा रंग पकड़ता है

सावन के अंधे को सब हरा ही हरा दिखता है

Unit 4 In the Market

In this unit you will learn the following skills:

- Identifying things you like and things you need.
- Expressing hobbies and interests.
- Expressing desires and impressions.
- Choosing items while shopping.
- Asking and reporting prices.
- Carrying out simple shopping transactions.

In addition, you will become familiar with South Asian food and clothing, as well as everyday shopping and eating customs.

18

Expressing Likes, Needs, and Desires

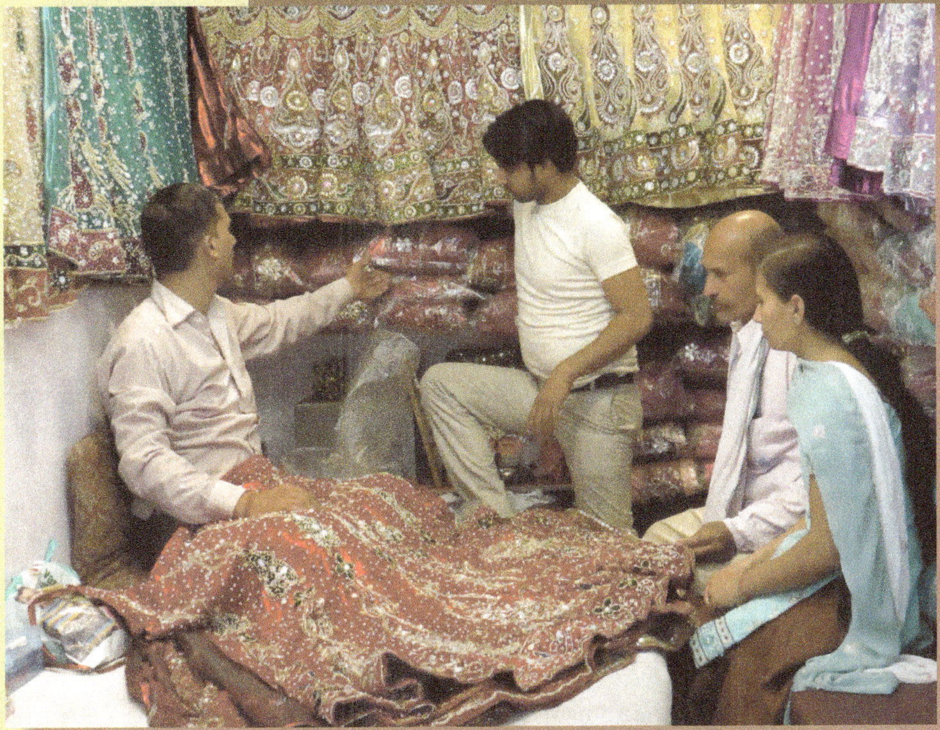

One of the first things that many English-speaking students notice when shopping in South Asia is that the layout of South Asian shops differs from what they are used to seeing at home. In traditional South Asian shops, the customer generally sits or stands in one place telling the shopkeeper what he or she needs while the shopkeeper shows the customer his merchandise. Being able to express what one likes and needs is therefore an essential survival skill in South Asia.

Expressing Likes and Needs

Likes and needs are commonly expressed in English using simple sentences such as these:

I like ice cream.

We need more rice.

Though much less natural to English, one could also express what one likes using an alternative sentence pattern like the following:

Ice cream is pleasing to me.

In Hindi, likes, needs, and many other notions are expressed through structures that more closely parallel this second pattern. In this chapter you will learn how to use these structures, called *indirect constructions*, to express likes, needs, and many other types of information. Before beginning, take a look at the following Hindi expression; how does it differ from the equivalent English expression, *I like ice cream*?

मुझको	आइसक्रीम	पसंद है।
mujh ko	*āiskrīm*	*pasand hai.*
To me	ice cream	is pleasing.

Indirect Constructions

The most common expressions for stating likes and needs belong to a class of structures called indirect constructions. Take a look at some examples of these expressions.

X *ko* Y *pasand honā*	**for X to like Y**
आपको किस तरह का खाना पसंद है?	What type of food do you like?
मुझको हर तरह का खाना पसंद है।	I like every type of food.
समीर को मुर्ग़ी बहुत पसंद है।	Sameer likes chicken a lot.

X *ko* Y *cāhie*	**for X to need Y**
आपको क्या चाहिए?	What do you need?
मुझको दाल चाहिए।	I need daal (lentils).
उसको पानी चाहिए।	She needs water.

Note that in both of these constructions the subject is marked with a postposition. This is one of the essential characteristics of indirect constructions. The other essential structural characteristic is that the verb agrees with the element that corresponds to the English object.

As a general rule, a verb can only agree with a noun or pronoun in the direct case, so a postposition marking the subject effectively blocks agreement with the verb. Note how the verb takes the plural number in the following sentences to reflect agreement with the thing that is liked.

क्या आपको संतरे पसंद हैं?	Do you like oranges?
मुझको केले बहुत पसंद हैं।	I like bananas a lot.

When the item that is needed in the *cāhie* construction is plural in number, the final –*e* of *cāhie* becomes nasalized (*cāhiẽ*). Note the agreement in the following sentences:

हमको छह अंडे चाहिएँ।	We need six eggs.
उसको कितने टमाटर चाहिएँ?	How many tomatoes does he need?

Some speakers treat unnasalized *cāhie* as an invariable form and use it for both singular and plural items needed.

हमको बाज़ार से कुछ चीज़ें चाहिए।	We need some things from the market.

Additional Common Indirect Constructions

Expressions for stating likes and needs are only two examples of indirect constructions. Many more indirect constructions exist, and, in fact, many of Hindi's most common expressions are indirect constructions. Here are some examples:

X *ko* Y *mālūm honā*	**for X to know Y**
राज को हमारा पता मालूम है।	Raj knows our address.
क्या किसी को पूरी कहानी मालूम है?	Does anyone know the entire story?
क्या उसको हमारे नाम मालूम हैं?	Does he know our names? (*honā* agrees with *nām*, 'names')

X *ko* Y *yād honā*	**for X to remember Y**
क्या आपको वह घटना याद है?	Do you remember that incident?
क्या किसी को उसका नाम याद है?	Does anyone remember his name?
क्या आपको उनके नाम याद हैं?	Do you remember their names? (*honā* agrees with *nām*, 'names')

One of the most important verbs that requires an indirect construction is *lagnā*, 'to strike (as), to seem.' The indirect construction with *lagnā* often translates best with the phrase, 'to find (as).' When used with *acchā*, 'good,' *lagnā* can be translated using 'to like.'

X *ko lagnā*	**to seem to X, to strike X as…, for X to find…(as…)**
सब लोगों को यह क्लास अच्छी लगती है।	Everyone likes this class (finds it to be good).
आपको यह किताब कैसी लगती है?	How do you find this book? How do you like…
तुमको यह शहर कैसा लगता है?	How do you like this city?
मुझको यह शहर उबाऊ लगता है।	I find this city boring.

As illustrated by the constructions introduced above, the most common postposition used to mark the subject in indirect constructions is *ko*. Indirect constructions with *ko* are often referred to as *ko constructions.*

Additional Points

Negation: The verb *honā* is dropped from many indirect constructions when negated. It is generally dropped from the *mālūm honā, yad honā,* and *pasand honā* constructions when negated.

विवेक को चीनी खाना पसंद नहीं।	Vivek doesn't like Chinese food.
मनीषा को तुम्हारा पता मालूम नहीं।	Manisha doesn't know your address.
मुझको उसका नाम याद नहीं।	I don't remember his name.

Reflexive pronouns: The same rules regarding the use of reflexive pronouns apply in indirect constructions as in direct constructions. The second mention of a subject (the main element about which the sentence provides information) in a single clause is replaced with *apnā* or *xud*. This rule is sometimes not observed in casual conversation.

मुझको अपनी गाड़ी चाहिए।	I need my car.
उसको अपनी क्लास पसंद है।	He likes his class.
मुझको अपना घर सबसे अच्छा लगता है।	I like my own home the most.

Learning indirect constructions: Most indirect constructions feature the subject in the role of experiencer rather than as an agent (or doer). However, not all expressions related to experiencing require indirect constructions. In general, there is no way to definitively predict whether a given expression will take the form of an indirect construction or not. Each indirect construction must therefore be memorized individually as it is encountered.

Vocabulary 1

Food Items

अंगूर	*angūr* (m.)	grape
अंडा	*aṇḍā* (m.)	egg
अदरक	*adrak* (m.)	ginger
आटा	*āṭā* (m.)	flour
आम	*ām* (m.)	mango
आलू	*ālū* (m.)	potato
केला	*kelā* (m.)	banana
गरम मसाला	*garam masālā* (m.)	a popular and ubiquitous mix of spices
गाजर	*gājar* (f.)	carrot
गोभी	*gobhī* (f.)	cauliflower
गोश्त / माँस	*gośt/mā̃s* (m.)	meat
चावल	*cāval* (m.)	rice
टमाटर	*ṭamāṭar* (m.)	tomato
तेल	*tel* (m.)	oil
दही	*dahī* (m.)	yogurt
दाल	*dāl* (f.)	lentils
दूध	*dūdh* (m.)	milk
धनिया	*dhaniyā* (m./f.)	cilantro

Food Items (cont'd)

नमक	*namak* (m.)	salt
पनीर	*panīr* (m.)	paneer
पालक	*pālak* (m.)	spinach
प्याज़	*pyāz* (f.)	onion
फल	*phal* (m.)	fruit
बकरा	*bakrā* (m.)	goat (*bakre kā gośt*, goat meat; also called *maṭan*)
बर्फ़ी	*barfī* (f.)	a popular Indian sweet
बैंगन	*baĩgan* (m.)	eggplant
मटर	*maṭar* (f.)	peas
मसाला	*masālā* (m.)	spice
मसालेदार	*masāledār*	spicy
मिठाई	*miṭhāī* (f.)	a sweet
मिर्च	*mirc* (f.)	pepper
मुग़लई	*mug̲h̲laī*	Mughlai, a style of North Indian cuisine
मुर्ग़ी	*murg̲h̲ī* (f.)	chicken
लड्डू	*laḍḍū* (m.)	a popular ball-shaped Indian sweet
लहसुन	*lahsun* (m.)	garlic
लाल मिर्च	*lāl mirc* (f.)	red pepper
शिमला मिर्च	*śimlā mirc* (f.)	bell pepper
संतरा	*santarā* (m.)	orange
सब्ज़ी	*sabzī* (f.)	vegetable; vegetable dish

साग	*sāg* (m.)	greens
सादा	*sādā*	plain, simple
सेब	*seb* (m.)	apple

Additional Words

अगर...तो...	*agar...to...*	if...then...
अलग-अलग	*alag-alag*	different, various
क़साई	*qasāī*	butcher
किराने की दुकान	*kirāne kī dukān* (f.)	general store, dry goods and staples store
X के यहाँ	X *ke yahā̃*	at X's (place) (e.g., *phalvāle ke yahā̃*, 'at the fruit seller's')
चंद	*cand*	some, a few
ना	*nā*	Isn't it so? Right?
पता	*patā* (m.)	address
फलवाला	*phalvālā* (m.)	fruit seller
फ़िल्म	*film* (f.)	film, movie
बस	*bas* (colloq.)	just, only
भाषा, ज़बान	*bhāṣā, zabān* (f.)	language (also *zabān*, f. tongue)
मनपसंद, पसंदीदा	*manpasand, pasandīdā* (inv.)	favorite
मार-धाड़ वाली फ़िल्म	*mār-dhāṛ vālī film* (f.)	action film (*mār-dhāṛ*, f. [colloq.] violence)
मिलना-जुलना	*milnā-julnā* (v.i.)	to look alike; to socialize
शास्त्रीय	*śāstrīy*	classical

Additional Words (cont'd)

शौक़	*śauq* (m.)	hobby, interest
संगीत	*sangīt* (m.)	music
सब्ज़ीवाला	*sabzīvālā* (m.)	vegetable seller
साबुन	*sābun* (m.)	soap
हलवाई	*halvāī* (m.)	sweet maker

Indirect Constructions

आना	*ānā* (v.i.)	to come
X को Y आना	X *ko* Y *ānā*	for X to know Y (a language or skill)
चाहिए, चाहिएँ	*cāhie, cāhiẽ*	is/are needed
X को Y चाहिए	X *ko* Y *cāhie*	X needs Y
पसंद	*pasand* (f.)	liking
X को Y पसंद होना	X *ko* Y *pasand honā*	for X to like Y
मालूम	*mālūm*	known
X को (Y) मालूम होना	X *ko* (Y) *mālūm honā*	for X to know (Y—a piece of information)
मिलना	*milnā* (v.i.)	to get; to meet; to be available; to be similar
X को Y मिलना	X *ko* Y *milnā*	for X to get Y
X से मिलना	X *se milnā*	to meet X, to see X socially
याद	*yād* (f.)	a memory
X को (Y) याद होना	X *ko* (Y) *yād honā*	for X to remember Y
लगना	*lagnā*	to strike, to seem
X को लगना	X *ko lagnā*	to seem to X, to strike X as…, for X to find (something to be…)
समझ	*samajh* (f.)	understanding
X की समझ में आना	X *kī samajh mẽ ānā*	to make sense to X

Notes:

- *patā* is also used in a construction similar to X *ko mālūm honā*. X *ko patā honā*, for X to know.
- *pasandīdā* is an invariable adjective. In general, adjectives ending in *–īdā* are invariable.
- *milnā:* Earlier we explained that impersonal sentences can be produced by dropping the subject and placing the verb in the third person masculine form. For example, *is śabd ko kaise likhte haĩ*, 'How do you write this word/How does one write this word?' Impersonal sentences with *ko* constructions can be produced by merely dropping the 'X *ko*' portion. The verb still agrees with the Y element. The meaning of 'to be available,' is actually the impersonal form of X *ko* Y *milnā*. For example, *us ko ye kahā̃ miltā hai?* 'Where does he get this.' *ye kahā̃ miltā hai?* 'Where does one get this,' and by extension, 'Where is this available?'
- *sādā*: We use the word *sādā* as a variable adjective. Some speakers use *sādā* as an invariable adjective.

Exercise 1 G

Fill in the Blanks

Subjects and verbs have been deleted from the sentences below. Supply the missing words, and then write out the complete sentences and their translations. The missing subjects have been provided in parentheses; make any changes necessary to them as you add them to the sentences.

X *ko* Y *pasand honā*

१. ____________ (मेरे पिता) हर तरह का खाना ____________।

२. ____________ (मैं) ज़्यादातर सब्ज़ियाँ ____________।

३. ____________ (आप) खाने में क्या-क्या ____________?

४. ____________ (मेरा दोस्त) शास्त्रीय संगीत बहुत ____________।
५. ____________ (वह) पुरानी बालीवुड फ़िल्में ____________।

X ko lagnā

६. ____________ (आप) भारतीय खाना कैसा ____________?
७. ____________ (आप) भारतीय खाने में कौन-कौन सी चीज़ें अच्छी ____________?
८. ____________ (मैं) बालीवुड फ़िल्में बहुत उबाऊ ____________।
९. ____________ (वह) बालीवुड फ़िल्में पसंद नहीं लेकिन बालीवुड गाने बहुत अच्छे ____________।

X *ko* Y *cāhie*

१०. ____________ (हम) किराने की दुकान से क्या-क्या ____________?
११. ____________ (आप) कितने सेब ____________?
१२. क्या ____________ (आप) कुछ और ____________?
१३. ____________ (मैं) कुछ फल और सब्ज़ियाँ ____________।
१४. क्या ____________ (कोई) पानी ____________?

X *ko* Y *mālūm honā*

१५. ____________ (मैं) इस सवाल का जवाब ____________ नहीं।
१६. क्या ____________ (तुम) उन लड़कियों के नाम ____________?

X *ko* Y *yād honā*

१७. ____________ (वह) मेरी बात ____________ नहीं।
१८. ____________ (मैं) तुम्हारा सवाल ____________।

X *ko* Y *ānā*

१८. क्या ____________ (आप) स्पैनिश ____________?
१९. ____________ (आप) कौन-कौन सी भाषाएँ ____________?
२०. ____________ (मैं) सिर्फ़ हिन्दी ____________।

Exercise 2

G

Translate into Hindi.

1. What do you need?
2. Do you need anything?
3. I need lentils and rice.

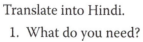

4. I don't need anything else.
5. What does Rohit need from the market?
6. What does he need from the general store?
7. He needs soap and oil.
8. Does he need anything from the butcher?
9. Yes, he needs chicken.
10. Does Shikha need anything from the vegetable seller's?
11. She needs carrots and tomatoes.
12. She also needs apples and bananas from the fruit seller's.
13. What does Salmaan like to eat? ("What does Salmaan like in eating?")
14. Does he like Mughlai food?
15. He likes Mughlai food a lot.
16. Does he like Indian sweets?
17. How does Sushma like (find) spicy food?
18. She likes plain food better.
19. What is your favorite food?
20. My favorite food is...

Exercise 3

Role Play

In recent years, supermarket-style stores have begun to appear in large cities in South Asia. Though smaller in size than American supermarkets, these stores sell a variety of different products. The majority of shopping, however, is still done from traditional markets with small stores and vendors selling a very specialized range of products.

Role 1: You have just recently arrived in India and you need to buy some items from your local traditional market. Your partner will play the role of a local resident. Find out where the following items can be found.

तेल	मटन	पनीर	संतरे	अंगूर	चावल	गोभी	मुर्ग़ी
दाल	मटर	सेब	आम	पालक	साबुन	केले	मिठाइयाँ

Role 2: Answer your partner's questions about where the above items can be found.

उदाहरण

क. तेल कहाँ मिलता है?
ख. तेल किराने की दुकान पर मिलता है।
क. गाजर कहाँ मिलती है?
ख. गाजर सब्ज़ीवाले के यहाँ मिलती है।

Exercise 4

You are at the market. Your cousin Alka calls you and leaves a voicemail for you asking to buy some items for her and some for your other cousin, Saumya. Listen to the voicemail and sort the items based on where you can get them and according to whose items they are so that you can deliver them to the right person.

Note: *lete āo* is similar to *le āo*, meaning 'Bring!'

अलग-अलग दुकानें	अलका	सौम्या
सब्ज़ीवाला		
फलवाला		
किराने की दुकान		
हलवाई		
गोश्त की दुकान		

भैया, तुम बाज़ार में हो तो मेरे और सौम्या के लिए भी कुछ चीज़ें लेते आओ| मुझे बाज़ार से आलू, कुछ लहसुन, और टमाटर चाहिएँ| इनके अलावा बासमती चावल, मुर्गी का गोश्त, नहाने का साबुन, सेब, और लड्डू भी चाहिएँ| सौम्या को भी कुछ चीज़ें चाहिएँ| उसको प्याज़, पालक, बकरे का गोश्त, केले, संतरे, बर्फ़ी, पनीर, और चने की दाल चाहिए|

Exercise 5

Using the shopping lists you made for Alka and Saumya in the previous activity, confirm with a partner what Alka and Saumya need from different places in the market. Ask and answer all questions in complete Hindi sentences.

उदाहरण

अलका को सब्ज़ी की दुकान से क्या चाहिए?
सौम्या को हलवाई के यहाँ से क्या चाहिए?

Exercise 6

Sarita and Seema are friends. Seema is interested in knowing more about one of Sarita's cousins, Madhu. Listen to Sarita and Seema's conversation and note what Madhu likes and dislikes. Check your findings with a partner in Hindi.

मधु को ये चीज़ें पसंद हैं|	उसको ये चीज़ें पसंद नहीं|

सीमा मुझको तुम्हारी कज़िन मधु से मिलकर बहुत अच्छा लगा| उसके बारे में कुछ और बताओ| उसको क्या-क्या पसंद है?

सरिता मधु को बहुत चीज़ें पसंद हैं|

सीमा क्या उसको फ़िल्में पसंद हैं?

सरिता हाँ उसको फ़िल्में बहुत पसंद हैं|

सीमा उसको कैसी फ़िल्में पसंद हैं?

सरिता उसको हिन्दी फ़िल्में पसंद हैं|

सीमा क्या उसको किताबें पसंद हैं?

सरिता नहीं उसको किताबें पसंद नहीं|

सीमा उसको कैसा खाना पसंद है?

सरिता उसको हिंदुस्तानी खाना पसंद है|

सीमा क्या उसको संगीत पसंद है?

सरिता हाँ उसको संगीत बहुत पसंद है|

सीमा उसको किस तरह का संगीत पसंद है?

सरिता उसको अमरीकी संगीत पसंद है|

सीमा लगता है कि हमारे शौक़ काफ़ी मिलते-जुलते हैं|

Exercise 7

Role Play

Role 1: You are going to meet the cousin of a friend of yours for the first time this afternoon. You want to find out some information about the cousin beforehand. Ask questions about the items in the list below to determine what the cousin likes and dislikes.

हिंदुस्तानी खाना, अमरीकी खाना, फ़्राँसीसी खाना, मेक्सिकन खाना, गोश्त, सब्ज़ियाँ, टमाटर, आलू, गोभी, बैंगन, मिठाइयाँ, फल, सेब, संतरे, केले, चावल, खेल, किताबें, बॉलीवुड फ़िल्में, अमरीकी फ़िल्में, पढ़ाई, टीवी, संगीत

Role 2: The chart below shows what your cousin likes and dislikes. Listen to your partner's questions and answer in complete sentences.

कज़िन का नाम	उसको ये चीज़ें पसंद हैं।	उसको ये चीज़ें पसंद नहीं।
कबीर	हिंदुस्तानी खाना, अमरीकी खाना, सब्ज़ियाँ, टमाटर, आलू, गोभी, बैंगन, फल, सेब, संतरे, खेल, किताबें, पढ़ाई	फ़्राँसीसी खाना, मेक्सिकन खाना, गोश्त, मिठाइयाँ, केले, चावल, सब फ़िल्में, टीवी, संगीत

Switch roles and repeat.

Role 1: Please reuse the list above.

Role 2:

कज़िन का नाम	उसको ये चीज़ें पसंद हैं।	उसको ये चीज़ें पसंद नहीं।
माया	हिंदुस्तानी खाना, फ़्राँसीसी खाना, गोश्त, सब्ज़ियाँ, टमाटर, आलू, बैंगन, फल, सेब, संतरे, खेल, अमरीकी फ़िल्में, संगीत	अमरीकी खाना, मेक्सिकन खाना, गोभी, मिठाइयाँ, केले, चावल, किताबें, बालीवुड फ़िल्में, पढ़ाई, टीवी

Contracted *ko* Pronoun Forms

When an oblique pronoun is used with the postposition *ko*, the oblique pronoun plus *ko* can optionally be replaced with a shorter form, which we will call the *contracted ko* form. The pronoun *āp* has no contracted *ko* form—the only possible form is *āp ko.*

Contracted *ko* Forms of Pronouns

	singular	plural
1	मुझे *mujhe* (= *mujh ko*)	हमें *hamẽ* (= *ham ko*)
2	तुझे *tujhe* (= *tujh ko*)	तुम्हें *tumhẽ* (= *tum ko*)
3	इसे / उसे *ise* (= *is ko*) *use* (= *us ko*)	इन्हें / उन्हें *inhẽ* (= *in ko*) *unhẽ* (= *un ko*)

The interrogative word *kaun* also has contracted *ko* forms. These are *kise* (sg.) and *kinhẽ* (pl.). The form *kinhẽ* is used when the expected answer to the question *who* is either a group of people or a person requiring a respectful plural form.

किसे	*kise* (= *kis ko*; *kaun*, sg., + *ko*)
किन्हें	*kinhẽ* (= *kin ko*; *kaun*, pl., + *ko*)

Examples:

मुझे भारतीय खाना पसंद है।	I like Indian food.
तुम्हें किस तरह की फ़िल्में पसंद हैं?	What sort of movies do you like?
क्या उन्हें मालूम है?	Does he know?
हमें बाज़ार से कुछ चीज़ें चाहिएँ।	We need some things from the market.
क्या उसे हिन्दी आती है?	Does he know Hindi?
मुझे बताओ।	Tell me.
उसे देखो।	Look at him.
किसे / किन्हें मालूम है।	Who knows / Who (all) knows?

Don't confuse contracted *ko* forms with oblique forms. Contracted *ko* forms only replace oblique pronouns + *ko*. If a pronoun is used with any of the other postpositions *par, se, tak,* or *mẽ,* the only possible form is: oblique pronoun + postposition. Students often mistake *ise* and *use* for contractions of *is se* and *us se*. *ise* and *use* are only contractions of *is ko* and *us ko,* never *is se* and *us se.*

Exercise 8 G

Fill in the Blanks

Replace the words in parentheses with contracted *ko* forms. Write the complete resulting sentences in Hindi and translate them into English.

१. ____________ (तुमको) किस तरह का खाना पसंद है?

२. ____________ (मुझको) हर तरह का मसालेदार खाना पसंद है।

३. क्या ____________ (उसको) बॉलीवुड फ़िल्में पसंद हैं?

४. तुम्हारे पिता को कौन-कौन सी सब्ज़ियाँ पसंद हैं? ____________ (उनको) आलू-गोभी और मटर-पनीर पसंद है।

५. ______________ (हमको) सब्ज़ीवाले के यहाँ से टमाटर, आलू, और प्याज़ चाहिए|
६. यहाँ ______________ (किसको) पानी चाहिए?
७. क्या ______________ (तुमको) पंजाबी आती है?
८. नहीं, ______________ (मुझको) सिर्फ़ अंग्रेज़ी और हिन्दी आती है|

Exercise 9

Natasha and Sudha are roommates. Listen to a phone conversation between them and then answer the questions about it.

नताशा	हलो सुधा, मैं नताशा बोल रही हूँ| मैं बाज़ार में हूँ| क्या यहाँ से कुछ चाहिए?
सुधा	हाँ, असल में हमें बहुत चीज़ें चाहिएँ|
नताशा	एक मिनट रुको, मैं लिख रही हूँ ... हाँ, तो हमें क्या-क्या चाहिए?
सुधा	हमें आलू, प्याज़, और टमाटर चाहिएँ|
नताशा	अच्छा, और क्या हमें लहसुन-अदरक चाहिए?
सुधा	हमें लहसुन नहीं चाहिए| वह हमारे पास है, लेकिन अदरक लेना मत भूलना*|
नताशा	अच्छा, जल्दी बताओ क्या किराने की दुकान से भी कुछ चाहिए?
सुधा	हाँ, हाँ हमें तेल और चावल चाहिए| और हाँ, साबुन भी चाहिए|
नताशा	अच्छा, इसके अलावा कुछ और चाहिए?
सुधा	नहीं, मेरे ख़याल में और कुछ नहीं चाहिए|
नताशा	ठीक है|

*मत भूलना, 'Don't forget.'

सवाल

१. नताशा कहाँ से फ़ोन करती है?
२. नताशा सुधा से क्या पूछती है?
३. नताशा और सुधा को खाने में क्या-क्या चाहिए?
४. उनको क्या नहीं चाहिए?
५. उनको खाने के अलावा और कुछ चाहिए? अगर हाँ, तो क्या?

Exercise 10  

Role Play

Role 1: You are making a shopping list and need the help of your roommate to determine what you have in your apartment and what you need. Your partner will play the role of your roommate. Ask your partner questions to determine what to add to your list. You might want to sequence your questions in terms of places where various items are sold.

उदाहरण

क. हमें किराने की दुकान से क्या चाहिए?

ख. हमें तेल चाहिए|

क. हमें सब्ज़ियों में क्या-क्या चाहिए?

ख. हमें ...

Role 2: Answer your partner's questions in complete sentences. The illustration below contains the things that you need from the market.

गोभी

टमाटर

प्याज़

आलू

आटा

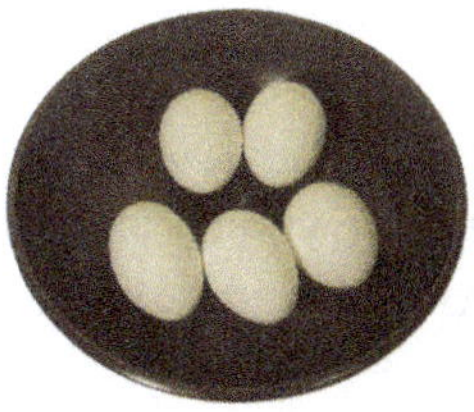

अंडा

चावल

मिर्च

दूध

गरम मसाला

When you are finished, switch roles and repeat using the following illustration:

धनिया

शिमला मिर्च

बैंगन

टमाटर

नमक

चावल

लाल मिर्च

तेल

गोश्त / माँस

दही

Exercise 11

Interview a classmate to determine what he or she likes and dislikes. Feel free to talk about food, weather, movies, books, music, or anything else you can think of. Try to identify at least three similarities and three differences in what you like and dislike.

उदाहरण

क. क्या तुम्हें हिंदुस्तानी खाना पसंद है?

ख. हाँ मुझे हिंदुस्तानी खाना बहुत पसंद है|

क. अच्छा, मुझे भी पसंद है| क्या तुम्हें चिकन टिक्का पसंद है?

ख. हाँ, मुझे बहुत पसंद है|

क. क्या तुम्हें यहाँ का मौसम पसंद है?

ख. मुझे गर्मियों में यहाँ का मौसम पसंद है लेकिन मुझे सर्दियों में यहाँ का मौसम पसंद नहीं|

Additional Uses of the Infinitive

Earlier you learned how to use infinitives with postpositions to sequence actions. Here are a few additional uses of infinitives.

Expressing Likes and Interests with Activities: Infinitives in *ko* Constructions

When discussing likes and dislikes, it is common to talk about not only physical items, but also activities that one likes or dislikes doing. As seen in chapters 5 and 14, the infinitive form of the verb refers to the action of doing something and can be translated both as *to* V (*to eat, to sleep, to work*) and V-*ing* (*eating, sleeping, working*).

Infinitives can be inserted into *ko* constructions such as X *ko* Y *pasand honā* and X *ko lagnā* to express likes, dislikes, interests, and other impressions about activities.

X *ko* V-*nā pasand honā*	**for X to like to V/to like V-ing**
मुझे किताबें पढ़ना पसंद है।	I like reading books.
तुम्हें वीकेंड पर क्या-क्या करना पसंद है?	What do you like to do on the weekend?

X *ko lagnā*	**to seem to X, for X to find…to be…**
मुझे भाषाएँ सीखना मज़ेदार लगता है।	I find learning languages fun.
उसे फ़िल्में देखना उबाऊ लगता है।	He finds watching movies boring

The construction X *ko* V-*ne kā śauq honā*, 'for X to enjoy V-ing (as a hobby),' is also common when talking about likes and interests.

X *ko* V-*ne kā śauq honā*	**for X to enjoy V-ing (as a hobby)**
क्या तुम्हें फ़िल्में देखने का शौक़ है?	Do you enjoy watching movies?
मुझे गिटार बजाने का शौक़ है।	I enjoy playing the guitar/I play guitar as a hobby.

Infinitives are often used with the construction X *ko ānā* to express the idea of knowing how to do something.

X *ko* V-*nā ānā*	**for X to know how to V (a skill)**
मुझे खाना पकाना आता है।	I know how to cook.

When the object of the infinitive in the V-*nā ānā* construction is not masculine singular, both the infinitive and *ānā* follow an unusual agreement pattern.

क्या तुम्हें गाड़ी चलानी आती है?	Do you know how to drive?

In this construction, the infinitive inflects like an adjective to agree with the direct object, and the verb *ānā* also agrees with the direct object. Some speakers keep the infinitive in its regular form for this construction (i.e. *kyā tumhẽ gāṛī calānā ātā hai*).

Infinitives with X *ko cāhie*: Infinitives can be used with many *ko* constructions. Use caution, however, when using infinitives with the X *ko cāhie* construction. The *cāhie* construction produces an unexpected meaning with infinitives, which will be covered in unit 6.

Using the Infinitive as the Subject of a Sentence

An infinitive functioning as a verbal noun can also be used as the subject of a sentence when talking abstractly about activities.

मेरे लिए जल्दी उठना मुश्किल है|	Getting up early is difficult for me.
भाषा सीखना आसान नहीं है|	Learning a language is not easy.
आमलेट बनाना आसान है|	Making omelets is easy.
पढ़ाई करना ज़रूरी है|	Studying is necessary.

Sentences of this structure can also be phrased in an alternative manner in English. This alternative phrasing is not possible in Hindi.

It is difficult to get up early.
It is a difficult task to learn a language.
It's easy to cook eggs.
It's necessary to study.

When translating English expressions of this form into Hindi, beginning students often find it easier to first convert the expressions into the equivalent English form, which is closer in structure to the Hindi form.

It is difficult to get up early.
↓
Getting up early is difficult.
↓
जल्दी उठना मुश्किल है|

Expressing What One Wants to Do

A desire to do an activity can be expressed using the verb *cāhnā*, 'to want,' preceded by an infinitive.

V-*nā cāhnā*	**to want to V**
मैं बाज़ार जाना चाहता हूँ|	I want to go to the market.
हम लोग खाना खाना चाहते हैं|	We want to eat.
क्या तुम फ़िल्म देखना चाहते हो?	Do you want to see a movie?

The Oblique Infinitive with Verbs of Motion

An oblique infinitive with a verb of motion (i.e. V-*ne jānā*, V-*ne ānā*) is used to express the notion of going or coming somewhere for the purpose of performing an action.

मैं सब्ज़ियाँ ख़रीदने बाज़ार जा रहा हूँ।	I'm going to the market to buy some vegetables.

Additional Points

Negation: The negative particle *na* is used to negate an infinitive.

वह हमेशा कुछ कहना चाहता है। उसके लिए न बोलना मुश्किल है।	He always wants to say something. Not speaking is difficult for him.

Subjects of infinitives: Infinitives also retain their ability as verbs to take a subject. The subject, if animate, is marked with the postposition *kā*, which agrees with the infinitive.

तुम्हारा सिग्रेट पीना अच्छी आदत नहीं है।	Your smoking cigarettes is not a good habit.
उसके आने से पहले कमरा साफ़ करो।	Clean the room before he gets here. ("before his coming")

If the subject is inanimate, the postposition *kā* is optional.

फ़िल्म शुरू होने से पहले मैं एक कोल्ड ड्रिंक ख़रीदना चाहता हूँ। फ़िल्म के शुरू होने से पहले मैं एक कोल्ड ड्रिंक ख़रीदना चाहता हूँ।	I want to buy a soft drink before the movie starts.

Vocabulary 2

Words that Describe Activities

अहम, महत्त्वपूर्ण	*aham, mahattv-pūrṇ*	important
आसान	*āsān*	easy
उबाऊ	*ubāū*	boring
ग़ैरज़रूरी, अनावश्यक	*ghairzarūrī, anāvaśyak*	unnecessary

Words that Describe Activities (cont'd)

ज़रूरी, आवश्यक	*zarūrī, āvaśyak*	necessary
दिलचस्प, रोचक	*dilcasp, rocak*	interesting
मज़ेदार	*mazedār* (adj.)	fun, amusing; tasty
मुश्किल, कठिन	*muśkil, kaṭhin*	difficult (also *muśkil, kaṭhināī,* f. 'difficulty')

Some Words Related to Habits, Hobbies, and Recreation

आदत	*ādat* (f.)	habit
ख़रीदारी करना	*xarīdārī karnā* (v.t.)	to shop
ख़र्च करना	*xarc karnā* (v.t.)	to spend
घूमना	*ghūmnā* (v.i.)	to roam, to travel
चलाना	*calānā* (v.t.)	to drive, to operate, to ride (a bike)
तैरना	*tairnā* (v.i.)	to swim
दिलचस्पी	*dilcaspī* (f.)	interest (X *ko* Y *mẽ dilcaspī honā*, for X to be interested in Y, have an interest in Y)
नाचना	*nācnā* (v.i.)	to dance
नियमित रूप से, पाबंदी से	*niyamit rūp se, pābandī se*	regularly
पीना	*pīnā* (v.t.)	to drink; to smoke
फ़ुर्सत	*fursat* (f.)	free time, leisure time
बचाना	*bacānā* (v.t.)	to save
बिताना, गुज़ारना	*bitānā, guzārnā* (v.t.)	to pass (*vaqt guzārnā*, to pass time)
मज़ा	*mazā* (m.)	fun
मनोरंजन	*manoranjan* (m.)	fun, recreation
साज़	*sāz* (m.)	musical instrument
सिलना	*silnā* (v.t.)	to sew

Additional Words

असल में	*asal mẽ*	actually, in fact
एकदम	*ekdam*	completely; suddenly
कमाना	*kamānā* (v.t.)	to earn
ख़रीदना	*xarīdnā* (v.t.)	to buy
ख़ाली	*xālī*	free, unoccupied; empty (*xālī samay*, free time)
चाहना	*cāhnā* (v.t.)	to want
ज़िंदगी, जीवन	*zindagī* (f.), *jīvan* (m.)	life (cf. *zindā*, 'alive.')
तबियत	*tabiyat* (f.)	current state of health
थोड़ा-बहुत	*thoṛā-bahut*	a fair amount (of)
बनना	*bannā*(v.i.)	to become
बेचना	*becnā* (v.t.)	to sell
भरपूर	*bharpūr*	complete, full
राय	*rāy* (f.)	opinion (*merī rāy mẽ*, in my opinion)
विचार, ख़्याल	*vicār*, *xayāl* (m.)	thought, idea (*mere vicār mẽ*, in my view)
शादी	*śādī* (f.)	wedding, marriage
शादी करना	*śādī karnā* (v.t.)	to marry, to get married
शौक़	*śauq* (m.)	hobby, interest X *ko* V-*ne kā śauq honā*, for X to enjoy V-ing (as a hobby)
सचमुच	*sacmuc*	really
सहमत	*sahmat*	in agreement, agreeing (X *se sahmat honā*, to agree with X)
सेहत, स्वास्थ्य	*sehat* (f.), *svāsthy* (m.)	health
सेहतमंद, स्वस्थ	*sehatmand*, *svasth*	healthy

Exercise 12

Read aloud and translate.

१. तुम्हें किन चीज़ों का शौक़ है? २. मुझे क्रिकेट खेलने का शौक़ है| ३. मुझे किताबें पढ़ने का शौक़ है| ४. क्या तुम्हें खाना पकाना आता है? ५. मुझे खाना खाने का बहुत शौक़ है लेकिन पकाना बिल्कुल नहीं आता| ६. तुम्हें ख़ाली समय में क्या-क्या करना पसंद है? ७. मुझे टीवी देखना पसंद है| ८. मुझे दोस्तों के साथ सिनेमाघर जाना पसंद है| मुझे फ़िल्में देखने का बड़ा शौक़ है| ९. हम लोगों को घूमना और नई जगहें देखना पसंद है| १०. भारत और पाकिस्तान में ज़्यादातर लड़कों को क्रिकेट खेलना आता है| ११. क्या तुम्हें भाषाएँ सीखने का शौक़ है? १२. हाँ, मुझे भाषाएँ सीखना बहुत पसंद है| १३. आपको कितनी भाषाएँ बोलनी आती हैं? १४. क्या आपको संस्कृत पढ़नी आती है? १५. क्या तुम आज दोपहर को फ़िल्म देखना चाहते हो? १६. आज मेरी तबियत ठीक नहीं है, मैं घर पर रहना चाहता हूँ| १७. मैं कुछ ख़रीदारी करना चाहती हूँ| १८. हर रोज़ इतना पैसा ख़र्च करना ठीक नहीं है| १९. पैसा बचाना अच्छी आदत है| २०. लेकिन ज़िंदगी में कुछ मज़ा करना भी ज़रूरी है|

Exercise 13

Translate into Hindi.

1. I like getting up early.
2. I like to run in the morning.
3. What do you like to do on the weekend?
4. What do you like more, staying at home or going out?
5. Do you know how to play tennis?
6. What things do you know how to cook?
7. What do you want to do this afternoon?
8. Do you want to go to the mall with me?
9. I want to buy some new clothes.
10. I find going to the mall boring. Do you want to do something else?
11. After learning Hindi, I want to learn Urdu too.
12. Learning a language is not an easy task (work).

Exercise 14

Ajay and Hemant have just met through a mutual friend and are getting to know each other. Listen to their conversation and then answer the questions about it.

हेमन्त	तो अजय बताओ, तुम्हारे क्या-क्या शौक़ हैं?
अजय	मुझे संगीत बहुत पसंद है|
हेमन्त	अच्छा, क्या तुम्हें कोई साज़ बजाना आता है?
अजय	नहीं मुझे बजाना तो नहीं आता| बस सुनना पसंद है|
हेमन्त	अच्छा, मुझे भी संगीत सुनना पसंद है|
अजय	क्या तुम्हें खेल पसंद हैं|
हेमन्त	हाँ मुझे क्रिकेट बहुत पसंद है| और टीवी पर बास्केटबॉल देखने का शौक़ है|
अजय	अच्छा, क्या तुम्हें बास्केटबॉल खेलना भी आता है?
हेमन्त	हाँ मुझे थोड़ा-बहुत आता है|
अजय	अच्छा, तो तुम्हारे और क्या-क्या शौक़ हैं?
हेमन्त	मुझे खाना पकाने का शौक़ है| मैं असल में शेफ़ बनना चाहता हूँ|
अजय	सचमुच? तुम्हें क्या-क्या पकाना आता है?
हेमन्त	मुझे हिंदुस्तानी खानों में कई चीज़ें पकानी आती हैं| लेकिन चीनी खाना पकाना मुझे सबसे ज़्यादा पसंद है|
अजय	अच्छा, क्या तुम्हें चाउमिन पकाना आता है?
हेमन्त	हाँ चाउमिन बहुत आसान है| मुझे अच्छी तरह आता है|

सवाल

१. अजय को क्या-क्या पसंद है?

२. अजय को कौन सा साज़ बजाना आता है?

३. हेमन्त क्या बनना चाहता है?

४. हेमन्त को कौन-कौन से खेल पसंद हैं?

५. हेमन्त को कौन-कौन से खाने पकाने आते हैं?

Exercise 15

Role Play

Role 1: A friend of yours wants to introduce you to another friend. Before meeting the friend, you want to find out some basic information about him or her. Ask questions to determine who the friend is (name, age, profession, residence) and if the friend likes the following things:

फ़िल्में देखना, टीवी देखना, बाग़ में टहलना, ख़रीदारी करना, जापानी खाना खाना, चीनी खाना खाना, बातें करना, नए लोगों से मिलना

Role 2: Choose a person who you know well in real life (such as a good friend). Answer all of your partner's questions by giving information about the person.

Switch roles and repeat.

Role 1:

मैक्सिकी रेस्टोरेंट जाना, हिंदुस्तानी रेस्टोरेंट में खाना खाना, क्रिकेट खेलना, बास्केटबॉल खेलना, अंग्रेज़ी फ़िल्में देखना, बातें करना, बॉलीवुड फ़िल्में देखना, ख़रीदारी करना

Exercise 16

Role Play: You are trying to make plans with a friend for the coming weekend. Pair up with a classmate, who will play the role of your friend. Try to find at least five things that both of you want to do this weekend. You can talk about the following activities and/or any others that you are able to think of.

फ़िल्म देखना, पार्क जाना, मॉल जाना / ख़रीदारी करना, लाइब्रेरी जाना / पढ़ाई करना, बाहर खाना खाना (कहाँ), कॉफ़ी हाउस जाना / कॉफ़ी पीने जाना, पार्टी में जाना, जिम जाना / कसरत करना, अजायबघर जाना, बास्केटबॉल (या कोई और खेल) खेलना

Exercise 17

Pair up with a classmate. Alternate reading aloud to each other the statements below. After each statement your partner reads, indicate whether you agree or disagree with it by saying one of the following sentences:

मैं इससे सहमत हूँ।	I agree with this.
मैं इससे सहमत नहीं हूँ।	I do not agree with this.

छात्र १:

१. मुझे हिन्दी सीखना बहुत मुश्किल लगता है|
२. मुझे खाना पकाना आसान लगता है|
३. मुझे लगता है कि भरपूर जीवन के लिए शादी करना ज़रूरी है|
४. मेरे विचार में दुनिया देखना महत्त्वपूर्ण है|
५. मुझे लगता है कि पैसा कमाना अहम है लेकिन कुछ चीज़ें पैसा कमाने से ज़्यादा अहम हैं|

छात्र २:

१. अच्छी सेहत के लिए कसरत करना ज़रूरी है|
२. शराब पीना बुरी आदत है|
३. मेरी राय में रोज़ अख़बार पढ़ना अहम है|
४. इस क्लास के लिए पढ़ाई करना ज़रूरी नहीं है|
५. जल्दी उठना अच्छी आदत है|

Exercise 18

Write ten opinions about the activities mentioned below. When called upon by your teacher, read one of your sentences aloud. As you listen to your classmates' statements, be prepared to say whether you agree or disagree with each statement if asked by your teacher to do so.

Which of the following things are easy to do and which are difficult?

नई भाषा सीखना, हिन्दी सीखना, खाना पकाना, पाँच मील दौड़ना, जल्दी उठना, ख़ुश रहना, नए लोगों से मिलना

Which of the following things are important to do in life? Which are necessary? Which are unnecessary?

बहुत पैसा कमाना, शादी करना, प्यार करना, सेहतमंद रहना, दुनिया देखना, कोई और भाषा सीखना, पढ़ाई करना

Which of the following do you think are good and bad habits? Which are good for one's health and which are not? Which aren't necessary?

रोज़ आठ गिलास पानी पीना, पाबंदी से कसरत करना, दौड़ना, जल्दी उठना, अच्छा खाना खाना, ज़्यादा गोश्त न खाना, शराब पीना, सिग्रेट पीना, अख़बार पढ़ना

Exercise 19

Bingo

Move around your classroom and mingle with your classmates. Ask questions to find people for whom the statements in the table below are true. When you find a person for whom a statement is true, record their name under the statement. Your teacher will tell you how much time you will be given. Points will be awarded as follows:

- 5 points for each completed row or column.
- 10 points for each completed row or column in which no two adjacent squares have the same person's name written.
- 12 points for each category completed (Of the three categories: 1) I know how to..., 2) I like to..., 3) I want to...).

I know how to cook Indian food.	I like to travel.	I can't (don't know how to) dance.	I know how to ride a bike.	I like to play basketball.
I like shopping.	I like listening to music.	I know how to write Urdu.	I like dancing.	I want to learn Sanskrit.
I find learning languages difficult.	I know how to play an instrument (which one?).	I like watching Bollywood films.	I like reading novels (उपन्यास).	I know how to drive a motorcycle.
I know how to make chai.	I want to go to sleep.	I know how to speak Spanish.	I want to learn how to play ("learn to play") an instrument.	After learning Hindi, I want to go to India.
I know how to play cricket.	I want to take Hindi next year.	I want to learn to write Urdu.	I don't know how to swim.	I want to travel the world.

19

Choosing Items and Expressing Measures

In this chapter you will learn two essential skills for communicating with shopkeepers, choosing items and talking about measures.

Using *vālā* to Indicate an Item

When communicating with a shopkeeper, it is often necessary to single out one item from among many similar ones. In English, this is often done with phrases such as the following:

this one

that one

the red one

the big one

the one with a collar

the one with buttons

the one on top

All of these phrases can be expressed in Hindi using the word *vālā*, which generally translates best using the word 'one.'

Using *vālā* with *ye* and *vo*

With the words *ye* and *vo*, *vālā* means 'this one' or 'that one.'

यह वाला	this one
वह वाला	that one

The word *vālā* is a variable adjective, so it inflects to agree in gender and number with the item it refers to.

मुझे वह साड़ी पसंद नहीं, लेकिन यह वाली अच्छी है।	I don't like that sari, but *this one* (*sāṛī*, f.) is nice.
ये जूते अच्छे नहीं लगते। मुझे वे वाले दिखाइए।	I don't like these shoes. Show me *those ones* (*jūte*, m.pl.).

Using *vālā* with Adjectives

Added to an adjective, *vālā* means 'a...one' or 'the...one.'

सस्ता वाला	a/the cheap one
महँगा वाला	a/the expensive one

आपको कौन सी क़मीज़ पसंद है, सस्ती वाली या महँगी वाली?	Which shirt do you like, *the cheap one* or *the expensive one*?
यह कपड़ा बहुत मोटा है। मुझे इससे हल्का वाला चाहिए।	This cloth is too thick; I need *one that is lighter than this*.

Using *vālā* with Adverbs and Postpositional Phrases

Used with an adverb of a postpositional phrase (a postposition plus its object), *vālā* has a similar meaning.

ऊपर वाला	the one above/on top
इसके बग़ल वाला	the one next to it

मुझे यह कपड़ा पसंद नहीं। वह ऊपर वाला दिखाइए।	I don't like this cloth. Show me that *one on top*.
इस क़मीज़ पर दाग़ हैं। इसके बग़ल वाली दिखाइए।	This shirt has stains on it. Show me *the one next to it*.

Using *vālā* with Nouns

Added to nouns, *vālā* means '(the) one with...' or 'a/the ...-ed one.'

कॉलर वाला	a/the collared one, (the) one with a collar
आस्तीन वाला	a/the sleeved one, (the) one with sleeves

मुझे कॉलर वाले कुर्ते पसंद नहीं।	I don't like *kurtas* with collars.
मैं गाँव में लम्बी आस्तीनों वाली क़मीज़ें पहनती हूँ।	In the village I wear long-sleeved shirts.

As can be seen in the second example above, the presence of *vālā* causes the noun that it follows to take the oblique case.

Vendors and other service providers are often identified by their ware or service using *vālā*.

रिक्शेवाला	rickshaw driver
फलवाला	fruit seller
सब्ज़ीवाला	vegetable seller

Using *vālā* with Infinitive Verbs

Added to an oblique infinitive, *vālā* forms an agentive noun, 'one who V-s' or 'a V-er.'

काम करनेवाला	a worker (m.)
सफ़ाई करनेवाली	one who cleans (f.), a cleaning woman
फल बेचनेवाला	a fruit seller (m.)

In addition, *vālā* with the oblique infinitive can mean 'about to V' or 'on the verge of V-ing.'

बारिश होनेवाली है।	It's about to rain.
रेलगाड़ी पहुँचनेवाली है।	The train is about to arrive.

Vocabulary 1

Clothing

आस्तीन	*āstīn* (f.)	sleeve
कढ़ाई	*kaṛhāī* (f.)	embroidery

कपड़ा	*kapṛā* (m.)	cloth
क़मीज़	*qamīz* (f.)	shirt, top
कुर्ता	*kurtā* (m.)	tunic
कॉलर	*kālar* (m.)	collar
गहरा	*gahrā*	deep, dark
गाढ़ा	*gāṛhā*	dark, thick (in consistency)
चप्पल	*cappal* (f.)	sandal
चश्मा	*caśmā* (m.)	glasses
जूता	*jūtā* (m.)	shoe
जेब	*jeb* (f.)	pocket
टोपी	*ṭopī* (f.)	hat
ढीला	*ḍhīlā*	loose
तंग	*tang*	tight
दाग़	*dāgh* (m.)	stain, blemish
दुपट्टा	*dupaṭṭā* (m.)	scarf
धारी	*dhārī* (f.)	stripe
पतलून	*patlūn* (f.)	a pair of pants
पाजामा	*pājāmā* (m.)	drawstring pants (worn with a kurta)
महीन	*mahīn*	fine
मोज़ा	*mozā* (m.)	sock
मोटा	*moṭā*	thick, heavy (cloth); fat
शलवार	*śalvār* (f.)	a type of loose, drawstring pants worn with various tops
शाल	*śāl* (f.)	shawl
शेरवानी	*śervānī* (f.)	a type of long, formal dress coat
साड़ी	*sāṛī* (f.)	sari
हल्का	*halkā*	light (in color or weight)

Additional Words

अलग	*alag*	separate
गहना, ज़ेवर	*gahnā*, *zevar* (m.)	jewel/s; jewelry (pl.)
दिखाना	*dikhānā* (v.t.)	to show
पसंद	*pasand* (f.)	liking (e.g., *merī pasand kī cīz*, 'a thing of my liking')
बग़ैर	*baghair*	without (X *ke baghair*/*baghair* X *ke*, without X)
बिना	*binā*	without (X *ke binā*/*binā* X *ke*, without X)
मगर	*magar*	but (= *lekin*)
महँगा	*mahãgā*	expensive
रिक्शा	*rikśā* (m.)	rickshaw
रिक्शेवाला	*rikśevālā* (m.)	rickshaw driver
वही	*vahī*	that very (= *vo* + *hī*)
सस्ता	*sastā*	inexpensive, cheap

Exercise 1

Do an internet image search for any of the following items that you are unfamiliar with (you can use the Roman spellings given):

"kurta pajama," "shalwar kameez," "sherwani," "sari," "dupatta."

Exercise 2

Read aloud and translate.

१. यह वाला आपको कैसा लगता है? २. क्या आपको वह वाला पसंद है? ३. आपको यह वाला ज़्यादा पसंद है या वह वाला? ४. मुझे यह वाला उस वाले से ठीक लगता है। ५. आपको कैसी पतलून चाहिए? मुझे कोई हल्के रंग वाली चाहिए। ६. मुझे ढीली वाली भी ठीक लगती है। ७. तुम्हें मेरे नए जूते कैसे लगते हैं? ८. यह कुर्ता आकाश के लिए ठीक नहीं, उसको सिर्फ़ लम्बी आस्तीनों वाले कुर्ते पसंद हैं। ९. यह वाली क़मीज़ मुझे अच्छी नहीं लगती। मुझे कोई सादी क़मीज़ दिखाइए। १०. लगता है उसे अपनी लाल वाली क़मीज़ बहुत पसंद है। वह हर पार्टी में वही क़मीज़ पहनती है।

Exercise 3

Translate into Hindi.

(Nos. 1-4: assume you are speaking of *patlūn*, f. 'a pair of pants')

1. Show me a loose one.
2. Do you have a red one?
3. I need one with pockets (a pocketed one).
4. I don't like blue ones.

(Nos. 5- 8: *kapṛā*, m. 'cloth')

5. Do you have a(ny) yellow one?
6. How do you like this striped one?
7. Show me that one above.
8. No, not that one, show me the one behind that.

(Nos. 9-12: *qamīz*, f. 'shirt')

9. I need a short-sleeved one.
10. Do you like this one?
11. No, I don't like green ones.
12. Show me another one.

Exercise 4

You are planning a trip to India in the next few weeks. A friend of yours has asked you to bring an article of clothing back for him. Read his request and identify an item that he will like from among all of the pictures provided in the next chapter.

मुझे एक नया कुर्ता चाहिए। मुझे सादे वाले कुर्ते पसंद हैं, धारी वाले नहीं। मुझे हल्के रंग वाले और गाढ़े रंग वाले दोनों ठीक लगते हैं। मुझे कॉलर वाले पसंद हैं लेकिन खड़े कॉलर वाले ज़्यादा पसंद हैं। मुझे सिर्फ़ जेब वाला कुर्ता चाहिए। मैं जेब में अपना चश्मा रखता हूँ।

Exercise 5

Listen to the dialogue and compose sentences noting: a) what the customer is shopping for, b) what she likes and what she does not like, c) what the outcome of the dialogue is.

ग्राहक	भैया, मुझे कुछ शलवार क़मीज़ के सूट दिखाइए।
दुकानदार	यह लीजिए मैडम, यह बिल्कुल नए फ़ैशन का है।

ग्राहक	नहीं, मुझे यह पसंद नहीं। इसका रंग बहुत गाढ़ा है। कोई और दिखाइए।
दुकानदार	तो यह लीजिए, यह हल्के रंग का है।
ग्राहक	हाँ, मुझे उसका रंग तो पसंद है मगर इसमें कढ़ाई कुछ ज़्यादा है।
दुकानदार	अच्छा, तो आपको हल्की कढ़ाई वाला चाहिए?
ग्राहक	हाँ हल्की कढ़ाई वाला या बग़ैर कढ़ाई वाला भी ठीक है।
दुकानदार	अच्छा, तो यह देखिए मैडम, इसका रंग भी हल्का है और इसमें कढ़ाई भी हल्की है।
ग्राहक	हाँ, यह तो अच्छा लगता है मगर इसकी क़मीज़ बिना आस्तीन की है। कोई इसी तरह का आस्तीनों वाला सूट दिखाइए।
दुकानदार	अच्छा, यह लीजिए। बिल्कुल आप की पसंद के मुताबिक़। इसका रंग भी हल्का है, कढ़ाई भी हल्की है और इसमें आस्तीनें भी हैं।
ग्राहक	हाँ, यह वाला मुझे पसंद है। यह अलग रख दीजिए।*

*यह अलग रख दीजिए, 'please set this aside.' The form *rakh dījie* is an example of a compound verb. Please see unit 40 for a more detailed explanation of compound verbs.

Exercise 6

Using the following dialogue as a model, act out the role play below with a classmate. Prior to beginning the role play, read the following dialogue aloud with your partner.

क. मुझे कुर्ता चाहिए।

ख. आपको कैसा कुर्ता चाहिए?

क. मुझे लम्बा वाला चाहिए।

ख. यह वाला देखिए।

क. मुझे यह वाला पसंद नहीं। क्या आपके पास सफ़ेद वाला है?

ख. हाँ, यह वाला देखिए। आपको कैसा लगता है?

क. हाँ, यह ठीक है। यह वाला अलग रखिए। और कोई जेब वाला भी दिखाइए।

ख. यह वाला देखिए। यह वाला बहुत अच्छा है, ना?

क. नहीं, मुझे कॉलर वाले पसंद नहीं।

ख. ...

Role Play

Teacher: Prior to class, photocopy the pictures of pants, kurtas, and shirts in the next chapter. Cut the photocopied pictures so that only one image appears on each slip of paper. Provide students playing the role of shopkeeper with the set of pictures appropriate to their activity.

A. Role 1: You are shopping for a pair of pants. Read aloud the sentences below in order to request to see various types of pants.

१. मुझे पतलून चाहिए| मुझे कोई गाढ़े रंग वाली दिखाइए|
२. मुझे सफ़ेद वाली दिखाइए|
३. क्या आपके पास कोई ढीली वाली है? मुझे दिखाइए|
४. मुझे कोई तंग वाली दिखाइए|
५. मुझे जेब वाली दिखाइए|
६. मुझे बिना जेब वाली दिखाइए|
७. क्या आपके पास बिना जेब और गाढ़े रंग वाली है? मुझे दिखाइए|
८. अगर आपके पास कोई सफ़ेद रंग की जेब वाली है तो वह भी दिखाइए|
९. मुझे ढीली सफ़ेद वाली चाहिए|

Role 2: You are an employee at a clothing store. Your partner will play the role of a customer. Show her the items that she requests to see. For each request, show her all of the items that match the qualities that she wants to see. Your teacher will provide you with pictures of pants to show your customer.

B. Switch roles and repeat the previous exercise. This time the customer wants to buy a *kurtā*.

१. मुझे एक कुर्ता चाहिए| मुझे कोई सफ़ेद रंग वाला दिखाइए|
२. मुझे जेब वाले दिखाइए|
३. क्या आपके पास बिना कॉलर वाले हैं? दिखाइए|
४. क्या आपके पास कॉलर वाले हैं? सादे कॉलर वाले और खड़े कॉलर वाले दोनों दिखाइए|
५. कुछ धारी वाले भी दिखाइए|
६. कुछ गाढ़े रंग वाले भी दिखाइए|
७. कोई सफ़ेद धारी वाला दिखाइए|
८. जेब वाला लेकिन बिना कॉलर वाला दिखाइए|
९. गाढ़ा धारी वाला दिखाइए|
१०. ठीक है| मुझे सादा सफ़ेद खड़े कॉलर वाला कुर्ता चाहिए|

C. Repeat the same activity, this time discussing shirts. The sentences will now be given in English, so the person playing the role of customer will have to translate them into Hindi. After completing the first round, switch roles and repeat.

Round 1:

a. I need a shirt. Show me some dark-colored ones.
b. Do you have any light-colored ones? Show me those, too.
c. Show me ones with pockets.
d. How many (ones) do you have without pockets?
e. Do you have any dark ones without pockets?
f. OK. I want the light one without a pocket.

Round 2:

a. I need a shirt. Show me some long-sleeved ones.
b. How many short-sleeved ones do you have? Please show them to me.
c. Do you have any striped shirts? Please show me.
d. How many (ones) do you have without stripes?
e. Show me a white, short-sleeved shirt.
f. OK. I want the dark, long-sleeved one.

Measures

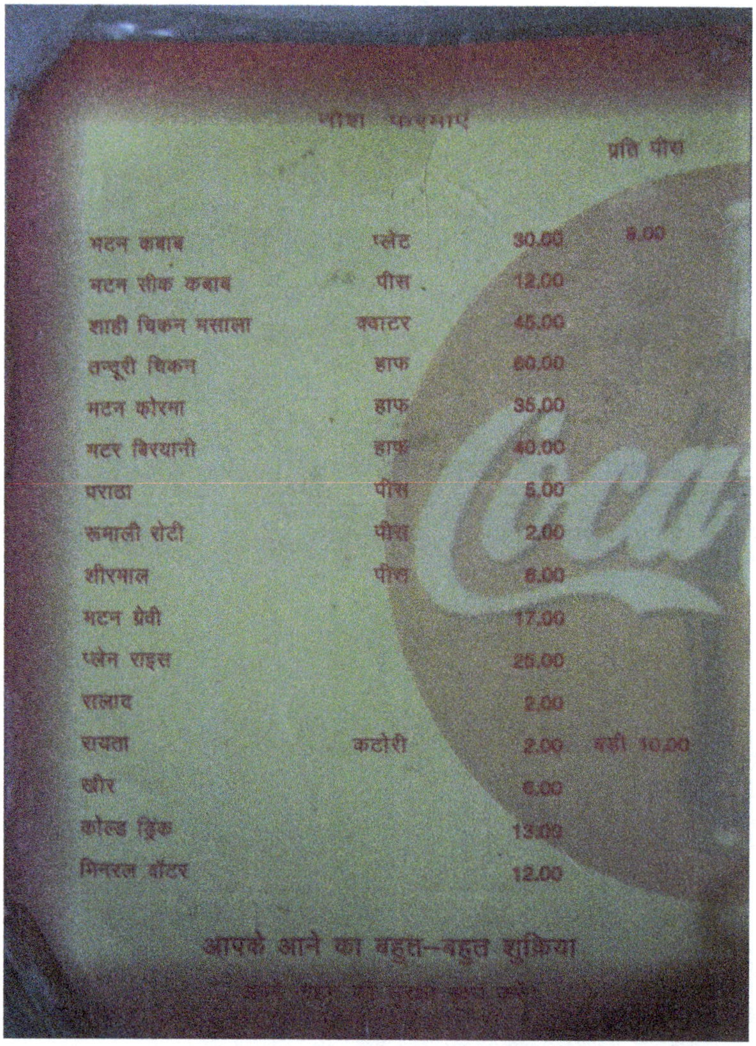

India follows the metric system. When reporting measures, no word corresponding to 'of' is used in Hindi.

एक किलो गोश्त	one kg. of meat
एक पाव प्याज़	one-quarter kg. of onions
आधा किलो मटर	one-half kg. of peas
एक कप चाय	one cup of tea
आधा कप दूध	half a cup of milk
दो चम्मच चीनी	two spoonfuls of sugar
ढाई मीटर कपड़ा	two-and-one-half meters of cloth
पौन मीटर रेशम	three-quarters of a meter of silk
एक जोड़ी जूते	one pair of shoes
तीन जोड़े कपड़े	three sets of clothes

Vocabulary 2

आँच	*ā̃c* (f.)	flame (e.g., of a gas stove)
आधा	*ādhā*	half
इलायची	*ilāycī* (f.)	cardamom
उंडेलना	*unḍelnā* (v.t.)	to pour
उबलना	*ubalnā* (v.i.)	to boil
उबालना	*ubālnā* (v.t.)	to boil
कपड़ा	*kapṛā* (m.)	cloth
किलो, किलोग्राम	*kilo, kilogrām*	kilogram
गुच्छा, गड्डी	*gucchā* (m.), *gaṭṭhī* (f.)	bunch, small tied bundle (e.g. of herbs)
ग्राहक	*grāhak*	customer
चीनी	*cīnī* (f.)	sugar
छन्नी	*channī* (f.)	strainer
छानना	*chānnā* (v.t.)	to strain, to sift
जूता	*jūtā* (m.)	shoe
जोड़ना	*joṛnā* (v.t.)	to join, to add (up)
जोड़ा	*joṛā* (m.)	set (e.g., of clothes)

जोड़ी	*joṛī* (f.)	pair, couple
डालना	*ḍālnā* (v.t.)	to put in (*mẽ*)
तैयार	*taiyār* (*tayyār*)	ready
दर्जन	*darjan*	dozen
दुकानदार	*dukāndār*	shopkeeper
धीमा	*dhīmā*	low (in intensity), slow
पत्ती	*pattī* (f.)	small leaf (i.e. *cāy pattī, cāy kī pattī*, tea leaves)
पाव	*pāv*	one quarter part; ¼ kg.
मीटर	*mīṭar*	meter
रेशम	*reśam* (m.)	silk
विधि, तरकीब	*vidhi, tarkīb* (f.)	method
शीशी	*śīśī* (f.)	small bottle
सामग्री	*sāmagrī* (f.)	ingredients, material
स्वाद	*svād* (m.)	taste

Note:

- *dukāndār*: *dukān*, f. 'store, shop'; *-dār*, 'possessor of'

Exercise 7 G

Read aloud and translate.

१. हमें बाज़ार से एक पाव चाय की पत्ती चाहिए। २. मुझे एक बोतल पानी चाहिए। ३. उसके पास सिर्फ़ दो जोड़े कपड़े हैं। ४. तुम्हारे पास कितने जोड़ी जूते हैं? ५. मैं कॉफ़ी में एक चम्मच चीनी लेता हूँ। ६. मुझे आधा किलो आटा दीजिए। ७. चार कप चाय लाओ। ८. मुझे ढाई किलो आलू चाहिए। ९. हमें एक दर्जन अंडे चाहिएँ। १०. पतलून बनाने के लिये ढाई मीटर कपड़ा चाहिए। ११. उसमें दो कप दूध और दो कप पानी डालिए।

Exercise 8 G

Translate into Hindi.

1. I need one kg. of apples.
2. We need a quarter kg. of sugar.
3. I just need one cup of tea.
4. I need two bottles of water.

5. I only have one bottle of water.
6. Give me one-half kg. of oranges.
7. Give us one-and-a-half kg. of rice.
8. Put one spoonful of oil in it.
9. Boil four cups of water.
10. We need one-half spoonful of garam masala.

Exercise 9

An American friend of yours is interested in making authentic North Indian tea but hasn't been able to find a good recipe. You have found the following recipe online. Read the recipe and then translate it for your friend.

चाय बनाने की विधि

सामग्री:
दो कप दूध, दो छोटे चम्मच चीनी, दो चम्मच चाय की पत्ती, दो हरी इलायची

विधि:

१. दो कप दूध उबालिए|
२. दूध उबलने से थोड़ा पहले उसमें दो छोटे चम्मच चाय की पत्ती, दो चम्मच चीनी और दो हरी इलायची डालिए|
३. धीमी आँच पर एक मिनट उबालिए|
४. चाय तैयार है| चाय को छननी से छानिए| और कप में उंडेलिए|
५. गरम-गरम चाय पीजिए|

Exercise 10

You are an assistant at a dry goods store in India. Listen to the conversation between the shop owner and the customer. As you listen, note all of the items that are needed and the amount needed so that you will be able to retrieve what the customer needs.

दुकानदार	भाई साहब, आपको क्या चाहिए?
ग्राहक	मुझे तीन किलो चावल चाहिए|
दुकानदार	और?
ग्राहक	एक-एक किलो मूँग और मसूर की दालें भी दे दीजिए*|
दुकानदार	और क्या चाहिए?
ग्राहक	क्या आपके पास सरसों का तेल है?

दुकानदार	जी हाँ, सरसों का तेल भी है।
ग्राहक	एक शीशी वह भी दे दीजिए। और चीनी भी एक पाव दे दीजिए*।
दुकानदार	जी अच्छा, और कुछ?
ग्राहक	आधा दर्जन नहाने का साबुन भी दे दीजिए*।
दुकानदार	जी, यह लीजिए नहाने का साबुन। और कुछ?
ग्राहक	नहीं, बस इतना ही। पैसे जोड़ दीजिए*।

*The phrases *de dījiye* and *joṛ dījiye* are examples of compound verbs. When used with imperative forms, compound verbs are often more polite than simple verbs. Compound verbs are formed by adding one of the verbs *denā, lenā,* or *jānā* the the stem of the main verb to form a new stem, and then conjugating it as one normally would. *Jānā* is generally used with intransitive verbs. *Lenā* and *denā* are used with transitive verbs. *Lenā* gives a sense of the subject of the sentence doing the action for his or her own benefit. *Denā* gives the sense of doing the action for the benefit of another. Please see chapter 40 for more information on compound verbs.

20

Discussing Prices

In this chapter you will learn another essential skill when shopping—the ability to talk about prices. This skill is all the more important in South Asia, where prices are often not fixed and negotiating is a common practice.

Price Constructions

Price per Item

The most common way to ask how much an item costs is X *kitne kā hai*, '(of) how much is X.' The postposition *kā* and the verb *honā* change in form to agree with the item being discussed; the word *kitne* always appears ending in *-e*.

X *kitne kā hai*?	**how much is X?**
यह क़मीज़ कितने की है?	How much is this shirt (f.)?
वह कुर्ता कितने का है?	How much is that kurta (m.)?
ये साड़ियाँ कितने की हैं?	How much are these saris (f.pl.)?
ये कपड़े कितने के हैं?	How much are these clothes (m.pl.)?

To answer the question of how much a countable item costs, merely replace the question word *kitne* with the price. In this construction as well, both the postposition *kā* and the verb *honā* agree with the item.

X [price] *kā hai*.	**X is [price].**
यह क़मीज़ तीन सौ रुपये की है।	This shirt is 300 rupees.
यह कुर्ता साढ़े तीन सौ रुपये का है।	This kurta is 350 rupees.

Note: The plural word *rupaye* is commonly used without the plural oblique suffix *–õ*.

Price per Unit of Measure

The construction below can be used to ask how much an item is per unit of measure. The verb *honā* agrees with the item being asked about.

X *kyā hisāb / bhāv hai*?	**How much is X per unit?**
ये आलू क्या हिसाब हैं?	How much are these potatoes (i.e. per kg.)?
बासमती चावल क्या भाव है?	How much is the basmati rice?

To report the price of something per unit of measure, no word for 'per' is needed:

# *rupaye* [unit]	**# rupees per [unit]**
ये आलू पंद्रह रुपये किलो हैं।	These potatoes are 15 rupees a kilo.
बासमती चावल चालीस रुपये किलो है।	Basmati rice is 40 rupees a kilo.

Translating 'for' with Prices

Generally, the English phrase 'for [a price]' corresponds to [price] *mẽ* in Hindi.

बीस रुपये में	for 20 rupees
एक सौ रुपये में	for 100 rupees
मुफ़्त में	for free
कम पैसे में	for less money

बीस रुपये में कितने समोसे मिलते हैं?	How many samosas can you get for 20 rupees?
मुफ़्त में कुछ नहीं मिलता।	You don't get anything for free.
यही सामान उस दुकान में कम पैसे में मिलता है।	You can get the same stuff in that store for less money.

Vocabulary 1

अकेला	*akelā*	alone, only
अनुभव, तजुर्बा	*anubhav, tajurbā* (m.)	experience
अनोखा	*anokhā*	unique
असली	*aslī*	true, genuine
क़ीमत	*qīmat* (f.)	value, price
दरअसल	*darasal*	actually, in fact (= *asal mẽ*)

दाम	*dām* (m.)	price
निर्भर	*nirbhar*	dependent (upon X; X *par nirbhar honā*, to depend on X)
परहेज़ करना	*parhez karnā* (v.t.)	to refrain (from, *se*)
पसंद करना	*pasand karnā* (v.t.)	to like; to choose something one likes
फ़र्क़, अंतर	*farq*, *antar* (m.)	difference
माँगना	*mā̃gnā* (v.t.)	to ask for
मुफ़्त	*muft*	free (in price)
मोल-भाव	*mol-bhāv* (m.)	bargaining, haggling
रिवाज	*rivāj* (m.)	custom, practice
रुपया	*rupayā* (m.)	rupee (unit of currency)
हिसाब	*hisāb* (m.)	price per unit of measurement; calculation

Additional Food-Related Words

These words will be used in the unit activities.

अदद	*adad* (m.)	one number of
कड़वा	*kaṛvā*	bitter; (too) spicy
क़ीमा	*qīmā* (m.)	ground meat
खट्टा	*khaṭṭā*	sour
खीरा	*khīrā* (m.)	cucumber
घी	*ghī* (m.)	ghee, clarified butter
ज़ीरा	*zīrā* (m.)	cumin

तलना	*talnā* (v.t.)	to fry
तेज़ पत्ता, तेज पत्ता	*tez pattā, tej pattā* (m.)	bay leaf
तौलना	*taulnā* (v.t.)	to weigh
दालचीनी	*dālcīnī* (f.)	cinnamon
नमकीन	*namkīn*	salty
पुदीना	*pudīnā* (m.)	mint
भिंडी	*bhinḍī* (f.)	okra
मक्खन	*makkhan* (m.)	butter
मीठा	*mīṭhā*	sweet
रोटी	*roṭī* (f.)	bread, (esp. flat bread)
लौंग	*laung* (f.)	clove
साग	*sāg* (m.)	greens
स्याह ज़ीरा	*syāh zīrā* (m.)	black cumin (*syāh*, black)

Exercise 1 G

Read aloud and translate.

१. यह पतलून कितने की है? २. और यह नीली वाली कितने की है? ३. ये कपड़े कितने के हैं? ४. क़मीज़ चार सौ रुपये की है और पतलून छह सौ की है| ५. टमाटर क्या भाव है? ६. छोटे वाले बीस रुपये किलो हैं और बड़े वाले पच्चीस रुपये किलो हैं| ७. यह कपड़ा कितने रुपये मीटर है? ८. यह कपड़ा दो सौ रुपये मीटर है| ९. इन जूतों का दाम पाँच सौ रुपये क्यों है? वे वाले सिर्फ़ चार सौ रुपये के हैं| दोनों में फ़र्क़ क्या है? १०. बासमती चावल क्या हिसाब है? ११. यह वाला तीस रुपये किलो है| १२. उस दुकान में दो जोड़ी जूते ख़रीदने पर एक जोड़ी जूते मुफ़्त मिलते हैं|

Exercise 2

Translate into Hindi.

1. How much are these pants?
2. They are 350 rupees.
3. How much is this shirt?
4. It is 230 rupees.
5. How much is this *kurtā*?
6. It is 335 rupees.
7. How much are these tomatoes (by weight)?
8. They are 30 rupees a kilo.
9. How much are the oranges?
10. They are 33 rupees a kilo.
11. I need one and a half pounds.
12. How much is the garlic?
13. It's 40 rupees a kilo.
14. I need one-quarter kg.
15. How much is one bottle of water?

Exercise 3

Role Play

Teacher: Prior to class, make photocopies of the pictures of pants, kurtas, and shirts below. Make sure that the prices do not appear on the photocopies that you make. Distribute the appropriate pictures to the students playing the role of shopper in each role play.

Role 1: You are shopping for a pair of pants. Refer to the pictures of pants that your teacher distributes to you. Your partner will play the role of the shopkeeper. Ask how much the different pairs of pants cost. Note the answers and then confirm them with your partner orally when finishing.

Role 2: You are a shopkeeper of a clothing store. Help your customer by telling him or her the price of each of the items he or she asks about. Under each picture is the item's price.

क़ीमतें

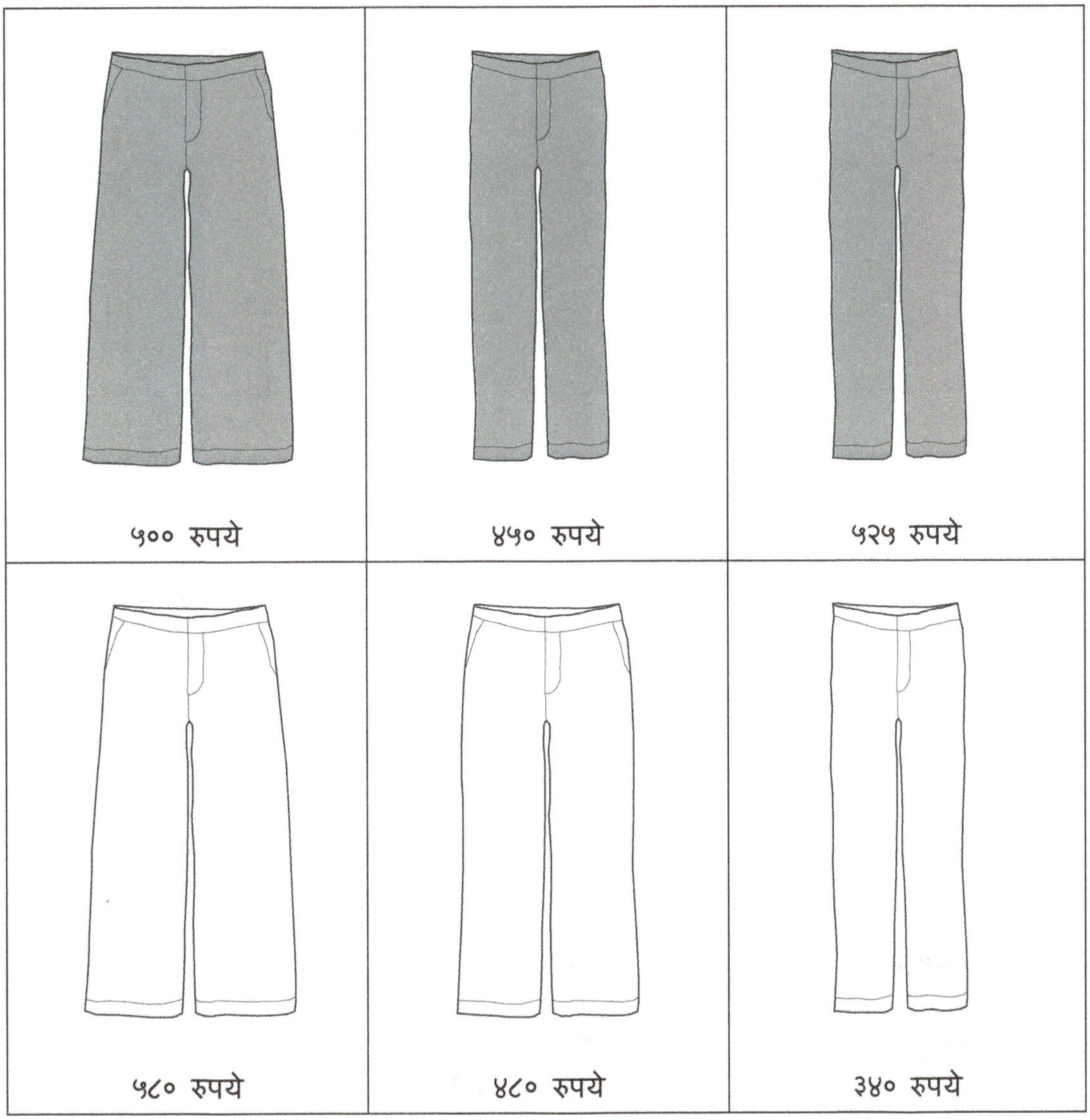

उदाहरण

क. यह पतलून कितने की है?

ख. यह चार सौ रुपये की है।

क. यह वाली कितने की है?

ख. यह वाली साढ़े चार सौ की है।

क. और यह जेब वाली? यह कितने की है?

ख. यह पाँच सौ रुपये की है।

Switch roles and repeat the role play with *kurtās* and shirts.

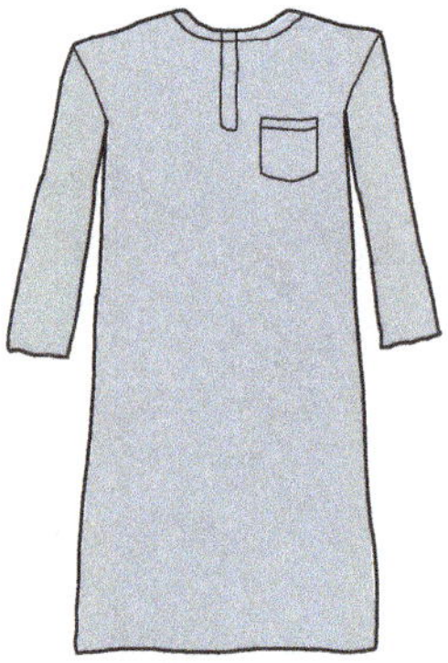

२१५ रुपये

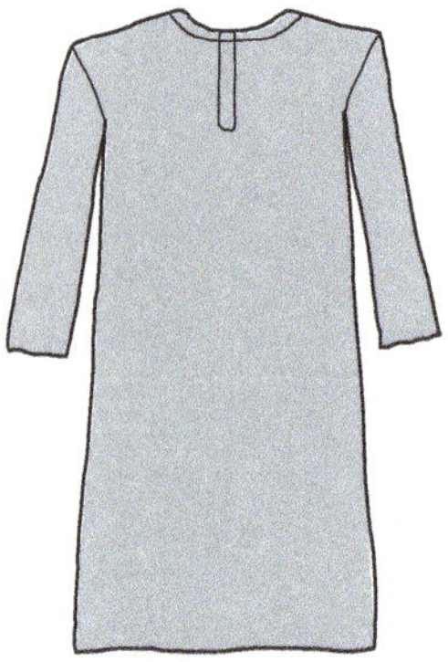

१९५ रुपये

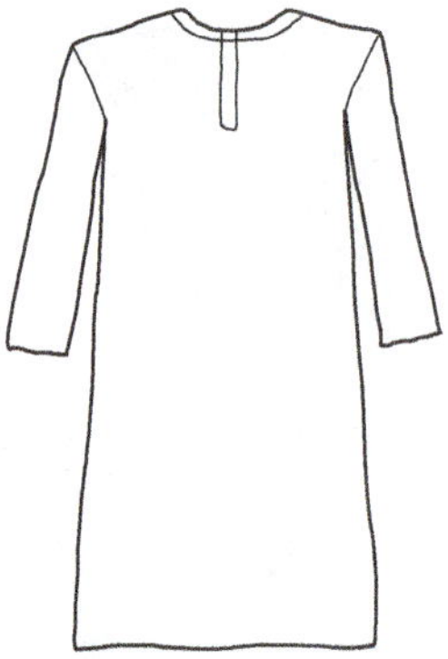

२९० रुपये

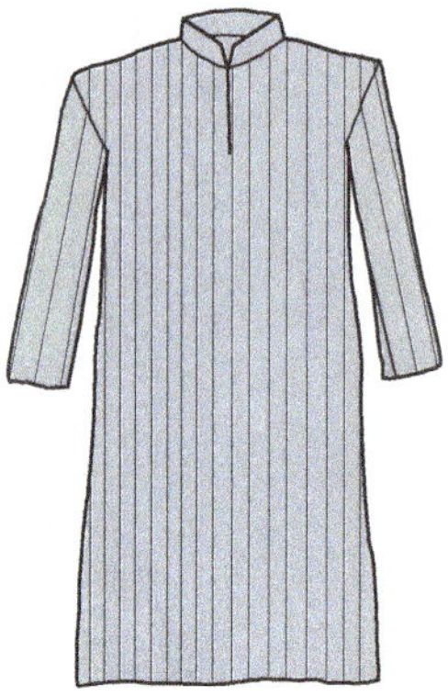

३०५ रुपये

३५० रुपये

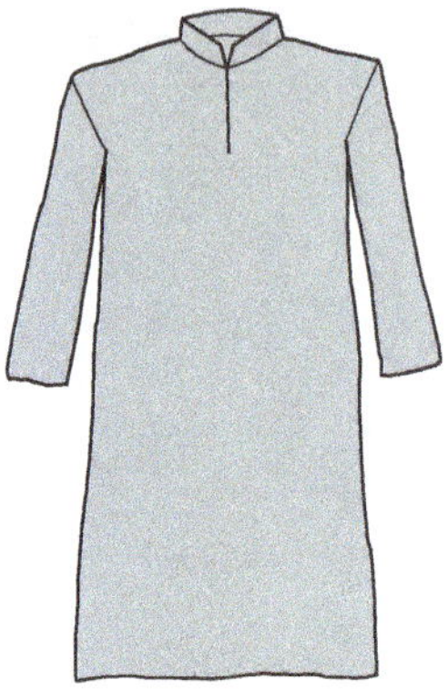

२५० रुपये

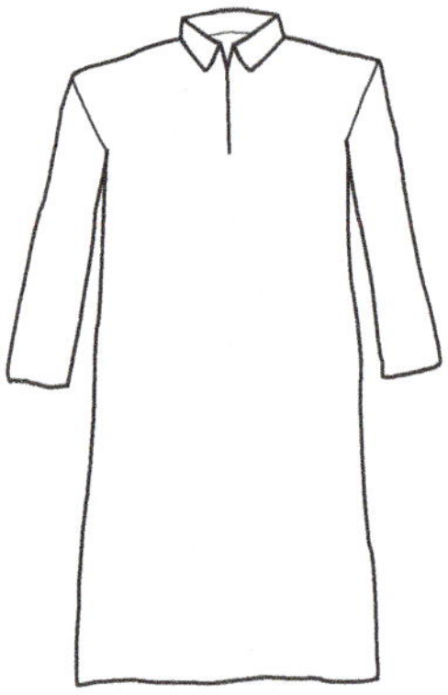

१७५ रुपये

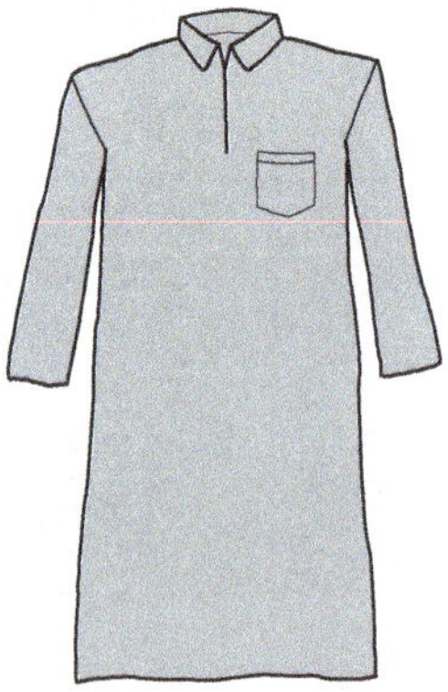

१८० रुपये

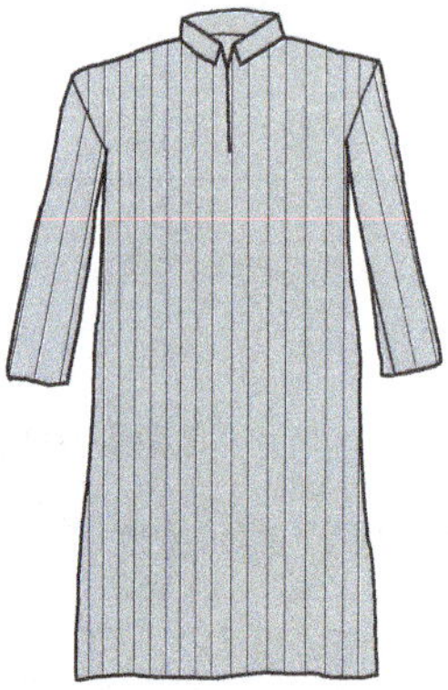

२३५ रुपये

४८५ रुपये	४६५ रुपये	४५५ रुपये

४१५ रुपये	३९५ रुपये	३३५ रुपये

Exercise 4

Buying Produce

Listen to the dialogue and note all of the items that are bought, the price that is originally asked for each, the price that is given in the end, and the amount of each item that is bought.

Item	Price Requested	Price Paid	Amount Purchased

क. हाँ भैया, ये आलू क्या हिसाब हैं?

ख. भाई साहब! आलू पंद्रह रुपये किलो हैं|

क. ठीक है, मुझे एक किलो दे दो|

ख. ठीक है, और कुछ?

क. हाँ, टमाटर कैसे हैं?

ख. टमाटर बीस रुपये किलो हैं|

क. मुझे लगता है यह कुछ ज़्यादा है|

ख. ठीक है, उन्नीस रुपये किलो दे दीजिए|

क. ठीक है, मुझे आधा किलो चाहिए|

ख. और कुछ?

क. हाँ, प्याज़ क्या भाव है?

ख. प्याज़ अट्ठारह रुपये किलो है|

क. यह कुछ ज़्यादा महँगी है|

ख. नहीं भाई साहब, यह एकदम ठीक दाम है|

क. अच्छा ठीक है, डेढ़ किलो दे दो|

...

Exercise 5

Role Play

Useful Phrases:

ठीक-ठीक बताओ|	Tell me an appropriate price.
तुम ज़्यादा माँग / बता रहे हो|	You are asking for too much.
यह कुछ ज़्यादा है|	This is a bit too much (expensive).
यह कुछ ज़्यादा महँगा है|	This is a bit too expensive.
यह एकदम ठीक दाम है|	This price is completely fine.

दे दो।*	Please give me… (with *tum*)
दे दीजिए।	Please give me… (with *āp*)

*The phrases *de do* and *de dījie* are slightly more polite than *do* and *dījie*. These are examples of compound verbs. Compound verbs consist of a main verb, in stem form, followed by one of the verbs *jānā*, *lenā*, or *denā*, which bear verbal inflections and supply additional nuances. Please see unit 8 for more information on compound verbs.

Role 1: You are in a bazaar in Delhi shopping for fruits and vegetables. Before purchasing items, find out what the prices are per item or per kg. Ask the vendor how much each of the items below costs. If the item meets the price you would like to pay, purchase it. If not, try to get the vendor to lower the price. Mark the items that you purchase by placing a check in the appropriate box.

Item	सेब	टमाटर	मटर	भिंडी	बैंगन	आलू	लहसुन	अदरक	प्याज़
Amount needed	1 kg	1.5 kg	0.5 kg	0.5 kg	0.5 kg	1 kg	0.25 kg	0.25 kg	1 kg
Price you can pay per kg	rs. 25	rs. 20	rs. 20	rs. 18	rs. 30	rs. 15	rs. 19	rs. 21	rs. 17
Bought?									

Role 2: You are a fruit and vegetable vendor in a market in Delhi. The chart below shows the price that you would like to get for each item as well as the lowest price that you can possibly accept. Your partner will play the role of your customer. Try to sell your items for the highest possible price to your customer. If your customer decides to buy an item, place a checkmark in the bottom row and indicate the amount of the item that your customer needs.

Item	सेब	टमाटर	मटर	भिंडी	बैंगन	आलू	लहसुन	अदरक	प्याज़
Asking price per kg.	rs. 25	rs. 20	rs. 20	rs. 20	rs. 31	rs. 16	rs. 20	rs. 22	rs. 17
Lowest price you will accept	rs. 24	rs. 19	rs. 19	rs. 18	rs. 29	rs. 15	rs. 19	rs. 21	rs. 16
Bought?									

21

Unit 4 Review Activities

The goal of this chapter is to review the content of unit 4 and provide additional opportunities to synthesize all of the content presented up to this point.

G

1. Grammar Review

- What are the two essential structural differences between indirect constructions and the corresponding English expressions?
- Write the complete table of contracted *ko* pronoun forms from memory.
- Give three new uses of the infinitive learned in this unit.
- How do phrases with the word *vālā* generally translate into English? Give some examples.

2. Tips for Increasing Fluency: Speaking Drills

You can increase your speaking fluency by regularly performing the following speaking drills. The first few times you carry out each drill, focus on accuracy; then focus on speed as you become able to use the structure more automatically.

A. X *ko* Y *pasand honā*

a. Form questions for each of the following items of the form 'Do you like...?' Use *āp* first and then repeat using *tum*.

भारतीय खाना, चीनी खाना, मिठाइयाँ, फल, सब्ज़ियाँ, गोश्त, किताबें, फ़िल्में

b. Go through the preceding list of items and state what things you like and what things you dislike. Once you become comfortable discussing these items, create your own list of additional items and repeat.

c. Repeat drill b, but this time make sentences about a friend or acquaintance of yours.

d. Make sentences describing what sorts of the above items you like and what sorts you dislike.

B. V-*nā cāhnā*

a. What do you want to do this evening? State ten things in close succession that you want to or do not want to do.

b. Repeat discussing things you want to do this weekend.

c. Make a list of verbs and verb phrases for eight activities that you do often with friends. Go through the list and create questions for each verb that you could ask a friend in order to find out if he or she wants to do the activity this weekend.

C. *X ko V-nā pasand honā*

a. Create questions that you could ask a person to determine if he or she likes doing the activities below. First ask using *āp*, and then repeat with *tum*.

पढ़ाई करना, बाहर रेस्टोरेंटों में खाना खाना, फ़ोन पर बातें करना, दोस्तों के साथ वक़्त गुज़ारना, नए लोगों से मिलना, कपड़े ख़रीदना, टीवी देखना, फ़िल्में देखना

b. Which of the above activities do you like doing and which do you not like?

c. Repeat drill 2 describing the activities that a person you know likes and does not like to do.

3. Personalization Questions

Pair up with a partner. Take turns asking and answering the following questions. Answer in complete sentences.

१. आपको किस तरह का खाना सबसे ज़्यादा पसंद है?

२. आपका मनपसंद खाना कौन सा है?

३. आपको ख़ाली समय में क्या-क्या करना पसंद है?

४. आपको किन विषयों में दिलचस्पी है?

५. क्या आपको ... आता है?*

गाड़ी चलाना, खाना पकाना, क्रिकेट खेलना, स्पैनिश बोलना, हिन्दी पढ़ना, नाचना, गाना गाना, तैरना, कोई साज़ बजाना

६. अपने घर वालों के बारे में कुछ बताइए। उनको क्या-क्या पसंद है?

७. अपने दोस्तों के बारे में कुछ बताइए। उनके शौक़ क्या-क्या हैं?

८. मैं क्लास के बाद बाज़ार जा रहा हूँ। क्या आपको वहाँ से कुछ चाहिए?

*Some changes might be necessary here based on the gender of the direct object.

4. Shopping in South Asia is often quite a different experience from shopping in America. Read the text and in the table below note all of the differences that are mentioned.

दक्षिण एशिया में ख़रीदारी करना एक अनोखा अनुभव है। अमरीका में ज़्यादातर दुकानों में एक ही दाम होता है। दक्षिण एशिया में ऐसा नहीं है। असल में भारत में मोल-भाव करने का बड़ा रिवाज है, इसलिए यह जानना ज़रूरी है कि असली दाम क्या है। अगर दुकानदार को लगता है कि किसी ग्राहक को असली दाम मालूम नहीं तो वह अक्सर ज़्यादा पैसा माँगता है।

ज़्यादातर दक्षिण एशियाई दुकानें अमरीकी डिपार्टमेंट स्टोर्ज़ की तरह नहीं हैं| आमतौर पर अमरीकी दुकानों में ग्राहक अकेले घूमता है, चीज़ें ख़ुद देखता है, और ख़ुद पसंद करता है| बहुत कम दक्षिण एशियाई दुकानों में ऐसा होता है| आमतौर पर ग्राहक एक जगह पर बैठता है और दुकान वाला उसको सामान दिखाता है|

कुछ बड़े शहरों में एक-दो सुपरमार्केटें हैं लेकिन ज़्यादातर लोग मुहल्ले के बाज़ार से खाने-पीने का सामान ख़रीदते हैं| फल फलवाले से ख़रीदते हैं, सब्ज़ियाँ सब्ज़ीवाले से ख़रीदते हैं और चावल, तेल और दूसरी ऐसी चीज़ें किराने की दुकान से ख़रीदते हैं|

दक्षिण एशिया में ख़रीदारी	अमरीका में ख़रीदारी

5. You are helping a friend plan a dinner tomorrow night. Your friend has invited an acquaintance, Jameel, and his family for dinner and is trying to decide what to cook based on the foods that the guests like. Listen to your friend's conversation with Jameel. Note everything you hear about the likes and dislikes of Jameel and his family members.

मेज़बान	मुझे ख़ुशी है कि आप और आपके घर वाले कल मेरे यहाँ डिनर पर तशरीफ़ ला रहे हैं । ज़रा मुझे बताइए कि आपको खाने में क्या-क्या पसंद है|
जमील	मुझे गोश्त वाली सब चीज़ें पसंद हैं|
मेज़बान	और आपके पिता को क्या पसंद है?
जमील	उनकी कोई ख़ास पसंद नहीं, मगर वे दूध और दही वाली चीज़ों से परहेज़ करते हैं|
मेज़बान	और आपकी मम्मी?
जमील	उनको सब्ज़ियाँ बहुत पसंद हैं|
मेज़बान	सब्ज़ियाँ तो मुझे भी बहुत पसंद हैं| जमील, आपके भाई और बहन को खाने में क्या पसंद है?
जमील	मेरे भाई को मेरी तरह गोश्त वाली डिशें पसंद हैं| मेरी बहन को गोश्त और सब्ज़ियाँ दोनों पसंद हैं मगर भिंडी पसंद नहीं|
मेज़बान	बहुत शुक्रिया, जमील| अब मेरा काम काफ़ी आसान हो गया| ठीक है, कल मिलेंगे|
जमील	जी अच्छा, नमस्ते|
मेज़बान	नमस्ते|

6. You are thinking of serving the following items. Based on what you learned in the previous activity, which of these items could you serve and which would it not make sense to serve? Identify the recipes that you could and couldn't serve. Compare your conclusions with those of a partner and explain your rationale for reaching them.

शामी कबाब	बिरयानी	आलू-गोभी की सब्ज़ी	भिंडी की सूखी सब्ज़ी
सामग्री	सामग्री	सामग्री	सामग्री
क़ीमा	बासमती चावल	आलू	भिंडी
चने की दाल	गोश्त	गोभी	प्याज़
लहसुन	प्याज़	प्याज़	नमक
अदरक	लहसुन	टमाटर	मिर्च
काली मिर्च	अदरक	अदरक	तेल
लाल मिर्च	हरी मिर्च	नमक	ज़ीरा
बड़ी इलायची	हरा धनिया	लाल मिर्च	
छोटी इलायची	पुदीना	गरम मसाला	
लौंग	गरम मसाला	पानी	
नमक	लाल मिर्च	तेल	
पानी	नमक		
प्याज़	स्याह ज़ीरा		
हरा धनिया	दालचीनी		
तेल तलने के लिये	लौंग		
	छोटी इलायची		
	तेज़ पत्ता		
	दही		
	तेल या घी		
	पीला रंग		
	पानी		

7. Role Play

Role 1: You have decided to serve Shami Kabab. You will need some of the ingredients listed above. Your partner will play the role of one of your family members who knows which items you have at your house. Find out from your partner which of the items listed in the recipe you need and which you already have; note the items that you need. Review your results verbally with your partner when you have finished.

Role 2: The list below shows the items that you have at home. Your partner will play the role of a family member. He needs to do some shopping and is trying to determine which items he needs to buy and which you already have. Refer to the list below and answer your partner's questions in complete sentences.

लहसुन, काली मिर्च, बड़ी इलायची, नमक, पानी, हरा धनिया

Switch roles and repeat the activity.

Role 1: You want to cook Aloo Gobhi.

Role 2: Here is the list of things you have in your home:

प्याज़, अदरक, गरम मसाला, पानी

8. Your sister is going to the market later in the day. Write a note to her explaining that you need some food items and asking her to pick them up from the market. Use the items that you determined were needed from the previous activity.

9. You have not been to the market for a long time, so you are not familiar with current prices. You decide that in order to gain a basic idea, you should listen in for a couple minutes as other people shop. Listen to the dialogue and note all of the items that are bought as well as the prices paid for them.

ग्राहक	भैया सब्ज़ी वाले, ये आलू क्या भाव हैं?
दुकानदार	आलू बहन जी, दस रुपये किलो हैं|
ग्राहक	दस रुपये किलो तो तुम बहुत ज़्यादा बता रहे हो|
दुकानदार	तो आप नौ दे दीजिए| कितना चाहिए?
ग्राहक	एक किलो|
दुकानदार	और बताइए, क्या चाहिए?
ग्राहक	हरी मटर कितने रुपये किलो दे रहे हो?
दुकानदार	वैसे दाम तो बारह रुपये किलो है मगर आप पुरानी ग्राहक हैं, आप दस दे दीजिए|
ग्राहक	दस भी बहुत ज़्यादा हैं| आठ में दो|
दुकानदार	नहीं बहन जी, दस से कम नहीं|
ग्राहक	अच्छा ठीक है, आधा किलो दे दो और एक पाव टमाटर भी तौल दो|
दुकानदार	यह लीजिए| और कुछ?
ग्राहक	एक गुच्छा हरा धनिया भी रख दो| और भैया जल्दी करो| बताओ कितने पैसे हुए?
दुकानदार	जी आलू के नौ रुपये, मटर आधा किलो - पाँच रुपये, टमाटर के चार रुपये और एक रुपये का हरा धनिया| आपके हुए कुल उन्नीस रुपये|
ग्राहक	यह लो बीस रुपये और एक रुपये का नींबू भी दे दो|
दुकानदार	जी अच्छा, यह लीजिए|

10. Role Play

Role 1: You now know what shopping you need to do for your dinner party. You are now at the market and the items you need are listed below. Your partner will play the role of the vendor from whom you are purchasing the items. You have known the vendor for a long time and can assume that he will give you a fair price. Your aims are to: (1) communicate what you need, (2) find out how much each item costs, and (3) communicate how much of each item you need.

item	आलू	टमाटर	प्याज़	लहसुन	गोभी	धनिया
amount	डेढ़ किलो	आधा किलो	आधा किलो	१५० ग्राम	एक अदद	एक गुच्छा
price?						

Role 2: You are a vendor in a market. Your partner is a regular customer of yours who would like to buy some food items from you. Your aims are to: (1) determine what your customer needs, (2) determine how much, and (3) tell her the proper price based on your price list below. Note how much of each item your partner needs as you find out. When you have finished the activity, compare your results with those of your partner.

item	आलू	टमाटर	प्याज़	लहसुन	गोभी	धनिया
amount?						
price in rupees	10/kg.	20/kg.	14/kg.	30/kg.	14/pc.	2/bunch

Switch roles and repeat.

Role: 1:

item	भिंडी	बैंगन	अदरक	पुदीना	गाजर	खीरा
amount	आधा किलो	आधा किलो	१०० ग्राम	एक गुच्छा	आधा किलो	तीन अदद
price?						

Role 2:

item	भिंडी	बैंगन	अदरक	पुदीना	गाजर	खीरा
amount?						
price in rupees	9/kg.	16/kg.	25/kg.	2/bunch	8/kg.	1.5/piece

11. Here are the names of some common South Asian foods that are mentioned in the passage that follows. Do an internet image search on each food item that you are unfamiliar with. You can use the English spellings given below for your search.

अचार	achar
चपाती / रोटी	chapati/ roti
दाल	daal
पकौड़ा	pakora
पराठा	paratha
पूड़ी	poori
बिरयानी	biryani
शामी कबाब	shami kabab
सूजी का हलवा	sooji ka halwa

12. Study the vocabulary and then read the passage about food culture in India and write a similar passage for a South Asian audience about eating habits in America.

Vocabulary

उबलना	*ubalnā* (v.i.)	to boil
उबालना	*ubālnā* (v.t.)	to boil
कच्चा	*kaccā*	raw, uncooked; unfinished (opp. of *pakkā*)
खिलाना	*khilānā* (v.t.)	to feed, to serve food
ख़ुशी	*xuśī* (f.)	happiness
चीनी, शक्कर	*cīnī* (f.), *śakkar* (m.)	sugar
जूस	*jūs* (m.)	juice
टुकड़ा	*ṭukṛā* (m.)	piece
नींबू	*nī̃bū* (m.)	lemon

पक्का	*pakkā*	definite; firm, finished
बिस्कुट	*biskuṭ* (m.)	cookie, cracker
मौक़ा	*mauqā* (m.)	occasion; opportunity
वग़ैरह	*vag͟haira*	et cetera
शराब	*śarāb* (f.)	liquor
शाकाहारी	*śākāhārī*	vegetarian
स्वादिष्ट, लज़ीज़	*svādiṣṭ, lazīz*	delicious

चलिए, आज हम हिंदुस्तानी खाने के बारे में बात करते हैं|

हम हर सुबह उठने के बाद चाय पीते हैं| चाय में चाय की पत्ती, चीनी, और दूध होता है| फिर हम नाश्ता करते हैं| नाश्ते में पूड़ी या पराठे के साथ सब्ज़ी खाते हैं| अक्सर लोग आलू या गोभी के पराठे खाते हैं| कभी-कभी सूजी का हलवा भी खाते हैं|

दोपहर के खाने में लोग दाल, सब्ज़ी, रोटी, और चावल खाते हैं| लोग अचार भी बड़े शौक़ से खाते हैं| ज़्यादातर आम या नींबू का अचार होता है| दोपहर के बाद शाम को फिर एक बार चाय पीते हैं| हमारे यहाँ लोग दिन में कई बार चाय पीते हैं| चाय के साथ बिस्कुट या पकौड़े भी खाते हैं| भारत में रात के खाने में भी सब्ज़ी, दाल, और रोटी, वग़ैरह खाते हैं|

अक्सर लोग खाने में सब्ज़ी और दाल के अलावा गोश्त भी खाते हैं| बहुत से लोग गोश्त नहीं खाते हैं| उनको शाकाहारी कहते हैं|

हम भारत में बहुत मिठाइयाँ खाते हैं| कभी-कभी खाने के बाद मिठाई खाते हैं लेकिन ख़ुशी के मौक़े पर तो ख़ासतौर पर मिठाइयाँ खाते और खिलाते हैं|

Sayings and Proverbs

ऊँट के मुँह में ज़ीरा
घर की मुर्ग़ी दाल बराबर
यह मुँह और मसूर की दाल
बाप भला न भैया, सब से बड़ा रुपैया
ऊंची दुकान फीके पकवान
अपना पैसा खोटा तो परखैया का क्या दोष
आदमी जाने बसे, सोना जाने कसे

Unit 5 My Childhood

In this unit you will learn the following skills:

- Describing past scenes and circumstances.
- Describing buildings and surroundings.
- Describing your life in previous stages.
- Describing your childhood.
- Describing ongoing events in the past.
- Locating events accurately in various time frames.

In addition, you will learn important information on life as a child in South Asia as well as the layout of South Asian homes.

22

My Childhood Home

In this chapter you will learn how to describe past places and circumstances such as those from your childhood.

Describing Past Circumstances

Earlier in the book you learned how to describe your home using statements such as these:

मेरे घर में तीन सोने के कमरे हैं।	My home has three bedrooms.
रसोईघर बैठक के बग़ल में है।	The kitchen is next to the drawing room.

Describing a building or space known in the past is very similar. It involves replacing simple present forms of *honā* with equivalent past forms. Take a look at these examples:

मेरे घर में तीन सोने के कमरे थे।	My home had three bedrooms.
रसोईघर बैठक के बग़ल में था।	The kitchen was next to the drawing room.

The Verb *honā* in the Simple Past

The preceding examples contain simple past forms of *honā,* which correspond to English 'was' and 'were.' Simple past forms of *honā* can be used to describe circumstances at either a particular point in the past or over an extended period in the past.

Forms: The simple past forms of *honā* are *thā, the, thī,* and *thī̃.* The endings that these forms bear are identical to the variable adjective endings (*acchā, acche, acchī*) with the exception of the feminine plural form, which is nasalized.

Simple Past Forms of *honā*

	singular	plural
masculine	था	थे
feminine	थी	थीं

Simple past forms of *honā* can be used in most contexts in which 'was' and 'were' are used in English. For example, in addition to describing a childhood home, they can also be used to describe past circumstances such as where one was at various points in the past few days.

कल तुम कहाँ थे?	Where were you (m.) yesterday?
मैं घर पर था। तुम कहाँ थीं?	I (m.) was at home. Where were you (f.)?
मैं काम पर थी।	I (f.) was at work.

Vocabulary 1

Home

ऊपरी	*ūprī*	upper
खुला	*khulā*	open (cf. *khulnā*, v.i. to open)
गलियारा	*galiyārā* (m.)	hallway
गुलदान	*guldān* (m.)	flower vase
चबूतरा	*cabūtrā* (m.)	platform
छज्जा	*chajjā* (m.)	eaves (of a roof); balcony
निचला	*niclā*	low, lower
बरामदा, दालान	*barāmdā, dālān* (m.)	veranda
मंज़िल	*manzil* (f.)	storey; destination
# मंज़िला	# *manzilā*	# storeyed
रोशनदान	*rośandān* (m.)	an opening high on a wall to allow air and light in

In addition, please review the home-related vocabulary covered in unit 2.

Village and Country

कच्चा	*kaccā*	unfinished (of roads, etc.; opposite of *pakkā*); unripe
क़स्बा	*qasbā* (m.)	town
किनारा	*kinārā* (m.)	edge, bank (*ke kināre*, on the edge/bank of)
खेत	*khet* (m.)	field (for farming) (*khetī*, f. farming)
गाँव	*gā̃v* (*gā̃õ*) (m.)	village
गाय	*gāy* (f.)	cow
जानवर	*jānvar* (m.)	animal

Village and Country (cont'd)

तालाब	*tālāb* (m.)	pond, reservoir
पक्का	*pakkā*	finished, concrete (of roads, etc.); certain
पेड़	*peṛ* (m.)	tree
फूल	*phūl* (m.)	flower
बंदर	*bandar* (m.)	monkey
बकरा	*bakrā* (m.)	goat (*bakrī*, f. she-goat)
बेल	*bel* (f.)	vine
भैंस	*bhaĩs* (f.)	water buffalo
मछली	*machlī* (f.)	fish

Additional Words

अमरूद	*amrūd* (m.)	guava
अलग-अलग	*alag-alag*	different; various
कल	*kal*	yesterday; tomorrow
के बीचों-बीच	*ke bīcõ-bīc*	right in the middle of
छुट्टी	*chuṭṭī* (f.)	break, day off, weekend, holiday, vacation time
दाख़िल होना	*dāxil honā*	to enter (= अंदर जाना)
V-ने पर	V-*ne par*	upon V-ing
परसों	*parsõ*	two days ago; the day after tomorrow
पहले	*pahle*	ago; previously; first

पिछला	*pichlā*	last, previous
प्यारा	*pyārā*	cute, dear
बचपन	*bacpan* (m.)	childhood
भीड़	*bhīṛ* (f.)	crowd, state of there being a crowd
यानी	*yānī*	that is to say
रंग-बिरंगा	*rang-birangā*	colorful
लौटना	*lauṭnā* (v.i.)	to return (come/go back)

Important Expressions

जब...तब / तो...	*jab...tab / to...*	when...(then)...*
बचपन में	*bacpan mẽ*	In childhood, as a kid
# साल की उम्र में	*# sāl kī umr mẽ*	at the age of #
# साल पहले	*# sāl pahle*	# years ago

*Unlike English, in which the word 'then' is generally dropped from the second clause of this construction, the Hindi word *to* is generally included. The word *tab*, which also means 'then' can also be used to mark the second clause. Similar are expressions such as *agar...,to...*, 'if..., then...,' *cũki...*, *isliye...*, 'since, therefore,' and *hālā̃ki...*, *lekin...*, 'although..., still...,' in which the second clause is generally marked in Hindi, while in English it is not.

Exercise 1 G

Read aloud and translate. Indicate whether the subject of each sentence is masculine or feminine.

१. कल दो बजे आप कहाँ थे? २. कल पूरी दोपहर मैं घर पर था| ३. तुम आज सुबह आठ बजे कहाँ थीं? ४. मैं यहाँ थी| तुम कहाँ थे? ५. आप लोग यहाँ आने से पहले कहाँ थे? ६. हम पुस्तकालय में थे| ७. तुम्हारे साथ कौन-कौन था? ८. मेरे साथ आशा और सीमा थीं| ९. तुम सोमवार को क्लास में क्यों नहीं थे? १०. सोमवार को मेरी तबियत ठीक नहीं थी, इसलिए मैं क्लास में नहीं था| ११. आपके बचपन वाले घर में कितने कमरे थे? १२. मेरा बचपन वाला घर बहुत छोटा था| उसमें सिर्फ़ दो कमरे थे|

Exercise 2

Translate into Hindi.

1. Where was Sarah yesterday?
2. She wasn't feeling well.
3. Was Raj in class two days ago?
4. Yes, he was here.
5. Why wasn't Sandeep at work last week?
6. He was on vacation.
7. My childhood home was in Old Lucknow.
8. It was a big three-story house.
9. It had a big courtyard.
10. My room had big windows.

Exercise 3

Pair up with a classmate. Imagine that you are the investigator of a crime and that your classmate is a suspect. The crime is believed to have been committed in the library by a lone person. Find out all of the places where your classmate was and whom he or she was with during the times below so that you can determine whether to follow up with further questioning later. When finished, switch roles and repeat.

last (yesterday) night	yesterday afternoon	yesterday morning
two days ago in the evening	two days ago, afternoon	two days ago, morning

Exercise 4

Read the passage, give it an appropriate Hindi title, and then translate it into English.

बचपन में मेरा घर गाँव में था| वहाँ हमारी ज़िंदगी अच्छी थी| मेरा गाँव ज़्यादा बड़ा नहीं था| उसमें लगभग बीस घर थे| गाँव की सड़कें पक्की नहीं थीं| सड़कों पर हमेशा बहुत से जानवर होते थे| सबसे ज़्यादा गायें, भैंसें और बकरियाँ होती थीं, लेकिन उनके अलावा दूसरे जानवर भी होते थे| गाँव में एक बड़ा तालाब था| वह तालाब काफ़ी ख़ूबसूरत था| तालाब के किनारे एक बड़ा पेड़ था| उसपर बहुत बंदर रहते थे| वहाँ बहुत से पौधे भी थे| गाँव के चारों तरफ़* खेत थे|

* के चारों तरफ़, 'in all directions,' 'all around.' चारों, *cārõ*, 'all four.' In general, [number] + *-õ* means 'all [number].' For example, तीनों, *tīnõ*, 'all three'; पाँचों, *pā̃cõ*, 'all five.'

Please see the end of the chapter for a list of additional wildlife-related vocabulary.

Exercise 5

The questions below are about the passage, an excerpt from a memoir. In the excerpt the writer describes the first time he saw a memorable building. Translate the questions into Hindi, and then read the excerpt. When finished, return to the questions and answer them in complete sentences.

a. Where was the narrator standing?
b. How many stories did the building have?
c. What colors ('of what color') were the doors and windows?
d. What was in the windows?
e. Where were the red flowers?

मुझे याद है, वह शाम का समय था। मौसम सुहावना था। मैं एक बाज़ार के बीच खड़ा था। वहाँ बहुत भीड़ थी। मेरे सामने एक ख़ूबसूरत इमारत थी। यह इमारत दो मंज़िला थी। इमारत का रंग हल्का नीला था। निचली मंज़िल पर दीवार के बीच में एक बहुत बड़ा दरवाज़ा था। उस दरवाज़े के दोनों तरफ़ दो-दो खिड़कियाँ थीं। खिड़कियाँ काफ़ी बड़ी-बड़ी* थीं। खिड़कियों में रंग-बिरंगे फूलों के गुलदान थे। उन खिड़कियों के ऊपर रोशनदान थे। खिड़कियों और दरवाज़े का रंग बैंगनी था। ऊपरी मंज़िल पर दोनों तरफ़ दो छोटे कमरे थे। उन कमरों के बीच खुली छत थी। उन कमरों और छत के आगे छज्जा था। छज्जे पर एक लाल फूलों वाली बेल थी।

*Repeating an adjective in this manner intensifies the meaning ('very big'). In some cases, repeating a word can also have a distributive meaning. For example, *do-do khiṛkiyā̃,* in the previous sentence means 'two windows each" ("on each side").

Exercise 6

Listen to the dialogue and draw the layout of the house where Prakash lived as a kid.

अमित	प्रकाश, बचपन में तुम कहाँ रहते थे?
प्रकाश	मैं बचपन में भारत में रहता था।
अमित	क्या तुम्हारा घर शहर में था?
प्रकाश	नहीं, मेरा घर एक क़स्बे में था।
अमित	तुम्हारा घर कैसा था?
प्रकाश	मेरा घर काफ़ी सादा और छोटा था।

अमित	बाहर से देखने में* वह कैसा था?
प्रकाश	बाहर से भी वह काफ़ी सादा था| सामने दीवार के बीच में एक दरवाज़ा था| दरवाज़े के दोनों तरफ़ एक-एक खिड़की थी| उनके सामने एक चबूतरा था| चबूतरे के सामने दो सीढ़ियाँ थीं|
अमित	अंदर से वह कैसा था?
प्रकाश	दरवाज़े से अंदर जाने पर एक पतला गलियारा था| गलियारे के दोनों तरफ़ एक-एक कमरा था| कमरे और गलियारे के आगे एक बरामदा था|
अमित	क्या तुम्हारे घर में कोई आँगन भी था?
प्रकाश	हाँ, दालान के आगे एक आँगन था| उसके बीचों-बीच अमरूद का एक पेड़ था| आँगन के दूसरी तरफ़ रसोईघर था|
अमित	यानी आँगन दालान और रसोईघर के बीच में था?
प्रकाश	जी हाँ, और आँगन के दाईं तरफ़ गुसलख़ाना था|

* देखने में, 'in appearance.'

Exercise 7

Pair up with a classmate. Take turns and describe the layout of a bedroom in a former residence. Draw a blueprint of your partner's room as you listen to the description. When drawing, feel free to ask your partner Hindi questions to clarify any points that are unclear. When finished share the blueprint with your partner for verification.

Vocabulary 2

Wildlife

Here are some additional wildlife-related words that are useful to know.

उल्लू	*ullū* (m.)	owl; fool
ऊँट	*ū̃ṭ* (m.)	camel
कीड़ा	*kīṛā* (m.)	insect, microbe
ख़तरनाक	*xatarnāk*	dangerous
गधा	*gadhā* (m.)	donkey; fool
गुलाब	*gulāb* (m.)	rose
घास	*ghās* (f.)	grass
घोड़ा	*ghoṛā* (m.)	horse
चिड़िया, परिंदा	*ciṛiyā* (f.) *parindā* (m.)	bird
चींटी	*cī̃ṭī* (f.)	ant
चूहा	*cūhā* (m.)	mouse, rat
छिपकली	*chipkalī* (f.)	gecko, small lizard
जंगल	*jangal* (m.)	jungle, uncultivated land
जंगली	*janglī*	wild
जान	*jān* (f.)	life, life force
तितली	*titlī* (f.)	butterfly
तोता	*totā* (m.)	parrot
पतंगा	*patangā* (m.)	moth
पौधा	*paudhā* (m.)	plant

Wildlife (cont'd)

फूल	*phūl* (m.)	flower
बेल	*bel* (f.)	vine
बैल	*bail* (m.)	bull
भालू	*bhālū* (m.)	bear
भेड़	*bheṛ* (f.)	sheep
मक्खी	*makkhī* (f.)	fly
मगरमच्छ	*magarmacch* (m.)	crocodile
मच्छर	*macchar* (m.)	mosquito
लोमड़ी	*lomṛī* (f.)	fox
शेर	*śer* (m.)	lion
साँप	*sā̃p* (m.)	snake
हाथी	*hāthī* (m.)	elephant
हिरन	*hiran* (m.)	deer

23

Describing One's Childhood

In this chapter you will learn how to describe previous periods in your life, such as childhood.

The Past Habitual Verb Tense

Discussions of childhood often involve statements about general circumstances, such as where one lived, as well as statements about activities one regularly engaged in. Here are some examples:

आप बचपन में कहाँ रहते थे?	Where did you live as a kid?
मैं भारत में रहता था|	I lived in India.
जब मैं बच्ची थी तो मैं बहुत कहानियाँ पढ़ती थी|	When I was a child I read a lot of stories.
मैं बचपन में बहुत क्रिकेट खेलता था|	I played a lot of cricket as a child.

The verb forms in these examples belong to the past habitual verb tense, which is the past tense equivalent of the present habitual. Like the present habitual, the past habitual describes circumstances over an extended period of time. The past habitual is not appropriate for recounting anecdotes or describing discrete events that happened in the past. On the other hand, it is appropriate when describing circumstances over a broad period of time, such as during one's childhood or one's former life in another town.

Formation: The past habitual verb tense is the past tense equivalent of the present habitual in form as well as function. The past habitual is formed by adding the adjectival suffix *–tā* to the verb stem and then appending the simple past forms of *honā*, which are written separately. Here is the full conjugation of the verb *jānā* in the past habitual:

The Past Habitual Verb Tense

	singular	plural
masculine	जाता था	जाते थे
feminine	जाती थी	जाती थीं

Here are some additional examples of the past habitual in use:

यहाँ आने से पहले हम भारत में रहते थे|	Before coming here, we lived in India.
मेरे माँ-बाप, चाचा-चाची, दादा-दादी, सब एक ही घर में रहते थे|	My parents, uncle and aunt, grandparents—everyone lived in the same house.
तुम बचपन में कौन-कौन से खेल खेलते थे?	What games/sports did you play as a kid?
मेरी दादी मुझे बहुत कहानियाँ सुनाती थीं|	My grandmother read/told me a lot of stories.

Additional Points

'Used to': The English 'used to' construction can be expressed by using *pahle*, 'before, previously,' with the past habitual if the past time frame is not otherwise clear.

तुम पहले कहाँ रहते थे?	Where did you used to live?
वह पहले बैंक में काम करता था।	He used to work in a bank.

A Word of Caution: Not all English simple past tense sentences correspond to past habitual sentences in Hindi. Consider these sentences:

I played tennis when I was a kid.
I played tennis yesterday.

These sentences employ the same verb tense despite the fact that they assume different time frames. The first sentence refers to an extended period of time (childhood), whereas the second describes an event that took place at a discrete point in time.

Hindi requires that different verb tenses be used to express these different time frames. As already mentioned, the past habitual is appropriate for describing circumstances over an extended period of time. Events that occur as discrete instances can be described using another verb tense, the perfective, which will be introduced in unit 8.

Vocabulary 1

अंधेरा	*andherā* (m.)	darkness
अजनबी	*ajnabī*	stranger
अब	*ab*	now
अलग	*alag*	different, separate
अलग-अलग	*alag-alag*	separate, various; separately
इतिहास, तारीख़	*itihās* (m.), *tārīx* (f.)	history (also *tārīx*, calendar date)
उड़ाना	*uṛānā* (v.t.)	to fly, to cause to fly (*patang uṛānā*, to fly a kite)
कहानी	*kahānī* (f.)	story
ख़ूब	*xūb*	a lot; good
ख़याल, ख़्याल, विचार	*xayāl, vicār* (m.)	idea, thought

गुड़िया	*guṛiyā* (f.)	doll
चौराहा	*caurāhā* (m.)	intersection
छड़ी	*chaṛī* (f.)	stick, rod, cane
ज़माना	*zamānā* (m.)	era
ज़रूर	*zarūr*	certainly
जवान	*javān*	young
जवानी	*javānī* (f.)	youth
जैसे	*jaise*	as
जो	*jo* (rel.)	who, which
(X से) डरना	(X *se*) *ḍarnā* (v.i.)	to fear X
डाँटना	*ḍā̃ṭnā* (v.t.)	to scold
X के दौरान	X *ke daurān*	during X
पकड़ना	*pakaṛnā* (v.t.)	to catch
पड़ोस	*paṛos* (m.)	neighborhood
पतंग	*patang* (m.)	kite
परी	*parī* (f.)	fairy
प्यार, मुहब्बत	*pyār* (m.), *muhabbat* (f.)	love
प्रकार	*prakār* (m.)	type, manner (= *tarah*, f.)
बेहतरीन	*behtarīn*	best (*behtar*, better)
X भर	X *bhar*	throughout X (*din bhar*, for the entire day, *duniyā bhar*, throughout the world)
भूत	*bhūt* (m.)	ghost
मज़ा	*mazā* (m.)	fun (*mazedār*, adj. fun, enjoyable)
मनोरंजन	*manoranjan* (m.)	entertainment, recreation
मारना	*mārnā* (v.t.)	to strike, to hit; *mār ḍālnā,* to kill
मुहल्ला	*muhallā* (m.)	quarter (of town)

मेहनत	*mehnat* (f.)	hard work
राजा	*rājā* (m.)	king
रानी	*rānī* (f.)	queen
वग़ैरह	*vag̲h̲aira*	et cetera
वहीं	*vahī̃* (*vahā̃* + *hī*)	right there
विज्ञान	*vijñān* (*vigyān*) (m.)	science
शतरंज	*śatranj* (f.)	chess
सख़्त, कठोर	*saxt, kaṭhor*	strict, hard, harsh
साहित्य	*sāhity* (m.)	literature
सुनाना	*sunānā* (v.t.)	to recite, to read aloud
ही	*hī*	just, only

Notes:

- The word *jo* is a relative pronoun. Unlike English, which employs interrogatives as relative words, Hindi has a special set of relative words that are used to mark relative phrases. All relative words begin with the letter ज. Please see the supplementary grammar section at the end of the book for more information on relative words and clauses.
- The word *hī* functions like *bhī*, adding emphasis to the word that it follows. Unlike *bhī*, which adds inclusive emphasis ('also'), *hī* adds exclusive emphasis ('only'). The word *hī* produces new forms when used with certain pronouns and adverbs. For example:

वहाँ	+	ही	→	वहीं	*vahī̃*
यहाँ	+	ही	→	यहीं	*yahī̃*
वह	+	ही	→	वही	*vahī*
यह	+	ही	→	यही	*yahī*
इस	+	ही	→	इसी	*isī*
उस	+	ही	→	उसी	*usī*
मुझ	+	ही	→	मुझी	*mujhī*
तुझ	+	ही	→	तुझी	*tujhī*

हम	+	ही	→	हमीं	*hamī̃*
तुम	+	ही	→	तुम्हीं	*tumhī̃*
इन	+	ही	→	इन्हीं	*inhī̃*
उन	+	ही	→	उन्हीं	*unhī̃*

Exercise 1 G

Read aloud and translate.

१. आप बचपन में कहाँ रहती थीं? २. मैं इलाहाबाद के पास एक छोटे गाँव में रहती थी| वहाँ मेरी ज़िंदगी बहुत अच्छी थी| ३. गाँव में सिर्फ़ एक स्कूल था| गाँव के सब बच्चे वहीं पढ़ते थे| ४. मैं स्कूल में अलग-अलग विषय पढ़ती थी| ५. मुझे हिन्दी सबसे ज़्यादा पसंद थी, लेकिन इतिहास भी दिलचस्प लगता था| ६. गर्मियों की छुट्टियों में मैं बहुत कहानियाँ पढ़ती थी| ७. ज़्यादातर कहानियों में रानी और राजा होते थे जो एक दूसरे से प्यार करते थे| ९. आम के मौसम में शाम को सब लोग आँगन में बैठते थे और आम खाते थे| १०. मेरे भाई पतंग उड़ाते थे| ११. हमारे पास ज़्यादा चीज़ें नहीं थीं लेकिन ज़िंदगी अच्छी थी और सब लोग ख़ुश थे| १२. उस ज़माने की ज़िंदगी आज की ज़िंदगी से बहुत अलग थी|

Exercise 2

Translate the questions into Hindi and then answer them in complete sentences.

1. Where did you live as a child?
2. Where did you go to school?
3. Did you play sports? What games/sports did you play?
4. Did your parents read you stories? What kind of stories did you like?
5. What sorts of food did you eat?
6. Did your friends live in your neighborhood?
7. What did you do with your friends?

Exercise 3

Read the following passage and compose Hindi questions that can be answered by reading it. When finished, pair up with a classmate and exchange your questions verbally. Answer all questions in complete Hindi sentences.

मेरे बचपन में कोई टीवी नहीं था। टीवी तो दूर की बात, हमारे गाँव में ज़्यादातर लोगों के पास रेडियो भी नहीं था। हम सब बच्चे दिन में स्कूल जाते थे जैसे अब तुम लोग जाते हो। लेकिन हमारा स्कूल बहुत छोटा था। उस स्कूल में सिर्फ़ तीन छोटे कमरे थे। हमारे मास्टर काफ़ी सख़्त थे। वे हमें डाँटते थे और छड़ी से मारते थे। मैं उनसे बहुत डरता था। हमारा स्कूल गाँव के मेन चौराहे पर था और मेरे ख़याल से वह अभी भी वहीं है।

Exercise 4

Listen to the dialogue, and then answer the questions in complete Hindi sentences.

विमल	सूरज, आप बचपन में कहाँ रहते थे?
सूरज	विमल, मैं बचपन में न्यू जर्सी में रहता था।
विमल	आपके साथ कौन-कौन रहता था?
सूरज	मेरे साथ मेरे माता-पिता और दो भाई रहते थे।
विमल	आप कौन से स्कूल जाते थे?

सूरज	मैं एक पब्लिक स्कूल जाता था।
विमल	क्या आप स्कूल में कोई खेल खेलते थे?
सूरज	जी हाँ, मैं स्कूल में बॉस्केटबॉल खेलता था।
विमल	क्या आप ख़ूब पढ़ाई करते थे?
सूरज	मैं कोर्स की किताबें कम पढ़ता था, लेकिन मैं दूसरी किताबें पढ़ता था।
विमल	आप किस तरह की किताबें पढ़ते थे?
सूरज	मैं ज़्यादातर भूतों की कहानियाँ और कॉमिक्स पढ़ता था।
विमल	स्कूल में आपके मनपसंद विषय कौन-कौन से थे?
सूरज	स्कूल में मेरे मनपसंद विषय इतिहास और विज्ञान थे।
विमल	क्या आप बचपन में किसी चीज़ से डरते थे?
सूरज	मैं भूतों से डरता था।
विमल	शायद भूतों की कहानियाँ पढ़ने की वजह से।
सूरज	हाँ, ज़रूर इसी वजह से।

सवाल

१. सूरज बचपन में कहाँ रहता था?
२. सूरज कौन से स्कूल जाता था?
३. वह कौन से खेल खेलता था?
४. वह किस तरह की किताबें पढ़ता था?
५. वह किस चीज़ से डरता था?

Exercise 5

Talk to a classmate and find out what his or her childhood was like. Where did your classmate live? Where did he or she go to school? Did he or she play sports? Which ones? Did he or she study a lot? What was his or her favorite subject? Was he or she afraid of anything as a kid? If so what? Note the details that your classmate tells you and then report them to a different classmate.

24

Describing a Scene in the Past

In this chapter you will learn how to describe scenes from the past as well as how to state what you were doing at various points of time in the past.

The Past Continuous Verb Tense

In addition to describing circumstances over an extended period in the past, it is also possible to depict events as having been in progress during a particular moment in the past. This is useful when describing a scene in the past.

तेज़ बारिश हो रही थी|	It was raining heavily.
सब लोग सो रहे थे|	Everyone was sleeping.
मैं एक उपन्यास पढ़ रहा था|	I was reading a novel.

The verb tense in these sentences is the past continuous. This tense corresponds in most contexts to the English past continuous, which has the form *was/were V-ing* (e.g. *I was sleeping. We were waiting for you*). Like its English counterpart, the Hindi past continuous is used to indicate that an action or event was in progress at a particular moment in the past.

Formation: The past continuous is formed according to the following formula:

V + ***rahā / rahe / rahī*** → ***honā* [past]**

Here is the full conjugation of the verb *jānā*, 'to go,' in the past continuous:

The Past Continuous Verb Tense

	singular	plural
masculine	जा रहा था	जा रहे थे
feminine	जा रही थी	जा रही थीं

In this chapter you will use the past continuous to describe scenes seen in the past as well as to describe what you and others were doing at particular times in the past. In addition, you will learn how to use this verb tense to describe scenes observed in the past.

Examples:

कल पाँच बजे तुम क्या कर रहे थे?	What were you doing at five yesterday?
मैं तुमको बार-बार फ़ोन कर रही थी|	I was calling you over and over again.

तुम फ़ोन क्यों नहीं उठा रहे थे?	Why weren't you picking up the phone?
मैं नहा रहा था|	I was bathing.
तुम फ़ोन क्यों कर रही थीं?	Why were you calling?

Vocabulary 1

आपस में	*āpas mẽ*	among themselves, yourselves, ourselves
कोना	*konā* (m.)	corner
खींचना	*khĩcnā* (v.t.)	to pull (*tasvīr khĩcnā*, to take a picture)
गतिविधि	*gatividhi* (f.)	activity
टहलना	*ṭahalnā* (v.i.)	to stroll
ढूँढना	*ḍhū̃ḍhnā* (v.t.)	to search for
दृश्य, मंज़र	*driśy, manzar* (m.)	scene
नालायक़	*nālāyaq*	good for nothing
बजना	*bajnā* (v.i.)	to play (i.e., for music to play)
बहस करना	*bahas karnā* (v.t.)	to have a discussion; to debate (*bahas*, f. discussion, debate)
बार-बार	*bār-bār*	repeatedly
भीड़	*bhīṛ* (f.)	crowd, crowded state
मज़ाक़	*mazāq* (m.)	joke
मज़ा	*mazā* (m.)	fun, enjoyment
X का मज़ा लेना	X *kā mazā lenā*	to enjoy X
महक	*mahak* (f.)	smell, fragrance
माहौल	*māhaul* (m.)	atmosphere, environment
शोर-शराबा	*śor-śarābā* (m.)	noise
संगीत	*sangīt* (m.)	music
सहेली	*sahelī* (f.)	female friend of a female
सीरियल	*sīriyal* (m.)	television series
हँसी	*hãsī* (f.)	laughter (cf. *hãsnā*, to laugh)
हँसी-मज़ाक़ करना	*hãsī-mazāq karnā*	to joke around

Exercise 1

Read aloud and translate.

१. कल दोपहर साढ़े पाँच बजे मैं एक कॉफ़ी हाउस में थी| २. मैं वहाँ अपनी दोस्त के साथ कॉफ़ी पी रही थी| ३. मौसम काफ़ी सुहाना था| ४. हल्की हवा चल रही थी और ज़्यादा सर्दी भी नहीं थी| ५. कॉफ़ी हाउस में हल्का संगीत बज रहा था| ६. कुछ लोग आपस में बातें कर रहे थे और कुछ किताबें पढ़ रहे थे| ७. एक कोने में कुछ लड़के बैठे थे और आपस में हँसी-मज़ाक़ कर रहे थे| ८. कॉफ़ी हाउस के बाहर लोग अपने बच्चों के साथ टहल रहे थे| ९. कोई पानी-बताशे खा रहा था तो कोई आइसक्रीम का मज़ा ले रहा था| १०. माहौल में हर तरफ़ ख़ुशी थी|

Exercise 2

Translate the questions below into Hindi. When finished, listen to the dialogue and answer the questions in complete sentences.

a. What was Simran doing this morning?
b. Where was Zeba, and what was she doing this morning?
c. What was Shabana doing a little while ago?
d. What were Zeba and Shabana doing last night?
e. How was Ahmad's party and what was going on (happening) there?

सिमरन	अरे ज़ेबा, तुम यहाँ हो| मैं तुम्हें आज सुबह लाइब्रेरी में ढूँढ रही थी|
ज़ेबा	सुबह तो मैं शबाना के साथ थी|
सिमरन	तुम लोग सुबह क्या कर रही थीं?
ज़ेबा	हम लोग अपने फ़्लैट की सफ़ाई कर रहे थे|
सिमरन	शबाना इस समय कहाँ है?
ज़ेबा	मुझे मालूम नहीं| थोड़ी देर पहले वह टीवी पर अपना मनपसंद सीरियल देख रही थी|
सिमरन	तुम दोनों कल शाम को अहमद की पार्टी में भी नहीं थीं| तुम कहाँ थीं?
ज़ेबा	कल शाम को हम सब शीला के फ़्लैट में थे|

सिमरन क्या वहाँ भी कोई पार्टी थी?

ज़ेबा नहीं, हम लोग शाहरुख़ ख़ान की नई फ़िल्म देख रहे थे| तुम बताओ, अहमद की पार्टी कैसी थी?

सिमरन अहमद की पार्टी में हमेशा की तरह बहुत शोर-शराबा था| कुछ लोग नाच रहे थे और बाक़ी ज़ोर-ज़ोर से बहस कर रहे थे| और तुम्हारी फ़िल्म कैसी थी?

ज़ेबा फ़िल्म बहुत मज़ेदार थी|

Exercise 3

Yesterday afternoon a crime was committed. The police have interrogated a number of suspects concerning their whereabouts at the time of the crime. Below are some excerpts from their interrogation transcripts. Read aloud and translate the sentences.

पुलिस कल दोपहर को चार बजे तुम कहाँ थे और क्या कर रहे थे?

आनन्द मैं घर पर था| मैं अपने परिवार के साथ टीवी देख रहा था|

पुलिस कल दोपहर को तुम कहाँ थे?

जय कितने बजे?

पुलिस चार बजे?

जय मैं काम पर था| मैं पूरी दोपहर काम में व्यस्त था|

पुलिस कल दोपहर चार बजे तुम कहाँ थे और क्या कर रहे थे?

फ़ारिस हम लोग लाइब्रेरी में पढ़ रहे थे|

पुलिस कल दोपहर को चार बजे तुम कहाँ थे?

कबीर मैं काम पर था| मैं हमेशा उस समय काम पर होता हूँ|

पुलिस कल दोपहर चार बजे तुम कहाँ थीं, किसके साथ थीं और क्या कर रही थीं?

शीतल मैं अपनी सहेलियों के साथ थी| हम सब सिनेमाघर में फ़िल्म देख रहे थे|

Exercise 4

The police have interviewed additional people to attempt to corroborate the suspects' stories. Listen to the excerpts from the interviews and compare them with the suspects' own statements. Determine which of the suspects can be ruled out and which require further attention.

कल दोपहर को चार बजे आनन्द कहाँ था?

कल चार बजे आनन्द हमारे साथ घर पर था| हम सब टीवी पर एक सीरियल देख रहे थे|

हाँ साहब, क्या आप जय को जानते हैं?

हाँ, क्यों?

कल चार बजे वह यहाँ था?

हाँ, उस समय वह यहाँ था| वह नालायक़ अक्सर काम पर नहीं आता है लेकिन कल वह यहाँ था|

क्या कल दोपहर को तुम फ़ारिस के साथ थे?

हाँ, आज हमारा इम्तिहान था, इसलिए हम लोग कल लाईब्रेरी में पढ़ाई कर रहे थे| फ़ारिस हमारे साथ था|

क्या आप कबीर को जानते हैं?

हाँ, वह यहाँ काम करता है| मैं उसको अच्छी तरह जानता हूँ| क्यों? कोई बात है?

क्या आप जानते हैं कि कल दोपहर चार बजे वह कहाँ था?

कल कबीर की तबियत ठीक नहीं थी, इसलिए शायद वह अपने घर पर था|

कल दोपहर को चार बजे आप लोग कहाँ थीं और क्या कर रही थीं?

कल हम लोग सिनेमाघर में एक फ़िल्म देख रहे थे।

क्या शीतल आप के साथ थी?

जी हाँ, वह हमारे साथ थी।

Exercise 5

Role Play

Teacher: Have the students count off as 'ones' and twos.' Have students form pairs of ones and twos for Part I. Assign each pair of students a letter (Pair A, Pair B, Pair C, etc.) by which you will be able to identify them.

Part I

You and a friend are major suspects in a crime that was committed on campus yesterday. You must work with your friend to come up with a consistent account of what you were doing yesterday from 12:00 to 5:00 pm. Work with your partner to come up with a common story for what you were doing. Fill out the table below with the places where you were, the activities that you were doing, and the other people you were with.

समय	जगह	गतिविधि	किन लोगों के साथ?
12:00			
1:00			
2:00			
3:00			
4:00			
5:00			

When finished, silently review what you have come up with. You will need to memorize your account for the next part of the activity.

Part II

With the exception of Pair A, the class will now form two large groups, 'ones' in the first group, and 'twos' in the second. The groups will work as independent investigatory committees to interview the members of each pair of students and attempt to find discrepancies in their accounts of what they were doing between 12:00 and 5:00 yesterday.

The two groups should move to different sides of the classroom, or different rooms if possible. Group One will interrogate one member of Pair A while Group Two interrogates the other member. Once both groups have finished interrogating one member, the members of Pair A should switch to be interrogated by the other group. Each group should attempt to find discrepancies in the stories of the two members.

When finished, repeat for Pair B and as many other pairs as time permits.

25

Expressions of Time

This chapter summarizes the many points regarding expressions of time covered thus far and also introduces a few new ones. It is intended primarily for reference.

Clock-Related Time Expressions

Telling Time

Increments of 15 minutes: Earlier you learned how to tell the time in increments of 15 minutes. To review, for times with the number one as their reference, including *ḍeṛh*, 'one and a half,' the form is *bajā hai.*

एक बजा है।	It's 1:00
सवा एक बजा है।	It's a quarter past one.
पौन बजा है / पौने एक बजा है।	It's a quarter to one.
डेढ़ बजा है।	It's half past one.

For all other times, the form is *baje haĩ.*

दो बजे हैं।	It's 2:00.
सात बजे हैं।	It's 7:00.
सवा तीन बजे हैं।	It's a quarter past three.
ढाई बजे हैं।	It's 2:30.
पौने दो बजे हैं।	It's a quarter to two.
साढ़े चार बजे हैं।	It's 4:30.

Time by the exact minute: The phrases *bajne mẽ*, 'till,' and *bajkar*, 'past,' can be used to tell the time by the exact minute. The phrase *bajne mẽ* literally means 'in ringing,' whereas *bajkar* means 'having rung' (see chapter 37 for details on the verb stem + *kar* construction). The verb *honā* agrees with the number of minutes.

चार बजने में पाँच मिनट हैं।	It's 3:55.
आठ बजने में दस मिनट हैं।	It's 7:50.
बारह बजने में सात मिनट हैं।	It's 11:53.
ग्यारह बजकर तीन मिनट हैं।	It's 11:03.
चार बजकर चौदह मिनट हैं।	It's 4:14.
दो बजकर एक मिनट है।	It's 2:01.

Segment of the day: Clock times can be reported in relation to a segment of the day using the postposition *ke.*

दोपहर के चार बजे हैं।	It's 4:00 in the afternoon.
रात के ग्यारह बजे हैं।	It's 11:00 at night.

Stating the Time at Which Something Happens

Increments of 15 minutes: The word *baje* can be used to describe the time *at which* something happens for all times told in increments of 15 minutes (i.e. using the words: *savā, sāṛhe, paune, paun, ḍeṛh,* and *ḍhāī*).

वे लोग एक बजे आ रहे हैं।	They're coming at 1:00.
तुम कल साढ़े चार बजे कहाँ थीं?	Where were you yesterday at 4:30?
परसों डेढ़ बजे मैं घर पर था।	Two days ago at 1:30 I was at home.
बच्चे रोज़ सुबह साढ़े सात बजे स्कूल जाते हैं।	The kids go to school every morning at 7:30.

Smaller increments of time: The postposition *par,* 'at' is generally used for times that employ *bajne mẽ* or *bajkar.*

आप आठ बजने में दस मिनट पर कहाँ थे?	Where were you at 7:50?
जया सात बजकर बीस मिनट पर कहाँ थी?	Where was Jaya at 7:20?

The Verb *bajnā*

The verb *bajnā* means 'to ring,' or '[for an hour] to strike.' In addition to the forms in which it has already been introduced, *bajnā* can also be used in many other verb forms. Here are some examples:

चार बज रहे हैं।	It's striking 4:00.
चार बजनेवाले हैं।	It's about to strike 4:00.
चार बज गये हैं।	It's already 4:00.*

*See unit 8 for details on this construction.

Non–Clock-Based Time Expressions

The Order of Dates in Hindi

In Hindi, dates are listed in the following order: date, month, year

पंद्रह अगस्त १९४७	August 15, 1947
छब्बीस जनवरी १९५०	January 26, 1950
दो अक्तूबर १८६९	October 2, 1869

Expressing 'in,' 'on,' 'at,' and 'during' with Time Expressions

Expressing 'on' with dates: The postposition *ko* is also used for "on" with dates.

मेरा जन्मदिन २१ फ़रवरी को है।	My birthday is on February 21st.
तुम १० जून को कहाँ थे?	Where were you on June 10th?
मेरा भाई १५ तारीख़ को आ रहा है।	My brother is coming on the 15th.

Note the use of the word *tārīx*, f. 'date' in the preceding and following examples.

आठ तारीख़ को	on the 8th (of the current month)
तेरह तारीख़ को	the 13th

Expressing 'in' with times of the day: The postposition that is generally used to express "in" with times of the day is *ko*. However, *ko* is omitted when the time of day is *subah* and can also be omitted when the day is mentioned (e.g., *āj dopahar, kal śām, parsõ rāt*).

मैं सुबह काम पर जाता हूँ।	I go to work in the morning.
तुम शाम को घर कितने बजे लौटते हो?	What time do you return home in the evening?
आज दोपहर (को) हम लोग चाय पर मिल रहे हैं।	We're meeting for tea this afternoon.

Expressing 'on' with days of the week: The postposition *ko* is also used to express "on" with days of the week.

पिछले सोमवार को तुम कहाँ थे?	Where were you last Monday?
आप रविवार को कितने बजे उठते हैं?	What time do you get up on Sunday?
हम लोग शुक्रवार को फ़िल्म देखने जा रहे हैं। तुम भी हमारे साथ चलो।	We're going to see a movie on Friday. Why don't you come with us?

Locating an event 'in' a month or year: As in English, the postposition *mẽ*, 'in,' is used to locate an event within a month or a calendar year.

हर साल बरसात जून या जुलाई में शुरू होती है।	The rainy season starts every year in June or July.
मैं २०१४ में हिन्दी पढ़ने भारत जा रहा हूँ।	I'm going to India to study Hindi in 2014.

Expressing 'at' or 'during' a time: Many time expressions in which "at" or "during" is understood occur in the oblique case without a postposition. Sometimes phrases that occur in the oblique case without a postposition are described as having an implied postposition, or "ghost-position."

इस समय मैं व्यस्त हूँ।	I'm busy now ("at this time").
क्या आप अगले हफ़्ते कुछ कर रहे हैं?	Are you doing anything next week?
पिछले साल हम लोग भारत में थे।	We were in India last year.

Expressing 'for' a time: Most expressions corresponding to English "for [a duration of time]" can be translated with or without *ke liye*. When used without *ke liye*, the time expression occurs in the direct case if the unit of time is plural; if the time expression is singular, either the direct or oblique case is acceptable.

दो मिनट यहाँ रुकिए।	Wait here for two minutes.
मैं थोड़ी देर आराम करना चाहता हूँ।	I want to rest for a little bit.
वह सारे दिन / सारा दिन काम करती है।	She works (for) the entire day.
मैं एक घंटे / घंटा वहाँ खड़ा था।	I was standing there for an hour.

Expressing the construction 'to have been V-ing since/for': English expressions of the forms "have been V-ing since/for," and "have V-ed since/for," employ present-tense verb forms (simple present forms of *honā*, present habitual, present continuous) with the postposition *se* corresponding to "for" and "since." Please see unit 8 for more information on these structures.

मैं उसे कई साल से जानता हूँ।	I've known him for several years.
तुम कितने दिन से हिन्दी सीख रहे हो?	How long have you been learning Hindi?

Expressing 'by' and 'until': The postposition *tak* is used for both "by" and "until."

दो बजे तक यहाँ रहो।	Stay here until 2:00.
दो बजे तक काम ख़त्म करो।	Finish the work by 2:00.

Expressing 'in': English "in," meaning "after a duration of...," is rendered in Hindi with *mẽ*. In some cases, *bād* or *ke bād* can also be appropriate. The postposition *mẽ* gives a sense of "in, but not later than" whereas *bād* gives the sense of "in, but not sooner than." The postposition *ke bād* gives the sense of "not before," or "not earlier than."

मैं १५ मिनट में आ रहा हूँ।	I'm coming in 15 minutes.
बीस मिनट में / बाद / के बाद आइये।	Come in (after) 20 minutes.

Expressing 'ago': The phrase [duration of time] *pahle* means "[duration of time] ago."

चार साल पहले मैं हिंदुस्तान में था।	Four years ago I was in India.
एक घंटे पहले आप कहाँ थे?	Where were you an hour ago?

Oblique Forms with Expressions of Time

One peculiarity of plural expressions of time is that when governed by postpositions they can occur without the oblique ending *–õ*.

मैं तीन हफ़्ते के लिए भारत जा रही हूँ।	I'm going to India for three weeks.

As can be seen in the above example as well as several other examples given in this chapter, the relationship between oblique case endings and postpositions is slightly messy with expressions of time. We offer the following points to summarize the important information.

- Singular nouns always occur in the oblique case when used with postpositions.
- When expressions of time denoted by singular nouns are used in an adverbial sense, but without a postposition, they generally occur in the oblique case, though in some instances the direct case is acceptable.
- Adverbial expressions of time denoted by plural nouns do not generally take the oblique ending *–õ* without a postposition.[*]
- Adverbial expressions of time denoted by plural nouns often do not take the oblique ending *–õ*, even when used with postpositions.

[*]An exception is *in dinõ,* 'these days.'

Vocabulary 1

Please review numbers, given in appendix 1.

Exercise 1

Pair up with a classmate. Take turns asking each other what time it is and answering using the times given below. Answer in complete sentences.

Set I	Set II	Set III
A 12:45	A 8:00 p.m.	A 11:10
B 1:30	B 5:30 a.m.	B 7:55
C 6:00	C 1:00 p.m.	C 9:59
D 4:30	D 2:30 p.m.	D 5:01
E 2:30	E 7:15 a.m.	E 3:20
F 7:15	F 10:45 p.m.	F 6:40

Exercise 2

Translate the sentences into Hindi.

a. I eat dinner at 6:00 in the evening.
b. What time do you go to school in the morning?
c. Where was your friend last evening?
d. I get up at 10:00 on Sunday.
e. We watch a Hindi film every Saturday.
f. My birthday is on January 15.
g. Where were you on January 10?
h. Where were you on the 5th last month?
i. He is coming in 10 minutes.
j. We are going to a party on Thursday.

Exercise 3

Use the following phrases in sentences and then translate them into English. When finished, pair up with a classmate. Read your sentences aloud to each other. Listen and translate orally.

दो साल पहले, थोड़ी देर, पूरे दिन, चार हफ़्ते के लिए, तीन बजे तक, दस मिनट बाद, पाँच मिनट में, अगले महीने

26

Unit 5 Review Activities

The goal of this chapter is to review the content of unit 5 and provide additional opportunities to synthesize all of the content presented up to this point.

G

1. Grammar Review

- What is the Hindi equivalent of "was/were?" What are its four forms?
- Which Hindi verb tense can be used to describe one's past routine? How is this verb tense formed? Give an example of a past tense English sentence that could *not* be expressed using this verb tense.
- What is the Hindi equivalent of the verb tense in sentences such as "I was sleeping?" How is this Hindi verb tense formed?
- How do you say 'on' a day or date?

2. Tips for Increasing Fluency: Speaking Drills

These drills are designed to promote both accuracy and fluency. When going through them, it is a good idea to write key words on a piece of paper prior to starting so that you can then run through all of the sentences rapidly without pausing. When carrying out the exercises, focus first on accuracy, and then as you repeat the activities and they become more automatic, focus on speed. The aim is to be able to speak about everyday life in an accurate and automatic manner.

Simple Past Forms of *honā*

- Make sentences describing everywhere you were over the past 48 hours, and the time of day that you were in each place.
- Take a minute to recall a memorable person or building that you encountered recently. Describe the person or building's appearance (in the form, "He had brown hair," "It was tall.").

Past Continuous

- Where were you and what were you doing during each of the last 24 hours? Write sentences accounting for each hour or block of hours.
- Describe a memorable scene that you recently witnessed. Where were you? What was happening? What was everybody doing?

Past Habitual

- Describe your daily routine wherever you lived before beginning your current job or course of study.

3. Personalization Questions

Pair up with a partner. Take turns asking and answering the following questions. Answer in complete sentences.

१. आप कल इस समय कहाँ थे / थीं?

२. कल का मौसम कैसा था?

३. पाँच साल पहले आप कहाँ रहते थे और क्या करते थे / रहती थीं और करती थीं?

४. आप बचपन में किस शहर में रहते थे / रहती थीं?

५. आप बचपन में कौन से खेल खेलते थे / खेलती थीं?

६. दस साल पहले आपके माता-पिता क्या करते थे?

७. दो साल पहले आप क्या करते थे / करती थीं?

4. Read the passage aloud and translate it orally with a partner line by line. Next, using the passage as a model, tell your partner about any memorable scene that you have witnessed. Describe everything that was happening around you in the scene.

Note to teacher: Students can be reminded one day in advance to think of a memorable scene so that they will be ready to describe it in class.

चलना-फिरना	*calnā-phirnā* (v.i.)	to wander around
पश्चिमी	*paścimī*	western
पर्यटक	*paryaṭak*	tourist, traveler

पिछले साल गर्मियों में मैं दिल्ली में था| मेरा होटल पुराने शहर के मेन बाज़ार में था| मुझे होटल की खिड़की से बाहर का दृश्य अच्छी तरह याद है| बाज़ार में बहुत भीड़ थी| बहुत से लोग चल-फिर रहे थे| औरतें ख़रीदारी कर रही थीं| एक-दो पश्चिमी पर्यटक भी थे| वे तस्वीरें खींच रहे थे| वहाँ एक चाय की दुकान थी| चाय की दुकान पर कुछ लोग चाय पी रहे थे और हिन्दी अख़बार पढ़ रहे थे| एक कोने पर कबाब की दुकान थी| वहाँ से बहुत अच्छी महक आ रही थी| कुछ लड़के कबाब खा रहे थे और आपस में हँसी-मज़ाक़ कर रहे थे| मैं बहुत ख़ुश था कि मैं दिल्ली में हूँ|

5. Mr. Prakash is a great Hindi writer. He is 75 years old. A children's magazine has asked him to write a note about his childhood for its readers. Study the vocabulary thoroughly and then read Mr. Prakash's note and answer the questions.

क्योंकि	*kyõki*	because
छपना	*chapnā* (v.i.)	to be published
जीवन	*jīvan* (m.)	life
पत्रिका	*patrikā* (f.)	magazine
बेहतरीन	*behtarīn*	best
मगर	*magar*	but (= *lekin*)
महत्त्व, अहमियत	*mahattv* (m.), *ahamiyat* (f.),	importance
महत्त्वपूर्ण, अहम	*mahattvpūrṇ, aham*	important
राजा, बादशाह	*rājā, bādśāh* (m.)	king
व्यक्ति	*vyakti* (m.)	person
शायद	*śāyad*	perhaps
शिकार	*śikār* (m.)	hunting

मेरे बचपन के दिन मेरे जीवन के बेहतरीन दिन थे| अब यह मानना मुश्किल है कि हम भी एक दिन बच्चे थे| जब मैं छोटा था तो एक बड़े घर में, एक बड़े परिवार के साथ रहता था| मेरे दादा और दादी भी हमारे साथ रहते थे| मैं ज़्यादातर वक़्त अपने दादा-दादी के साथ गुज़ारता था| हमारे घर में एक बड़ा आँगन था और सब बच्चे दिन भर उसमें खेलते थे| उनके खेल अजीब और मज़ेदार थे| उस समय घरों में टीवी नहीं था मगर हमारे घर में बहुत किताबें थीं| मैं किताबें पढ़ता था और कभी-कभी शतरंज खेलता था| मैं ज़्यादातर कहानियों की किताबें पढ़ता था लेकिन कभी-कभी इतिहास की किताबें भी पढ़ता था| मेरी दादी रोज़ मुझे कहानियाँ सुनाती थीं| ज़्यादातर कहानियाँ परियों और राजाओं की होती थीं| छुट्टियों में मैं अपने दादा और पिताजी के साथ चिड़ियों के शिकार पर भी जाता था| हम गर्मी की छुट्टियों में गाँव जाते थे| मैं बारह साल की उम्र में छोटी-छोटी कहानियाँ लिखता था| वे कहानियाँ बच्चों की पत्रिकाओं में छपती थीं| वे कहानियाँ अच्छी नहीं थीं लेकिन मैं कहानियाँ लिखना चाहता था क्योंकि मेरे दादा हर कहानी के लिए मुझे एक आइसक्रीम देते थे| मैं अब भी बहुत आइसक्रीम खाता हूँ| मेरे लिए मेरा बचपन बहुत महत्त्वपूर्ण है| शायद हर व्यक्ति के लिए उसका बचपन महत्त्व रखता है|

१. बचपन में प्रकाशजी के साथ कौन-कौन रहता था?

२. प्रकाश जी बचपन में ज़्यादा समय किसके साथ गुज़ारते थे?

३. वे कैसी किताबें पढ़ते थे?

४. छुट्टियों में प्रकाश जी क्या करते थे?

५. प्रकाशजी कहानियाँ क्यों लिखना चाहते थे?

6. Listen to the dialogue. You may listen to it several times if necessary. Compose five questions in Hindi that can be answered by listening to the dialogue. When finished, pair up with a classmate and exchange questions orally. Answer in complete Hindi sentences.

शालिनी	स्नेहा, आप कहाँ रहती हैं?
स्नेहा	मैं ऐन आर्बर, मिशिगन में रहती हूँ।
शालिनी	क्या आप हमेशा से अमरीका में रहती हैं?
स्नेहा	नहीं, मैं बचपन में भारत में रहती थी।
शालिनी	अच्छा, क्या आपका पूरा परिवार भारत में रहता था?
स्नेहा	जी हाँ, मेरा पूरा परिवार वहाँ रहता था।
शालिनी	आप बचपन में क्या करती थीं?
स्नेहा	मैं खेलती थी और स्कूल जाती थी।
शालिनी	आप क्या खेलती थीं?
स्नेहा	मैं ज़्यादातर घर में गुड़ियाँ वग़ैरह खेलती थी।
शालिनी	और आपके भाई क्या खेलते थे?
स्नेहा	वे बाहर क्रिकेट खेलते थे। मेरे बड़े भाई शतरंज भी खेलते थे।
शालिनी	आपके बड़े भाई उस समय क्या करते थे?
स्नेहा	वे उस समय दिल्ली यूनिवर्सिटी में पढ़ते थे।
शालिनी	अब वे कहाँ हैं?
स्नेहा	अब वे न्यू यॉर्क में रहते हैं। मेरा पूरा परिवार अब अमरीका में है।

7. Write a paragraph about your childhood. Describe where you lived, what you studied, who your friends were, what sports you played, what foods you liked and disliked, and what you liked and disliked doing.

Sayings and Proverbs

आप भला तो जग भला

आँख ओझल पहाड़ ओझल

मेरी बिल्ली मुझी से म्याऊँ

पूत के पाँव पालने में ही नज़र आ जाते हैं

वो ज़माने गुज़र गये जब ख़लील ख़ाँ फ़ाख़्ता उड़ाते थे

मुँह में राम बग़ल में छुरी

हाथी चलता है कुत्ते भौंकते हैं

अपनी अज्ञानता का ज्ञान ही ज्ञान की पहली सीढ़ी है

Unit 6 Rules and Responsibilities

In this unit you will learn the following skills:

- Discussing rules: What you can and cannot do.
- Expressing compulsion: What you should and need to do.
- Making suggestions.
- Giving instructions.

In addition, you will learn some basic norms of behavior that are commonly observed in South Asian societies.

27

Rules and Regulations

In this chapter you will learn how to describe what you can and cannot do in school and at your residence.

The Verb *saknā*

Stating what one is and is not allowed to do often involves using the verb *can* in English. The Hindi verb *saknā* is the equivalent of *can/to be able to*. This chapter will focus on using *saknā* to express what you can and cannot do in your classroom and your residence.

हम क्लास में सिर्फ़ हिन्दी बोल सकते हैं।	We can only speak Hindi in class.
क्या तुम अपने हॉस्टल में कुत्ता रख सकते हो?	Can you have a dog in your dormitory?
नहीं, हम हॉस्टल में कुत्ता नहीं रख सकते।	No, we can't keep a dog in the dormitory.

Form: Verb phrases with *saknā* are formed by (a) placing the main verb, or the verb denoting the action that can be done, in stem form, (b) appending *saknā*, which is written separately from the main verb stem, and (c) conjugating *saknā* by adding the endings of the appropriate verb tense.

For example, if you need to say "He can speak," the main verb is *bolnā*, 'to speak.' The verb *bolnā* therefore occurs in stem form and is followed by *saknā*: *bol saknā*, 'to be able to speak.' Verb tense endings must then be added to *saknā*. In this case, 'can' is a present-tense verb form, which translates using the present habitual in Hindi.

वह बोल सकता है।	He can speak.

By contrast, "He could have spoken," and "He could (previously) speak," are expressed by using the endings of the past habitual verb tense.

वह बोल सकता था।	He could (previously) speak /He could have spoken.

The verb *saknā* can be used in any verb tense except the present and past continuous. It cannot, however, be used without a main verb as it can in English (e.g. "Yes we can").

Negation: When *saknā* is negated, the negation word can either immediately precede the main verb or *saknā*.

वह नहीं नाच सकता।	He can't dance.
वह नाच नहीं सकता।	He can't dance.

V-*ne denā*

The construction V-*ne denā*, the oblique infinitive followed by the verb *denā*, means 'to let V, to allow to V.' Here are some examples:

हमारे अध्यापक हमें क्लास में खाना खाने देते हैं।	Our teacher lets us eat food in class.
बच्चों को कॉफ़ी मत पीने दो।	Don't let the children drink coffee.
मेरी माँ मुझे हर रोज़ सिर्फ़ आधा घंटा टीवी देखने देती थीं।	My mother would only let me watch TV for half an hour a day.

Vocabulary 1

अंदर	*andar* (adv.)	inside (X *ke andar*, ppn. inside X)
अंधेरा	*andherā* (m.)	darkness
अगरबत्ती	*agarbattī* (f.)	incense
अलग-अलग	*alag-alag*	separate, various; separately
आग	*āg* (f.)	fire (*āg lagnā*, for a fire to start)
आवाज़	*āvāz* (f.)	voice, sound
कब	*kab*	when
क़ानून	*qānūn* (m.)	law
कुत्ता	*kuttā* (m.)	dog
कूड़ा	*kūṛā* (m.)	trash
चलाना	*calānā* (v.t.)	to drive, to operate
जलाना	*jalānā* (v.t.)	to burn
जाँच	*jā̃c* (f.)	inspection
जागना	*jāgnā* (v.i.)	to be awake, to wake up
जो	*jo* (rel.)	who
ठहरना	*ṭhaharnā* (v.i.)	to stop, to stay
तनख़्वाह	*tanxāh* (f.)	salary
तय करना	*tay karnā*	to set; to determine
तय होना	*tay honā*	to be set; to be determined

तैरना	*tairnā* (v.i.)	to swim
दाख़िल होना	*dāxil honā*	to enter
दाख़िला लेना	*dāxilā lenā* (v.t.)	to enroll in
दूर	*dūr*	distant, far
देर	*der* (f.)	a while; delay (X *ko der honā*, for X to be late; *der lagnā*, for there to be a delay)
(X का) ध्यान / ख़याल रखना	(X *kā*) *dhyān / xayāl rakhnā*	to pay due attention to X, keep X in mind, look after X
नियम	*niyam* (m.)	rule, law
X को नींद आना	X *ko nīd̃* (f.) *ānā*	for X to be/get sleepy
पालना	*pālnā* (v.t.)	to rear (i.e. an animal, a child)
पीना	*pīnā* (v.t.)	to drink, to smoke
फैलाना	*phailānā* (v.t.)	to spread
फ़्रांसीसी	*frānsīsī* (f.)	French
बंदूक़	*bandūq* (f.)	rifle
बिल्ली	*billī* (f.)	cat
भाषण	*bhāṣaṇ* (m.)	speech (*bhāṣaṇ denā*, to give a speech)
मना	*manā*	forbidden
मरम्मत	*marammat* (f.)	repair (X *kī marammat karnā*, to repair X)
मोमबत्ती	*mombattī* (f.)	candle
लगातार	*lagātār*	continuously
शराब	*śarāb* (f.)	alcoholic beverage
शोर	*śor* (m.)	noise (*śor karnā*, to make noise)
सख़्त	*saxt*	strict; (*saxt manā*, strictly forbidden)
साज़	*sāz* (m.)	musical instrument
सिग्रेट	*sigreṭ* (f.)	cigarette (*sigreṭ pīnā*, to smoke a cigarette)
हॉस्टल	*hāsṭal* (m.)	dorm, hostel

Exercise 1 G

Read aloud and translate.

१. आप क्लास में कॉफ़ी पी सकते हैं लेकिन खाना नहीं खा सकते| २. हमारे अध्यापक हमें क्लास में कॉफ़ी नहीं पीने देते, लेकिन पानी पीने देते हैं| ३. तुम क्लास में अपना कुत्ता नहीं ला सकतीं| ४. क्या मैं अंदर आ सकता हूँ? ५. ज़रूर| आइए, बैठिए| हम थोड़ी देर बात कर सकते हैं| ६. हम यह काम घर पर कर सकते हैं| ७. क्या मैं थोड़ी दूर तुम्हारे साथ चल सकता हूँ? ८. हम अपने फ़्लैट में ऊँची आवाज़ में संगीत नहीं बजा सकते| ९. क्लास में अंग्रेज़ी बोलना मना है| यहाँ पर हम सिर्फ़ हिन्दी बोल सकते हैं| १०. मुझे बताइए कि हम हॉस्टल में क्या-क्या नहीं कर सकते| ११. आप अपने कमरे में अगरबत्ती या मोमबत्ती नहीं जला सकते| उससे आग लग सकती है| १२. उसके माँ-बाप उसे अंधेरा होने के बाद बाहर नहीं जाने देते|

Exercise 2 G

Translate into Hindi.

1. Can you explain the rules of the dorm to me?
2. Can he smoke cigarettes in his room?
3. Can we eat or drink anything in class?
4. Eating is forbidden, but you can drink water in class.
5. Our teachers only let us speak English in school.
6. Can I keep my bicycle in the hallway?
7. Keeping a dog in one's room is forbidden, but you can keep a cat.
8. Making noise after 10:00 is strictly forbidden.
9. You can't drink alcohol inside the dorm.
10. They don't let us do anything.

Exercise 3

Read the passage, give it an appropriate Hindi title, and answer the questions in complete sentences in Hindi.

हमारे हॉस्टल में बहुत नियम हैं| हम अपने कमरे में कोई जानवर नहीं रख सकते| हम अपने कमरे में कूड़ा नहीं फैला सकते| वार्डन जाँच के लिए कभी भी आ सकते हैं| हम कमरे में फ़्रिज रख सकते हैं लेकिन फ़्रिज में सिर्फ़ कोल्ड ड्रिंक वग़ैरह रख सकते हैं| कमरे में शराब रखना सख़्त मना है| हमारे सोने का कोई समय तय नहीं है लेकिन रात नौ बजे के बाद हम संगीत नहीं बजा सकते| हॉस्टल में लड़कों और लड़कियों के सेक्शन अलग-अलग हैं| लड़कियाँ लड़कों के सेक्शन में जब चाहे* जा सकती हैं लेकिन लड़के शाम सात बजे के बाद लड़कियों के सेक्शन में दाख़िल नहीं हो सकते| लड़कियों के सेक्शन में एक बैठक है| लड़के लड़कियों से वहाँ मिल सकते हैं|

१. क्या कमरे में कुत्ता रख सकते हैं?
२. कमरे के अंदर कूड़ा क्यों नहीं फैला सकते?
३. क्या कमरे में रात को पार्टी कर सकते हैं?
४. लड़के लड़कियों के कमरों में कब जा सकते हैं और कब नहीं जा सकते?
५. क्या लड़कियाँ लड़कों के कमरों में जा सकती हैं?

*जब चाहे, 'at will,' 'whenever one wants.'

Exercise 4

Compare the rules of your dorm or residence with those of a classmate's. Try to find as many commonalities as possible in terms of what you can and can't do. Feel free to discuss the activities below and any other additional ones that you can think of.

सिग्रेट पीना, कुत्ता पालना, बिल्ली पालना, कोई और पालतू जानवर रखना, फ़्रिज रखना, माईक्रोवेव रखना, चूल्हा रखना, कॉफ़ी मशीन रखना, अगरबत्ती जलाना, मोमबत्ती जलाना, संगीत ज़ोर से बजाना, किसी भी समय बाहर जाना

The Verb *pānā*

The verb *pānā*, 'to be able to,' overlaps with *saknā* in both meaning and usage. When used with a main verb occurring in stem form, *pānā* adds the sense that the subject is 'able,' 'capable,' or 'having the capacity' to perform the action of the main verb.

क्या तुम हिन्दी बोल पाते हो?	Are you able to speak Hindi?
मैं सिर्फ़ भारतीय खाना पका पाती हूँ।	I'm only able to cook Indian food.

The verb *pānā* can also add the sense of 'managing' to perform the action of the main verb, often with the understanding that the action presents some challenge, barrier, or obstacle to be overcome.

ज़ाकिर हुसैन तबला इतनी तेज़ कैसे बजा पाते हैं?	How does Zakir Hussein manage to play the tabla so fast?
लगता है कि तुम्हें बहुत काम है। क्या तुम आ पाओगे?*	You seem to have a lot of work. Will you be able to come?

*The word *pāoge* is a future form; please see unit 7 for more information on this form.

The verb *pānā* occurs with all verb tenses, including the present and past continuous.

मैं तुम्हारी किताब नहीं ढूँढ पा रही हूँ।	I'm not able to find your book (despite my best efforts). I haven't been able to find your book.

The present continuous verb tense in the above example gives the sense that the act of searching for the book is still in progress, or that the subject has not yet ceased looking for it.

Using the Verb *pānā* Independently

The verb *pānā* used as an independent verb expresses a different meaning. As an independent verb *pānā* means 'to get, to obtain, to find.'

वह हर महीने बीस हज़ार रुपये पाता है।	He gets 20,000 rupees a month.
मेरा भाई बड़ी अच्छी तनख़्वाह पा रहा है।	My brother is getting a very good salary.

Exercise 5 G

Read aloud and translate. Also tell whether each statement is true or false for you.

१. मैं ज़्यादातर पियानो बजाता / बजाती हूँ लेकिन थोड़ा गिटार भी बजा पाता / पाती हूँ। २. मैं खाना नहीं पका पाता / पाती हूँ। ३. मैं साइकल चला पाता / पाती हूँ। ४. मैं थोड़ी स्पैनिश बोल पाता / पाती हूँ। ५. मैं तीन मील दौड़ पाता / पाती हूँ। ६. मैं यह क्लास लेने से पहले थोड़ी हिन्दी बोल पाता था / पाती थी। ७. हिन्दी क्लास में दाख़िला लेने से पहले मैं थोड़ी हिन्दी पढ़ पाता था / पाती थी लेकिन मुझे लिखना नहीं आता था। ८. बारह बजे से पहले मुझे बिल्कुल नींद नहीं आती। मैं नहीं सो पाता / पाती।

Exercise 6

Translate the sentences into Hindi.

1. The students are trying, but they're not able to learn (they are having difficulty learning).
2. Why aren't you able to (why are you having difficulty) understand what I'm saying.
3. I can speak Hindi but I'm unable to write it.
4. Can you read and write Hindi?
5. Six months ago I couldn't speak Hindi at all, but now I can speak well.

Exercise 7

Bingo: Mingle with your classmates. Ask questions to identify people who meet the descriptions given. Each time you identify a classmate who fits the description, write their name in the cell containing that description. The first student to get five in a row wins.

क्या कोई है जो गिटार बजा सकता है?	क्या कोई है जो तीन भाषाएँ जानता है?	क्या कोई है जो बंदूक़ चला पाता है?	क्या कोई है जो भारतीय खाना पका सकता है?	क्या कोई है जो तीन मील दौड़ सकता है?
क्या कोई है जो गाड़ी नहीं चला पाता?	क्या कोई है जो गा सकता है?	क्या कोई है जो मोटरसाइकिल चला सकता है?	क्या कोई है जो गोल्फ़ खेल सकता है?	क्या कोई है जो कोई हिंदुस्तानी साज़ बजा सकता है?
क्या कोई है जो फ़्रांसीसी समझ सकता है?	क्या कोई है जो क्रिकेट खेल सकता है?	क्या कोई है जो मेक्सिकन खाना पका सकता है?	क्या कोई है जो नहीं तैर सकता?	क्या कोई है जो हिन्दी लिख सकता है?
क्या कोई है जो दो घंटे लगातार बोल सकता है?	क्या कोई है जो नाच सकता है?	क्या कोई है जो स्पैनिश बोल सकता है?	क्या कोई है जो चीनी खाना पका सकता है?	क्या कोई है जो मसालेदार खाना पका पाता है?
क्या कोई है जो गाड़ी की मरम्मत कर सकता है?	क्या कोई है जो सारी रात जाग सकता है?	क्या कोई है जो भाषण दे सकता है?	क्या कोई है जो संस्कृत पढ़ पाता है?	क्या कोई है जो तस्वीर बना सकता है?

28

Expressing Compulsion

In this chapter you will learn how to express things that you need to, have to, and ought to do.

मुझे अभी क्लास जाना है।	I need to go to class now.
वह अच्छी क्लास है, लेकिन उसमें बहुत मेहनत करनी पड़ती है।	It's a good class but you have to work really hard in it.
तुम्हें यह सवाल प्रोफ़ेसर से पूछना चाहिए।	You should ask the professor this question.

Expressions of Compulsion

Expressions conveying meanings of 'should,' 'ought to,' 'need to,' and 'have to' are collectively referred to as *expressions of compulsion*. In Hindi, compulsion is expressed through various indirect constructions. Hindi has three main compulsion expressions; these are, in order of increasing intensity:

X *ko* V-*nā cāhiye*	X should V, X ought to V
X *ko* V-*nā honā*	for X to have to V, for X to need to V
X *ko* V-*nā paṛnā*	for X to have/need to V, for X to have no option but to V, for X to be forced to V

X *ko* V-*nā cāhie*

Earlier the construction X *ko cāhie* was introduced. This construction is used to express needs when used with nouns. With infinitives the construction expresses the meaning 'should/ought to.'

देर हो रही है। हमें चलना चाहिए।	It's getting late. We should go.
तुम्हें बोलने से पहले सोचना चाहिए।	You should think before speaking.

'Should have' and 'ought to have' can be expressed by appending the simple past form of *honā*, *thā*, to *cāhie*.

तुम्हें बोलने से पहले सोचना चाहिए था।	You should have thought before speaking.

X *ko* V-*nā honā*

आज शाम मुझे बहुत काम है। मुझे एक निबंध लिखना है।	I have a lot of work this evening. I have to write an essay.
क्या तुम्हें कुछ करना है?	Do you need to do anything?
मुझे तुमसे कुछ पूछना था।	I needed to ask you something.

X *ko* V-*nā paṛnā*

मैं अपने दफ़्तर से बहुत दूर रहता हूँ, इसलिए मुझे रोज़ जल्दी उठना पड़ता है।	I live very far from my office so I have to wake up early every morning.
जब मैं बच्चा था तो स्कूल पहुँचने के लिए मुझे रोज़ पाँच मील पैदल चलना पड़ता था।	When I was a kid, I had to walk five miles a day to get to school.

Agreement Patterns

All three expressions of compulsion follow an unusual pattern of agreement: the infinitive behaves like an adjective; the final *–ā* changes to *–e* and *–ī* to agree with the direct object, and the compulsion verb also agrees with the direct object.

In the *cāhie* construction, the final vowel of the word *cāhie* is nasalized (*cāhiẽ*) when the direct object is plural in number. Many speakers treat *cāhie* as an invariable form with both singular and plural direct objects.

आपको कुछ नई किताबें ख़रीदनी चाहिएँ।	You should buy some new books.
मुझे इस हफ़्ते दो निबंध लिखने हैं।	I need to write two essays this week.
मुझे अपनी बीमारी की वजह से बहुत सी दवाएँ लेनी पड़ती हैं।	I have to take a lot of medicines because of my illness.

Vocabulary 1

ओढ़ना	*oṛhnā* (v.t.)	to cloak with, cover with
(बाल) कटाना	(*bāl*) *kaṭānā* (v.t.)	to get (one's hair) cut
के अनुसार, के मुताबिक़	*ke anusār, ke mutābiq*	according to
ख़र्च करना	*xarc karnā*	to spend
गुज़रना	*guzarnā* (v.i.)	to pass
गर्मी	*garmī* (f.)	heat (X *ko garmī lagnā*, for X to be hot)
चला जाना	*calā jānā* (v.i.)	to leave
चूँकि...इसलिए...	*cũki...islie...*	since... therefore...

जन्मदिन, सालगिरह	*janm-din* (m.), *sālgirah* (f.)	birthday
जल्द से जल्द	*jald se jald*	as soon as possible
ढकना	*ḍhaknā* (v.t.)	to cover
तमीज़	*tamīz* (f.)	manners (X *ko tamīz honā*, for X to have manners)
तैयारी	*taiyārī* (*tayyārī*) (f.)	preparation(s)
तोहफ़ा	*tohfā* (m.)	gift
दर्द	*dard* (m.)	pain
दुपट्टा	*dupaṭṭā* (m.)	scarf
धार्मिक, मज़हबी	*dhārmik, mazhabī*	religious
X का ध्यान रखना	X *kā dhyān rakhnā*	to keep X in mind, give due attention to X
नाराज़	*nārāz*	angry
निबंध	*nibandh* (m.)	essay
पेट	*peṭ* (m.)	stomach
प्यास	*pyās* (f.)	thirst (X *ko pyās lagnā*, for X to be thirsty)
बीमारी	*bīmarī* (f.)	illness
बोरियत	*boriyat* (f.)	boredom
भूख	*bhūkh* (f.)	hunger (X *ko bhūkh lagnā*, for X to be hungry)
मसला, समस्या	*maslā* (m.), *samasyā* (f.)	problem
रिश्तेदार	*riśtedār* (m.)	relative
लिबास	*libās* (m.)	clothing, attire
शरीर	*śarīr* (m.)	body
सर्दी	*sardī* (f.)	cold (X *ko sardī lagnā*, for X to be cold)

सलाह	*salāh* (f.)	advice
साफ़-सुथरा	*sāf-suthrā*	clean and tidy
सिर, सर	*sir, sar* (m.)	head
सुबह-सवेरे	*subah-savere*	early in the morning
हल	*hal* (m.)	solution
हालाँकि...लेकिन / फिर भी	*hālā̃ki...lekin / phir bhī*	although / even though... still...
हो जाना	*ho jānā*	to become

Notes:

- Earlier the two-clause expressions *agar...to*, 'if..., then,' and *jab...to*, 'when..., then' were introduced. The expressions *cū̃ki...islie*, 'since..., therefore,' and *hālā̃ki...lekin*, 'although... still...' are similar in that the second clause is generally explicitly marked.
- *ho jānā* is an example of a compound verb. Compound verbs consist of the verb stem of the main verb, which supplies the basic meaning, and an additional verb, most often *jānā*, *lenā*, or *denā*, which adds additional nuances. *jānā* is the most common verb used with intransitive verbs (those that can't take an object). With verbs like *honā* and *sonā*, which can either describe a static state ('being,' 'sleeping') or a change in state ('happening, becoming'; 'falling asleep'), the use of the compound verb *jānā* indicates a change in state. Please see unit 8 for more details.

Exercise 1 G

Read aloud and translate into English.

१. अगर तुम्हारी तबियत ठीक नहीं है तो तुम्हें आराम करना चाहिए| २. अगर तुम्हारा पेट ख़राब है तो तुम्हें सादा खाना खाना चाहिए| ३. उनको अपने बच्चों को कुछ तमीज़ सिखानी चाहिए| ४. मुझे देर हो रही है, मुझे घर जाना है| ५. कल मेरा इम्तिहान है, मुझे पढ़ाई करनी है| प्लीज़ शोर मत करो| ६. मुझे इन छुट्टियों में बाल कटाने हैं| ७. आपको आज शाम को क्या-क्या करना है? ८. हमें सारा काम रात आठ बजे तक ख़त्म करना है| ९. अली को दो नौकरियाँ करनी पड़ती हैं| १०. मेरे गाँव में रोज़ रात आठ बजे लाइट चली जाती है, इसलिए मुझे अपना घर का काम उससे पहले ख़त्म करना पड़ता है| ११. भारत में अध्यापक के क्लास में दाख़िल होने पर बच्चों को खड़ा होना पड़ता है| १२. हमें यह काम जल्द से जल्द ख़त्म करना है| १३. चूँकि हमें आज ही काम ख़त्म करना है, इसलिए हमें अभी शुरू करना चाहिए| १४. मुझे सात बजे से पहले दफ़्तर पहुँचना होता है, इसलिए मुझे सुबह पाँच बजे उठना पड़ता है| १५. आपको भारत में खाने का ख़ास ध्यान रखना चाहिए| आपको सिर्फ़ बोतलवाला पानी पीना चाहिए| १६. आपको शरीर को अच्छी तरह ढकनेवाले कपड़े पहनने चाहिएँ और दुपट्टा ओढ़ना चाहिए|

Exercise 2

Translate into Hindi.

1. I need to wash the dishes.
2. You ought to study more.
3. I'm going to the market. Do you need to do any shopping?
4. I don't have a car. I therefore have to (have no option but to) walk everywhere.
5. We're going to see a movie. You should come with us.
6. You seem sick. You should take care of yourself.
7. I'm busy now. I have to go to work. Can we talk later?
8. I don't know what I should do. Can you give me some advice?

Exercise 3

Read to the problems described in the left column and match them with the most appropriate solutions in the column on the right.

समस्या	हल
मेरी तबियत ठीक नहीं है।	आपको गरम कपड़े पहनने चाहिएँ।
मुझे बोरियत हो रही है।	आपको हर रोज़ बजट के मुताबिक़ ख़र्च करना चाहिए।
मैं दुबला होना चाहती हूँ।	आप को डॉक्टर के पास जाना* चाहिए।
मेरे पति का जन्मदिन है।	आपको कोई फ़िल्म देखनी चाहिए।
मुझे सर्दी लग रही है।	आपको कम खाना चाहिए और हर रोज़ व्यायाम करना चाहिए।
मेरे पैसे महीना ख़त्म होने से पहले ख़त्म हो जाते हैं।	आपको कुछ खाना चाहिए।
मुझे भूख लग रही है।	आपको एक तोहफ़ा ख़रीदना चाहिए।

*X के पास जाना, 'to go to X [a person], go to see X'

Exercise 4

Role Play: Pair up with a classmate and alternate playing the following roles. Switch after each four statements.

Role 1: You have a set of statements describing various problems. Read each statement aloud and wait for your partner's response. Your partner will make appropriate suggestions. Feel free to ask follow-up questions or make additional statements.

Role 2: Do not read any statements while playing this role. Listen as your partner reads various statements describing problems, and then offer advice (what your partner should do) for each problem mentioned. Try to offer as many solutions as possible for each problem.

Set 1:

मुझे भूख लग रही है|
मुझे सर्दी लग रही है|
मेरा सिर दुख रहा है|
मैं थका हुआ / थकी हुई हूँ|

Set 2:

मुझे प्यास लग रही है|
मुझे गर्मी लग रही है|
मेरे पेट में दर्द हो रहा है|
मुझे बोरियत हो रही है|

Set 3:

मेरा / मेरी दोस्त मुझ से नाराज़ है|
मेरे पैसे महीने के ख़त्म होने से पहले ख़त्म हो जाते हैं|
मेरे इम्तिहान में हमेशा ख़राब मार्क्स आते हैं|
मुझे मालूम नहीं कि आजकल दुनिया में क्या हो रहा है|

Set 4:

मेरी तबियत ठीक नहीं है|
मेरा / मेरी रूममेट बहुत शोर करता है / करती है|
आजकल पेट्रोल बहुत महँगा है|
मैं भारत के बारे में ज़्यादा नहीं जानता| मैं और जानना चाहता हूँ|

Exercise 5

Interview a classmate. Find out if or when your classmate has to do the following activities:

- go to his or her next class
- go to work (*kām par jānā*)
- shopping (for what?)
- go to the library
- study for a test
- write a paper
- call parents
- pay rent (*kirāyā*)
- get hair cut

Record your classmate's responses and then be prepared to report them.

29

Giving and Following Instructions

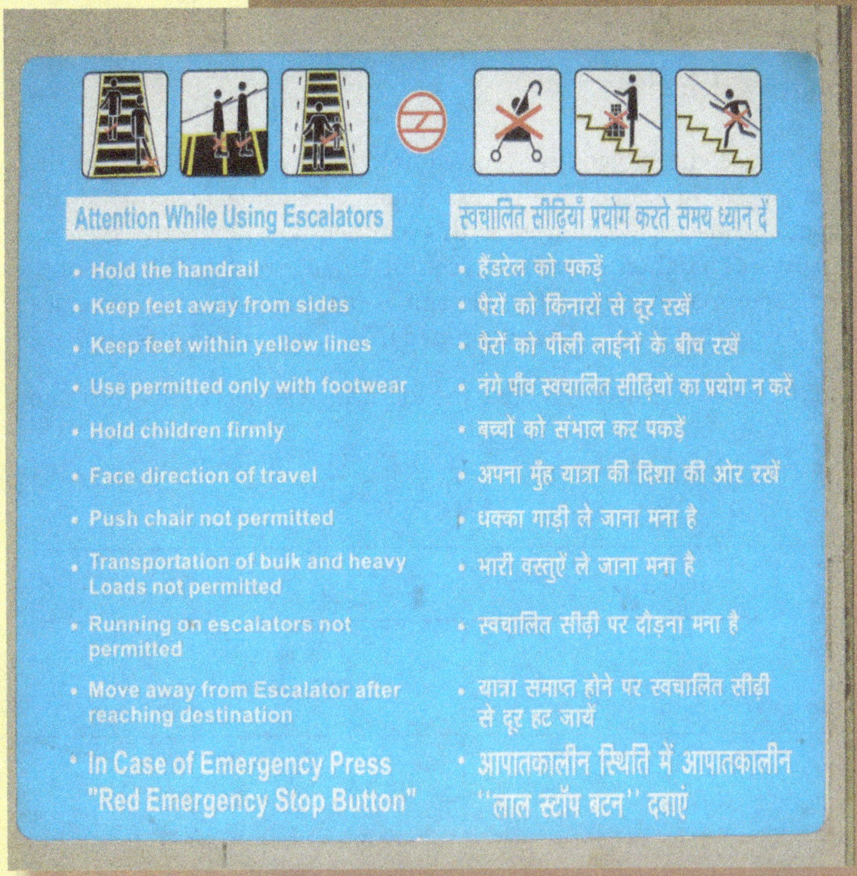
Attention While Using Escalators
• Hold the handrail
• Keep feet away from sides
• Keep feet within yellow lines
• Use permitted only with footwear
• Hold children firmly
• Face direction of travel
• Push chair not permitted
• Transportation of bulk and heavy Loads not permitted
• Running on escalators not permitted
• Move away from Escalator after reaching destination
• In Case of Emergency Press "Red Emergency Stop Button"
स्वचालित सीढ़ियाँ प्रयोग करते समय ध्यान दें
• हैंडरेल को पकड़ें
• पैरों को किनारों से दूर रखें
• पैरों को पीली लाईनों के बीच रखें
• नंगे पाँव स्वचालित सीढ़ियों का प्रयोग न करें
• बच्चों को संभाल कर पकड़ें
• अपना मुँह यात्रा की दिशा की ओर रखें
• धक्का गाड़ी ले जाना मना है
• भारी वस्तुएँ ले जाना मना है
• स्वचालित सीढ़ी पर दौड़ना मना है
• यात्रा समाप्त होने पर स्वचालित सीढ़ी से दूर हट जायें
• आपातकालीन स्थिति में आपातकालीन ''लाल स्टॉप बटन'' दबाएं

In this chapter you will learn an important way of giving instructions and stating rules. The structure that is used for this purpose is also used to express a desire or will that an action be performed or an event or state come to be.

Here are examples of the types of instructions that you will learn to express and understand:

छात्र ठीक समय पर क्लास में आएँ।	Students shall come to class on time.
कोई छात्र देर से न आए।	No student shall come late.

The Subjunctive: Introduction

As shown in the examples above, the subjunctive is often used to state general rules, norms, or instructions, particularly those intended for a general audience, such as recipes and rules posted or announced in public places. When used in this manner, the subjunctive is similar to the imperative, but expresses a lighter command, request, or suggestion. This use of the subjunctive is sometimes easier to understand if one imagines that each sentence is prefaced by a statement such as "It is expected that...," "It is suggested that...," or "It is requested that..."

Formation: The subjunctive can be formed by adding the following endings to the verb stem:

Subjunctive Endings

	singular	plural
1	-ऊँ (*maĩ*) -*ũ*	-एँ (*ham*) -*ẽ*
2	-ए (*tū*) -*e*	-ओ (*tum*) -*o*
		-एँ (*āp*) -*ẽ*
3	-ए (*vo*) -*e*	-एँ (*vo*) -*ẽ*

A useful way to remember these forms is that they are nearly identical to the simple present forms of *honā*, minus the initial *h-*. The only difference is that wherever *–ai* and *–aĩ* occur in simple present forms of *honā*, *–e* and *–ẽ* occur in the subjunctive endings. Here is the conjugation of the verb *jānā*, 'to go,' in the subjunctive verb form:

The Subjunctive Verb Form

	singular		plural	
1	मैं जाऊँ	I shall go.	हम जाएँ	We shall go.
2	तू जाए	You shall go.	तुम जाओ	You shall go.
			आप जाएँ	You shall go.
3	वह जाए	He/she shall go.	वे जाएँ	They shall go.

If the stem ends in a consonant, add the *mātrā* vowel sign (मैं करूँ, हम करें, etc.) rather than the full vowel form.

Using the Subjunctive

Keep in mind that 'shall' is only one of several English forms that the subjunctive corresponds to. For example, the subjunctive also corresponds to English 'may,' expressing a wish or statement of will.

आप हमेशा ख़ुश रहें।	May you always be happy.
भगवान आपका भला करे।	May God watch out for you.

The subjunctive is also often used to elicit feedback from the person being addressed on a proposed course of action. In English, this use is accomplished using forms such as 'Shall I…,' 'Should I…,' 'Shall we…,' etc.

मैं आपके साथ चलूँ?	Shall I come along with you?
हम खाना खाएँ?	Shall we eat? What shall we eat?
(हम) चलें?	Shall we go?

A closely related use of the subjunctive is asking permission.

हम लोग अंदर आएँ?	May we come in?
मैं एक बात पूछूँ?	May I ask something?

Of course the verb *saknā* can also be used to ask permission similar to English.

क्या हम लोग अंदर आ सकते हैं?	Can we come in?

English expressions with "Let's..." are expressed using the subjunctive with the phrases *āie/āo/calie/calo.*

आइए खाना खाएँ।	Let's eat.
चलो फ़िल्म देखें।	Let's see a movie.

Negation: Subjunctive verbs are generally negated with the negation word *na* (न).

छात्र क्लास में खाना न खाएँ।	Students shall not eat food in class.
छात्र क्लास में शोर न करें।	Students shall not be loud in class.
(आप) हॉस्टल में सिग्रेट या शराब न पिएँ।	Don't smoke or drink in the hostel.

Most of the meanings of the subjunctive introduced here are expressed when the subjunctive is used independently, or without the help of any supporting phrase. The subjunctive is capable of expressing many additional nuances. However, these nuances require the concurrent use of supporting phrases, called *subordinating expressions.* These phrases will be introduced in later sections.

Verbs with Irregular Subjunctive Forms

The verbs *lenā* 'to take', *denā* 'to give', and *honā* 'to be' are formed irregularly in the subjunctive.

लेना	singular	plural
1	*lū̃* लूँ	*lẽ* लें
2	*le* ले	*lo* लो
		lẽ लें
3	*le* ले	*lẽ* लें

देना	singular	plural
1	*dū̃* दूँ	*dẽ* दें
2	*de* दे	*do* दो
		dẽ दें
3	*de* दे	*dẽ* दें

होना	singular	plural
1	*hoū̃* होऊँ*	*hõ* हों
2	*ho* हो	*ho* हो
		hõ हों
3	*ho* हो	*hõ* हों

*Many speakers use the form *hū̃* for the first-person singular subjunctive form of *honā*.

Additional Peculiarities

Verbs with stems that end in ई and ऊ shorten the final vowel to इ and उ before the subjunctive endings are added. The letter य is also sometimes written between the final इ of the stem and the subjunctive ending.

Examples:

जीना, 'to live': मैं जिऊँ / जियूँ; तू, वह जिए / जिये; हम, आप, वे जिएँ / जियें; तुम जियो
छूना, 'to touch': मैं छुऊँ; तू, वह छुए; हम, आप, वे छुएँ; तुम छुओ

Expressing What One Wants Others to Do

A construction involving the subjunctive is used to express the desire that another person perform an action, or that an event or state come to be.

X चाहता है कि Y ... X wants Y to ...

This construction literally means, 'X wants that Y should...' The verb that X wants Y to perform occurs in the subjunctive.

मेरे अध्यापक चाहते हैं कि मैं और मेहनत करूँ। My teacher wants me to work harder.
उसके माता-पिता चाहते हैं कि वह डॉक्टर बने। His parents want him to become a doctor.

This construction is appropriate when one person wants another to do something. When the subject of a sentence wants to do something him or herself, the construction V-*nā cāhnā* is more common.

मैं थोड़ी देर आराम करना चाहता हूँ। I want to rest for a little bit.
वह पंजाबी सीखना चाहती है। She wants to learn Panjabi.

Vocabulary 1

अभ्यास	*abhyās* (m.)	practice, exercise
आइए / चलिए ...	*āie/calie...* + subj.	Let's...
इज़्ज़त, आदर	*izzat* (f.), *ādar* (m.)	respect, dignity, honor (X *kī izzat karnā* / X *kā ādar karnā,* to treat X with respect)
उड़ान	*uṛān* (f.)	flight
कंबल	*kambal* (m.)	blanket
क़तार	*qatār* (f.)	line, queue
कामयाब, सफल	*kāmyāb, saphal*	successful (*kāmyābī, saphaltā,* f. success)
क्यों न...	*kyõ na*	how about..., why not... (introduces a suggestion in the subjunctive)
जब भी	*jab bhī*	whenever
X का जी चाहना कि...	X *kā jī cāhnā ki* + subj.	for X to feel like...; X *kā* V-*ne kā jī cāhnā,* for X to feel like V-ing
ताकि	*tāki* (conj.)	so that...(+subj.)
दर्द	*dard* (m.)	pain
दवा	*davā* (f.)	medicine
पेटी	*peṭī* (f.)	belt

बरताव	*bartāv* (*bartāo*) (m.)	behavior (*bartāv karnā*, to behave)
बाँधना	*bā̃dhnā* (v.t.)	to tie, to fasten
भगवान, ख़ुदा	*bhagvān, xudā* (m.)	God (*bhagvān / xudā kare*, God willing)
भरोसा	*bharosā* (m.)	trust, belief in
भाग, हिस्सा	*bhāg, hissā* (m.)	part
यात्रा, सफ़र	*yātrā* (f.), *safar* (m.)	journey (*yātrā / safar karnā*, to travel, to take a journey)
यात्री, मुसाफ़िर	*yātrī, musāfir*	traveler
वाक्य	*vāky* (m.)	sentence
शरीक होना	*śarīk honā* (v.i.)	to participate
संस्कृति	*sanskriti* (f.)	culture
व्यवहार, सलूक	*vyavhār, salūk* (m.)	behavior
हवाई अड्डा	*havāī aḍḍā* (m.)	airport
हवाई जहाज़	*havāī jahāz* (m.)	airplane

Exercise 1 G

Fill in the blanks: Complete the Hindi sentences by translating the English phrases.

१. मेरे माता-पिता चाहते हैं कि मैं... (become a doctor)

२. हमारे अध्यापक चाहते हैं कि हम... (speak Hindi in class)

३. मैं नहीं चाहता कि तू... (sit near me)

४. हम चाहते हैं कि तुम... (bring coffee for us)

५. मैं चाहता हूँ कि आप... (come to our party)

६. मेरा दोस्त चाहता है कि वह लड़की... (dance with him)

७. हम चाहते हैं कि वह लड़का... (play with us)

८. हम नहीं चाहते कि वे लोग... (eat this ice cream)

९. सब लोग चाहते हैं कि शाहरुख़ ख़ान... (dance)

१०. हम चाहते हैं कि सिराज और सीमा... (sing a song)

Exercise 2

Read aloud and translate these classroom instructions posted on a bulletin board:

१. क्लास में ठीक समय पर आएँ|
२. क्लास में न सोएँ|
३. क्लास में सिर्फ़ हिन्दी बोलें|
४. हमेशा पूरे वाक्य बोलें|
५. जब भी कोई सवाल हो तो अध्यापक से पूछें|
६. हर अभ्यास में भाग लें और पूरी कोशिश करें|
७. अध्यापक और उनकी संस्कृति की इज़्ज़त करें|
८. अध्यापक के क्लास में आने पर खड़े हो जाएँ|
९. सब सहपाठियों के साथ अच्छा व्यवहार करें|
१०. खाने की चीज़ें क्लास में न लाएँ|

Exercise 3

Imagine that you are the resident assistant in a dormitory. You have a new batch of students coming to move in next week. Write rules for the dorm that can be distributed to the new students. Your rules should address these violations:

- Students play music loudly at night, disturbing others.
- Students burn incense and candles, which is a fire hazard.
- Students smoke cigarettes in the dorm, which is prohibited.
- Students leave trash and personal items in common areas.
- Students do not lock their rooms and thefts can occur.
- Students keep food in their rooms, which attracts ants.
- Students do not clean their rooms regularly.
- Visitors do not sign the visitors' register.

Exercise 4

Match each suggestion with an appropriate situation:

मेरा चाय पीने का जी चाह रहा है|	क्या मैं कंबल दूँ?
बहुत बोरियत हो रही है|	मैं तुम्हें जूस दूँ?
मुझे सर्दी लग रही है|	मैं चाय बनाऊँ?
मुझे प्यास लग रही है|	मैं तुम्हें अख़बार दूँ?
मनीष के पेट में दर्द हो रहा है|	क्या हम फ़िल्म देखने चलें?
मेरा सिर दुख रहा है|	हम उसे साफ़ करें?
मैं कुछ पढ़ना चाहती हूँ|	क्या हम उसे दवा दें?
हमारा कमरा बहुत गंदा है|	मैं टीवी बंद करूँ?

Exercise 5

You are at a Indian airport with your American friends who do not speak Hindi. Listen to the announcements and translate them in writing.

१. यात्री अपने सामान का ध्यान ख़ुद रखें|
२. अपना सामान ठीक जगह पर रखें|
३. हवाई अड्डे पर कूड़ा न फैलाएँ|
४. किसी अजनबी पर भरोसा न करें|
५. काउंटर के सामने क़तार में खड़े हों|
६. हवाई जहाज़ में सिग्रेट न पियें|
७. उड़ान के दौरान अपनी कुर्सी की पेटी बाँधे रखें|*

*V-ए रखना, 'to keep V-ed,' for example, बाँधे रखना, *bā̃dhe rakhnā*, 'to keep fastened.'

30

Unit 6 Review Activities

The goal of this chapter is to review the content of unit 6 and provide additional opportunities to synthesize all of the content presented up to this point.

G

1. Grammar Review

- How do you say that somebody can or cannot do something? Give one example of each.
- What are the constructions for 'for X to need to V,' 'X should V,' and 'for X to have no option but to V?' Give the constructions and one example of each.
- What is unusual about the behavior of infinitives in expressions of compulsion?
- Name at least two uses of the subjunctive other than giving commands, suggestions, or requests.
- Conjugate any verb in its entirety in the subjunctive.

2. Tips for Increasing Fluency: Speaking Drills

These drills are designed to promote both accuracy and fluency. When going through them, it is a good idea to write key words on a piece of paper prior to starting so that you can run through all of the sentences rapidly without pausing. When carrying out the exercises, focus first on accuracy, then as you repeat the activities and they become more automatic, focus on speed. The aim is to be able to speak about everyday life in an accurate and automatic manner.

saknā

- Create 8–10 questions that you could ask an acquaintance to determine what he or she can and can't do in class, at work, at his or her residence.
- Form responses to the questions that you created in the previous drill.

Expressions of Compulsion

- Make a list of 8–10 chores that people perform regularly. Create questions that you could ask to determine if an acquaintance has to do each action, or when they next have to carry out the action.
- Make 8–10 sentences describing things that you have to do this week.
- Create sentences that you might offer as advice to people who have the following problems:
    - A friend wants to lose weight.
    - A friend wants to become rich.
    - A classmate wants to learn Hindi well.
    - A classmate wants to get better grades on tests.

Subjunctive

- Give rules of behavior for your classroom or dorm.
- Explain how to prepare a simple food or drink item.

3. Personalization Questions

Pair up with a partner. Take turns asking and answering the following questions. Answer in complete sentences.

१. आज दोपहर को तुम्हें क्या-क्या करना है?
२. क्या तुम्हें किसी को फ़ोन करना है?
३. तुम्हें आज कितने घंटे पढ़ाई करनी है?
४. तुम्हें इस वीकेंड क्या-क्या करना है?
५. क्या तुम्हें बाज़ार से कुछ ख़रीदना है? क्या?
६. तुम्हें अपना कमरा महीने में कितनी बार साफ़ करना पड़ता है?
७. तुमको अपने माता-पिता के घर जाने में कितने घंटे सफ़र करना पड़ता है?
८. तुमको बचपन में ऐसा क्या करना पड़ता था जो तुम्हें पसंद नहीं था?
९. मैं एक नई भाषा सीखना चाहता हूँ। मैं कैसे सीखूँ?

4. A Letter to a Friend

Translate the questions below into Hindi, read the letter that Kabir has written to his friend, and then answer the questions. Write your answers in complete Hindi sentences.

उम्मीद	*ummīd* (f.)	hope, expectation
ख़ैरियत	*xairiyat* (f.)	state of being well (*xairiyat se honā*, to be well; *sab xairiyat hai*, all is well)
जल्द से जल्द	*jald se jald*	as quickly as possible
X को नमस्ते कहना	X *ko namaste kahnā*	to say 'hello' to X
पर	*par*	but (=*lekin*)
मम्मी-पापा	*mammī-pāpā*	parents
हालाँकि	*hālā̃ki*	although

A. What does Kabir think of his Indian relatives?
B. Why does Kabir have to get up early in the morning in India?
C. Why is Kabir unable to see new places in India?

D. What are Kabir plans for his coming vacation?
E. What does Kabir want from Sameer?

प्रिय समीर,

उम्मीद है कि तुम ख़ैरियत से होगे| अगली छुट्टियों के दौरान मैं हिंदुस्तान जा रहा हूँ| हिंदुस्तान में मेरे बहुत से रिश्तेदार रहते हैं| मैं जब अपने माता-पिता के साथ हिंदुस्तान जाता हूँ तो ज़्यादातर अपने रिश्तेदारों के साथ ठहरता हूँ| लेकिन इस बार मैं उनके साथ नहीं ठहरना चाहता| मेरे रिश्तेदार बहुत अच्छे हैं लेकिन उनके साथ बहुत सी चीज़ों का ध्यान रखना पड़ता है| वे लोग सुबह-सवेरे उठते हैं इसलिए मुझे भी जल्दी उठना पड़ता है| वे रोज़ मेरे लिए ख़ास खाने पकाते हैं तो मुझे उनके साथ खाना पड़ता है, हालाँकि मैं बाहर खाना चाहता हूँ| वे लोग शराब नहीं पीते तो मैं भी नहीं पी सकता| उनके यहाँ हमेशा लोग मिलने आते रहते हैं* तो मुझे उनसे बातें करनी पड़ती हैं| मैं नई जगहें देखना चाहता हूँ पर सारा समय रिश्तेदारों से मिलने में गुज़र जाता है| इस बार मैं अपने तौर पर हिंदुस्तान देखना चाहता हूँ और अपनी छुट्टियाँ आज़ादी से गुज़ारना चाहता हूँ| मैं चाहता हूँ कि इस बार तुम भी मेरे साथ हिंदुस्तान चलो| अगर तुम मेरे साथ चलना चाहते हो तो जल्द से जल्द बताओ ताकि हम तुरंत तैयारी शुरू कर सकें| हमें काफ़ी तैयारी करनी है| अच्छा अपने मम्मी-पापा को नमस्ते कहना|**

तुम्हारा दोस्त,
कबीर चौधरी

*लोग मिलने आते रहते हैं, people keep on coming to meet.
**The infinitive can also function as an imperative form.

5. What were your responsibilities at home when you were a child? What chores did you have to do? What were the rules of the house? Were your parents strict? What could you and couldn't you do? Write a paragraph addressing these questions.

उदाहरण

मैं हर रोज़ सिर्फ़ आधा घंटा टीवी देख सकता था|
मुझे हर रोज़ बर्तन धोने पड़ते थे|

6. In this passage, Amy, an American student, seeks advice from her Indian acquaintance, Rama. Listen to the passage and then write the answers to the questions in complete Hindi sentences.

शुभकामना	*śubhkāmnā*	good wish (शुभकामनाएँ, best wishes)

A. What is Amy asking Rama for suggestions about?
B. Where is Amy planning to go in India?
C. According to Rama, what is the difference between cities and villages in terms of what a woman can wear?
D. What does Rama tell Amy to be careful about in religious sites?
E. What suggestions does Rama give Amy about food and drink?

एमी	रमा, अगले महीने मैं भारत जा रही हूँ। मुझे मालूम नहीं कि मुझे क्या तैयारी करनी चाहिए। क्या आप कुछ सलाह दे सकती हैं कि मुझे वहाँ क्या करना चाहिए और क्या नहीं करना चाहिए?
रमा	अच्छा एमी, आप हिंदुस्तान में कहाँ जा रही हैं?
एमी	मैं सीधे दिल्ली जा रही हूँ लेकिन वहाँ से राजस्थान और दूसरी जगहें भी जाना है।
रमा	मर्दों के लिए तो कोई मुश्किल नहीं है लेकिन चूँकि आप औरत हैं तो आपको अपने कपड़ों का थोड़ा ध्यान रखना चाहिए।
एमी	तो क्या मैं भारत में पश्चिमी कपड़े बिल्कुल नहीं पहन सकती?
रमा	दिल्ली, मुंबई और दूसरे बड़े शहरों में पहन सकती हैं लेकिन फिर भी अच्छा है कि शरीर को अच्छी तरह ढकनेवाले कपड़े पहनें।
एमी	और गाँव वग़ैरह में क्या पहनूँ?
रमा	भारतीय कपड़े पहनें या कम से कम क़मीज़ के साथ दुपट्टा ओढ़ें।
एमी	ठीक है, और क्या करूँ?
रमा	अगर किसी मंदिर, मस्जिद या दूसरी धार्मिक जगह जाएँ तो अपना सिर ढकें।
एमी	खाने-पीने के बारे में भी कोई सलाह है?
रमा	हाँ, सड़क के किनारे से ख़रीदकर* कुछ न खाएँ। अच्छे साफ़ सुथरे रेस्टोरेंट में खाएँ या लोगों के घरों में खाएँ। पानी भी सिर्फ़ बोतलवाला पियें।
एमी	आपकी सलाह के लिए बहुत-बहुत शुक्रिया।
रमा	कोई बात नहीं। मेरी शुभकामना है कि आपका सफ़र अच्छा हो।

*ख़रीदकर, 'having bought'

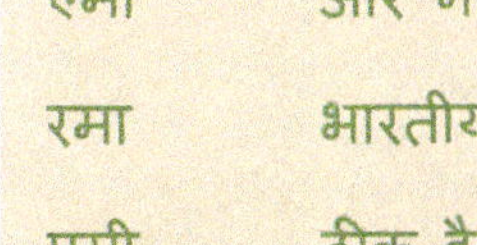

7. **Role Play:** Your teacher will assign to you one of the roles below. Pair up with a classmate and carry out the role play scenario. Make sure that you speak only in complete Hindi sentences.

Role 1: You are an Indian student who is about to travel to America to study. In this role, you are planning to study at your current (real-life) school. You have met an American (your partner) who is from this school and is studying in India. Ask your partner questions to seek advice about what will make living in America easier for you. Find out about the following things:

- Where to shop for clothing, and food
- What to wear and what clothes to buy to be comfortable in various weather
- Where to meet people
- What fun things there are to do
- How to get around the city without a car
- Where to live in the city
- What else to see and do when in America.

Role 2: You are an American living in India. You have met a young Indian student who is going to be moving to America soon to study at your university. Answer your partner's questions by giving him advice that will make his transition to America easier.

Sayings and Proverbs

बिन माँगे मोती मिले, माँगे मिले न भीख

अकेला चना भाड़ नहीं फोड़ सकता

खाए सो पछताए, न खाए सो पछताए

नाच न जाने आँगन टेढ़ा

पढ़ें फ़ारसी बेचें तेल, यह देखो कुदरत का खेल

बंदर क्या जाने अदरक का स्वाद

Unit 7 A Trip to South Asia

In this unit you will learn the following skills:

- Narrating future events.
- Accepting and declining invitations.
- Discussing travel plans, definite and possible.
- Booking travel tickets.
- Arranging lodging.
- Giving and following directions.
- Seeking information about tourist destinations.
- Planning and discussing travel itineraries.

In addition, you will learn about some of the famous places of South Asia.

31

My Plans

In this chapter you will learn how to describe your plans using sentences such as these:

मैं इस शुक्रवार को शिकागो जाऊँगा।	I'm going to go to Chicago this Friday.
मेरा हवाई जहाज़ छह बजे रवाना होगा।	My plane will depart at 6:00.
आज शाम मैं और मेरे दोस्त एक फ़िल्म देखेंगे।	Tonight my friends and I are going to see a movie.

You will also learn how to extend, accept, and decline invitations to make plans.

The Future Verb Tense

The sentences in the examples above employ the future verb tense, which describes events that will be realized at some point in the future. This verb form corresponds to the English forms 'will' and 'am/is/are going to' (e.g., He will arrive at 5:00, We are going to come by train).

Formation: The future verb tense is formed by adding to subjunctive forms the suffix *–gā/–ge/–gī*, which agrees with the subject in gender and number like a variable adjective.

subjunctive forms + ***–gā / –ge / –gī***

Here is the full conjugation of the verb *jānā* in the future verb tense:

		singular			plural		
masculine	1	जाऊँगा	*jāū̃gā*	I will go	जाएँगे	*jāẽge*	We will go
	2	जाएगा	*jāegā*	You will go	जाओगे	*jāoge*	You will go
					जाएँगे	*jāẽge*	You will go
	3	जाएगा	*jāegā*	He will go	जाएँगे	*jāẽge*	They will go
feminine	1	जाऊँगी	*jāū̃gī*	I will go	जाएँगी	*jāẽgī**	We will go
	2	जाएगी	*jāegī*	You will go	जाओगी	*jāogī*	You will go
					जाएँगी	*jāẽgī*	You will go
	3	जाएगी	*jāegī*	She will go	जाएँगी	*jāẽgī*	They will go

*As is the case with all verb tenses, groups of females using the *ham* form tend to use the masculine form (*jāẽge*) rather than the feminine.

Note that the structure of the future conjugation table is similar to that of the present habitual and present continuous, both covered in unit 3. This similarity results from the future form's two sets of endings, the first of which follows a person/number agreement pattern, and the second of which—the suffix *–gā/-ge/-gī*—follows the gender/number agreement pattern of adjectives.

	singular	plural
masculine	-गा	-गे
feminine	-गी	-गी

Here are some additional examples of the future verb tense in use:

आज शाम को मैं घर की सफ़ाई करूँगा।	This evening I'm going to clean my house.
मैं कल के इम्तिहान के लिए पढ़ाई करूँगा।	I'm going to study for tomorrow's test.
मैं फ़िल्म देखने जा रहा हूँ। मेरे साथ चलोगी?	I'm going to see a movie. Would you like to (will you) come with me?
मैं अगले महीने अपने परिवार के साथ भारत जाऊँगा।	Next month I'm going to go to India with my family.

Using the Future vs. the Present Continuous

As in English, the present continuous verb tense can also be used to describe a future event when the speaker wishes to depict the event as already determined or planned, or having already been set in motion.

मैं कल भारत जा रहा हूँ।	I am going to India tomorrow.
इसकी ट्रेन पंद्रह मिनट में आ रही है।	His train is coming in 15 minutes.

Invitations and Plans

Various structures that have already been introduced can be used when proposing plans or extending and accepting invitations. Here are some examples of possible exchanges that could occur.

क.	मुझे बहुत भूख लगी है। क्यों न हम चाट खाने चलें?	I'm really hungry. Why don't we go and eat chat?
ख.	ठीक है। चलो।	OK. Let's go.

क.	मेरे साथ फ़िल्म देखने चलोगे?	Would you like to go see a film with me?
ख.	कौन सी फ़िल्म?	Which film?
क.	मैं आमिर ख़ान की नई फ़िल्म देखना चाहता हूँ।	I want to see the new Amir Khan film.
ख.	हाँ, क्यों नहीं। कितने बजे? ...	Sure, why not? What time? ...

क.	अगले रविवार रात के खाने पर हमारे घर तशरीफ़ लाइए।	Please come to our house for dinner next Sunday night.
ख.	क्यों नहीं, ज़रूर। क्या कोई ख़ास मौक़ा है?	Certainly, why not? Is it a special occasion?
क.	जी, मेरी बेटी का दूसरा जन्मदिन है।	Yes, it's my daughter's second birthday.
ख.	बहुत बहुत मुबारक हो। भई यह तो बहुत ख़ुशी का मौक़ा है। हम ज़रूर आएँगे।	Congratulations! This is a very happy occasion. I will definitely come.

Turning down invitations politely is also essential when making plans. The verb *pānā* is one structure that can be used effectively for this purpose. As seen earlier, the verb *pānā* carries the meaning of 'to be able to,' and is used to express cabability and a sense of 'managing' to perform an action. In negative sentences, *pānā* can convey the idea that despite one's best wishes or efforts, one is unable to carry out an action ('I will not be able to...'). It is therefore frequently used to decline invitations and other proposed plans.

माफ़ कीजिए, मैं कल शाम आप के घर नहीं आ पाऊँगा। मुझे कुछ काम है।	I'm sorry, I won't be able to come to your house tomorrow evening. I have some work.
मुझे अफ़सोस है लेकिन हम आपकी पार्टी में नहीं आ पाएँगे। हमारे यहाँ ख़ुद कुछ मेहमान आ रहे हैं।	I'm sorry, but we won't be able to come to your party. We are having some guests ourselves.

Vocabulary 1

अगला	*aglā*	next
अफ़सोस	*afsos* (m.)	sorrow, regret (X *ko afsos honā*, for X to feel sorrow/regret)
अरे	*are*	interjection used to express surprise or to catch attention
इरादा	*irādā* (m.)	Intention X *kā* V-*ne kā irādā honā* / X *kā irādā honā ki...*, for X to intend/plan to V
उपन्यास	*upanyās* (m.)	novel
घुमाना	*ghumānā* (v.t.)	to show around
ज़रूर	*zarūr*	certainly
ठहरना	*ṭhaharnā* (v.i.)	to stop, to stay
दावत	*dāvat* (f.)	invitation; social gathering with food, reception, party (*dāvat denā*, to invite)
परेशानी	*pareśānī* (f.)	trouble, distress
X को Y पसंद आना	X *ko pasand* Y *ānā* (v.i.)	for X to like Y...(after experiencing it)
प्रोग्राम	*progrām* (m.)	program, what one plans to do (i.e. for the day)
फ़ुरसत	*fursat* (f.)	free time (X *ko fursat honā*, for X to be free—not busy)

भविष्य	*bhaviṣy* (m.)	future
माफ़ करना	*māf karnā* (v.t.)	to forgive, excuse (*māf kījie*, excuse me/I'm sorry)
मिलाना	*milānā* (v.t.)	to introduce (X *se*, to X)
मुबारक हो, बधाई हो	*mubārak , badhāī ho*	congratulations (*dīvālī mubārak ho*, Happy Diwali)
मौक़ा	*mauqā* (m.)	occasion, opportunity
योजना	*yojnā* (f.)	plan
रवाना होना	*ravānā honā* (v.i.)	to depart
व्यस्त	*vyast*	busy
शुभकामनाएँ	*śubhkāmnāẽ*	best wishes
संबंध, सिलसिला	*sambandh, silsilā* (m.)	connection (*is sambandh mẽ*, in this connection); *silsilā*, m. connection, sequence

Notes:

- The verb *ṭhaharnā* is similar to *baiṭhnā* and *kharā honā* in its use in the present continuous. The form *ṭhahrā huā / ṭhahre hue / ṭhahrī huī* is used for sentences such as *āp kahā̃ ṭhahre hue haĩ*, 'Where are you staying (currently).' The variable form V-*ā (huā)* is the past participle. For more information on this form please see the supplementary grammar section at the end of the book.

Exercise 1 G

Read aloud and translate the passage into English.

इस सप्ताहांत मैं बहुत व्यस्त रहूँगा| मैं कल दोपहर दोस्तों के साथ फ़िल्म देखूँगा| उसके बाद हम चाइनीज़ रेस्टोरेंट में खाना खाएँगे| कल मेरी एक दोस्त का जन्मदिन है| शाम को उसके यहाँ पार्टी होगी| मुझे उसके लिए तोहफ़ा ख़रीदना है| मैं उसके लिए एक किताब ख़रीदूँगा| एक उपन्यास है जो मुझे लगता है उसे पसंद आएगा| परसों सुबह मैं अपने कुछ दोस्तों से कॉफ़ी हाउस में नाश्ते पर मिलूँगा| उसके बाद हम लोग टेनिस खेलने जाएँगे| सोमवार को मेरी साहित्य की क्लास में इम्तिहान है, इसलिए परसों शाम को मुझे कुछ पढ़ाई करनी पड़ेगी|

Exercise 2

Translate the sentences into Hindi using the future tense.

1. This afternoon I'm going to go to the library.
2. I'm going to stay there until 6:00.
3. After that, I'll go home. Then I'll cook dinner.
4. After dinner, my friends are going to come to my house.
5. We are going to watch a movie.
6. Would you like to come watch it with us? (Will you come watch it with us)?
7. Tomorrow it's going to rain.
8. I'm going to stay home.
9. The day after tomorrow the weather will be nice.
10. I'm sorry, I won't be able to meet you tomorrow. I have to go to class.
11. We won't be able to come to your party. We're going to India next week. We will be there for a month.

Exercise 3

You and a friend have been talking about meeting up tomorrow. You have received this note from your friend. Write a response explaining your plans for the entire day and when you might be free to meet.

कल मैं छह बजे उठूँगा| मैं नाश्ता करने के बाद क्लास जाऊँगा| मेरी क्लासें साढ़े ग्यारह बजे तक चलेंगी, फिर मैं दोपहर का खाना खाऊँगा| अगर तुम चाहो तो मुझसे दोपहर के खाने पर मिल सकते हो| मैं एक अच्छा रेस्टोरेंट जानता हूँ| यह रेस्टोरेंट कैंपस के पास है| दोपहर के खाने के बाद मेरी एक और क्लास होगी, जो दो बजे ख़त्म होगी| क्लास के बाद मैं दो घंटे लाइब्रेरी में पढ़ाई करूँगा| फिर मैं अपने फ़्लैट वापस जाऊँगा| उसके बाद मैं जिम जाऊँगा| मुझे दोपहर को एक घंटा कसरत करना पसंद है| उसके बाद अगर तुम चाहो तो हम शाम का खाना साथ खा सकते हैं और खाने के बाद कोई फ़िल्म देख सकते हैं| तुम्हारा कल का प्रोग्राम क्या है? तुम्हें किस समय फ़ुरसत होगी?

Exercise 4

Listen to the dialogue between two friends, Rohan and Nitin, and answer the questions about it in complete sentences.

रोहन	नितिन, कल मैं एक हिन्दी फ़िल्म देखने जा रहा हूँ। क्या तुम भी मेरे साथ चलोगे?
नितिन	नहीं यार, कल मैं पूरे दिन व्यस्त हूँ।
रोहन	क्यों, क्या कर रहे हो?
नितिन	मेरे मम्मी-पापा कल मुझसे मिलने आ रहे हैं।
रोहन	अच्छा! वे कितने दिन यहाँ रहेंगे?
नितिन	सिर्फ़ एक दिन।
रोहन	अच्छा, वे गाड़ी से आ रहे हैं कि* ट्रेन से?
नितिन	ट्रेन से। उनकी ट्रेन सुबह नौ बजे आएगी। मैं उनसे स्टेशन पर मिलूँगा, फिर उनको अपने अपार्टमेंट ले जाऊँगा। वहाँ हम लोग नाश्ता करेंगे, फिर मैं उनको थोड़ी देर आराम करने दूँगा।
रोहन	क्या तुम उनको कैम्पस भी दिखा पाओगे?
नितिन	हाँ, वे पहली बार यहाँ आ रहे हैं, इसलिए मैं उनको कैम्पस घुमाऊँगा और उन्हें अपने कुछ प्रोफ़ेसरों से भी मिलाऊँगा।
रोहन	अच्छा, यह उनको बहुत अच्छा लगेगा। तो तुम लोग दोपहर को क्या करोगे?
नितिन	मेरे मम्मी-पापा को थाई खाना बहुत पसंद है, इसलिए मेरा इरादा है कि मैं उनको थाई रेस्टोरेंट ले जाऊँ। उसके बाद मुझे कुछ ख़रीदारी करनी है तो हम लोग मॉल चलेंगे।
रोहन	क्या वे कल रात यहाँ ठहरेंगे?
नितिन	हाँ, वे कल रात मेरे साथ ठहरेंगे, फिर परसों सुबह वापस जाएँगे।
रोहन	अच्छा।
नितिन	तो मैं कल व्यस्त हूँ लेकिन परसों मेरे पास समय होगा।

रोहन ठीक है, तो हम परसों फ़िल्म देख सकते हैं।

नितिन हाँ, परसों बिल्कुल ठीक है मेरे लिए।

रोहन ठीक है, तो परसों मिलते हैं। अच्छा, नितिन, अपने माता-पिता को मेरी तरफ़ से नमस्ते कहना।

नितिन ज़रूर। अच्छा, फिर परसों मिलते हैं।

रोहन ठीक है, बाय।

*कि can be used colloquially to mean 'or.'

सवाल

१. नितिन के माता-पिता कितने दिन उसके पास ठहरेंगे?
२. नितिन कल सुबह क्या-क्या करेगा?
३. नितिन अपने माता-पिता को कैंपस क्यों ले जाएगा?
४. कल दोपहर को नितिन के माता-पिता क्या-क्या करेंगे?
५. नितिन और रोहन हिन्दी फ़िल्म देखने कब जाएँगे?

Exercise 5

Pair up with a partner. Interview your partner to find out what he or she is going to do this afternoon. Is he or she going to do the following activities today and if so, at what time?

- wash clothes
- cook
- read a book
- study
- meet up with any friends
- watch television
- listen to music
- exercise

Ask about any additional activities that come to mind. Note what your partner tells you and be prepared to report it.

Exercise 6

Listen to the dialogue and write the gist of it.

मिश्रा जी	श्रीवास्तव जी, कल शाम आप हमारी दावत में आ रहे हैं, ना?
श्रीवास्तव जी	माफ़ कीजिएगा*, कल शाम तो मैं नहीं आ पाऊँगा। असल में मेरे कुछ रिश्तेदार आजकल मेरे यहाँ ठहरे हुए हैं तो मैं उनके साथ व्यस्त हूँ।
मिश्रा जी	तो कोई बात नहीं, आप अपने रिश्तेदारों को भी ले आइए।
श्रीवास्तव जी	अरे नहीं, आपको परेशानी होगी।
मिश्रा जी	अरे परेशानी की कोई बात नहीं। आप आएँगे तो हमें अच्छा लगेगा।
श्रीवास्तव जी	ठीक है, मैं अपने रिश्तेदारों से बात करूँगा फिर मैं इस संबंध में आपको शाम तक फ़ोन करूँगा।
मिश्रा जी	ठीक है, अच्छा, नमस्ते।
श्रीवास्तव जी	नमस्ते।

*कीजिएगा, is an alternative ultra-polite imperative form.

Exercise 7

Role Play:

Pair up with a classmate. Carry out the role that your teacher assigns to you.

Role 1: Imagine that you are trying to befriend your classmate. Express interest in doing the activities below. You can use statements/questions of the forms: Do you want to...? Would you like to...? Shall we...? Why don't we ...?

- go to drink coffee
- play basketball this afternoon
- watch a movie this weekend
- travel to India next year
- go on a picnic on Saturday
- watch my dog tomorrow so that I can go shopping

Role 2: Politely turn down your partner's invitations by saying "I'm sorry, I won't be able to… I have to…" (Make up an excuse). Feel free to use the expression *māf kījiye*, or *mujhe afsos hai*, "I'm sorry…"

Switch roles and repeat. The student playing role 1 can ask about the following activities:

- talk after class
- come to my house for tea
- study together in the library this evening
- go to the gym with me
- go to a party with me and my friends this weekend
- come to my house to play computer games

32

My Travel Plans: Definite and Possible

In this chapter you will learn how to discuss definite and possible travel plans. As seen in the previous chapter, definite future plans can be expressed using the future verb tense, or in some cases, the present continuous.

अगले महीने मैं दिल्ली जा रहा हूँ।	Next month I'm going to Delhi.
मैं वहाँ अपने रिश्तेदारों से मिलूँगा।	I'll see my relatives there.
मैं एक हफ़्ते के लिए मथुरा भी जाऊँगा।	I'm also going to go to Mathura for a week.

When making and discussing future plans, it is also useful to be able to say what one might do, or what it is possible that one will do. The subjunctive verb form can be employed for this purpose.

शायद मैं आगरा भी जाऊँ।	Perhaps I'll go to Agra too.
अगर मैं वहाँ जाऊँ तो मैं ताज महल देखूँगा।	If I go there, I'll see the Taj Mahal. (Subjunctive is in the 'if' clause.)
हो सकता है कि मैं मुंबई भी जाऊँ।	It's possible that I'll go to Mumbai too.
लेकिन मुमकिन है कि मुझे दिल्ली में ही रहना पड़े।	But I might just have to stay in Delhi.

Using the Subjunctive with Subordinating Expressions

In the sentences above, the subjunctive is employed in conjunction with introductory phrases that express contingency or a lesser degree of certainty about the outcome of the future event. Phrases such as these— *agar*, 'if,' *śāyad*, 'perhaps,' *ho saktā hai ki* and *mumkin hai ki*, 'it's possible that'—are examples of *subordinating expressions*.

Subordinating expressions are a set of short words and phrases that drastically expand the expressive power of the subjunctive. With the help of these phrases, the subjunctive is not limited to suggestions and expressions of desire or will; it can also express contingency, uncertainty, doubt, necessity, purpose, fear, and other nuances.

Some Important Subordinating Expressions

use	subordinating expression	example
possibility	हो सकता है कि... It's possible that..., might	हो सकता है कि रेलगाड़ी देर से आए। The train might come late.
	संभव / मुमकिन है कि... It's possible that..., might	संभव है कि आज दोपहर बारिश हो। It might rain this afternoon.
	शायद maybe, perhaps	शायद कल मौसम बेहतर हो। Perhaps tomorrow the weather will be better.

necessity	ज़रूरी है कि... It's necessary that...	ज़रूरी है कि हम चार बजे से पहले स्टेशन पहुँचें। It's necessary for us to arrive at the station before 4:00.
	X को चाहिए कि... It's necessary for X to..., What X needs to do is...	उसको चाहिए कि वह आराम करे। What he needs to do is rest. He needs to rest.
longing	काश If only..., Would that..., I hope	काश उसकी उड़ान ठीक समय पर पहुँचे। I hope his flight arrives on time.
purpose	...ताकि... ...so that..., ...in order to...	हमें आगरा जाना चाहिए ताकि हम ताज महल देख सकें। We should go to Agra so that we can see the Taj Mahal.
contingency	अगर... तो... If...(then)	अगर आप भारत जाएँ तो आप को ताज महल ज़रूर देखना चाहिए। If you go to India, you should definitely see the Taj Mahal.
fear/ apprehension	कहीं ऐसा न हो कि... May it not be that..., I hope that...(not)	कहीं ऐसा न हो कि हमारी ट्रेन छूट जाए। I hope our train doesn't leave (without us).
	X को डर है कि... X is afraid that...	मुझे डर है कि हमारी ट्रेन देर से न आए। I'm afraid our train will come late. ("I have the fear: May our train not come late.")

Additional Points

Not all subordinating expressions require that the subjunctive be used in all circumstances. For instance, *śāyad* and *agar* can be used with other verb tenses. If the action or event described is a future one, the subjunctive is most common, though other tenses, such as the future verb tense, are also possible.

शायद हमारा हवाई जहाज़ देर से पहुँचेगा।	Our plane may arrive late.
अगर हमारी ट्रेन देर से आएगी तो हम क्या करेंगे?	If our train arrives late, what will we do?

Using the future in these sentences paints the actions as real, definite, or more vivid possibilities. Using the subjunctive in either sentence would be appropriate when depicting the actions as hypothetical, or as less vivid possibilities.

It is often useful to think of the subjunctive as a qualified form of the future verb tense. Both the subjunctive and the future verb tense describe actions that will be realized at a later point in time. The two verb forms differ mainly in terms of the speaker's *mood*, or stance toward the statement. The future asserts that an action *will* occur, whereas the subjunctive typically suggests that it *could* occur or that its occurrence would be of subjective significance to the speaker (in terms of being desired, feared, etc.).

It is important to remember that the time frame of a dependent subjunctive verb is determined not by the time in which the sentence is spoken, but by the time frame established in the main clause. When a subjunctive verb is introduced by a phrase that ends in the word *ki*, 'that,' the time frame of the introductory phrase serves as the reference point for the clause that follows *ki*. Consider the following sentence:

वे चाहते थे कि हम उनके साथ चलें लेकिन हमें कहीं और जाना था।	They wanted us to go with them but we had to go somewhere else.

In this sentence the verb *calnā*, 'to go' is unrealized within the time frame of the verb of the main clause *cāhnā*, 'to want.' The subjunctive is thus appropriate from the perspective of the subject of that verb at the time of the performance of the verb (at the time of "wanting").

Vocabulary 1

Travel

इंतज़ाम, प्रबंध	*intazām, prabandh* (m.)	arrangement
उड़ान	*uṛān* (f.)	flight
किराया	*kirāyā* (m.)	rent, fare
क़िला	*qilā* (m.)	fort
खंडहर	*khanḍhar* (m.)	ruins
गाड़ी	*gāṛī* (f.)	car
घूमना	*ghūmnā* (v.i.)	to roam, to travel

छूटना	*chūṭnā*	to depart, to leave (without)
जमा करना	*jamā karnā*	to submit (a form, an application); to collect, amass
टिकट	*ṭikaṭ* (m./f.)	ticket
ट्रेन	*ṭren* (f.)	train
डिब्बा	*ḍibbā* (m.)	box; train car
तैयार	*taiyār*	ready, prepared
दरगाह	*dargāh* (f.)	shrine or tomb of a Muslim saint
फ़ैसला	*faislā* (m.)	decision ([V-*ne*] *kā faislā karnā*, to decide [to V])
बुक करना	*buk karnā*	to book
भरना	*bharnā* (v.i./v.t.)	to fill, to fill out (*fārm bharnā*, to fill out a form)
मंज़िल	*manzil* (f.)	destination; storey
X का मज़ा लेना	X *kā mazā lenā*	to enjoy X
महल	*mahal* (m.)	palace
रवाना होना	*ravānā honā*	to depart
रेलगाड़ी	*relgāṛī* (f.)	train
वापसी	*vāpsī* (f.)	return
सवारी	*savārī* (f.)	passenger
सीट	*sīṭ* (f.)	seat
सैर	*sair* (f.)	tour
स्टेशन	*sṭeśan* (m.)	station

Additional Words

आशा	*āśā* (f.)	hope (X *ko āśā honā ki*, for X to hope that [+ future tense])
उम्मीद	*ummīd* (f.)	expectation, hope (X *ko ummīd honā ki*, for X to have an expectation/hope that [+ future tense])
कहीं	*kahī̃*	anywhere, somewhere (*kahī̃ aisā na ho ki*, may it not be that…)
V-ने को	V-*ne ko*	to V (e.g. *kyā kuch khāne ko hai*, 'Is there anything to eat?')
जहाँ	*jahā̃* (rel.)	where
जी चाहना	*jī cāhnā*	to feel like… (X *kā jī cāhnā ki*; X *kā* V-*ne kā jī cāhnā*, for X to feel like…)
डर	*ḍar* (m.)	fear
ताकि	*tāki*	so that…, in order to…
दरअसल, वास्तव में	*dar-asal, vāstav mẽ*	actually, in fact (=*asal mẽ*)
दिल चाहना	*dil cāhnā*	to feel like… (X *kā dil cāhnā ki*, for X to feel like…)
पक्का	*pakkā*	definite, certain
मंगलमय	*mangalmay*	good, auspicious (e.g. *yātrā mangalmay ho*, [May you] have a pleasant journey)
मन करना	*man karnā*	to feel like… (X *kā* V-*ne kā man karnā*, for X to feel like V-ing; X *kā man karnā ki…*, for X to feel like…)
मन होना	*man honā*	to feel like… (X *kā* V-*ne kā man honā*, for X to feel like V-ing)
लायक़, योग्य	*lāyaq, yogy*	worthy (X *ke lāyaq / yogy*, worthy of X; V-*ne lāyaq / yogy*, worth V-ing)
संभव, मुमकिन	*sambhav, mumkin*	possible
संभावना	*sambhāvnā* (f.)	possibility

Note:

- The phrases with *āśā*, 'hope,' and *ummīd*, 'expectation/hope' introduce a phrase in the future tense, and not the subjunctive.

Exercise 1

Read aloud and translate.

१. हो सकता है कि मैं अगले साल भारत जाऊँ| २. अगर मैं भारत जाऊँ, तो शायद मैं मुंबई देख सकूँ| ३. यह ज़रूरी है कि तुम रवाना होने से पहले सफ़र का इंतज़ाम अच्छी तरह करो| ४. हमें फ़ौरन स्टेशन जाना है| कहीं ऐसा न हो कि हमारी ट्रेन छूट जाए (छूटे)| ५. हमें जल्द से जल्द हवाई अड्डे पहुँचना है ताकि हमारी उड़ान न छूटे| ६. रेलगाड़ी लखनऊ कितने बजे पहुँचेगी? ७. उनकी ट्रेन किस प्लेटफ़ार्म पर आएगी? ८. आपकी मंज़िल इस स्टेशन के बाद आएगी| ९. मुझे पटना जाना है, मुझे टिकट कहाँ मिलेगा? १०. आपको यह फ़ार्म भरना है फिर खिड़की नंबर पाँच पर इसे जमा कीजिए| टिकट आपको वहाँ मिलेगा| ११. एक सीट का किराया कितना होगा? १२. आप कितने दिन के लिए होटल बुक करेंगे?

Exercise 2

Translate into Hindi.

1. My family is going to go to Lucknow in a couple of months.
2. We are going to visit relatives.
3. We will stay at my (paternal) grandparents' house.

4. Our plane will depart from New York on October 4. We will arrive in Delhi the next morning.
5. We will take a train to Lucknow the next day.
6. Our train will depart at 6:00 and will arrive at 12:00 in the afternoon.
7. My uncle will come to meet us at the station.
8. It's possible that other people will come too.
9. We will then go to my grandparents' house so that we can rest.
10. It's possible that we won't be able to rest. Other relatives will certainly come to see us.

Exercise 3

G

Add phrases to the following sentences to add the sense that the events described are less than certain possibilities. Write out the complete resulting sentences.

उदाहरण

मैं एक और दिन जयपुर में रहूँगा। → शायद मैं एक और दिन जयपुर में रहूँ।

१. इन गर्मियों में मेरी पूरी हिन्दी की क्लास दक्षिण एशिया जाएगी। २. सब लोग भारत जाएँगे। ३. कुछ लोग नेपाल जाएँगे। ४. मैं अपने रिश्तेदारों से मिलूँगा। ५. मेरा एक दोस्त मुंबई और गोवा घूमेगा। ६. लखनऊ में मैं असली मुग़लई खाना खाऊँगा। ७. कुछ लोग बीमार हो जाएँगे। ८. हमें हिन्दी का इस्तेमाल करने के बहुत मौक़े मिलेंगे।

Exercise 4

Match the statements on the left with the most appropriate statements on the right.

मैं मोहनजोदड़ो और हड़प्पा जाना चाहता हूँ...	ताकि तुम अपनी मंज़िल पर जल्दी पहुँच सको।
हमें फ़ौरन रेलवे स्टेशन जाना चाहिए...	ताकि मैं खंडहर देखूँ।
तुम्हें हवाई जहाज़ से जाना चाहिए...	ताकि तुम हैदराबाद भी घूम सको।
तुम्हें दक्षिण भारत भी जाना चाहिए...	ताकि हमारी ट्रेन न छूटे।
हम आगरा के बाद फ़तेहपुर सीकरी जाएँगे...	ताकि आपकी यात्रा के दौरान मौसम अच्छा रहे।
आपको फ़रवरी-मार्च में हिंदुस्तान जाना चाहिए...	ताकि हम वहाँ की पुरानी मुग़ल इमारतें देखें।

Exercise 5

Pair up with a classmate.

Student 1: Your partner is planning a trip to South Asia. Find out where he or she is going to go and the reason why he or she will visit each place.

उदाहरण

क. आप सबसे पहले कहाँ जाएँगे?

ख. सबसे पहले मैं दिल्ली जाऊँगा|

क. आप दिल्ली क्यों जाएँगे?

ख. ताकि मैं कुतुब मीनार देखूँ|

क. उसके बाद आप कहाँ जाएँगे?

ख. दिल्ली के बाद मैं हिमाचल प्रदेश जाऊँगा|

Student 2: You are planning a trip to South Asia. Below is your basic itinerary listing the places that you will visit and the purpose for visiting each place. Answer your partner's questions in the manner indicated in the example above.

Destination	**Attraction**
Delhi	See Qutub Mīnār.
Agra	See Tāj Mahal.
Jaipur	See the desert and stay in old havelis.
Mumbai	Meet Bollywood film stars. (*filmī sitāre*)
Goa	See old Portuguese forts.
Hyderabad	Eat Haidarābādī biryani.
Kerala	Do a boat tour. (*nāv kī sair*)

Switch roles and repeat.

Destination	**Attraction**
Delhi	See old Delhi.
Kashmir	See Dal lake.
Kathmandu	Do trekking in the mountains.
Lucknow	Buy clothing with *cikan* embroidery; eat famous kabobs.
Lahore	See the famous Badshahi mosque
Karachi	Stroll on Clifton Beach

Exercise 6

You are planning a trip to India. Your travel agent has sent you the following note about your itinerary. Read the note and answer the questions.

आपके सफ़र का पूरा इंतज़ाम हो गया है*| आपकी उड़ान तीस अप्रैल को शिकागो से होगी| चौदह घंटे बाद आप दिल्ली पहुँचेंगे| दिल्ली में आप एक रात रहेंगे| वहाँ आप अशोक गेस्टहाउस में ठहरेंगे| अगले दिन आप ट्रेन से आगरा जाएँगे जहाँ आप ताज महल देखेंगे| ताज महल देखने के बाद आप फ़तेहपुर सीकरी जाएँगे| वह आगरा से ज़्यादा दूर नहीं है| फ़तेहपुर सीकरी में पुराने महल और सलीम चिश्ती की दरगाह देखने के बाद आप आगरा वापस जाएँगे और एक रात मुमताज़ गेस्टहाउस में ठहरेंगे| अगली सुबह दस बजे आप ट्रेन से लखनऊ के लिए रवाना होंगे| आप वहाँ लगभग चार बजे पहुँचेंगे| लखनऊ में आप दो दिन रहेंगे| वहाँ आप नवाब गेस्टहाउस में ठहरेंगे| लखनऊ में आप बड़ा इमामबाड़ा, छोटा इमामबाड़ा और दूसरी पुरानी इमारतें देख सकेंगे और लखनऊ के खानों का मज़ा ले सकेंगे| लखनऊ के बाद आप दिल्ली वापस आएँगे| आप अपनी वापसी की उड़ान से पहले दो दिन दिल्ली घूम सकते हैं| दिल्ली में बहुत सी चीज़ें देखने लायक़ हैं| मेरी शुभकामना है कि आपकी यात्रा मंगलमय हो| सात मई को आप हवाई जहाज़ से अमरीका वापस जाने के लिए रवाना होंगे|

१. भारत के लिए आपकी उड़ान किस तारीख़ को और कहाँ से होगी?

२. दिल्ली में आप कुल कितने दिन रहेंगे और वहाँ कहाँ ठहरेंगे?

३. आप अपनी यात्रा के दौरान भारत के कौन-कौन से शहर देखेंगे?

४. ताज महल देखने के तुरंत बाद आप क्या करेंगे?

५. आप अमरीका वापस कब आएँगे?

*हो गया है, 'has been completed.'

The Tomb of the saint Salim Chishti, Fatehpur Sikri, India

Exercise 7

Translate the questions into Hindi, listen to the dialogue, and then answer the questions in complete sentences.

a. Where is Pushpa going and for how long?
b. Who is she visiting?
c. What will she do during her vacation?
d. How is she traveling?
e. What does she ask Sandhya to do?

संध्या	पुष्पा, इन छुट्टियों के लिए तुम्हारा क्या इरादा है?
पुष्पा	मैं न्यूयॉर्क सिटी जा रही हूँ। मेरी एक सहेली वहाँ पढ़ती है।
संध्या	अच्छा? तुम न्यूयॉर्क में कितने दिन रहोगी?
पुष्पा	मैं दो दिन वहाँ रहूँगी। रविवार को वापस आऊँगी।
संध्या	तो तुम वहाँ क्या-क्या करोगी?
पुष्पा	न्यूयॉर्क में बहुत से अच्छे रेस्टोरेंट हैं। हम अच्छे खाने खाएँगे और घूमेंगे।
संध्या	तुम लोग कहाँ घूमोगी? कोई ख़ास इरादा है?
पुष्पा	हम न्यूयॉर्क सेंट्रल पार्क देखेंगे। फिर शायद कुछ अजायबघर देखें।
संध्या	तुम न्यूयॉर्क कैसे जाओगी?
पुष्पा	मैं हवाई जहाज़ से जाऊँगी। मेरी उड़ान कल शाम को है और रविवार को छह बजे वापसी होगी।
संध्या	अच्छा।
पुष्पा	संध्या, दरअसल मुझे तुमसे यह पूछना था कि अगर तुम्हें रविवार को फ़ुरसत हो, तो क्या तुम मुझे लेने आ सकोगी?
संध्या	हाँ, ज़रूर, लेकिन हम कहाँ मिलेंगे।
पुष्पा	बैगेज क्लेम में?
संध्या	हाँ, ठीक है।

33

Arranging Transportation and Lodging

In this chapter you will learn how to arrange transportation and lodging. Here are some examples of sentences you will learn to say:

पटना जाने में कितना समय लगेगा?	How long will it take to get to Patna?
वहाँ जाने में कितने पैसे लगेंगे?	How much will it cost to get there?
फ़ैज़ाबाद जानेवाली बस किस प्लेटफ़ार्म से चलेगी?	From which platform will the bus to Faizabad leave?
ट्रेन नंबर ४३५ चलनेवाली है।	Train number 435 is about to leave.
ताज होटल में एक रात ठहरने में कितना पैसा लगेगा?	How much will it cost to to stay for one night in the Taj Hotel?

How Long It Takes and How Much It Costs

The construction V-*ne mẽ...lagnā* can be used to state both how much it will cost to do something and how long it will take.

V-*ne mẽ* [*paisā*] *lagnā*	**for it to cost [money] to V**
वहाँ जाने में कितना पैसा लगेगा?	How much will it cost to get there?
बस से सफ़र करने में चार सौ रुपये लगेंगे।	It will cost 400 rupees to travel by bus.

V-*ne mẽ* [*samay*] *lagnā*	**for it to take [time] to V**
दिल्ली पहुँचने में कितना समय लगेगा?	How long will it take to get to Delhi?

Imminent Events

As mentioned briefly in unit 4, chapter 19, the word *vālā* with an oblique infinitive gives two senses. The basic sense is as an agentive noun or adjective ("a V-er," "one that V-s").

V-*ne vālā*	**one that V-s, a V-er**
लखनऊ जानेवाली ट्रेन का किराया कितना है?	What is the fare for the train going to Lucknow? (the train that goes to Lucknow)
आगरा से आनेवाली बस कब पहुँचेगी?	When will the bus coming from Agra arrive?
सफ़ाई करनेवाली कितने बजे आती है?	What time does the cleaning woman come?

The other use of the oblique infinitive with *vālā*, which will be the focus in this chapter, is to express imminence ("about to V," or "on the verge of V-ing.").

V-*ne vālā*	about to V, on the verge of V-ing
हमारी ट्रेन छूटनेवाली है।	Our train is about to leave.
उसका हवाई जहाज़ अभी आनेवाला है।	His airplane is about to come right now.
एक बजनेवाला है।	It's almost one o'clock.

Vocabulary 1

चलना	*calnā* (v.i.)	to move; to depart (i.e. a train); to go with
चाबी, चाभी	*cābī*, *cābhī* (f.)	key
X को देर होना / हो जाना	X *ko der honā/ho jānā*	for X to be/get late (*der se*, adv. 'late')
पहचान पत्र	*pahcān patr* (m.)	identification card (*pahcān*, f. identity)
फ़रमाना	*farmānā* (v.i.)	to speak
रवानगी, प्रस्थान	*ravāngī* (f.), *prasthān* (m.)	departure
सवारी	*savārī* (f.)	passenger
सेवा	*sevā* (f.)	service (X *kī sevā karnā*, to serve X)

Note:

- *farmānā* is equivalent to *bolnā* but is more polite. It can be used to refer to other people's speech but not one's own.

Exercise 1 G

Read aloud and translate.

१. मुंबई से आनेवाला हवाई जहाज़ तीन घंटे देर से आएगा| २. लखनऊ से हैदराबाद जानेवाली गाड़ी प्लेटफ़ार्म नंबर चार पर आएगी| ३. मैं चार बजे वाली गाड़ी से जा रहा हूँ| ४. दिल्ली से मुंबई हवाई जहाज़ से जाने में ढाई घंटे लगते हैं| ५. यहाँ से दिल्ली हवाई जहाज़ से जाने में २००० रुपये लगेंगे| ६. ट्रेन से जाने में सिर्फ़ ३०० रुपये लगेंगे| ७. ट्रेन से जाने में कितना वक़्त लगेगा?

Exercise 2 G

Translate into Hindi.

1. The train coming from Hyderabad will arrive on platform number four.
2. The plane going to London is (standing) at gate number 13.
3. Which is the bus that goes to Jodhpur?
4. It's that one. It's about to leave right now.
5. Train number 345 is about to arrive on platform number seven.
6. How much does it cost to get to New York from here?
7. How long does it take to get to Los Angeles?
8. How much will it cost to go to Boston by train?
9. How long will it take to get to Bhopāl?
10. It will take quite a while to travel there.

Exercise 3

Answer the questions based on the information in the schedule below. Answer in complete Hindi sentences. Work in pairs: one student should read the first four sentences aloud and the other listen and then answer without reading the questions. Then switch roles and repeat with the remaining four sentences.

कहाँ तक	छूटने का समय	प्लेटफ़ार्म	
जयपुर	6:00	५	–
आगरा	7:15	९	२ घंटे देर से छूटेगी
मुंबई	7:45	६	–
लखनऊ	8:30	४	–
शिमला	9:30	१०	२० मिनट देर से छूटेगी

कहाँ से	पहुँचने का समय	प्लेटफ़ार्म	
चंडीगढ़	5:45	२	१ घंटा देर से पहुँचेगी
अमृतसर	6:30	८	–
जोधपुर	8:45	१	१० मिनट जल्दी पहुँचेगी
वाराणसी	9:30	७	–
कोलकाता	10:00	३	–

१. जयपुर जानेवाली रेलगाड़ी कितने बजे चलेगी?
२. प्लेटफ़ार्म नंबर २ पर आनेवाली रेलगाड़ी किस शहर से आ रही है?
३. कौन सी तीन ट्रेनें देर से चल रही हैं?
४. लखनऊ जानेवाली ट्रेन कब और किस प्लेटफ़ार्म से चलेगी?
५. चंडीगढ़ से आनेवाली ट्रेन कितने बजे पहुँचेगी?
६. कौन सी ट्रेन पहले आएगी, अमृतसर से आनेवाली या जोधपुर से आनेवाली?
७. आगरा जानेवाली ट्रेन कितने बजे चलेगी?
८. कौन सी ट्रेन सबसे आख़िर में पहुँचेगी? कितने बजे और किस प्लेटफ़ार्म पर पहुँचेगी?

Exercise 4

Role Play

Student 1: Imagine that you are a customer in a travel agency and your partner is a travel agent. Find out how long and how much time it will take to get to the places listed in the table. Note your findings and then check them with your partner when finished.

Destination	Flight Duration (hours)	Fare (rupees)
दिल्ली		
जयपुर		
चेन्नई		
मुंबई		
लखनऊ		
काठमांडू		
बंगलुरु		

Student 2: You are a travel agent. Answer your partner's questions based on the information given in the table.

Destination	Flight Duration (hours)	Fare (rupees)
दिल्ली	1:00	2000
जयपुर	1:15	2500
चेन्नई	2:05	4000
मुंबई	1:45	3700
लखनऊ	0:30	1500
काठमांडू	1:30	3200
बंगलुरु	2:00	4050

Switch roles and repeat.

Student 1:

Destination	Flight Duration (hours)	Fare (rupees)
दिल्ली		
इलाहाबाद		
हैदराबाद		
मुंबई		
लखनऊ		
वाराणसी		
कोलकाता		

Student 2:

Destination	Flight Duration (hours)	Fare (rupees)
दिल्ली	2:00	5100
इलाहाबाद	1:00	2800
हैदराबाद	0:45	2300
मुंबई	0:30	1700
लखनऊ	1:15	3400
वाराणसी	1:45	4200
कोलकाता	2:30	5600

Exercise 5

Listen to the dialogue and answer the questions in complete sentences.

क. मुझे दिल्ली से आगरा के लिए एक टिकट चाहिए|

ख. कौन सी तारीख़ के लिए|

क. आज के लिए|

ख. आज तो बस एक ट्रेन है जो दिल्ली से शाम चार बजे छूटती है|

क. वह आगरा कितने बजे पहुँचेगी?

ख. साढ़े छह बजे|

क. ठीक है तो उसी ट्रेन के लिए एक टिकट दे दीजिए|

ख. आपको कौन सी क्लास में सीट चाहिए?

क. जनरल क्लास ठीक है| बस सीट रिज़र्व होनी चाहिए| किराया कितना होगा?

ख. साढ़े पाँच सौ रुपये|

क. जी अच्छा, यह लीजिए ये छह सौ रुपये हैं|

ख. यह लीजिए आपके पचास रुपये और यह आपका टिकट|

क. शुक्रिया|

सवाल

१. यात्री को कहाँ जाना है?
२. वहाँ पहुँचने में कितना समय लगेगा?
३. कितने पैसे लगेंगे?
४. यात्री कौन सी क्लास का टिकट ख़रीदता है?

Exercise 6

You are working for a travel book publisher. You have been asked to compile a Hindi phrase book covering important travel situations. Listen to the dialog and note the essential phrases related to booking a hotel room. Share your phrases with a partner.

क. जी फ़रमाइए, मैं आपकी क्या सेवा कर सकता हूँ?

ख. मुझे आपके होटल में एक कमरा चाहिए।

क. आपको कमरा कितने दिनों के लिए चाहिए?

ख. मुझे एक दिन के लिए कमरा चाहिए। एक दिन का किराया कितना होगा?

क. हमारे होटल में एक दिन का किराया ८०० रुपये है।

ख. कमरे में ए-सी भी है?

क. जी हाँ, कमरे में ए-सी है।

ख. ठीक है, तो एक कमरा बुक कर दीजिए।

क. आपका नाम क्या है?

ख. समीर खन्ना।

क. कोई पहचान पत्र है आपके पास?

ख. जी हाँ, यह लीजिए, मेरा पासपोर्ट।

क. ठीक है, यहाँ साइन कर दीजिए।

...

क. यह रहा आप का पासपोर्ट और यह कमरे की चाबी। हमारे यहाँ चेक-आउट टाइम सुबह ११ बजे है।

ख. ठीक है।

Exercise 7

Role Play: Booking a Room in a Guest House

In this activity feel free to use any of the useful phrases that you noted in the previous activity.

Role 1: You need a room in a guest house for two nights, tonight and tomorrow night. You will need it for yourself and a traveling companion. You will need two beds. You would like a room with air conditioning, but don't need anything else. Find out what the rate is and book a room.

Role 2: You work at the front desk at a guest house. Help your guest find a suitable room. Your rates are 550 rupees a night for single rooms and 700 rupees a night for double rooms. Rooms with air conditioning are an extra 150 rupees a night. Rooms with TVs are an extra 50 rupees a night.

Goa, India

34

Finding One's Way

Giving and Following Directions

In this chapter you will learn how to carry out one of the most essential tasks when traveling, asking for and following directions.

Adverbs

Hindi does not have any single structure equivalent to the adverbial suffix *–ly* in English (e.g. *directly, quickly*). A couple of the most common patterns for forming adverbs are given below.

Using adjectives as adverbs: Adjectives are words that describe qualities of nouns and answer questions such as *of what type, of what qualities, in what state*. Adverbs answer questions such as *where, when,* and *in what manner.* Many adjectives in Hindi can also be used as adverbs. Variable adjectives used as adverbs take the masculine singular oblique ending, *-e*.

Examples:

सीधा	*sīdhā*, straight, direct (adj.)
सीधे	*sīdhe*, straight, directly (adv.)
यह सीधा रास्ता है।	This is the direct way.
इसी रास्ते पर सीधे जाइए।	Go straight on this road.

The adjectives *bāyā̃* and *dāyā̃* have a final nasalized vowel, but otherwise behave as regular variable adjectives: *bāyā̃/bāyẽ/bāyī̃* and *dāyā̃/dāyẽ/dāyī̃*. In addition, the letter **य** can optionally be dropped from the forms other than the masculine singular direct form: *bāyā̃/bāẽ/bāī̃, dāyā̃/dāẽ/dāī̃*.

बायाँ	*bāyā̃*, left (adj.)
बाएँ	*bāẽ*, to the left (adv.)
इस चौराहे से बाएँ मुड़ो।	Turn (to the) left at this intersection.
दायाँ	*dāyā̃*, right (adj.)
दाएँ।	*dāẽ*, to the right (adv.)
अगली सड़क पर दाएँ मुड़िए।	Turn (to the) right on the next road.

Here are some additional contrasting examples of adjectives and adverbs in use:

आपका सफ़र कैसा था?	How was (what were the qualities of—adj.) your journey?
आप कैसे सफ़र करेंगे?	How (in what manner—adv.) will you travel?
मैं अकेला हूँ।	I am alone (state—adj.).
मैं अकेले सफ़र कर रहा हूँ।	I am traveling alone (manner—adv.).

Using a noun plus the postposition *se*: As mentioned above, there is no single structure in Hindi that corresponds to English adverbs; however, another common equivalent is Hindi postpositional phrases consisting of a noun plus the postposition *se*.

देर से	late
ट्रेन देर से आएगी।	The train will come late.

Perspective in Directions

Whereas it is common when giving directions in English to describe the landmarks from the perspective of the questioner or "asker" ("You will come to a brick building," "You will see a gas station"), the Hindi phrasing of such sentences differs significantly.

थोड़ी दूर पर एक पार्क आएगा।	After a little distance, you'll come to a park. ("A park will come.")
उसके बाद आपको एक स्कूल दिखाई देगा।	After that, you'll see a school. ("A school will become visible to you.")
फिर आपको एक ऊँची लाल इमारत दिखेगी।	Then you'll see a tall red building. ("A tall red building will appear to you.")

Subjunctive and Imperative Usage

Note that both the imperative and subjunctive can be used when giving directions and instructions.

यहाँ से सीधे जाइए।	Go straight from here.
यहाँ से सीधे जाएँ।	Go straight from here.
वहाँ से बाएँ मुड़िए।	Turn left there.
वहाँ से बाएँ मुड़ें	Turn left there.

Vocabulary 1

आगे	*āge*	ahead
उल्टा हाथ	*ulṭā hāth*	left hand (*ulṭe hāth par*, on the left side)
चौराहा	*caurāhā* (m.)	intersection
तरफ़	*taraf* (f.)	direction
X की तरफ़	X *kī taraf*	in the direction of X
थाना	*thānā* (m.)	police station
दायाँ	*dāyā̃* (adj.)	right
दाहिना	*dāhinā* (adj.)	right
दिखना	*dikhnā* (v.i.)	to appear to, to look, to seem
दिखाई देना	*dikhāī denā* (v.i.)	to appear to, to become visible to (X *ko*)
दूर	*dūr*	distant
नज़दीक	*nazdīk*	nearby (X *ke nazdīk*, near to X)
पटरी	*paṭrī* (f.)	(rail) track
पार करना	*pār karnā* (v.t.)	to cross
पुल	*pul* (m.)	bridge
पेट्रोल पंप	*peṭrol pamp* (m.)	gas station
बायाँ	*bāyā̃* (adj.)	left
मुड़ना	*muṛnā* (v.i.)	to turn (X *se muṛnā*, to turn at/from X; X *par muṛnā*, to turn on to X)
रास्ता	*rāstā* (m.)	way, road (*rāstā pūchnā*, to ask for directions; *rāstā batānā*, to give directions)
सड़क	*saṛak* (f.)	road
सीधा	*sīdhā*	straight, direct

सीधा हाथ	*sīdhā hāth*	right hand (*sīdhe hāth par*, on the right side)
स्टेशन	*sṭeśan* (m.)	station (*relve sṭeśan*)
हाथ	*hāth* (m.)	hand

Exercise 1 G

Read aloud and translate.

१. पेट्रोल पंप से दाएँ मुड़िए। २. मेडिकल कॉलेज रोड पर बाएँ मुड़िए। ३. एक चौराहा पार कीजिए फिर अगले चौराहे से दाहिनी तरफ़ मुड़िए। ४. एक डाकघर आएगा, उसके ठीक बाद बाएँ मुड़िए। ५. यहाँ से सीधे जाइए। तीन चौराहों के बाद आपकी मंज़िल इसी रोड पर आएगी। ६. सफ़दर जंग रोड पार कीजिए फिर ज़रा और आगे जाने के बाद सिनेमाघर दाएँ हाथ पर आएगा। ७. रेलवे स्टेशन की तरफ़ जाइए। स्टेशन से कुछ आगे जाइए फिर एक बाज़ार आएगा। ८. अगले चौराहे से बाएँ मुड़िए फिर लगभग एक मील सीधे जाइए।

Exercise 2 G

Write the Hindi equivalents of the sentences below. Note that some sentences might require a change in perspective (e.g., *You will come to...* vs. *A...will come*).

1. Go up to that intersection.
2. Then turn left from there.
3. You will come to a traffic signal.
4. You will see a yellow building.
5. You will come to the zoo on the right side.
6. When you see the library, turn right from there.
7. After walking (going) for a little distance, you'll see a restaurant.
8. There will be a movie theater next to it.
9. Go into the restaurant.
10. I will meet you there.

Exercise 3

A. Start at point number 1 marked on the map below and follow the directions to the destination. Identify the destination when you reach it.

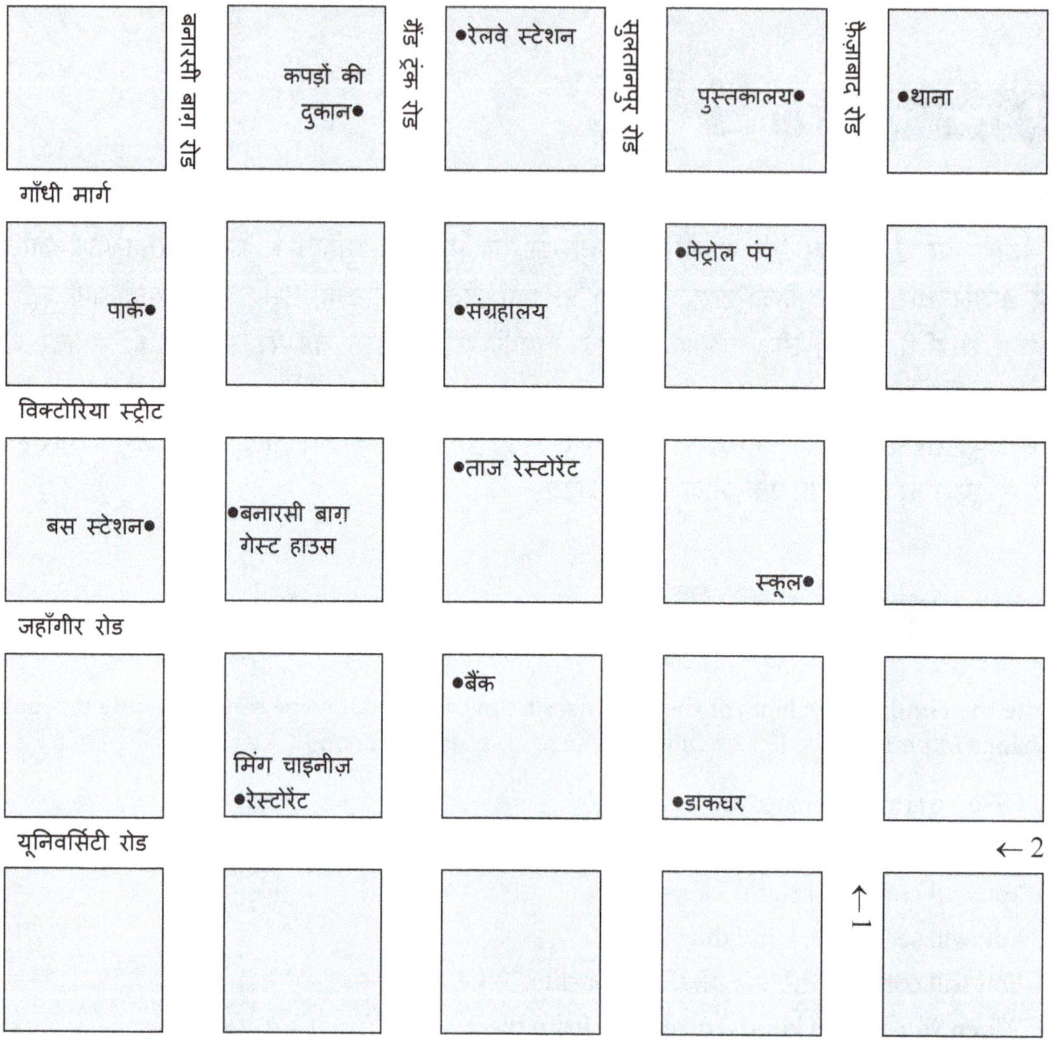

यहाँ से सीधे जाइए। अगले चौराहे पर आपको एक स्कूल दिखाई देगा। वहाँ से बाएँ मुड़िए। फिर उसके तुरंत बाद दाएँ मुड़िए। थोड़ी देर बाद पेट्रोल पंप आएगा। उसके बाद बायीं तरफ़ मुड़िए। फिर ग्रैंड ट्रंक रोड आएगी। उसपर दाएँ मुड़िए। दाएँ मुड़ने के ठीक बाद आपकी मंज़िल वहीं दाहिने हाथ पर होगी।

B. Start at point number 2 marked on the map above and follow the directions given in the audio passage to reach the destination. Identify the destination when you reach it.

> यहाँ से सीधे जाइए, डाकघर की तरफ़। डाकघर वाले चौराहे से दाएँ मुड़िए। जहाँगीर रोड पर फिर बाएँ मुड़िए। उसके बाद अगले ही चौराहे से दाएँ मुड़िए। आपको थोड़ी दूर बाद ताज रेस्टोरेंट दिखाई देगा। ताज रेस्टोरेंट वाले चौराहे से बाएँ मुड़िए, फिर उसके फ़ौरन बाद एक बार फिर बाएँ मुड़िए। आपकी मंज़िल वहीं बायीं तरफ़ होगी।

C. Pair up with a classmate. Mark a starting location on a fresh copy of the map. Trace a route to one of the locations on the map. Your partner will also have a blank map. Mark the starting location and direction on his or her map with an arrow and then give directions to the destination that you have chosen. When finished, switch roles and repeat.

Exercise 4

How do you get from your residence to class? Write the directions that you follow each day (in the tense that would be appropriate for routine actions).

Exercise 5

Pair up with a classmate. Choose a place in your city that your classmate is likely to know about. Give directions to the location from your current location. Your partner will draw a map to the destination and then identify what the destination is.

Aminabad, Lucknow, India

35

Seeking Information for Travel Plans

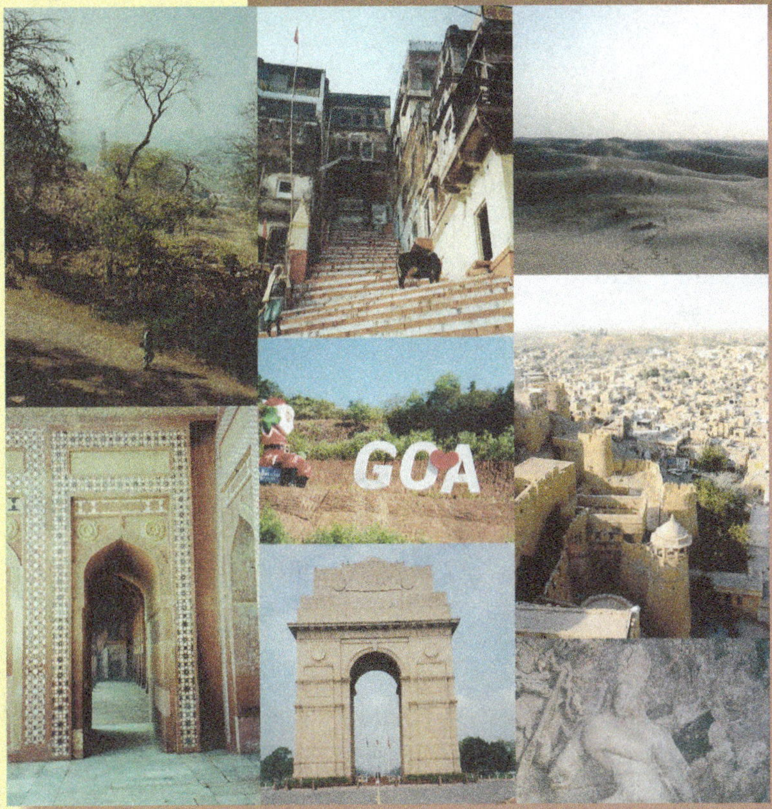

A very essential skill when traveling is seeking information. One structure that commonly occurs in requests for information, and in general when talking about information that one knows, remembers, perceives, etc., is the conjunction *ki*, 'that.'

क्या आपको मालूम है कि दिल्ली में क्या-क्या करने को है?	Do you know what there is to do in Delhi?
क्या आप बता सकते हैं कि इस शहर में क्या-क्या देखना चाहिए?	Can you tell me what one should see in this city?

The Conjunction *ki*

As the sentences above illustrate, there are important differences in usage between *ki* and its English counterpart. Some of the most essential differences are detailed below.

Omission of *ki*: In English, the word 'that' is omitted in many contexts. The word *ki* is less frequently omitted in similar Hindi contexts.

मेरा ख़याल है कि तुम्हें मसूरी ज़रूर जाना चाहिए।	I think (that) you should definitely go to Mussoorie.

Indirect and direct speech: In English, 'that' generally introduces indirect speech, or a paraphrase of the idea being referred to. Hindi *ki* can introduce either indirect speech or *direct speech*. Direct speech is a restatement of the words of a person as they might have been spoken by that person. Generally, the context makes clear whether *ki* introduces direct or indirect speech.

वह सोचता है कि मैं बहुत होशियार हूँ।	He thinks that he is very smart. He thinks: "I am very smart." [OR] He thinks that I am very smart.

Additional differences in the phrasing of the second clause: In English, statements such as 'I don't know...,' 'He doesn't remember...,' and 'Can you tell me...' generally introduce relative clauses such as '...who he is,' '...when they are coming,' '...where the money is.' In Hindi, the information that is known, remembered, perceived, understood, told, etc. is stated in the form of a question rather than as a relative clause.

क्या तुम्हें मालूम है कि वाराणसी में कौन-कौन सी जगहें देखने लायक़ हैं।	Do you know what things are worth seeing in Varanasi?
क्या तुम्हें पता है कि दिल्ली में लोटस टेंपल कहाँ है?	Do you know where in Delhi the Lotus Temple is?
मुझे याद नहीं कि हमारी रवानगी कब है।	I don't remember when our departure is.
उसको याद नहीं कि उसके होटल का नाम क्या है।	She doesn't remember what her hotel's name is.

Tense sequencing: English has tense sequencing rules that determine the tense of the clause introduced by 'that.' For example, if the main clause occurs in the past tense, the clause introduced by 'that' often occurs in the past tense as well. In Hindi, which does not have these types of tense sequencing rules, the clause introduced by *ki* generally occurs in the tense in which the idea was originally told, stated, perceived, etc.

मुझे मालूम नहीं था कि जेन भारत में है।	I didn't know Jane was in India.
उन्हें मालूम था कि मैं भी भारत जा रहा हूँ लेकिन वे मेरे साथ नहीं जाना चाहते थे।	They knew I was going to India too, but they didn't want to go with me.

Vocabulary 1

Geography and General Knowledge

आबादी, जनसंख्या	*ābādī, jansankhyā* (f.)	population
एशिया	*eśiyā*	Asia; *eśiyāī*, Asian
उपमहाद्वीप	*upmahādvīp* (m.)	subcontinent
ओर, जानिब	*or, jānib* (f.)	side
भूगोल	*bhūgol* (m.)	geography
भाग, हिस्सा	*bhāg, hissā* (m.)	part
राजधानी	*rājdhānī* (f.)	capital
दुनिया	*duniyā* (f.)	world
राज्य, प्रदेश, सूबा	*rājy, pradeś, sūbā* (m.)	province
इलाक़ा, क्षेत्र	*ilāqā, kśetr* (m.)	region
स्थित	*sthit*	situated, located
प्रधान मंत्री	*pradhān mantrī*	prime minister

Physical Features

खाड़ी	*khāṛī* (f.)	bay
घाटी, वादी	*ghāṭī, vādī* (f.)	valley
चट्टान	*caṭṭān* (f.)	large rock, boulder
चोटी	*coṭī* (f.)	peak
ज़मीन, धरती	*zamīn, dhartī* (f.)	land; Earth
झरना	*jharnā* (m.)	waterfall
झील	*jhīl* (f.)	lake
टापू, द्वीप	*ṭāpū, dvīp* (m.)	island
टीला	*ṭīlā* (m.)	dune, mound, hillock
तट, किनारा	*taṭ, kinārā* (m.)	bank, shore
दरिया	*dariyā* (m.inv.)	river
देहात	*dehāt* (m.)	countryside
नदी	*nadī* (f.)	river, stream
नहर	*nahar* (f.)	canal, irrigation channel
पर्वत शृंखला	*parvat śrinkhalā* (f.)	mountain chain (*parvat*, m. mountain = *pahāṛ*)
पहाड़	*pahāṛ* (m.)	mountain
पहाड़ी	*pahāṛī* (f.)	hill; adj. mountainous
प्रकृति	*prakriti* (f.)	nature
प्राकृतिक	*prākritik*	natural
मैदान	*maidān* (m.)	plain, field
रेगिस्तान	*registān* (m.)	desert
रेत, बालू	*ret, bālū* (f.)	sand
समुद्र	*samudr* (m.)	ocean; sea

Sunset over the Arabian Sea

Additional Words

V-ने को	V-*ne ko*	to V (e.g., *what is there to do, what is there to see?*)
ज़िंदा	*zindā*	alive
V-ने लायक़, V-ने योग्य	V-*ne lāyaq*, V-*ne yogy*	worth V-ing
शामिल	*śāmil*	included
शायर, कवि	*śāyar, kavi* (m.)	poet
शायरी, कविता	*śāyrī, kavitā* (f.)	poetry

In addition, please review the cardinal directions given in chapter 7.

Notes:

- The suffix *–ī* forms both nouns from adjectives and adjectives from nouns. Some examples of adjectives from nouns are: *paścimī* (fr. *paścim*), *eśiyāī* (fr. *eśiyā*). Some examples of nouns from adjectives are: *ābādī* (fr. *ābād*, 'populated, inhabited.') *śāyrī* (fr. *śāyar*). When the base adjective ends in *–a*, the suffix takes the form *–gī*: *zindagī* (fr. *zindā*), *ravāngī* (fr. *ravānā*).
- The feminine suffix *–tā* forms nouns in Sanskrit loanwords: *kavitā*, 'poetry,' (fr. *kavi*, 'poet'); *sundartā*, 'beauty,' (fr. *sundar*, 'beautiful').

Exercise 1

Read aloud and translate.

१. क्या आपको मालूम है कि ताज महल किस शहर में है? २. नहीं, मुझे मालूम नहीं कि वह कहाँ है| ३. लेकिन मुझे मालूम है कि वह हिंदुस्तान में है| ४. क्या तुम जानते हो कि बनारस दुनिया का सबसे पुराना शहर है और यह भारत में है? ५. कौन बता सकता है कि भारत के उत्तरी भाग में कौन सी पर्वत शृंखला है? ६. क्या आपको पता है कि दुनिया में सबसे ज़्यादा बारिश चेरापूंजी में होती है और यह जगह पूर्वी भारत में है? ७. मुझे याद नहीं कि पाकिस्तान के कितने सूबे हैं| ८. मुझे मालूम नहीं कि मुझे दक्षिण एशिया जाने का मौक़ा कब मिलेगा, लेकिन मैं एक दिन वहाँ ज़रूर जाऊँगा|

Exercise 2

Translate into Hindi.

1. Do you know where in the world people speak Hindi?
2. Can you tell me what the capital of India is?
3. Who knows which countries are to the east of India?
4. Do you know how many rivers there are in the Panjab?
5. Does anyone know what the world's biggest mountain is?
6. Does anybody know where in India Hyderabad is?
7. Does anybody know who the biggest Hindi poets are?
8. I know Ghalib is a great poet, but I don't remember when he lived.
9. Do you know what the word "Panjab" means?
10. Do you know the names of the major rivers of South Asia?

Exercise 3

Read aloud the following questions and find the answers to them. When you are finished, your teacher will repeat the questions aloud; listen to the questions and share your answers if called upon.

१. क्या आपको मालूम है कि पाकिस्तान की राजधानी क्या है?
२. क्या आपको मालूम है कि भारत के कितने राज्य हैं?
३. क्या कोई बता सकता है कि भारत में कितनी भाषाएँ हैं?
४. क्या आप जानते हैं कि भारत के पश्चिमी भाग में कौन सा रेगिस्तान है?
५. क्या आप बता सकते हैं कि पाकिस्तान के पश्चिमी ओर कौन-कौन से देश हैं?
६. क्या कोई बता सकता है कि भारत के दक्षिणी तरफ़ कौन सा समुद्र है?

७. क्या आपको पता है कि दक्षिण एशिया में कौन-कौन से देश शामिल हैं?
८. क्या कोई जानता है कि पाकिस्तान का प्रधान मंत्री कौन है?
९. क्या आपको मालूम है कि हिंदुस्तान और पाकिस्तान की आबादी कितनी है?
१०. क्या कोई जानता है कि हिन्दी के मशहूर कवि कौन-कौन हैं?

Exercise 4

Below is additional vocabulary that will be used in the unit activities. Learn the vocabulary and then translate the sentences that follow.

Vocabulary 2

अनोखा	*anokhā*	unique
अहमियत, महत्त्व	*ahamiyat* (f.), *mahattv*	importance (cf. *aham*, important)
ऐतिहासिक	*aitihāsik*	historical, historic
कला	*kalā* (f.)	art
कहलाना	*kahlānā* (v.i.)	to be called, to cause to be called
केंद्र	*kendr* (m.)	center
के आधार पर	X *ke ādhār par*	on the basis of X (*ādhār*, m. basis)
के द्वारा	*ke dvārā*	by, by means of
के माध्यम से, के ज़रिए	*ke mādhyam se, ke zarie*	by means of
चिकन	*cikan*	a style of fine embroidery
जानकारी, मालूमात	*jānkārī* (f.), *mālūmāt* (m.pl.)	information
जुड़ना	*juṛnā* (v.i.)	to be linked to, to connect (be connected) to
जुड़ा हुआ	*juṛā huā*	connected, linked

ज़ेवर	*zevar* (m.)	piece of jewelry (*zevarāt*, jewelry)
झील	*jhīl* (f.)	lake
तारीफ़	*tārīf* (f.)	praise (X *kī tārīf karnā*, to praise X)
दुनिया भर	*duniyā-bhar*	throughout the world
पर्यटन स्थल	*paryaṭan-sthal* (m.)	tourist destination
प्राकृतिक	*prākritik*	natural
बेहद	*behad*	without limit (*had*, f. limit)
मशहूर, प्रसिद्ध	*maśhūr, prasiddh*	famous
महल	*mahal* (m.)	palace
माध्यम, ज़रिया	*mādhyam, zariyā* (m.)	a means
मुग़लई	*mughlaī*	a style of South Asian food
राजपूती	*rājpūtī*	relating to Rajputs
लोकप्रिय	*lokpriy*	popular
संस्कृति	*sanskriti* (f.)	culture
सभ्यता, तहज़ीब	*sabhytā, tahzīb* (f.)	civilization, refinement, culture
सांस्कृतिक	*sānskritik*	cultural
साहित्य	*sāhity* (m.)	literature
साहित्यिक	*sāhityik*	literary
स्वतंत्रता, आज़ादी	*svatantrtā, āzādī* (f.)	freedom, independence
स्वादिष्ट, लज़ीज़	*svādiṣṭ, lazīz*	delicious
हवेली, कोठी	*havelī* (m.), *koṭhī* (f.)	mansion

हाकिम	*hākim* (m.)	ruler

Note:

- *juṛā huā:* the form V-*ā huā* is the perfective participle. It corresponds to the English form 'V-ed' or 'V-en.' For example, *thakā huā*, 'tired' (from *thaknā*, 'to tire'), *marā huā*, 'dead' (from *marnā*, 'to die'), *bacā huā*, 'left(over)' (from *bacnā*, 'to be saved, to be left over'). Both portions of this form inflect as variable adjectives: *thakā huā, thake hue, thakī huī; marā huā, mare hue, marī huī*; etc.

Now translate these sentences using the vocabulary you just learned.

१. क्या आपको मालूम है कि लखनऊ को उर्दू का साहित्यिक और सांस्कृतिक केंद्र क्यों कहते हैं? २. क्या आप बता सकते हैं कि इस शहर में क्या देखने लायक़ है? ३. यहाँ के खंडहर पश्चिमी पर्यटकों के बीच काफ़ी लोकप्रिय हैं| ४. यहाँ की ऐतिहासिक इमारतें, क़िले, और हवेलियाँ भी देखने लायक़ हैं| ५. क्या आपको मालूम है कि इस मुहल्ले की इमारतें कितनी पुरानी हैं? यहाँ की इमारतें स्वतंत्रता से पहले की हैं| उस ज़माने में अंग्रेज़ भारत के हाकिम थे| ७. आपके ख़्याल में भारत में सफ़र करने का सब से आसान तरीक़ा क्या है? ८. भारत के सब शहर एक दूसरे से रेल के माध्यम से जुड़े हुए हैं, इसलिए रेल से सफ़र करना सब से आसान है| ९. क्या कोई बता सकता है कि भारत की आबादी कितनी है? १०. क्या आपको मालूम है कि श्री लंका के रहनेवाले क्या कहलाते हैं? श्री लंका के रहनेवाले सिंहली कहलाते हैं| ११. अगर तुम लखनऊ जाओ तो तुम्हें टुंडे कबाब ज़रूर खाना चाहिए| लोग उस कबाब की बेहद तारीफ़ करते हैं| १२. आपके ख़याल में एक अच्छा चिकन की कढ़ाई वाला कुर्ता ख़रीदने के लिए मुझे कहाँ जाना चाहिए? १३. आपको मालूम होगा कि दक्षिण एशिया की संस्कृति में परिवार और शादी की बेहद अहमियत है| १४. इस पूरी जानकारी के लिए धन्यवाद| अब इसके आधार पर यह फ़ैसला करना आसान होगा कि मैं कहाँ जाऊँ और क्या देखूँ|

Exercise 5

Read the following sentences describing Delhi. When you are finished, write five sentences in Hindi about one of the South Asian cities listed below and share them with your class.

दिल्ली भारत की राजधानी है| उसे भारत का दिल भी कहते हैं| दिल्ली उत्तर भारत में स्थित है| दिल्ली में बहुत सी शानदार इमारतें देखने लायक़ हैं| पुरानी दिल्ली में बहुत अच्छा मुग़लई खाना मिलता है|

मुंबई लखनऊ वाराणसी अमृतसर जयपुर कोलकाता बंगलुरु लाहौर

36

Unit 7 Review Activities

The goal of this chapter is to review the content of unit 7 and provide additional opportunities to synthesize all of the content presented up to this point.

1. Grammar Review

- Which English verb forms does the Hindi future verb tense most often correspond to?
- How is the future verb tense formed? Conjugate any verb in its entirety in the future.
- How can possible future actions be expressed? Give some examples.
- How do you say how long it will take or how much it will cost to get somewhere? Give two Hindi examples.

2. Tips for Increasing Fluency: Speaking Drills

These drills are designed to promote both accuracy and fluency. When going through them, it is a good idea to write key words on a piece of paper prior to starting so that you can run through all of the sentences rapidly without pausing. When carrying out the exercises, focus first on accuracy, then as you repeat the activities and they become more automatic, focus on speed. The aim is to be able to speak about everyday life in an accurate and automatic manner.

A. Future

- Make a list of 8–10 activities that people typically perform on a daily basis. Create questions asking, "Are you going to...today," and "When will you next...?"
- Narrate what you are going to do for the rest of the day.
- Narrate what you are going to do this weekend.

B. Expressing Inclinations

- Make a list of 8–10 activities that you feel like doing. Make sentences of the type, "I feel like..."

C. Subjunctive

- State eight things that you might do this week but aren't completely sure about.
- State eight things that you want others to do.

D. *vaqt/paisā lagnā*

- Make a list of ten cities, some in your geographic region and others across the country. State how long it takes to get to each from your current city by different modes of transportation.
- Make sentences describing how much (approximately) it costs/will cost to get to these cities.

3. Personalization Questions

Pair up with a partner. Take turns asking and answering the following questions. Answer in complete sentences.

१. आप आज शाम को क्या-क्या करेंगे / करेंगी?
२. आप अगले सप्ताहांत क्या-क्या करेंगे / करेंगी?
३. आप अगली ख़रीदारी के दौरान क्या-क्या ख़रीदेंगे / ख़रीदेंगी?
४. आप अगली लम्बी छुट्टियों के दौरान कहाँ-कहाँ जाएँगे / जाएँगी?
५. अगले साल कॉलेज में आप कौन-कौन से विषय पढ़ेंगे / पढ़ेंगी?
६. आप पढ़ाई ख़त्म करने के बाद क्या काम करेंगे / करेंगी?
७. अगर आप भारत जाएँ तो वहाँ क्या-क्या देखेंगे / देखेंगी?
८. अगर आप नेपाल जाएँ तो वहाँ क्या-क्या देखेंगे / देखेंगी?

4. Booking a Train Ticket: Listen to the dialogue and then answer the questions.

पहुँचाना	*pahũcānā* (v.t.)	to deliver (e.g. a person to his/her destination)
मेहरबानी	*meharbānī* (f.)	kindness, act of kindness (*baṛī meharbānī hogī*, it will be a big act of kindness, I would appreciate it)

मुसाफ़िर	मुझे दिल्ली के लिए दो टिकट चाहिएँ।
क्लर्क	आपको टिकट कहाँ से चाहिएँ?
मुसाफ़िर	मुझे लखनऊ से चाहिएँ।
क्लर्क	टिकट कब के लिए और कौन सी ट्रेन के लिए चाहिएँ?
मुसाफ़िर	जी, मैं कल ही दिल्ली जाना चाहता हूँ। क्या कल दोपहर के लिए कोई ट्रेन मिलेगी?
क्लर्क	कल शताब्दी एक्सप्रेस में सिर्फ़ एक सीट मिल सकती है।
मुसाफ़िर	नहीं, मुझे तो दो चाहिएँ। क्या कोई और ट्रेन है?

क्लर्क	या तो परसों के लिए शताब्दी के दो टिकट ले लीजिए या मैं देखता हूँ कि कल रात वाली गाड़ी में कोई जगह है या नहीं।
मुसाफ़िर	जी, शुक्रिया। ज़रा देख दीजिए, बड़ी मेहरबानी होगी।
क्लर्क	रात को दस बजे लखनऊ मेल लखनऊ से दिल्ली के लिए छूटती है। वह आपको दूसरे दिन सुबह सात बजे दिल्ली पहुँचा देगी। उसमें कल के लिए दो सीटें मिल जाएँगी।
मुसाफ़िर	ठीक है, किराया कितना होगा?
क्लर्क	आपको ए-सी वाले डिब्बे में सीटें चाहिएँ या बिना ए-सी वाले में?
मुसाफ़िर	जी, मुझे ए-सी वाले में चाहिएँ। उसका किराया कितना होगा?
क्लर्क	एक आदमी का किराया १२०० रुपये है।
मुसाफ़िर	ठीक है, यह लीजिए २४०० रुपये।
क्लर्क	जी, पहले फ़ॉर्म भर दीजिए। फिर उसके साथ रुपये जमा कीजिए।
	...
मुसाफ़िर	जी, यह लीजिए फ़ॉर्म और २४०० रुपये।
क्लर्क	जी, ठीक है। यह लीजिए, ये आप के टिकट।
मुसाफ़िर	जी, थैंकयू।

सवाल

१. मुसाफ़िर को टिकट कहाँ से कहाँ के लिए चाहिएँ?
२. मुसाफ़िर शताब्दी एक्सप्रेस से क्यों नहीं जा सकता?
३. लखनऊ मेल लखनऊ से कितने बजे छूटती है?
४. मुसाफ़िर को कौन से डिब्बे में सीटें चाहिएँ और उनका किराया कितना है?

5. Guided Conversation: Buying a Bus Ticket

Student 1: You are a traveler in India and need to buy a bus ticket. Go through the following steps to buy the ticket.

- Say that you need to go to Chandigarh (चंडीगढ़).
- Ask how many buses there are today.
- Find out when each of the buses leaves. Note the times.
- Ask questions (one question per bus) to determine when each of the buses arrives.
- Ask questions (one question per bus) to determine whether each bus has air conditioning or not.
- Ask questions to determine the fare for each bus.
- Choose the air conditioned bus that arrives closest to 8:00 pm and buy three tickets.

You can fill out the following table with the information that you find.

Destination	Departure	Arrival	Fare	A/C
Chandigarh				
Chandigarh				
Chandigarh				
Chandigarh				

Student 2: You are a clerk in a bus station. Answer your customer's questions in complete sentences and help him or her to buy a ticket.

Bus No.	Destination	Departure	Arrival	Fare	A/C
305	Chandigarh	5:05 am	11:00 am	400	yes
290	Chandigarh	6:55 am	1:00 pm	225	no
165	Chandigarh	12:30 pm	6:00 pm	250	no
208	Chandigarh	2:45 pm	9:00 pm	450	yes

Switch roles and repeat.

Student 1: You are a traveler in India and need to buy a bus ticket. Go through the following steps to buy the ticket.

- Say that you need to go to Jaipur (जयपुर).
- Ask how many buses there are today.
- Find out when each of the buses leaves. Note the times.
- Ask questions (one question per bus) to determine when each of the buses arrives.
- Ask questions (one question per bus) to determine whether each bus has air conditioning or not.
- Ask questions to determine the fare for each bus.
- Choose the air conditioned bus with the shortest travel time and buy one ticket.

You can fill out the following chart with the information that you find.

Destination	Departure	Arrival	Fare	A/C
Jaipur				
Jaipur				
Jaipur				
Jaipur				

Student 2: You are a clerk in a bus station. Answer your customer's questions in complete sentences and help him or her to buy a ticket.

Bus No.	Destination	Departure	Arrival	Fare	A/C
315	Jaipur	5:00 am	4:30 pm	410	no
465	Jaipur	7:00 am	6:15 pm	390	no
609	Jaipur	12:00 pm	7:30 pm	755	yes
512	Jaipur	3:00 pm	11:30 pm	685	yes

6. Role Play: Buying a Train Ticket

Student 1: You are traveling in South Asia and need to buy a train ticket. You are standing at the ticket window in the Lucknow train station and need two tickets to New Delhi. You need to arrive by 8:00 tonight. Find out how many trains there are, when they leave, and when they arrive. You don't need tickets for the air-conditioned compartment, but if the price is not much more than non-air conditioned, you can buy them. Find out the necessary information and then purchase a ticket.

Student 2: You are a clerk at the railway station ticket counter. Here is the information about today's trains:

First class has air conditioning; second class does not. Fares that are crossed out represent seats that are not available.

Train No.	Destination	Departure	Arrival	Fare	
				First class	Second class
104	Varanasi	5:00 pm	11:00 pm	830	420
135	Varanasi	10:00 pm	tomorrow 6:00 am	830	420
450	Kolkata	6:00 am	tomorrow 3:00 am	2020	610
440	Kolkata	11:30 am	tomorrow 8:30 am	~~2020~~	610
485	Kolkata	3:45 pm	tomorrow 2:00 pm	~~2020~~	~~610~~
790	New Delhi	8:00 am	2:00 pm	1205	450
712	New Delhi	12:00 pm	6:45 pm	~~1205~~	450
730	New Delhi	2:30 pm	8:15 pm	1205	450
245	Mumbai	6:15 am	tomorrow 4:45 am	2125	875

Switch roles and repeat.

Student 1: You are traveling in South Asia and need to buy train tickets. You are standing at the ticket window in the Lucknow train station and need three tickets to Kolkata (*kolkātā*). You need to arrive by tomorrow at 2:00 pm. Find out how many trains there are, when they leave, and when they arrive. You need tickets for the air-conditioned compartment. Find out the necessary information and then purchase the three tickets.

Student 2: You are a clerk at the railway station ticket counter. Use the information given in the table above to help your customer purchase the ticket that she or he needs.

7. **Booking a Hotel Room:** Listen to the dialogue and then answer the questions.

होटल कर्मचारी	हलो ताज प्लाज़ा होटल। मैं आप की क्या सेवा कर सकता हूँ?
बाबर	जी, मझे आपके होटल में एक कमरा चाहिए। क्या आपके यहाँ कोई कमरा ख़ाली है?
होटल कर्मचारी	आपको कमरा कब चाहिए और कितने दिनों के लिए?
बाबर	जी, मुझे चार जुलाई को दो दिनों के लिए कमरा चाहिए।
होटल कर्मचारी	ठीक है। आपको सिंगल बेड वाला कमरा चाहिए या डबल बेड वाला?
बाबर	मुझे डबल बेड वाला चाहिए। उसका किराया कितना होगा?
होटल कर्मचारी	जी, ए-सी वाले डबल बेड कमरे का किराया एक दिन का २००० रुपये होगा।
बाबर	क्या आपके होटल में बिना ए-सी वाले कमरे भी हैं?
होटल कर्मचारी	जी हाँ, बिना ए-सी वाले कमरे भी हैं। उनमें कूलर लगे हैं।
बाबर	अच्छा तो बिना ए-सी वाले कमरे का किराया कितना है?
होटल कर्मचारी	जी, बिना ए-सी वाले कमरों का एक दिन का किराया १२०० रुपये है।
बाबर	अच्छा तो एक बिना ए-सी वाला कमरा दो दिन के लिए बुक कर दीजिए।
होटल कर्मचारी	जी, ज़रूर। कमरा किसके नाम पर बुक होगा?
बाबर	मेरा नाम लिख लीजिए। बाबर अहमद।
होटल कर्मचारी	ठीक है तो आप कितने बजे चेक इन कीजिएगा*?
बाबर	११ और १२ बजे के बीच।
होटल कर्मचारी	असल में हमारे यहाँ चेक आउट टाइम साढ़े बारह बजे है।
बाबर	ठीक है, तो हम साढ़े बारह बजे आएँगे।

होटल कर्मचारी	जी, ठीक है। मैं आपके नाम एक बिना ए-सी वाला डबल बेड कमरा चार जुलाई के लिए बुक कर दूँ?
बाबर	जी, हाँ, बुक कर दीजिए।
होटल कर्मचारी	एक ज़रूरी बात। जब आप आएँ तो अपना पासपोर्ट या कोई और पहचान पत्र ज़रूर साथ लेते आइएगा।
बाबर	ठीक है, बाय।

*"What time would you like to check in?"

सवाल

१. बाबर को कमरा कब और कितने दिनों के लिए चाहिए?

२. ए-सी वाले कमरे का किराया कितना है और बिना ए-सी वाले कमरे का किराया कितना है?

३. बाबर कब चेक इन करना चाहता है?

४. वह कब चेक इन करेगा?

8. Role Play

A. Student 1: You need to book a room in a guest house. You need a double-bed room. You need the room for two people. You would like a room with air conditioning. Find out what other amenities the room has. Book a room for tonight. You only need the room for one night.

Student 2: You are the clerk in the guest house. Help your customer book a room. All rooms have a phone, TV, fan, and hot water. The rates are as follows:

single bed w/ A/C	700 rupees	available
single bed w/o A/C	600 rupees	available
double bed w/ A/C	1000 rupees	unavailable
double bed w/o A/C	900 rupees	available

Switch roles and repeat.

B. Student 1: You need to book a room in a guest house for next Monday. You will be staying for three nights. You are the only guest. It is the winter so air conditioning is not necessary. Find out what other amenities the room has and then book the room.

Student 2: You are the clerk in the guest house. Help your customer book a room. All rooms have a phone, TV, fan, and hot water. There is an internet café in the lobby and a rooftop restaurant. The rates are as follows:

single bed w/ A/C	800 rupees	available
single bed w/o A/C	600 rupees	unavailable
double bed w/ A/C	1000 rupees	unavailable
double bed w/o A/C	700 rupees	available

9. The following passage is an excerpt from a travel brochure about Udaipur, India. Translate the questions first, then read the passage. When finished, answer the questions in complete Hindi sentences.

कला	*kalā* (f.)	art
के द्वारा	*ke dvārā*	by, by means of
झील	*jhīl* (f.)	lake
पर्यटन स्थल	*paryaṭan-sthal* (m.)	tourist destination
प्राकृतिक	*prākritik*	natural
मशहूर	*maśhūr*	famous
महल	*mahal* (m.)	palace
राजपूती	*rājpūtī*	relating to Rajputs

1. Where is Udaipur situated in India?
2. What is its importance in India?
3. What kinds of places can one see in Udaipur?
4. What buildings are worth seeing in Udaipur?
5. What do the people of Udaipur like that has made Udaipur famous?

उदयपुर भारत के सबसे सुंदर शहरों में से एक है| यह एक लोकप्रिय पर्यटन स्थल है| यह भारत के एक पश्चिमी राज्य राजस्थान में स्थित है| उदयपुर में कई झीलें हैं और इस वजह से इसे 'झीलों का शहर' भी कहते हैं|

उदयपुर राजपूती कला और संस्कृति का एक केंद्र भी है| यहाँ की इमारतें देखने लायक़ हैं| दूर-दूर से लोग यहाँ के महल, हवेलियाँ, और मंदिर देखने आते हैं| आजकल ज़्यादातर महलों में शानदार होटल हैं| उदयपुर में एक चिड़ियाघर और कई अजायबघर भी हैं| उनमें एक भारतीय लोककला का संग्रहालय भी है| उदयपुर में कई सुंदर बाग़ हैं जिन में 'सहेलियों की बाड़ी' काफ़ी मशहूर है| यहाँ की सुंदर इमारतों और प्राकृतिक सुंदरता के कारण लोग फ़िल्मों की शूटिंग के लिए भी आते हैं| उदयपुर हवाई जहाज़, रेल, और सड़क के द्वारा भारत के सभी बड़े शहरों से जुड़ा हुआ है|

Udaipur, India

10. Review the vocabulary and listen to the dialogue about Lucknow, India, then answer the questions.

आधार	*ādhār* (m.)	basis
कढ़ाई	*kaṛhāī* (f.)	embroidery
कहलाना	*kahlānā* (v.i.)	to be called, to be known as
कुंदन	*kundan*	a type of glasswork used in jewelry
खंडहर	*khanḍhar* (m.)	(archeological) ruins
ख़ासियत	*xāsiyat* (f.)	specialty, special quality

ज़माना	*zamānā* (m.)	era
जानकारी	*jānkārī* (f.)	knowledge of a thing
ज़ेवरात	*zevrāt* (m.)	jewelry
तहज़ीब	*tahzīb* (f.)	(high) culture, refinement
तारीफ़	*tārīf* (f.)	praise (X *kī tārīf karnā*, to praise X)
निभाना	*nibhānā* (v.t.)	to carry out (a role)
पुकारना	*pukārnā* (v.t.)	to call (e.g. to call something by the name of…)
भूमिका	*bhūmikā* (f.)	role
मक़बरा	*maqbarā* (m.)	tomb, mausoleum
मेल	*mel* (m.)	coming together, meeting, mixture
राजधानी	*rājdhānī* (f.)	capital
लोकप्रिय	*lokpriy*	popular
लोकप्रियता	*lokpriytā* (f.)	popularity
संस्कृति	*sanskriti* (f.)	culture
साहित्यिक	*sāhityik*	literary (*sāhity*, m. literature)
सांस्कृतिक	*sānskritik*	cultural
स्थित	*sthit*	located
स्वादिष्ट, लज़ीज़	*svādiṣṭ, lazīz*	delicious
हाकिम	*hākim* (m.)	ruler

सारा मैं इस साल के आख़िर में हिंदुस्तान जा रही हूँ। मैं लखनऊ भी जाना चाहती हूँ। आप लखनऊ से हैं तो लखनऊ के बारे में कुछ बताइए।

फ़ौज़िया अच्छा, कहाँ से शुरू करूँ? लखनऊ एक बेहद दिलचस्प शहर है। यह हिंदुस्तान के सबसे ज़्यादा आबादी वाले राज्य उत्तर प्रदेश की राजधानी है। लखनऊ को लोग अवध या नवाबों का शहर भी कहते हैं।

सारा उसे नवाबों का शहर क्यों कहते हैं?

फ़ौज़िया लखनऊ के हाकिम नवाब कहलाते थे। उन नवाबों ने लखनऊ को एक साहित्यिक और सांस्कृतिक केंद्र बनाने में बड़ी भूमिका निभाई, इसलिए इसे नवाबों का शहर कहते हैं।

सारा	लोग लखनऊ की तहज़ीब की बहुत तारीफ़ करते हैं। कुछ वहाँ की तहज़ीब के बारे में बताइए।
फ़ौज़िया	लखनऊ की तहज़ीब गंगा-जमुनी तहज़ीब कहलाती है। यहाँ की संस्कृति में हिन्दुस्तानी और ईरानी संस्कृतियों का अनोखा मेल देख सकते हैं।
सारा	लखनऊ की क्या-क्या चीज़ें मशहूर हैं।
फ़ौज़िया	लखनऊ अपनी तहज़ीब और उर्दू ज़बान के लिए सब से ज़्यादा मशहूर है। मगर इसकी लोकप्रियता में यहाँ की शायरी, संगीत, और खानों का भी बहुत महत्त्व है।
सारा	मुझे स्वादिष्ट खानों का बहुत शौक़ है। लखनऊ के खानों में कौन-कौन से खाने सबसे ज़्यादा लोकप्रिय हैं?
फ़ौज़िया	लखनऊ में कई तरह के क़ोरमे, बिरयानी, कबाब, और रोटियाँ ख़ास हैं। जब आप लखनऊ जाएँ तो वहाँ टुंडे कबाब ज़रूर खाएँ।
सारा	और वहाँ कौन-कौन सी इमारतें देखने लायक़ हैं?
फ़ौज़िया	बड़ा इमामबाड़ा, छोटा इमामबाड़ा, शाह नजफ़ इमामबाड़ा, रूमी दरवाज़ा, बारादरी, और सआदत अली ख़ान का मक़बरा देखने लायक़ हैं। अगर आप के पास वक़्त हो तो लखनऊ यूनिवर्सिटी की इमारतें भी देखिएगा। और हाँ, अंग्रेज़ों के ज़माने में लखनऊ में ब्रिटिश रेज़ीडेंसी भी थी। आप रेज़ीडेंसी के खंडहर भी देख सकती हैं।
सारा	मुझे ख़रीदारी करना बहुत पसंद है। मैं लखनऊ से अपने दोस्तों के लिए क्या तोहफ़े ख़रीद सकती हूँ?
फ़ौज़िया	आप लखनऊ से चिकन की कढ़ाई के कुर्ते और कुंदन के ज़ेवरात ख़रीद सकती हैं। वहाँ अच्छे नागरे जूते भी मिलते हैं।
सारा	जी, बहुत बहुत शुक्रिया। मैं लखनऊ ज़रूर जाऊँगी और मुझे यक़ीन है कि इन जानकारियों के आधार पर मेरा सफ़र बहुत आसान होगा।
फ़ौज़िया	शुक्रिया की कोई बात नहीं। मुझे ख़ुशी होगी अगर आप मेरा शहर देखें।

सवाल

१. लखनऊ भारत के किस राज्य में स्थित है और लोग उसे किन दूसरे नामों से पुकारते हैं?

२. लखनऊ की तहज़ीब की क्या ख़ासियत है?

३. लखनऊ किन चीज़ों के लिए मशहूर है?

४. लखनऊ की कौन-कौन सी इमारतें देखने लायक़ हैं?

५. हम लखनऊ से तोहफ़े के तौर पर क्या ख़रीद सकते हैं?

Bara Imambara, Lucknow, India

11. Project (Two Parts):

a. Choose a location from the following list of places in South Asia or choose another place in South Asia if there is a particular place that you are interested in researching that is not on the list.

Delhi	Agra/Fatehpur Sikri	Mumbai
Jaipur/Rajasthan	Varanasi	Panjab
Kolkata	Kashmir	Darjeeling
Mohenjo Daro/Harappa	Karachi	Himachal Pradesh
Uttaranchal	Kathmandu	Goa
Hyderabad	Kerala	Tamil Nadu

Prepare a presentation in Hindi on the place you selected. What is it famous for? What is there to see, do, and eat there? Where is it located and what other interesting cities are nearby? What is the best way to reach your location? Deliver your presentation to your class. While others are presenting, note the essential information that they mention.

b. Based on the information that you collected from your classmates' reports, work with a partner to create a three week itinerary for a trip to South Asia. Where will you go? How will you get there? How long will you stay in each place? What will you see and do? Once you have decided on an itinerary, write separate reports on your entire itinerary.

Jodhpur, India

Sayings and Proverbs

पढ़ोगे लिखोगे बनोगे नवाब, खेलोगे कूदोगे होगे ख़राब

न रहेगा बाँस, न बजेगी बाँसुरी

बकरे की माँ कब तक ख़ैर मनाएगी

मियाँ बीवी राज़ी तो क्या करेगा क़ाज़ी

रानी रूठेंगी अपना सुहाग लेंगी

नाई नाई कितने बाल? ए जजमान आगे आएँगे

Unit 8 Past Events and Experiences

In this unit you will learn the following skills:

- Describing past events.
- Giving background information to past narratives.
- Describing professional experience, life experiences, and accomplishments.
- Seeing a doctor, describing symptoms and ailments.
- Reading and listening to simple news items.

In addition, you will learn how to give detailed and extended narrations of your past experiences.

37

My Weekend

In this chapter you will learn how to narrate simple sequences of past events. The focus will be on describing things that you did during recent periods of free time, such as after school or work, or on a recent weekend or vacation.

Here are some examples of things you will be able to say after completing this chapter:

कल मैं साढ़े आठ बजे उठा|	Yesterday I got up at 8:30.
उसके बाद मैंने कॉफ़ी पी और नाश्ता किया|	After that, I had coffee and breakfast.
फिर मैं ४५ मिनट पार्क में दौड़ा|	Then I ran in the park for 45 minutes.

The Perfective Verb Tense

The verb form used in the examples above is the perfective verb tense. As the examples show, the closest English equivalent is the simple past tense. The perfective should not be confused with the past habitual, which also corresponds to the English simple past in some contexts. Unlike the perfective, the past habitual depicts events as general circumstances over an extended period of time in the past. Please review chapter 23 for additional information on the distinction between the past habitual and the perfective.

Formation: The perfective is formed by adding the endings *–ā* (masc, sg.), *-e* (masc. pl.), *-ī* (fem. sg.), and *-ī̃* (fem. pl.) directly to the verb stem. The endings are identical to the variable adjective endings with the exception of the feminine plural ending, which is nasalized.

Here is a sample conjugation with the verb *uṭhnā* 'to rise, get up.' All of the forms mean 'rose,' or 'got up.'

	singular	plural
masculine	उठा *uṭhā*	उठे *uṭhe*
feminine	उठी *uṭhī*	उठीं *uṭhī̃*

Here are some additional examples of the perfective in use:

मैं ७ बजे उठा|	I (m.) got up at 7:00.
मैं ८ बजे उठी|	I (f.) got up at 8:00.
आप कितने बजे उठे?	When did you (m.pl.) get up?
तुम कितने बजे उठीं?	When did you (f.pl.) get up?
पापा देर से उठे|	Papa got up late.

सारा आज जल्दी उठी।	Sarah got up early today.
सब लोग यहाँ कितने बजे पहुँचे?	What time did everybody get here?
उसकी ट्रेन कल रात ९ बजे पहुँची।	His train arrived at 9:00 last night.

Peculiarities in the Formation of the Perfective

Irregular verbs *honā, jānā, karnā, lenā,* and *denā*: The verbs, *honā*, 'to be,' *jānā*, 'to go,' *karnā*, 'to do,' *lenā*, 'to take,' and *denā*, 'to give' have irregular conjugations in the perfective.

The Verb *honā* in the Perfective

होना	singular	plural
masculine	हुआ *huā*	हुए *hue*
feminine	हुई *huī*	हुईं *huī̃*

The Verb *jānā* in the Perfective

जाना	singular	plural
masculine	गया *gayā*	गए *gae*
feminine	गई *gaī*	गईं *gaī̃*

The Verb *karnā* in the Perfective

करना	singular	plural
masculine	किया *kiyā*	किए *kie*
feminine	की *kī*	कीं *kī̃*

The Verb *denā* in the Perfective

देना	singular	plural
masculine	दिया *diyā*	दिए *die*
feminine	दी *dī*	दीं *dī̃*

The Verb *lenā* in the Perfective

लेना	singular	plural
masculine	लिया *liyā*	लिए *lie*
feminine	ली *lī*	लीं *lī̃*

Note that the masculine plural forms गये, किये, दिये, and लिये are also possible as are the feminine forms गयी and गयीं.

Additional points: Note also the following peculiarities.

Verbs with stems ending in long –आ (e.g., आना, 'to come,):

य is inserted in the masculine singular form and is optionally inserted in the other forms. While य may optionally be written in the other forms, it is not pronounced.

आया, आए (or आये), आई (or आयी), आईं (or आयीं)

Stems ending in –ओ (e.g., सोना, 'to sleep'):

य is inserted in the masculine singular form obligatorily and is optionally inserted in the other forms, though य is uncommon in forms other than the masculine singular. While य may occasionally be found written in these other forms, it is never pronounced.

सोया, सोए, सोई, सोईं (the following forms are also possible but less common: सोये, सोयी, सोयीं)

Stems ending in long –ई (e.g., पीना, 'to drink'):

The long ई is shortened in the masculine forms; य is inserted obligatorily in the masculine singular and optionally in the masculine plural form. The ई belonging to the stem is deleted in both feminine forms.

पिया, पिए (or पिये), पी, पीं

Stems ending in long –ऊ (e.g., छूना, 'to touch'):

The ऊ is shortened to उ before the endings are added.

छुआ, छुए, छुई, छुईं

Vocabulary 1

जन्म	*janm* (m.)	birth
ठीक होना	*ṭhīk honā*	to get better
निकलना	*nikalnā* (v.i.)	to exit, to emerge from (*se*)
परवरिश	*parvariś* (f.)	upbringing
पलना	*palnā* (v.i.)	to be raised/reared
पलना-बढ़ना	*palnā-baṛhnā* (v.i.)	to grow up, to be raised
पैदा होना	*paidā* (inv.) *honā*	to be born
बड़ा होना	*baṛā honā*	to grow up
बढ़ना	*baṛhnā* (v.i.)	to increase, to grow
बीमार	*bīmār*	sick, ill
लेटना	*leṭnā* (v.i.)	to lie down

Note:

- The verb *leṭnā* is similar to *baiṭhnā* when used with the present continuous verb tense. *vo leṭ rahā hai,* with the the present continuous, means 'He is (in the process of) lying down.' *vo leṭā* (*huā*) *hai,* means 'He is (in the state of) lying down.'

Exercise 1

Read aloud and translate.

१. आज सुबह मैं सात बजे उठा| २. तुम कितने बजे उठीं? ३. मैं पाँच बजे उठी| मुझे कुछ पढ़ाई करनी थी इसलिए मुझे जल्दी उठना पड़ा| ४. तुम घर से कितने बजे निकलीं? ५. मैं आठ बजे निकली और यहाँ नौ बजे पहुँची| ६. सड़क पर गाड़ियों की बहुत भीड़ थी, इसलिए यहाँ आने में थोड़ी देर लगी| ७. आप अपने घर वालों से पिछली बार कब मिले? ८. हम पिछली बार दो महीने

पहले मिले जब मैं लम्बी छुट्टियों के लिए घर गया| ९. आप यहाँ आने से पहले कहाँ रहती थीं और यहाँ कब आईं? १०. यहाँ आने से पहले मैं हैदराबाद में रहती थी| मैं लगभग दो साल पहले यहाँ आई| ११. मैं भारत में पैदा हुआ| मेरा परिवार यहाँ आया जब मैं छोटी थी| १२. आप कहाँ और किस साल पैदा हुए? १३. मैं १९९१ में दिल्ली में पैदा हुआ| १४. आप कहाँ पली-बढ़ीं? १५. मेरी परवरिश यहाँ अमरीका में हुई| १६. क्या आप शादीशुदा हैं? आपकी शादी कब हुई? १७. मेरी शादी २००५ में हुई|

Exercise 2

Translate into Hindi.

1. I got up early this morning.
2. It rained yesterday.
3. What happened? Why are you crying?
4. Why didn't you bathe this morning?
5. When did Sarah and Priya come?
6. Where did Javed and Abhay go?
7. What time did you go to sleep last night?
8. Yesterday afternoon I met my friend to drink coffee.
9. Then we walked for a little while in the park.
10. After that I went back home and lay down on the couch.

Exercise 3

Personalization Questions

१. आज सुबह आप कितने बजे उठे / उठीं?
२. आज सुबह आप घर से कितने बजे निकले / निकलीं?
३. आप यहाँ क्लास में कितने बजे पहुँचे / पहुँचीं?
४. आप कल रात कितने बजे सोए / सोईं? क्या आप हमेशा इतने बजे सोते हैं / सोती हैं?
५. आप अपने घर वालों से पिछली बार कब मिले / मिलीं?
६. आप कहाँ पैदा हुए / हुईं?
७. आप कहाँ पले-बढ़े / पली-बढ़ीं?

Transitive and Intransitive Verbs

The distinction between transitive and intransitive verbs is essential to understand in Hindi, as transitive verbs require a special construction in the perfective and related verb tenses. Transitive verbs are those that are capable of taking a direct object. Intransitive verbs, on the other hand, are those that are incapable of taking a direct object.

Transitive verbs describe actions in which the subject acts upon some external object, whereas intransitive verbs describe the subject existing in a state or undergoing an action. For example, 'to raise' is a transitive verb. In a sentence such as "John is raising the flag," the subject "John" acts upon the direct object, "the flag," causing it to undergo a change in state. The verb 'to rise,' on the other hand does not imply any external agent; in a sentence such as "The temperature is rising," the subject of the sentence, "the temperature" itself undergoes the action of 'rising' rather than acting upon an external object.

Some Common Transitive and Intransitive Verbs

transitive		intransitive	
करना	to do	होना	to be
खाना	to eat	आना	to come
देखना	to see, look (at)	जाना	to go
सुनना	to hear, listen (to)	रहना	to remain, stay
लिखना	to write	बैठना	to sit
कहना	to say	सोना	to sleep

There is a simple and generally effective test that can be used to determine if a verb is transitive or intransitive. Insert the verb you wish to test into the question "What did he...?" Most transitive verbs will produce grammatical sentences (e.g. *What did he do? What did he eat?*), whereas most intransitive verbs will not (e.g. **What did he be?* **What did he come?*). Take a minute to test the remaining verbs given in the table above.

Differentiated Transitive/Intransitive Verb Pairs

English possesses many verbs that function both transitively and intransitively. Many such individual English verbs correspond to differentiated transitive and intransitive verb pairs in Hindi.

उबलना	*ubalnā*, intransitive (v.i.)	to boil ("The water is boiling.")
उबालना	*ubālnā*, transitive (v.t.)	to boil ("He is boiling some water.")
खुलना	*khulnā* (v.i.)	to open ("The door opened.")
खोलना	*kholnā* (v.t.)	to open ("She opened the door.")
टूटना	*ṭūṭnā* (v.i.)	to break ("The vase broke.")
तोड़ना	*toṛnā* (v.t.)	to break ("He broke the vase.")
दिखना	*dikhnā* (v.i.)	to look (to appear)
देखना	*dekhnā* (v.t.)	to look at (to see, to watch)
फैलना	*phailnā* (v.i.)	to spread ("Word is spreading.")
फैलाना	*phailānā* (v.t.)	to spread ("They are spreading the word.")
रुकना	*ruknā* (v.i.)	to stop ("The car stopped.")
रोकना	*roknā* (v.t.)	to stop ("He stopped the car.")
शुरू होना	*śurū honā* (v.i.)	to begin, to start ("Class is starting.")
शुरू करना	*śurū karnā* (v.t.)	to begin, to start ("The professor is starting class.")

Examples:

पानी उबल रहा है।	The water is boiling.
वह पानी उबाल रही है।	She is boiling water.
क्लास शुरू हो रही है।	Class is starting.
अध्यापक क्लास शुरू कर रहे हैं।	The teacher is starting class.

The conjunct verbs *śurū honā* and *śurū karnā* illustrate an important characteristic of conjunct verbs, which is that *honā* and *karnā* are often found in related transitive and intransitive conjunct verb pairs.

The Perfective of Transitive Verbs

One reason for being able to tell whether a verb is transitive or intransitive is that it is necessary for using differentiated pairs of transitive and intransitive verbs appropriately. However, there is another equally, if not more, essential reason why it is important to know whether a verb is transitive or intransitive. As will be explained in this section, transitive verbs follow an unusual agreement pattern when used in the perfective and related verb tenses.

The *ne* Construction

Hindi intransitive verbs function as one might expect in the perfective—the verb agrees with the subject, which appears in the direct case. On the other hand, transitive verbs follow a pattern that resembles that of indirect constructions—the subject is marked with a postposition and the verb agrees with the direct object. The subject is marked with the postposition *ne*, which only occurs in this construction and cannot be translated into English. Nouns and adjectives that directly precede *ne* take the oblique case, as they do with other postpositions. Pronouns take special forms with *ne*. These will be introduced below.

Form: Transitive verbs in the perfective take the same endings as intransitive verbs—the endings *-ā*, *-e*, *-ī*, and *-ī̃*, which are added directly to the verb stem. Unlike intransitive verbs, however, transitive verbs agree with the direct object. Take a look at the following examples:

कबीर ने सेब खाया।	Kabir ate an apple (m.).
कबीर ने कुछ मिठाइयाँ खाईं।	Kabir ate some sweets (f.pl.).
सारा ने सेब खाया।	Sarah ate an apple.
सारा ने कुछ मिठाइयाँ खाईं।	Sarah ate some sweets.

In some cases, the direct object is either not mentioned or is itself marked by a postposition (for example, a specific human direct object is always marked by *ko*). When this is the case, the verb takes its default form, which is the masculine singular.

पीटर ने राबर्ट को देखा।	Peter saw Robert.
पीटर ने सारा को देखा।	Peter saw Sarah.
सारा ने पीटर को देखा।	Sarah saw Peter.
सारा ने प्रीति को देखा।	Sarah saw Preeti.

Here are a few additional examples of perfective transitive verbs in use:

पिछले हफ़्ते मैंने एक अच्छी फ़िल्म देखी।	Last week I saw a good movie.
तुमने वीकेंड के दौरान क्या-क्या किया?	What did you do over the weekend?
हमने एक अच्छा नया रेस्टोरेंट ढूँढा।	We found a good new restaurant.
मैंने पिछले साल पूरे भारत की सैर की।	Last year I traveled through all of India.
कल मैंने अपने माता-पिता से फ़ोन पर बात की।	Yesterday I talked with my parents on the phone.

The key points to keep in mind when using transitive verbs used in the perfective verb tense are as follows:

- The special postposition *ne* is used to mark the subject of the sentence.
- The verb agrees with the direct object.
- If the direct object is also marked by a postposition, the verb takes the masculine singular form by default.

Pronoun Forms with *ne*

Pronouns take special forms with the postposition *ne*. The first and second-person forms are identical to the direct forms. The third-person singular forms are identical to the oblique forms. Third-person plural forms are unique to *ne*.

	singular	plural
1	मैंने *maĩ ne*	हमने *ham ne*
2	तूने *tū ne*	तुमने *tum ne*
		आपने *āp ne*
3	इसने, उसने *is ne, us ne*	इन्होंने, उन्होंने *inhõ ne, unhõ ne*

The word *koī* takes the form *kisī* with *ne*. The interrogative word *kaun* takes the forms *kis ne* (sg.) and *kinhõ ne* (pl.)

Examples:

मैंने कल एक फ़िल्म देखी।	I saw a movie yesterday.
तुमने खाना कब खाया?	When did you eat?
उसने कब फ़ोन किया?	When did he call?
हमने कुछ बात की।	We talked a little bit.
क्या आपने काम ख़त्म किया?	Did you finish the work?
उन्होंने एक अच्छा चुटकुला सुनाया।	He told a good joke.

Additional Points

There are a few additional points regarding the use of the perfective that are important to understand.

Verbs that behave irregularly with regard to *ne*: A few verbs that are transitive in meaning, such as X *se milnā*, 'to meet X,' *lānā*, 'to bring,' and *bhūlnā* (usually used in the form *bhūl jānā*), 'to forget,' do not take *ne*.

मैं आज सुबह तरुण से मिला।	This morning I met Tarun.
मैं कुछ मिठाइयाँ लाया।	I brought some sweets.
माफ़ कीजिए, मैं आपका नाम भूल गया।	I'm sorry, I forgot your name.

Conjunct verbs: When using conjunct verbs in the perfective, it is only necessary to consider the verb portion of the conjunct verb to determine whether *ne* must be used. The meaning of the conjunct verb as a whole does not matter. For example, *ārām karnā*, 'to rest,' and *kasrat karnā*, 'to exercise,' both require *ne* due to the fact that the verb portion, *karnā*, 'to do,' is transitive. The fact that the meanings 'rest' and 'exercise' are intransitive does not matter.

मैंने काम के बाद कसरत की।	I exercised after work.
उसके बाद मैंने आराम किया।	After that I rested.

Note that the noun portion of both of these verbs functions grammatically as the direct object of the verb. This is the case with many, but not all conjunct verbs.

As seen earlier, some noun-based conjunct verbs function as if the noun and verb are an undivided grammatical unit. Examples of this type of conjunct verb are *śurū honā*, 'to start, begin (intransitive),' *śurū karnā*, 'to start, begin (transitive),' and *istemāl karnā*, 'to use.'

आज क्लास देर से शुरू हुई|	Class started late today.
अध्यापक ने क्लास देर से शुरू की|	The teacher started class late.
मैंने तुम्हारी किताब इस्तेमाल की|	I used your book.

As explained earlier, the verb *istemāl karnā* can optionally be used in an alternative manner in which the noun *istemāl* functions as the direct object of *karnā*.

मैंने तुम्हारी किताब का इस्तेमाल किया|	I used your book.

The verbs *saknā* and *pānā*: Complex verb phrases containing *saknā* and *pānā* are always treated as intransitive—*ne* is never used to mark the subject.

वह नहीं आ पाया|	He wasn't able to come.
मैं तुम्हारी पूरी बात नहीं सुन पाया|	I wasn't able to hear everything you said.
हमारी मुलाक़ात नहीं हो सकी|	We weren't able to meet.

Indirect constructions never take *ne*.

मुझे कुछ पैसे मिले|	I got some money.
मुझे आपका खाना बहुत पसंद आया|	I enjoyed your food a lot.
आपको यह बात कैसे पता चली?	How did you find that out?

Vocabulary 2

ख़राब	*xarāb*	bad, gone bad
खाँसी	*khā̃sī* (f.)	coughing (X *ko khā̃sī ānā*, for X to have a cough, for X to be afflicted by coughing)
ख़ूब	*xūb*	a lot
खेल	*khel* (m.)	game, sport; trick (*jādū kā khel*)
खोना	*khonā* (v.i./v.t.)	to lose, to get lost
चाँदनी	*cā̃dnī* (f.)	moonlight
चुटकुला	*cuṭkulā* (m.)	joke
जादू	*jādū* (m.)	magic
जादूगर	*jādūgar*	magician
ताश	*tāś* (m.)	playing cards
थैला	*thailā* (m.)	bag
पछताना	*pachtānā*	to regret
X को पता चलना	X *ko patā calnā*	for X to find out
पत्ता	*pattā* (m.)	leaf, sheet
(X को) पसंद आना	(X *ko*) *pasand ānā*	(for X) to like, enjoy (after trying)
पार	*pār* (m.)	far bank, shore; opposite side (*ke us pār*, on the opposite side of)
पैक करना	*paik karnā*	to pack
प्रवेश	*praveś* (m.)	entrance, admission (*praveś lenā*, to gain admission, enroll in)
बुलाना	*bulānā* (v.t.)	to invite
बेकार	*bekār*	useless
भूलना / भूल जाना	*bhūlnā/bhūl jānā* (v.i.)	to forget
X को मज़ा आना	X *ko mazā ānā* (v.i.)	for X to have a good time, enjoy oneself
मनाना	*manānā*	to celebrate (a holiday, festival), to carry out (a diversional activity)

महसूस करना	*mahsūs karnā*	to feel
मुलाक़ात	*mulāqāt* (f.)	meeting
रहना	*rahnā* (v.i.)	to remain; to proceed, to go (perfective) (e.g., *kaisā rahā*, "How did it go?")
लेख	*lekh* (m.)	article
विषय	*viṣay* (m.)	subject
शानदार	*śāndār*	splendid, magnificent (*śān*, f. magnificence, majesty)
सचमुच	*sacmuc*	truly
सुझाव	*sujhāv* (m.)	suggestion (+ *denā*, to suggest)
सुनाई देना	*sunāī denā* (v.i.)	to become audible to
सो जाना	*so jānā*	to fall asleep

Notes:

- There are a handful of verbs that can be used either transitively or intransitively. When used transitively they take *ne*, when used intransitively, they do not. A few examples are: *badalnā*, 'to change,' *bharnā*, 'to fill,' *khonā*, 'to lose, to get lost,' *paṛhnā*, 'to read, to study.' *us ne śādī ke bād apnā nām nahī̃ badlā*, 'She didn't change her name after marriage'; *vo bīs sāl mẽ zarā nahī̃ badle*, 'He hasn't changed the least bit in twenty years.'
- There are a few exceptions to the rule that the verb portion of a conjunct verb always determines whether *ne* must be used. These exceptions include: *dikhāī denā*, 'to be(come) visible to,' *sunāī denā*, 'to be(come) audible to,' *man karnā/jī cāhnā*, 'to feel like..., to get the urge to...' These verbs do not take *ne*. *mujhe ek baṛī imārat dikhāī dī*, 'I saw a big building. A big building came into my view'; *mujhe ek ajīb āvāz sunāī dī*, 'I heard a strange sound. A strange sound became audible to me'; *merā man kiyā ki maĩ kuch mīṭhā khāū̃*, 'I got the urge to eat something sweet'; *merā jī cāhā ki maĩ zor se cīxū̃*, 'I felt like screaming loudly.'
- *so jānā* is an example of a compound verb. Please see chapter 33 for more details.

Exercise 4

Fill in the blanks to complete Raj's account of his day yesterday. Supply *ne* where it is needed and give the correct form of each verb given in parentheses.

मैं _____ लगभग छह बजे __________ (उठना)| फिर नहाने के बाद मैं _____ कपड़े __________ (पहनना) और नाश्ता __________ (करना)| फिर बस पकड़कर* मैं _____ कैम्पस __________ (पहुँचना)| मेरी तीन क्लासें थीं| सारी क्लासें सुबह थीं| आख़िरी क्लास के बाद मैं _____ एक दोस्त के साथ दोपहर का खाना __________ (खाना)| उसके बाद मैं _____ पुस्तकालय __________ (जाना)| मैं _____ वहाँ एक सहपाठी से __________ (मिलना) और हम _____ शाम तक एक प्रोजेक्ट पर काम __________ (करना)| उसके बाद मैं _____ अपने फ़्लैट वापस __________ (जाना)| फिर शाम का खाना खाने के बाद मैं _____ थोड़ी देर आराम __________ (करना)| फिर मैं _____ थोड़ी देर टीवी __________ (देखना) और एक दोस्त से फ़ोन पर बात __________ (करना)| उसके बाद मैं _____ हिन्दी क्लास के लिए एक लेख __________ (पढ़ना)| फिर मैं _____ थोड़ी देर किताब पढ़ने की कोशिश __________ (करना) लेकिन मुझे नींद बहुत ज़ोर से आ रही थी, इसलिए मैं _____ जल्दी __________ (सोना)|

*बस पकड़कर, 'having caught the bus'

Exercise 5

Personalization Questions

१. क्या आज सुबह आपने नाश्ता किया? आपने नाश्ते में क्या-क्या खाया?
२. क्या आपने नाश्ते के साथ कॉफ़ी पी? कितने कप?
३. कल आपने अपने दाँत कितनी बार साफ़ किए?
४. आपने कल कितनी देर पढ़ाई की? आपने पढ़ाई कहाँ की?
५. आपने पिछली बार सिनेमाघर में फ़िल्म कब देखी? आपने कौन सी फ़िल्म देखी?
६. आप पिछली बार कहाँ घूमने गए? आपने वहाँ क्या-क्या देखा? आपको कैसा लगा?
७. आपने इस यूनिवर्सिटी / कॉलेज में किस साल प्रवेश लिया?
८. आपने अपने माता-पिता से पिछली बार कब बात की?

९. आपने पिछली बार कौन सी किताब पढ़ी? वह कैसी थी?
१०. आपने पिछली बार कब ख़रीदारी की? क्या ख़रीदा?

Exercise 6

Read the following journal entry by Tom about his weekend and answer the given questions.

पिछला वीकेंड बहुत मज़ेदार रहा| शुक्रवार को हमारे इम्तिहान ख़त्म हुए और शुक्रवार की शाम को हम सब दोस्त एक फ़िल्म देखने गए| फ़िल्म के बाद हमने एक अच्छे रेस्टोरेंट में खाना खाया| फिर हम झील के किनारे टहलने गए| चाँदनी रात में झील का दृश्य और भी सुंदर था| हमारी दोस्त सीमा ने हमें एक ख़ूबसूरत गाना सुनाया| मैंने थोड़ी देर गिटार बजाया| हम सब कुछ देर नाचे भी| हमारा एक दोस्त डेविड जादूगर है| उसने हमें दो-चार खेल दिखाए| उसने जेन को ताश के चार पत्ते दिए| जेन ने वे पत्ते अपने थैले में रखे| डेविड ने कुछ शब्द जैसे “अबरा का डबरा” वग़ैरह कई बार बोले और ताश के पत्ते जेन के थैले के बजाए पीटर की जेब से नकले| आधी रात के बाद हम सब अपन-अपने घर वापस गए|

दूसरे दिन शनिवार को हम झील के उस पार पहाड़ी पर घूमने गए| हमने पहाड़ी पर बहुत अच्छी पिकनिक मनाई| हमारा इरादा था कि हम रात पहाड़ी पर ही गुज़ारें मगर हम अपने साथ कैंपिंग का सामान नहीं ले गए थे|* हमने सोचना शुरू किया कि हमें क्या करना चाहिए| डेविड ने सुझाव दिया कि हम शिकागो चलें| शिकागो यहाँ से दो घंटे दूर है| हमें यह ख़याल पसंद आया और शाम ७ बजे हम शिकागो के लिए रवाना हुए| ९ बजे हम शिकागो पहुँचे| वहाँ भी हमें बहुत मज़ा आया| इतवार की शाम को हम सब शिकागो से वापस आए और अगली दोपहर तक सोए| यह सचमुच बहुत मज़ेदार वीकेंड था|

*...नहीं ले गए थे, '...hadn't brought..."

सवाल

१. शुक्रवार की शाम को टॉम ने अपने दोस्तों के साथ क्या-क्या किया?
२. सीमा ने क्या किया?
३. किसको कौन सा साज़ बजाना आता है?
४. टॉम के दोस्तों में कौन जादूगर है? उसने क्या जादू दिखाया?
५. शनिवार को टॉम और उसके दोस्तों ने क्या-क्या किया?
६. टॉम और उसके दोस्त पहाड़ी पर रात क्यों नहीं गुज़ार सके?
७. वे शिकागो से कब वापस आए और फिर उन्होंने क्या किया?

Exercise 7

Listen to the dialogue between two Indian friends living in America and answer the questions about it.

अमर	और सुनाओ रमा, क्या हाल है?
रमा	सब ठीक है। तुम बताओ, तुम कैसे हो?
अमर	मैं ठीक हूँ। पिछले वीकेंड मैंने तुम्हें राहुल की पार्टी में नहीं देखा! लगता है तुम्हारा कोई और ख़ास प्रोग्राम था।
रमा	हाँ, मेरा पिछला वीकेंड बहुत शानदार था।
अमर	अच्छा! तुमने क्या-क्या किया?
रमा	शुक्रवार को हमने बहुत अच्छा खाना खाया फिर झील के किनारे सैर की।
अमर	तुम्हारे साथ कौन-कौन था?
रमा	मेरी हिन्दी क्लास से मेरे सब दोस्त। मेरी सहेली ज़ेबा भी न्यू यार्क से आई थी*।
अमर	अच्छा फिर तो तुम्हें बहुत मज़ा आया होगा।
रमा	हाँ, हमने बहुत बातें कीं। ज़ेबा बहुत अच्छा गाना गाती है। उसे पुराने हिन्दी गाने पसंद हैं। उसने हमें कई गाने भी सुनाए। शनिवार को मैं और ज़ेबा ख़रीदारी करने गए।
अमर	तुमने क्या-क्या ख़रीदा?
रमा	हमने बहुत कपड़े ख़रीदे और कुछ बेकार चीज़ें भी।
अमर	शनिवार को तुमने और क्या किया?
रमा	शनिवार की शाम को जोसेफ़ के घर में पार्टी थी। वहाँ बहुत मज़ा आया। रविवार को मैं बहुत थकी हुई थी इसलिए पूरा दिन सोई। सचमुच यह शानदार वीकेंड था।

*आई थी, 'had come.'

सवाल

१. रमा ने शुक्रवार किस-किस के साथ गुज़ारा? उन्होंने क्या-क्या किया?

२. ज़ेबा कौन है और कहाँ रहती है?

३. वीकेंड में किस-किस के घर में पार्टी थी?

४. रमा ने शनिवार को क्या-क्या किया?

५. रविवार को रमा ने क्या-क्या किया?

Exercise 8

Write a paragraph about what you did last weekend.

Exercise 9

Pair up with a classmate. Interview each other to find out what you did last weekend. When speaking, do not read from the paragraph that you wrote earlier. Take notes on what your partner tells you; make sure you find out at least ten activities. Report your findings in Hindi to your class.

38

Narrating a Story

In this chapter you will learn additional tools that will aid in narrating events in a natural way. In the first section of this chapter you will learn how to explain background events to a main storyline. In the second section you will learn an additional way to sequence events.

The Past Perfect

The past perfect verb tense in Hindi corresponds most closely to the English past perfect, which is the verb tense in sentences such as "He had left a note on the door," and "The train had left before we even arrived." One of the most common uses of the past perfect is giving background events to the main storyline in past narration.

Formation: The past perfect is formed by appending simple past forms of *honā* to perfective verb forms; the simple past forms of *honā* are written separately from the main verb. The feminine plural perfective ending, *–ī̃*, loses its nasalization when *thī̃* is added.

perfective forms + ***honā* [simple past]**

Here is the conjugation of the verb *pahũcnā* in the past perfect, all forms of which mean 'had arrived.'

	singular	plural
masculine	पहुँचा था *pahũcā thā*	पहुँचे थे *pahũce the*
feminine	पहुँची थी *pahũcī thī*	पहुँची थीं *pahũcī thī̃*

Past perfect transitive and intransitive verbs follow the same patterns of agreement and *ne* usage as the perfective. The postposition *ne* marks the subject of a transitive verb; the verb agrees with the direct object unless the direct object is marked by a postposition, in which case the verb takes the masculine singular form. Intransitive verbs agree with the subject.

Using the Past Perfect

The past perfect is used to describe a past occurrence that is relevant in understanding a subsequent occurrence or state of affairs that also existed (at least partially) in the past. In many contexts, the Hindi past perfect (corresponding to 'had done' in English) is used where the simple past (I did...) would be more common in English. Take a look at the following examples. The sentences in parentheses have been given to provide context for the past perfect examples.

(मेरा पेट कल रात से ख़राब है।)	(My stomach has been upset since last night.)
आपने कल दिन में क्या खाया था?	What did you eat yesterday?

(तुम इम्तिहान के लिए तैयार क्यों नहीं थे?) (Why weren't you ready for the test?)

अध्यापक ने हमें पहले से नहीं बताया था| The teacher didn't tell us beforehand.

The past perfect generally implies some intervening reference point or period of relevance between the time of the past perfect action and the present. In some cases, however, the past perfect is used when a past reference point is not immediately evident from the context. In such cases, the past perfect signals that the action is not immediately relevant in the present, or that the period of relevance (which might not be explicitly defined) has ended.

Exercise 1

G

Read aloud and translate the following sentences. The first sentence in each set provides the context for the remaining sentences.

मेरी किताब कहाँ है?

मैंने अभी एक घंटे पहले कहीं देखी थी|

तुमने अपने बैग में रखी थी| शायद वहाँ हो|

मैं सुबह से बीमार महसूस कर रहा हूँ|

आपने कल क्या खाया था?

तुमने इतनी ज़्यादा मिठाइयाँ क्यों खाई थीं?

क्या तुमने कल बहुत शराब पी थी?

इम्तिहान में मेरे बहुत ख़राब नंबर आए हैं|

क्या तुमने इम्तिहान की पूरी तैयारी की थी?

इम्तिहान से पहले वाली रात तुम कितना सोई थीं?

मैंने कॉफ़ी पी थी इसलिए मुझे दो बजे तक नींद नहीं आई|

कल रात को तुम हमारे साथ फ़िल्म देखने क्यों नहीं आए? फ़िल्म बहुत मज़ेदार थी|

मैंने वह फ़िल्म पिछले हफ़्ते देखी थी| फिर से देखने का मन नहीं था|

मेरे माता-पिता मुझसे मिलने आए थे| मैं उनके साथ व्यस्त था|

मेरा फ़ोन ठीक नहीं था| दरअसल मुझे आज ही सुबह पता चला कि तुमने फ़ोन किया था|

Exercise 2 G

Translate into Hindi.

1. He had told me that I didn't have to come yesterday.
2. I had understood that the day before yesterday was a day off.
3. We had decided that we would go to the park, but then it started raining.
4. I hadn't eaten so I was hungry.
5. You really should see this film. You will like it a lot. Really? I had heard that it wasn't very good.
6. I had gone to sleep half an hour earlier. Then the phone rang.
7. Before leaving, I had left some money on the table. Did you get it?
8. I had cooked dinner, but then my stomach started hurting (*dukhne lagā*) so I didn't eat.

The *kar* Construction

The construction V + *kar*, means 'having V-ed.' It is used to sequence two verbs within a single sentence, both of which have the same subject. The subject need only be mentioned once in the sentence.

जाकर	having gone
खाकर	having eaten
नहाकर	having bathed
सोचकर	having thought

मैं घर जाकर आराम करना चाहता हूँ।	I want to go home and rest. ("Having gone home I want to rest.")
तुम घर पहुँचकर मुझे फ़ोन करो।	Call me when you get home. ("Having arrived at home call me.")

Using *kar* with the *ne* construction: When the *kar* construction is used with a main verb that is in the perfective, the main (conjugated) verb determines the use of *ne*.

तुमने वहाँ जाकर क्या किया?	What did you go there and do? ("What did you do having gone there?")
मैं खाना खाकर गया था इसलिए मैंने वहाँ कुछ नहीं खाया।	I ate before going so I didn't eat anything there.
मैंने फूल ख़रीदकर गाड़ी में रखे।	I bought flowers and put them in the car.

The verb *karnā* takes the form *karke* in this construction. It never takes the form **karkar*.

मैं वह फ़ैसला करके बहुत पछताया।	I really regretted having made that decision.
काम ख़त्म करके मैंने थोड़ी देर आराम किया।	Having finished the work, I rested for a bit.

In colloquial speech, the form V + *ke* can be used in place of V + *kar* for other verbs as well.

तुमने वहाँ पहुँचके क्या किया?	What did you do after arriving there?

Additional Points

The *kar* is sometimes dropped from the construction, leaving the verb in bare stem form. The verbs *le jānā*, 'to take away,' and *le ānā*, 'to bring,' are actually examples of the *kar* construction in which the *kar* portion has been dropped. The long forms of these verbs are *le kar jānā*, 'to go/leave having taken something,' and *le kar ānā*, 'to come having taken something.'

In some cases the verb that appears in the *kar* construction is used adverbially to describe the manner in which the main verb is carried out.

वह जो भी बोलता है, मुस्कराकर बोलता है।	Whatever he says, he says with a smile.
संभलकर चलिए।	Walk carefully.

Note the following idiomatic expressions with the *kar* construction:

(से) होकर	via, by way of
सोच-समझकर	having deliberated, having given due consideration
जान-बूझकर	intentionally; knowingly

Vocabulary 1

अंगूठी	*angūṭhī* (f.)	ring
अनगिनत	*an-ginat*	countless
असली	*aslī*	true, authentic
इजाज़त	*ijāzat* (f.)	permission (*ijāzat denā*, to give permission)
इनाम	*inām* (m.)	reward, prize
इशारा	*iśārā* (m.)	sign, indication (*iśārā karnā*, to point); signal
ऐतिहासिक	*aitihāsik*	historical, historic (cf. *itihās*, m. 'history')
क़दम	*qadam* (m.)	step, foot (*qadmõ mẽ gir paṛnā*, to fall to someone's feet)
क़बूल करना	*qabūl karnā* (v.t.)	to accept, to admit
काटना	*kāṭnā* (v.t.)	to cut
क़िस्सा	*qissā* (m.)	tale, story
क़ीमती	*qīmtī*	valuable
ग़ायब	*g̱hāyab* (adj.)	disappeared
गिरना	*girnā* (v.i.)	to fall (*gir paṛnā*, same)
गुज़ारना	*guzārnā* (v.t.)	to pass (time)
चुराना	*curānā* (v.t.)	to steal
चोर	*cor*	thief
चोरी	*corī* (f.)	theft
ज़बरदस्त	*zabardast*	forceful; (colloq.) awesome, great
जवाहरात	*javāharāt* (m.pl.)	jewels
जान-बूझकर	*jān-būjhkar*	intentionally, knowingly
जिस	*jis* (rel.)	whom, which (oblique of *jo*)
ढेर सारा	*ḍher sārā*	(colloq.) a ton of

दरबार	*darbār* (m.)	royal court
देखभाल	*dekhbhāl* (f.)	looking after, caring after (X *kī dekhbhāl karnā*, to look after X)
धूम-धाम	*dhūm-dhām* (f.)	pomp and show
पकड़ना	*pakaṛnā* (v.t.)	to catch
परेशान	*pareśān*	worried, troubled
बढ़ना	*baṛhnā* (v.i.)	to increase, to grow
बनवाना	*banvānā* (v.t.)	to have (something) made
बादशाह	*bādśāh* (m.)	king, emperor
बुलाना	*bulānā* (v.t.)	to call, invite, summon
मुस्कराना	*muskarānā* (v.i.)	to smile
X में से	X *mẽ se*	among X, from among X
रस्म	*rasm* (f.)	ceremony
रोना	*ronā* (v.i.)	to cry
लकड़ी	*lakṛī* (f.)	wood
लम्बाई	*lambāī* (f.)	length
शरीक होना	*śarīk honā* (v.t.)	to participate (*mẽ*, in)
शादी	*śādī* (f.)	wedding, marriage
संभलना	*sambhalnā* (v.i.)	to steady oneself (so as not to fall)
स्वीकार करना	*svīkār karnā* (v.t.)	to accept, to admit
हाज़िर	*hāzir*	present, in attendance
हीरा	*hīrā* (m.)	diamond
(से) होकर	(*se*) *hokar*	via, by way of
सोच-समझकर	*soc-samajhkar*	having deliberated, having given due consideration
होशियारी	*hośiyārī* (f.)	cleverness; intelligence

Exercise 3

Join the pairs of sentences using the *kar* construction and then translate the resulting sentences.

उदाहरण

मैं घर गया = मैं सोया + मैं घर जा कर सोया|

वाक्य १	**वाक्य २**
मैं पुस्तकालय गया|	मैंने इम्तिहान के लिए पढ़ाई की|
मैं घर वापस आई|	मैं सोई|
वे लड़कियाँ वहाँ पहुँचीं|	उन्होंने अपने माँ-बाप को फ़ोन किया|
मैं घर गई|	मैंने खाना पकाना शरू किया|
मेरे पिता कुछ देर किताब पढ़ेंगे|	वे सो जाएँगे|
मैं अपने माता-पिता के घर जाऊँगी|	मैं आराम करूँगी|
राहुल अपने परिवार के साथ बैठा|	उसने रात का खाना खाया|
हम सुबह-सुबह* उठे|	हम सफ़र के लिए तैयार हुए|

*सुबह-सुबह, 'early in the morning.'

Exercise 4

Faisal has written a diary entry about his weekend. Read the entry and write questions that can be answered based on the information that it contains. When you are finished, pair up with a classmate and exchange your questions orally, answering in complete sentences.

मेरी पिछली छुट्टियाँ काफ़ी अच्छी रहीं| शुक्रवार को क्लास के बाद मैंने अपने दोस्तों के साथ एक भारतीय रेस्टोरेंट में खाना खाया| खाना खाकर हमने शाहरुख़ ख़ान की नई फ़िल्म देखी| मैंने इससे पहले शाहरुख़ ख़ान की कोई फ़िल्म कभी नहीं देखी थी| मुझे यह फ़िल्म कुछ ख़ास नहीं

लगी लेकिन वह मेरे दोस्तों को काफ़ी पसंद आई। शनिवार की सुबह मैं ग्यारह बजे तक सोया। मैं उठने के बाद एक दोस्त से मिला। हमने साथ नाश्ता किया। नाश्ता करके हम मॉल में घूमे। मैंने एक पतलून ख़रीदी और मेरे दोस्त ने भी कुछ ख़रीदारी की। शनिवार की रात को मैं एक पार्टी में गया। पार्टी काफ़ी शानदार थी। मैं दो बजे तक वहाँ रहा। रविवार की सुबह मैंने जल्दी उठकर पूरे फ़्लैट की सफ़ाई की। मैंने पिछली बार दो हफ़्ते पहले सफ़ाई की थी इसलिए फ़्लैट काफ़ी गंदा था। पूरी दोपहर मैंने पुस्तकालय में पढ़ाई की फिर मैं अपने फ़्लैट वापस जाकर सो गया।

Exercise 5

Match the background events given in the left-hand column with the events in the right-hand column.

उसने जाने से पहले कबाब पराठे खाए थे।	मैंने इस वीकेंड सिर्फ़ घर में आराम किया।
मैंने शाम को चार कप काफ़ी पी थी।	मैं दिल्ली जानेवाला था, लेकिन नहीं जा सका।
उसने एक बहुत लोकप्रिय टीवी सीरियल में काम किया था।	उसने अर्जुन के यहाँ कुछ नहीं खाया।
मैंने पिछले हफ़्ते बहुत काम किया था।	उसको शहर का बच्चा-बच्चा जानता था।
मेरी गाड़ी छूट गई थी।	मैं सारी रात नहीं सोया।

Exercise 6

Akbar-Birbal stories are very popular in India. Akbar was a Mughal emperor and Birbal was one of his famous "nine jewels" (*nau ratn*) of the court. Read the following story and answer the given questions.

बीरबल अकबर के नौ रत्नों में से थे। वे अपनी होशियारी के लिए दूर-दूर तक मशहूर थे। अकबर बादशाह के पास अनगिनत क़ीमती लिबास और हीरे-जवाहरात थे। बादशाह के महल में आठ ख़ास नौकर थे जो उनके लिबास और ज़ेवरात की देखभाल करते थे और वे ही उन्हें दरबार के लिए तैयार करते थे। किसी और को बादशाह के कमरे में जाने की इजाज़त नहीं थी।

अकबर बादशाह के पास बहुत सी क़ीमती अंगूठियाँ थीं लेकिन एक ख़ास अंगूठी बादशाह को बेहद पसंद थी| एक दिन बादशाह ने नौकरों से अपनी मनपसंद अंगूठी पहनने के लिए माँगी| मालूम हुआ कि अंगूठी अपनी जगह से ग़ायब है| अकबर के नौकरों ने अंगूठी सब जगह ढूँढी लेकिन किसी को अंगूठी नहीं मिली| अकबर ने परेशान होकर बीरबल को बुलवाया और अंगूठी की चोरी का क़िस्सा सुनाया|

बीरबल ने महल के आठों नौकरों को बुलाकर उन्हें लकड़ी की एक-एक छड़ी दी| सब छड़ियाँ लम्बाई में बराबर थीं| बीरबल ने नौकरों से कहा कि दूसरे दिन सब अपनी-अपनी छड़ी लेकर दरबार में हाज़िर हों| उन्होंने नौकरों से कहा कि जिसने अंगूठी चुराई है उसकी छड़ी दूसरे दिन दरबार में पहुँचकर एक इंच लम्बी हो जाएगी|

अगले दिन सब नौकर अपनी-अपनी छड़ी लेकर दरबार में आए और अपनी छड़ियाँ बीरबल को दीं| बीरबल ने एक नौकर की तरफ़ इशारा करके कहा कि अंगूठी इसने चुराई है| वह नौकर अकबर के क़दमों में गिर पड़ा और उसने रोकर स्वीकार किया कि अंगूठी उसी ने चुराई थी|

बादशाह बहुत हैरान हुए| उन्होंने बीरबल से पूछा कि उन्होंने चोर को कैसे पकड़ा| बीरबल ने जवाब दिया कि चोर ने अपनी छड़ी काटकर एक इंच छोटी कर दी थी| उसने सोचा कि वह दरबार में पहुँचकर एक इंच बढ़ जाएगी|

अकबर बादशाह बीरबल की होशियारी से बहुत ख़ुश हुए और उन्होंने बीरबल को भारी इनाम दिया|

सवाल

१. बीरबल किसलिए मशहूर थे?

२. अकबर के महल में कितने नौकर थे और वे क्या काम करते थे?

३. अकबर ने बीरबल को क्यों बुलवाया?

४. बीरबल ने नौकरों को क्या दिया?

५. बीरबल ने चोर को कैसे पकड़ा?

Exercise 7

Neeta is meeting her friend Pinky after a month. Listen to their conversation and answer the questions that follow.

नीता	जब मैं तुमसे पिछले महीने मिली थी तो तुमने बताया था कि तुम भारत जानेवाली हो। तो कैसा रहा तुम्हारा भारत का सफ़र?
पिंकी	बहुत ही अच्छा। मैं भारत अपनी कज़िन की शादी के लिए गई थी लेकिन मुझे वहाँ काफ़ी घूमने का मौक़ा भी मिला।
नीता	अच्छा! तो तुम कहाँ-कहाँ घूमीं?
पिंकी	मेरी कज़िन की शादी चंडीगढ़ में थी तो चंडीगढ़ में कई दिन गुज़ारे। वहाँ काफ़ी जगहें देखीं। वहाँ ख़ूब शॉपिंग की। शादी के बाद मैंने अपने कज़िन्ज़ के साथ जयपुर और दिल्ली की भी सैर की।
नीता	वाह! लगता है कि तुमने इंडिया में बहुत मज़ा किया। पहले यह बताओ कि शादी कैसी हुई।
पिंकी	शादी बहुत अच्छी थी। असली भारतीय शादी थी। बहुत धूम-धाम थी। ढेर सारी रस्में हुईं। ख़ूब गाना-बजाना हुआ।
नीता	तुम्हारे पास शादी की तस्वीरें हैं?
पिंकी	मेरे पास तस्वीरें नहीं हैं, लेकिन वहाँ दूल्हेवालों ने पूरी शादी की वीडियो बनवायी थी। मेरे पास वह वीडियो है। मैं तुम्हें किसी दिन दिखाऊँगी।
नीता	अगले हफ़्ते मुझे कोई काम नहीं है। क्यों न हम अगले हफ़्ते शादी की वीडियो देखें?
पिंकी	हाँ, अगले हफ़्ते देख सकते हैं।
नीता	और जयपुर और दिल्ली में तुमने क्या-क्या किया?
पिंकी	जयपुर में हम पुराने शहर में ठहरे और हमने वहाँ बहुत सी ऐतिहासिक इमारतें देखीं। दिल्ली में हमने लाल क़िला देखा और हम लोधी गार्डन भी गए।
नीता	तुमने इंडिया में बहुत अच्छा वक़्त गुज़ारा। मैं भी अगले साल इंडिया जाना चाहती हूँ।

सवाल

१. पिंकी भारत क्यों गई थी?

२. चंडीगढ़ में क्या हुआ? पिंकी ने वहाँ क्या-क्या किया?

३. भारत में पिंकी किसके साथ घूमी?

४. जयपुर और दिल्ली में पिंकी ने क्या किया?

५. अगले हफ़्ते पिंकी और नीता क्या करेंगी?

39

My Experience and Accomplishments

In this chapter you will learn how to describe your work and life experience using sentences such as these:

मैंने भारत से बी.ए. किया है।	I did my B.A. from India.
मैंने अलग-अलग नौकरियाँ की हैं।	I have worked in various jobs.
मैंने भारत और अमरीका दोनों जगहों की कंपनियों के लिए काम किया है।	I have worked for both Indian and American companies.
मैं पूरा दक्षिण एशिया घूमा हूँ।	I have traveled all of South Asia.
मैंने सब मशहूर जगहें देखी हैं।	I have seen all of the famous places.
मैंने पूर्वी एशिया की भी सैर की है।	I have also traveled through East Asia.

The Present Perfect Verb Tense

The sentences in the examples above employ the present perfect verb tense, which corresponds to the English present perfect, or the verb tense with the form 'has/have V-ed.' (e.g., "He has arrived," "They have eaten.")

Formation: In Hindi, the present perfect is formed by appending the simple present forms of *honā* to the perfective forms. The perfective forms and the simple present forms of *honā* are written separately.

perfective forms + ***honā* [simple present]**

The feminine plural perfective ending, *-ī̃*, loses its nasalization when *honā* is added. Here is the complete conjugation of the intransitive verb *pahũcnā*, 'to arrive':

		singular		plural	
masculine	1	मैं पहुँचा हूँ	I have arrived	हम पहुँचे हैं	We have arrived
	2	तू पहुँचा है	You have arrived	तुम पहुँचे हो	You have arrived
				आप पहुँचे हैं	You have arrived
	3	वह पहुँचा है	He has arrived	वे पहुँचे हैं	They have arrived
feminine	1	मैं पहुँची हूँ	I have arrived	हम पहुँची हैं	We have arrived
	2	तू पहुँची है	You have arrived	तुम पहुँची हो	You have arrived
				आप पहुँची हैं	You have arrived
	3	वह पहुँची है	She has arrived	वे पहुँची हैं	They have arrived

Present perfect transitive and intransitive verbs follow the same patterns of agreement and *ne* usage as the perfective.

Using the Present Perfect

The present perfect is generally appropriate when describing a past event that is relevant in explaining some state of affairs that exists in the present.

Here are some important functions in which you will practice using the present perfect in this chapter:

- Explaining why a present state of affairs exists (The questions in parentheses are given to provide context for the examples with present perfect verbs):

(समीर कहाँ है?)	Where is Sameer?
वह बाज़ार गया है।	He has gone to the market.
(क्या खाने को कुछ है?)	Is there anything to eat?
हाँ, मैंने खाना पकाया है।	Yes, I have cooked some food.
(आप चाय क्यों बना रही हैं)	Why are you making tea?
कुछ मेहमान आए हैं।	Some guests have come.

- Recounting life experiences:

आप भारत में कहाँ-कहाँ घूमे हैं?	Where in India have you traveled?
मैंने लगभग हर जगह का खाना खाया है।	I have eaten the food of just about every place.

- Enumerating things one has done over a period of time up to the present:

आपने इस महीने कितनी फ़िल्में देखी हैं?	How many movies have you seen this month?
तुमने अपने माता-पिता से इस महीने कितनी बार बात की है?	How many times have you spoken with your parents this month?
तुमने सुबह से कितने कप कॉफ़ी पी है?	How many cups of coffee have you had since this morning?

- Describing professional experience and achievements:

आपने कहाँ तक पढ़ाई की है?	To what level have you completed your education?
मैंने लखनऊ यूनिवर्सिटी से बी. ए. किया है।	I have done a B.A from Lahore University.
मैंने शिकागो से एम. ए. किया है।	I have done an M.A. from Chicago.
आपने कहाँ-कहाँ नौकरी की है?	Where have you worked?
मैंने अपने पिता की कंपनी में काम किया है।	I have worked in my father's company.
मैंने एक बैंक में काम किया है।	I have worked in a bank.

Stating How Long You Have Been Doing Something

When describing one's experience, it is also common to include what one is currently doing and how long one has been doing it. Consider the following sentences:

हम लोग दो साल से हिन्दी सीख रहे हैं।	We have been learning Hindi for two years.
मैं सन् २००७ से इस कंपनी के लिए काम करती हूँ।	I have worked in this company since 2007.
मैं यहाँ तीन साल से काम कर रहा हूँ।	I have been working here for three years.
हमारी कंपनी कई साल से इस शहर में है।	Our company has been in this city for several years.

In general, English sentences of the form *has/have...since/for...*, are expressed in Hindi with present tense verb forms. The postposition *se* is used corresponding to English *since* and *for*.

Parallel constructions with past tense verb forms are also possible. These have the general form *had...since/for...* in English.

वह दो दिन से बीमार था।	He had been sick for two days.
वह मंगलवार से बीमार था।	He had been sick since Tuesday.
मैं उसको सिर्फ़ एक महीने से जानता था।	I had known him for only a month.
मैं एक साल पहले से हिन्दी पढ़ रही थी।	I had been studying Hindi for one year.

The Verb *cuknā*

Hindi has no adverb corresponding to English *already*. In contexts where *already* is used in English, Hindi generally employs the verb *cuknā*. This structure is also often used to talk about accomplishments.

मैं हाई स्कूल पास कर चुका हूँ।	I have already graduated from high school.
वह कोर्सवर्क पूरा कर चुका है। पिछले सेमेस्टर से अपना शोधपत्र लिख रहा है।	He has already finished his coursework. He has been writing his dissertation since last semester.
इतनी कम उम्र में वह तीन किताबें लिख चुका है।	At such a young age he has already written three books.

Form: The verb *cuknā* is used with a main verb in stem form to add a sense of completion to the main verb that generally corresponds to English 'already.' The *cuknā* construction can be used with any tense except the present and past continuous (as an action in progress is inherently incomplete). The verb *cuknā* never takes the *ne* construction.

The verb *cuknā* is sometimes used to state experiences in contexts in which *already* would not be appropriate in English.

मैं हिंदुस्तान घूम चुका हूँ।	I have traveled through India. I have been to India.
मैं ताज महल देख चुका हूँ।	I have seen the Taj Mahal.
मैं पाकिस्तान में तीन साल रह चुका हूँ।	I have lived in Pakistan for three years. (I have spent three years living in Pakistan.)

The verb *cuknā* and English "already" do not correspond in all circumstances. The phrase *pahle se* (*hī*) can be used to convey the idea that an action or state that was already in effect continues to be in effect.

मैं पहले से ही यहाँ था।	I was already here.
मुझे पहले से ही थोड़ी हिन्दी आती थी।	I already knew a little Hindi.
मैं पहले से भारत के बारे में काफ़ी जानता था।	I already knew quite a bit about India.

Vocabulary 1

अंतर्राष्ट्रीय	*antarrāṣṭrīy*	international
अनुभव, तजुर्बा	*anubhav, tajurbā* (m.)	experience
इनाम	*inām* (m.)	prize, reward
कम से कम	*kam se kam*	at least
कुल मिलाकर	*kul milākar*	altogether
ख़बर	*xabar* (f.)	news, news item
ग़ैर-सरकारी	*ghair-sarkārī*	non-governmental
जी लगाकर	*jī lagākar*	(adverbial) diligently, putting one's heart into…
जीतना	*jītnā* (v.t./v.i.)	to win
तय होना	*tay honā* (v.i.)	to be determined, fixed, settled
V-ने को तैयार	V-*ne ko taiyār*	ready to V
दुर्घटना	*durghaṭnā* (f.)	accident
प्राप्त / हासिल करना	*prāpt / hāsil karnā*	to obtain
फ़ैसला	*faislā* (m.)	decision (*faislā karnā*, to decide)
बातचीत	*bātcīt* (f.)	conversation (*bātcīt karnā*, to talk, converse)
मुक़ाबला	*muqāblā* (m.)	competition
राजनीति, सियासत	*rājnīti, siyāsat* (f.)	politics (*rajnīti śāstr*, m. political science)
राष्ट्रीय	*rāṣṭrīy*	national (*rāṣṭr*, m. nation)
लिपि	*lipi* (f.)	script
विषय	*viṣay* (m.)	topic
वैसे तो... लेकिन...	*vaise to...lekin...*	while it is true that...still...
शिक्षा, तालीम	*śikṣā, tālīm* (f.)	education

संस्था	*sansthā* (f.)	institution, organization
सफलता, कामयाबी	*saphaltā, kāmyābī* (f.)	success (*saphal, kāmyāb*, successful)
समाचार	*samācār* (m.)	news, news item
हादसा	*hādsā* (m.)	accident
हारना	*hārnā* (v.i.)	to be defeated, to lose

Exercise 1 G

Read aloud and translate.

१. मैंने भारत से बी. ए. तक शिक्षा प्राप्त की है। २. उन्होंने हिन्दी साहित्य में पी. एच. डी. की है। ३. आपने कौन-कौन से विषय पढ़े हैं? ४. आपने कितने साल नौकरी की है? ५. मैंने कुल मिलाकर चार साल नौकरी की है। ६. मैंने अलग-अलग जगहों पर नौकरियाँ की हैं। ७. शर्मा जी ने इस विषय पर एक किताब लिखी है। ८. सीमा ने दो साल इस अख़बार के लिए काम किया है, लेकिन अब वह यहाँ काम नहीं करती। ९. वह अब कहाँ काम करती है और वहाँ कब से काम कर रही है? १०. तुम्हारे भाई ने कहाँ तक पढ़ाई की है? ११. उसने बी. ए. तक पढ़ाई की है। उसके बाद उसने कंप्यूटर कोर्स भी किया है। १२. तुम हिन्दी कब से सीख रहे हो? १३. मैं पिछले सितंबर से सीख रहा हूँ। १४. मैं लगभग सात महीनों से हिन्दी सीख रहा हूँ। १५. आप इस शहर में कितने साल से रह रहे हैं? १६. मैं बी. ए. पास कर चुका हूँ, लेकिन मैं अभी और पढ़ना चाहता हूँ। १७. मेरी बेटी बहुत होशियार है। वह अपने स्कूल के मुक़ाबलों में बहुत इनाम जीत चुकी है। १८. मैं निबंध का पहला हिस्सा पूरा कर चुका हूँ। १९. कौन-कौन यह कहानी पढ़ चुका है? २०. मैं यह वाली कहानी पढ़ चुकी हूँ लेकिन मुझे याद नहीं कि कहानी के आख़िर में क्या होता है।

Exercise 2 G

Translate into Hindi.

1. I have heard that Sanskrit is a difficult language.
2. I have read this book three times.
3. I have been to (gone to) India several times, but I have never been to Pakistan.
4. Have you seen the Himalaya Mountains?
5. I have done my M.A. from Delhi University.
6. She has worked in several large companies.

7. I have studied several languages, but I only know English and Hindi well.
8. We have been living in this city for several years.
9. Our class has been learning Hindi since last September.
10. We have already learned the script.
11. I have been studying here for one year.
12. I have already taken nine classes.

Exercise 3

Personalization Questions

१. आपने सुबह से कितने कप कॉफ़ी पी है?
२. आपने आज सुबह से लेकर अब तक क्या-क्या खाया है?
३. सुबह से लेकर अब तक आपने कितने लोगों को फ़ोन किया है?
४. आपने आज कितनी बार कपड़े बदले हैं?
५. आपने इस महीने कितनी किताबें पढ़ी हैं?
६. इस साल आपने कौन-कौन सी अच्छी फ़िल्में देखी हैं?
७. क्या आपने कभी कोई बॉलीवुड फ़िल्म देखी है?
८. क्या आपने कभी जापानी खाना खाया है? अगर हाँ, तो आप को कैसा लगा?
९. आप इस शहर में कब से रह रहे हैं?

१०. आपने अपनी ज़्यादातर ज़िंदगी किस शहर में गुज़ारी है?

११. क्या आप नौकरी करते हैं? अगर हाँ तो आप यह नौकरी कब से कर रहे हैं?

१२. आपने कहाँ-कहाँ नौकरी की है?

१३. आपने दुनिया में कहाँ-कहाँ की सैर की है?

१४. क्या आप कभी किसी मशहूर व्यक्ति से मिले हैं?

१५. आप हिन्दी कितने महीने से सीख रहे हैं?

Exercise 4

Your teacher will assign one of the sets of questions and statements below to you and one to a classmate. Take turns reading your sentences aloud. While one partner reads, the other should listen and respond to each statement in a complete sentence using *caknā*.

उदाहरण

क. क्या तुम अभी भी फ़ैसला कर रहे हो?
ख. नहीं, मैं फ़ैसला कर चुका हूँ|

Set I

१. क्या सब लोग खाना खा रहे हैं?

२. क्या अली सफ़ाई कर रहा है?

३. क्या मीना खाना पका रही है?

४. क्या प्रिया अभी भी तैयार हो रही है?

५. क्या तुम इन लोगों को फ़ोन करने जा रहे हो?

६. आप यह काम ख़त्म कर पाएँगे?

७. उसको इसके बारे में मत बताओ|

८. क्या आप हिन्दी बोलना सीखने के साथ देवनागरी लिपि भी सीख रहे हैं?

९. मेघना को उन लड़कों से कभी बात नहीं करनी चाहिए|

१०. यह खाना मत खाओ| यह परसों से यहाँ रखा है|

Set II

१. क्या पापा अख़बार पढ़ रहे हैं?
२. क्या मम्मी चाय बना रही हैं?
३. क्या बच्चे नहा रहे हैं?
४. क्या अमित अभी भी सोच रहा है?
५. क्या आप यह किताब पढ़ रहे हैं?
६. उस दुकान से कपड़े मत ख़रीदो। उसका सामान बहुत महँगा है।
७. क्या आप हमारे साथ यह फ़िल्म देखने चलेंगे?
८. आप मुझे मेरे पैसे कब देंगे? मुझे उनकी ज़रूरत है।
९. गीता कॉलेज कब ख़त्म करेगी?
१०. आज शुक्ला जी रिश्ता लेकर आए थे। तुम्हारी शादी तय हो गई है। तुम उनके बेटे से शादी करोगी।

Exercise 5

A. Form a group of three with two of your classmates. You are working on the hiring committee for your company with two of your coworkers. You have been given three applications to review. Each of you should read the excerpts from one application and then share the details with your committee members. Fill out the chart below with the important information that you learn.

कुमार अजय	अहमद जमील	संध्या नारायण

१. नाम: कुमार अजय
मैंने हिन्दी में एम. ए. किया है|
मैंने अपनी पूरी पढ़ाई हिन्दी माध्यम से की है|
मैं पिछले छह महीनों से एक कंप्यूटर कोर्स भी कर रहा हूँ|
मैंने दो साल अलग-अलग जगहों पर नौकरियाँ की हैं|
मैं सुबह, शाम किसी भी समय काम करने को तैयार हूँ|
मैं मेहनती हूँ और अपना काम जी लगाकर करूँगा|

२. नाम: अहमद जमील
मैंने अंग्रेज़ी में एम. ए. किया है|
कॉलेज में मेरे विषय हिन्दी, अंग्रेज़ी, और राजनीति शास्त्र थे|
मैंने चार साल नौकरी की है|
मैं एक बड़ी अंतर्राष्ट्रीय कंपनी के लिए भी काम कर चुका हूँ|
मैं सुबह ७ बजे से ८ बजे तक एक कोर्स ले रहा हूँ लेकिन उसके बाद मुझे कोई काम नहीं है|
मैं कंपनी की कामयाबी में अपनी कामयाबी समझूँगा|

३. नाम: संध्या नारायण
मैंने अंग्रेज़ी में पी. एच. डी. की है|
मैं अमरीका में पैदा हुई और मैंने अपनी सारी ज़िंदगी अमरीका में ही गुज़ारी है|
मैंने तीन साल जर्मनी में एक कंपनी के लिए काम किया है|
एक साल से मैं एक ग़ैरसरकारी संस्था के लिए काम कर रही हूँ|
मैंने जर्मन और हिन्दी में एक-एक साल का कोर्स किया है|
मुझे शाम को अपनी बच्ची की देखभाल करनी पड़ती है लेकिन मैं सुबह किसी भी समय काम शुरू कर सकती हूँ|

B. You have also received a voice message from your boss about the requirements for the job that you are hiring for. Listen to the voicemail and note all of the essential pieces of information. You may read the text of the voicemail afterwards to confirm what you have noted.

हमें कोई चाहिए जिसने कम से कम एम. ए. किया हो*। अगर उसने पी. एच. डी. की हो तो और भी अच्छा है। उसके पास तीन साल नौकरी का अनुभव भी होना चाहिए। अगर वह किसी बड़ी कंपनी में काम कर चुका हो तो और भी अच्छा है। यह ज़रूरी है कि वह अच्छी तरह अंग्रेज़ी और हिन्दी दोनों जानता हो। वैसे तो हमारे दफ़्तर का समय सुबह ९ बजे से शाम ५ बजे तक है लेकिन हमें ऐसा व्यक्ति चाहिए जो शाम को ओवरटाइम करने के लिए भी तैयार हो।

*Note how the subjunctive is used in the auxiliary verb. Please see the supplementary grammar section at the end of the book for more information on this structure.

C. Based on the information that you have, work with your partners to match the most qualified applicant to the position. Speak only in Hindi and be prepared to give the rationale for your decision.

40

At the Doctor

In this chapter you will learn how to discuss your health and describe symptoms of illnesses in order to communicate with a doctor.

Ailments and Physical Conditions

Many English expressions related to physical ailments contain the verb *to have*. Corresponding Hindi expressions generally take the following form:

X *ko* [ailment] *honā* **for X to have [ailment]**

Here are some common examples:

X *ko taklīf honā*	for X to have an ailment, for something to be troubling X
आपको क्या तकलीफ़ है?	What is troubling you? What ailment do you have?
मेरे पेट में बहुत तकलीफ़ हो रही है।	My stomach is hurting a lot.
X *ko buxār honā*	for X to have a fever
मुझे दो दिन से बुख़ार है।	I have had a fever for two days.
X *ko zukām honā*	for X to have a cold
उसको बहुत बुरा ज़ुकाम है।	He has a very bad cold.

Many ailment-related expressions are expressed through *ko* constructions with other verbs, such as *lagnā* and *ānā*.

X *ko cakkar ānā*	for X to feel dizzy, experience spells of dizziness
मुझे चक्कर आ रहे हैं।	I'm feeling dizzy.
X *ko coṭ lagnā*	for X to get injured
तुम्हें कहाँ चोट लगी?	Where did you get injured?

In general, many physical conditions are expressed through *ko* constructions.

X को भूख लगना	for X to be/get hungry
X को प्यास लगना	for X to be/get thirsty
X को सर्दी लगना	for X to be/get cold

X को गर्मी लगना	for X to be/get hot
X को नींद आना	for X to be/get sleepy

Expressing the Beginning of an Action

The construction V-*ne lagnā*, the oblique infinitive followed by *lagnā*, expresses the inception of an action, generally an unplanned one, or one that begins of its own accord.

वह उल्टी करने लगा।	He began to vomit.
मेरे पेट में दर्द होने लगा।	My stomach began to hurt.
मुझे सर्दी लगने लगी।	I began to feel cold.

Compound Verbs

Most of the verbs encountered till now have been simple verbs that consist of a single verb stem that supplies the meaning of the action and serves as a base for tense endings to be affixed. Such simple verbal constructions can be represented as follows:

V + -[tense endings]

However, a few verbal constructions have also been encountered in which two verb stems are used, the first of which occurs in stem form and provides the basic meaning, and the second of which bears tense endings and provides the main verb with an additional nuance. This pattern can be represented as follows (where V1 represents the main verb and V2 represents the second verb):

$$\mathbf{V_1 + V_2 + \text{-[tense endings]}}$$

Hindi possesses several additional verbal constructions that follow this pattern, and that unfortunately have no direct counterpart in English. These verbal constructions are collectively called *compound verbs*. Various verbs are used as the second verb in compound verb constructions, though the most common are *jānā, lenā,* and *denā*. Contrast the forms of the verbs in the following pairs of sentences.

simple verbs		compound verbs	
वह आया।	He came.	वह आ गया।	He (finally) came.
मैंने खाना खाया।	I ate.	मैंने खाना खा लिया।	I (already) ate.
मैंने उसको बताया।	I told him.	मैंने उसको बता दिया।	I (went ahead and) told him.

बच्चे सोए।	The children slept.	बच्चे सो गए।	The children fell asleep.
सब कुछ ठीक होगा।	Everything will be alright.	सब कुछ ठीक हो जाएगा।	Everything will be(come) alright.
मैं हिन्दी बोलती हूँ।	I speak Hindi.	मैं हिन्दी बोल लेती हूँ।	I (manage to) speak Hindi

As can be seen in these examples, the verb *jānā* is typically used with intransitive verbs, whereas either *denā* or *lenā* is used with transitive verbs. As can also be seen, compound verbs add subtle nuances to the meaning of the main verb. In general, compound verbs add the sense that the performance of the action brings about the completion of a previously existing state of affairs or the establishment of a new state of affairs.

In addition, the verbs *denā* and *lenā* indicate the direction of the effects of the action with respect to the subject. The verb *denā* indicates an action with effects directed away from the subject, whereas *lenā* indicates an action with effects directed toward the subject. The verb *lenā* can also add the sense of 'managing' to do something, similarly to the verb *pānā*.

Due to the fact that one of the basic meanings that compound verbs express is completion, they are typically not used with negation or with the continuous verb tenses, both of which are by definition incomplete. For the same reason, compound verbs are typically not found in the middle of a sequence of verbs in continuous narration, though they very well might be found at the end of the sequence.

A complete account of compound verbs would take up more space than is available here. At this stage, your goal should be to recognize compound verbs when you encounter them, and to develop a sense of the particular nuances that they add in each context.

Vocabulary 1

In addition to the words given here, please also refer to the list of body-related words given at the end of the chapter. Some of these might be needed to carry out the exercises of this chapter.

अचानक	*acānak*	all of a sudden
इलाज	*ilāj* (m.)	treatment (medical) (X *kā ilāj karnā*, to treat X)
उल्टी	*ulṭī* (f.)	vomit, vomiting (X *ko ulṭī ānā*, for X to feel nauseous; *ulṭī karnā*, to vomit)
कमज़ोर	*kamzor*	weak
कमज़ोरी	*kamzorī* (f.)	weakness, fatigue

खाँसी	*khā̃sī* (f.)	coughing, fits of coughing (*khānsī ānā*, to have a cough; *khā̃snā*, to cough)
ख़ुराक	*xurāk* (f.)	dose; diet
ख़ून	*xūn* (m.)	blood (*xūn bahnā*, to bleed)
गड़बड़	*gaṛbaṛ* (f.)	mess, unsettled state
गला	*galā* (m.)	throat
गोली	*golī* (f.)	pill, bullet
घबराना	*ghabrānā* (v.i.)	to be/get anxious, disconcerted
घायल	*ghāyal*	wounded
घाव	*ghāv* (m.)	wound
चक्कर	*cakkar* (m.pl.)	spells of dizziness (X *ko cakkar ānā*, for X to get/feel dizzy)
चोट	*coṭ* (f.)	injury (X *ko coṭ lagnā*, for X to get an injury)
छींक	*chī̃k* (f.)	sneeze (X *ko chī̃k ānā*, for X to sneeze, for X to have to sneeze; *chī̃knā*, to sneeze)
ज़ख़्म	*zaxm* (m.)	wound (*zaxmī*, wounded)
जल्द ही	*jald hī*	very quickly
जाँच	*jā̃c* (f.)	examination; investigation
ज़ुकाम	*zukām* (m.)	a cold (X *ko zukām honā*, for X to have a cold)
तकलीफ़	*taklīf* (f.)	discomfort
तेज़	*tez*	strong, sharp
थकान	*thakān* (f.)	tiredness
दर्द	*dard* (m.)	pain (*sirdard*, m. headache)
दवा / दवाई	*davā* / *davāī* (f.)	medicine
दस्त	*dast* (m.pl.)	diarrhea
दुखना	*dukhnā* (v.i.)	to hurt, be sore
दुबारा, दोबारा	*dubārā*, *dobārā*	again
दुर्घटना, हादसा	*durghaṭnā* (f.), *hādsā* (m.)	accident

निगलना	*nigalnā* (v.t.)	to swallow
नुस्ख़ा	*nusxā* (m.)	prescription
पट्टी	*paṭṭī* (f.)	bandage (to apply)
परहेज़	*parhez* (m.)	refraining from (X *se parhez karnā*, to refrain from X)
पसीना	*pasīnā* (m.)	sweat (X *ko pasīnā ānā*, for X to sweat)
बंद होना	*band honā*	to stop (w/ infinitive); to close
बहना	*bahnā* (v.i.)	to flow (*nāk bahnā*, for one's nose to run)
बाँधना	*bā̃dhnā* (v.t.)	to tie
बिस्कुट	*biskuṭ* (m.)	cracker, cookie
बुख़ार	*buxār* (m.)	fever (X *ko buxār honā*, for X to have a fever)
बेहोश	*behoś*	unconscious
भारी	*bhārī*	heavy (*tabiyat bhārī honā*, for one to not feel well)
मतली	*matlī* (f.)	nausea (X *ko matlī honā*, for X to be nauseous)
मरीज़	*marīz*	patient (medical)
महसूस करना	*mahsūs karnā*	to feel
X को महसूस होना	X *ko mahsūs honā*	for X to feel (+ noun)
मोच	*moc* (f.)	sprain (X *ke/kī…mẽ moc ānā*, for X's… to get sprained)
लेटना	*leṭnā* (v.i.)	to lie down
सूखना	*sūkhnā* (v.i.)	to dry out, to go dry
सूजन	*sūjan* (f.)	swelling (*sūjnā*, v.i. to swell), inflammation
होश	*hoś* (m.)	consciousness (*hoś mẽ ānā*, to return to consciousness)

Exercise 1

Read aloud and translate.

१. बच्ची को कल से तेज़ बुख़ार है| २. उसे डॉक्टर को दिखाना चाहिए| ३. डॉक्टर साहब, आज सुबह से मेरे पेट में दर्द हो रहा है| ४. क्या आपको मतली भी हो रही है? ५. मतली तो नहीं हो रही है मगर गला सूख रहा है| ६. कल रात भर में उसको पाँच उल्टियाँ हो चुकी हैं| ७. आज सुबह से मेरे सिर में हल्का दर्द हो रहा था, फिर शाम से चक्कर भी आने लगे| ८. मैंने सुबह वाली ख़ुराक खा ली है| ९. एक ही ख़ुराक में मेरी तबियत कुछ ठीक हो गई है| १०. मुझे प्यास लग रही है| मुझे कुछ पानी दे दीजिए|

Exercise 2

Translate the sentences into Hindi.

1. I have a cold and I have a cough too.
2. Is your nose also running?
3. No, but I have really severe pain in my head. Actually, my entire body is hurting.
4. I was feeling dizzy for a little while, then all of a sudden I went unconscious.
5. I had some ice cream from that shop and then I started feeling nauseous.
6. How many times have you vomited since the morning?
7. My stomach is upset and I'm sweating.
8. Your leg is bleeding. How did you get hurt?

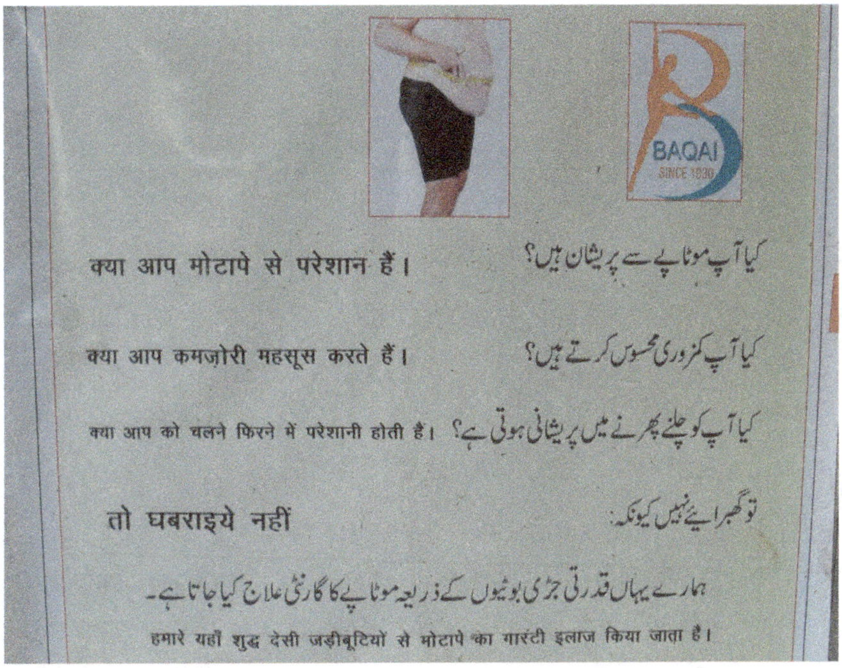

Exercise 3

You are volunteering at a health clinic in South Asia. The clerk has taken the following notes about three patients who need to see the doctor on duty.

Form a group of three students. Read one of the notes below. Note the essential pieces of information, and then in your own words share what you have read. As your partners share, note what they report in the table below. When finished, decide with your partners who should be sent to see the doctor first.

मरीज़ १	मरीज़ २	मरीज़ ३

मरीज़ १: मरीज़ को पेट में दर्द है| उसने कल रात मसालेदार खाना खाया था| उसके बाद उसको उल्टियाँ शुरू हो गईं| रात १२ बजे तक उसकी तबियत कुछ ठीक हो गई थी लेकिन सुबह यहाँ आने से पहले उसने दो उल्टियाँ की थीं|

मरीज़ २: मरीज़ को ज़ुकाम और बुख़ार है| उसको एक हफ़्ते से खाँसी आ रही थी लेकिन अब खाँसी कुछ बेहतर है| कल उसको चक्कर भी आ रहे थे लेकिन अब वह कुछ बेहतर महसूस कर रही है| कल सारा दिन उसकी तबियत ज़्यादा ख़राब थी इसलिए उसने कुछ नहीं खाया था लेकिन आज सुबह अस्पताल आने से पहले उसने कॉफ़ी पी थी और कुछ बिस्कुट खाए थे|

मरीज़ ३: मरीज़ के पैर में चोट लगी है| आज सुबह वह सीढ़ी से नीचे गिर गया था| हादसे के तुरंत बाद वह बेहोश हो गया था| उसके भाई ने उसके ज़ख़्म पर पट्टी बाँध दी थी और ख़ून बहना बंद हो गया था| लेकिन होश में आने के बाद जब उसने चलना शुरू किया तो ख़ून बहना दुबारा शुरू हो गया| इस समय ख़ून नहीं बह रहा है लेकिन मरीज़ बहुत कमज़ोरी महसूस कर रहा है|

Exercise 4

Shubhi has been feeling ill and has gone to see the doctor. Listen to the conversation between Shubhi and the doctor and answer the questions.

शुभि	नमस्ते डॉक्टर साहब|
डॉक्टर	नमस्ते शुभि| कहो, क्या तकलीफ़ है?
शुभि	बस कल से तेज़ बुख़ार है और सिर में दर्द भी है|
डॉक्टर	कल किस वक़्त से तबियत ख़राब है?
शुभि	असल में परसों सुबह से ही तबियत भारी थी| फिर शाम तक हल्का बुख़ार हो गया और कल शाम से तो बहुत तेज़ बुख़ार है|
डॉक्टर	अच्छा, परसों या उससे पहले तुमने क्या खाया था?
शुभि	कल शाम तो कुछ भारी नहीं खाया| कल रात को सिर्फ़ चाय पी थी और बिस्कुट खाए थे| हाँ, दो दिन पहले मैं एक दावत में गई थी और वहाँ काफ़ी चीज़ें खाई थीं|
डॉक्टर	अच्छा, क्या पेट में भी दर्द है?
शुभि	जी हाँ, पेट में भी कुछ दर्द हो रहा है| असल में पूरा बदन दुख रहा है और बहुत कमज़ोरी महसूस हो रही है|
डॉक्टर	ज़रा अपनी जीभ दिखाओ| अच्छा, अब इस बेंच पर लेट जाओ| मुझे तुम्हारे पेट की जाँच करनी है|
शुभि	जी, अच्छा|
डॉक्टर	क्या यहाँ दर्द है?
शुभि	जी हाँ हल्का दर्द हो रहा है|

डॉक्टर	घबराओ मत। मैं दवा दूँगा। दो दिन में बिल्कुल ठीक हो जाओगी। यह लो दवाओं का नुस्ख़ा। तीन दिन तक रोज़ तीन ख़ुराकें खानी हैं। उम्मीद है जल्द ही ठीक हो जाओगी। ज़्यादा मसालेदार खाने से परहेज़ करो। सादा खाना खाओ और ख़ूब पानी पियो।
शुभि	शुक्रिया डॉक्टर साहब। नमस्ते।
डॉक्टर	नमस्ते।

सवाल

१. शुभि को क्या तकलीफ़ है?

२. शुभि ने दो दिन पहले क्या खाया था?

३. शुभि को कितनी ख़ुराकें कितने दिन तक खानी हैं?

४. शुभि को किस चीज़ से परहेज़ करना है?

Exercise 5

Role Play

Student 1: You are the friend of an American in India who is not feeling well. Your friend does not know Hindi so you have offered to help communicate at the doctor's office. You have now arrived at the doctor's office and the clerk has some questions about your friend's condition. Answer the questions based on the following information:

Current symptoms?	Is he or she feeling any pain? Where?	When and how did it start?	Did he or she eat (had he or she eaten) anything before it started? What?	What has he or she eaten and drunk (has he or she eaten and drunk) since this morning?	Did he or she take (had he or she taken) any medicine before coming to the hospital?
stomach ache, dizziness	pain in the stomach and in the back	started at a party two days ago	kababs	nothing	a painkiller

Student 2: You are the clerk in a doctor's office. Find out the following information from your partner about the ill friend who does not speak Hindi.

Current symptoms?	Is he or she feeling any pain? Where?	When and how did it start?	Did he or she eat (had he or she eaten) anything before it started? What?	What has he or she eaten and drunk (has he or she eaten and drunk) since this morning?	Did he or she take (had he or she taken) any medicine before coming to the hospital?

Switch roles and repeat.

Student 1:

Current symptoms?	Is he or she feeling any pain? Where?	When and how did it start?	Did she eat (had he or she eaten) anything before it started? What?	What has he or she eaten and drunk (has he or she eaten and drunk) since this morning?	Did he or she take (had he or she taken) any medicine before coming to the hospital?
Fever, cold	Pain in the head and throat	Started three days ago. She had gone to visit her sister's kids	Doesn't remember	Tea and biscuits	Cold medicine

Vocabulary 2

Additional Body-Related Vocabulary

अंगूठा	*angūṭhā* (m.)	thumb
उंगली	*unglī* (f.)	finger
एड़ी	*eṛī* (f.)	heel
कंधा	*kandhā* (m.)	shoulder
कमर	*kamar* (f.)	waist
कलाई	*kalāī* (f.)	wrist
कुहनी	*kuhnī* (f.)	elbow
गर्दन	*gardan* (f.)	neck
गला	*galā* (m.)	throat
घुटना	*ghuṭnā* (m.)	knee
छाती	*chātī* (f.)	chest
जिस्म	*jism* (m.)	body
जीभ	*jībh* (f.)	tongue
टाँग	*ṭā̃g* (f.)	leg
त्वचा, चमड़ी	*tvacā, camṛī* (f.)	skin
दिल	*dil* (m.)	heart
धड़	*dhaṛ* (m.)	torso
नाख़ून	*nāxūn* (m.)	nail
पाँव	*pā̃v* (*pā̃õ*) (m.)	foot, leg
पिंडली	*pinḍlī* (f.)	calf
पीठ	*pīṭh* (f.)	back

पेट	*peṭ* (m.)	stomach
पैर	*pair* (m.)	leg, foot
फेफड़ा	*phephṛā* (m.)	lung
बाँह, बाज़ू	*bā̃h* (f.), *bāzū* (m.)	arm
भौंह, भौं	*bhaũh*, *bhaũ* (f.)	eyebrow
माथा	*māthā* (m.)	forehead
शरीर	*śarīr* (m.)	body
सिर, सर	*sir, sar* (m.)	head
सीना	*sīnā* (m.)	chest
हड्डी	*haḍḍī* (f.)	bone
हथेली	*hathelī* (f.)	palm
हाथ	*hāth* (m.)	hand, arm

41

Unit 8 Review Activities

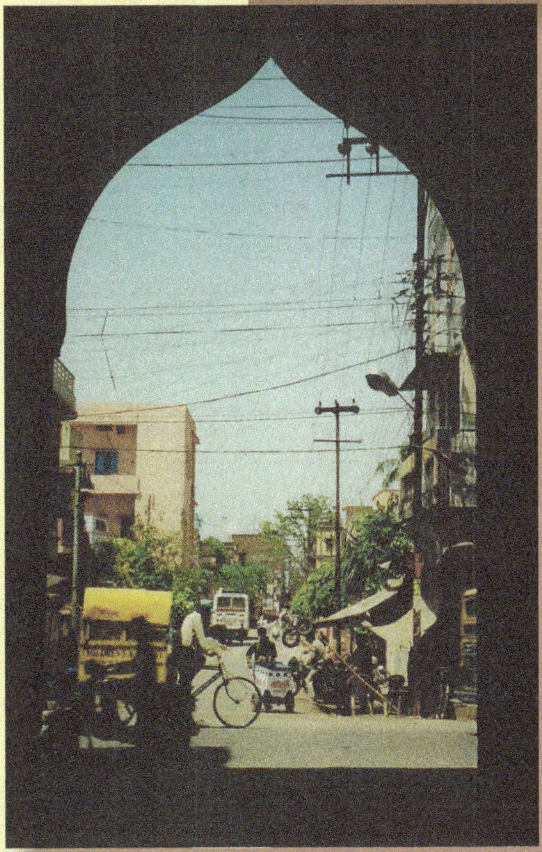

The goal of this chapter is to review the content of unit 8 and provide additional opportunities to synthesize all of the content presented throughout the book.

G

1. Grammar Review

- What is the difference between the perfective and past habitual in terms of usage?
- How is the perfective formed? Conjugate any verb in its entirety in this verb tense.
- Explain the unusual agreement pattern affecting the perfective, present perfect, and past perfect verb tenses.
- How is the present perfect formed? Conjugate any verb in its entirety in this verb tense.
- What English verb tense does the Hindi present perfect correspond most closely to? What is the primary purpose of the present perfect?
- How is the past perfect formed? Conjugate any verb in its entirety in this verb tense.
- What is the primary function of the past perfect in past narration?
- Give two examples of the use of the verb *cuknā*. What English word is usually used in the translation of this structure?
- What is another structure that is used to indicate completion of an action as well as a change in state resulting from its completion?

2. Tips for Increasing Fluency: Speaking Drills

- Make sure that you can ask and answer all of the general questions given throughout this unit.

A. Perfective

- Choose a recent day that was typical in terms of what you did from morning till evening. List all of the actions that you performed in chronological order (choose about 15 verbs). Narrate what you did on this day from beginning till end. Use the temporal conjunctions and other tools that you have learned to sequence the events.
- Describe the last time you went out of town. What did you do from the time you left to the time you returned?

B. Present Perfect

- List your education, work, and other accomplishments on a separate piece of paper in key-word form. Go through your list and explain your accomplishments as if you are talking to a prospective employer.

C. Past Perfect

- The verb tense is best practiced by giving background information on previous events prior to a main storyline.

D. *cuknā*

- Make a list of all of the chores and school assignments that you had to do in the past two weeks as well as those that you still need to do in the next week. Note each action in the form of a keyword. Go through your list and state what you have already done and what you still have to do.

3. Personalization Questions

Vocabulary 1

घटना	*ghaṭnā* (f./v.i.)	incident, event; घटना घटना, for an event to occur
विस्तार	*vistār* (m.)	extent, expanse (*vistār se*, in detail, at length)
समारोह	*samāroh* (m.)	function, celebratory occasion; ceremony
हाल में	*hāl mẽ*	recently
हैरान	*hairān*	surprised

१. क्या आपने कभी कोई दिलचस्प सफ़र किया है? उसके बारे में विस्तार से बताइए।
२. क्या कभी आपके साथ कोई दुर्घटना हुई? उसके बारे में विस्तार से बताइए।
३. क्या किसी घटना ने कभी आपको हैरान किया। उसके बारे में विस्तार से बताइए।
४. क्या आपने हाल में कोई दिलचस्प दिन गुज़ारा? उसके बारे में विस्तार से बताइए।
५. क्या आपने कभी किसी दिलचस्प समारोह में भाग लिया? उसके बारे में विस्तार से बताइए।

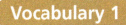

4. Form four groups students. Make up a story with your classmates by adding sentences turn by turn. Feel free to use all of the past-tense forms that you know as well as any other tenses that are appropriate. Remember to use the appropriate form for the function of your sentence. Below is a list of past-tense verb forms and their functions to help you out:

किरदार *kirdār* (m.) role

Main storyline	Perfective: What did the character do? / What happened?	किरदार ने क्या किया / क्या हुआ?
Background Information	Past Habitual: What did the character regularly do in the period in which the story takes place?	किरदार क्या करता था?
	Past Continuous: What was the character doing (i.e. when something else happened)?	किरदार क्या कर रहा था?
	Past Perfect: What had the character done before that is relevant to the main line of events? What had happened before?	किरदार ने उससे पहले क्या किया था / क्या हुआ था?

Write your own final version of the story. Feel free to add or subtract any details.

5. Read the following passage about an American student named Josh, and his first trip to India, and answer the questions.

Vocabulary 2

अनुभव, तजुर्बा	*anubhav, tajurbā* (m.)	experience
इन्चार्ज	*incārj*	head, in charge
गंदगी	*gandgī* (f.)	dirt; filth, grime
ग़लती	*ghalatī* (f.)	mistake
गली	*galī* (f.)	alley, lane

X से गुज़रना	X *se guzarnā*	to pass (by) X
जारी रखना	*jārī rakhnā*	to maintain
टेढ़ा-मेढ़ा	*ṭeṛhā-meṛhā*	crooked, winding
तंग	*tang*	tight
तलाश	*talāś* (f.)	search
दर्शन	*darśan* (m.)	view of (esp. of a deity during worship)
धर्म, मज़हब	*dharm* (m.), *mazhab* (m.)	religion
पल	*pal* (m.)	moment
पहनाना	*pahnānā* (v.t.)	to dress (another person)
बाँसुरी	*bā̃surī* (f.)	bamboo flute
भरपूर	*bharpūr*	full, complete
भिखारी	*bhikhārī*	beggar
माला	*mālā* (f.)	garland
माहौल	*māhaul* (m.)	atmosphere
रूमानी	*rūmānī*	romantic
सुकून	*sukūn* (m.)	peace, tranquility
हालत	*hālat* (f.)	condition

मेरा हिंदुस्तान का सफ़र

मैं पहली बार हिंदुस्तान २००० में गया| उस समय मुझे हिंदू धर्म में दिलचस्पी थी, इसलिए मैं भारत जाकर ख़ुद अनुभव करके उसके बारे में और जानना चाहता था| उससे एक साल पहले से मैं संस्कृत पढ़ रहा था और जाने से पहले गर्मियों में मैंने हिन्दी पढ़ना भी शुरू किया था| मुझे बहुत ख़ुशी थी कि वाराणसी में एक हिन्दी प्रोग्राम है क्योंकि वहाँ मैं अपनी हिन्दी और संस्कृत की पढ़ाई भी जारी रख सकता था और हिंदू धर्म को भी अच्छी तरह समझ सकता था| मुझे ख़ासतौर पर साधुओं में दिलचस्पी थी|

असल में भारत जाने से पहले भारत मेरे लिए सिर्फ़ एक रूमानी ख़्याल था| मुझे लगता था कि भारत मूँछ वाले राजाओं, साधुओं, और हाथियों का देश है| मुझे बिल्कुल मालूम नहीं था कि असली भारत क्या है|

तो मैं और मेरा ग्रुप सितंबर के शुरू में दिल्ली पहुँचे। वहाँ हवाई अड्डे पर हिन्दी प्रोग्राम की इन्चार्ज ट्रूडी हमारे लिए फूलों की मालाएँ लेकर आई थीं। जब हम हवाई अड्डे पर मिले तो उन्होंने हमें मालाएँ पहनाईं। हमने दिल्ली में दो-चार दिन गुज़ारे। हमने कुतुब मीनार और दूसरी इमारतें देखीं और बहुत मुग़लई खाना खाया।

उसके बाद हमने वाराणसी जानेवाली गाड़ी पकड़ी और हमें भारतीय रेलगाड़ी का भरपूर अनुभव हुआ। वाराणसी पहुंचने के बाद मुझे बड़ा कल्चर शॉक लगा। ट्रेन स्टेशन के बाहर बहुत भिखारी थे। उनकी हालत बहुत बुरी थी। इसके अलावा हर तरफ़ कूड़ा था और गंदगी थी। उस समय मैंने सोचा कि शायद भारत आकर मैंने ग़लती की है और मैं इस जगह आठ महीने कैसे रह सकता हूँ।

हम लोगों ने कुछ आराम किया और खाना खाया तो कुछ बेहतर लगने लगा। उसके बाद हम गंगा नदी देखने गए। वाराणसी की गलियाँ बहुत तंग और टेढ़ी-मेढ़ी हैं। उन गलियों से गुज़रने के बाद गंगाजी का दर्शन हुआ। उसी पल मैं समझ गया कि मैं यहाँ क्यों आया हूँ। वहाँ ठंडी हवा चल रही थी। कहीं दूर कोई बाँसुरी बजा रहा था। पेड़ों पर बंदर के बच्चे खेल रहे थे। माहौल में सुकून था। यह मेरा रूमानी हिंदुस्तान था जिसकी तलाश में मैं इतनी दूर आया था।

प्रश्न

१. जब जोश पहली बार भारत गये, उस समय उनको किस चीज़ में दिलचस्पी थी?
२. वे वाराणसी जाकर क्या जारी रखना चाहते थे?
३. हिंदुस्तान जाने से पहले उनका हिंदुस्तान के बारे में क्या विचार था?
४. जब वे और उनका ग्रुप ट्रूडी से मिले तो ट्रूडी ने क्या किया?
५. दिल्ली में जोश ने क्या-क्या किया?
६. वाराणसी की गलियाँ कैसी हैं?
७. गंगा के किनारे माहौल कैसा था?
८. जिस चीज़ की तलाश में जोश हिंदुस्तान गए थे क्या वह चीज़ उन्हें मिली?

Varanasi, India

6. Write an account of a memorable experience you have had. In addition to recounting the main line of events, be sure to set the stage by explaining the background circumstances behind your story. Feel free to write about a travel experience, your first day in college, a frightening experience, or any other subject of your own choosing.

7. Read the news story about an accident and answer the questions.

Vocabulary 3

आशंका	*āśankā* (f.)	fear; apprehension
एलान	*elān* (m.)	announcement
के क़रीब	X *ke qarīb*	around X
गत	*gat*	past
तभी	*tabhī*	right then
तय	*tay*	determined, fixed
दबना	*dabnā* (v.i.)	to be pressed down
दबा हुआ	*dabā huā* (v.i.)	pressed down (i.e., by rubble)
दुर्घटनास्थल	*durghaṭnā-sthal* (m.)	the site of an accident
पुल	*pul* (m.)	bridge
मरम्मत	*marammat* (f.)	repair
मलबा	*malbā* (m.)	rubble
मुआवज़ा	*muāvzā* (m.)	compensation
मौत	*maut* (f.)	death
राहतकर्मी	*rāhatkarmī*	relief worker
व्यक्ति	*vyakti* (m.)	individual

पुल रेलगाड़ी पर गिर गया, ३० व्यक्तियों की मौत

भारत के पूर्वी राज्य बिहार में एक पुल के रेलगाड़ी पर गिर जाने से ३० व्यक्तियों की मौत हो गयी| गत रविवार को शाम सात बजे के क़रीब जब एक यात्री ट्रेन एक पुल के नीचे से गुज़र रही थी, तभी पुल का एक हिस्सा टूटकर उस पर गिर गया| यह एक डेढ़ सौ साल पुराना पुल था जिसकी मरम्मत का काम अगले महीने होना तय था| इस दुर्घटना में अब तक ३० व्यक्तियों के मरने और १०० से ज़्यादा व्यक्तियों के घायल होने की ख़बर है| राहतकर्मी मलबे में दबे लोगों को बाहर निकालने का काम कर रहे हैं| आशंका है कि अभी भी काफ़ी लोग मलबे में दबे हुए हैं|

रेल मंत्री दुर्घटनास्थल पर पहुँच चुके हैं और उन्होंने मरनेवालों के परिवारों को ३ - ३ लाख रुपये और घायलों को ७५ हज़ार रुपये मुआवज़ा देने का एलान किया है|

1. How did people die in the Indian state of Bihar?
2. How old was the bridge?
3. What are relief workers doing?
4. What has the railway minister announced?

8. Listen to the news clip about an accident and answer the questions.

Vocabulary 4

अधिकारी	*adhikārī* (m.)	official
इलाक़ा, क्षेत्र	*ilāqā, kṣetr* (m.)	region
गंभीर	*gambhīr*	serious
ज़बरदस्त	*zabardast*	strong, powerful
पुलिस	*pulis* (f.)	police
मर्द	*mard* (m.)	man
शामिल	*śāmil*	included
स्वयंसेवक	*svayamsevak* (m.)	volunteer
हटाना	*haṭānā* (v.t.)	to move aside; to remove

कल रात हुई ज़बरदस्त बारिश में जमीलाबाद के क़रीब एक इलाक़े में दो घरों की दीवारें गिर गयीं| इस दुर्घटना में चार लोगों की मौत और पाँच के घायल होने की ख़बर है| घायलों को तुरंत अस्पताल पहुँचाया गया जहाँ उनका इलाज हो रहा है| घायलों में से एक की हालत गंभीर है| मरनेवालों में दो मर्द, एक औरत, और एक बच्चा शामिल हैं| इलाक़े के लोगों को आशंका है कि मलबे में अभी कुछ लोग और दबे हो सकते हैं| पुलिस अधिकारी और स्वयंसेवक मलबा हटाने और लोगों को ढूँढने में व्यस्त हैं|

सवाल

१. जमीलाबाद के क़रीब क्या दुर्घटना हुई?
२. इस दुर्घटना में कितने लोगों की मौत हुई और कितने लोग घायल हुए?
३. इलाक़े के लोगों को किस बात की आशंका है?
४. पुलिस अधिकारी और स्वयंसेवक क्या कर रहे हैं?

Sayings and Proverbs

रात गई बात गई

घर का भेदी लंका ढाए

खोदा पहाड़, निकली चुहिया

ब्याह न किया तो क्या, बारात तो गए हैं

रस्सी जल गयी, बल न गया

कौवा चला हंस की चाल, अपनी चाल भी भूल गया

अब पछताए होत क्या, जब चिड़ियाँ चुग गयीं खेत

न ख़ुदा ही मिला न विसाल-ए-सनम, न इधर के रहे न उधर के ही हम

कबिरा खड़ा बजार में मांगे सबकी खैर, न काहू से दोस्ती न काहू से बैर

Appendix 1: Numbers

Cardinal Numbers

०	शून्य	*śūny*	0
१	एक	*ek*	1
२	दो	*do*	2
३	तीन	*tīn*	3
४	चार	*cār*	4
५	पाँच	*pā̃c*	5
६	छह	*che*	6
७	सात	*sāt*	7
८	आठ	*āṭh*	8
९	नौ	*nau*	9
१०	दस	*das*	10
११	ग्यारह	*gyārah*	11
१२	बारह	*bārah*	12
१३	तेरह	*terah*	13
१४	चौदह	*caudah*	14
१५	पंद्रह	*pandrah*	15
१६	सोलह	*solah*	16
१७	सत्रह	*satrah*	17
१८	अठारह	*aṭhārah*	18
१९	उन्नीस	*unnīs*	19
२०	बीस	*bīs*	20
२१	इक्कीस	*ikkīs*	21
२२	बाईस	*bāīs*	22

२३	तेईस	*teīs*	23
२४	चौबीस	*caubīs*	24
२५	पच्चीस	*paccīs*	25
२६	छब्बीस	*chabbīs*	26
२७	सत्ताईस	*sattāīs*	27
२८	अट्ठाईस	*aṭṭhāīs*	28
२९	उनतीस	*untīs*	29
३०	तीस	*tīs*	30
३१	इकत्तीस	*ikattīs*	31
३२	बत्तीस	*battīs*	32
३३	तैंतीस	*taĩtīs*	33
३४	चौंतीस	*caũtīs*	34
३५	पैंतीस	*paĩtīs*	35
३६	छत्तीस	*chattīs*	36
३७	सैंतीस	*saĩtīs*	37
३८	अड़तीस	*aṛtīs*	38
३९	उनतालीस	*untālīs*	39
४०	चालीस	*cālīs*	40
४१	इकतालीस	*iktālīs*	41
४२	बयालीस	*bayālīs*	42
४३	तैंतालीस	*taĩtālīs*	43
४४	चवालीस	*cavālīs*	44
४५	पैंतालीस	*paĩtālīs*	45
४६	छियालीस	*chiyālīs*	46
४७	सैंतालीस	*saĩtālīs*	47
४८	अड़तालीस	*aṛtālīs*	48
४९	उनचास	*uncās*	49
५०	पचास	*pacās*	50
५१	इक्यावन	*ikyāvan*	51

५२	बावन	*bāvan*	52
५३	तिरपन	*tirpan*	53
५४	चौवन	*cauvan*	54
५५	पचपन	*pacpan*	55
५६	छप्पन	*chappan*	56
५७	सत्तावन	*sattāvan*	57
५८	अट्ठावन	*aṭṭhāvan*	58
५९	उनसठ	*unsaṭh*	59
६०	साठ	*sāṭh*	60
६१	इकसठ	*iksaṭh*	61
६२	बासठ	*bāsaṭh*	62
६३	तिरसठ	*tirsaṭh*	63
६४	चौंसठ	*caũsaṭh*	64
६५	पैंसठ	*paĩsaṭh*	65
६६	छियासठ	*chiyāsaṭh*	66
६७	सड़सठ	*saṛsaṭh*	67
६८	अड़सठ	*aṛsaṭh*	68
६९	उनहत्तर	*unhattar*	69
७०	सत्तर	*sattar*	70
७१	इकहत्तर	*ikhattar*	71
७२	बहत्तर	*bahattar*	72
७३	तिहत्तर	*tihattar*	73
७४	चौहत्तर	*cauhattar*	74
७५	पचहत्तर	*pachattar*	75
७६	छिहत्तर	*chihattar*	76
७७	सतहत्तर	*sathattar*	77
७८	अठहत्तर	*aṭhhattar*	78
७९	उन्यासी	*unyāsī*	79
८०	अस्सी	*assī*	80

८१	इक्यासी	*ikyāsī*	81
८२	बयासी	*bayāsī*	82
८३	तिरासी	*tirāsī*	83
८४	चौरासी	*caurāsī*	84
८५	पचासी	*pacāsī*	85
८६	छियासी	*chiyāsī*	86
८७	सत्तासी	*sattāsī*	87
८८	अट्ठासी	*aṭṭhāsī*	88
८९	नवासी	*navāsī*	89
९०	नब्बे, नव्वे	*nabbe, navve*	90
९१	इक्यानवे	*ikyānve*	91
९२	बानवे	*bānve*	92
९३	तिरानवे	*tirānve*	93
९४	चौरानवे	*caurānve*	94
९५	पचानवे	*pacānve*	95
९६	छियानवे	*chiyānve*	96
९७	सत्तानवे	*sattānve*	97
९८	अट्ठानवे	*aṭṭhānve*	98
९९	निन्यानवे	*ninyānve*	99
१००	सौ, एक सौ	*sau, ek sau*	100

Higher Numbers

हज़ार	*hazār*	1,000
लाख	*lākh*	100,000 (1,00,000)
करोड़	*karoṛ*	10,000,000 (1,00,00,000)
अरब	*arab*	1,000,000,000 (1,00,00,00,000)

Numbers higher than 100 are formed regularly from the above elements.

दो सौ	*do sau*, 200
तीन सौ पच्चीस	*tīn sau paccīs*, 325
सात सौ पचपन	*sāt sau pacpan*, 755
एक हज़ार तीन सौ / तेरह सौ	*ek hazār tīn sau / terah sau*, 1300
चार हज़ार दो सौ बारह	*cār hazār do sau bārah*, 4212
बीस हज़ार	*bīs hazār*, 20,000
एक लाख बीस हज़ार	*ek lākh bīs hazār*, 1,20,000
पाँच लाख पैंतीस हज़ार एक सौ बयालीस	*pā̃c lākh, paintīs hazār ek sau bayālīs*, 5,35,142

Ordinal Numbers

All ordinal numbers in Urdu are variable adjectives. Numbers one through four, six, and nine have irregular ordinal forms.

पहला	*pahlā*, first
दूसरा	*dūsrā*, second
तीसरा	*tīsrā*, third
चौथा	*cauthā*, fourth
छठा	*chaṭhā*, sixth
नवाँ	*navā̃*, ninth

Other ordinals are formed regularly by adding the variable suffix *–vā̃* (*-vẽ*/*-vī̃*) to the cardinal form.

पाँचवाँ	*pā̃cvā̃*, fifth
सातवाँ	*sātvā̃*, seventh
आठवाँ	*āṭhvā̃*, eighth
दसवाँ	*dasvā̃*, tenth
बीसवाँ	*bīsvā̃*, 20th
पच्चीसवाँ	*paccīsvā̃*, 25th

Appendix 2: Grammar Supplement

Causative Verbs

Hindi possesses a special class of verbs, called causatives, that express the notion of getting an action done through an intermediary. Causative verbs can be grouped in sets with related transitive and intransitive verb pairs of the type seen in Unit 8.

Intransitive		Non-causative Transitive		Causative	
उठना	*uṭhnā*, v.i., to rise	उठाना	*uṭhānā*, v.t., to raise	उठवाना	*uṭhvānā*, v.t. to have (sthg.) raised
रुकना	*ruknā*, v.i., to stop	रोकना	*roknā*, v.t., to stop	रुकवाना	*rukvānā*, v.t. to have (sthg.) stopped
खुलना	*khulnā*, v.i., to open	खोलना	*kholnā*, v.t., to open	खुलवाना	*khulvānā*, to have (sthg.) opened

All causative verbs are transitive and so require that *ne* be used in the perfective and related tenses. Most, though not all, causative verbs bear the ending –*vānā*. Most causatives are formed by affixing –*vānā* to either the intransitive stem or a weakened form of the transitive stem. Some causatives are formed with the suffix –*ānā*, though there are also many verbs ending in –*ānā* that are not causatives, for example, *banānā* and *uṭhānā*.

Here are some additional examples of causatives formed from stems already encountered.

बनवाना	*banvānā*, v.t., to have (sthg.) made (by somebody else)
पकवाना	*pakvānā*, v.t., to have (sthg.) cooked
पढ़वाना	*paṛhvānā*, v.t., to have (someone) taught
बुलवाना	*bulvānā*, v.t., to have (someone) summoned
धुलवाना	*dhulvānā*, v.t., to have (sthg.) washed

A few verb sets have two causatives—one in –*vānā* and the other in –*ānā*.

कराना	*karānā*, v.t., to have (sthg.) done
करवाना	*karvānā*, v.t., to have (sthg.) done
सिलाना	*silānā*, v.t., to have (sthg.) stitched, sewn
सिलवाना	*silvānā*, v.t., to have (sthg.) stitched, sewn

All causative verbs can be used in a special causative construction in which the intermediary is marked with the postposition *se*.

X से कराना	to have X do (sthg.)/get X to do (sthg.)
X से बनवाना	to have X make (sthg.)
X से धुलवाना	to have X wash (sthg.)
X से सिलवाना	to have X sew (sthg.)

Regardless of whether an intermediary is explicitly mentioned, the use of a causative verb always implies one.

मैं मज़दूरों से यह काम कराऊँगा।	I will have laborers do this work.
मैं यह काम कल कराऊँगा।	I will have this work done tomorrow.
उसने अपनी शादी में शहर के सबसे मशहूर रसोइये से खाना पकवाया।	She had the most famous cook in the city cook for her wedding.
उसने बहुत स्वादिष्ट खाना पकवाया।	She had very delicious food cooked.

Relative-Correlative Constructions

English interrogative words have two uses. In addition to their straightforward use in forming questions, they can also be used as relative words, marking relative clauses. For example, consider the following sentences, in which the underlined portions are relative clauses:

Where did the man <u>who was standing here</u> go.

<u>When we get there</u>, I'm going to take a nap.

There are a lot of parks in the city <u>where I live</u>.

Hindi forms relative clauses not with question words, but with distinct *relative* words. All relative words in Hindi begin with the letter ज.

जो	*jo*, who, which, that… (cf. *kaun/kyā, ye, vo*)
जब	*jab*, when… (cf. *kab, ab, tab/to*)
जहाँ	*jahā̃*, where… (cf. *kahā̃, yahā̃, vahā̃*)
जैसा	*jaisā*, adj., as, like, the type of… (cf. *kaisā, aisā, vaisā*)
जैसे	*jaise*, adv., as, the manner in which… (cf. *kaise, aise, vaise*)
जितना	*jitnā*, as much as… (cf. *kitnā, itnā, utnā*)
जिधर	*jidhar*, in the direction that… (cf. *kidhar, idhar, udhar*)

The relative pronoun *jo* also has the following forms, which correspond to the various forms of the interrogative *kaun*, 'who.'

जिस	*jis*, corresponds to *kis*
जिन	*jin*, corresponds to *kin*
जिसे	*jise*, corresponds to *kise*
जिन्हें	*jinhẽ*, corresponds to *kinhẽ*
जिन्होंने	*jinhõ ne*, corresponds to *kinhõ ne*

Here are some examples of Hindi relative words in use:

मैं एक आदमी को जानता हूँ जो बहुत अच्छा सितार बजाता है।	I know a man who plays really good sitar.
मैं तुम्हें बताऊँगा जब तुम मेरे घर आओगे।	I'll tell you when you come to my house.

In the examples above, the Hindi relative words are used similarly to Engish ones—the relative clauses are embedded within or follow the main clause. Hindi relative words are also commonly used in constructions with corresponding words called correlatives. Correlative words occur within the main clause and function as placeholders for the relative clause. The relative clause often precedes the main clause rather than following or being embedded within it

जो ... वह ...	*jo...vo*, that which...., that...; s/he who..., s/he...
जब ... तब / तो ...	*jab...tab/to*, when..., then...
जहाँ ... वहाँ ...	*jahā̃...vahā̃*, where..., there...
जैसा ... वैसा ...	*jaisā...vaisā*, the type of..., that type...
जैसे ... वैसे ...	*jaise...vaise*, in which manner..., in that manner...
जितना ... उतना ...	*jitnā...utnā*, as much as..., that much...
जिधर ... उधर ...	*jidhar...udhar*, in which direction..., in that direction...

Examples:

जो आदमी बाहर खड़ा है, वह कौन है?	Who is the man who is standing outside? "The man who is standing outside, who is he?"
जब मैं घर पहुँचूँगा, तो मैं थोड़ी देर आराम करूँगा।	When I arrive home, I'm going to rest for a little while. "When I arrive home, then I'm going to rest for a little while."

जहाँ वह काम करता है, वहाँ उसकी पत्नी भी काम करती है।	His wife also works where he works. "Where he works, there his wife also works."
जैसी क़मीज़ तुमने पहनी है, मैं वैसी ख़रीदना चाहती हूँ।	I want to buy a shirt like the one you are wearing.
जैसे मैंने किया तुम भी वैसे करो।	Do it the way that I did it.
जितने छात्र तुम्हारी क्लास में हैं, उतने हमारी क्लास में नहीं हैं।	There aren't as many students in our class as yours.
तुम कल जिस लड़की से बात कर रहे थे, वह कौन थी?	Who was the girl you were talking with yesterday.

The word *bhī* used with relative words gives the sense of 'ever,' as in 'whoever,' 'whenever,' etc.

जो भी कहना है, सबके सामने कहो।	Whatever you have to say, say it in front of everyone.
जब भी आप आते हैं, वह यहाँ नहीं होता।	Whenever you come, he's not here.

A similar sense can be conveyed by merely repeating some relative words.

जो-जो जाना चाहता है, वह जा सकता है।	Whoever wants to go can go.
जहाँ-जहाँ शिक्षा की कमी है, वहाँ वहाँ ग़रीबी है।	Wherever there's a lack of education, there's poverty.

Additional Constructions with Relative Pronouns

The construction *jab tak..., tab tak...* means 'as long as,' or 'by the time.' The construction *jab tak* (+neg.)..., *tab tak...* means 'until.'

जब तक वे लोग आएँगे, तब तक मैं अपना काम ख़त्म कर लूँगा।	I'll finish my work by the time they get here.
जब तक वह वहाँ रहेगा, तब तक मैं वहाँ नहीं जाऊँगा।	I will not go there as long as he remains there.
जब तक काम ख़त्म नहीं होगा, तब तक हम यहाँ रहेंगे।	We'll stay here until the work is finished.

The construction *jaise hī..., vaise hī...* means 'as soon as.'

जैसे ही मैं घर पहुँचूँगा, वैसे ही मैं आपको फ़ोन करूँगा।	I'll call you as soon as I get home.

The phrase *jahā̃ tak* means 'as far as.'

जहाँ तक मैं जानता हूँ, यह बात बिल्कुल सही है।	As far as I know, that's absolutely correct.
जहाँ तक पैसे का सवाल है, मैं इस नौकरी से संतुष्ट हूँ।	As far as money is concerned, I'm satisfied with this job.

The Contrafactual Verb Form

Contrafactual verb forms express notions such as *If...had been the case, ...would have happened.* In Hindi, the contrafactual form of the verb is identical to the present habitual verb form minus the auxiliary verb *honā*. The contrafactual is generally negated using *na*, though *nahī̃* is also found in colloquial speech.

अगर मुझे यह बात मालूम होती तो मैं उससे कुछ न कहता।	If I had known this, I wouldn't have said anything to him.
अगर हम घर से ज़रा पहले चलते तो हमारी ट्रेन न छूटती।	If we had left home a little earlier, we wouldn't have missed our train.

Additional Meanings and Uses of *honā*

The Presumptive Form of *honā*

The future forms of the verb *honā*, in addition to conveying future meanings, can also express presumptions corresponding to 'must' or 'probably' in English.

इस समय सब बच्चे स्कूल में होंगे।	All the children are probably at school now.
आप बहुत थकी हुई होंगी। थोड़ी देर आराम कीजिए।	You must be very tired. Please rest a little.

The form *rahā hogā* can be used to make presumptions about the past. The form *rahā* inflects adjectivally—*rahe hõge, rahī hogī*, etc.

जून में हिंदुस्तान में बहुत गर्मी रही होगी।	It must have been hot in India in June.

The Verb *honā* in the Subjunctive

Like other verbs in the subjunctive, the verb *honā* in the subjunctive can be used to express possibility, uncertainty, etc. about future circumstances. Unlike other verbs, however, *honā* can also express possibility and uncertainty with regard to circumstances in other time frames.

पता नहीं कि वह काम पर क्यों नहीं आया। हो सकता है कि वह बीमार हो।	I'm not sure why he's not at work today. Maybe he's sick.

The form *rahā ho* is often used to express possibility or uncertainty about the past.

हो सकता है कि वह वहाँ रहा हो, लेकिन मैंने उसको नहीं देखा।	It's possible that he was there, but I didn't see him.

Uses of Alternative Auxiliary Forms of *honā*

Presumptive, subjunctive, and contrafactual forms of *honā* can replace the indicative forms that are used as auxiliary verbs in various verb tenses.

वे लोग अभी आ रहे होंगे।	They are probably coming now.
हो सकता है कि वे लोग अभी आ रहे हों।	It's possible that they're coming now.
अगर वे लोग आ रहे होते तो वे हमें बताते।	If they were coming, they would have told us.

The Passive Voice

Up to this point all verbs have been presented in the *active voice*, which can be thought of as the default way of presenting an action. In the active voice, actions are depicted as being performed by a subject. When a verb occurs in the *passive voice*, on the other hand, it loses its ability to take the original subject, and the object is promoted to subject position.

For example, 'John ate the apple,' is an active sentence; the corresponding passive sentence is, 'The apple was eaten.' Similarly, 'The guards will see him,' is an active sentence; the corresponding passive sentence is, 'He will be seen.'

In Hindi, the passive voice is formed by placing the verb in perfect participle form and appending the verb *jānā*. The perfect participle is identical to the perfective form (minus nasalization in the feminine plural form).

Active Form	Meaning	Passive Form	Meaning
करना	to do	किया जाना	to be done
देखना	to see	देखा जाना	to be seen
बताना	to tell	बताया जाना	to be told
बनाना	to make	बनाया जाना	to be made
कहना	to say	कहा जाना	to be said

The perfect participle plus *jānā* forms a new stem, which can then be conjugated in the various verb tenses as an active verb would be.

भारत में मेहमानों को आमतौर पर चाय पिलाई जाती है।	In India, guests are generally served tea.
प्राचीन भारत में संस्कृत बोली जाती थी।	In ancient India, Sanskrit was spoken.
मेहमानों को खाना खिलाया जा रहा है।	The guests are being fed/served.
मेहमानों को खाना खिलाया जा रहा था।	The guests were being fed/served.
दोषियों को सज़ा दी जाए।	Let the guilty be punished.
दोषियों को सज़ा दी जाएगी।	The guilty will be punished.
दोषियों को सज़ा दी गई।	The guilty were punished.
दोषियों को सज़ा दी गई है।	The guilty have been punished.
मुझे बताया गया था कि आज आने की ज़रूरत नहीं।	I had been told that it wasn't necessary to come today.

Participial Forms

Basic Forms

Participles are adjectival forms of verbs. Hindi has two main participial forms, *imperfective participles* and *perfective participles*. Both of these occur in long and short forms.

Imperfective participles have the short form V-*tā* and long form V-*tā huā*. These forms correspond to English participles of the form 'V-ing.' Both parts (V-*tā* and *huā*) inflect to agree with the noun being described.

रोता (हुआ) बच्चा	a crying baby
चलती (हुई) गाड़ी	a moving vehicle
उबलता (हुआ) पानी	boiling water

Perfective participles have the short form V-*ā* and long form V-*ā huā*. These forms correspond to English participles of the form 'V-ed,' 'V-en,' and other irregular forms. Both parts (V-*ā* and *huā*) inflect to agree with the noun being described.

उबला (हुआ) पानी	boiled water
कटी (हुई) प्याज़	cut up onion
रुकी (हुई) गाड़ी	a stopped car

Perfective and imperfective participles are found in various constructions, some of the most common of which are listed below.

V-*te hue*, While V-ing

The invariable form V-*te hue* is an adverbial use of the imperfective participle, meaning 'while V-ing.'

मैंने दौड़ते हुए आपको देखा / दौड़ते हुए मैंने आपको देखा।	I saw you while (I was) running.
मैंने आपको दौड़ते हुए देखा।	I saw you while (you were) running.

V-*te samay* / V-*te vaqt*, While V-ing, at the Time of V-ing

The form V-*te* is invariable in this construction.

गाड़ी चलाते समय फ़ोन पर बात न करें।	Don't talk on the phone while driving.
होमवर्क करते वक़्त टीवी मत देखो।	Don't watch TV while doing your homework.

V-*te hī*, As Soon as...

The form V-*te* is invariable in this construction.

मैं घर पहुँचते ही तुम्हें फ़ोन करूँगा।	I'll call you as soon as I get home.
वह लेटते ही सो गया।	He fell asleep as soon as he lay down.

V-*e binā* / V-*e ba<u>gh</u>air*, Without V-ing

The form V-*e* is invariable in this construction.

उसने मुझसे पूछे बिना मेरा क़लम ले लिया।	He took my pen without asking me.
वह हमें बताए बग़ैर चली गई।	She left without telling us.

V-*te rahnā* / V-*te jānā*, to Keep on V-ing

The form V-*tā* is variable in both of these constructions. The V-*te jānā* construction is often appropriate when the action increases in intensity.

देखते रहिए।	Keep on watching.
मैं कोशिश करता रहूँगा।	I'll keep on trying.
जब तक बरसात शुरू नहीं होगी तब तक गर्मी बढ़ती जाएगी।	It's going to keep getting hotter and hotter until the rains start.

V-*e rakhnā*, to Keep (sthg.) V-ed

The form V-*e* is invariable in this construction.

दरवाज़ा खोले रखिए।	Keep the door open.
अपनी कुर्सी की पेटी बाँधे रखें।	Keep your seatbelt fastened.

V-*e* (*hue*)

This invariable form gives a still image of the subject engaged in the action, or being in the state resulting from having performed the action. The meaning of this form is active, and only transitive verbs occur in it.

तुम यह संदूक़ लिए हुए कहाँ जा रहे हो?	Where are you going carrying this trunk?
वह किस तरह के कपड़े पहने हुए थी।	What kind of clothes was she wearing?

Appendix 3: Additional Information for Teachers

1. Suggested contact hours for each chapter:

Unit	Chapter	Activities Section	Suggested Class Hours
1 Me and My School	1 Introductions	1	.5
		2	.25
		3	.5
		4	.25
		5	.75
	2 Me and My Classmates		1
	3 My Classroom	1	.25
		2	.75
		3	.5
	4 Describing Classroom Items	1	.75
		2	.5
		3	.25
	5 Giving Commands and Making Requests	1	.25
		2	.5
	6 Unit 1 Review Activities		2
2 My Family and My Home	7 Locating Places and Objects	1	.75
		2	.75
		3	.75
		4	1
	8 Identifying Family Members	1	.5
		2	.5
		3	1
	9 Describing Family Members	1	1
		2	1
		3	.75
	10 My Home, My Possessions	1	1
		2	1
	11 Making Comparisons	1	1
		2	1
	12 Unit 2 Review Activities		3

3 Daily Life	13 My Daily Routine	1	2
		2	.75
		3	.5
	14 My Day	1	.75
		2	1
	15 What's Happening: Reporting Live	1	1
		2	.5
	16 Weather and Climate	1	.5
		2	1
	17 Unit 3 Review Activities		3
4 In the Market	18 Expressing Likes, Needs, and Desires	1	2
		2	.75
		3	1.5
	19 Choosing Items and Expressing Measures		1.5
	20 Discussing Prices		.75
	21 Unit 4 Review Activities		3
5 My Childhood	22 My Childhood Home		1.5
	23 Describing One's Childhood		1.5
	24 Describing a Scene in the Past		2
	25 Expressions of Time		.75
	26 Unit 5 Review Activities		2
6 Rules and Responsibilities	27 What We Can and Can't Do	1	1
		2	.5
	28 Expressing Compulsion		1.5
	29 Giving and Following Instructions		1
	30 Unit 6 Review Activities		2
7 A Trip to South Asia	31 My Plans		1.5
	32 My Travel Plans: Definite and Possible		1.5
	33 Arranging Transportation and Lodging	1	1.5
		2	
	34 Finding One's Way		1.5
	35 Sharing Information about Locations in South Asia		1
	36 Unit 7 Review Activities		4

8 My Experiences	37 My Weekend	1	1
		2	1.5
	38 Narrating a Story	1	.5
		2	1.5
	39 My Experience and Accomplishments		2
	40 At the Doctor's		1.5
	41 Unit 8 Review Activities		3

2. Notes to the teacher about specific exercises:

Sound and Script 2, exercise 3

We have included this activity to provide students with an extra step between recognizing individual letters in isolation and reading complete words with connected letter forms.

Chapter 7, exercise 6

Read aloud the place names listed under Exercise 1 above.

Chapter 20, exercise 6

Prior to class, photocopy the pictures of pants, kurtas, and shirts that appear in the next chapter. Cut up the photocopied pictures so that only one image appears on each slip of paper. Provide students playing the role of shopkeeper with the set of pictures appropriate to their activity.

Chapter 21, exercise 3

Prior to class, make photocopies of the pictures of pants, kurtas, and shirts. Make sure that the prices do not appear on the photocopies that you make. Distribute the appropriate pictures to the students playing the role of shopper in each role play.

Chapter 35, Exercise 3

Make three photocopies per student of the map and distribute a fresh map to each student before each of the next three exercises.

Hindi–English Glossary

अंगूठा	*angūṭhā* (m.)	thumb
अंगूठी	*angūṭhī* (f.)	ring
अंगूर	*angūr* (m.)	grape
अंग्रेज़ी	*angrezī* (f.)	English
अंडा	*anḍā* (m.)	egg
अण्डाकार	*anḍākār*	oval shaped
अंत	*ant* (m.)	end
अंतर	*antar* (m.)	difference
अंतर्राष्ट्रीय	*antarrāṣṭrīy*	international
अंदर	*andar* (adv.)	inside
अंधेरा	*andherā* (m.)	darkness
अकेला	*akelā*	alone, only
अक्तूबर/ अक्टूबर	*aktūbar/ akṭūbar* (m.)	October
अक़्लमंद	*aql-mand*	intelligent, having common sense
अक्सर	*aksar*	often
अख़बार	*axbār* (m.)	newspaper
अगर...तो...	*agar…to…*	if…then…
अगरबत्ती	*agarbattī* (f.)	incense
अगला	*aglā*	next
अगस्त	*agast* (m.)	August
अचानक	*acānak*	all of a sudden
अच्छा	*acchā*	good; Really! Is that so! (excl.)
अजनबी	*ajnabī*	stranger
अजायबघर	*ajāyabghar*(m.)	museum
अजीब	*ajīb*	strange
अदद	*adad* (m.)	one number of
अदरक	*adrak* (m.)	ginger
अधिकारी	*adhikārī* (m.)	official

अध्यापक	*adhyāpak* (m.)	teacher
अध्यापिका	*adhyāpikā* (f.)	teacher
अनगिनत	*an-ginat*	countless
अनावश्यक	*anāvaśyak*	unnecessary
अनुभव	*anubhav* (m.)	experience
अनोखा	*anokhā*	unique
अपना	*apnā*	one's own (reflexive)
अपने से	*apne se*	one one's own, without outside influence
अप्रैल	*aprail* (m.)	April
अफ़ग़ानी	*afghānī*	Afghani
अफ़सोस	*afsos* (m.)	sorrow, regret (X *ko afsos honā*, for X to feel sorrow/regret)
अब	*ab*	now
अब्बा	*abbā* (m.)	father
अब्बू	*abbū* (m.)	father
अभी	*abhī*	right now, at this moment (*ab*, 'now' + *hī*)
अभ्यास	*abhyās* (m.)	practice, exercise
अमरीकी	*amrīkī*	American
अमरूद	*amrūd* (m.)	guava
अमीर	*amīr*	rich
अम्मा	*ammā* (f.)	mother
अम्मी	*ammī* (f.)	mother
अरे	*are*	interjection used to express surprise or to catch attention
अर्थ	*arth* (m.)	meaning
अर्थशास्त्र	*arthśāstr* (m.)	economics
अलग	*alag*	different, separate
अलग-अलग	*alag-alag*	different, various, separate; separately
अलमारी	*almārī* (f.)	wardrobe, closet, cupboard; shelving unit
असल में	*asal mẽ*	actually, in fact
असली	*aslī*	true, genuine
अस्पताल	*aspatāl* (m.)	hospital
अहम	*aham*	important
अहमियत	*ahamiyat* (f.)	importance
आँख	*ā̃kh* (f.)	eye

आँगन	*ā̃gan* (m.)	courtyard
आँच	*ā̃c* (f.)	flame (e.g., of a gas stove)
आख़िर	*āxir* (m.)	end
आग	*āg* (f.)	fire (*āg lagnā*, for a fire to start)
आगे	*āge*	ahead
आज	*āj*	today
आजकल	*ājkal*	these days
आज़ादी	*āzādī* (f.)	freedom, independence
आटा	*āṭā* (m.)	flour
आदत	*ādat* (f.)	habit
आदमी	*ādmī* (m.)	man
आधा	*ādhā*	half
आधार	*ādhār* (m.)	basis
आना	*ānā* (v.i.)	to come
आना (X को Y)	X *ko* Y *ānā*	for X to know Y (a language or skill)
आपका	*āp kā*	your, yours
आपस में	*āpas mẽ*	mutually, together, with each other
आबादी	*ābādī* (f.)	population
आम	*ām*	common, commonplace; (m.) mango
आमतौर पर	*ām taur par*	usually, generally
आयताकार	*āyatākār*	rectangular
आराम करना	*ārām karnā* (v.t.)	to rest
आरामदेह	*ārāmdeh*	comfortable
आलसी	*ālsī*	lazy
आलू	*ālū* (m.)	potato
आवश्यक	*āvaśyak*	necessary
आवश्यकता	*āvaśyaktā* (f.)	necessity
आवाज़	*āvāz* (f.)	voice, sound
आशंका	*āśankā* (f.)	fear; apprehension
आशा	*āśā* (f.)	hope (X *ko āśā honā ki*, for X to hope that [+ future tense])
आस-पास	*ās-pās*	nearby
आसमान	*āsmān* (m.)	sky
आसान	*āsān*	easy

आस्तीन	*āstīn* (f.)	sleeve
इंतज़ाम	*intazām* (m.)	arrangement
इंतज़ार	*intizār* (m.)	wait, act of waiting
इंतज़ार करना (X का)	X *kā intizār karnā*	to wait for X
इजाज़त	*ijāzat* (f.)	permission (*ijāzat denā*, to give permission)
इज़्ज़त	*izzat* (f.)	respect, dignity, honor (X *kī izzat karnā*, to treat X with respect)
इतना	*itnā*	this much, so much
इतवार	*itvār* (m.)	Sunday
इतिहास	*itihās* (m.)	history
इनाम	*inām* (m.)	prize, reward
इन्चार्ज	*incārj*	head, in charge
इन्सान	*insān* (m.)	human being
इमारत	*imārat* (f.)	building
इम्तिहान	*imtihān* (m.)	test, examination
इरादा	*irādā* (m.)	intention (X *kā* V-*ne kā irādā honā* / X *kā irādā honā ki*..., for X to intend/plan to V)
इलाक़ा	*ilāqā* (m.)	region
इलाज	*ilāj* (m.)	treatment (medical) (X *kā ilāj karnā*, to treat X)
इलायची	*ilāycī* (f.)	cardamom
इशारा	*iśārā* (m.)	sign, indication (*iśārā karnā*, to point); signal
इस्तेमाल	*istemāl* (m.)	use
इस्तेमाल करना (X का)	X (*kā*) *istemāl karnā*	to use X
ईमानदार	*īmāndār*	honest
ईरानी	*īrānī*	Iranian
उंगली	*unglī* (f.)	finger
उंडेलना	*unḍelnā* (v.t.)	to pour
उठना	*uṭhnā* (v.i.)	to get up
उड़ान	*uṛān* (f.)	flight
उड़ाना	*uṛānā* (v.t.)	to fly, to cause to fly (*patang uṛānā*, to fly a kite)
उतना	*utnā*	that much, so much
उतारना	*utārnā* (v.t.)	to take off (*kapṛe utārnā*, to get undressed)
उत्तर	*uttar* (m.)	answer; north
उत्तरी	*uttarī*	northern

उदास	*udās*	unhappy, melancholy
उदाहरण	*udāharaṇ* (m.)	example
उपन्यास	*upanyās* (m.)	novel
उपमहाद्वीप	*upmahādvīp* (m.)	subcontinent
उबलना	*ubalnā* (v.i.)	to boil
उबाऊ	*ubāū*	boring
उबालना	*ubālnā* (v.t.)	to boil
उम्मीद	*ummīd* (f.)	expectation, hope (X *ko ummīd honā ki*, for X to have an expectation/hope that [+ future tense])
उम्र	*umr* (f.)	age
उल्टा हाथ	*ulṭā hāth*	left hand (*ulṭe hāth par*, on the left side)
उल्टी	*ulṭī* (f.)	vomit, vomiting (X *ko ulṭī ānā*, for X to feel nauseous; *ulṭī karnā*, to vomit)
उल्लू	*ullū* (m.)	owl; fool
ऊँचा	*ū̃cā*	high
ऊँट	*ū̃ṭ* (m.)	camel
ऊपर	*ūpar*	up
ऊपरी	*ūprī*	upper
एकदम	*ekdam*	completely; suddenly
एक-दूसरे	*ek-dūsre*	each other (reciprocal)
एड़ी	*eṛī* (f.)	heel
एलान	*elān* (m.)	announcement
एशिया	*eśiyā*	Asia; *eśiyāī*, Asian
ए-सी	*e-sī* (m.)	air conditioner, air conditioning
ऐतिहासिक	*aitihāsik*	historical, historic (cf. *itihās*, m. 'history')
ऐसा	*aisā*	like this, of this type
ओढ़ना	*oṛhnā* (v.t.)	to cloak with
ओर	*or* (f.)	side
और	*aur*	and; else; more, additional
औरत	*aurat* (f.)	woman
कंधा	*kandhā* (m.)	shoulder
कंप्यूटर	*kampyūṭar* (m.)	computer
कंबल	*kambal* (m.)	blanket

कई	*kaī*	several
कक्षा	*kakṣā* (f.)	class, classroom
कच्चा	*kaccā*	raw, uncooked; unfinished (opp. of *pakkā*)
कटाना (बाल)	(*bāl*) *kaṭānā* (v.t.)	to get (one's hair) cut
कटोरी	*kaṭorī* (f.)	small bowl
कठिन	*kaṭhin*	difficult
कठोर	*kaṭhor*	strict, hard, harsh
कड़वा	*kaṛvā*	bitter; (too) spicy
कढ़ाई	*kaṛhāī* (f.)	embroidery
क़तार	*qatār* (f.)	line, queue
क़द	*qad* (m.)	height
क़दम	*qadam* (m.)	step, foot (*qadmõ mẽ gir paṛnā*, to fall to someone's feet)
कपड़ा	*kapṛā* (m.)	cloth
कपड़े	*kapṛe* (m.pl.)	clothes
कब	*kab*	when
क़बूल करना	*qabūl karnā* (v.t.)	to accept, to admit
कभी-कभार	*kabhī-kabhār*	once in a while
कभी-कभी	*kabhī-kabhī*	sometimes
कम	*kam*	less, fewer; little, few
कम करना	*kam karnā*	to lower, to lessen, to decrease
कम से कम	*kam se kam*	at least
कमज़ोर	*kamzor*	weak
कमज़ोरी	*kamzorī* (f.)	weakness, fatigue
कमर	*kamar* (f.)	waist
कमरा	*kamrā* (m.)	room (in a building)
कमाना	*kamānā* (v.t.)	to earn
क़मीज़	*qamīz* (f.)	shirt, top
क़रीब	*qarīb* (adv.)	near, about (cf. *taqrīban*, 'approximately')
क़रीब	*qarīb*	approximately
कर्मचारी	*karmcārī*	employee
कल	*kal*	yesterday; tomorrow
क़लम	*qalam* (m., f.)	pen
कला	*kalā* (f.)	art

कलाई	*kalāī* (f.)	wrist
कवि	*kavi* (m.)	poet
कविता	*kavitā* (f.)	poetry
कसरत करना	*kasrat karnā*	to exercise
क़साई	*qasāī*	butcher
क़स्बा	*qasbā* (m.)	town
कहना	*kahnā* (v.t.)	to say, call (by name), (X *se kahnā*, to say to X)
कहलाना	*kahlānā* (v.i.)	to be called, to cause to be called, to be known as
कहाँ	*kahā̃*	where
कहानी	*kahānī* (f.)	story
कहीं	*kahī̃*	anywhere, somewhere (*kahī̃ aisā na ho ki*, may it not be that…)
काँटा	*kā̃ṭā* (m.)	fork
का	*kā*	of
काग़ज़	*kāg̲h̲az* (m.)	paper
काग़ज़ात	*kāg̲h̲zāt* (m.pl.)	papers
काटना	*kāṭnā* (v.t.)	to cut
कान	*kān* (m.)	ear
क़ानून	*qānūn* (m.)	law
कॉपी	*kāpī* (f.)	notepad, blank book for writing
काफ़ी	*kāfī*	quite, rather; enough
काम	*kām* (m.)	work, task
काम करना	*kām karnā* (v.t.)	to work; to do a task
कामयाब	*kāmyāb*	successful
कामयाबी	*kāmyābī* (f.)	success
कारण	*kāraṇ* (m.)	reason
कार्यालय	*kāryālay* (m.)	office
कॉलर	*kālar* (m.)	collar
काला	*kālā*	black
क़ालीन	*qālīn* (f.)	carpet
कि	*ki* (conj.)	that
कितना	*kitnā*	how much, how many
कितने बजे	*kitne baje*	at what time
किताब	*kitāb* (f.)	book

किनारा	*kinārā* (m.)	edge, bank (*ke kināre*, on the edge/bank of)
किराने की दुकान	*kirāne kī dukān* (f.)	general store, dry goods and staples store
किराया	*kirāyā* (m.)	rent, fare
क़िला	*qilā* (m.)	fort
किलो	*kilo*	kilogram
किसका	*kis kā*	whose
क़िस्सा	*qissā* (m.)	tale, story
की तरफ़	*kī taraf*	in the direction of
की तरह	*kī tarah*	like, in the manner of (*tarah*, f. manner)
की वजह से	*kī vajah se*	because of
कीड़ा	*kīṛā* (m.)	insect, microbe
क़ीमत	*qīmat* (f.)	value, price
क़ीमती	*qīmtī*	valuable
क़ीमा	*qīmā* (m.)	ground meat
कुछ	*kuch*	some, something; a bit (+ adj.)
कुत्ता	*kuttā* (m.)	dog
कुर्ता	*kurtā* (m.)	tunic
कुर्सी	*kursī* (f.)	chair
कुल मिलाकर	*kul milākar*	altogether
कुहनी	*kuhnī* (f.)	elbow
कुहरा	*kuhrā* (m.)	fog
कूड़ा	*kūṛā* (m.)	trash
कूड़ेदान	*kūṛedān* (m.)	wastebasket, trash can
केंद्र	*kendr* (m.)	center
के अनुसार	*ke anusār*	according to
के अलावा	*ke alāvā*	apart from, in addition to
के आगे	*ke āge*	ahead of, beyond
के आधार पर	*ke ādhār par*	on the basis of
के ऊपर	*ke ūpar*	on top of, above
के क़रीब	*ke qarīb*	around
के कारण	*ke kāraṇ*	because of
के ज़रिए	*ke zarie*	by means of
के दरमियान	*ke darmiyān*	between, in the middle/midst of
के दाईं तरफ़	*ke dāī̃ taraf*	to the right of

के दाहिनी तरफ़	*ke dāhinī taraf*	to the right of
के दौरान	*ke daurān*	during
के द्वारा	*ke dvārā*	by, by means of
के नीचे	*ke nīce*	under, below
के पास	*ke pās*	near; in the possession of
के पीछे	*ke pīche*	behind
के बग़ल में	*ke baghal mẽ*	next to
के बजाय	*ke bajāy*	instead of
के बाईं तरफ़	*ke bāī̃ taraf*	to the left of
के बाद	*ke bād*	after
के बारे में	*ke bāre mẽ*	about
के बावजूद	*ke bāvjūd*	in spite of
के बीच	*ke bīc*	between (also *ke bīc mẽ*, between, in the middle of)
के बीचों-बीच	*ke bīcõ-bīc*	right in the middle of
के माध्यम से	*ke mādhyam se*	by means of
के मुताबिक़	*ke mutābiq*	according to
के यहाँ	X *ke yahā̃*	at X's (place)
के लिए / के लिये	*ke lie / ke liye*	for
के साथ	*ke sāth*	with, accompanying (*sāth sāth / ek sāth*, adv., together)
के सामने	*ke sāmne*	in front of, facing, opposite from
केमिस्ट की दुकान	*kemisṭ kī dukān* (f.)	medicine shop
केला	*kelā* (m.)	banana
केवल	*keval*	only, just
क़ैंची	*qaĩcī* (f.)	scissors
कैसा	*kaisā*	how, in what state; of what kind
को लेकर	*ko lekar*	including; regarding
को, V-ने को	V-*ne ko*	to V (e.g. *kyā kuch khāne ko hai*, 'Is there anything to eat?')
कोई	*koī*	some, someone; any, anyone
कोठी	*koṭhī* (f.)	mansion
कोना	*konā* (m.)	corner
कोशिश	*kośiś* (f.)	effort
कोशिश करना (V-ने की)	V-*ne kī kośiś karnā*	to try to V

कौन	*kaun*	who
कौन सा	*kaun sā*	which
क्या	*kyā*	what
क्यों	*kyõ*	why
क्यों न...	*kyõ na*	how about..., why not...
क्योंकि	*kyõki*	because
क्लास	*klās* (f.)	class
क्षेत्र	*kṣetr* (m.)	region
खंडहर	*khanḍhar* (m.)	(archeological) ruins
खट्टा	*khaṭṭā*	sour
खड़ा	*khaṛā*	standing
खड़ा होना	*khaṛā honā* (v.i.)	to stand
ख़तरनाक	*xatarnāk*	dangerous
ख़त्म करना	*xatm karnā* (v.t.)	to finish
ख़त्म होना	*xatm honā* (v.i.)	to end, to finish
ख़बर	*xabar* (f.)	news, news item
ख़याल	*xayāl* (m.)	thought, idea
ख़याल रखना (X का)	(X *kā*) *xayāl rakhnā*	to pay due attention to X, keep X in mind, look after X
ख़राब	*xarāb*	bad, spoiled, in a bad state
ख़रीदना	*xarīdnā* (v.t.)	to buy
ख़रीदारी करना	*xarīdārī karnā* (v.t.)	to shop
ख़र्च करना	*xarc karnā* (v.t.)	to spend
खाँसी	*khā̃sī* (f.)	coughing (X *ko khā̃sī ānā*, for X to have a cough, for X to be afflicted by coughing)
खाड़ी	*khāṛī* (f.)	bay
खाना	*khānā* (v.t.)	to eat; m., food (*khānā khānā*, to eat)
ख़ाली	*xālī*	empty, available; free, not occupied
ख़ास	*xās*	special
ख़ासतौर पर	*xās-taur par*	especially, particularly
ख़ासियत	*xāsiyat* (f.)	specialty, special quality
खिड़की	*khiṛkī* (f.)	window
खिलाना	*khilānā* (v.t.)	to feed, to serve food
खींचना	*khī̃cnā* (v.t.)	to pull (*tasvīr khī̃cnā*, to take a picture)

खीरा	*khīrā* (m.)	cucumber
ख़ुद	*xud*	oneself; myself, yourself, himself, etc.
ख़ुद-बख़ुद	*xud-baxud*	one one's own, without outside influence
ख़ुदा	*xudā* (m.)	God
ख़ुराक	*xurāk* (f.)	dose; diet
खुलना	*khulnā* (v.i.)	to open
खुला	*khulā*	open (cf. *khulnā*, v.i. to open)
ख़ुश	*xuś*	happy
ख़ुशमिज़ाज	*xuśmizāj*	fun-loving
ख़ुशी	*xuśī* (f.)	happiness
ख़ून	*xūn* (m.)	blood (*xūn bahnā*, to bleed)
ख़ूब	*xūb*	a lot; good
ख़ूबसूरत	*xūbsūrat*	beautiful, handsome
खेत	*khet* (m.)	field (for farming)
खेल	*khel* (m.)	game, sport; (*jādū kā khel*) trick
खेलना	*khelnā* (v.t.)	to play
ख़ैरियत	*xairiyat* (f.)	state of being well
खोना	*khonā* (v.i./v.t.)	to lose, to get lost
खोलना	*kholnā* (v.t.)	to open
गंजा	*ganjā*	bald
गंदगी	*gandgī* (f.)	dirt; filth, grime
गंदा	*gandā*	dirty
गंभीर	*gambhīr*	serious
गुज़रना	*guzarnā* (v.i.)	to pass
गड्डी	*gaṭṭhī* (f.)	bunch, small tied bundle (e.g. of herbs)
गड़बड़	*gaṛbaṛ* (f.)	mess, unsettled state
गणित	*gaṇit* (m.)	mathematics
गत	*gat*	past
गतिविधि	*gatividhi* (f.)	activity
गधा	*gadhā* (m.)	donkey; fool
गमला	*gamlā* (m.)	flower pot
गरम मसाला	*garam masālā* (m.)	a popular and ubiquitous mix of spices
ग़रीब	*g͟harīb*	poor
गर्दन	*gardan* (f.)	neck

गर्म	*garm* (adj.)	hot
गर्मियाँ	*garmiyā̃* (f.pl.)	hot season, summer
गर्मी	*garmī* (f.)	heat (X *ko garmī lagnā*, for X to be hot)
ग़लत	*g͟halat*	wrong, false
ग़लती	*g͟halatī* (f.)	mistake
गला	*galā* (m.)	throat
गलियारा	*galiyārā* (m.)	hallway
गली	*galī* (f.)	alley, lane
गहना	*gahnā* (m.)	jewel/s; jewelry (pl.)
गहरा	*gahrā*	deep, dark (with colors)
गाँव	*gā̃v* (*gā̃õ*) (m.)	village
गाजर	*gājar* (f.)	carrot
गाड़ी	*gāṛī* (f.)	vehicle, car
गाढ़ा	*gāṛhā*	dark, thick (in consistency)
गाना	*gānā* (m.)	song; to sing (v.t.)
गाय	*gāy* (f.)	cow
ग़ायब	*g͟hāyab* (adj.)	disappeared
गाल	*gāl* (m.)	cheek
गिनना	*ginnā* (v.t.)	to count
गिरजाघर	*girjāghar* (m.)	church
गिरना	*girnā* (v.i.)	to fall (*gir paṛnā*, same)
गिलास	*gilās* (m.)	glass for drinking
गुच्छा	*gucchā* (m.)	bunch, small tied bundle (e.g. of herbs)
गुज़रना (X से)	X *se guzarnā*	to pass (by) X
गुज़ारना	*guzārnā* (v.t.)	to pass (time)
गुड़िया	*guṛiyā* (f.)	doll
गुरुवार	*guruvār* (m.)	Thursday
गुलदान	*guldān* (m.)	flower vase
गुलाब	*gulāb* (m.)	rose
गुलाबी	*gulābī*	pink
ग़ुसलख़ाना	*g͟husalxānā* (m.)	bathroom, washroom
ग़ैरज़रूरी	*g͟hairzarūrī*	unnecessary
ग़ैरज़िम्मेदार	*g͟hairzimmedār*	irresponsible
ग़ैर-सरकारी	*g͟hair-sarkārī*	non-governmental

गोभी	*gobhī* (f.)	cauliflower
गोरा	*gorā*	light-skinned, fair in complexion
गोल	*gol*	round
गोली	*golī* (f.)	pill, bullet
गोश्त	*gośt* (m.)	meat
ग्राहक	*grāhak*	customer
घंटा	*ghanṭā* (m.)	hour
घटना	*ghaṭnā* (f./v.i.)	incident, event; *ghaṭnā ghaṭnā*, for an event to occur
घड़ी	*ghaṛī* (f.)	clock, watch
घना	*ghanā*	thick, dense
घबराना	*ghabrānā* (v.i.)	to be/get anxious, disconcerted
घर	*ghar* (m.)	home, house
घाटी	*ghāṭī* (f.)	valley
घायल	*ghāyal*	wounded
घाव	*ghāv* (m.)	wound
घास	*ghās* (f.)	grass
घी	*ghī* (m.)	ghee, clarified butter
घुँघराला	*ghũghrālā*	curly
घुटना	*ghuṭnā* (m.)	knee
घुमाना	*ghumānā* (v.t.)	to show around
घूमना	*ghūmnā* (v.i.)	to roam, to travel
घोड़ा	*ghoṛā* (m.)	horse
चंद	*cand*	some, a few
चक्कर	*cakkar* (m.pl.)	spells of dizziness (X *ko cakkar ānā*, for X to get/feel dizzy)
चट्टान	*caṭṭān* (f.)	large rock, boulder
चढ़ना	*caṛhnā* (v.i.)	to climb (X *par*), to ascend
चप्पल	*cappal* (f.)	sandal
चबूतरा	*cabūtrā* (m.)	platform
चमड़ी	*camṛī* (f.)	skin
चम्मच / चमचा	*cammac/camcā* (m.)	spoon
चलना	*calnā* (v.i.)	to move, go, accompany; to run, operate; depart
चलना-फिरना	*calnā-phirnā* (v.i.)	to wander around
चला जाना	*calā jānā* (v.i.)	to leave

चलाना	*calānā* (v.t.)	to drive, to operate, to ride (a bike)
चश्मा	*caśmā* (m.)	glasses
चहल-क़दमी	*cahal-qadmī* (f.)	walk, stroll
चाँदनी	*cā̃dnī* (f.)	moonlight
चाक़ू	*cāqū* (m.)	knife
चाचा	*cācā* (m.)	paternal uncle (father's younger brother)
चाची	*cācī* (f.)	father's younger brother's (*cācā*'s) wife
चादर	*cādar* (f.)	sheet, bedsheet
चाबी, चाभी	*cābī* (f.), *cābhī* (f.)	key
चाय	*cāy* (f.)	tea
चारदीवारी	*cārdīvārī* (f.)	enclosure wall
चालाक	*cālāk*	cunning
चावल	*cāval* (m.)	rice
चाहना	*cāhnā* (v.t.)	to want (V-*nā cāhnā*, to want to V)
चाहिए (X को Y)	X *ko* Y *cāhie*	X needs Y
चाहिए/चाहिएँ	*cāhie/cāhiẽ*	is/are needed
चिंता	*cintā* (f.)	worry, thought, preoccupation
चिंता करना	*cintā karnā*	to worry (about X, X *kī*)
चिकन	*cikan*	a style of fine embroidery
चिड़िया	*ciṛiyā* (f.)	bird
चिड़ियाघर	*ciṛiyāghar* (m.)	zoo
चींटी	*cī̃ṭī* (f.)	ant
चीज़	*cīz* (f.)	thing
चीनी	*cīnī*	Chinese; (f.) sugar
चुटकुला	*cuṭkulā* (m.)	joke
चुराना	*curānā* (v.t.)	to steal
चूँकि... इसलिए...	*cū̃ki... islie...*	Since… therefore…
चूल्हा	*cūlhā* (m.)	stove
चूहा	*cūhā* (m.)	mouse, rat
चेहरा	*cehrā* (m.)	face
चोट	*coṭ* (f.)	injury (X *ko coṭ lagnā*, for X to get an injury)
चोटी	*coṭī* (f.)	peak
चोर	*cor*	thief
चोरी	*corī* (f.)	theft

चौक	*cauk* (m.)	square, central market
चौकोर	*caukor*	square in shape
चौड़ा	*cauṛā*	wide
चौराहा	*caurāhā* (m.)	intersection
छज्जा	*chajjā* (m.)	eaves (of a roof); balcony
छड़ी	*chaṛī* (f.)	stick, rod, cane
छत	*chat* (f.)	ceiling, roof
छन्नी	*channī* (f.)	strainer
छपना	*chapnā* (v.i.)	to be published
छाती	*chātī* (f.)	chest
छात्र	*chātr* (m.)	student
छात्रा	*chātrā* (f.)	student
छानना	*chānnā* (v.t.)	to strain, to sift
छिपकली	*chipkalī* (f.)	gecko, small lizard
छींक	*chī̃k* (f.)	sneeze (X *ko chī̃k ānā*, for X to sneeze, for X to have to sneeze; *chī̃knā*, to sneeze)
छुट्टी	*chuṭṭī* (f.)	break, day off, weekend, holiday, vacation time
छूटना	*chūṭnā*	to depart, to leave (without)
छोटा	*choṭā*	small
छोड़ना	*choṛnā* (v.t.)	to leave; to drop off
जंगल	*jangal* (m.)	jungle, uncultivated land
जंगली	*janglī*	wild
ज़ख़्म	*zaxm* (m.)	wound (*zaxmī*, wounded)
जगह	*jagah* (f.)	place; space
जनवरी	*janvarī* (f.)	January
जनसंख्या	*jansankhyā* (f.)	population
जन्म	*janm* (m.)	birth
जन्मदिन	*janm-din* (m.)	birthday
जब भी	*jab bhī*	whenever
जब... तब/तो...	*jab... tab/to...*	when...(then)...
ज़बरदस्त	*zabardast*	forceful, strong; (colloq.) awesome, great
ज़बान	*zabān* (f.)	language, tongue
जमा करना	*jamā karnā*	to submit (a form, an application); to collect, amass
ज़माना	*zamānā* (m.)	era

ज़मीन	*zamīn* (f.)	land; Earth
ज़रिया	*zariyā* (m.)	a means
ज़रूर	*zarūr*	certainly
ज़रूरत	*zarūrat* (f.)	necessity
ज़रूरी	*zarūrī*	necessary
जलवायु	*jalvāyu* (f.)	climate
जलाना	*jalānā* (v.t.)	to burn
जल्द से जल्द	*jald se jald*	as soon as possible, as quickly as possible
जल्द ही	*jald hī*	very quickly
जल्दी	*jaldī*	early; quickly (*jaldī mẽ*, in a hurry)
जवान	*javān*	young
जवानी	*javānī* (f.)	youth
जवाब	*javāb* (m.)	answer
जवाब देना	*javāb denā* (v.t.)	to reply, respond, answer
जवाहरात	*javāharāt* (m.pl.)	jewels
जहाँ	*jahā̃ (rel.)*	where
जाँच	*jā̃c* (f.)	examination; investigation
जागना	*jāgnā* (v.i.)	to be awake, to wake up
जाड़ा	*jāṛā* (m.)	winter
जादू	*jādū* (m.)	magic
जादूगर	*jādūgar*	magician
जान	*jān* (f.)	life, life force
जानकारी	*jānkārī* (f.)	information, knowledge of a thing
जानना	*jānnā* (v.t.)	to know
जान-बूझकर	*jān-būjhkar*	intentionally, knowingly
जानवर	*jānvar* (m.)	animal
जाना	*jānā* (v.i.)	to go
जानिब	*jānib* (f.)	side
जारी रखना	*jārī rakhnā*	to maintain
ज़िंदगी	*zindagī* (f.)	life
ज़िंदा	*zindā*	alive
ज़िक्र	*zikr* (m.)	mention
ज़िक्र करना (X का)	X *kā zikr karnā*	to mention X (to, *se*)
ज़िम्मेदार	*zimmedār*	responsible

जिस	*jis* (rel.)	whom, which (oblique of *jo*)
जिस्म	*jism* (m.)	body
जी	*jī*	yes; an honorific marker appended to names to show respect
जी चाहना (X का)	X *kā jī cāhnā*	for X to feel like…; (X *kā jī cāhnā ki*; X *kā* V-*ne kā jī cāhnā*, for X to feel like…)
जी लगाकर	*jī lagākar*	(adverbial) diligently, putting one's heart into…
जी हाँ	*jī hā̃*	yes
जीतना	*jītnā* (v.t./v.i.)	to win
जीभ	*jībh* (f.)	tongue
ज़ीरा	*zīrā* (m.)	cumin
जीवन	*jīvan* (m.)	life
ज़ुकाम	*zukām* (m.)	a cold (X *ko zukām honā*, for X to have a cold)
जुड़ना	*juṛnā* (v.i.)	to be linked to, to connect (be connected) to
जुड़ा हुआ	*juṛā huā*	connected, linked
जुलाई	*julāī* (f.)	July
जूता	*jūtā* (m.)	shoe
जून	*jūn* (m.)	June
जूस	*jūs* (m.)	juice
जेब	*jeb* (f.)	pocket
ज़ेवर	*zevar* (m.)	piece of jewelry
ज़ेवरात	*zevrāt* (m.pl.)	jewelry
जैसे	*jaise*	like, as
जो	*jo* (rel.)	who, which
जोड़ना	*joṛnā* (v.t.)	to join, to add (up)
जोड़ा	*joṛā* (m.)	set (e.g., of clothes), pair
जोड़ी	*joṛī* (f.)	pair, couple
ज़ोर	*zor* (m.)	force (*zor se*, loudly, forcefully)
ज़्यादा	*zyādā* (adv.)	more, too much (*zyādā...nahī̃*, not very…, not many…)
ज़्यादातर	*zyādātar*	most, mostly
झरना	*jharnā* (m.)	waterfall
झाड़ू लगाना	*jhāṛū lagānā*	to sweep
झील	*jhīl* (f.)	lake
टमाटर	*ṭamāṭar* (m.)	tomato

टहलना	*ṭahalnā* (v.i.)	to stroll
टाँग	*ṭā̃g* (f.)	leg
टापू	*ṭapū* (m.)	island
टिकट	*ṭikaṭ* (m./f.)	ticket
टीला	*ṭīlā* (m.)	dune, mound, hillock
टीवी	*ṭīvī* (m.)	TV
टुकड़ा	*ṭukṛā* (m.)	piece
टूटना	*ṭūṭnā* (v.i.)	to break
टेढ़ा-मेढ़ा	*ṭeṛhā-meṛhā*	crooked, winding
टोपी	*ṭopī* (f.)	hat
ट्रेन	*ṭren* (f.)	train
ट्वायलेट	*ṭvāyleṭ* (m.)	toilet, bathroom
ठंड/ठंडक	*ṭhanḍ/ṭhanḍak* (f.)	cold weather; cold
ठंडा	*ṭhanḍā* (adj.)	cold
ठहरना	*ṭhaharnā* (v.i.)	to stop, to stay
ठीक	*ṭhīk*	fine, OK; right, immediately (with certain compound postpositions)
ठीक होना	*ṭhīk honā*	to get better
ठीक-ठाक	*ṭhīk-ṭhāk*	alright, so-so
ठुड्डी	*ṭhuḍḍī* (f.)	chin
ठेला	*ṭhelā* (m.)	cart
डर	*ḍar* (m.)	fear
डरना (X से)	(X *se*) *ḍarnā* (v.i.)	to fear X
डाँटना	*ḍā̃ṭnā* (v.t.)	to scold
डाकघर	*ḍākghar* (m.)	post office
डालना	*ḍālnā* (v.t.)	to put in (*mẽ*)
डिब्बा	*ḍibbā* (m.)	box, container; train car
डेढ़	*ḍeṛh*	half past one; one and a half
ड्रॉइंग रूम	*ḍrāing rūm* (m.)	drawing room
ढकना	*ḍhaknā* (v.t.)	to cover
ढाई	*ḍhāī*	half past two; two and a half
ढाबा	*ḍhābā* (m.)	an open-air, no-frills roadside restaurant
ढीला	*ḍhīlā*	loose
ढूँढना	*ḍhū̃ḍhnā* (v.t.)	to search for

ढेर सारा	*ḍher sārā*	(colloq.) a ton of
तंग	*tang*	tight
तंदुरुस्त	*tandurust*	healthy, fit
तक	*tak* (ppn.)	up till, until; by (time) (...*se lekar...tak*, from...to...)
तक़रीबन	*taqrīban*	approximately
तकलीफ़	*taklīf* (f.)	discomfort
तकिया	*takiyā* (m.)	pillow
तजुर्बा	*tajurbā* (m.)	experience
तट	*taṭ* (m.)	bank, shore
तनख़्वाह	*tanxāh* (f.)	salary
तबियत	*tabiyat* (f.)	current state of health
तभी	*tabhī*	right then
तमीज़	*tamīz* (f.)	manners (X *ko tamīz honā*, for X to have manners)
तय	*tay*	determined, fixed
तय करना	*tay karnā*	to set; to determine
तय होना	*tay honā* (v.i.)	to be determined, fixed, settled
तरकीब	*tarkīb* (f.)	method
तरफ़	*taraf* (f.)	direction
तरह	*tarah* (f.)	manner
तलना	*talnā* (v.t.)	to fry
तलाक़	*talāq* (f.)	divorce
तलाक़शुदा	*talāq-śudā* (inv.)	divorced
तलाश	*talāś* (f.)	search
तशरीफ़ रखना	*taśrīf rakhnā* (v.i.)	to sit down
तशरीफ़ लाना	*taśrīf lānā* (v.i.)	to come
तश्तरी	*taśtarī* (f.)	plate
तस्वीर	*tasvīr* (f.)	picture
तहज़ीब	*tahzīb* (f.)	civilization, refinement, culture
ताई	*tāī* (f.)	wife of *tāū*
ताऊ	*tāū* (m.)	paternal uncle (father's older brother)
ताकि	*tāki*	so that…, in order to…
तारीख़	*tārīx* (f.)	calendar date; history
तारीफ़	*tārīf* (f.)	praise (X *kī tārīf karnā*, to praise X)

तालाब	*tālāb* (m.)	pond, reservoir
तालीम	*tālīm* (f.)	education
ताश	*tāś* (m.)	playing cards
तिकोना	*tikonā*	triangular
तितली	*titlī* (f.)	butterfly
तिब्बती	*tibbatī*	Tibetan
तिल	*til* (m.)	mole
तुम्हारा	*tumhārā*	your, yours
तुरंत	*turant*	immediately
तूफ़ान	*tūfān* (m.)	storm
तेज़	*tez*	sharp, quick, fiery (of people); strong, quick (of things)
तेज़ पत्ता	*tez pattā* (m.)	bay leaf
तेल	*tel* (m.)	oil
तैयार	*taiyār*	ready, prepared
तैयार (V-ने को)	V-*ne ko taiyār*	ready to V
तैयारी	*taiyārī* (f.)	preparation(s)
तैरना	*tairnā* (v.i.)	to swim
तोंद	*tõd* (f.)	belly, gut
तो	*to*	so, then; indeed [emphatic particle]
तोड़ना	*toṛnā* (v.t.)	to break
तोता	*totā* (m.)	parrot
तोहफ़ा	*tohfā* (m.)	gift
तौलना	*taulnā* (v.t.)	to weigh
तौलिया	*tauliyā* (m.)	towel
त्वचा	*tvacā* (f.)	skin
थका हुआ	*thakā huā*	tired (both words inflect)
थकान	*thakān* (f.)	tiredness
थाना	*thānā* (m.)	police station
थाली	*thālī* (f.)	metal plate
थैला	*thailā* (m.)	bag
थोड़ा	*thoṛā*	a little, a bit
थोड़ा बहुत	*thoṛā bahut*	a fair amount (of)
दक्षिण	*dakṣiṇ* (m.)	south

दक्षिणी	*dakṣiṇī*	southern
दफ़्तर	*daftar* (m.)	office
दबना	*dabnā* (v.i.)	to be pressed down
दबा हुआ	*dabā huā*	pressed down (i.e., by rubble)
दरअसल	*dar-asal*	actually, in fact
दरगाह	*dargāh* (f.)	shrine or tomb of a Muslim saint
दरबार	*darbār* (m.)	royal court
दरमियाना	*darmiyānā*	belonging to the middle, medium
दरवाज़ा	*darvāzā* (m.)	door
दरिया	*dariyā* (m. type 2)	river
दरी	*darī* (f.)	carpet, rug
दर्जन	*darjan*	dozen
दर्द	*dard* (m.)	pain (*sirdard*, m. headache)
दर्शन	*darśan* (m.)	view of (esp. of a deity during worship)
दवा/दवाई	*davā/davāī* (f.)	medicine
दस्त	*dast* (m.pl.)	diarrhea
दही	*dahī* (m.)	yogurt
दाँत	*dā̃t* (m.)	tooth
दाख़िल होना	*dāxil honā*	to enter
दाग़	*dāgh* (m.)	stain, blemish
दाढ़ी	*dāṛhī* (f.)	beard
दादा	*dādā* (m.)	paternal grandfather
दादी	*dādī* (f.)	paternal grandmother
दाम	*dām* (m.)	price
दायाँ	*dāyā̃*	right (direction, side)
दाल	*dāl* (f.)	lentils
दालचीनी	*dālcīnī* (f.)	cinnamon
दालान	*dālān* (m./f.)	veranda
दावत	*dāvat* (f.)	invitation; social gathering with food, reception, party (*dāvat denā*, to invite)
दाहिना	*dāhinā*	right (direction, side)
दिखना	*dikhnā* (v.i.)	to appear to, to look, to seem
दिखाई देना	*dikhāī denā* (v.i.)	to appear to, to become visible to (X *ko*)
दिखाना	*dikhānā* (v.t.)	to show

दिन	*din* (m.)	day
दिनचर्या	*dincaryā* (f.)	daily routine
दिल	*dil* (m.)	heart
दिल चाहना	*dil cāhnā*	to feel like… (X *kā dil cāhnā ki*, for X to feel like…)
दिलचस्प	*dilcasp*	interesting
दिलचस्पी	*dilcaspī* (f.)	interest
दिलचस्पी होना (X को Y में)	X *ko* Y *mẽ dilcaspī honā*	for X to be interested in Y, have an interest in Y
दिसंबर	*disambar* (m.)	December
दीदी	*dīdī* (f.)	title for older sister
दीवार	*dīvār* (f.)	wall
दुकान	*dukān* (f.)	store, shop
दुकानदार	*dukāndār*	shopkeeper
दुखना	*dukhnā* (v.i.)	to hurt, be sore
दुखी	*dukhī*	unhappy
दुनिया	*duniyā* (f.)	world
दुनिया भर	*duniyā-bhar*	throughout the world
दुपट्टा	*dupaṭṭā* (m.)	scarf
दुबला	*dublā*	skinny, thin (people)
दुबला-पतला	*dublā-patlā*	skinny, thin (people)
दुबारा/दोबारा	*dubārā/dobārā*	again
दुर्घटना	*durghaṭnā* (f.)	accident
दुर्घटनास्थल	*durghaṭnā-sthal* (m.)	the site of an accident
दुल्हन	*dulhan* (f.)	bride
दूध	*dūdh* (m.)	milk
दूर	*dūr*	distant, far
दूल्हा	*dūlhā* (m.)	groom
दूसरा	*dūsrā*	other; second
दृश्य	*driśy* (m.)	scene
देखना	*dekhnā* (v.t.)	to look at
देखने में	*dekhne mẽ*	in appearance
देखभाल	*dekhbhāl* (f.)	looking after, caring after (X *kī dekhbhāl karnā*, to look after X)
देर	*der* (f.)	a (short) while, length of time; delay

देर से	*der se*	late
देर होना (X को)	X *ko der honā*	for X to be/get late
देश	*deś* (m.)	country
देहात	*dehāt* (m.)	countryside
दैनिक	*dainik*	daily
दोनों	*donõ*	both
दोपहर	*dopahar* (f.)	afternoon (*dopahar ko*, in the afternoon)
दोस्त	*dost*	friend
दौड़ना	*dauṛnā* (v.i.)	to run
द्वीप	*dvīp* (m.)	island
धड़	*dhaṛ* (m.)	torso
धनिया	*dhaniyā* (m./f.)	cilantro
धन्यवाद	*dhanyavād*	thank you
धरती	*dhartī* (f.)	land; Earth
धर्म	*dharm* (m.)	religion
धारी	*dhārī* (f.)	stripe
धार्मिक	*dhārmik*	religious
धीमा	*dhīmā*	low (in intensity), slow
धीरे	*dhīre*	slowly (also *dhīre dhīre*)
धूप	*dhūp* (f.)	sunshine
धूम-धाम	*dhūm-dhām* (f.)	pomp and show
धोना	*dhonā* (v.t.)	to wash
धोबी	*dhobī* (m.)	washerman
ध्यान रखना (X का)	(X *kā*) *dhyān rakhnā*	to pay due attention to X, keep X in mind, look after X
न...न...	*na...na...*	neither...nor...
नक़्शा	*naqśā* (m.)	map
नज़दीक	*nazdīk*	nearby (X *ke nazdīk*, near to X)
नदी	*nadī* (f.)	river, stream
नफ़रत	*nafrat* (f.)	hatred
नफ़रत करना (X से)	X *se nafrat karnā*	to hate X
नमक	*namak* (m.)	salt
नमकीन	*namkīn*	salty
नमस्कार	*namaskār*	Hello / Goodbye

नमस्ते कहना (X को)	*X ko namaste kahnā*	to say 'hello' to X
नया	*nayā*	new
नवंबर	*navambar* (m.)	November
नहर	*nahar* (f.)	canal, irrigation channel
नहाना	*nahānā* (v.i.)	to bathe
नहीं	*nahī̃*	no; not
ना	*nā*	Isn't it so? Right?
नाक	*nāk* (f.)	nose
नाख़ून	*nāxūn* (m.)	nail
नाचना	*nācnā* (v.i.)	to dance
नाज़ुक	*nāzuk*	delicate
नाटा	*nāṭā*	short (of people)
नाती/नातिन	*nātī/nātin*	grandson/granddaughter (daughter's children)
नाना	*nānā* (m.)	maternal grandfather, mother's father
नानी	*nānī* (f.)	maternal grandmother, mother's mother
नारंगी	*nārangī*	orange
नाराज़	*nārāz*	angry
नालायक़	*nālāyaq*	good for nothing
नाश्ता करना	*nāśtā karnā* (v.t.)	to have breakfast
निकलना	*nikalnā* (v.i.)	to exit, to emerge from (*se*)
निकाह	*nikāh* (m.)	Islamic wedding
निगलना	*nigalnā* (v.t.)	to swallow
निचला	*niclā*	low, lower
निबंध	*nibandh* (m.)	essay
निभाना	*nibhānā* (v.t.)	to carry out (a role)
नियम	*niyam* (m.)	rule, law
नियमित	*niyamit*	restricted, controlled (*niyamit rūp se*, regularly)
निर्भर	*nirbhar*	dependent (upon X; X *par*)
निवास	*nivās* (m.)	residence
नींद आना (X को)	*X ko nī̃d* (f.) *ānā*	for X to be/get sleepy
नींबू	*nī̃bū* (m.)	lemon
नीचा	*nīcā*	low
नीचे	*nīce*	down, downstairs, in the lower part
नीला	*nīlā*	blue

नुस्ख़ा	*nusxā* (m.)	prescription
नेपाली	*nepālī*	Nepali
नौकर	*naukar*	servant, employee
नौकरी	*naukrī* (f.)	job
पंखा	*pankhā* (m.)	fan
पकड़ना	*pakaṛnā* (v.t.)	to catch
पकाना	*pakānā* (v.t.)	to cook
पक्का	*pakkā*	definite, certain; firm, finished
पछताना	*pachtānā*	to regret
पटरी	*paṭrī* (f.)	(rail) track
पट्टी	*paṭṭī* (f.)	bandage (to apply)
पड़ना	*paṛnā* (v.i.)	to fall, to befall
पड़ोस	*paṛos* (m.)	neighborhood
पढ़ाई	*paṛhāī* (f.)	study
पढ़ाई करना	*paṛhāī karnā* (v.t.)	to study
पढ़ाकू	*paṛhākū*	studious
पढ़ाना	*paṛhānā* (v.t.)	to teach
पतंग	*patang* (m.)	kite
पतंगा	*patangā* (m.)	moth
पतझड़	*patjhaṛ* (m.)	fall (season)
पतला	*patlā*	thin
पतलून	*patlūn* (f.)	a pair of pants
पता	*patā* (m.)	address, whereabouts
पता करना (X का)	(X *kā*) *patā karnā*	to find out (about X)
पता चलना (X को)	X *ko patā calnā*	for X to find out
पति	*pati* (m.)	husband
पत्ता	*pattā* (m.)	leaf, sheet
पत्ती	*pattī* (f.)	small leaf (i.e. *cāe pattī*, tea leaves)
पत्नी	*patnī* (f.)	wife
पत्रिका	*patrikā* (f.)	magazine
पनीर	*panīr* (m.)	paneer
पर	*par*	but; on, at
पर, V-ने पर	V-*ne par*	upon V-ing
परदा	*pardā* (m.)	curtain

परवरिश	*parvariś* (f.)	upbringing
परसों	*parsõ*	two days ago; the day after tomorrow
परहेज़	*parhez* (m.)	refraining from (X *se parhez karnā*, to refrain from X)
परहेज़ करना	*parhez karnā* (v.t.)	to refrain (from, *se*)
परिंदा	*parindā* (m.)	bird
परिवार	*parivār* (m.)	family
परी	*parī* (f.)	fairy
परीक्षा	*parīkṣā* (f.)	test, examination
परेशान	*pareśān*	worried, troubled, distressed
परेशान करना	*pareśān karnā*	to bother
परेशानी	*pareśānī* (f.)	trouble, distress
पर्यटक	*paryaṭak*	tourist, traveler
पर्यटन स्थल	*paryaṭan-sthal* (m.)	tourist destination
पर्वत शृंखला	*parvat śrinkhalā* (f.)	mountain chain (*parvat*, m. mountain = *pahāṛ*)
पलंग	*palang* (m.)	bed, bedframe
पल	*pal* (m.)	moment
पलना	*palnā* (v.i.)	to be raised/reared
पलना-बढ़ना	*palnā-baṛhnā* (v.i.)	to grow up, to be raised
पश्चिम	*paścim* (m.)	west
पश्चिमी	*paścimī*	western
पसंद	*pasand* (f.)	liking
पसंद आना (X को Y)	X *ko pasand* Y *ānā* (v.i.)	for X to like Y…(after experiencing it)
पसंद करना	*pasand karnā* (v.t.)	to like; to choose something one likes
पसंद होना (X को Y)	X *ko* Y *pasand honā*	for X to like Y
पसंदीदा	*pasandīdā* (inv.)	favorite
पसीना	*pasīnā* (m.)	sweat (X *ko pasīnā ānā*, for X to sweat)
पहचान	*pahcān* (f.)	identity
पहचान पत्र	*pahcān patr* (m.)	identification card (*pahcān*, f. identity)
पहनना	*pahannā* (v.t.)	to put on (*kapṛe pahannā*, to get dressed)
पहनाना	*pahnānā* (v.t.)	to dress (another person)
पहले	*pahle*	ago; previously; first
पहाड़	*pahāṛ* (m.)	mountain
पहाड़ी	*pahāṛī* (f.)	hill; adj. mountainous

पहुँचना	*pahũcnā* (v.i.)	to arrive; to reach (somewhere)
पहुँचाना	*pahũcānā* (v.t.)	to deliver (e.g. a person to his/her destination)
पाँव	*pā̃v* (*pāõ*) (m.)	foot, leg
पाकिस्तान	*pākistān*	Pakistan
पाकिस्तानी	*pākistānī*	Pakistani
पाजामा	*pājāmā* (m.)	drawstring pants (worn with a kurta)
पानी	*pānī* (m.)	water
पानी की बोतल	*pānī kī botal* (f.)	water bottle
पापा	*pāpā* (m.)	father
पाबंदी	*pābandī* (f.)	restriction, control; regularity (*pābandī se*, regularly)
पार	*pār* (m.)	far bank, shore; opposite side (*ke us pār*, on the opposite side of)
पार करना	*pār karnā* (v.t.)	to cross
पार्क	*pārk* (m.)	park
पालक	*pālak* (m.)	spinach
पालतू	*pāltū* (adj.)	pet (i.e. pet dog, pet cat)
पालना	*pālnā* (v.t.)	to rear (i.e. an animal, a child)
पाव	*pāv*	one quarter part; ¼ kg.
पिंडली	*pinḍlī* (f.)	calf
पिछला	*pichlā*	last, previous
पिता	*pitā* (m.)	father
पीछे	*pīche*	behind
पीठ	*pīṭh* (f.)	back
पीना	*pīnā* (v.t.)	to drink; to smoke
पीला	*pīlā*	yellow
पुकारना	*pukārnā* (v.t.)	to address as, call as
पुदीना	*pudīnā* (m.)	mint
पुराना	*purānā*	old
पुल	*pul* (m.)	bridge
पुलिस	*pulis* (f.)	police
पुस्तकालय	*pustakālay* (m.)	library
पूछना	*pūchnā* (v.t.)	to ask (someone, X se)
पूरा	*pūrā*	completed, complete; entire
पूरा करना	*pūrā karnā*	to complete

पूर्व	*pūrv* (m.)	east
पूर्वी	*pūrvī*	eastern
पेंसिल	*pensil* (f.)	pencil
पेट	*peṭ* (m.)	stomach
पेटी	*peṭī* (f.)	belt
पेट्रोल पंप	*peṭrol pamp* (m.)	gas station
पेड़	*peṛ* (m.)	tree
पेशा	*peśā* (m.)	profession; occupation
पैक करना	*paik karnā*	to pack
पैदल	*paidal*	on foot, by foot
पैदा होना	*paidā* (inv.) *honā*	to be born
पैर	*pair* (m.)	leg, foot
पैसा	*paisā* (m.)	money
पोता/पोती	*potā/potī*	grandson/granddaughter (son's children)
पौधा	*paudhā* (m.)	plant
पौने	*paune*	quarter to; number minus a quarter
प्याज़	*pyāz* (f.)	onion
प्यार	*pyār* (m.)	love; affection
प्यार करना (X से)	X *se pyār karnā*	to love X
प्यारा	*pyārā*	cute, dear
प्याला	*pyālā* (m.)	bowl
प्याली	*pyālī* (f.)	cup
प्यास	*pyās* (f.)	thirst (X *ko pyās lagnā*, for X to be thirsty)
प्रकार	*prakār* (m.)	type, manner (= *tarah*, f.)
प्रकृति	*prakriti* (f.)	nature
प्रदेश	*pradeś* (m.)	state
प्रधान मंत्री	*pradhān mantrī*	prime minister
प्रबंध	*prabandh* (m.)	arrangement
प्रवेश	*praveś* (m.)	entrance, admission (*praveś lenā*, to enroll in)
प्रश्न	*praśn* (m.)	question
प्रसिद्ध	*prasiddh*	famous
प्राकृतिक	*prākritik*	natural
प्राप्त करना	*prāpt karnā*	to obtain
प्रोग्राम	*progrām* (m.)	program, what one plans to do (i.e. for the day)

प्लेट	*pleṭ* (f.)	plate
फ़रमाना	*farmānā* (v.i.)	to speak
फ़रवरी	*farvarī* (f.)	February
फ़र्क़	*farq* (m.)	difference
फ़र्श	*farś* (m.)	floor
फल	*phal* (m.)	fruit
फलवाला	*phalvālā* (m.)	fruit seller
फ़िक्र	*fikr* (f.)	worry, thought, preoccupation
फ़िक्र करना	*fikr karnā*	to worry (about X, X *kī*)
फिर	*phir*	then; again
फ़िल्म	*film* (f.)	film, movie
फ़ुरसत	*fursat* (f.)	free time (X *ko fursat honā*, for X to be free—not busy)
फूफा	*phūphā* (m.)	husband of *buā*
फूल	*phūl* (m.)	flower
फेफड़ा	*phephṛā* (m.)	lung
फैलना	*phailnā* (v.i.)	to spread
फैलाना	*phailānā* (v.t.)	to spread
फ़ैसला	*faislā* (m.)	decision (V-*ne kā faislā karnā*, to decide to V)
फ़ोन	*fon* (m.)	phone
फ़ोन करना	*fon karnā* (v.t.)	to call (by phone)
फ़ौरन	*fauran*	immediately
फ़्रांसीसी	*frānsīsī* (f.)	French
बंग्लादेशी	*banglādeśī*	Bangladeshi
बंद	*band*	closed
बंद करना	*band karnā*	to close, to stop (discontinue doing sthg.)
बंद होना	*band honā*	to stop (w/ infinitive); to close
बंदर	*bandar* (m.)	monkey
बंदूक़	*bandūq* (f.)	rifle
बकरा	*bakrā* (m.)	goat (*bakrī*, f. she-goat)
बग़ैर	*baghair*	without (X *ke baghair*/*baghair* X *ke*, without X)
बचपन	*bacpan* (m.)	childhood
बचपन में	*bacpan mẽ*	In childhood, as a kid
बचाना	*bacānā* (v.t.)	to save

बच्चा	*baccā* (m.)	child (male)
बच्ची	*baccī* (f.)	child (female)
बजना	*bajnā* (v.i.)	to sound, resound, be struck (a bell); to play (i.e., for music to play)
बजा है	...*bajā hai*	It's...o'clock (with times based on 'one')
बजाना	*bajānā* (v.t.)	to play (an instrument); to make ring
बजे	...*baje*	at...o'clock
बजे हैं	...*baje haĩ*	It's...o'clock
बड़ा	*baṛā*	big
बड़ा होना	*baṛā honā*	to grow up
बढ़ना	*baṛhnā* (v.i.)	to increase, to grow
बढ़िया	*baṛhiyā* (inv.)	excellent
बदतमीज़	*badtamīz*	ill-mannered
बदन	*badan* (m.)	body
बदमाश	*badmāś*	wicked, villainous; naughty
बदलना	*badalnā* (v.t./v.i.)	to change (*kapṛe badalnā*, to change clothes, get dressed)
बदसूरत	*badsūrat*	ugly
बधाई हो	*badhāī ho*	congratulations
बनना	*bannā* (v.i.)	to become
बनवाना	*banvānā* (v.t.)	to have (something) made
बनाना	*banānā* (v.t.)	to make
बरताव	*bartāv* (m.)	behavior (*bartāv karnā*, to behave)
बरबाद	*barbād*	ruined
बरबाद करना	*barbād karnā* (v.t.)	to ruin; to waste (e.g., *vaqt*, m. time)
बरसात	*barsāt* (f.)	rains, rainy season
बराबर	*barābar*	equal, equally
बरामदा	*barāmdā* (m.)	veranda
बर्तन	*bartan* (m.)	pots and pans; a cooking or eating vessel
बर्फ़	*barf* (f.)	snow, ice
बर्फ़ पड़ना	*barf paṛnā* (v.i.)	to snow
बर्फ़ी	*barfī* (f.)	a popular Indian sweet
बसंत	*basant* (m.)	spring
बस	*bas* (colloq.)	just, only
बहन	*bahan* (f.)	sister

बहना	*bahnā* (v.i.)	to flow (*nāk bahnā*, for one's nose to run)
बहस	*bahas* (f.)	discussion, debate
बहस करना	*bahas karnā* (v.t.)	to have a discussion; to debate
बहुत	*bahut*	a lot (of); very
बहुत सा	*bahut sā*	many, a lot of
बाँधना	*bā̃dhnā* (v.t.)	to tie, to fasten
बाँसुरी	*bā̃surī* (f.)	bamboo flute
बाँह	*bā̃h* (f.)	arm
बाक़ी	*bāqī*	the rest of, the remaining
बाग़	*bāgh* (m.)	garden
बाज़ार	*bāzār* (m.)	market
बाज़ू	*bāzū* (m.)	arm
बात	*bāt* (f.)	utterance, a thing that is or has been spoken; a significant thing
बात करना (X से Y की)	X *se* (Y *kī*) *bāt karnā* (v.t.)	to talk to X (about Y)
बातचीत	*bātcīt* (f.)	conversation (*bātcīt karnā*, to talk, converse)
बातूनी	*bātūnī*	talkative
बाथरूम	*bāthrūm* (m.)	bathroom, washroom
बादल	*bādal* (m.)	cloud
बादशाह	*bādśāh* (m.)	king, emperor
बाप	*bāp* (m.)	father (informal, can be disrespectful)
बायाँ	*bāyā̃*	left (side, direction)
बार	*bār* (f.)	time (i.e., one time, two times)
बार-बार	*bār-bār*	repeatedly
बारिश	*bāriś* (f.)	rain
बारिश होना	*bāriś honā* (v.i.)	to rain
बारीक	*bārīk*	fine, thin, threadlike; minute
बाल	*bāl* (m.)	a strand of hair
बालू	*bālū* (f.)	sand
बाहर	*bāhar*	outside
बिताना	*bitānā* (v.t.)	to pass
बिना	*binā*	without (X *ke binā*/*binā* X *ke*, without X)
बिल्कुल	*bilkul*	completely, absolutely

बिल्ली	*billī* (f.)	cat
बिस्कुट	*biskuṭ* (m.)	cookie, cracker
बिस्तर	*bistar* (m.)	bedding
बीमार	*bīmār*	ill, sick
बीमारी	*bīmārī* (f.)	illness
बुआ	*buā* (f.)	paternal aunt
बुक करना	*buk karnā*	to book
बुख़ार	*buxār* (m.)	fever (X *ko buxār honā*, for X to have a fever)
बुद्धिमान	*buddhimān*	intelligent, having common sense
बुधवार	*budhvār* (m.)	Wednesday
बुरा	*burā*	bad
बुलाना	*bulānā* (v.t.)	to invite, call, summon
बृहस्पतिवार	*brihaspativār* (m.)	Thursday
बेकार	*bekār*	useless
बेचना	*becnā* (v.t.)	to sell
बेडरूम	*beḍrūm* (m.)	bedroom
बेल	*bel* (f.)	vine
बेवक़ूफ़	*bevaqūf*	foolish, a fool
बेहतर	*behtar*	better
बेहतरीन	*behtarīn*	best
बेहद	*behad*	without limit (*had*, f. limit)
बेहोश	*behoś*	unconscious
बैंगन	*baĩgan* (m.)	eggplant
बैंगनी	*baĩgnī*	purple
बैठक	*baiṭhak* (f.)	drawing room
बैठना	*baiṭhnā* (v.i.)	to sit down
बैठा	*baiṭhā*	seated
बैल	*bail* (m.)	bull
बोतल	*botal* (f.)	bottle
बोरियत	*boriyat* (f.)	boredom
भगवान	*bhagvān* (m.)	God
भतीजा/भतीजी	*bhatījā/bhatījī*	nephew/niece (brother's children)
भर	X *bhar*	throughout X

भरना	*bharnā* (v.i./v.t.)	to fill, to fill out (*fārm bharnā*, to fill out a form)
भरपूर	*bharpūr*	complete, full
भरा	*bharā*	full
भरोसा	*bharosā* (m.)	trust, belief in
भरोसा करना (X पर)	X *par bharosā karnā*	to trust X; have faith (not religious) in X
भविष्य	*bhaviṣy* (m.)	future
भाँजा/भाँजी	*bhā̃jā/bhā̃jī*	nephew/niece (sister's children)
भाई	*bhāī* (m.)	brother
भाई-बहन	*bhāī-bahan* (m.pl.)	siblings, brothers and sisters
भाग	*bhāg* (m.)	part
भाभी	*bhābhī* (f.)	sister-in-law (brother's wife)
भारत	*bhārat*	India
भारतीय	*bhāratīy*	Indian
भारी	*bhārī*	heavy (*tabiyat bhārī honā*, for one to not feel well)
भालू	*bhālū* (m.)	bear
भाषण	*bhāṣaṇ* (m.)	speech (*bhāṣaṇ denā*, to give a speech)
भाषा	*bhāṣā* (f.)	language
भिंडी	*bhinḍī* (f.)	okra
भिखारी	*bhikhārī*	beggar
भी	*bhī*	also, too, either; even (+ negation)
भीड़	*bhīṛ* (f.)	crowd, crowded state
भूख	*bhūkh* (f.)	hunger (X *ko bhūkh lagnā*, for X to be hungry)
भूगोल	*bhūgol* (m.)	geography
भूत	*bhūt* (m.)	ghost
भूमिका	*bhūmikā* (f.)	role
भूरा	*bhūrā*	brown
भूलना/भूल जाना	*bhūlnā/bhūl jānā* (v.i.)	to forget
भेड़	*bheṛ* (f.)	sheep
भैंस	*bhaĩs* (f.)	water buffalo
भैया	*bhaiyā* (m.)	brother
भोजनालय	*bhojnālay* (m.)	traditional vegetarian restaurant
भौंह/भौं	*bhaũh/bhaũ* (f.)	eyebrow
मंगलमय	*mangalmay*	good, auspicious

मंगलवार	*mangalvār* (m.)	Tuesday
मंज़र	*manzar* (m.)	scene
मंज़िल	*manzil* (f.)	destination; storey
मंज़िला	# *manzilā*	# storeyed
मंदिर	*mandir* (m.)	temple
मई	*maī* (f.)	May
मक़बरा	*maqbarā* (m.)	tomb, mausoleum
मकान	*makān* (m.)	house
मक्खन	*makkhan* (m.)	butter
मक्खी	*makkhī* (f.)	fly
मगर	*magar*	but (= *lekin*)
मगरमच्छ	*magarmacch* (m.)	crocodile
मच्छर	*macchar* (m.)	mosquito
मछली	*machlī* (f.)	fish
मज़बूत	*mazbūt*	strong, solid (in build)
मज़हब	*mazhab* (m.)	religion
मज़हबी	*mazhabī*	religious
मज़ा	*mazā* (m.)	fun, enjoyment
मज़ा आना (X को)	X *ko mazā ānā* (v.i.)	for X to have a good time, enjoy oneself
मज़ा लेना (X का)	X *kā mazā lenā*	to enjoy X
मज़ाक़	*mazāq* (m.)	joke
मज़ेदार	*mazedār* (adj.)	fun, amusing; tasty
मटर	*maṭar* (f.)	peas
मतलब	*matlab* (m.)	meaning
मतली	*matlī* (f.)	nausea (X *ko matlī honā*, for X to be nauseous)
मदद	*madad* (f.)	help
मदद करना (X की)	X *kī madad karnā*	to help X
मन करना	*man karnā*	to feel like... (X *kā* V-*ne kā man karnā*, for X to feel like V-ing; X *kā man karnā ki*..., for X to feel like...)
मन होना	*man honā*	to feel like... (X *kā* V-*ne kā man honā*, for X to feel like V-ing)
मनपसंद	*manpasand*	favorite
मना	*manā*	forbidden
मनाना	*manānā* (v.t.)	to celebrate (a holiday, festival), to carry out (a diversional activity)

मनुष्य	*manuṣy* (m.)	human being
मनोरंजन	*manoranjan* (m.)	entertainment, recreation
मम्मी	*mammī* (f.)	mother
मम्मी-पापा	*mammī-pāpā*	parents
मरम्मत	*marammat* (f.)	repair (X *kī marammat karnā*, to repair X)
मरीज़	*marīz*	patient (medical)
मर्द	*mard* (m.)	man
मलबा	*malbā* (m.)	rubble
मशहूर	*maśhūr*	famous
मसला	*maslā* (m.)	problem
मसाला	*masālā* (m.)	spice
मसालेदार	*masāledār*	spicy
मस्जिद	*masjid* (f.)	mosque
महँगा	*mahãgā*	expensive
महक	*mahak* (f.)	smell, fragrance
महत्त्व	*mahattv* (m.)	importance
महत्त्वपूर्ण	*mahattvpūrṇ*	important
महल	*mahal* (m.)	palace
महसूस करना	*mahsūs karnā*	to feel
महसूस होना (X को)	X *ko mahsūs honā*	for X to feel (+ noun)
महीन	*mahīn*	fine
महीना	*mahīnā* (m.)	month
माँ	*mā̃* (f.)	mother
माँगना	*mā̃gnā* (v.t.)	to ask for
माँ-बाप	*mā̃-bāp* (m.pl.)	parents
माँस	*mā̃s* (m.)	meat
माता	*mātā* (f.)	mother
माता-पिता	*mātā-pitā* (m.pl.)	parents
माथा	*māthā* (m.)	forehead
माध्यम	*mādhyam* (m.)	a means
मानना	*mānnā* (v.t.)	to believe; to regard
माफ़	*māf*	excused; forgiven
माफ़ करना	*māf karnā* (v.t.)	to forgive, excuse (*māf kījiye*, excuse me/I'm sorry)

मामा	*māmā* (m.)	maternal uncle
मामी	*māmī* (f.)	wife of *māmā*
मायका	*māykā* (m.)	parent's home (of a married woman)
मार-धाड़ वाली फ़िल्म	*mār-dhāṛ vālī film* (f.)	action film
मारना	*mārnā* (v.t.)	to strike, to hit; *mār ḍālnā*, to kill
मार्ग	*mārg* (m.)	road (esp. in proper street names)
मार्च	*mārc* (m.)	March
माला	*mālā* (f.)	garland
मालूम	*mālūm*	known
मालूम होना (X को Y)	X *ko* (Y) *mālūm honā*	for X to know (Y—a piece of information)
मालूमात	*mālūmāt* (m.pl.)	information
माहिर	*māhir*	expert
माहौल	*māhaul* (m.)	atmosphere, environment
मिज़ाज	*mizāj* (m.)	temperament, disposition
मिठाई	*miṭhāī* (f.)	a sweet
मिनट	*minaṭ* (m.)	minute
मिर्च	*mirc* (f.)	pepper
मिलनसार	*milansār*	friendly
मिलना (X को Y)	X *ko* Y *milnā*	for X to get Y
मिलना (X से)	X *se milnā*	to meet X, to see X socially
मिलना-जुलना	*milnā-julnā* (v.i.)	to look alike; to socialize
मिलाना	*milānā* (v.t.)	to introduce (X *se*, to X)
मिसाल	*misāl* (f.)	example
मीटर	*mīṭar*	meter
मीठा	*mīṭhā*	sweet
मील	*mīl* (m.)	mile
मुँह	*mũh* (m.)	mouth, face
मुआवज़ा	*muāvzā* (m.)	compensation
मुक़ाबला	*muqāblā* (m.)	competition
मुग़लई	*mughlaī*	Mughlai, a style of North Indian cuisine
मुड़ना	*muṛnā* (v.i.)	to turn (X *se muṛnā*, to turn at/from X; X *par muṛnā*, to turn on to X)
मुफ़्त	*muft*	free (in price)

मुबारक हो	*mubārak ho*	congratulations (*dīvālī mubārak ho*, Happy Diwali)
मुमकिन	*mumkin*	possible
मुर्ग़ी	*murghī* (f.)	chicken
मुलाक़ात	*mulāqāt* (f.)	meeting
मुल्क	*mulk* (m.)	country
मुश्किल	*muśkil*	difficult; (f.) difficulty
मुसाफ़िर	*musāfir*	traveler
मुस्कराना	*muskarānā* (v.t.)	to smile
मुहब्बत	*muhabbat* (f.)	love
मुहल्ला	*muhallā* (m.)	quarter (of town)
मूँछें	*mũchẽ* (f.pl.)	moustache
में	*mẽ*	in
X में से	X *mẽ se*	among X, from among X
मेज़	*mez* (f.)	table, desk
मेज़पोश	*mezpoś* (m.)	table cloth
मेज़बान	*mezbān*	host
मेरा	*merā*	my, mine
मेल	*mel* (m.)	coming together, meeting, mixture
मेहनत	*mehnat* (f.)	hard work
मेहनती	*mehantī*	hard working
मेहमान	*mehmān*	guest
मेहरबानी	*meharbānī* (f.)	kindness, act of kindness (*baṛī meharbānī hogī*, it will be a big act of kindness, I would appreciate it)
मैदान	*maidān* (m.)	plain, field
मॉल	*māl* (m.)	mall (also, **माल**, m. goods)
मोच	*moc* (f.)	sprain (X *ke/kī...mẽ moc ānā*, for X's…to get sprained)
मोज़ा	*mozā* (m.)	sock
मोटा	*moṭā*	fat, heavyset; thick
मोमबत्ती	*mombattī* (f.)	candle
मोल-भाव	*mol-bhāo* (m.)	bargaining, haggling
मौक़ा	*mauqā* (m.)	occasion; opportunity
मौत	*maut* (f.)	death

मौसम	*mausam* (m.)	season; weather
मौसा	*mausā* (m.)	husband of *mausī*
मौसी	*mausī* (f.)	maternal aunt
यक़ीन	*yaqīn* (m.)	certainty, confidence
यक़ीन करना	*yaqīn karnā*	to believe
यह	*ye*	this, it
यहाँ	*yahā̃*	here, over here
या	*yā*	or
यात्रा	*yātrā* (f.)	journey (*yātrā karnā*, to travel, to take a journey)
यात्री	*yātrī*	traveler
याद	*yād* (f.)	a memory
याद होना (X को Y)	X *ko* (Y) *yād honā*	for X to remember Y
यानी	*yānī*	that is to say
योग्य	*yogy*	worthy
योग्य, V-ने योग्य	V-*ne yogy*	worth V-ing
योजना	*yojnā* (f.)	plan
रंग	*rang* (m.)	color
रंग-बिरंगा	*rang-birangā*	colorful
रखना	*rakhnā* (v.t.)	to put, to place; to keep
रवानगी	*ravāngī* (f.)	departure
रवाना होना	*ravānā honā* (v.i.)	to depart
रविवार	*ravivār* (m.)	Sunday
रसोईघर	*rasoīghar* (m.)	kitchen
रस्म	*rasm* (f.)	ceremony, custom
रहना	*rahnā* (v.i.)	to live, reside; to remain
राजधानी	*rājdhānī* (f.)	capital
राजनीति	*rājnīti* (f.)	politics
राजनीति शास्त्र	*rajnīti śāstr* (m.)	political science
राजपूती	*rājpūtī*	relating to Rajputs
राजमार्ग	*rājmārg* (m.)	highway
राजा	*rājā* (m.)	king
राज्य	*rājy* (m.)	state
रात	*rāt* (f.)	night (*rāt ko*, at night)
रानी	*rānī* (f.)	queen

राय	*rāy* (f.)	opinion
राष्ट्रीय	*rāṣṭrīy*	national (*rāṣṭr*, m. nation)
रास्ता	*rāstā* (m.)	way, road (*rāstā pūchnā*, to ask for directions; *rāstā batānā*, to give directions)
राहतकर्मी	*rāhatkarmī*	relief worker
रिक्शा	*rikśā* (m.)	rickshaw
रिक्शेवाला	*rikśevālā* (m.)	rickshaw driver
रिवाज	*rivāj* (m.)	custom, practice
रिश्तेदार	*riśtedār*	a relative
रुकना	*ruknā* (v.i.)	to stop, halt
रुपया	*rupayā* (m.)	rupee (unit of currency)
रूमानी	*rūmānī*	romantic
रेगिस्तान	*registān* (m.)	desert
रेत	*ret* (f.)	sand
रेलगाड़ी	*rel gāṛī* (f.)	train
रेलवे स्टेशन	*relve sṭeśan* (m.)	train station
रेशम	*reśam* (m.)	silk
रेस्टोरेंट	*resṭorenṭ* (m.)	restaurant
रोकना	*roknā* (v.t.)	to stop
रोचक	*rocak*	interesting
रोज़/रोज़ाना	*roz/rozānā*	daily
रोटी	*roṭī* (f.)	bread, (esp. flat bread)
रोना	*ronā* (v.i.)	to cry
रोशनदान	*rośandān* (m.)	an opening high on a wall to allow air and light in
लकड़ी	*lakṛī* (f.)	wood
लगना (X को)	X *ko lagnā*	to seem to X, to strike X as…, for X to find (something to be…)
लगभग	*lagbhag*	approximately
लगातार	*lagātār*	continuously
लगाना	*lagānā* (v.t.)	to put on, apply to, attach to (*par/se*)
लज़ीज़	*lazīz*	delicious
लड़का	*laṛkā* (m.)	boy
लड़की	*laṛkī* (f.)	girl
लड्डू	*laḍḍū* (m.)	a popular ball-shaped Indian sweet
लम्बा	*lambā*	long, tall

लम्बाई	*lambāī* (f.)	height, length
लम्बा-चौड़ा	*lambā-cauṛā*	big and sturdily built
लहसुन	*lahsun* (m.)	garlic
लाना	*lānā* (v.i.)	to bring (also *le ānā*)
लापरवाह	*lāparvāh*	careless
लायक़	*lāyaq*	worthy (X *ke lāyaq*, worthy of X; V-*ne lāyaq*, worth V-ing)
लायक़, V-ने लायक़	V-*ne lāyaq*	worth V-ing
लाल	*lāl*	red
लाल मिर्च	*lāl mirc* (f.)	red pepper
लिपि	*lipi* (f.)	script
लिबास	*libās* (m.)	clothing, attire
लिहाफ़	*lihāf* (m.)	thick blanket, comforter
ले चलना	*le calnā* (v.i.)	to take with
ले जाना	*le jānā* (v.i.)	to take (someone/something somewhere)
लेकिन	*lekin*	but
लेटना	*leṭnā* (v.i.)	to lie down
लॉन	*lān* (m.)	lawn
लोकप्रिय	*lokpriy*	popular
लोकप्रियता	*lokpriytā* (f.)	popularity
लोग	*log* (m.pl.)	people
लोमड़ी	*lomṛī* (f.)	fox
लौंग	*laung* (f.)	clove
लौटना	*lauṭnā* (v.i.)	to return (come/go back)
वक़्त	*vaqt* (m.)	time
वग़ैरह	*vaghaira*	et cetera
वज़न	*vazan* (m.)	weight
वजह	*vajah* (f.)	reason
वर्ष	*varṣ* (m.)	year
वर्षा	*varṣā* (f.)	rain
वह	*vo*	that, it
वहाँ	*vahā̃*	there, over there
वहीं	*vahī̃*	right there
वही	*vahī*	that very

वाक्य	*vāky* (m.)	sentence
वादी	*vādī* (f.)	valley
वापस	*vāpas*	back
वापसी	*vāpsī* (f.)	return
वास्तव में	*vāstav mẽ*	actually, in fact
विचार	*vicār* (m.)	thought, idea
विज्ञान	*vijñān* (*vigyān*) (m.)	science
विद्यार्थी	*vidyārthī* (m./f.)	student
विधि	*vidhi* (f.)	method
विवाह	*vivāh* (m.)	wedding
विवाहित	*vivāhit*	married
विश्वास	*viśvās* (m.)	certainty, confidence
विश्वास करना	*viśvās karnā*	to believe
विषय	*viṣay* (m.)	essay, subject
विस्तार	*vistār* (m.)	extent, expanse (*vistār se*, in detail, at length)
वैसा	*vaisā*	like that, of that type
वैसे तो... लेकिन...	*vaise to...lekin...*	while it is true that...still...
व्यक्ति	*vyakti* (m./f.)	person, individual
व्यवसाय	*vyavasāy* (m.)	profession; vocation
व्यवहार	*vyavhār* (m.)	behavior
व्यस्त	*vyast*	busy
व्यायाम करना	*vyāyām karnā*	to exercise
शक्कर	*śakkar* (m.)	sugar
शक्ल	*śakl* (f.)	appearance; face; shape
शख़्स	*śaxs* (m./f.)	person, individual
शतरंज	*śatranj* (f.)	chess
शताब्दी	*śatābdī* (f.)	century
शनिवार	*śanivār* (m.)	Saturday
शब्द	*śabd* (m.)	word
शब्दकोश	*śabdkoś* (m.)	dictionary
शराब	*śarāb* (f.)	alcoholic beverage
शरारती	*śarārtī*	naughty
शरीक होना	*śarīk honā* (v.t.)	to participate (*mẽ*, in)
शरीर	*śarīr* (m.)	body

शर्मीला	*śarmīlā*	shy
शलवार	*śalvār* (f.)	a type of loose, drawstring pants worn with various tops
शहर	*śahar* (m.)	city
शाकाहारी	*śākāhārī*	vegetarian
शादी	*śādī* (f.)	wedding, marriage
शादी करना	*śādī karnā* (v.t.)	to marry, to get married
शादीशुदा	*śādī-śudā* (inv.)	married
शानदार	*śāndār*	splendid, magnificent
शाबाश	*śābāś*	Bravo! Good job!
शाम	*śām* (f.)	evening (*śām ko*, in the evening)
शामिल	*śāmil*	included
शायद	*śāyad*	perhaps, maybe
शायर	*śāyar* (m.)	poet
शायरी	*śāyrī* (f.)	poetry
शाल	*śāl* (f.)	shawl
शास्त्रीय	*śāstrīy*	classical
शिकार	*śikār* (m.)	hunting
शिक्षक	*śikṣak* (m.)	instructor
शिक्षा	*śikṣā* (f.)	education
शिक्षिका	*śikṣikā* (f.)	instructor
शिमला मिर्च	*śimlā mirc* (f.)	bell pepper
शीशी	*śīśī* (f.)	small bottle
शुक्रवार	*śukrvār* (m.)	Friday
शुक्रिया	*śukriyā*	thank you
शुभकामनाएँ	*śubhkāmnāẽ*	best wishes
शुरू	*śurū* (m.)	beginning
शुरू करना	*śurū karnā* (v.t.)	to begin, to start
शुरू होना	*śurū honā* (v.i.)	to begin, to start
शेर	*śer* (m.)	lion
शेरवानी	*śervānī* (f.)	a type of long, formal dress coat
शोर	*śor* (m.)	noise (*śor karnā*, to make noise)
शोर मचाना	*śor-macānā*	to make a lot of noise
शोर-शराबा	*śor-śarābā* (m.)	noise

शौक़	*śauq* (m.)	hobby, interest
शौक़ होना (X को V-ने का)	X *ko* V-*ne kā śauq honā*	for X to enjoy V-ing (as a hobby)
शौचालय	*saucālay* (m.)	toilet, bathroom
संगीत	*sangīt* (m.)	music
संग्रहालय	*sangrahālay* (m.)	museum
संजीदा	*sanjīdā* (inv.)	serious
संतरा	*santarā* (m.)	orange
संबंध	*sambandh* (m.)	connection (*is sambandh mẽ*, in this connection)
संभलना	*sambhalnā* (v.i.)	to steady oneself (so as not to fall)
संभव	*sambhav*	possible
संभावना	*sambhāvnā* (f.)	possibility
संस्कृति	*sanskriti* (f.)	culture
संस्था	*sansthā* (f.)	institution, organization
सख़्त	*saxt*	strict, hard, harsh (*saxt manā*, strictly forbidden)
सच	*sac*	true
सचमुच	*sacmuc*	really, truly
सड़क	*saṛak* (f.)	road
सदी	*sadī* (f.)	century
सप्ताह	*saptāh* (m.)	week
सप्ताहांत	*saptāhānt* (m.)	weekend
सफ़र	*safar* (m.)	journey (*safar karnā*, to travel, to take a journey)
सफल	*saphal*	successful
सफलता	*saphaltā* (f.)	success
सफ़ाई	*safāī* (f.)	cleaning
सफ़ाई करना (X की)	X *kī safāī karnā*	to clean X
सफ़ेद	*safed*	white
सब	*sab*	all
सब्ज़ी	*sabzī* (f.)	vegetable; vegetable dish
सब्ज़ीवाला	*sabzīvālā* (m.)	vegetable seller
सभ्यता	*sabhytā* (f.)	civilization
समझ	*samajh* (f.)	understanding
समझ में आना (X की)	X *kī samajh mẽ ānā*	to make sense to X
समझना	*samajhnā* (v.i./v.t.)	to understand

समय	*samay* (m.)	time
समस्या	*samasyā* (f.)	problem
समाचार	*samācār* (m.)	news, news item
समाचार पत्र	*samācār patr* (m.)	newspaper
समारोह	*samāroh* (m.)	function, celebratory occasion; ceremony
समुद्र	*samudr* (m.)	ocean; sea
सर	*sar* (m.)	head
सरकारी	*sarkārī*	governmental (*sarkār*, f. 'government')
सर्दियाँ	*sardiyā̃* (f.pl.)	cold season, winter
सर्दी	*sardī* (f.)	cold (X *ko sardī lagnā*, for X to be cold)
सलाह	*salāh* (f.)	advice
सलूक	*salūk* (m.)	behavior
सवा	*savā*	quarter past; number plus a quarter
सवारी	*savārī* (f.)	passenger
सवाल	*savāl* (m.)	question
ससुर	*sasur* (m.)	father-in-law
ससुराल	*sasurāl* (m.)	in-laws' (home)
सस्ता	*sastā*	inexpensive, cheap
सहपाठी	*sahpāṭhī*	classmate
सहमत	*sahmat*	in agreement, agreeing (with X, X *se*)
सही	*sahī*	correct, true
सहेली	*sahelī* (f.)	female friend of a female
साँप	*sā̃p* (m.)	snake
साँवला	*sā̃vlā*	dark or dusky in complexion
सांस्कृतिक	*sānskritik*	cultural
साइकिल	*sāikil* (f.)	bicycle
साग	*sāg* (m.)	greens
साज़	*sāz* (m.)	musical instrument
साड़ी	*sāṛī* (f.)	sari
साढ़े	*sāṛhe*	half past; number plus one half
सादा	*sādā*	plain, simple
साफ़	*sāf*	clear, clearly; clean
साफ़ करना	*sāf karnā* (v.t.)	to clean
साफ़-सुथरा	*sāf suthrā*	neat and clean, clean and tidy

साबुन	*sābun* (m.)	soap
सामग्री	*sāmagrī* (f.)	ingredients, material
सामान	*sāmān* (m.sg.)	stuff, things
साल	*sāl* (m.)	year
सालगिरह	*sālgirah* (f.)	birthday
सास	*sās* (f.)	mother-in-law
साहब	*sāhab*	an honorific marker appended to male names
साहित्य	*sāhity* (m.)	literature
साहित्यिक	*sāhityik*	literary (*sāhity*, m. literature)
सिग्रेट	*sigreṭ* (f.)	cigarette (*sigreṭ pīnā*, to smoke a cigarette)
सितंबर	*sitambar* (m.)	September
सिनेमाघर	*sinemāghar* (m.)	cinema, theatre
सियासत	*siyāsat* (f.)	politics
सिर	*sir* (m.)	head
सिर्फ़	*sirf*	only, just
सिलना	*silnā* (v.t.)	to sew
सिलसिला	*silsilā* (m.)	connection, sequence
सीट	*sīṭ* (f.)	seat
सीढ़ी	*sīṛhī* (f.)	stair
सीधा	*sīdhā*	simple, ingenuous (of people); straight, direct (of things)
सीधा हाथ	*sīdhā hāth*	right hand (*sīdhe hāth par*, on the right side)
सीधा-सादा	*sīdhā-sādā*	simple, plain, ingenuous
सीना	*sīnā* (m.)	chest
सीरियल	*sīriyal* (m.)	television series
सुंदर	*sundar*	beautiful, handsome
सुकून	*sukūn* (m.)	peace, tranquility
सुझाव	*sujhāv* (m.)	suggestion (+ *denā*, to suggest)
सुनहरा	*sunharā / sunahrā*	golden, blond (of hair)
सुनाई देना	*sunāī denā* (v.i.)	to become audible to
सुनाना	*sunānā* (v.t.)	to recite, to read aloud
सुबह	*subah* (f.)	morning, in the morning
सुबह-सवेरे	*subah-savere*	early in the morning
सुस्त	*sust*	lazy; sluggish, slow

सुहावना/सुहाना	*suhāvnā/suhānā*	pleasant
सूखना	*sūkhnā* (v.i.)	to dry out, to go dry
सूजन	*sūjan* (f.)	swelling (*sūjnā*, v.i. to swell), inflammation
सूरज	*sūraj* (m.)	sun
से	*se*	from, than, by
से दूर	*se dūr*	far from, distant from
से पहले	*se pahle* (ppn.)	before
सेब	*seb* (m.)	apple
सेवा	*sevā* (f.)	service (X *kī sevā karnā*, to serve X)
सेहत	*sehat* (f.)	health
सेहतमंद	*sehatmand*	healthy
सैर	*sair* (f.)	tour
सो जाना	*so jānā*	to fall asleep
सोच-समझकर	*soc-samajhkar*	having deliberated, having given due consideration
सोना	*sonā* (v.i.)	to sleep (*so jānā*, to fall asleep, go to sleep)
सोने का कमरा	*sone kā kamrā* (m.)	bedroom
सोफ़ा	*sofā* (m.)	sofa
सोमवार	*somvār* (m.)	Monday
स्कूल	*skūl* (m.)	school
स्टेशन	*sṭeśan* (m.)	station (*relve sṭeśan*)
स्थान	*sthān* (m.)	place
स्थित	*sthit*	situated, located
स्याह ज़ीरा	*syāh zīrā* (m.)	black cumin
स्लेटी	*sleṭī*	gray
स्वतंत्रता	*svatantrtā* (f.)	freedom, independence
स्वभाव	*svabhāv* (m.)	temperament, disposition
स्वयं	*svayam*	oneself; myself, yourself, himself, etc.
स्वयंसेवक	*svayamsevak* (m.)	volunteer
स्वस्थ	*svasth*	healthy
स्वाद	*svād* (m.)	taste
स्वादिष्ट	*svādiṣṭ*	delicious
स्वास्थ्य	*svāsthy* (m.)	health
स्वीकार करना	*svīkār karnā* (v.t.)	to accept, to admit

हँसमुख	*hãsmukh*	fun-loving
हँसी	*hãsī* (f.)	laughter (cf. *hãsnā*, to laugh)
हँसी-मज़ाक़ करना	*hãsī-mazāq karnā*	to joke around
हटाना	*haṭānā* (v.t.)	to move aside; to remove
हड्डी	*haḍḍī* (f.)	bone
हथेली	*hathelī* (f.)	palm
हफ़्ता	*haftā* (m.)	week
हमेशा	*hameśā*	always
हर	*har*	each, every
हर तरह का	*har tarah kā*	all types of, "of all types"
हरा	*harā*	green
हल	*hal* (m.)	solution
हलवाई	*halvāī* (m.)	sweet maker
हल्का	*halkā*	light (in color or weight)
हवा	*havā* (f.)	wind; air
हवाई अड्डा	*havāī aḍḍā* (m.)	airport
हवाई जहाज़	*havāī jahāz* (m.)	airplane
हवेली	*havelī* (m.)	mansion
हाँ	*hā̃*	yes
हाकिम	*hākim* (m.)	ruler
हाज़िर	*hāzir*	present, in attendance
हाथ	*hāth* (m.)	hand; arm
हाथी	*hāthī* (m.)	elephant
हादसा	*hādsā* (m.)	accident
हारना	*hārnā* (v.i.)	to be defeated, to lose
हाल में	*hāl mẽ*	recently
हालत	*hālat* (f.)	condition
हालाँकि...लेकिन/ फिर भी	*hālā̃ki...lekin/phir bhī*	although / even though… still…
हासिल करना	*hāsil karnā*	to obtain
हिंदुस्तान	*hindustān*	India
हिंदुस्तानी	*hindustānī*	Indian
हिरन	*hiran* (m.)	deer
हिसाब	*hisāb* (m.)	price per unit of measurement; calculation
हिस्सा	*hissā* (m.)	part

ही	*hī*	just, only
हीरा	*hīrā* (m.)	diamond
हैरान	*hairān*	surprised
हॉस्टल	*hāsṭal* (m.)	dorm, hostel
होंठ	*hõṭh* (m.)	lip
हो जाना	*ho jānā*	to become
होकर, से होकर	(*se*) *hokar*	via, by way of
होटल	*hoṭal* (m.)	hotel; restaurant
होश	*hoś* (m.)	consciousness (*hoś mẽ ānā*, to return to consciousness)
होशियार	*hośiyār*	smart, clever
होशियारी	*hośiyārī* (f.)	cleverness; intelligence

English–Hindi Glossary

about	के बारे में, *ke bāre mẽ*
absolutely	बिल्कुल, *bilkul*
accept	to accept, to admit: स्वीकार करना, *svīkār karnā* (v.t.), क़बूल करना, *qabūl karnā* (v.t.)
accident	दुर्घटना, *durghaṭnā* (f.), हादसा, *hādsā* (m.)
accident site	दुर्घटनास्थल, *durghaṭnā-sthal* (m.)
according to	के अनुसार, *ke anusār*, के मुताबिक़, *ke mutābiq*
activity	गतिविधि, *gatividhi* (f.)
actually	असल में, *asal mẽ*, दरअसल, *dar-asal*, वास्तव में, *vāstav mẽ*
add	to add (up), to join to: जोड़ना, *joṛnā* (v.t.)
additional	और, *aur*
address	पता, *patā* (m.); to address as, call: पुकारना, *pukārnā* (v.t.)
admission	प्रवेश, *praveś* (m.); *praveś lenā*, to enroll in
advice	सलाह, *salāh* (f.)
Afghani	अफ़ग़ानी, *afghānī*
after	के बाद, *ke bād*
afternoon	दोपहर, *dopahar* (f.); *dopahar ko*: in the afternoon
again	फिर से, *phir se*; दुबारा / दोबारा, *dubārā / dobārā*
age	उम्र, *umr* (f.)
ago	पहले, *pahle*
agree	to agree with X: X से सहमत होना, X *se sahmat honā*
ahead	आगे, *āge*; ahead of: के आगे, *ke āge*
air	हवा, *havā* (f.)
air conditioning	ए-सी, *e-sī* (m.)
airplane	हवाई जहाज़, *havāī jahāz* (m.)
airport	हवाई अड्डा, *havāī aḍḍā* (m.)
alcohol	alcoholic beverage: शराब, *śarāb* (f.)

alive	ज़िंदा, *zindā*
all	सब, *sab*
all of a sudden	अचानक, *acānak*
alley	गली, *galī* (f.)
alone	अकेला, *akelā*
alright, so-so	ठीक-ठाक, *ṭhīk-ṭhāk*
also	भी, *bhī*
although	हालाँकि, *hālā̃ki* (*...lekin/phir bhī...*, still...)
altogether	कुल मिलाकर, *kul milākar*
always	हमेशा, *hameśā*
American	अमरीकी, *amrīkī*
among X	X में से, X *mẽ se*
amusing	मज़ेदार, *mazedār* (adj.)
and	और, *aur*
angry	नाराज़, *nārāz*
animal	जानवर, *jānvar* (m.)
announcement	एलान, *elān* (m.)
answer	जवाब, उत्तर, *javāb* (m.), *uttar* (m.); to answer: जवाब देना, *javāb denā* (v.t.)
ant	चींटी, *cī̃ṭī* (f.)
any	some, someone; any, anyone: कोई, *koī*
anywhere	कहीं, *kahī̃*
apart from	के अलावा, *ke alāvā*
appear	to appear to, to become visible to (X *ko*): दिखाई देना, *dikhāī denā* (v.i.), दिखना, *dikhnā* (v.i.); to appear to, to look, to seem: दिखना, *dikhnā* (v.i.), लगना, *lagnā* (v.i.)
appearance	appearance, face: शक्ल, *śakl* (f.); in appearance: देखने में, *dekhne mẽ*
apple	सेब, *seb* (m.)
apprehension	fear; apprehension: आशंका, *āśankā* (f.)
approximately	लगभग, *lagbhag*, क़रीब, *qarīb*, तक़रीबन, *taqrīban*,
April	अप्रैल, *aprail* (m.)

arm	बाँह, *bā̃h* (f.), बाज़ू, *bāzū* (m.)
around, near, in the vicinity of	के क़रीब, *ke qarīb*
arrangement	इंतज़ाम, *intazām* (m.), प्रबंध, *prabandh* (m.)
arrive	to arrive; to reach (somewhere): पहुँचना, *pahũcnā* (v.i.)
art	कला, *kalā* (f.)
Asia	एशिया, *eśiyā* (*eśiyāī*, Asian)
ask	पूछना, *pūchnā* (v.t.) (someone, X se); ask for: माँगना, *mā̃gnā* (v.t.)
asleep	fall asleep: सो जाना, *so jānā*
at	on, at: पर, *par*
atmosphere	माहौल, *māhaul* (m.)
audible	to become audible to सुनाई देना, *sunāī denā* (v.i.)
August	अगस्त, *agast* (m.)
aunt	paternal aunt: बुआ, *buā* (f.), maternal aunt: मौसी, *mausī* (f.), father's younger brother's (*cācā*'s) wife: चाची, *cācī* (f.), wife of *māmā*: मामी, *māmī* (f.), wife of *tāū*: ताई, *tāī* (f.)
available	available; free, not occupied: ख़ाली, *xālī*
awake	to be awake, to wake up: जागना, *jāgnā* (v.i.)
back	पीठ, *pīṭh* (f.); (go/come) back: वापस, *vāpas*; वापस आना, *vāpas ānā*, to come back; वापस जाना, *vāpas jānā*, to go back, to give back: वापस करना, *vāpas karnā*
bad	बुरा, *burā*; in a bad state, gone bad, spoiled: ख़राब, *xarāb*
bag	थैला, *thailā* (m.)
bald	गंजा, *ganjā*
bamboo flute	बाँसुरी, *bā̃surī* (f.)
banana	केला, *kelā* (m.)
bandage	पट्टी, *paṭṭī* (f.)
Bangladeshi	बंग्लादेशी, *banglādeśī*
bank	bank, shore: किनारा, *kinārā* (m.), तट, *taṭ* (m.); *ke kināre*, on the edge/bank of; far bank, shore; opposite side: पार, *pār* (m.); *ke us pār*, on the opposite side of
bargaining	मोल-भाव, *mol-bhāv* (m.)
basis	आधार, *ādhār* (m.); on the basis of: के आधार पर, *ke ādhār par*
bathe	नहाना, *nahānā* (v.i.)

bathroom	bathroom, washroom: ग़ुसलख़ाना, *ghusalxānā* (m.); bathroom, toilet: ट्वायलेट, *tvāyleṭ* (m.), शौचालय, *saucālay* (m.)
bay	खाड़ी, *khāṛī* (f.)
bay leaf	तेज़ पत्ता, *tez pattā* (m.)
bear	भालू, *bhālū* (m.)
beard	दाढ़ी, *dāṛhī* (f.)
beautiful	ख़ूबसूरत, *xūbsūrat*, सुंदर, *sundar*
because	क्योंकि, *kyõki*; because of: के कारण, *ke kāraṇ*, की वजह से, *kī vajah se*
become	to become: बनना, *bannā* (v.i.), हो जाना, *ho jānā*
bed	bed, bedframe: पलंग, *palang* (m.); bedding: बिस्तर, *bistar* (m.)
bedroom	सोने का कमरा, *sone kā kamrā* (m.), बेडरूम, *beḍrūm* (m.)
bedsheet	चादर, *cādar* (f.)
before	से पहले, *se pahle* (ppn.)
beggar	भिखारी, *bhikhārī*
begin	शुरू करना, *śurū karnā* (v.t.), शुरू होना, *śurū honā* (v.i.)
beginning	शुरू, *śurū* (m.); शुरुआत, *śuruāt* (f.)
behavior	व्यवहार, *vyavhār* (m.), सलूक, *salūk* (m.), बरताव, *bartāv* (m.); to behave: व्यवहार करना, बरताव करना, etc.
behind	behind, in the back: पीछे, *pīche*; behind X: X के पीछे, X *ke pīche*
believe	विश्वास करना, *viśvās karnā*, यक़ीन करना, *yaqīn karnā*; to believe; to regard: मानना, *mānnā* (v.t.)
bell pepper	शिमला मिर्च, *śimlā mirc* (f.)
belly	तोंद, *tõd* (f.)
below	के नीचे, *ke nīce*
belt	पेटी, *peṭī* (f.)
best	बेहतरीन, *behtarīn*
best wishes	शुभकामनाएँ, *śubhkāmnāẽ*
better	बेहतर, *behtar*; to get better: ठीक होना, *ṭhīk honā*
between X	X के बीच, X *ke bīc*; in the middle of: *ke bīc mẽ*
beyond X	X के आगे, X *ke āge*
bicycle	साइकिल, *sāikil* (f.)
big	बड़ा, *baṛā*
bird	चिड़िया, *ciṛiyā* (f.), परिंदा, *parindā* (m.)

birth	जन्म, *janm* (m.)
birthday	जन्मदिन, *janm-din* (m.), सालगिरह, *sālgirah* (f.)
black	काला, *kālā*
black cumin	स्याह ज़ीरा, *syāh zīrā* (m.)
blanket	कंबल, *kambal* (m.); thick blanket, comforter: लिहाफ़, *lihāf* (m.)
blond	सुनहरा, *sunharā / sunahrā*
blood	ख़ून, *xūn* (m.); *xūn bahnā*, to bleed
blue	नीला, *nīlā*
body	बदन, *badan* (m.), शरीर, *śarīr* (m.), जिस्म, *jism* (m.)
boil	उबलना, *ubalnā* (v.i.), उबालना, *ubālnā* (v.t.)
bone	हड्डी, *haḍḍī* (f.)
book	किताब, *kitāb* (f.); to book: बुक करना, *buk karnā*
boredom	बोरियत, *boriyat* (f.)
boring	उबाऊ, *ubāū*
born	to be born: पैदा होना, *paidā* (inv.) *honā*
both	दोनों, *donõ*
bother	परेशान करना, *pareśān karnā*
bottle	बोतल, *botal* (f.); small bottle: शीशी, *śīśī* (f.)
bowl	प्याला, *pyālā* (m.); small bowl: कटोरी, *kaṭorī* (f.)
boy	लड़का, *laṛkā* (m.)
Bravo!	शाबाश, *śābāś*
bread	bread, (esp. flat bread): रोटी, *roṭī* (f.)
break	break, day off, weekend, holiday, vacation time: छुट्टी, *chuṭṭī* (f.); to break: टूटना, *ṭūṭnā* (v.i.), तोड़ना, *toṛnā* (v.t.)
breakfast	breakfast, snack: नाश्ता, *nāśtā* (m.); to have breakfast: नाश्ता करना, *nāśtā karnā* (v.t.)
bride	दुल्हन, *dulhan* (f.)
bridge	पुल, *pul* (m.)
bring	लाना, *lānā* (v.i.)
brother	भाई, *bhāī* (m.); diminutive: भैया, *bhaiyā* (m.); brothers and sisters: भाई-बहन, *bhāī-bahan* (m.pl.)
brown	भूरा, *bhūrā*
building	इमारत, *imārat* (f.)

bull	बैल, *bail* (m.)
bunch	bunch, small tied bundle: गुच्छा, *gucchā* (m.), गट्ठी, *gaṭṭhī* (f.)
burn	जलाना, *jalānā* (v.t.); जलना, *jalnā* (v.i.)
busy	व्यस्त, *vyast*
but	लेकिन, *lekin*, पर, *par*, मगर, *magar*
butcher	क़साई, *qasāī*
butter	मक्खन, *makkhan* (m.); ghee, clarified butter: घी, *ghī* (m.)
butterfly	तितली, *titlī* (f.)
buy	ख़रीदना, *xarīdnā* (v.t.)
by	by, by means of: से, *se*; with passive voice: के द्वारा, *ke dvārā*; by (time): तक, *tak* (ppn.)
by means of	के माध्यम से, *ke mādhyam se*, के ज़रिए, *ke zarie*; by, by means of: के द्वारा, *ke dvārā*
by way of	होकर, से होकर, (*se*) *hokar*
calf	पिंडली, *pinḍlī* (f.)
call	to call, summon: बुलाना, *bulānā* (v.t.); to call (by name): कहना, *kahnā* (v.t.); to address as, call: पुकारना, *pukārnā* (v.t.); to call by phone: फ़ोन करना, *fon karnā* (v.t.); to be called, to cause to be called, to be known as: कहलाना, *kahlānā* (v.i.)
camel	ऊँट, *ũṭ* (m.)
canal	canal, irrigation channel: नहर, *nahar* (f.)
candle	मोमबत्ती, *mombattī* (f.)
capital	राजधानी, *rājdhānī* (f.)
car	गाड़ी, *gāṛī* (f.)
cardamom	इलायची, *ilāycī* (f.)
cards	playing cards: ताश, *tāś* (m.)
careless	लापरवाह, *lāparvāh*
carpet	carpet, rug: क़ालीन, *qālīn* (f.), दरी, *darī* (f.)
carrot	गाजर, *gājar* (f.)
carry out	to carry out (a role): निभाना, *nibhānā* (v.t.)
cart	ठेला, *ṭhelā* (m.)
cat	बिल्ली, *billī* (f.)
catch	पकड़ना, *pakaṛnā* (v.t.)

cauliflower	गोभी, *gobhī* (f.)
ceiling	छत, *chat* (f.)
celebrate	to celebrate (a holiday, festival): मनाना, *manānā* (v.t.)
center	केंद्र, *kendr* (m.)
century	शताब्दी, *śatābdī* (f.), सदी, *sadī* (f.)
ceremony	रस्म, *rasm* (f.)
certain	निश्चित, *niścit*; (colloq.) definite, certain; firm, finished: पक्का, *pakkā*
certainly	ज़रूर, *zarūr*
certainty	certainty, confidence; विश्वास, *viśvās* (m.), यक़ीन, *yaqīn* (m.)
chair	कुर्सी, *kursī* (f.)
change	बदलना, *badalnā* (v.t./v.i.); *kapṛe badalnā*, to change clothes, get dressed
charge	in charge, head: इन्चार्ज, *incārj*
cheap	inexpensive, cheap: सस्ता, *sastā*
cheek	गाल, *gāl* (m.)
chess	शतरंज, *śatranj* (f.)
chest	सीना, *sīnā* (m.), छाती, *chātī* (f.)
chicken	मुर्ग़ी, *murghī* (f.)
child	child, male child: बच्चा, *baccā* (m.); female child: बच्ची, *baccī* (f.)
childhood	बचपन, *bacpan* (m.); in childhood, as a kid: बचपन में, *bacpan mẽ*
chin	ठुड्डी, *ṭhuḍḍī* (f.)
Chinese	चीनी, *cīnī*
choose	चुनना, *cunnā* (v.t.), to choose something one likes; to like: पसंद करना, *pasand karnā* (v.t.)
church	गिरजाघर, *girjāghar* (m.)
cigarette	सिग्रेट, *sigreṭ* (f.); *sigreṭ pīnā*, to smoke a cigarette
cilantro	धनिया, *dhaniyā* (m./f.)
cinema	सिनेमाघर, *sinemāghar* (m.)
cinnamon	दालचीनी, *dālcīnī* (f.)
city	शहर, *śahar* (m.)
civilization	सभ्यता, *sabhytā* (f.); civilization, refinement, culture: तहज़ीब, *tahzīb* (f.)
class	क्लास, *klās* (f.); class, classroom: कक्षा, *kakṣā* (f.)

classical	शास्त्रीय, *śāstrīy*
classmate	सहपाठी, *sahpāṭhī*
clean	(adj.): साफ़, *sāf*; to clean: साफ़ करना, *sāf karnā* (v.t.), X की सफ़ाई करना, X *kī safāī karnā*
cleaning	सफ़ाई, *safāī* (f.)
clear	clear, clearly: साफ़, *sāf*, स्पष्ट, *spaṣṭ*
clever	clever, smart: होशियार, *hośiyār*
cleverness	होशियारी, *hośiyārī* (f.)
climate	जलवायु, *jalvāyu* (f.)
climb	चढ़ना, *caṛhnā* (v.i.)
cloak with	ओढ़ना, *oṛhnā* (v.t.)
clock	घड़ी, *ghaṛī* (f.)
close	बंद करना, *band karnā*
closed	बंद, *band*
closet	अलमारी, *almārī* (f.)
cloth	कपड़ा, *kapṛā* (m.)
clothes	clothes, clothing: कपड़े, *kapṛe* (m.pl.); clothing, attire: लिबास, *libās* (m.)
cloud	बादल, *bādal* (m.)
clove	लौंग, *laung* (f.)
cold	cold (adj.): ठंडा, *ṭhanḍā*; cold, cold weather (noun): सर्दी, *sardī*, ठंड / ठंडक, *ṭhanḍ / ṭhanḍak* (f.); for X to be cold: X *ko sardī lagnā*; cold season, winter: सर्दियाँ, *sardiyā̃* (f.pl.); cold, illness: ज़ुकाम, *zukām* (m.); X *ko zukām honā*, for X to have a cold
collect	to collect, amass: जमा करना, *jamā karnā*
color	रंग, *rang* (m.)
colorful	रंग-बिरंगा, *rang-birangā*
come	आना, *ānā* (v.i.); तशरीफ़ लाना, *taśrīf lānā* (v.i.)
comfortable	आरामदेह, *ārāmdeh*
common	common, commonplace: आम, *ām*
compensation	मुआवज़ा, *muāvzā* (m.)
competition	मुक़ाबला, *muqāblā* (m.)

complete	complete, completed: पूरा, *pūrā*; complete, full, thorough: भरपूर, *bharpūr*; to complete: पूरा करना, *pūrā karnā*
computer	कंप्यूटर, *kampyūṭar* (m.)
condition	हालत, *hālat* (f.)
congratulations	बधाई हो, *badhāī ho*, मुबारक हो, *mubārak ho*
connected	connected, linked: जुड़ा हुआ, *juṛā huā*
connection	संबंध, *sambandh* (m.); *is sambandh mẽ*, in this connection
consciousness	होश, *hoś* (m.); *hoś mẽ ānā*, to return to consciousness
container	डिब्बा, *ḍibbā* (m.)
continuously	लगातार, *lagātār*
conversation	बातचीत, *bātcīt* (f.); *bātcīt karnā*, to talk, converse
cook	पकाना, *pakānā* (v.t.)
cookie	बिस्कुट, *biskuṭ* (m.)
corner	कोना, *konā* (m.)
correct	सही, *sahī*
coughing	खाँसी, *khā̃sī* (f.); X *ko khā̃sī ānā*, for X to have a cough, for X to be afflicted by coughing
count	गिनना, *ginnā* (v.t.)
countless	अनगिनत, *an-ginat*
country	देश, *deś* (m.), मुल्क, *mulk* (m.); country, countryside: देहात, *dehāt* (m.)
court	royal court: दरबार, *darbār* (m.)
courtyard	आँगन, *ā̃gan* (m.)
cover	ढकना, *ḍhaknā* (v.t.)
cow	गाय, *gāy* (f.)
cracker	बिस्कुट, *biskuṭ* (m.)
crocodile	मगरमच्छ, *magarmacch* (m.)
crooked	crooked, winding: टेढ़ा-मेढ़ा, *ṭeṛhā-meṛhā*
cross	to cross: पार करना, *pār karnā* (v.t.)
crowd	crowd, crowded state: भीड़, *bhīṛ* (f.)
cry	रोना, *ronā* (v.i.)
cucumber	खीरा, *khīrā* (m.)
culture	संस्कृति, *sanskriti* (f.); cultural: सांस्कृतिक, *sānskritik*

cumin	ज़ीरा, *zīrā* (m.)
cunning	चालाक, *cālāk*
cup	प्याली, *pyālī* (f.), कप, *kap* (m.)
cupboard	अलमारी, *almārī* (f.)
curly	घुँघराला, *ghũghrālā*
curtain	परदा, *pardā* (m.)
custom	custom, practice: रिवाज, *rivāj* (m.)
customer	ग्राहक, *grāhak*
cut	to cut: काटना, *kāṭnā* (v.t.); to get (one's hair) cut: (बाल) कटाना, (*bāl*) *kaṭānā* (v.t.)
cute	प्यारा, *pyārā*
daily	(adj.): दैनिक, *dainik*; (adv.) रोज़/रोज़ाना, *roz/rozānā*; daily routine: दिनचर्या, *dincaryā* (f.)
dance	to dance: नाचना, *nācnā* (v.i.)
dangerous	ख़तरनाक, *xatarnāk*
dark	dark (with colors): गाढ़ा, *gāṛhā*, गहरा, *gahrā*; dark complexioned: साँवला, *sā̃vlā*
darkness	अंधेरा, *andherā* (m.)
date	calendar date: तारीख़, *tārīx* (f.)
day	दिन, *din* (m.); daily: (adj.): दैनिक, *dainik*; (adv.) रोज़/रोज़ाना, *roz/rozānā*; these days: आजकल, *ājkal*
dear	(adj.): प्यारा, *pyārā*
death	मौत, *maut* (f.)
debate	बहस, *bahas* (f.); to have a discussion; to debate: बहस करना, *bahas karnā* (v.t.)
December	दिसंबर, *disambar* (m.)
decision	फ़ैसला, *faislā* (m.); V-*ne kā faislā karnā*, to decide to V
decrease	कम करना, *kam karnā*
deep	गहरा, *gahrā*
deer	हिरन, *hiran* (m.)
defeated	to be defeated, to lose: हारना, *hārnā* (v.i.)
definite	definite, certain; firm, finished: पक्का, *pakkā*
delay	देर, *der* (f.)

delicate	नाज़ुक, *nāzuk*
delicious	स्वादिष्ट, *svādiṣṭ*, लज़ीज़, *lazīz*
deliver	to deliver पहुँचाना, *pahũcānā* (v.t.)
dense	thick, dense: घना, *ghanā*
depart	रवाना होना, *ravānā honā* (v.i.); to depart, to leave (without): छूटना, *chūṭnā*; depart, set out: चलना, *calnā* (v.t.)
departure	रवानगी, *ravāngī* (f.), प्रस्थान, *prasthān* (m.)
dependent	निर्भर, *nirbhar* (upon X; X *par*)
desert	रेगिस्तान, *registān* (m.)
desk	मेज़, *mez* (f.)
destination	मंज़िल, *manzil* (f.)
detail	in detail, at length: विस्तार से, *vistār se*
determined	determined, fixed: तय, *tay*; to be determined, fixed, settled: तय होना, *tay honā* (v.i.)
diamond	हीरा, *hīrā* (m.)
diarrhea	दस्त, *dast* (m.pl.)
dictionary	शब्दकोश, *śabdkoś* (m.)
difference	फ़र्क़, *farq* (m.), अंतर, *antar* (m.)
different	different, separate: अलग, *alag*; different, various, separate, separately (adj./adv.): अलग-अलग, *alag-alag*
difficult	मुश्किल, *muśkil*, कठिन, *kaṭhin*; difficulty: मुश्किल, *muśkil* (f.)
dignity	respect, dignity, honor: इज़्ज़त, *izzat* (f.); X *kī izzat karnā*, to treat X with respect
direction	तरफ़, *taraf* (f.); in the direction of X: की तरफ़, X *kī taraf*
directions	to ask for directions: रास्ता पूछना, *rāstā pūchnā*; to give directions: रास्ता बताना, *rāstā batānā*
dirty	गंदा, *gandā*
disappeared	ग़ायब, *<u>gh</u>āyab* (adj.)
discomfort	तकलीफ़, *taklīf* (f.)
discussion	discussion, debate: बहस, *bahas* (f.); to have a discussion; to debate: बहस करना, *bahas karnā* (v.t.)
disposition	स्वभाव, *svabhāv* (m.), मिज़ाज, *mizāj* (m.)
distant	दूर, *dūr*
divorce	तलाक़, *talāq* (f.); divorced: तलाक़शुदा, *talāq-śudā* (inv.)

dizziness	spells of dizziness: चक्कर, *cakkar* (m.pl.)
dog	कुत्ता, *kuttā* (m.)
doll	गुड़िया, *guṛiyā* (f.)
donkey	गधा, *gadhā* (m.)
door	दरवाज़ा, *darvāzā* (m.)
dorm	dorm, hostel: हॉस्टल, *hāsṭal* (m.)
dose	ख़ुराक, *xurāk* (f.)
down	नीचे, *nīce* (adv.)
dozen	दर्जन, *darjan*
drawing room	बैठक, *baiṭhak* (f.), ड्रॉइंग रूम, *ḍrāing rūm* (m.)
dress	to dress (another person): पहनाना, *pahnānā* (v.t.); to get dressed: कपड़े बदलना, *kapṛe badalnā*, कपड़े पहनना, *kapṛe pahannā*
drink	पीना, *pīnā* (v.t.)
drive	to drive, to operate: चलाना, *calānā* (v.t.)
drop off	to leave; to drop off: छोड़ना, *choṛnā* (v.t.)
dry	to dry out, to go dry: सूखना, *sūkhnā* (v.i.)
dune	टीला, *ṭīlā* (m.)
during	के दौरान, *ke daurān*
each	हर, *har*
each other	एक-दूसरे, *ek-dūsre* (reciprocal)
ear	कान, *kān* (m.)
early	जल्दी, *jaldī*
earn	कमाना, *kamānā* (v.t.)
east	पूर्व, *pūrv* (m.)
eastern	पूर्वी, *pūrvī*
easy	आसान, *āsān*
eat	खाना, *khānā* (v.t.); *khānā khānā*, to eat; food: *khānā* (m.)
economics	अर्थशास्त्र, *arthśāstr* (m.)
edge	किनारा, *kinārā* (m.); *ke kināre*, on the edge/bank of
education	शिक्षा, *śikṣā* (f.), तालीम, *tālīm* (f.)
effort	कोशिश, *kośiś* (f.)
egg	अंडा, *anḍā* (m.)
eggplant	बैंगन, *baĩgan* (m.)

either	either…, or…: या..., या..., *yā…, yā…*; (not) either, neither: भी, *bhī* (+ neg.)
elbow	कुहनी, *kuhnī* (f.)
elephant	हाथी, *hāthī* (m.)
else	और, *aur*
embroidery	कढ़ाई, *kaṛhāī* (f.)
emerge	to exit, to emerge from (*se*): निकलना, *nikalnā* (v.i.)
employee	कर्मचारी, *karmcārī*; employee, servant: नौकर, *naukar*
empty	empty, available; free, not occupied: ख़ाली, *xālī*
enclosure wall	चारदीवारी, *cārdīvārī* (f.)
end	अंत, *ant* (m.), आख़िर, *āxir* (m.); ख़त्म होना, *xatm honā* (v.i.), ख़त्म करना, *xatm karnā* (v.t.)
English	अंग्रेज़ी, *angrezī* (f.)
enjoy	for X to like Y, enjoy Y: X को Y पसंद होना, X *ko* Y *pasand honā* for X to enjoy V-ing (as a hobby): X को V-ने का शौक़ होना, X *ko* V-*ne kā śauq honā*; for X to have a good time, enjoy oneself: X को मज़ा आना, X *ko mazā ānā* (v.i.); to enjoy X, take pleasure in X: मज़ा लेना (X का), X *kā mazā lenā*
enough	काफ़ी, *kāfī*
enter	दाख़िल होना, *dāxil honā*; अंदर जाना, *andar jānā*
entertainment	entertainment, recreation: मनोरंजन, *manoranjan* (m.)
environment	माहौल, *māhaul* (m.)
equal	equal, equally: बराबर, *barābar*
era	ज़माना, *zamānā* (m.)
especially	ख़ासतौर पर, *xās taur par*
essay	निबंध, *nibandh* (m.)
et cetera	वग़ैरह, *vaghaira*
even	भी, *bhī*
even though	हालाँकि, *hālā̃ki* (*...lekin/phir bhī…*, still…)
evening	शाम, *śām* (f.); *śām ko*, in the evening
event, incident	घटना, *ghaṭnā* (f./v.i.); *ghaṭnā ghaṭnā*, for an event to occur
every	हर, *har*
examination	examination; investigation: जाँच, *jā̃c* (f.); test, examination: इम्तिहान, *imtihān* (m.); परीक्षा, *parīkṣā* (f.)

example	उदाहरण, *udāharaṇ* (m.); मिसाल, *misāl* (f.)
excellent	बढ़िया, *baṛhiyā* (inv.)
excuse	to forgive, excuse: माफ़ करना, *māf karnā* (v.t.); *māf kījiye*, excuse me/I'm sorry
exercise	an exercise, practice: अभ्यास, *abhyās* (m.); व्यायाम करना, *vyāyām karnā*, कसरत करना, *kasrat karnā*
exit	to exit, to emerge from (*se*): निकलना, *nikalnā* (v.i.)
expectation	expectation, hope: उम्मीद, *ummīd* (f.); X *ko ummīd honā ki*, for X to have an expectation/hope that [+ future tense]
expensive	महँगा, *mahãgā*
experience	अनुभव, *anubhav* (m.), तजुर्बा, *tajurbā* (m.)
expert	माहिर, *māhir*
eye	आँख, *ãkh* (f.)
eyebrow	भौंह/भौं, *bhaũh/bhaũ* (f.)
face	मुँह, *mũh* (m.), चेहरा, *cehrā* (m.)
facing	in front of, facing: के सामने, *ke sāmne*
fact, in fact	असल में, *asal mẽ*, दरअसल, *dar-asal*, वास्तव में, *vāstav mẽ*
fairy	परी, *parī* (f.)
fall	to fall: गिरना, *girnā* (v.i.) (*gir paṛnā*, same); to fall, to befall: पड़ना, *paṛnā* (v.i.); fall (season): पतझड़, *patjhaṛ* (m.)
false	ग़लत, *ghalat*
family	परिवार, *parivār* (m.)
famous	मशहूर, *maśhūr*, प्रसिद्ध, *prasiddh*
fan	पंखा, *pankhā* (m.)
far	दूर, *dūr*; far from: से दूर, *se dūr*
fare	fare, rent: किराया, *kirāyā* (m.)
fat	fat, heavyset: मोटा, *moṭā*
father	पिता, *pitā* (m.), पापा, *pāpā* (m.), अब्बा, *abbā* (m.), अब्बू, *abbū* (m.); father (informal, can be disrespectful): बाप, *bāp* (m.)
father-in-law	ससुर, *sasur* (m.)
favorite	मनपसंद, *manpasand*; पसंदीदा, *pasandīdā* (inv.)
fear	डर, *ḍar* (m.); fear; apprehension: आशंका, *āśankā* (f.); to fear X: X से डरना, *ḍarnā* (v.i.)

February	फ़रवरी, *farvarī* (f.)
feed	खिलाना, *khilānā* (v.t.)
feel	महसूस करना, *mahsūs karnā*; for X to feel (+ noun): X को महसूस होना, X *ko mahsūs honā*; to feel like (doing something): जी चाहना, *jī cāhnā*, दिल चाहना, *dil cāhnā*, मन होना, *man honā*, मन करना, *man karnā*
fever	बुख़ार, *buxār* (m.); X *ko buxār honā*, for X to have a fever
few	few, fewer: कम, *kam*; a few: चंद, *cand*
field	field (for farming): खेत, *khet* (m.); field, plain: मैदान, *maidān* (m.)
fill	भरना, *bharnā* (v.i./v.t.); fill out: भरना, *bharnā* (v.i./v.t.)
film	फ़िल्म, *film* (f.)
filth	filth, grime: गंदगी, *gandgī* (f.)
find	for X to find (something to be…), to seem to X, to strike X as…: X को लगना, X *ko lagnā*; to find after searching: ढूँढना, *ḍhū̃ḍhnā* (v.t.)
find out	for X to find out: X को पता चलना, X *ko patā calnā* (v.i.); to find out (about X): (X का) पता करना, (X *kā*) *patā karnā* (v.t.)
fine	fine, OK: ठीक, *ṭhīk*; fine, not rough: महीन, *mahīn*; fine, thin, threadlike; minute: बारीक, *bārīk*
finger	उंगली, *unglī* (f.)
finish	ख़त्म होना, *xatm honā* (v.i.), ख़त्म करना, *xatm karnā* (v.t.)
fire	आग, *āg* (f.); *āg lagnā*, for a fire to start
first	पहले, *pahle*
fish	मछली, *machlī* (f.)
fit	healthy, fit: तंदुरुस्त, *tandurust*
fixed	determined, fixed: तय, *tay*
flame	आँच, *ā̃c* (f.)
flight	उड़ान, *uṛān* (f.)
floor	फ़र्श, *farś* (m.); floor, story: मंज़िल, *manzil* (f.)
flour	आटा, *āṭā* (m.)
flow	बहना, *bahnā* (v.i.); *nāk bahnā*, for one's nose to run
flower	फूल, *phūl* (m.)
flower pot	गमला, *gamlā* (m.)
flower vase	गुलदान, *guldān* (m.)

fly	fly, insect: मक्खी, *makkhī* (f.); to fly (to cause to fly): उड़ाना, *uṛānā* (v.t.); *patang uṛānā*, to fly a kite
fog	कुहरा, *kuhrā* (m.)
fool	fool, a fool; foolish: बेवक़ूफ़, *bevaqūf*; donkey; fool: गधा, *gadhā* (m.); owl; fool: उल्लू, *ullū* (m.)
foot	पाँव, *pā̃v* (*pā̃õ*) (m.); leg, foot: पैर, *pair* (m.); on foot, by foot: पैदल, *paidal*
for	के लिए / के लिये, *ke lie / ke liye*
forbidden	मना, *manā*
forehead	माथा, *māthā* (m.)
forget	भूलना/भूल जाना, *bhūlnā/bhūl jānā* (v.i.)
forgive	माफ़ करना, *māf karnā* (v.t.); *māf kījiye*, excuse me/I'm sorry
fork	काँटा, *kā̃ṭā* (m.)
fort	क़िला, *qilā* (m.)
fox	लोमड़ी, *lomṛī* (f.)
fragrance	महक, *mahak* (f.)
free	free (in price): मुफ़्त, *muft*; free time, leisure time: फ़ुरसत, *fursat* (f.); X *ko fursat honā*, for X to be free—not busy
freedom	freedom, independence: आज़ादी, *āzādī* (f.), स्वतंत्रता, *svatantrtā* (f.)
French	फ़्रांसीसी, *frānsīsī* (f.)
Friday	शुक्रवार, *śukrvār* (m.)
friend	दोस्त, *dost*, मित्र, *mitr*; female friend of a female: सहेली, *sahelī* (f.)
friendly	मिलनसार, *milansār*
from	से, *se*
front	in front of, facing: के सामने, *ke sāmne,* in front of, ahead of: के आगे, *ke āge*
fruit	फल, *phal* (m.)
fruit seller	फलवाला, *phalvālā* (m.)
fry	तलना, *talnā* (v.t.)
full	भरा, *bharā*
fun	fun, enjoyment; मज़ा, *mazā* (m.); fun (adj.): मज़ेदार, *mazedār* (adj.)
function	function, celebratory event: समारोह, *samāroh* (m.)
fun-loving	हँसमुख, *hā̃smukh*, ख़ुशमिज़ाज, *xuśmizāj*

future	भविष्य, *bhaviṣy* (m.)
game	खेल, *khel* (m.)
garden	बाग़, *bāgh* (m.)
garland	माला, *mālā* (f.)
garlic	लहसुन, *lahsun* (m.)
gas station	पेट्रोल पंप, *peṭrol pamp* (m.)
gecko	छिपकली, *chipkalī* (f.)
generally	आमतौर पर, *ām taur par*
geography	भूगोल, *bhūgol* (m.)
get	for X to get, obtain Y: X को Y मिलना, X *ko* Y *milnā*
get up	उठना, *uṭhnā* (v.i.)
ghee	ghee, clarified butter: घी, *ghī* (m.)
ghost	भूत, *bhūt* (m.)
gift	तोहफ़ा, *tohfā* (m.)
ginger	अदरक, *adrak* (m.)
girl	लड़की, *laṛkī* (f.)
glass	for drinking: गिलास, *gilās* (m.), glass (the material): शीशा, *śīśā* (m.)
glasses	चश्मा, *caśmā* (m.)
go	जाना, *jānā* (v.i.); to go with, accompany; depart: चलना, *calnā* (v.i.)
goat	बकरा, *bakrā* (m.)
God	भगवान, *bhagvān* (m.); ख़ुदा, *xudā* (m.)
golden	सुनहरा, *sunahrā*
good	अच्छा, *acchā*; good, auspicious: मंगलमय, *mangalmay*
good for nothing	नालायक़, *nālāyaq*
Good job!	शाबाश, *śābāś*
goodbye	hello / goodbye: नमस्ते, *namaste*, नमस्कार, *namaskār*
goods	माल, *māl* (m.)
governmental	सरकारी, *sarkārī*; *sarkār*, f. government
grandchild	grandson/granddaughter (son's children): पोता/पोती, *potā/potī*; grandson/granddaughter (daughter's children): नाती/नातिन, *nātī/nātin*
grandfather	paternal grandfather: दादा, *dādā* (m.), maternal grandfather, mother's father: नाना, *nānā* (m.)

grandmother	paternal grandmother: दादी, *dādī* (f.), maternal grandmother, mother's mother: नानी, *nānī* (f.)
grape	अंगूर, *angūr* (m.)
grass	घास, *ghās* (f.)
gray	स्लेटी, *sleṭī*
green	हरा, *harā*
greens	साग, *sāg* (m.)
groom	दूल्हा, *dūlhā* (m.)
ground meat	क़ीमा, *qīmā* (m.)
grow	उगना, *ugnā* (v.i.); to grow up: बड़ा होना, *baṛā honā* (v.i.); to grow up, be raised: पलना-बढ़ना, *palnā-baṛhnā* (v.i.); to increase, to grow: बढ़ना, *baṛhnā* (v.i.)
guava	अमरूद, *amrūd* (m.)
guest	मेहमान, *mehmān*
gut	तोंद, *tõd* (f.)
habit	आदत, *ādat* (f.)
hair	बाल, *bāl* (m.)
half	आधा, *ādhā*; half past, number plus one half: साढ़े, *sāṛhe*; half past one, डेढ़, *ḍeṛh*; half past two, ढाई, *ḍhāī*
hallway	गलियारा, *galiyārā* (m.)
hand	हाथ, *hāth* (m.)
handsome	ख़ूबसूरत, *xūbsūrat*, सुंदर, *sundar*
happiness	ख़ुशी, *xuśī* (f.)
happy	ख़ुश, *xuś*
hard work	मेहनत, *mehnat* (f.); hard working: मेहनती, *mehantī*
harsh	सख़्त, *saxt*, कठोर, *kaṭhor*
hat	टोपी, *ṭopī* (f.)
hate	to hate X: X से नफ़रत करना, X *se nafrat karnā*
hatred	नफ़रत, *nafrat* (f.)
head	सिर, *sir* (m.), सर, *sar* (m.)
health	स्वास्थ्य, *svāsthy* (m.); सेहत, *sehat* (f.); health, current state of health: तबियत, *tabiyat* (f.)
healthy	स्वस्थ, *svasth*; सेहतमंद, *sehatmand*; healthy, fit: तंदुरुस्त, *tandurust*

heart	दिल, *dil* (m.)
heat	heat, warmth: गर्मी, *garmī* (f.); X *ko garmī lagnā*, for X to be hot
heavy	भारी, *bhārī*
heel	एड़ी, *eṛī* (f.)
height	क़द, *qad* (m.), लम्बाई, *lambāī* (f.)
hello	hello / goodbye: नमस्ते, *namaste*, नमस्कार, *namaskār*
help	मदद, *madad* (f.); to help X: X की मदद करना, X *kī madad karnā*
here	here, over here: यहाँ, *yahā̃*
high	ऊँचा, *ū̃cā*
highway	राजमार्ग, *rājmārg* (m.)
hill	पहाड़ी, *pahāṛī* (f.)
historical	historical, historic: ऐतिहासिक, *aitihāsik*
history	इतिहास, *itihās* (m.), तारीख़, *tārīx* (f.)
hit	to strike, to hit: मारना, *mārnā* (v.t.)
hobby	शौक़, *śauq* (m.)
home	घर, *ghar* (m.)
honest	ईमानदार, *īmāndār*
honor	respect, dignity, honor: इज़्ज़त, *izzat* (f.); X *kī izzat karnā*, to treat X with respect
hope	आशा, *āśā* (f.), उम्मीद, *ummīd* (f.); X *ko ummīd honā ki*, for X to have an expectation/hope that [+ future tense], X *ko āśā honā ki*, for X to hope that [+ future tense]
horse	घोड़ा, *ghoṛā* (m.)
hospital	अस्पताल, *aspatāl* (m.)
host	मेज़बान, *mezbān*
hot	गर्म, *garm* (adj.); X को गर्मी लगना, for X to be/get hot
hotel	होटल, *hoṭal* (m.)
hour	घंटा, *ghanṭā* (m.)
house	मकान, *makān* (m.)
how	कैसा, *kaisā* (adj.); कैसे, *kaise* (adv.)
how about…	क्यों न…, *kyõ na*
how many	कितना, *kitnā*
how much	कितना, *kitnā*

human being	इन्सान, *insān* (m.), मनुष्य, *manuṣy* (m.)
hunger	भूख, *bhūkh* (f.); X *ko bhūkh lagnā*, for X to be hungry
hunting	शिकार, *śikār* (m.)
hurt	to hurt, be sore: दुखना, *dukhnā* (v.i.)
husband	पति, *pati* (m.)
idea	विचार, *vicār* (m.), ख़याल, *xayāl* (m.)
identity	पहचान, *pahcān* (f.); identification card: पहचान पत्र, *pahcān patr* (m.)
if…then…	अगर…तो…, *agar…to…*
ill	बीमार, *bīmār*
ill-mannered	बदतमीज़, *badtamīz*
illness	बीमारी, *bīmārī* (f.)
immediately	तुरंत, *turant*, फ़ौरन, *fauran*
importance	अहमियत, *ahamiyat* (f.), महत्त्व, *mahattv* (m.)
important	महत्त्वपूर्ण, *mahattvpūrṇ*, अहम, *aham*
in	में, *mẽ*; inside of: के अंदर, *ke andar*, के भीतर, *ke bhītar*
in addition to	के अलावा, *ke alāvā*
in spite of	के बावजूद, *ke bāvjūd*
incense	अगरबत्ती, *agarbattī* (f.)
incident	घटना, *ghaṭnā* (f./v.i.); *ghaṭnā ghaṭnā*, for an incident to occur
included	शामिल, *śāmil*
including	including; regarding: को लेकर, *ko lekar*
increase	बढ़ना, *baṛhnā* (v.i.); बढ़ाना, *baṛhānā* (v.t.)
independence	independence, freedom: आज़ादी, *āzādī* (f.), स्वतंत्रता, *svatantrtā* (f.)
India	भारत, *bhārat*; हिंदुस्तान, *hindūstān*
Indian	भारतीय, *bhāratīy*, हिंदुस्तानी, *hindustānī*
indication	sign, indication: इशारा, *iśārā* (m.); *iśārā karnā*, to point
individual	person, individual: व्यक्ति, *vyakti* (m./f.), शख़्स, *śaxs* (m./f.)
inexpensive	सस्ता, *sastā*
inflammation	सूजन, *sūjan* (f.); *sūjnā*, v.i. to swell
information	सूचना, *sūcnā* (f.), मालूमात, *mālūmāt* (m.pl.); information, knowledge of a thing: जानकारी, *jānkārī* (f.)
ingredients	ingredients, material: सामग्री, *sāmagrī* (f.)
injury	चोट, *coṭ* (f.); X *ko coṭ lagnā*, for X to get an injury

in-laws' home	ससुराल, *sasurāl* (m.)
insect	कीड़ा, *kīṛā* (m.)
inside	अंदर, *andar* (adv.); inside of: के अंदर, *ke andar*
instead of	के बजाय, *ke bajāy*
institution	institution, organization: संस्था, *sansthā* (f.)
instructor	शिक्षक, *śikṣak* (m.); शिक्षिका, *śikṣikā* (f.)
intelligent	intelligent, having common sense: अक़्लमंद, *aql-mand*, बुद्धिमान, *buddhimān*
intention	इरादा, *irādā* (m.); X *kā* V-*ne kā irādā honā* / X *kā irādā honā ki*..., for X to intend/plan to V
intentionally	जान-बूझकर, *jān-būjhkar*
interest	दिलचस्पी, *dilcaspī* (f.)
interested	for X to be interested in Y, have an interest in Y: X को Y में दिलचस्पी होना, X *ko* Y *mẽ dilcaspī honā*
interesting	दिलचस्प, *dilcasp*, रोचक, *rocak*
international	अंतर्राष्ट्रीय, *antarrāṣṭrīy*
intersection	चौराहा, *caurāhā* (m.)
introduce	to introduce (X *se*, to X): मिलाना, *milānā* (v.t.)
investigation	examination; investigation: जाँच, *jā̃c* (f.)
invitation	invitation; social gathering with food, reception, party: दावत, *dāvat* (f.); *dāvat denā*, to invite
invite	to invite, call, summon: बुलाना, *bulānā* (v.t.)
Iranian	ईरानी, *īrānī*
irresponsible	ग़ैरज़िम्मेदार, *ghairzimmedār*
island	टापू, *ṭapū* (m.), द्वीप, *dvīp* (m.)
it	वह, *vo*, यह, *ye*
January	जनवरी, *janvarī* (f.)
jewelry	ज़ेवरात, *zevrāt* (m.); jewel/s; jewelry (pl.): गहना, *gahnā* (m.); jewels: जवाहरात, *javāharāt* (m.pl.)
job	नौकरी, *naukrī* (f.)
joke	मज़ाक़, *mazāq* (m.); चुटकुला, *cuṭkulā* (m.); joke around: हँसी-मज़ाक़ करना, *hā̃sī-mazāq karnā*
journey	सफ़र, *safar* (m.), यात्रा, *yātrā* (f.); to travel, to take a journey: *safar karnā*, *yātrā karnā*

juice	जूस, *jūs* (m.)
July	जुलाई, *julāī* (f.)
June	जून, *jūn* (m.)
jungle	जंगल, *jangal* (m.)
just	just, only: सिर्फ़, *sirf*, केवल, *keval*, बस, *bas* (colloq.), ही, *hī* (emphatic particle)
keep	to keep; to put, to place: रखना, *rakhnā* (v.t.)
key	चाबी, *cābī* (f.), चाभी, *cābhī* (f.)
kill	मारना, *mārnā* (v.t.), मार डालना, *mār ḍālnā* (v.t.)
kilogram	किलो, *kilo*
kindness	kindness, act of kindness: मेहरबानी, *meharbānī* (f.); *baṛī meharbānī hogī*, it will be a big act of kindness, I would appreciate it
king	राजा, *rājā* (m.); king, emperor: बादशाह, *bādśāh* (m.)
kitchen	रसोईघर, *rasoīghar* (m.)
kite	पतंग, *patang* (m.)
knee	घुटना, *ghuṭnā* (m.)
knife	चाक़ू, *cāqū* (m.)
know	जानना, *jānnā* (v.t.); for X to know (Y—a piece of information): X को Y मालूम होना, X *ko* (Y) *mālūm honā*; for X to know Y (a language or skill): X को Y आना, X *ko* Y *ānā*; intentionally, knowingly: जान-बूझकर, *jān-būjhkar*
lake	झील, *jhīl* (f.)
land	ज़मीन, *zamīn* (f.), धरती, *dhartī* (f.)
language	भाषा, *bhāṣā* (f.); language, tongue: ज़बान, *zabān* (f.)
last	last, previous: पिछला, *pichlā*; last, final: आख़िरी, *āxirī*
late	देर से, *der se*: for X to be/get late: X को देर होना, X *ko der honā*
laugh	to laugh: हँसना, *hãsnā* (v.i.)
laughter	हँसी, *hãsī* (f.)
law	क़ानून, *qānūn* (m.); law, rule: नियम, *niyam* (m.)
lazy	आलसी, *ālsī*; lazy; sluggish, slow: सुस्त, *sust*
leaf	leaf, sheet: पत्ता, *pattā* (m.); small leaf (i.e. *cāe pattī*, tea leaves): पत्ती, *pattī* (f.)
least	at least: कम से कम, *kam se kam*

leave	to depart, to leave (without): छूटना, *chūṭnā*; छोड़ना, *choṛnā* (v.t.); चला जाना, *calā jānā* (v.i.)
left	left (direction): बायाँ, *bāyā̃*; left hand: उल्टा हाथ, *ulṭā hāth*; *ulṭe hāth par*, on the left side; to the left of: के बाईं तरफ़, *ke bāī̃ taraf*
leg	leg, foot: पैर, *pair* (m.); टाँग, *ṭā̃g* (f.)
lemon	नींबू, *nī̃bū* (m.)
length	लम्बाई, *lambāī* (f.)
lentils	दाल, *dāl* (f.)
less	कम, *kam*
library	पुस्तकालय, *pustakālay* (m.)
lie down	लेटना, *leṭnā* (v.i.)
life	ज़िंदगी, *zindagī* (f.), जीवन, *jīvan* (m.); life, life force: जान, *jān* (f.)
light	light (in color or weight): हल्का, *halkā*; light-skinned, fair in complexion: गोरा, *gorā*
like	for X to like Y: X को Y पसंद होना, X *ko* Y *pasand honā*; for X to like Y…(after experiencing it): X को Y पसंद आना, X *ko* Y *pasand ānā* (v.i.); to like; to choose something one likes: पसंद करना, *pasand karnā* (v.t.)
like	like, in the manner of: की तरह, *kī tarah*; like this, of this type: ऐसा, *aisā*; like that, of that type: वैसा, *vaisā*; like, as: जैसे, *jaise*
line	क़तार, *qatār* (f.)
linked	connected, linked: जुड़ा हुआ, *juṛā huā*; to be linked to, to connect (be connected) to: जुड़ना, *juṛnā* (v.i.)
lion	शेर, *śer* (m.)
lip	होंठ, *hõṭh* (m.)
literary	साहित्यिक, *sāhityik*
literature	साहित्य, *sāhity* (m.)
little	little (e.g., very little): कम, *kam*; little, a little: थोड़ा, *thoṛā*; little, small: छोटा, *choṭā*
live	to live, reside: रहना, *rahnā* (v.i.); live, be alive: जीना, *jīnā* (v.i.)
located	स्थित, *sthit*
long	लम्बा, *lambā*
look	to look at: देखना, *dekhnā* (v.t.); to appear to, to look, to seem: दिखना, *dikhnā* (v.i.)

looking after	देखभाल, *dekhbhāl* (f.); X *kī dekhbhāl karnā*, to look after X
loose	ढीला, *ḍhīlā*
lose	to lose, to get lost: खोना, *khonā* (v.i./v.t.); to be defeated, to lose: हारना, *hārnā* (v.i.)
lot	lot, a lot (of): बहुत, *bahut*
love	प्यार, *pyār* (m.), मुहब्बत, *muhabbat* (f.); to love X: X से प्यार करना, X *se pyār karnā*
low	नीचा, *nīcā*; low, lower: निचला, *niclā*; low in intensity: धीमा, *dhīmā*
lower, reduce	कम करना, *kam karnā*
lung	फेफड़ा, *phephṛā* (m.)
magazine	पत्रिका, *patrikā* (f.)
magic	जादू, *jādū* (m.)
magician	जादूगर, *jādūgar*
magnificent	शानदार, *śāndār*
maintain	जारी रखना, *jārī rakhnā*
make	बनाना, *banānā* (v.t.); to have something made: बनवाना, *banvānā* (v.t.)
mall	मॉल, *māl* (m.)
man	आदमी, *ādmī* (m.), मर्द, *mard* (m.)
mango	आम, *ām* (m.)
manner	तरह, *tarah* (f.), प्रकार, *prakār* (m.)
manners	तमीज़, *tamīz* (f.); X *ko tamīz honā*, for X to have manners
mansion	हवेली, *havelī* (m.), कोठी, *koṭhī* (f.)
many	many, a lot of: बहुत सा, *bahut sā*; how many: see 'how'
map	नक़्शा, *naqśā* (m.)
March	मार्च, *mārc* (m.)
market	बाज़ार, *bāzār* (m.); square, central market: चौक, *cauk* (m.)
marriage	शादी, *śādī* (f.)
married	शादीशुदा, *śādī-śudā* (inv.), विवाहित, *vivāhit*
marry	शादी करना, *śādī karnā* (v.t.)
material	सामग्री, *sāmagrī* (f.)
mathematics	गणित, *gaṇit* (m.)
matter	matter, spoken thing, utterance: बात, *bāt* (f.)

mausoleum	मक़बरा, *maqbarā* (m.)
May	मई, *maī* (f.)
meaning	मतलब, *matlab* (m.), अर्थ, *arth* (m.)
means	means, a means: माध्यम, *mādhyam* (m.), ज़रिया, *zariyā* (m.)
meat	गोश्त, *gośt* (m.), माँस, *mā̃s* (m.)
medicine	दवा/दवाई, *davā/davāī* (f.)
medicine shop	केमिस्ट की दुकान, *kemisṭ kī dukān* (f.)
medium	दरमियाना, *darmiyānā*
meet	to meet X, to see X socially: X से मिलना, X *se milnā*
meeting	मुलाक़ात, *mulāqāt* (f.)
memorize	याद करना, *yād karnā* (v.t.)
memory	याद, *yād* (f.)
mention	ज़िक्र, *zikr* (m.); to mention X: X का ज़िक्र करना, X *kā zikr karnā* (to, *se*)
mess	mess, unsettled state: गड़बड़, *gaṛbaṛ* (f.)
metal plate	थाली, *thālī* (f.)
meter	मीटर, *mīṭar*
method	विधि, *vidhi* (f.), तरकीब, *tarkīb* (f.)
microbe	कीड़ा, *kīṛā* (m.)
middle	in the middle of: के बीच में, *ke bīc mẽ*
mile	मील, *mīl* (m.)
milk	दूध, *dūdh* (m.)
mint	पुदीना, *pudīnā* (m.)
minute	minute, fine, thin, threadlike: बारीक, *bārīk*
minute	मिनट, *minaṭ* (m.)
mistake	ग़लती, *ghalatī* (f.)
mole	तिल, *til* (m.)
moment	पल, *pal* (m.)
Monday	सोमवार, *somvār* (m.)
money	पैसा, *paisā* (m.)
monkey	बंदर, *bandar* (m.)
month	महीना, *mahīnā* (m.)
moonlight	चाँदनी, *cā̃dnī* (f.)

more	और, *aur*; ज़्यादा, *zyādā*
morning	morning, in the morning: सुबह, *subah* (f.); early in the morning: सुबह-सवेरे, *subah-savere*
mosque	मस्जिद, *masjid* (f.)
mosquito	मच्छर, *macchar* (m.)
most	most, mostly: ज़्यादातर, *zyādātar*
moth	पतंगा, *patangā* (m.)
mother	माँ, *mā̃* (f.), माता, *mātā* (f.), मम्मी, *mammī* (f.), अम्मा, *ammā* (f.), अम्मी, *ammī* (f.)
mother-in-law	सास, *sās* (f.)
mountain	पहाड़, *pahāṛ* (m.)
mountain chain	पर्वत शृंखला, *parvat śrinkhalā* (f.)
mountainous	पहाड़ी, *pahāṛī*
mouse	mouse, rat: चूहा, *cūhā* (m.)
moustache	मूँछें, *mū̃chẽ* (f.pl.)
mouth	मुँह, *mũh* (m.)
move	to move, go: चलना, *calnā* (v.i.); move aside: हटाना, *haṭānā* (v.t.); हटना, *haṭnā* (v.i.)
movie	फ़िल्म, *film* (f.)
much	too much: ज़्यादा, *zyādā* (adv.); that much, so much: उतना, *utnā*; this much, so much: इतना, *itnā*
museum	संग्रहालय, *sangrahālay* (m.), अजायबघर, *ajāyabghar* (m.)
music	संगीत, *sangīt* (m.)
musical instrument	साज़, *sāz* (m.)
mutually	आपस में, *āpas mẽ*
my	my, mine: मेरा, *merā*
nail	नाख़ून, *nāxūn* (m.)
national	राष्ट्रीय, *rāṣṭrīy*
natural	प्राकृतिक, *prākritik*
nature	प्रकृति, *prakriti* (f.)
naughty	शरारती, *śarārtī*
nausea	मतली, *matlī* (f.); X *ko matlī honā*, for X to be nauseous
near	near, about: क़रीब, *qarīb* (adv.); nearby: आस पास, *ās pās*; nearby: नज़दीक, *nazdīk*; near to: X *ke nazdīk*, near to X

neat and clean	साफ़-सुथरा, *sāf-suthrā*
necessary	ज़रूरी, *zarūrī*, आवश्यक, *āvaśyak*
necessity	ज़रूरत, *zarūrat* (f.), आवश्यकता, *āvaśyaktā* (f.)
neck	गर्दन, *gardan* (f.)
need	X needs Y: X को Y चाहिए, X *ko* Y *cāhie*
neighborhood	पड़ोस, *paṛos* (m.)
neither…nor…	न…न…, *na…na…*
Nepali	नेपाली, *nepālī*
nephew	nephew/niece (brother's children): भतीजा/भतीजी, *bhatījā/bhatījī*; nephew/niece (sister's children): भाँजा/भाँजी, *bhā̃jā/bhā̃jī*
new	नया, *nayā*
news, news item	ख़बर, *xabar* (f.), समाचार, *samācār* (m.)
newspaper	अख़बार, *axbār* (m.), समाचार पत्र, *samācār patr* (m.)
next	अगला, *aglā*
next to	के बग़ल में, *ke baghal mẽ*
niece	nephew/niece (brother's children): भतीजा/भतीजी, *bhatījā/bhatījī*; nephew/niece (sister's children): भाँजा/भाँजी, *bhā̃jā/bhā̃jī*
night	रात, *rāt* (f.) (*rāt ko*, at night)
no	नहीं, *nahī̃*
noise	शोर-शराबा, *śor-śarābā* (m.); शोर, *śor* (m.); *śor karnā*, to make noise; to make a lot of noise: शोर मचाना, *śor macānā*
non-governmental	ग़ैर-सरकारी, *ghair-sarkārī*
north	उत्तर, *uttar* (m.)
northern	उत्तरी, *uttarī*
nose	नाक, *nāk* (f.)
not	नहीं, *nahī̃*, न, *na*, मत, *mat*
notepad	कॉपी, *kāpī* (f.)
novel	उपन्यास, *upanyās* (m.)
November	नवंबर, *navambar* (m.)
now	अब, *ab*; right now: अभी, *abhī*
o'clock	It's...o'clock: बजे हैं, *...baje haĩ*; It's...o'clock (with times based on 'one'), बजा है, *...bajā hai*; at...o'clock: बजे, *...baje*
obtain	प्राप्त करना, *prāpt karnā*, हासिल करना, *hāsil karnā*

ocean	समुद्र, *samudr* (m.)
October	अक्तूबर/ अक्टूबर, *aktūbar/ akṭūbar* (m.)
of	का, *kā*
office	दफ़्तर, *daftar* (m.), कार्यालय, *kāryālay* (m.)
official	अधिकारी, *adhikārī* (m.)
often	अक्सर, *aksar*
oil	तेल, *tel* (m.)
okra	भिंडी, *bhinḍī* (f.)
old	पुराना, *purānā*; old (of people): बुज़ुर्ग, *buzurg*; बूढ़ा, *būṛhā*
on	on, at: पर, *par*
on top of, above	के ऊपर, *ke ūpar*
once in a while	कभी-कभार, *kabhī-kabhār*
one and a half	डेढ़, *ḍeṛh*
onion	प्याज़, *pyāz* (f.)
only	just, only: सिर्फ़, *sirf*, केवल, *keval*, बस, *bas* (colloq.), ही, *hī* (emphatic particle)
open	open (adj.) खुला; to open: खुलना, *khulnā* (v.i.); खोलना, *kholnā* (v.t.)
operate	to drive, to operate: चलाना, *calānā* (v.t.)
opinion	राय, *rāy* (f.)
opportunity	मौक़ा, *mauqā* (m.)
opposite from	facing, opposite from: के सामने, *ke sāmne*
or	या, *yā*
orange	orange (in color): नारंगी, *nārangī*; orange (fruit): संतरा, *santarā* (m.)
organization	संस्था, *sansthā* (f.), संगठन, *sangaṭhan* (m.)
other	दूसरा, *dūsrā*
outside	बाहर, *bāhar*
oval shaped	अण्डाकार, *anḍākār*
owl	उल्लू, *ullū* (m.)
pain	दर्द, *dard* (m.); *sirdard*, m. headache
pair	pair, couple: जोड़ी, *joṛī* (f.)
Pakistan	पाकिस्तान, *pākistān*
Pakistani	पाकिस्तानी, *pākistānī*
palace	महल, *mahal* (m.)

palm	हथेली, *hathelī* (f.)
paneer	पनीर, *panīr* (m.)
pants	पतलून, *patlūn* (f.); drawstring pants: पाजामा, *pājāmā* (m.)
paper	काग़ज़, *kāghaz* (m.); papers: काग़ज़ात, *kāghzāt* (m.pl.)
parents	माता-पिता, *mātā-pitā* (m.pl.), माँ-बाप, *mā̃-bāp* (m.pl.), मम्मी-पापा, *mammī-pāpā*
park	पार्क, *pārk* (m.)
parrot	तोता, *totā* (m.)
part	भाग, *bhāg* (m.), हिस्सा, *hissā* (m.)
participate	to participate (in X): (X में) शरीक होना, (X *mẽ*) *śarīk honā* (v.t.)
particularly	ख़ासतौर पर, *xās taur par*
pass	to pass (e.g., time): बिताना, *bitānā* (v.t.), गुज़ारना, *guzārnā* (v.t.); to pass by X: X से गुज़रना, X *se guzarnā* (v.i.)
passenger	सवारी, *savārī* (f.)
past	गत, *gat*
patient (medical)	मरीज़, *marīz*
peace	peace, tranquility: सुकून, *sukūn* (m.)
peak	चोटी, *coṭī* (f.)
peas	मटर, *maṭar* (f.)
pen	क़लम, *qalam* (m., f.)
pencil	पेंसिल, *pensil* (f.)
people	लोग, *log* (m.pl.)
pepper	मिर्च, *mirc* (f.); red pepper: लाल मिर्च, *lāl mirc* (f.); bell pepper: शिमला मिर्च, *śimlā mirc* (f.)
perhaps	शायद, *śāyad*
permission	इजाज़त, *ijāzat* (f.); *ijāzat denā*, to give permission
person	person, individual: व्यक्ति, *vyakti* (m./f.), शख़्स, *śaxs* (m./f.)
pet	पालतू, *pāltū* (adj.)
phone	फ़ोन, *fon* (m.)
picture	तस्वीर, *tasvīr* (f.)
piece	टुकड़ा, *ṭukṛā* (m.)
pill	गोली, *golī* (f.)
pillow	तकिया, *takiyā* (m.)

pink	गुलाबी, *gulābī*
place	स्थान, *sthān* (m.); place; space: जगह, *jagah* (f.); to place, to put; to keep: रखना, *rakhnā* (v.t.)
plain	plain, field: मैदान, *maidān* (m.); plain, simple: सादा, *sādā*
plan	योजना, *yojnā* (f.)
plant	पौधा, *paudhā* (m.)
plate	तश्तरी, *taśtarī* (f.), प्लेट, *pleṭ* (f.)
platform	चबूतरा, *cabūtrā* (m.)
play	खेलना, *khelnā* (v.t.); to play (an instrument): बजाना, *bajānā* (v.t.)
playing cards	ताश, *tāś* (m.)
pleasant	सुहावना/सुहाना, *suhāvnā/suhānā*
pocket	जेब, *jeb* (f.)
poet	शायर, *śāyar* (m.), कवि, *kavi* (m.)
poetry	कविता, *kavitā* (f.), शायरी, *śāyrī* (f.)
police	पुलिस, *pulis* (f.)
police station	थाना, *thānā* (m.)
political science	राजनीति शास्त्र, *rajnīti śāstr* (m.)
politics	राजनीति, *rājnīti* (f.), सियासत, *siyāsat* (f.)
pomp and show	धूम-धाम, *dhūm-dhām* (f.)
pond	pond, reservoir: तालाब, *tālāb* (m.)
poor	ग़रीब, *g̲h̲arīb*
popular	लोकप्रिय, *lokpriy*
popularity	लोकप्रियता, *lokpriytā* (f.)
population	आबादी, *ābādī* (f.), जनसंख्या, *jansankhyā* (f.)
possibility	संभावना, *sambhāvnā* (f.)
possible	संभव, *sambhav*, मुमकिन, *mumkin*
post office	डाकघर, *ḍākghar* (m.)
potato	आलू, *ālū* (m.)
pots and pans	बर्तन, *bartan* (m.)
pour	उंडेलना, *unḍelnā* (v.t.)
practice	practice doing something: अभ्यास, *abhyās* (m.); custom, practice: रिवाज, *rivāj* (m.)
praise	तारीफ़, *tārīf* (f.); X *kī tārīf karnā*, to praise X

preparation(s)	तैयारी, *taiyārī* (f.)
prepared	ready, prepared, तैयार, *taiyār*; ready to V: तैयार (V-ने को), V-*ne ko taiyār*
prescription	नुस्ख़ा, *nusxā* (m.)
present	present, in attendance: हाज़िर, *hāzir*
pressed down	दबा हुआ, *dabā huā*; to be pressed down: दबना, *dabnā* (v.i.)
previously	पहले, *pahle*
price	दाम, *dām* (m.); price per unit of measurement: भाव (m.), हिसाब, *hisāb* (m.)
prime minister	प्रधान मंत्री, *pradhān mantrī*
prize	इनाम, *inām* (m.)
problem	समस्या, *samasyā* (f.), मसला, *maslā* (m.)
profession	व्यवसाय, *vyavasāy* (m.), पेशा, *peśā* (m.)
program	program, what one plans to do (i.e. for the day): प्रोग्राम, *progrām* (m.)
published	to be published: छपना, *chapnā* (v.i.)
pull	खींचना, *khī̃cnā* (v.t.); *tasvīr khī̃cnā*, to take a picture
purple	बैंगनी, *baĩgnī*
put	to put (on), to place (on); to keep: रखना, *rakhnā* (v.t.); to put in: डालना, *ḍālnā* (v.t.); to put on, apply to, attach to (*par/se*): लगाना, *lagānā* (v.t.); to put on, wear: पहनना, *pahannā* (v.t.); *kapṛe pahannā*, to get dressed
quarter	quarter (of town): मुहल्ला, *muhallā* (m.); quarter past; number plus a quarter: सवा, *savā*; quarter to; number minus a quarter: पौने, *paune*
queen	रानी, *rānī* (f.)
question	सवाल, *savāl* (m.), प्रश्न, *praśn* (m.)
quick	quick, sharp: तेज़, *tez*
quickly	जल्दी, *jaldī*; *jaldī mẽ*, in a hurry; very quickly: जल्द ही, *jald hī*; as quickly as possible: जल्द से जल्द, *jald se jald*
quite	काफ़ी, *kāfī*
rain	बारिश, *bāriś* (f.), वर्षा, *varṣā* (f.); rains, rainy season: बरसात, *barsāt* (f.); to rain: बारिश होना, *bāriś honā* (v.i.)
raised	to be raised/reared: पलना, *palnā* (v.i.)
rather, quite	काफ़ी, *kāfī*

raw	कच्चा, *kaccā*
reach	to arrive; to reach (somewhere): पहुँचना, *pahũcnā* (v.i.)
read	पढ़ना, paṛhnā (v.t.); to recite, read aloud for others to hear: सुनाना, *sunānā* (v.t.)
ready	तैयार, *taiyār*; ready to V: V-ने को तैयार, V-*ne ko taiyār*
really	सचमुच, *sacmuc*
rear	पालना, *pālnā* (v.t.)
reason	कारण, *kāraṇ* (m.), वजह, *vajah* (f.); because of: के काराण / की वजह से, *ke kāraṇ / kī vajah se*
recently	हाल में, *hāl mẽ*
recite	सुनाना, *sunānā* (v.t.)
recreation	entertainment, recreation: मनोरंजन, *manoranjan* (m.)
rectangular	आयताकार, *āyatākār*
red	लाल, *lāl*
reduce	कम करना, *kam karnā*
refrain	to refrain (from, *se*): परहेज़ करना, *parhez karnā* (v.t.)
regard	मानना, *mānnā* (v.t.)
regarding	को लेकर, *ko lekar*
region	इलाक़ा, *ilāqā* (m.), क्षेत्र, *kṣetr* (m.)
regret	sorrow, regret: अफ़सोस, *afsos* (m.); X *ko afsos honā*, for X to feel sorrow/regret; to regret: पछताना, *pachtānā* (v.i.)
regularly	नियमित रूप से, *niyamit rūp se*, पाबंदी से, *pābandī se*
relative	रिश्तेदार, *riśtedār*
relief	राहत, *rāhat* (f.) relief worker: राहतकर्मी, *rāhatkarmī*
religion	धर्म, *dharm* (m.), मज़हब, *mazhab* (m.)
religious	धार्मिक, *dhārmik*, मज़हबी, *mazhabī*
remain	रहना, *rahnā* (v.i.)
remaining	the rest of, the remaining: बाक़ी, *bāqī*
remember	for X to remember Y: X को Y याद होना, X *ko* (Y) *yād honā*
remove	हटाना, *haṭānā* (v.t.), दूर करना, *dūr karnā* (v.t.)
rent	rent, fare: किराया, *kirāyā* (m.)
repair	मरम्मत, *marammat* (f.); X *kī marammat karnā*, to repair X
repeatedly	बार-बार, *bār-bār*

reply	जवाब देना, *javāb denā* (v.t.)
reservoir	pond, reservoir: तालाब, *tālāb* (m.)
residence	निवास, *nivās* (m.)
respect	इज़्ज़त, *izzat* (f.); X *kī izzat karnā*, to treat X with respect
respond	जवाब देना, *javāb denā* (v.t.)
responsible	ज़िम्मेदार, *zimmedār*
rest	the rest of, the remaining: बाक़ी, *bāqī*; to rest: आराम करना, *ārām karnā* (v.t.)
restaurant	रेस्टोरेंट, *restorenṭ* (m.); होटल, *hoṭal* (m.); roadside restaurant: ढाबा, *ḍhābā* (m.); traditional vegetarian restaurant: भोजनालय, *bhojnālay* (m.)
return	वापसी, *vāpsī* (f.); to return (come/go back): लौटना, *lauṭnā* (v.i.)
reward	इनाम, *inām* (m.)
rice	चावल, *cāval* (m.)
rich	अमीर, *amīr*
rickshaw	रिक्शा, *rikśā* (m.); rickshaw driver: रिक्शेवाला, *rikśevālā* (m.)
rifle	बंदूक़, *bandūq* (f.)
right	right (direction): दायाँ, *dāyā̃*, दाहिना, *dāhinā*; right hand: सीधा हाथ, *sīdhā hāth*; *sīdhe hāth par*, on the right side; to the right of: के दाईं तरफ़, *ke dāī̃ taraf*, के दाहिनी तरफ़, *ke dāhinī taraf;* right, correct: सही, *sahī*
ring	अंगूठी, *angūṭhī* (f.)
river	नदी, *nadī* (f.), दरिया, *dariyā* (m. type 2)
road	सड़क, *saṛak* (f.); road (esp. in proper street names): मार्ग, *mārg* (m.); way, road: रास्ता, *rāstā* (m.)
roam	घूमना, *ghūmnā* (v.i.)
rock, stone	पत्थर, *patthar* (m.); large rock, boulder: चट्टान, *caṭṭān* (f.)
rod	छड़ी, *chaṛī* (f.)
role	भूमिका, *bhūmikā* (f.)
romantic	रूमानी, *rūmānī*
roof	छत, *chat* (f.)
room	room (in a building): कमरा, *kamrā* (m.); room, space: जगह, *jagah* (f.)
rose	गुलाब, *gulāb* (m.)
round	गोल, *gol*

routine, daily routine	दिनचर्या, *dincaryā* (f.)
rubble	मलबा, *malbā* (m.)
rug, carpet	carpet, rug: क़ालीन, *qālīn* (f.), दरी, *darī* (f.)
ruin	बरबाद करना, *barbād karnā* (v.t.)
ruined	बरबाद, *barbād*
ruins	खंडहर, *khanḍhar* (m.)
rule	rule, law: नियम, *niyam* (m.)
ruler	हाकिम, *hākim* (m.)
run	दौड़ना, *dauṛnā* (v.i.); to run, operate: चलना, *calnā* (v.i.); चलाना, *calānā* (v.t.)
rupee	रुपया, *rupayā* (m.)
salary	तनख़्वाह, *tanxāh* (f.)
salt	नमक, *namak* (m.)
salty	नमकीन, *namkīn*
sand	बालू, *bālū* (f.), रेत, *ret* (f.)
sandal	चप्पल, *cappal* (f.)
sari	साड़ी, *sāṛī* (f.)
Saturday	शनिवार, *śanivār* (m.)
save	बचाना, *bacānā* (v.t.)
say	कहना, *kahnā* (v.t.); X *se kahnā*, to say to X
scarf	दुपट्टा, *dupaṭṭā* (m.)
scene	दृश्य, *driśy* (m.), मंज़र, *manzar* (m.)
school	स्कूल, *skūl* (m.)
science	विज्ञान, *vijñān* (*vigyān*) (m.)
scissors	क़ैंची, *qaĩcī* (f.)
scold	डाँटना, *ḍā̃ṭnā* (v.t.)
script	लिपि, *lipi* (f.)
sea	समुद्र, *samudr* (m.)
search	तलाश, *talāś* (f.); ढूँढना, *ḍhū̃ḍhnā* (v.t.)
season	season; weather: मौसम, *mausam* (m.)
seat	सीट, *sīṭ* (f.)
seated	बैठा, *baiṭhā*
second	दूसरा, *dūsrā*

see	to see, watch, look at, देखना, *dekhnā* (v.t.) to see X socially, to meet X: X से मिलना, X *se milnā*
seem	to seem to X, to strike X as…, for X to find (something to be…): X को लगना, X *ko lagnā*; to appear to, to look, to seem: दिखना, *dikhnā* (v.i.)
self (reflexive)	अपना, *apnā*, ख़ुद, *xud*, स्वयं, *svayam*
sell	बेचना, *becnā* (v.t.)
sense	to make sense to X: X की समझ में आना, X *kī samajh mẽ ānā*
sentence	वाक्य, *vāky* (m.)
separate	different, separate: अलग, *alag*; different, various, separate, separately (adj./adv.): अलग-अलग, *alag-alag*
September	सितंबर, *sitambar* (m.)
serious	गंभीर, *gambhīr*, संजीदा, *sanjīdā* (inv.)
servant	नौकर, *naukar*
service	सेवा, *sevā* (f.); X *kī sevā karnā*, to serve X
set	set (e.g., of clothes): जोड़ा, *joṛā* (m.); to set, determine (a time): तय करना, *tay karnā*
settled	to be determined, fixed, settled: तय होना, *tay honā* (v.i.)
several	कई, *kaī*
sew	सिलना, *silnā* (v.t.)
sharp	sharp, quick: तेज़, *tez*
shawl	शाल, *śāl* (f.)
sheep	भेड़, *bheṛ* (f.)
sheet	sheet, bedsheet: चादर, *cādar* (f.)
shelves	shelves, shelving unit: अलमारी, *almārī* (f.)
shirt	क़मीज़, *qamīz* (f.)
shoe	जूता, *jūtā* (m.)
shop	दुकान, *dukān* (f.); to shop: ख़रीदारी करना, *xarīdārī karnā* (v.t.)
shopkeeper	दुकानदार, *dukāndār*
short	short (of people): नाटा, *nāṭā*
shoulder	कंधा, *kandhā* (m.)
show	दिखाना, *dikhānā* (v.t.); to show around: घुमाना, *ghumānā* (v.t.)
shrine	shrine or tomb of a Muslim saint: दरगाह, *dargāh* (f.)

shy	शर्मीला, *śarmīlā*
siblings	भाई-बहन, *bhāī-bahan* (m.pl.)
sick	बीमार, *bīmār*
sickness	बीमारी, *bīmārī* (f.)
side	ओर, *or* (f.), जानिब, *jānib* (f.)
sign	sign, indication: इशारा, *iśārā* (m.); *iśārā karnā*, to point
silk	रेशम, *reśam* (m.)
simple	simple, plain (of people): सीधा, *sīdhā*, सीधा-सादा, *sīdhā-sādā*
Since… therefore…	चूँकि… इसलिए…, *cū̃ki…islie…*
sing	to sing: गाना, *gānā* (v.t.) (also 'song,' m.)
sir	sir, honorific marker: जी, *jī*, साहब, *sāhab*
sister	बहन, *bahan* (f.); older sister: दीदी, *dīdī* (f.)
sister-in-law	(brother's wife): भाभी, *bhābhī* (f.)
sit down	बैठना, *baiṭhnā* (v.i.), तशरीफ़ रखना, *taśrīf rakhnā* (v.i.)
situated	स्थित, *sthit*
skin	त्वचा, *tvacā* (f.), चमड़ी, *camṛī* (f.)
skinny	दुबला, *dublā*, दुबला-पतला, *dublā-patlā*
sky	आसमान, *āsmān* (m.)
sleep	सोना, *sonā* (v.i.); *so jānā*, to fall asleep, go to sleep
sleepy	for X to be/get sleepy: X को नींद आना, X *ko nī̃d* (f.) *ānā*
sleeve	आस्तीन, *āstīn* (f.)
slow	धीमा, *dhīmā*
slowly	धीरे, *dhīre* (also *dhīre dhīre*)
small	छोटा, *choṭā*
smart	smart, clever: होशियार, *hośiyār*
smell	smell, fragrance: महक, *mahak* (f.)
smile	मुस्कराना, *muskarānā* (v.t.)
smoke	पीना, *pīnā* (v.t.)
snake	साँप, *sā̃p* (m.)
sneeze	छींक, *chī̃k* (f.); X *ko chī̃k ānā*, for X to sneeze, for X to have to sneeze; *chī̃knā*, to sneeze
snow	बर्फ़, *barf* (f.); to snow: बर्फ़ पड़ना, *barf paṛnā* (v.i.)
so	तो, *to*

so much	that much, so much: उतना, *utnā*; this much, so much: इतना, *itnā*
so that…	so that…, in order to…: ताकि, *tāki*
soap	साबुन, *sābun* (m.)
sock	मोज़ा, *mozā* (m.)
sofa	सोफ़ा, *sofā* (m.)
solid	strong, solid (in build): मज़बूत, *mazbūt*
solution	हल, *hal* (m.)
some	some, something; a bit (+ adj.): कुछ, *kuch*; some, a few: चंद, *cand*; some, someone; any, anyone: कोई, *koī*
someone	someone, some; any, anyone: कोई, *koī*
something	some, something; a bit (+ adj.): कुछ, *kuch*
sometimes	कभी-कभी, *kabhī-kabhī*
somewhere	कहीं, *kahī̃*
song	गाना, *gānā* (m.) (also, 'to sing,' v.t.)
soon	as soon as possible: जल्द से जल्द, *jald se jald*
sore	to hurt, be sore: दुखना, *dukhnā* (v.i.)
sorrow	sorrow, regret: अफ़सोस, *afsos* (m.); X *ko afsos honā*, for X to feel sorrow/regret
so-so	ठीक-ठाक, *ṭhīk-ṭhāk*
sound	आवाज़, *āvāz* (f.)
sour	खट्टा, *khaṭṭā*
south	दक्षिण, *dakṣiṇ* (m.)
southern	दक्षिणी, *dakṣiṇī*
speak	बोलना, *bolnā* (v.t./v.i.); फ़रमाना, *farmānā* (v.i.)
special	ख़ास, *xās*; specialty, special quality: ख़ासियत, *xāsiyat* (f.)
speech	भाषण, *bhāṣaṇ* (m.); *bhāṣaṇ denā*, to give a speech
spend	ख़र्च करना, *xarc karnā* (v.t.)
spice	मसाला, *masālā* (m.)
spicy	मसालेदार, *masāledār*; spicy, too spicy: कड़वा, *kaṛvā*
spinach	पालक, *pālak* (m.)
splendid	शानदार, *śāndār*
spoiled	spoiled, in a bad state: ख़राब, *xarāb*
spoon	चम्मच / चमचा, *cammac/camcā* (m.)

sport	खेल, *khel* (m.)
sprain	मोच, *moc* (f.); X *ke/kī...mẽ moc ānā*, for X's...to get sprained
spread	फैलना, *phailnā* (v.i.), फैलाना, *phailānā* (v.t.)
spring	बसंत, *basant* (m.)
square	square, central market: चौक, *cauk* (m.)
square in shape	चौकोर, *caukor*
stain	दाग़, *dāgh* (m.)
stair	सीढ़ी, *sīṛhī* (f.)
stand	खड़ा होना, *khaṛā honā* (v.i.)
standing	खड़ा, *khaṛā*
start	शुरू करना, *śurū karnā* (v.t.), शुरू होना, *śurū honā* (v.i.)
state	राज्य, *rājy* (m.), प्रदेश, *prades* (m.)
station	स्टेशन, *sṭeśan* (m.); *relve sṭeśan*, train station
stay at	to stay at: ठहरना, *ṭhaharnā* (v.i.)
steady oneself	संभलना, *sambhalnā* (v.i.)
steal	चुराना, *curānā* (v.t.)
step	क़दम, *qadam* (m.); *qadmõ mẽ gir paṛnā*, to fall to someone's feet
stomach	पेट, *peṭ* (m.)
stop	to stop, halt: रुकना, *ruknā* (v.i.); रोकना, *roknā* (v.t.); ठहरना, *ṭhaharnā* (v.i.); to stop V-ing: V-ना बंद करना, V-*nā band karnā*
store	दुकान, *dukān* (f.); general store, dry goods and staples store: किराने की दुकान, *kirāne kī dukān* (f.)
storey	मंज़िल, *manzil* (f.); storeyed: मंज़िला, *manzilā*
storm	तूफ़ान, *tūfān* (m.)
story	कहानी, *kahānī* (f.); tale, story: क़िस्सा, *qissā* (m.)
stove	चूल्हा, *cūlhā* (m.)
strain	छानना, *chānnā* (v.t.)
strainer	छननी, *channī* (f.)
strange	अजीब, *ajīb*
stranger	अजनबी, *ajnabī*
stream	river, stream: नदी, *nadī* (f.)
strict	सख़्त, *saxt*
strike	to strike, to hit: मारना, *mārnā* (v.t.)

stripe	धारी, *dhārī* (f.)
stroll	टहलना, *ṭahalnā* (v.i.)
strong	strong, solid (in build): मज़बूत, *mazbūt*
student	छात्र, *chātr* (m.), छात्रा, *chātrā* (f.); विद्यार्थी, *vidyārthī* (m./f.)
studious	पढ़ाकू, *paṛhākū*
study	पढ़ाई, *paṛhāī* (f.); to study: पढ़ाई करना, *paṛhāī karnā* (v.t.)
stuff	stuff, things: सामान, *sāmān* (m.sg.)
sturdy	sturdily built: लम्बा-चौड़ा, *lambā-cauṛā*
subcontinent	उपमहाद्वीप, *upmahādvīp* (m.)
subject	विषय, *viṣay* (m.)
submit	to submit (a form, an application): जमा करना, *jamā karnā*
success	सफलता, *saphaltā* (f.), कामयाबी, *kāmyābī* (f.)
successful	सफल, *saphal*, कामयाब, *kāmyāb*
suddenly	अचानक *acānak*; एकदम, *ekdam*
sugar	चीनी, *cīnī* (f.), शक्कर, *śakkar* (m.)
suggestion	सुझाव, *sujhāv* (m.); *sujhāv denā*, to suggest
summer	गर्मियाँ, *garmiyā̃* (f.pl.)
sun	सूरज, *sūraj* (m.)
Sunday	रविवार, *ravivār* (m.), इतवार, *itvār* (m.)
sunshine	धूप, *dhūp* (f.)
surprised	हैरान, *hairān*
swallow	निगलना, *nigalnā* (v.t.)
sweat	पसीना, *pasīnā* (m.); X *ko pasīnā ānā*, for X to sweat
sweep	झाड़ू लगाना, *jhāṛū lagānā*
sweet	मीठा, *mīṭhā*; sweet maker: हलवाई, *halvāī* (m.); a sweet: मिठाई, *miṭhāī* (f.)
swelling	सूजन, *sūjan* (f.); *sūjnā*, v.i. to swell
swim	तैरना, *tairnā* (v.i.)
table	मेज़, *mez* (f.)
table cloth	मेज़पोश, *mezpoś* (m.)
take	to take (someone/something somewhere): ले जाना, *le jānā* (v.i.); to take with: ले चलना, *le calnā* (v.i.); to take off: उतारना, *utārnā* (v.t.); *kapṛe utārnā*, to get undressed

tale	tale, anecdote: क़िस्सा, *qissā* (m.)
talk	to talk to (converse with) X (about Y): X से बात करना (Y की), X *se* (Y *kī*) *bāt karnā* (v.t.)
talkative	बातूनी, *bātūnī*
tall	लम्बा, *lambā*
taste	स्वाद, *svād* (m.)
tasty	मज़ेदार, *mazedār* (adj.)
tea	चाय, *cāy* (f.)
teach	पढ़ाना, *paṛhānā* (v.t.)
teacher	अध्यापक, *adhyāpak* (m.), अध्यापिका, *adhyāpikā* (f.)
television series	सीरियल, *sīriyal* (m.)
temperament	स्वभाव, *svabhāv* (m.), मिज़ाज, *mizāj* (m.)
temple	मंदिर, *mandir* (m.)
test	test, examination: इम्तिहान, *imtihān* (m.); परीक्षा, *parīkṣā* (f.)
than	से, *se*
thank you	धन्यवाद, *dhanyavād*, शुक्रिया, *śukriyā*
that	कि, *ki* (conj.); वह, *vo*; that very: वही, *vahī*; that much: उतना, *utnā*
that is to say	यानी, *yānī*
theatre	movie theatre: सिनेमाघर, *sinemāghar* (m.)
theft	चोरी, *corī* (f.)
then	then, in that case: तो, *to*; then, after that: फिर, *phir*, तब, *tab*; right then: तभी, *tabhī*
there	there, over there: वहाँ, *vahā̃*; right there: वहीं, *vahī̃*
these days	आजकल, *ājkal*
thick	मोटा, *moṭā*; thick in consistency: गाढ़ा, *gāṛhā*; thick, dense: घना, *ghanā*
thief	चोर, *cor*
thin	पतला; (of people) दुबला, *dublā*, दुबला-पतला, *dublā-patlā*
thing	चीज़, *cīz* (f.); stuff, things: सामान, *sāmān* (m.sg.)
thirst	प्यास, *pyās* (f.); X *ko pyās lagnā*, for X to be thirsty
this	यह, *ye*; this much, so much: इतना, *itnā*
thought	विचार, *vicār* (m.), ख़याल, *xayāl* (m.)
throat	गला, *galā* (m.)

throughout	throughout X: भर, X *bhar*; throughout the world: दुनिया भर, *duniyā-bhar*
thumb	अंगूठा, *angūṭhā* (m.)
Thursday	गुरुवार, *guruvār* (m.), बृहस्पतिवार, *brihaspativār* (m.)
Tibetan	तिब्बती, *tibbatī*
ticket	टिकट, *ṭikaṭ* (m./f.)
tie	बाँधना, *bā̃dhnā* (v.t.)
tight	तंग, *tang*
time	समय, *samay* (m.), वक़्त, *vaqt* (m.); (i.e., one time, two times): बार, *bār* (f.); time, era: ज़माना, *zamānā* (m.); at what time: कितने बजे, *kitne baje*
tired	थका हुआ, *thakā huā*
tiredness	थकान, *thakān* (f.)
today	आज, *āj*
tomato	टमाटर, *ṭamāṭar* (m.)
tomb	मक़बरा, *maqbarā* (m.); shrine or tomb of a Muslim saint: दरगाह, *dargāh* (f.)
tomorrow	कल, *kal*
tongue	जीभ, *jībh* (f.)
too	भी, *bhī*
tooth	दाँत, *dā̃t* (m.)
top	shirt, top: क़मीज़, *qamīz* (f.)
torso	धड़, *dhaṛ* (m.)
tour	सैर, *sair* (f.)
tourist	पर्यटक, *paryaṭak*; tourist destination: पर्यटन स्थल, *paryaṭan-sthal* (m.)
towel	तौलिया, *tauliyā* (m.)
town	क़स्बा, *qasbā* (m.)
track	पटरी, *paṭrī* (f.)
train	रेलगाड़ी, *rel gāṛī* (f.), ट्रेन, *ṭren* (f.)
train car	डिब्बा, *ḍibbā* (m.)
train station	रेलवे स्टेशन, *relve sṭeśan* (m.)
trash	कूड़ा, *kūṛā* (m.); trash can: कूड़ेदान, *kūṛedān* (m.)
travel	to travel, to take a journey: सफ़र करना, *safar karnā*, यात्रा करना, *yātrā karnā*; to roam, to travel: घूमना, *ghūmnā* (v.i.)

traveler	यात्री, *yātrī*, मुसाफ़िर, *musāfir*; tourist, traveler: पर्यटक, *paryaṭak*
treatment	treatment (medical): इलाज, *ilāj* (m.): X *kā ilāj karnā*, to treat X
tree	पेड़, *peṛ* (m.)
triangular	तिकोना, *tikonā*
trouble	trouble, distress: परेशानी, *pareśānī* (f.)
true	सच, *sac*; true, genuine: असली, *aslī*; correct, true: सही, *sahī*
truly	सचमुच, *sacmuc*
trust	trust, belief in: भरोसा, *bharosā* (m.); to trust X; have faith (not religious) in X: X पर भरोसा करना, X *par bharosā karnā*
try	to try to V: V-ने की कोशिश करना, V-*ne kī kośiś karnā*
Tuesday	मंगलवार, *mangalvār* (m.)
tunic	कुर्ता, *kurtā* (m.)
turn	मुड़ना, *muṛnā* (v.i.); X *par muṛnā*, to turn on to X; X *se muṛnā*, to turn at/from X
TV	टीवी, *ṭīvī* (m.)
two and a half	ढाई, *ḍhāī*
type	तरह, *tarah* (f.), प्रकार, *prakār* (m.); like that, of that type: वैसा, *vaisā*; like this, of this type: ऐसा, *aisā*
ugly	बदसूरत, *badsūrat*
uncle	paternal uncle (father's older brother) ताऊ, *tāū* (m.); paternal uncle (father's younger brother): चाचा, *cācā* (m.); maternal uncle: मामा, *māmā* (m.); husband of *buā*: फूफा, *phūphā* (m.); husband of *mausī*: मौसा, *mausā* (m.)
unconscious	बेहोश, *behoś*
uncooked	कच्चा, *kaccā*
under	के नीचे, *ke nīce*
understand	समझना, *samajhnā* (v.i./v.t.)
understanding	समझ, *samajh* (f.)
unfinished	(opp. of *pakkā*): कच्चा, *kaccā*
unhappy	दुखी, *dukhī*; unhappy, melancholy: उदास, *udās*
unique	अनोखा, *anokhā*
unnecessary	ग़ैरज़रूरी, *g̲hairzarūrī*, अनावश्यक, *anāvaśyak*
until	तक, *tak* (ppn.); (...*se lekar*...*tak*, from...to...)

up	ऊपर, *ūpar*; up till, until: तक, *tak* (ppn.); (*...se lekar...tak*, from...to...)
upbringing	परवरिश, *parvariś* (f.)
upon	upon V-ing: V-ने पर, V-*ne par*
upper	ऊपरी, *ūparī*
use	इस्तेमाल, *istemāl* (m.); to use: X (का) इस्तेमाल करना, X (*kā*) *istemāl karnā*
useless	बेकार, *bekār*
usually	आमतौर पर, *ām taur par*
vacation time	break, day off, weekend, holiday, vacation time: छुट्टी, *chuṭṭī* (f.)
valley	घाटी, *ghāṭī* (f.), वादी, *vādī* (f.)
valuable	क़ीमती, *qīmtī*
value	value, price: क़ीमत, *qīmat* (f.)
vase	गुलदान, *guldān* (m.)
vegetable	vegetable; vegetable dish: सब्ज़ी, *sabzī* (f.)
vegetable seller	सब्ज़ीवाला, *sabzīvālā* (m.)
vegetarian	शाकाहारी, *śākāhārī*
vehicle	गाड़ी, *gāṛī* (f.)
veranda	बरामदा, *barāmdā* (m.), दालान, *dālān* (m./f.)
very	बहुत, *bahut*
via	होकर, से होकर, (*se*) *hokar*
village	गाँव, *gā̃v* (*gā̃õ*) (m.)
vine	बेल, *bel* (f.)
visible	to appear to, to become visible to (X *ko*): दिखाई देना, *dikhāī denā* (v.i.)
voice	आवाज़, *āvāz* (f.)
volunteer	स्वयंसेवक, *svayamsevak* (m.)
vomit	vomit, vomiting: उल्टी, *ulṭī* (f.); *ulṭī karnā*, to vomit; X *ko ulṭī ānā*, for X to feel nauseous
waist	कमर, *kamar* (f.)
wait	wait, act of waiting: इंतज़ार, *intizār* (m.); to wait for X: X का इंतज़ार करना, X *kā intizār karnā*
wake up	to be awake, to wake up: जागना, *jāgnā* (v.i.)
walk	walk, stroll: चहल-क़दमी, *cahal-qadmī* (f.)

wall	दीवार, *dīvār* (f.)
wander	to wander around: चलना-फिरना, *calnā-phirnā* (v.i.)
want	चाहना, *cāhnā* (v.t.); V-*nā cāhnā*, to want to V
wardrobe	अलमारी, *almārī* (f.)
wash	धोना, *dhonā* (v.t.)
washerman	धोबी, *dhobī* (m.)
washroom	ग़ुसलख़ाना, *ghusalxānā* (m.)
waste	बरबाद करना, *barbād karnā* (v.t.) (e.g., *vaqt*, m. time)
watch	घड़ी, *ghaṛī* (f.)
water	पानी, *pānī* (m.); water bottle: पानी की बोतल, *pānī kī botal* (f.)
water buffalo	भैंस, *bhaĩs* (f.)
waterfall	झरना, *jharnā* (m.)
way	way, road: रास्ता, *rāstā* (m.); *rāstā pūchnā*, to ask for directions; *rāstā batānā*, to give directions
weak	कमज़ोर, *kamzor*
weakness	कमज़ोरी, *kamzorī* (f.)
wear	to put on, wear: पहनना, *pahannā* (v.t.); *kapṛe pahannā*, to get dressed
weather	weather; season: मौसम, *mausam* (m.)
wedding	शादी, *śādī* (f.), विवाह, *vivāh* (m.); Islamic wedding: निकाह, *nikāh* (m.)
Wednesday	बुधवार, *budhvār* (m.)
week	हफ़्ता, *haftā* (m.), सप्ताह, *saptāh* (m.)
weekend	सप्ताहांत, *saptāhānt* (m.)
weigh	तौलना, *taulnā* (v.t.)
weight	वज़न, *vazan* (m.)
west	पश्चिम, *paścim* (m.)
western	पश्चिमी, *paścimī*
what	क्या, *kyā*
when	कब, *kab*; when…(then)…: जब… तब/तो…, *jab… tab/to…*
whenever	जब भी, *jab bhī*
where	कहाँ, *kahā̃*; जहाँ, *jahā̃* (rel.)
which	कौन सा, *kaun sā*; which (relative): जो, *jo*
while	while, length of time: देर, *der* (f.); once in a while: कभी-कभार, *kabhī-kabhār*

white	सफ़ेद, *safed*
who	who (interrogative): कौन, *kaun*; who, which (relative): जो, *jo*
whose	किसका, *kis kā*
why	क्यों, *kyõ*
why not...	क्यों न..., *kyõ na*
wide	चौड़ा, *caurā*
wife	पत्नी, *patnī* (f.)
wild	जंगली, *janglī*
win	जीतना, *jītnā* (v.t./v.i.)
wind	हवा, *havā* (f.)
winding	टेढ़ा-मेढ़ा, *ṭeṛhā-meṛhā*
window	खिड़की, *khiṛkī* (f.)
winter	जाड़ा, *jāṛā* (m.)
wish	best wishes: शुभकामनाएँ, *śubhkāmnāẽ*
with	with, accompanying: के साथ, *ke sāth* (*sāth sāth* / *ek sāth*, adv., together)
without	बिना, *binā*, बग़ैर, *bag͟hair*; without X: X *ke binā*/*binā* X *ke*, X *ke bag͟hair*/*bag͟hair* X *ke*
woman	औरत, *aurat* (f.)
wood	लकड़ी, *lakṛī* (f.)
word	शब्द, *śabd* (m.)
work	काम, *kām* (m.); to work; to do a task: काम करना, *kām karnā* (v.t.)
world	दुनिया, *duniyā* (f.)
worried	परेशान, *pareśān*
worry	worry, thought, preoccupation: चिंता, *cintā* (f.), फ़िक्र, *fikr* (f.); to worry about X: X की चिंता करना, X *kī cintā karnā*, X की फ़िक्र करना, X *kī fikr karnā*
worth V-ing	V-ने लायक़, V-*ne lāyaq*, V-ने योग्य, V-*ne yogy*
worthy	लायक़, *lāyaq*, योग्य, *yogy*; X *ke lāyaq/yogy*, worthy of X; V-*ne lāyaq*, worth V-ing
wound	घाव, *ghāv* (m.), ज़ख़्म, *zaxm* (m.)
wounded	घायल, *ghāyal*, ज़ख़्मी, *zaxmī*
wrist	कलाई, *kalāī* (f.)

wrong	ग़लत, *ghalat*
year	साल, *sāl* (m.), वर्ष, *varṣ* (m.)
yellow	पीला, *pīlā*
yes	जी, *jī*, हाँ, *hā̃*, जी हाँ, *jī hā̃*
yesterday	कल, *kal*
yogurt	दही, *dahī* (m.)
young	छोटा, *choṭā* जवान, *javān*
your	your, yours: आपका, *āp kā*, तुम्हारा, *tumhārā*
youth	जवानी, *javānī* (f.)
zoo	चिड़ियाघर, *ciṛiyāghar* (m.)

Beginning Hindi
Credits

All images have been used by permission. Those not credited below were taken by the authors or created by Georgetown University Press.

The Sound System and Script of Hindi

	Pages 1, 13	Farhan Farooqui
Chapter 1		
	Page 45	Farhan Farooqui
Chapter 2		
	Page 63	Urfia Farooqui
Chapter 3		
	Page 73	Urfia Farooqui
Chapter 5		
	Page 95	Azza Cohen
Chapter 6		
	Page 103	Urfia Farooqui
Chapter 7		
	Pages 111, 118	Urfia Farooqui
Chapter 8		
	Page 141	Azza Cohen
Chapter 10		
	Page 175	Farhan Farooqui
Chapter 11		
	Page 177	Subuhi Firdaus

Chapter 13		
	Page 199	Urfia Farooqui
Chapter 14		
	Page 221	Urfia Farooqui
Chapter 15		
	Page 231	Azza Cohen
Chapter 16		
	Page 252	Farhan Farooqui
Chapter 17		
	Pages 257	Farhan Farooqui
Chapter 18		
	Pages 265, 273	Farhan Farooqui
Chapter 19		
	Page 293	Urfia Farooqui
	Page 296	Farhan Farooqui
Chapter 20		
	Page 306	Urfia Farooqui
Chapter 21		
	Pages 319, 323	Farhan Farooqui
	Page 325	Urfia Farooqui
Chapter 23		
	Page 343	Farhan Farooqui
	Page 348	Urfia Farooqui
Chapter 24		
	Page 353	Natalie Aguayo
	Page 360	Farhan Farooqui
Chapter 25		
	Page 361	Subuhi Firdaus

Chapter 26		
	Page 369	Urfia Farooqui
Chapter 27		
	Pages 377, 382	Farhan Farooqui
Chapter 28		
	Page 385	Farhan Farooqui
Chapter 29		
	Page 393	Farhan Farooqui
Chapter 30		
	Page 403	Farhan Farooqui
Chapter 31		
	Page 411	Farhan Farooqui
Chapter 33		
	Page 437	Farhan Farooqui
Chapter 34		
	Page 447	Subuhi Firdaus
	Page 454	Farhan Farooquii
Chapter 36		
	Page 465	Natalie Aguayo
	Page 478	Urfia Farooqui
Chapter 38		
	Page 501	Natalie Aguayo
Chapter 39		
	Page 513	Subuhi Firdaus
Chapter 40		
	Page 525	Farhan Farooqui
	Page 531	Urfia Farooqui